# Children's Language

## VOLUME 2

*Edited by*

## KEITH E. NELSON
The Pennsylvania State University

GARDNER PRESS, INC., NEW YORK

Distributed by Halsted Press
Division of John Wiley & Sons, Inc.

NEW YORK • LONDON • SYDNEY • TORONTO

# Children's Language

*The Thought-Fox* (page    ) is part of the collection,
*Selected Poems, 1957-1967,* by Ted Hughes, published
in London in 1972 by Faber and Faber.

GARDNER PRESS, INC.
19 Union Square West
New York, New York 10003

Distributed solely by the Halsted Press
Division of John Wiley & Sons, Inc., New York


Library of Congress Cataloging in Publication Data
Main entry under title:

Children's language

    1.   Children—Language—Addresses, essays, lec-
tures.   I.   Nelson, Keith E.
LB1139.L3C45      372.6      77-26226
ISBN 0-470-99385-5 Volume 1
      0470-26716-X Volume 2 ✓

Printed in the United States of America

# PREFACE

This series, *Children's Language,* was born when it became clear that extensive work on entirely new fronts along with a great deal of reinterpretation of old-front data would be necessary before any persuasive and truly orderly account of language development could be assembled. For all volumes in the series there is a common scheme of operation with two tactics. First, to give authors sufficient planning time and freedom to arrive at a chapter-length account of their area of thinking which vividly shows both the progress and the problems in that area, with the author of each chapter free to find a workable proportion of new experimental contributions, review, and theory. This flexible approach means that formats vary among chapters and that author and editor require considerable patience of each other before the final organization of a chapter is realized. It also insures that none of the chapters will simply be reviews, and that none of the volumes will be "handbooks" or "reviews" or introductory texts. Rather, the volumes will try to capture the excitement and complexity of thinking and research at the growing, advancing edges of this broad field of children's language. The second tactic concerns the selection of topics for each volume. Again eschewing the general handbook or review approach there is no stress placed on representing all facets of children's language in one volume. The chapters placed within one volume are chosen because there are some common themes that tie subsets of them together and because each chapter is "due" in the following sense—the author's theoretical and experimental program has come to a point where a systematic account will be stimulating and perhaps catalytic to the work of other investigators.

In this second volume of *Children's Language* the topics covered diverge, as will the topics of many later volumes, from the traditional core of children's language studies. That core, the normal child's spoken words, sentences, and conversations, served well for Volume 1. However, it has become evident that to understand "language" and to understand how children acquire language, it is wise to look also at language forms other than speech and language acquirers who are not children—to wit, chimpanzees and gorillas. Further, it is appropriate to look at the kinds of in-context representations and communications that precede linguistic representations for the same contexts and events, as well as at the nature of cognitive and linguistic factors in acquisition of more than one language by an individual. These are the main angles of approach in Volume 2. Within these approaches are a subset of related theoretical questions.

A dual question runs through most of the chapters. How does the language-learner represent linguistic rules and categories, and how does the theorist represent the transitions in development from communication without certain rules to communication with the rules? In de Villiers' opening chapter provocative analyses are pursued which relate semantic and syntactic processes in acquisition. Maratsos and Chalkley look at these questions from a different perspective, encompassing evidence from cross-cultural acquisition and considerations of the child's memory and information-processing. Similarly, in bilingual acquisition Lindholm searches out cognitive components in the children's use of more than one spoken code. Greenfield and Dent address yet another edge of the cognition-language territory—how a child in a certain context chooses what to express linguistically and what to treat as less essential or less informative.

Still different perspectives arise when the symbols, phrases, and sentences used by nonhuman primates are examined. There may be a first blush of amazement when one reads that utterances such as the following have been produced by language-learners whose biological parents are chimpanzees or gorillas: "Angry bad sorry hug please" or "More me apple eat" (Nim); "Cereal want eat Koko" and "Lady eyemakeup there" (Koko); Adult —"What we play?" answered by "Me chase" (Moja); "Sherman want bread" (Sherman). Once the fact of such communication has been absorbed, a detailed analysis of utterances and their contexts is in order. And here we find again a concern with those dual questions of what cognitive processes lie behind the utterances and how can we account for transitions from less to more complexly structured utterances.

Another focus of recent theory concerns "input" language and the transition from early infant-caretaker exchanges in which the child primarily takes part by acting, to two-way communication in which both partners rely equally on language. Wells discusses how mothers can facilitate the child's progress in discourse and syntax. This kind of analysis is likely to be applied more and more in the future, and to both early and late stages of communicative growth for all modes of language and for all varieties of language-learners. Wells's own data on mother-child exchanges centers on the period between 15 and 42 months for the children. Beyond this, Wells presents some highly interesting longitudinal outcomes of early differences in language.

Modes, modes, modes! Any broad theory of language use and acquisition must be able to deal with the work of the past six years on the variety of forms which function well for linguistic communication. This volume begins, and the next two volumes in this series continue, an exploration of this general question by active researchers. Our theories need to include explanations of why some hearing children are better able to learn to communicate in sign language or printed visual symbols than in speech. More broadly, the play of cognitive, emotional, and linguistic factors in language acquisition in any mode by normal and exceptional children and by non-human language apprentices requires delineation. In the present volume, questions of similarities and differences between modes are directly and indirectly raised by the work with chimpanzees and gorillas. With their charges, Patterson (Koko), Terrace, Petitto, Sanders, and Bever (Nim), and the Gardners (Washoe, Moja, Pili, and Tatu) provide sign languge input and trace its acquisition. In contrast, Savage-Rumbaugh and Rumbaugh (Lana, Sherman, and Austin) place their language on sequences of visual computer keys. The language of input in this case receives a valuable separate analysis by Stahlke. Among the contrasting projects, a range of concerns, conclusions, and descriptive preferences is readily found, and the reader should give careful attention to the varied ways words like "symbol," "training," "spontaneous," and "imitation" are employed. These authors give fascinating treatment to such topics as ape-to-ape communication, inventiveness in language, and the structure of multisymbol utterances.

Overall, it is fair to say that the present contributors are working close to the border of advancing theory on language acquisition and the cognitive development enmeshed with language progress. Although no one can be certain just yet how a language-learner cracks the communicative code of his or her caretakers, and despite a consensus even on what "language" consists of, solid questions are being asked and crucial data are arriving month by month from researchers in vividly various modes. From this mix we are not likely to arrive soon at a unified theory, but we are getting close to some powerful and detailed competing models.

As the data and models evolve, they will be of interest to linguists, educators, psychologists, biologists, anthropologists, and many laypersons. More than that, much of the new information is likely to catch us off guard. For so long language was taken for granted, but now we see bracing progress in understanding the modes and variations of language and in specifying how memory, concepts, and linguistic skills unfold togeher developmentally. This is a period, to borrow from Ted Hughes's poem below, where much "else is alive" and will be arriving, in one form or another, to seize our attention and shake from us revised or newly born conclusions.

KEITH E. NELSON

*The Thought-Fox*

I imagine this midnight moment's forest
Something else is alive
Beside the clock's loneliness
And this blank page where my fingers move.

Through the window I see no star:
Something more near
Though deeper within darkness
Is entering the loneliness:

Cold, delicately as the dark snow
A fox's nose touches twig, leaf;
Two eyes serve a movement, that now
And again now, and now, and now

Sets neat prints into the snow
Between trees, and warily a lame
Shadow lags by stump and in hollow
Of a body that is bold to come

Across clearings, an eye,
A widening deepening greenness,
Brilliantly, concentratedly,
Coming about its own business

Till, with a sudden sharp hot stink of fox
It enters the dark hole of the head.
The window is starless still; the clock ticks,
The page is printed.

—Ted Hughes

# ACKNOWLEDGMENTS

Through some great luck, I have had the richest help when I needed it the most. Family thanks on many levels go to Madeline, Roena, Loide, and Craig Nelson, and to Ethel and Sam Coroniti.

Tutors and models have been numerous, but none more warmly appreciated than Bill Kessen. Finally, I think of all the support I have received from students, friends, and colleagues, with a special fondness for those who took professional risks to honor both personal relations and professional ethics.

K.E.N.

# CONTRIBUTORS

**T. G. BEVER**
*Department of Psychology, Columbia University, New York, New York*

**MARY ANNE CHALKLEY**
*Institute of Child Development, University of Minnesota, Minneapolis, Minnesota*

**CATHY HANKINS DENT**
*Department of Psychology, University of California, Los Angeles, California*

**JILL G. de VILLIERS**
*Department of Psychology, Smith College, Northampton, Massachusetts*

**R. ALLEN GARDNER**
*Department of Psychology, University of Nevada, Reno, Nevada*

**BEATRICE T. GARDNER**
*Department of Psychology, University of Nevada, Reno, Nevada*

**PATRICIA MARKS GREENFIELD**
*Department of Psychology, University of California, Los Angeles, California*

**KATHRYN J. LINDHOLM**
*Department of Psychology, University of California, Los Angeles, California*

**MICHAEL P. MARATSOS**
*Institute of Child Development, University of Minnesota, Minneapolis, Minnesota*

**FRANCINE G. PATTERSON**
*The Gorilla Foundation, 117820 Skyline Boulevard, Woodside, California*

**L. A. PETITTO**
*Department of Psychology, Columbia University, New York, New York*

**DUANE M. RUMBAUGH**
*Department of Psychology, Georgia State University, Atlanta, Georgia, Yerkes Regional Primate Research Center, Emory University, Atlanta, Georgia*

**R. J. SANDERS**
*Department of Psychology, Columbia University, New York, New York*

**E. SUE SAVAGE-RUMBAUGH**
*Yerkes Regional Primate Research Center, Emory University, Atlanta, Georgia*

**HERBERT F. W. STAHLKE**
*Department of English, Georgia State University, Atlanta, Georgia*

**H. S. TERRACE**
*Department of Psychology, Columbia University, New York, New York*

**GORDON WELLS**
*School of Education Research Unit, University of Bristol, Bristol, Wales, United Kingdom*

# CONTENTS

# 1

# THE PROCESS OF RULE LEARNING IN CHILD SPEECH: A NEW LOOK[1]

JILL G. DE VILLIERS

Recent years have witnessed a major change in the way psychologists view concept formation, and it has become increasingly clear that concepts once viewed as discrete or all-or-none instead possess internal structure. The implications of this change have carried over into the domain of language learning, where it appears that prototypes or best exemplars serve as focal points in learning the extension of words (Bowerman, 1977a). The present chapter will describe the theoretical and empirical work in these areas and raise the question: Might not grammatical categories also be viewed as having internal structure, with prototypes serving as focal points in the learning of grammatical rules? A speculative model of the process of rule learning will be explored as it relates to some preliminary empirical data.

## CONCEPT FORMATION

Traditionally, work in concept formation focused on artificial concepts whose attributes could be defined clearly: any instance having some predetermined concatenation of simple form or color attributes was a member of the category, such as "blue triangle with a red border" (Bruner, Goodnow, & Austin, 1956). The work in the laboratory was intended to provide a model for concepts in general, natural as well as artificial, but the lack of criterial attributes for concepts such as *dog* or *chair*—that is, features that were *always* present for category instances but *never* for members of other categories—led investigators to make up their own, better-behaved con-

1

cepts. There was the inherent belief that "real" concepts were merely less tractable concatenation of features, but not different in kind.

The revolution in the past decade has shown not only that the extension of such a model to natural concepts needs serious qualifications, but also the time-honored simple categories of form and color (and possibly even number) have internal psychological structure that the traditional approach fails to capture. Rosch (1975) describes the earlier approach as characterizing concepts as *digital*; that is, membership in a category is all-or-none. In contrast is her work demonstrating that many natural concepts are instead best considered *analog,* in that there are some very good examples, the prototype of the category, and other examples, not as good, which "surround" it. For natural concepts it makes sense to talk of degrees of membership in a category, and this internal structure has important consequences for learning and memory.

Posner and Keele (1968) were among the first to discuss concept formation in analog terms, though their experiments involved artificial concepts. These concepts were constructed by beginning with a simple dot pattern, say a triangle, then using a computer to generate distortions of the original by moving dots from their initial positions. The original pattern was the prototype for the set of patterns thus created, and the set had no discrete defining attributes. Subjects learned the resultant artificial concept on the basis of a set of examples varying in their "distance" from the prototype, and were then asked to judge the membership of new dot patterns that they had never seen. Some of the new examples were distortions even more remote than those that subjects had received in training, but the subjects proved capable of generalizing the concept to include them. If the initial training set had not included the prototype, subjects nevertheless saw it as an instance of the category when it was shown to them later. More strikingly, when asked to judge the exemplariness of instances, they found the initial pattern or prototype a better example than those on which they had been trained. Posner and Keele demonstrated that subjects were capable of abstracting a concept even when it was analog and had no defining attributes, and furthermore that the prototype—in this case the central tendency of the dot patterns—was an important organizer of the class and was considered the best example even if it was not one of the training stimuli.

Rosch's (1973, 1975) experiments were quite similar in methodology to this research, though she was dealing with natural concepts for which the prototype does not always coincide with the central tendency, where that notion is even meaningful. Her research began with the working hypothesis that there exist in the spectrum certain salient colors, coinciding with those areas that tend universally to be given names (Berlin & Kay, 1969). For the domain of form, the hypothesis was that there are certain "good" forms as in Gestalt psychology—the circle, square, and triangle—which attract attention, are more readily remembered, and so forth. The aim was to construct categories for an experiment on learning that either violated or capitalized upon the naturally occurring structure in the domains of color and form. The predictions were as follows:

1. It will be easier to learn categories when the variations center around a natural prototype than around an instance that is nonprototypical to the natural category.
2. The natural prototype will be learned first even if it is not central to the set of variations.
3. Subjects will consider the natural prototype the best example of the category even if it is not central.

As subjects in these learning experiments, Rosch used members of a Stone-Age culture, the Dani of New Guinea, whose language does not contain words for hues or for geometric forms. Each subject had to learn labels for eight categories constructed in a particular way. In one set, the central instance was the natural prototype—either the salient, focal color in that area of the spectrum, say a "true" red, or a good form such as a circle. In a different set, the central instance was a nonfocal color or form and the natural prototype was one of the variants on either side. In both domains the predictions were borne out. Categories that capitalized on the natural structure were learned consistently faster than those that did not. Natural prototypes were learned as exemplars more rapidly, and in the form domain they were more often chosen as the best examples even when they had not been central to the created categories. In the color domain the subjects found it impossible to make judgments of exemplariness.

Color and form categories seem to have internal structure that is universal and may be related to the physiology of our perceptual apparatus (McDaniel, 1974), but are the results of this research of any greater relevance to more complex concepts than was the older work on artificial concepts? For example, are semantic concepts such as *dog* or *chair* analog, with degrees of membership? Rosch's first experiment in semantic domains was designed to discover whether people in a given culture, in this case American college students, would consistently rank members of a category in the same way. The categories and names were taken from norms collected by Battig and Montague (1969) of the frequency with which an instance was given in response to the superordinate name. Subjects in their study had been asked to list all the examples they could think of for "flower," "furniture," "article of clothing," and so forth. In Rosch's study, subjects were asked to rate on a seven-point scale how well an instance reflected their "idea or image" of the category. Subjects showed substantial agreement, with "robin" overwhelmingly rated the "best" instance of a bird, "car" almost always the "best" vehicle, and so forth. However, the exemplariness ratings do not necessarily have anything to do with processing or using the category; they could be an interesting verbal by-product. In other experiments Rosch (1975) demonstrated that the rankings had predictive value for reaction times to statements such as, "A robin is a bird" versus "A penguin is a bird," finding that statements involving a prototype could be evaluated much more rapidly. In a second experiment, subjects were asked to judge whether or not a pair of instances was the same, and on some trials the category name was presented first as a prime. For example, the word *fruit* might be presented just before the pair *apple/apple*. The results indicated that priming facilitated time to judge *prototypical* instances, but actually delayed judgment for peripheral instances of the category. The implication is that the category name calls to mind the prototype rather than lists of criterial attributes. These are but two of the experiments Rosch has performed to demonstrate that the notions of prototype and degrees of membership have utility in describing concept formation and use not just for perceptual domains but also for semantic concepts.

The next question that must be addressed is: Where do prototypes come from? Why do concepts have the internal structure that they do? In the work of Posner (1969) and of Reed (1972), the prototype was constructed by the experimenter as the central tendency of the set of variations created by distorting an initial schematic form. In such cases the central tendency is the only prototype made available to the subjects. In the perceptual domains, it is suggested that the prototypes are salient because of the physiology of the human perceptual apparatus. In the semantic domain, it is likely that the culture has some influence; that is, prototypes may not be universally agreed upon but culture-specific, formed through principles of learning and information processing from the items given in a category. So, for instance, it might not be the case that South Sea Islanders and New Englanders would agree upon the same prototypical tree.

Rosch and Mervis (1975) explored the hypothesis that members of a category come to be viewed as prototypical of a category to the extent that they bear a family resemblance to (have attributes that overlap with) other members of the category. Conversely, the most prototypical instances of a category should overlap *least* with members of other categories, thus maximizing the separation between categories. Subjects in their experiment were asked to list the attributes of objects belonging to one of six categories: furniture, vehicles, fruit, weapons, vegetables, and clothing. It was found that few attributes were given that were true of all twenty members of a category. For example, *have pits* is not true of *all* fruits; neither is *round*. The rare attributes that were mentioned for all instances of a category—e.g., "you eat it" for all fruits—would not exclude members of other categories; in this case all foodstuffs. Thus, the attribute structure did not reveal criterial attributes common to all and only members of one category, but instead the attributes true of some but not all of the instances. Unique attributes were evenly distributed across each category; that is, they were as likely to be listed for prototypical instances as for peripheral ones. The majority of attributes listed demonstrated a family resemblance relationship for each of the six categories. This family resemblance structure proved to be highly correlated with prototypicality, such that the more an item had attributes in common with other members of the category, the more likely it was to be considered a "good" member of the category. A second experiment showed that prototypes shared the smallest number of attributes with members of contrasting categories. The importance of this research lies in the demonstration that "prototype" models of concept formation are not necessarily in conflict with cue validity models, in which the stimuli that gain control over behavior have the most *valid* attributes—that is, attributes that are most highly predictive of category membership. Prototypes are those items with the highest cue validity for a category; hence choosing them as the best representatives of a category is not arbitrary. The Rosch and Mervis paper is also an answer to critics who might view the initial findings on ratings or reaction times as reflecting only the labeling and association practices of one particular culture. There is a more basic reason for the primacy of some category members than, say, their frequency of association with the superordinate label.

A prediction that follows from this account of attribute structure is that new attributes should be seen as having greater cue validity if learned about the prototype than if learned about a peripheral instance. Specifically, if one taught a new property, teaching it with respect to the prototype should result in greater generalization within the category than teaching it about a peripheral instance, since prototypes share more attributes with other members than do peripheral instances. Rips (1976) tested that prediction in an experiment in which he taught subjects that either a prototypical member of a category, or a peripheral member, had a particular characteristic. In one version, the category was *birds;* the characteristic was affliction with a contagious disease. Subjects were asked to estimate the probability of other birds also contracting the disease, and it was found that the extent to which the characteristic was generalized was a function of the typicality of the bird for which it was taught, as well as the similarity between it and the other birds. Thus the similarity between two instances was weighted by their *typicality* to that category.

## Developmental Evidence for the Internal Structure of Concepts

Is there any evidence that the foregoing model of conceptual structure has value in accounting for the way children learn concepts and labels in the first place? Bornstein (1975) has shown that at as young an age as four to five months, infants spend more time looking at primary focal colors than at intermediate colors. Heider (1971) and Johnson (1977) both observed a fairly stable order of acquisition of basic color terms, the order for most children being: red, green, black, white, orange, yellow, blue, pink, brown, and purple. Most of the earliest color words are for focal colors, with the exception of orange, probably since it is also the name of a familiar fruit. Heider (1971) found better recognition of focal than non-focal colors by three-year-olds. The primacy of the focal color words in acquisition lends support to the idea that their saliency is somewhat independent of experience.

In semantic domains, it has become evident that children do not always extend their first words on the basis of defining features of the objects they denote. From a detailed study of the language of her two daughters, Christy and Eva, Bowerman (1977a) concluded that many of their early word uses were *complexive.* By this she meant that the children did not consistently regard any single attribute as criterial for the word's use; instead they shifted from one feature to another in successive uses of the word.

For example, the child might learn the word *doggie* for dog, then extend it to other furry things, such as blankets; to other four-legged things, such as horses; and to other moving things, such as spiders. This kind of complexive organization was noted earlier by Vygotsky (1962), Brown (1965), and Bloom (1973a), but these writers suggested that it was a primitive stage of word learning that is later replaced by the more systematic use of sets of defining features which apply to all instances named by a word. However, Bowerman points out that both types of word meaning seem to be present from the start in the child's vocabulary.

Bowerman (1977a) argued that the uses of the word clustered around a prototype which generally constituted the first referent for which the word was used. In addition, it was the referent for which the word had been introduced and most often modeled by the parents. Take, for example, Eva's word, *moon.* The prototype was the real moon, having the properties (a) *shape:* circular, crescent, or half moon; (b) *color:* yellow; (c) *surface:* shiny; (d) *viewing position:* seen at an angle from below; (e) *dimensionality:* flat; (f) *background:* broad expanse. Eva called the following other referents, among others, *moon:* a half grapefruit seen at an angle from below (properties a, b, d in common with prototype), a lemon slice (a, b, e), the dial on a dishwasher (a, c, d, e, f), a shiny leaf (a, c, e), circles on a wall hanging (a, d, e, f), half a cheerio cereal (a, [b?]), hangnails (a, e). Notice that the prototype shares one or more properties with all of the referents, but they share less in common with each other. In this case there was one constant feature of shape, but that was not always true for other categories. Hence the children's complexive word meanings are not unstructured chains of constantly shifting meanings; rather they seem to have internal structure characterized by a prototype and a set of variations around it, having an attribute structure much like the adult word use revealed by Rosch and Mervis (1975).

The question is left open at present as to how these prototypes arise. Bowerman (1977b) argues that for some cases, such as the real moon, the prototype might have had prelinguistic salience. In other cases the prototype might have been supplied by the adults, with frequency of exposure making some items salient in a not-yet-organized domain, hence influencing how the domain becomes structured. Brown (1977) suggested there might be a strong tendency for adults to supply a name first in connection with a prototypical referent; thus a collie, not a chihuahua, for the category *dog;* a chair, not a magazine rack, as examples of *furniture.* With the naturalistic data it is not possible to tease apart the variables of frequency of exposure and preexisting salience, or to distinguish their contribution to the process of forming prototypes on the basis of their representativeness of a set of instances, in terms of most overlapping attributes. One might imagine a teaching experiment with very young children in the process of learning their first words, some of whom would learn a word first in connection with the referent considered prototypical by adults, others of whom would learn it first in connection with a peripheral instance of the category. If new instances were then controlled in frequency for the two groups and extensions of the word followed closely, would the prototypes come to resemble one another, or would the categories become organized around distinct prototypes?

Other researchers have provided evidence for conceptual structure in children much like that in adults. Anglin (1977) found two- to four-year-old children in an experimental task were much more likely to use a category label for prototypical members and fail to use it for peripheral members of a category. For example, giraffes were more readily characterized as *animals* than were butterflies, despite the greater frequency of the latter in the child's experience. Mulford (1977) presented data that confirm the existence of internal structure in categories for three- to five-year-olds in a sorting task. Rosch (1973) performed an experiment with ten-year-olds which mirrored the one she had done with adults; namely, measuring reaction times to statements such as; "A robin is a bird." She found the same relationship existed between high prototypicality and low reaction time, and to a greater degree for children than for adults. This suggests prototypes are even more salient in children's concepts.

Work by Carey and Smith (1977) on children's developing knowledge of the concept of *animal* is suggestive of the role that prototypes play in the acquisiton of knowledge. Children were found to be more willing to attribute animal properties such as *eats, breathes,* or *has a heart,* to prototypical animals such as humans or mammals, than to fish or insects, which are not normally considered prototypical for the animal category. Prototypical animals were assigned many properties, peripheral animals only one or two, and none of the properties seemed criterial. To determine whether the prototype played any role in *learning* such properties, Carey and Smith taught a new property (e.g., *has a spleen*) about either a prototypical member (human) or a peripheral member (fly). Then they tested for generalization of this property to other animals. When taught about humans, the property *has a spleen* showed the same generalization gradient to other animals as had the untrained properties *eats, breathes, sleeps,* and so forth, lending credence to the hypothesis that they too had been learned first about the prototype. However, when learned about a fly, the property *has a spleen* showed minimal generalization. The experiment is similar to Rip's (1976) experiment on contagious disease and is convincing evidence that for young children as well as adults, prototypes in conceptual structure are foci for learning new attributes and for mediating their generalization.

A more direct demonstration comes from a study with children by Mervis (1976). She designed a category of toys designed to have a family resemblance structure, and taught it to children, using either good or poor exemplars in training. Her subjects learned the category much faster when taught with a good exemplar than with a peripheral one, and often generalized only minimally to a new exemplar when taught with the peripheral exemplar. Upon seeing the whole category, more than one child remarked, "If you'd only shown me *that* one [pointing to the prototype], I would have known what you meant!"

## GRAMMATICAL CATEGORIES

### Formal Approaches

The revolution in theories of concept formation and use has not yet led to a reconsideration by psychologists of categories in other domains that have traditionally been treated as all-or-none, such as grammatical rules. In this section, some assumptions about grammar will be explored and re-examined in the light of the work in concept formation.

Many writers have suggested that categories are defined ultimately by their function; that is, by the relationships into which the category members may enter. It is what *dogs* or *cats* either do or are used for that gives the individual instances their membership in the class. Once this is allowed, it does not make the problem of similarity disappear since functional equivalence still has to be recognized, though it is possible to allow changing sets of perceptual attributes as cues to an object's function (Nelson, 1974).

In the domain of grammatical "objects," categories are defined by their use; that is, notions such as *noun, noun phrase, subject,* or *sentence* cannot be defined in isolation but only in relation to other entities. They are defined by the relationships or rules into which they can enter, not by the properties they possess in isolation. Furthermore, according to traditional grammatical treatments, grammatical rules are all-or-none in their application: there can be no degrees of membership of categories such as *noun* or *sentence.* The logic of most grammars is thus discrete, as it was for earlier approaches to concepts in other domains.

According to the standard version of transformational grammer (Chomsky, 1965), rules operate on entities of a highly abstract nature that cannot be identified by either surface characteristics of sentences or by what they refer to in the world. For example, the passive transformation does not entail moving around the first and last words in a sentence, nor the first and last noun phrases; nor is it useful to summarize the operation as exchanging the noun phrases playing the semantic roles of *agent* and *patient.* Instead, the passive transformation permutes the deep structure entities of *subject* and *object,* which are defined formally in terms of the base phrase structure configuration. Similarly, some linguistic operations require postulating the category *subject* that is not isomorphic with any particular semantic role or set of semantic roles, but is more abstract, as in the following sentences where the subject is italicized and the semantic role of that noun phrase is shown in parentheses (after Fillmore, 1968):

| | |
|---|---|
| *John* opened the door. | (agent) |
| *The key* opened the door. | (instrument) |
| *The door* opened. | (object affected) |
| *John* heard the door open. | (experiencer) |

But if *subject,* for example, is defined by the relationships or rules into which it can enter, and if one can state the rules only by introducing the abstract category *subject,* is this not circular? How do speakers go beyond what they hear, to make creative extensions of rules to *new* subjects and so forth? The answer provided by Maratsos and Chalkley in Chapter 3 is that privileges of occurrence in linguistic environments are correlated; that is, they predict each other. Knowing that a form can be used in one construction allows us to infer that it can be used in another. Consider, for example, that we hear the word *flum* in a sentence such as, "I bought a flum." We can predict other potential uses: "The flum was great," "I really like your flum," "Flums are a godsend"; but not: "Have you flummed?" "Well, flum me!" or "What a flummy hat!"

In summary, formal approaches to language use privileges of occurrence, often defined in the abstract, to define categories independent of their meaning. Rules apply across the board; they do not permit degrees of membership.

## Semantic Approaches

Semantic approaches to grammar emphasize that much important information is lost by allowing only formal considerations—that it is necessary to preserve information such as whether the subject denotes an agent, beneficiary, experiencer, or the like. Fillmore (1968) argued that knowledge of semantic roles was critical to discussing the rules for sentence formation. Other linguists have argued that the level of formal deep structure is not necessary for describing grammar; that the deep structure of sentences might be directly semantic in nature (e.g., McCawley, 1968; Chafe, 1970). However, not all aspects of meaning are relevant to sentence formation. In describing the event "John pushed the car," the fact that John is an *agent* is relevant, but not that he is *male* or *human*. That push is an *action* has consequences for the grammmar, but that it involves *surface contact* does not, for example. In this way, generalization of rules would be a function of similarity along certain semantic dimensions, but not for other dimensions that have no effect upon sentence structure.

## Lexical Approaches

Quite recently several linguists have argued that the lexicon, given scant attention by standard transformational grammar, can be expanded in ways which have broad implications for grammatical analysis. The motivation for these changes came from a variety of sources and need not concern us here, but one major change that has taken place is that many structure-dependent transformations, such as the passive, have been eliminated in favor of an expanded lexicon. In the lexical approach of Bresnan (1978), the passive transformation disappears and passive verbs such as (be) *eat*(en) are separate entries in the lexicon from their active counterparts; in this case, *eat*. The lexicon incorporates information about the argument structure of individual verbs; that is, whether they have one-place relations such as *x sleep,* where *sleep* is intransitive, or two-place relations for transitive verbs such as *hit,* in *x hit y.* Also encoded next to individual verbs is information relevant to the functional structures into which they can enter; that is, the grammatical roles that their noun phrases play in sentences. For example, in the sentence $NP_1$ *hit* $NP_2$, $NP_1$ is the grammatical subject, and $NP_2$ is the object. Passive verbs are treated in the same way; they have separate entries in the lexicon and distinct functional structures allowing for the fact that the logical subject can be eliminated, as in the sentence, *John was hit.* The active-passive relation summarizes the relation between the active and passive entries of a set of verbs, but in no sense is the passive *derived* from an activelike base structure, as in traditional treatments.

For our present purposes we need mention only that much more information about syntactic possibilities is encoded in the lexicon, and major grammatical rules are no longer conceived of as operating in all-or-none fashion over all of a particular formally-defined class such as *noun* or *verb.* The implication is that there is a great deal of rote memorization at the individual word level, as opposed to highly formal analyses that are neutral with respect to the semantics of the individual words or other entities.

## DEVELOPMENTAL EVIDENCE
## OF THE NATURE OF GRAMMATICAL RULES

### Formal Approaches

The three approaches we have outlined have had their counterparts in the study of child language, often after a lag of several years. Investigation of grammatical development was given fresh impetus by Chomsky's (1957, 1965) proposals about the highly abstract and universal nature of human language, and many of the findings in child language seemed in keeping with those formulations. It was argued that since linguistic rules operate at an abstract level on entities that bear no simple relation to either surface forms or meanings, the child had to have hypotheses in advance of language learning that would narrow the possible grammars he would invent on the basis of the input. One such proposal (McNeill, 1966) was that the child should expect the major structural analysis of sentences to fall into relations such as *subject* and *predicate, modifier* and *noun, verb* and *object.* McNeill contended that Brown's (1973) three subjects, Adam, Eve, and Sarah, showed evidence in their earliest speech that they were constructing sentences on the basis of these abstract formulas. Their simple sentences seemed to be *verb + object* and *modifier + noun* constructions, but not *subject + predicate.* McNeill hypothesized that the children were "deleting" subjects from their sentences, and then the formulas seemed close to the abstract phrase structures of adult sentences.

Other investigators (Bowerman, 1973; Brown, 1973; Schlesinger, 1974) have argued that the evidence for abstract grammatical rules is lacking for early child speech. For instance, Bowerman (1973) pointed out that if children's sentences do reflect the abstract phrase structure of *subject* and *predicate,* one would expect at the very least that the subject noun phrase ought to show weaker links to the verb than the object noun phrase, as the latter two together form the verb phrase:

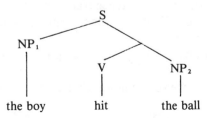

Bowerman performed a distributional analysis of data from several children and found no evidence that they observed that basic requirement, since there was a greater likelihood that they would produce the two constituents $NP_1 + V$ than the predicate $V + NP_2$. Thus, there is not distributional evidence to support a subject-predicate distinction in early child speech.

## Semantic Approaches

Other researchers have denied that the abstract notion of *subject* exists in child speech since rules that act on formally defined categories seem to be absent. At the beginning there is no evidence that rules generalize independently of semantic considerations. For instance, while it may be economical for adult grammar to propose a rule for ordering *subject* and then *verb,* rather than a host of particular rules for ordering agents, beneficiaries, experiencers, and the like, there is evidence that the child's rules are formulated with respect to these *semantic* relations. To give a concrete example: a child might have in his speech a large number of constructions such as *Daddy eat, Mommy drive, Me fall, Jimmy carry,* and so forth, which could be summarized by a rule such as: sentence = subject + verb. However, there might at the same time be no evidence of constructions such as *Daddy wear, Mommy see, I like,* suggesting that the generalizations the child is making are narrower in scope than *subject + verb* and are probably more accurately captured by the rule *agent + action,* which would not permit generalization to nonactions such as *wear, see,* or *like.*

Brown (1973) summarized the evidence on the earliest utterances of children learning many different languages and concluded that they begin by expressing a small set of semantic relations such as *agent + action, action + object* and *possessor + possessed,* and that these generalizations are in keeping with the child's cognitive development at age two years or so, when syntax begins to be used.

Formulations like the above are in keeping with the semantically based approaches to adult grammar of Fillmore (1968), Chafe (1970), and others. If, however, the true characterization of adult grammar relies on rules that are semantically independent, it remains a vexing problem to know how a child would arrive at the adult competence from such a beginning. Some investigators have proposed that just as rules such as *agent + action* are an economy compared to rules governing the placement of individual *words,* so when children learn major sentence transformations such as the passive, there is an economy in collapsing semantic rules into more formal generalizations (e.g., Bowerman, 1973). In that view, formal grammar may not be a good initial description, but it is the end point of the language learning process.

Is there any evidence for semantically based rules at a point beyond the very start of language learning? When the child begins to add inflections to his simple sentences, we have another source of evidence for the hypothesis that rules are semantically bound. One of the first pieces of data was presented by Gvozdev (1961) and highlighted by Bowerman (1973). The child studied by Gvozdev learned Russian, which has an accusative marker; that is, an inflection on the direct object. The child first learned to mark patients of action verbs such as *hit, push,* and *throw,* only later extending it to the objects of verbs such as *read* or *draw,* which entail a different semantic relationship between verb and object. This was evidence to suggest he had defined the scope of the grammatical marker more narrowly at first, to be a *semantic* marker.

Brown (1973) presented evidence from three children studied longitudinally, indicating that grammatical morphemes such as inflections do not enter speech in an all-or-none fashion; rather the probability of their use increases only gradually. Bloom, Lifter, and Tanouye (1977) studied the tense markers: the progressive, *ing,* regular and irregular forms of the past tense, and the third person singular *-s* as they emerged in six children observed over time. The main finding of their research was that the children's use of the inflections interacted in interesting ways with the semantics of the verbs to which they attach. The progressive *ing* was correctly used most often with action verbs that have continuous duration and no clear end result; for example, *singing.* Verbs that encode achievements that do have an end result and are punctual or momentary in duration were most frequently correctly inflected with the past tense; e.g., *he closed it.* The third person marker *-s* occurred most reliably with verbs that characterize the placement of an object; e.g., *goes, sits, fits.* It should be emphasized that the result is over and above any differences in the frequency of the *contexts* for use of the inflections. That is, at the same time that a child consistently supplied the past tense for a verb such as *close* or *eat,* he would fail to supply it where it was *obligatory* for such verbs as *sing* or *walk.* The grammatical markers were used at first over a limited semantic class; only later does that class become as diverse as that of verbs in adult speech.

Bloom et al. do not interpret the data in quite that way. They argue convincingly that the inflections do not mark tense at first, but are instead redundant aspect markers. That is, progressive *ing* does not mark present tense over a limited semantic range, but rather *duration* of the activity; the past tense is not used for *past* actions but for *brief* ones. A similar conclusion was reached by Bronckart and Sinclair (1973) in a study of how French children describe events. The experimenters showed the children events that varied as to the type of result, frequency, and duration of the action; e.g., a horse jumps over a fence, a truck slowly pushes a car into a garage, a fish swims in a basin. Afterward the children used the *passé composé* to describe actions with a clear result, the *présent* or *passé com-*

*posé* for actions with no intrinsic aim, and the *present* for actions that have no result. The conclusion was that children use the French verbal auxiliary to code aspect, not tense, until the age of six years.

What is needed is a detailed study of the broadening use of the inflections to a greater variety of verb types, to determine when the inflections become tense markers rather than aspect markers. Brown's three subjects reached 90 percent criterion of use in obligatory contexts well before age six, implying that the inflection was being used appropriately for the majority of verbs at that point regardless of their semantics. However, one would need to take a detailed look at the distribution of the obligatory contexts themselves to be sure that it was not heavily biased towards the easiest verb types for a given morpheme. For example, the majority of obligatory contexts for the past tense might denote brief actions, and the child might mark sufficient numbers of those verbs to reach criterion while still producing no past tenses on continuous action verbs.

As Maratsos (1978) points out, there is nothing inherent in the meaning of verbs that decides ultimately whether they can take a past tense morpheme. The fact that children are capable of crossing semantic categories and observing distributional rules is demonstrated by the child's overregularization of forms such as *seed* and *thinked,* neither of which are action verbs. So children do not maintain the hypothesis that only action verbs take the *-ed* ending, though it is possible that they begin with that strategy. Maratsos also cautions that one must distinguish the case of the semantic category forming the *basis* for generalization, from the case where the child is better able to analyze the past *meaning* for certain individual verbs than others. As a way of distinguishing these alternatives empirically, he suggests looking at naturalistic data for a child who had regular past tense endings for all semantic categories of verbs (presumably older children than in Bloom et al.'s [1977] study). Then one could study the overgeneralization of the *-ed* ending to irregular forms and determine whether it was semantically bounded; e.g., extended to action verbs as in *runned* or *bited* but not to nonaction verbs such as *thought* or *knew*. In this way, any limits on overgeneralization would not be due to a failure to recognize the meaning of pastness for certain semantic classes of verbs, but would indicate a semantic basis for generalization. Maratsos, Kuczaj, Fox, and Chalkley (in press) believe there is no good evidence for this strong claim.

When major structural transformations like the passive enter child speech, is there any evidence for across-the-board generalizations of a formal character? Maratsos et al. (in press) report that at first, children can understand action-verb passives such as "The dog was bitten by the cat," but not passives with nonaction verbs such as "The boy was remembered by the man," even when they controlled for the children's understanding of the verbs themselves. Therefore, the child's comprehension of this syntactic form is semantically bounded at first. There are other pertinent results with the passive which are best delayed until discussion of the lexical approach.

## Lexical Approaches

The idea that children begin syntax with formulae for combining *words* originated with Braine's (1963) notion of *pivot grammar.* A pivot grammar involved learning the position of certain key words, then forming sentences around them. Disagreement arose over the universality of that approach among children, and the extent to which it represented the true knowledge of those children whose data it did describe (Bloom, 1973b). Nevertheless, it remains the case that whenever stringent syntactic criteria are applied to the earliest sentences, some children appear to be learning formulas that are even narrower in scope than the semantic relations proposed by Brown (1973) and others (e.g., Leonard, 1976).

Braine (1976), for example, used data from several published sources as well as his own samples of child speech to decide upon the correct level of description of the first linguistic rules. He searched for distributional evidence that would permit subdivisions of broad semantic classifications, and frequently he found it. For example, a child might have a great many expressions involving the attributes of some object, as in: *little one, block red, truck blue, big dog, sock white.* Instead of describing this as a rule for expressing *attribute + entity,* with variable word order, Braine would subdivide the classification into, say, *size + entity* and *entity + color,* which do have fixed word order. Some of the formulae Braine discovered were even narrower than that, involving individual *words;* e.g., *hot X,* much as in pivot grammar. Bowerman (1976) likewise argues that for one of her children: "The early rules for combining words did not operate on *categories* of words, such as 'action' or 'modifier,' that could include more than one exemplar. Rather, each word was treated as a semantic isolate, in the sense that the ability to combine it with other words was not accompanied by a parallel ability to make two-word utterances with semantically related words" (p. 156). So Eva had formulas as *more X, want X* and so forth, and Bowerman could find no evidence that Eva proceeded at a later point to introduce economy into her rule system by using broad semantic classifications. Instead, she apparently went from a set of rules based on individual lexical items to a set of formal rules for sentence making.

There appear to be quite significant individual differences during this period in the scope of the generalizations children can make, and it would be interesting to know whether these differences are related to such variables as the age or cognitive development of the child at the beginning of sentence construction, or even the size of his vocabulary. One might guess, for instance, that children who go through a prolonged holophrastic period

scribe the more diverse events (experiencer, instrumental, and objective) by a two-word sentence with subject-verb word order? In other words, did children, despite their semantically limited training, learn a rule governing *subject-verb* placement? Inspection of Table I (from Leonard, 1975) reveals that they used subject-verb sentences for all events to the same degree as the children taught on the diverse relations.

Leonard's results are somewhat surprising given the conclusions for naturalistic data about rules of limited semantic scope. The group taught a semantically-bounded rule; in fact, entertained a broader rule for subject-verb constructions. Leonard offers some suggestions about why that might be so. The agentive relations included both action verbs (*walk, eat*) and nonaction verbs (*read, hold*), and thus was actually not as narrow as it might have been. Such experience might prepare the child quite well for relations of the experiencer kind in which an animate noun is combined with a verb denoting other than a physical action (e.g., girl sleep), and also for relations such as the instrumental, which is essentially an inanimate agent. Nevertheless, the fact that children extended the rule on the basis of these shared properties to the same degree as children trained on all four types, is impressive evidence that they went beyond the information given. Leonard asked whether the children might have generalized along the dimension physical action/event rather than the nature of the noun-verb relationship, since all relations included both physical activities (e.g., walk) and motionless events (e.g., sleep). However, the difference between the two classes of events failed to reach statistical significance.

One aspect of Leonard's data that he does not mention is the consistent order of difficulty of the four types of events: agent, experiencer, objective, and instrumental, an ordering that seems to be independent of the training received. Suppose another group of children had been trained just on instrumental events. Would their generalization be the same? To tempt the

**Table I**
**Mean Number of Subject-Verb Constructions Produced**
**by Children in Leonard's (1975) Experiment**

| | Type of Training | | |
|---|---|---|---|
| | **Situational** | **Situational** | **Nonsituational** |
| **Semantic Relations** | **Agentive only** | **All four semantic relations** | **All four semantic relations** |
| Agentive | 5.00 | 5.00 | 1.33 |
| Experiencer | 3.17 | 4.00 | 0.67 |
| Objective | 1.83 | 3.00 | 0.33 |
| Instrumental | 1.50 | 2.33 | 0.33 |

reader onward, and to make the first tentative link with the first section of this chapter, could the agentive relation constitute some kind of *prototype* for the subject-verb construction? Perhaps Leonard's choice of training materials was serendipitous, in that training about a prototype we know is more successful than training about a peripheral instance of a category. But what would it mean for grammatical constructs to have internal structure?

## NONCATEGORICAL GRAMMAR

In a series of recent papers, Ross (1972, 1974a) has made the proposal that the theory of grammar can be changed from a discrete theory to a non-discrete one. For instance, instead of requiring a grammar to partition strings of words into well-formed versus ill-formed, a grammar should only impose an ordering on those strings to the effect that A is *better* formed than B. In 1972, he offered evidence that formal categories such as *noun, adjective,* and *verb* are not discrete categories but rather have fuzzy boundaries, with some instances better than others. He proposed that a hierarchy relates those categories, based on observations that some syntactic processes apply more to verbs than to adjectives, some apply more to adjectives than to nouns, and so forth:

verb > present > perfect > passive > adjective > adjectival > noun
participle   participle   participle                      noun

As one example, he cites the rule permitting the placement of *it* before factive complements. The process is permitted following several verbs:

I { resent, hate, regret, appreciate, etc. } it that you used a hanky.

but possibly only one adjective: "I am aware of it that you didn't have to," and no nouns: "Her regret of it that you did was feigned."

Ross also described how some noun phrases are better than others, in that they enter into more constructions than others. Noun phrases such as *accurate tabs* in "Accurate tabs were kept on his account" are not readily used as an initial sentence topic: "Accurate tabs, they were kept on his account," unlike some "true" noun phrases: "Academia, it's greatly overrated." Ross argues that not only can noun phrases be ordered hierarchically from "best" to "worst" in terms of the number of rules they can enter, but the syntactic operations themselves can be ordered in terms of their "choosiness" in accepting noun phrases. So, in the above, the passive was less "choosy" than topicalization. Ross envisions noun phrases or other formal objects being assigned values on a scale of, say, *nouniness,* and syntactic operations requiring different thresholds of "nouniness" for the resultant sentence to be acceptable.

Ross has proposed a great many nondiscrete processes of the type described, which he has combined into a partial theory of their interrelationships (1974b). Basically it says that languages have a "center" and a "periphery," with syntactic processes applying more reliably to the center than the periphery. The logic is that while some processes *require* central instances—e.g., high values on "nouniness"—there are *no* processes that require peripheral instances. Some examples are:

1. There is no process that requires stative predicates, but there are some processes that require active predicates.
2. There are some processes that allow only true noun phrases; there are no processes that allow only fake noun phrases.
3. There are some processes that operate only within clauses; none that operate only across clauses.

As corollaries of this theoretical framework, Ross (1974b) proposed that the "center" of a language is learned first, that in historical change and in aphasia the periphery is the first to be lost, that variation in general is greater at the periphery, and so forth.

For our present purposes, note that Ross's (1974a) paper appeared with the title "Three batons for cognitive psychology," and asked psychologists, "Are there areas of investigation for which discrete systems have traditionally been assumed but for which nondiscrete treatment would make more sense?" It is time to assess the parallel between the proposals made by Ross for nondiscrete grammars, and those made for classification in general by Rosch.

## PARALLELS IN GRAMMATICAL
## AND NATURAL CATEGORIES

The premises of the two theories are virtually identical: that membership in a category (such as "noun phrase" or "animal") is by degrees rather than all-or-none; that the boundaries of categories are fuzzy rather than absolute. There is evidence in both cases that adults can rank category membership in a reliable fashion, though linguistics being what it is, the intuitions of Ross and his coworkers will have to be taken in lieu of the tabulated responses of four hundred college sophomores. Are there, however, any further parallels in grammar to the findings that the prototype is acquired first and serves as an organizer of experience, that teaching a category in which the prototype is central makes it easier to learn than teaching a category with a peripheral member central? To make the analogy more concrete, it is necessary to make a more detailed comparison of the two types of classification: in the case of grammar we would not be teaching a superordinate *name* for the category such as "animal" or "blue," but rather that the set of exemplars can enter into some superordinate rule; that is, be treated as equivalent for some higher order syntactic process. Thus the process of category formation is indirect in the case of grammar, the existence of the category being inferred from the generalization of the syntactic process. The difference may be more apparent than real, however, in non-laboratory learning.

To give an example, in Leonard's experiment the "category" to be acquired was the class of subject-verb sentences, and one would hypothesize that certain members of that class might be more representative or prototypical than others. Suppose animate agents are the best examples of subjects, and action verbs the best examples of verbs. That would account for why the children trained only on agentive constructions, the prototype, learned the category as well as children trained on all four constructions. It would also explain the fact that subject-verb production was easiest for agentive, next easiest for experiencer, and hardest for objective and instrumental even for children who received an equal amount of training on each type. Of course, Leonard's experiment was not designed to show this effect, so it is lacking in one important respect. No group received training only on the instances of the class hypothesized to be peripheral.

The experiment that follows was structured initially exactly like Leonard's, in that our purpose was to tease apart the child's learning of a semantically constrained rule versus his broad application after semantically limited training. In the course of conducting the experiment, the analogy between the work in concept formation and in grammar finally broke through to consciousness, and a final control group was added to the design. The results are preliminary at present, but so provocative as they stand that it is impossible not to report them. After discussing these results, some new directions are considered for the study of how grammatical rules are learned.

## A STUDY OF RULE LEARNING

### Design

The experiment was designed to examine generalization in children's spontaneous production of a rule following training, much like Leonard's experiment. The rules chosen were those for the passive—The boy is being pushed by the girl—and cleft constructions—It is the boy that the girl is pushing. These rules are not commonly present in the spontaneous speech of children of the age group 3–5 years who served as subjects. Whitehurst, Ironsmith, and Goldfein (1974) had used a modeling technique successfully to teach the passive to a group of 4–6-year-olds, but their experiment had two problems. One was the lack of a pretest of passive comprehension, so that one cannot be certain that some of their subjects did not already control the passive voice. The second problem was that Whitehurst et al. trained and tested passive sentences of the identical semantic type. They all described pictured events in which one animal performed an action on another animal, so generalization of the construction to different sorts of events could not be determined.

To correct these problems, the present experiment included a comprehension pretest and posttest on reversible passive and cleft sentences. Half of the children received training on clefts, and half on passives, so their diverging production skills could be contrasted (Nelson, 1977). As an additional interest, half of the children received imitation training, in which they were required to imitate sentences from the experimenter; and half received expansion training, in which the experimenter expanded their own attempts into a correct cleft or passive sentence.

The variable of real interest, however, was the semantics of the sentences trained and tested in generalization trials. The initial aim was to train children to produce passive (or cleft) sentences about pictured events that involved two animals and a reversible action (e.g., The pig hits the sheep—called here a *type A* event), then to test generalization to pictured events increasingly distant from that model; e.g., in which the patient is inanimate (The pig pulls the wagon—*type B* event), and finally in which the verb is less of an action (The lion reads the book—*type C* event). Would subjects form a semantically limited rule for the passive or cleft construction, and be incapable of producing that construction when the event semantics changed slightly? Within a short period of testing it was evident that this was the case, in that subjects restricted their use of the passive (or cleft) to type A events. It was obviously prudent to add a further group of subjects who received the opposite training, on type C events such as "The lion reads the book" to see if the children were constrained to an equal but opposite degree to produce only passives of *that* semantic type. In fact it will be shown that subjects trained on type C events instead preferred to use the passive for type A events, showing the same rather than the opposite generalization gradient. The asymmetry triggered the analogy between this work and the concept formation work which led to the present chapter. The details of the experiment are reported next, and then the question is raised: if these data do show asymmetry of generalization around a prototype, what kind of prototype could it be?

## Stimuli

Children received 40 pictures per session. Twenty of these constituted the training set, and the other 20 constituted the generalization trials or probes, pictures they had to describe spontaneously. For the 4 groups of children trained on type A events, the probe set consisted of 10 probes drawn from the same universe as the models (type A), 5 probes of type B and 5 of type C (see Table II). The fifth group of subjects who received training on type C events received 10 type C probes, 5 type B, and 5 type A probes (see Table III). Four out of five verbs in the probes had not been used in training; there was a single verb in common between training and probe examples.

## Subjects

The subjects were 37 children between the ages of 2.10 and 4.10 who were enrolled in nursery schools in the Boston area which drew from a variety of socioeconomic levels. Each child received a pretest of comprehension of 10 passives and 10 clefts of the reversible variety, and only children who scored less than 7 out of 10 on both clefts and passives were used as sub-

### Table II
### Stimuli for Subjects Trained on Type A Events

#### Type A training set

| | | | |
|---|---|---|---|
| boy lift kangaroo | sheep lick cow | horse push cow | kangaroo kiss horse |
| kangaroo lift boy | rabbit lick dog | cow push horse | boy kiss girl |
| gorilla lift elephant | dog lick rabbit | rabbit tickle pig | girl kiss boy |
| elephant lift gorilla | sheep push monkey | pig tickle rabbit | cow pull boy |
| cow lick sheep | monkey push sheep | horse kiss kangaroo | boy pull cow |

#### Probes

| Type A | Type B | Type C |
|---|---|---|
| monkey pat boy | pig pull cart | lion read book |
| boy pat monkey | horse lick cup | gorilla play piano |
| pig hit sheep | rabbit throws ball | dog smoke pipe |
| sheep hit pig | cat scratch tree | tiger smell flower |
| alligator bite monkey | dog bite chair | pig play trumpet |
| monkey bite alligator | | |
| rabbit lift frog | | |
| frog lift rabbit | | |
| pig squirt elephant | | |
| elephant squirt pig | | |

**Table III**
**Stimuli for Subjects Trained on Type C Events**

**Type C training set**

| | | | |
|---|---|---|---|
| bear read map | kangaroo play record | bird wear boot | elephant carry book |
| lion read book | dog play guitar | dog blow whistle | rabbit hold lamp |
| horse read magazine | elephant wear dress | tiger blow bubble | turtle hold kite |
| mouse read newspaper | pig wear pants | elephant blow candle | lion hold flag |
| alligator play drum | monkey wear hat | bear carry basket | kangaroo hold balloon |

**Phobes**

| Type C | Type B | Type A |
|---|---|---|
| rabbit paint picture | pig pull wagon | alligator bite monkey |
| alligator smoke cigarette | horse lick cup | rabbit lift frog |
| dog smoke pipe | rabbit throw ball | elephant squirt pig |
| pig play horn | cat scratch tree | pig hit sheep |
| gorilla play piano | dog bit chair | monkey pat boy |
| bear smell pie | | |
| sheep watch TV | | |
| lion hear telephone | | |
| tiger smell flower | | |
| dog paint fence | | |

jects. Children were assigned to 1 of 5 groups; with the average age equal for all groups (see Table IV).

## Procedure

The children received 5 training sessions each, ranging from 2 to 7 days apart, followed by a posttest of comprehension on both passives and clefts. In each session the experimenter explained that he or she had a pack of pictures that he would talk about, and for each picture the child would receive a marble to place in a puzzle-board which, when completed, formed the outline of an animal.[3] In the imitation groups, the experimenter used passive (or cleft) sentences about the 20 model pictures and the child was asked to imitate. On the randomly interspersed probe trials, themselves randomized as to type, the child was asked to describe the pictures. If he said only a word or two, he was gently guided by a nondirective question, such as "And what else?" or "What's happening?" All responses were transcribed during the session. In the expansion groups the experimenter asked the child to describe all 40 pictures, but expanded the sentences about the 20 models into either passives or clefts, giving no expansions for the probe trials. In all, responses were gathered for 20 probes over 5 sessions.

## Predictions

Before turning to the results, let us be precise about the ways they could shed light on the reality of the theories outlined earlier. To make things easier, the arguments will be made only for the case of the passive, but essentially the same ones could be made for clefts.

## 1. Abstract grammatical categories

It is a reasonable conjecture that by the age of three or four years, children have rules in their speech that would require postulating knowledge of abstract grammatical relations such as subject and object. Even researchers who hold the view that they do not constitute innate hypotheses sometimes grant that by then, children's speech seems to require those abstractions to introduce economy into their rule systems. If that is the case, then in the present experiment there should be no differences among the probes: the passive rule is introduced over a limited semantic domain but is perfectly in keeping with the more abstract formulation of a transformation acting on deep structure relationships in all-or-none fashion. Children should, therefore, as readily produce passives of the type, "The pipe is being smoked by the dog" as, "The sheep is being hit by the pig." The generalization gradient should be perfectly flat.

## 2. Semantically based rules

If children adopt a semantic approach to rule learning, the present training should accentuate that tendency. Children should learn only what they are taught; for example, that to produce a passive one inverts the order of the animate agent and animate patient of an action. Their hypothesis might be

**Table IV**
**Design of the Training Experiment**

| | Sentence Type Trained | | |
| --- | --- | --- | --- |
| | Clefts | Passives | Passives |
| Training Procedure | Type A training set | Type A training set | Type C training set |
| Imitation | N = 8 | N = 7 | N = 6 |
| Expansion | N = 10 | N = 6 | |

broad enough to incorporate also inanimate patients despite their training, but generalization should be less the more remote the event is from the training exemplars. If the rule is conceived of as all-or-none about a limited domain, individual children should show sharp cut-offs at the boundary of the category over which the rule applies.

## 3. Lexically based rules

An extreme version of the lexicalist position would be that children should only have set up passive verbs for items on which they were trained; for example, for the verbs *push, bite,* or *play.* A more reasonable version might argue that children would generalize on the grounds of verb semantics, in that the more similar the verbs to the training exemplars, the more generalization on the probe trials. One prediction might be that with training on type A, the number of passives for the types A and B would exceed that for type C, if the difference between the verb types is great enough, constrained as we were by picturable events. It is conceivable that the probe verbs are homogeneous enough that generalization will be across the board and only real nonactions, such as *know* or *believed,* or actions whose noun phrase roles are "tricky," such as *follow,* might not be included in the rule.

## 4. Prototypes in rule learning

The above three theories would make identical arguments regardless of the training exemplars, provided they were semantically bounded. The fourth theory, a prototype argument, would make competing predictions for the case where the training set was either prototypical or not. Suppose that type A events somehow constitute a prototype for the learning of the passive construction. One would expect learning to be facilitated when the training examples are prototypical, but slower when the training set is composed of nonprototypical, type C, events. Furthermore, the generalization gradient could be a different shape, for recall that in Rosch's experiments on color and form, the subjects regarded the focal colors and forms as the best examples even when they were not central to the training set.

The predictions are then:

a. Production of the passive should be greater for children trained on type A events than type C events, since learning about the prototype should facilitate learning.
b. Production of the passive should be maximal about the prototypical probes (type A) regardless of training.
c. The structure of the category should be the same for both groups of children.

## Results

Before turning to the results, let me describe the scoring procedure, for, as usual, children did not package their replies into the preconceived categories of "active," "passive," or "clefts." Some children adopted the reasonable hypothesis that to play the game one had to sprinkle one's speech with the morphemes *being* and *by,* so they would produce sentences of the sort "The sheep is being hit the pig" for the event *Sheep hit pig,* or "The dog is smoking by the pipe." Sometimes the two morphemes were used but with the active word order, so "The sheep is being hit by the pig" stood for *Sheep hit pig.* It was not clear whether that should be counted as a concatenation of the foregoing or as a real passive with reversed order. It was counted as the former because it neglects the major structural change that constitutes passivization; namely, a reversal of the subject and object noun phrases. Quite often, the children would mention the patient first, but then revert to an active; e.g., "The pig . . . the sheep's hitting him." In the light of the equal familiarity of the nouns and the linguistic sophistication of the children, this is probably an influence of the models. Table V indicates the proportion of responses in each category, normalized for the different numbers of opportunities over the three types of probes and for the different number of children in the groups. The data shown are for the expansion and imitation groups for the passive trained on type A events. They do not include the responses that maintained active word order and had no morpheme additions.

**Table V**
**Mean Number of Sentences Produced by Children**
**Taught the Passive about Type A Events***

| Scoring Categories | Imitation | | | Expansion | | |
|---|---|---|---|---|---|---|
| | Type A | Type B | Type C | Type A | Type B | Type C |
| Major Structural Change | | | | | | |
| Reversed Active | 0.43 | 0.00 | 0.00 | 0.50 | 0.00 | 0.00 |
| 2nd Noun First | 2.57 | 0.57 | 0.00 | 1.63 | 1.50 | 0.50 |
| Correct Passive | 5.14 | 0.57 | 0.00 | 3.25 | 0.25 | 0.25 |
| Minor Structural Change | | | | | | |
| Active plus *being* | 4.00 | 2.28 | 7.43 | 1.38 | 0.50 | 1.75 |
| Active plus *by* | 0.57 | 0.57 | 0.29 | 2.00 | 0.50 | 0.50 |
| Active plus both | 0.43 | 0.00 | 0.00 | 0.13 | 0.00 | 0.00 |
| Reversed Passive | 3.29 | 1.14 | 1.71 | 3.63 | 2.00 | 2.25 |

*Numbers have been adjusted to take account of the difference in opportunities for Type B and C events.

Another way to view the data would be to collapse across those scoring categories that seem to represent major structural modifications; i.e., rows 1, 2, and 3, and those that represent minor structural modifications; i.e., rows 4, 5, 6, and 7. These data are plotted in Figure 1-1.

The response in the cleft experimental groups fell into similar categories: the morphemes "its" and "that" were sprinkled about rather freely, and a very prevalent response was to add them both to the active sentence; e.g., "It's the sheep that's hitting the pig." However, the true equivalent to the reversed passive is the reversed cleft, "It's the sheep that the pig is hitting," since that is false about the event *Sheep hit pig,* although it retains the usual order of agent and patient. These data are shown in Table VI, and Figure 1-2 again shows the contrast between major versus minor structural modifications.

The pattern is reasonably clear-cut. Examining the data on major structural modifications in response to the probes, there is a rather steep generalization gradient that isolates type A from the others by a substantial margin. The pattern is the same for both passives and clefts and for both

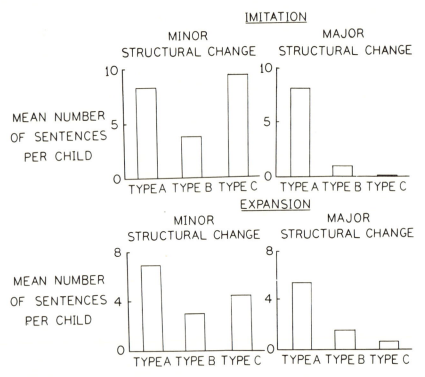

*Figure 1-1.* Generalization of children taught the passive about type A events.

**Table VI**
**Mean Number of Sentences Produced by Children**
**Taught the Cleft Form about Type A Events***

| Scoring Categories | Imitation | | | Expansion | | |
|---|---|---|---|---|---|---|
| | Type A | Type B | Type C | Type A | Type B | Type C |
| Major Structural Changes | | | | | | |
| Reversed Active | 0.66 | 0.00 | 0.00 | 0.70 | 0.00 | 0.00 |
| 2nd Noun First | 2.00 | 0.33 | 0.33 | 2.40 | 1.60 | 0.20 |
| Correct Cleft | 3.00 | 0.33 | 0.00 | 0.30 | 0.20 | 0.00 |
| Minor Structural Changes | | | | | | |
| Active plus *its* | 12.00 | 17.33 | 16.67 | 2.50 | 2.80 | 3.40 |
| Active plus *that* | 0.66 | 1.33 | 0.33 | 0.70 | 0.80 | 0.80 |
| Active plus both | 2.50 | 2.00 | 2.33 | 0.40 | 0.60 | 0.80 |
| Reversed Cleft | 8.33 | 6.33 | 6.67 | 0.00 | 0.00 | 0.00 |

*Numbers have been adjusted to take into account the different numbers of opportunities for Type B and C events.

imitation and expansion groups, though in one condition, cleft expansion, the children produced virtually no completely correct clefts. It was not the case that individual children either made major structural changes or made minor ones, which makes these data rather more difficult to explain. Presumably the child feels compelled to speak like the adult, but on any given occasion there are differing demands on his attention so that he comes out with varying degrees of approximation to the modeled sentences: sometimes the word order, sometimes the choice of subject, and sometimes only the morpheme such as "its" or "by," is correct. This idea of degrees of approximation to the model does not, however, account for the difference in the way major and minor structural changes are distributed across the different semantic types. Major structural changes occur with only some types of sentences; minor changes seem to occur equally with all types, suggesting that the processes underlying them may be distinct.

The critical data for interpreting the results come from the group of children taught the passive about type C events. Unfortunately children in this group made many fewer attempts at producing passives at all, which may bear out prediction a, but may also be a sampling artifact. As a result, the numbers are too small in the category of true passives for any meaningful comparison (see Table VII).

If, however, one collapses the responses into minor versus major structural modifications, the numbers are sufficiently large for comparison across probe types. These data are given in Figure 1-3.

It can be seen that the children in this group did *not* make the greatest

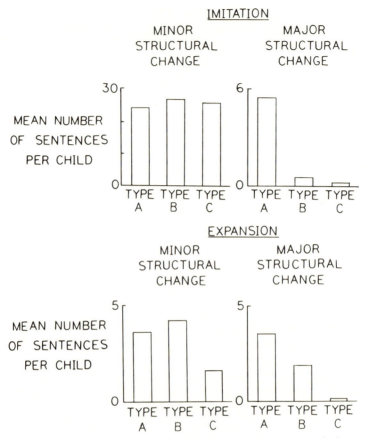

*Figure 1-2.* Generalization of children taught the cleft form about type A events.

number of major structural modifications to the sentence types on which they had been trained, but instead to those which might be hypothesized to represent the prototype.

## DISCUSSION

How might the various theories of rule learning accommodate these findings? The position that children at this age entertain abstract hypotheses about all-or-none grammatical rules does not seem to be borne out. The rules did not equally generalize to all exemplars. However, the theory that rules are semantically bound is not easily accommodated either, since for children trained on type C events the rule did not adhere to the

**Table VII**
**Mean Number of Sentences Produced by**
**Children Taught the Passive about**
**Type C events***

| Scoring Categories | Imitation | | |
|---|---|---|---|
| | Type A | Type B | Type C |
| Major Structural Change | | | |
|   Reversed Active | 1.00 | 0.67 | 0.17 |
|   2nd Noun First | 2.83 | 1.17 | 0.50 |
|   Correct Passive | 0.67 | 1.00 | 0.67 |
| Minor Structural Change | | | |
|   Active plus *being* | 0.33 | 1.00 | 0.50 |
|   Active plus *by* | 0.33 | 0.00 | 0.17 |
|   Active plus both | 0.00 | 0.33 | 1.00 |
|   Reversed Passive | 1.00 | 0.67 | 0.83 |

*Numbers have been adjusted to take into account the different number of opportunities for Type A and B events.

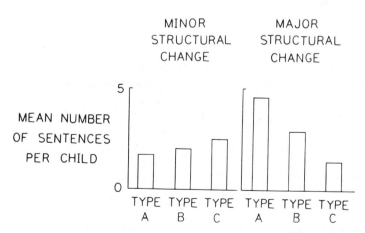

*Figure 1-3.* Generalization of children taught the passive about type C events.

events semantically closest to those on which it was trained. Theory 3, the lexical position, also has difficulty explaining the results if generalization across lexical items is governed by the semantic similarity of the verbs in some simple sense, but possibly not if the prototype model is incorporated into a theory of lexical organization.

The data exemplify one of the properties of prototype structures: asymmetry of generalization. However, at present a prototype theory is largely vacuous; it is an idea sparked by cross-domain comparisons at an abstract level. It is time to investigate what the notion "prototype" might mean when applied to the domain of grammar. Some alternative interpretations of the construct can be offered using the data from the present experiment not so much to decide among candidate theories as to provide illustrative material.

## A Frequency Explanation

The fact that Leonard's subjects responded in the same way regardless of the training set may mean that the training set comprised such a small proportion of their total exposure to subject-verb constructions that the difference in exposure of the form during the experiment had no significance. The same thing might be true of the present experiment. It may be that type A passives are much more frequent in the speech the child hears; thus the limited exposure to type C passives is insufficient to reverse the existing bias in frequency. Obviously the training was not insignificant in itself as the children did produce a limited number of correct forms. Although there is no baseline estimate for these children, it is unlikely that they would normally produce full passives, for two reasons: (*a*) other spontaneous or elicited speech data on children of this age (e.g., Horgan, 1978) show only around 10 percent of them use full passives; (*b*) no child trained on clefts spontaneously produced a passive sentence, and no child trained on passives spontaneously produced a cleft. Nevertheless, the biases in distribution may well have existed in the input prior to the experiment.

One argument against this is that passives and clefts are quite rare in the input, though we have no way of determining how frequently a form must be experienced in order for that exposure to cumulate and ultimately overcome the experimental exposure. We have no data available on the semantics of other passives the child might hear, though it is highly unlikely that type C passives outweigh type A, a result that is not uninteresting in itself. In the absence of the pertinent data on frequency this issue must remain unresolved.

## Prototypical Verbs

The first hypothesis to be explored is that the verbs used in training on type A events constitute some kind of prototype for the category of verbs.

There are two senses (at least) of prototypical that could be true. The one is semantic; that is, that certain verbs exemplify more common semantic attributes of the domain as a whole. Others share less in common. Along what attributes do verbs vary? Many different investigators have characterized verb semantics, and the variety of their analyses is overwhelming.

Verbs can be distinguished as being about enduring states (e.g., *know, love*) or about activities (*walk, hit*) which may be either punctual in duration (e.g., *jump*) or prolonged (e.g., *sing*); verbs may have an end result (e.g., *phone*) or not (e.g., *swim*); may express a causal relation between the noun phrases (e.g., *kill*) or not (e.g., *die*); may involve surface contact (e.g., *push*) or not (e.g., *hear*); designate actions that result in a creation (e.g., *build*) or not (e.g., *touch*); involve physical activity (e.g., *run*) or not (e.g., *overhear*); imply intention (e.g., *look at, listen*) or not (e.g., *see, forgot*), and so on. It is impossible to guess whether the verbs *push, hit,* and *pull* constitute a prototype of the verb class as a whole, but it is possible to ask whether they share more attributes in common than the other verbs in this experiment. As pictured, the verbs in the type A training set denoted actions having the following attributes: (*a*) intentionality, (*b*) physical action, (*c*) surface contact between the nouns, (*d*) action on an existing object rather than creation, (*e*) a change of state in the object, (*f*) punctual duration (though this entails an inference since the pictures are ambiguous with respect to aspect).

Type B probes consisted of the same set of verbs, but type C probes had more diversity. *Smell,* for instance, is not a physical action, at least in the same sense as *hit;* the duration is not punctual, there is no surface contact nor a change of state in the object, but it does involve intention. *Play,* for musical instruments, involves intention, surface contact, physical activity, nonpunctual duration, no real change of state in the object. *Read* involves intention, no physical action, questionable surface contact, nonpunctual duration, no change of state in the object. *Smoke* involves intention, no physical action, surface contact, nonpunctual duration, a questionable change of state in the object. Thus the probe verbs are linked to the training verbs by one or more attributes in common, though they are a heterogeneous collection in themselves. One attribute they all share is nonpunctual duration, which is not a picturable dimension.

The type C training set included other verbs (*blow, wear, carry, hold*) that share only nonpunctual duration with type C probes, and the new probes were expanded to include *paint, watch,* and *hear,* making the category even more semantically diverse.

Evidently, then, the physical actions did comprise a semantic prototype of the domain sampled in that they shared more attributes in common with the other verbs than the latter did with each other, with the exception of the feature of nonpunctual duration. It is curious that the children trained on type C ignored that feature and preferred to use the passive for punctual verbs (Type A) bearing other diverse similarities to the training set, though it is possible that the common element of nonpunctual duration was irrelevant because it could not be pictured.

To refer back to the discussion of Rosch and Mervis (1975), although prototypes in semantic categories shared more features with each other than with peripheral instances, it is not the case that all attributes have equal cue validity for the concept. For example, in the animal domain, *size* is an incidental feature which is not as helpful in delineating category membership as, say, *independent movement,* or even *eats grass.* In the domain of verbs, an attribute such as *surface contact* might be irrelevant for grammatical purposes, it may never be marked explicitly by inflection, and it may make no differences in rule application. On the other hand, causal versus noncausal might make a difference for certain rules and is, therefore, an attribute that should be weighted more heavily than others. What I am proposing is that the semantic characterization may not tell the whole story; that the distributional properties of verbs might render some semantic dimensions more relevant than others for the purposes of rule generalization.

What would it mean for some verbs to be more central in a *grammatical* sense than others? To refer again to Ross, one could hypothesize that some verbs would partake of more distributional privileges than others, with "good" verbs appearing in a great variety of constructions and "poor" verbs appearing only in nonchoosy constructions. For example, one such dimension is the active-stative dimension. According to Ross, there are no processes that require the predicates that undergo them to be only *stative,* but there are processes that require the predicates to be active. For example:

1. Action verbs can take the progressive; e.g., "He is going," "He is hitting the ball," but not "He is believing you" or "He is knowing the answer."
2. Action verbs can take the imperative; not many nonaction verbs can: "Hit the ball!" but not "Know the answer!"
3. Adjectives cannot enter the passive construction:
   John is being nice to people. → *People are being niced to by John.
   Neither can truly stative verbs:
   John is the quarterback. → *The quarterback is being been by John.
   Nor can some nonactions:
   The bottle contained shampoo. → *Shampoo was contained by the bottle.
   The man weighed 300 lbs. → *300 lbs. was weighed by the man.

Now the verbs in the present experiment might vary in terms of the breadth of constructions they typically enter. It is not necessary to claim that such uses be *forbidden* by the adult grammar, just that they be comparatively rare. So a child who has never heard the verb *smoke* used in the imperative might treat it grammatically the same as the verb *know*. Perhaps the child has observed that certain verbs that share semantic properties with *hit, push, touch* almost invariably enter grammatical rules: they can be used in the progressive and in imperatives, and are neutral with respect to animacy of agents and patients, and so forth. In contrast, verbs like *see, wear, have,* or *know* have probabilities of use ranging from 0 to 1.0 for different constructions. For the sake of argument, let us imagine it to be the case for the present domain of verbs that the action verbs of types A and B are seen by the child to have greater distributional possibilities than the verbs of type C. What would such knowledge imply about new rule learning?

If the child learns that a particular verb enters a new grammatical rule, he can apply that rule with confidence to other "good" verbs that enter many different constructions. However, he will be very cautious in using the rule with a verb that other constructions are "choosy" about, since he has no way of knowing from his limited training whether the new construction is choosy or not. In contrast, if he learns the rule with respect to a peripheral verb, he must again apply it with caution to other peripheral verbs, but there is a very strong likelihood that it can be used with "good" verbs, and he is likely to generalize to them with more confidence. Such a pattern would fit the data from the present experiment quite well.

The implication would be that only those semantic dimensions (e.g., actionness) that affect privileges of occurrence would be predictive of generalization. Furthermore, information about the wide or narrow opportunities of use of a verb would need to be encoded in the lexicon, which is a position closer to Bresnan (1978) than to either the traditional view of abstract grammar or the semantic approach.

## Distinguishing among prototypes

How could one decide which notion of prototype, semantic or grammatical, was the most applicable in the present case? I can think of one experiment that would be informative. In the semantic case it was proposed that the type A verbs had more attributes in common with each other and with the peripheral verbs than the latter did with each other. Hence generalization was maximal to the prototype. Unfortunately this latter inference has never been supported in the natural concept literature to date. Two experiments (Rips, 1976; Carey & Smith, 1977) have demonstrated that after training a new property about a peripheral instance, generalization was minimal compared to teaching it about a prototype. However, in each case they taught the property about a *single* peripheral instance. If Rips had instead taught, to take an example, that penguins, ostriches, eagles, and hummingbirds—that is, a variety of peripheral birds—all contracted a disease, I believe subjects would find it compelling to infer that indeed, robins and sparrows would contract it too. That would constitute the true parallel to the present experiment, wherein a variety of peripheral verbs were shown to enter into a relation; hence the prototypical verbs were seen as most likely to enter the construction too.

In the grammatical case, the number or variety of the peripheral verbs is irrelevant to the argument. According to Ross, the grammatical attribute structure of the verb class is not a family resemblance structure, but rather a strict hierarchy such that entry of even one peripheral verb into a relation *guarantees* the allowability of a prototypical verb. The two notions of prototype thus make competing predictions about the case of training on a semantically homogeneous set of peripheral verbs, or in the limit, on a single peripheral verb. There would not be any sense in which the type A verbs would constitute the center of a set of converging *semantic* attributes in that case, though the grammatical prototype notion would apply just as readily. This experiment remains to be done.

We might formulate a hypothesis: *Action verbs are prototypes of the verb category in that they serve as focal points in learning about verb markings and the grammatical roles played by verb arguments.* To review the evidence in keeping with this prediction:

1. Action verbs are learned earlier than state verbs in child speech (Bloom, Lightbown, & Hood, 1975; Leonard, 1976).

2. In Stage I, agent, which is a relation generally played by the subject of an action verb, occurs well before the relation *beneficiary* (verbs such as *have*), *possessor* (state verbs), and *experiencer* (e.g., *see, hear*) (Leonard, 1976).

3. In Russian, which has an inflection marking the direct object, the child studied by Gvozdev used the marker first for patients of action verbs, and only later for objects of nonaction verbs (Bowerman, 1973).

4. The passive is understood first in the case of *action* verbs, but only later for nonaction verbs (Maratsos et al., in press; Turner & Rommetveit, 1968).

This possibility deserves further exploration in the existing literature, but it cannot be the whole explanation of the present results. In four out of five conditions in the present experiment, children did not seem to generalize on the basis of the activity encoded by the verb. Instead, since there was such a dramatic difference between type A and type B probes, animacy of the *patient* seemed to be the important variable. It is difficult to handle the animacy of the patient as an important semantic feature of the verb, especially since it was optional for the verbs discussed here. Would one have separate entries in the lexicon for the same verb with either animate or inanimate patients? That may be a solution, but it is an inelegant one, for presumably it would depend upon the rule whether or not patient animacy were considered an important dimension of generalization. In the present case, there is a good reason why it is so significant: the patient of the action is being promoted to *surface subject* in the passive.

## Prototypical Subjects

It was mentioned in passing that perhaps agents represent the best sentence subjects. A similar hypothesis was proposed by Schlesinger (1974), who argued that grammatical rules might be learned first with respect to the notion of agent as a representative of the more abstract class of subject. This leads to a second hypothesis about prototypicality: *Agents serve as focal points in learning about the category subject.* What evidence supports such a contention? Clearly, learning first about *agents* might make action verbs more salient than verbs that entail other relations in subject position; hence the data that action verbs are learned before state verbs (Bloom et al., 1975) is easily accommodated by this hypothesis. It directly predicts the earlier emergence of agents than possessors, beneficiaries, and experiencers. Moreover, it predicts the earlier appearance of agents than instruments. Instruments are *inanimate* noun phrases typically involving action verbs; hence their late emergence (Leonard, 1976) is an embarrassment for the first hypothesis. Furthermore, in Leonard's (1975) experiment, the instrumental subject-verb expressions were the least readily produced by the children, despite the action verbs. In fact, verb activity was not a significant dimension of generalization in Leonard's experiment, but animacy-inanimacy of the subject did produce differences.

In the passive construction, however, agents *cannot* appear as surface subjects as the logical object occupies that position in the sentence. The passive thus appears an unnatural form in isolation from context, though it can be made plausible by appropriate contextual manipulation. Given this constraint, what features of the object in an isolated picture would render it salient enough to occupy such a privileged position in the sentence? One would predict animacy would be an important factor, and patients of action verbs should be more salient than those of nonaction verbs, since they are affected by the action to some degree. Thus, something that is *hit* or *pulled* should attract more attention than something that is seen as a static property of the agent; e.g., something *worn, smoked,* or *held.*

In the present experiment it is the case that the children have differential difficulty with producing the passive as a function of patient animacy and secondarily, the active character of the verb. On this account, then, verb semantics play a role only insofar as they accentuate the noun that occupies subject position in the passive voice. Moreover, this hypothesis provides a more plausible account of another persistent difficulty: the verb *follow* in the passive voice. The children in the study by Sinclair et al. (1971)

claimed it was difficult because the patient of the action goes in front; hence it determines the direction and pace of the agent. Furthermore, it does not involve physical contact in the same way as verbs like *push* or *kick*. Yet both of these semantic characteristics are shared by the verb *chase,* which is not reported to cause particular difficulty in the passive voice. It seems plausible to me that the difficulty with the verb *follow* resides in the fact that the patient is not so directly affected by the action, yet it certainly is affected by the action *chase.* For this reason, the patient of *follow* is a poor candidate for promoting to subject position.

If the second hypothesis is the correct explanation for the experimental results described above, then one might expect the generalization gradient to be much less steep if the context were manipulated in such a way as to accentuate the patient and make the passive construction more plausible for *all* the pictures (cf. Brown, 1976). When pictures are presented in isolation, the child has to rely upon his existing biases to decide which aspect of the event should be mentioned first. It is progressively more difficult to get him to pay attention to other than the agent if the alternative noun refers to an affected animate object, an affected inanimate object, or an unaffected inanimate object.

Braine and Wells (1978) have explored children's concepts of various cases such as *actor, instrument,* and *locative* in an ingenious task wherein the child must place token of a particular shape on the appropriate element in a picture. For example, a child might be taught to place a square token on the child must place a token of a particular shape on the appropriate element in cage.'' In one experiment in the series the researchers used two contrasting training sets: one that contained primarily inanimate actors, another consisting of primarily animate actors. After the children learned to place the tokens appropriately for the training set, generalization trials were run to see how broad their concepts were. Interestingly, regardless of the training set, both groups of children found the animate actors easiest to identify in the new pictures, making fewer errors on those trials than with inanimate actors. Braine and Wells conclude, ''Our interpretation of the results is that the children have a concept of 'actor' that includes inanimate actors, but that their prototype of an actor is nonetheless an animate actor; this prototype apparently influences the results even when almost all the training sentences use inanimate actors.'' These data provide indirect support for the contention that children bring certain biases to the task of forming grammatical categories; in this case, the underlying cognitive cases on which these categories are based.

It may be premature, however, to dispense with the hypothesis that verb semantics are important in rule generalization. Other investigators (e.g., Maratsos, 1978) have considered that dimension to be influential, and the range of verbs in the present experiment was very restricted. In particular, if the events had been acted out in the present study, the aspect of the actions might have proved important in generalization, as it has in other studies (Bloom et al., 1977; Bronckart & Sinclair, 1973). Also, if the technique could be modified to allow testing transfer to nonpicturable events, such as *know* or *love,* the action dimension might prove extremely important. It remains for future research to determine whether either or both of these proposals about prototypicality can be supported empirically.

## The Source of Prototypicality

Where might grammatical prototypes come from? Research in other domains has uncovered four possibilities:

1. The prototype is the central tendency of the exemplars (e.g., Posner & Keele, 1968).
2. The prototype has primacy because of the structure of the perceptual apparatus (Rosch, 1973).
3. The prototype is the most frequently experienced exemplar (Rosch, 1975).
4. The prototype possesses more shared attributes than peripheral instances, hence maximizing cue validity (Rosch & Mervis, 1975).

The two prototypes explored here might differentiate in terms of origin. Neither would seem to constitute the central tendency of the exemplars in any simple sense. It is possible that action verbs form a prototype of the verbs in the experimental task in the sense of sharing more semantic attributes than the other verbs. Furthermore, they might share more privileges of occurrence with each other than verbs that denote less actionlike events, hence maximizing the separability of verbs and, say, adjectives. They are not necessarily the most frequent verbs, though they might be more frequent in adult-to-child discourse. Nevertheless, there is evidence that they are salient in advance of learning their distributional privileges, since they constitute the earliest verb types in child speech (Bloom et al., 1975). It is possible that their salience predates syntax but is then accentuated by a combination of frequency, centrality in a semantic sense, and broad syntactic privileges. Despite the fast-accumulating data on the input to children, the research has not yet illuminated the process of syntactic generalization in child speech. However, detailed study of the distributional and semantic properties of verbs in the input could lead to firm predictions about a child's likely generalizations.[4]

With respect to the second prototype—namely, agents as the best exemplars of subjects—it seems likely that the salience of animate or moving objects as sentence topics is independent of linguistic experience. They constitute the most likely things to catch a child's attention and invoke a remark. Furthermore, there is evidence that mentioning the topic before the comment may not even have to be learned but may be an existing bias. An estimated 98 percent of the world's languages have word orders requiring the placement of subject before object (Greenberg, 1963). It has been argued (e.g., Clark & Clark, 1977) that this caters to a universal tendency in language processing to prefer given before new information. If so, then the prototype of the category *subject* might be a prototype akin to focal colors: it is salient because of the structure of our human processing system, independent of experience.

## CONCLUSION

The main purpose of the speculation about the existence of prototypes in grammatical rule learning was to bridge the gap between the work on general concept formation on the one hand and language learning in particular on the other. Some have argued that language learning involves special-purpose capacities that make it distinct from other learning, but the more we discover about learning in general the less special it may appear. While it is probable that there exist constraints on the form that linguistic rules will take which may be unique to that domain, it is difficult to argue that language learning does not also tap into our general capacities for rule induction and concept formation.

Nevertheless, analogies between distinct domains should only survive if they are useful. It was not my purpose to use the experiment as a strict test of competing theories of rule learning, but rather to explore what such theories would look like for concrete empirical data. The two candidate prototype models hold promise in that they tie together some existing loose ends in the literature and might stimulate further research to prove or disprove them. On a prototype account there is no necessity for linguistic rules to have strict semantic boundaries, though it does predict that rules might be semantically constrained at first. The insistence of traditional formulations that rules must be all-or-none rather than probabilistic might have hindered reporting of semantic biases that are not absolute because they seemed theoretically uninteresting. It is precisely these biases that become of primary interest for disclosing potential prototypes.

Ross's proposals about noncategorical grammars deserve greater attention, for they could further illuminate the process of rule generalization. It is a curious fact that children rarely make certain kinds of errors, even though they would seem overdetermined by traditional accounts. For example, one would expect children to say, "He is believing" or "Know the answer!" but they do not. Suppose however, that children learn early that certain semantically related items (e.g., action verbs) share extensive privileges of occurrence, whereas other items (e.g., verbs referring to mental states) are less reliable as representatives of that class in that they have more narrow distributional privileges. Both distributional and semantic information would enter into decisions about rule generalization, and the theory predicts a conservative approach to rule learning with *underextension* being a prevalent form of error.

In conclusion, there are fertile comparisons to be made between work on linguistic rule learning and concept formation. There are fundamental questions in common as to the nature of the categories, their internal representation and how they are most succesfully learned. Recent research has definitely uncovered the possibility that linguistic concepts too might have internal structure that leads to asymmetries of generalization and use.

## NOTES

[1]Preparation of this chapter was supported in part by NSF grant 3971X to Professor Roger Brown.

[2]Leonard (1975) refers to the *dative* case instead of the experiencer, following the example of Fillmore (1968). In a later account of the experiment in his book, *Meaning in Child Language* (1976), he changes the name of the case to the more usual *experiencer,* so that is the name we have adopted here.

[3]We have found this to be an invaluable technique for sustaining the child's interest over a large number (40) of stimuli. Once a child becomes interested in the game of completing the puzzle, the interest builds rather than declines as the end approaches, and we have not yet had a child who gave up playing our games with only 5 or so stimuli to go.

[4]We are currently undertaking such an investigation by tracing the use of verb inflections in the maternal input and the way the child subsequently attaches these inflections to particular verbs. Purely distributional evidence could lead to a ranking of verbs in terms of "goodness"; i.e., how many inflections they take, and inflections in terms of "choosiness"; i.e., how many verbs they attach to. We are examining the consequences of these properties in the child's beginning use of inflections.

## REFERENCES

Anglin, J. M. *Word, object and conceptual development.* New York: Norton, 1977.

Bandura, A., & Harris, M. Modification of syntactic style. *Journal of Experimental Child Psychology,* 1966, 4, 341–352.

Battig, W. F., & Montague, W. E. Category norms for verbal items in 56 categories: A replication and extension of the Connecticut category norms. *Journal of Experimental Psychology,* 1969, 80 (Monograph Supplement 3, Part 2).

Berlin, B., & Kay, P. *Basic color terms: Their universality and evolution.* Berkeley: University of California Press, 1969.

Bloom, L. *One word at a time: The use of single word utterances before syntax.* The Hague: Mouton, 1973a.

Bloom, L. Why not pivot grammar? *In* C. A. Ferguson & D. I. Slobin (Eds.), *Studies in child language development.* New York: Holt, Rinehart & Winston, 1973b.

Bloom, L., Lifter, K., & Tanouye, E. Semantic organization of verbs in child language and the acquisition of grammatical morphemes. Unpublished manuscript, 1977.

Bloom, L., Lightbown, P., & Hood, L. Structure and variation in child language. *Monographs of the Society for Research in Child Development,* 1975, 40 (2, Serial No. 160).

Bornstein, M. H. Qualities of color vision in infancy. *Journal of Experimental Child Psychology,* 1975, 19, 401–419.

Bowerman, M. L. Structural relationships in children's utterances: Syntactic or semantic? *In* T. M. Moore (Ed.), *Cognitive development and the acquisition of language* New York: Academic Press, 1973.

Bowerman, M. L. Semantic factors in the acquisition of word use and sentence construction *In* D. Morehead & A. Morehead (Eds.), *Directions in normal and deficient language.* Baltimore, Md.: University Park Press, 1976.

Bowerman, M. L. The acquisition of word meaning: An investigation of some current conflicts. *In* N. Waterson & C. Snow (Eds.), *The development of communication.* New York: Wiley, 1977a.

Bowerman, M. L. The structure and origin of semantic categories in the language learning child. Paper prepared in advance for the Burg Wartenstein symposium no. 74, *Fundamentals of Symbolism,* July 1977b.

Braine, M. D. S. The ontogeny of English phrase structure: The first phase. *Language,* 1963, 39(1), 1–14.

Braine, M. D. S. Children's first word combinations. *Monographs of the Society for Research in Child Development,* 1976, 41 (1, Serial No. 164).

Braine, M. D. S., & Wells, R. S. Case-like categories in children: The actor and some related categories. *Cognitive Psychology,* 1978, 10, 100–122.

Bresnan, J. A realistic transformational grammar. *In* M. Halle, J. Bresnan, & G. Miller (Eds.), *Linguistic theory and psychological reality.* Cambridge, Mass.: M.I.T. Press, 1978.

Bronckart, J. P., & Sinclair, H. Time, tense and aspect. *Cognition,* 1973, 2, 107–130.

Brown, I. Role of referent concreteness in the acquisition of passive sentence comprehension through abstract modeling. *Journal of Experimental Child Psychology,* 1976, 22, 185–199.

Brown, R. W. *Social psychology.* New York: Free press, 1965.

Brown, R. W. *A first language: The early stages.* Cambridge, Mass.: Harvard University Press, 1973.

Brown, R. W. Word from the language acquisition front. Paper presented at the Eastern Psychological Association Boston, April 1977.

Bruner, J. S., Goodnow, J. J., & Austin, G. A. *A study of thinking.* New York: Wiley, 1956.

Carey, S., & Smith, C. Productive thinking in preschool children. Grant proposal to NSF, 1977.

Chafe, W. L. *Meaning and the structure of language.* Chicago: University of Chicago Press, 1970.

Chomsky, N. *Syntactic structures.* The Hague: Mouton, 1957.

Chomsky, N. *Aspects of the theory of syntax.* Cambridge, Mass.: M.I.T. Press, 1965.

Chomsky, N. *Language and mind.* New York: Harcourt, Brace, Jovanovich, 1968.

Clark, H. H., & Clark, E. V. *Psychology and language: An introduction to psycholinguistics.* New York: Harcourt, Brace, Jovanovich, 1977.

Fillmore, C. The case for case. *In* E. Bach & R. T. Harms (Eds.), *Universals in linguistic theory.* New York: Holt, Rinehart, & Winston, 1968.

Fodor, J. A., Bever, T. G., & Garrett, M. *The psychology of language.* New York: McGraw-Hill, 1974.

Greenberg, J. H. Some universals of grammar with particular reference to the order of meaningful elements. *In* J. H. Greenberg (Ed.), *Universals of language,* Cambridge, Mass.: M.I.T. Press, 1963.

Gvozdev, A. N. *Voprozy izucheniia detskoi rechi* ("Problems in the language development of the child"). Moscow: Academy of Pediatric Science, 1961.

Heider, E. "Focal" color areas and the development of color names. *Developmental Psychology,* 1971, 4, 447–455.

Herrnstein, R. J., Loveland, D., & Cable, C. Natural concepts in pigeons. *Journal of Experimental Psychology: Animal Behavior Processes,* 1976, 2, 285–311.

Horgan, D. The development of the full passive. *Journal of Child Language,* 1978, 5, 65–80.

Johnson, E. G. The development of color knowledge in pre-school children. *Child Development,* 1977, 48, 308–311.

Leonard, L. B. The role of nonlinguistic stimuli and semantic relations in children's acquisition of grammatical utterances. *Journal of Experimental Child Psychology,* 1975, 19, 346–357.

Leonard, L. B. *Meaning in child language.* New York: Grune & Stratton, 1976.

McCawley, J. D. The role of semantics in a grammar. *In* E. Bach & R. T. Harms (Eds.), *Universals in linguistic theory.* New York: Holt, Rinehart, & Winston, 1968.

McDaniel, C. K. Basic color terms: Their neurophysiological basis. Paper presented at the American Anthropological Association Annual Meeting, Mexico City, 1974.

McNeill, D. Developmental psycholinguistics. *In* F. Smith & G. Miller (Eds.), *The genesis of language.* Cambridge, Mass.: M.I.T. Press, 1966.

Maratsos, M. P. How to get from words to sentences. *In* D. Aaronson & R. W. Rieber (Eds.), *Perspectives in psycholinguistics.* Hillsdale, N. J.: Lawrence Erlbaum, 1978.

Maratsos, M. P., Kuczaj, S. A. II, Fox, D. E. C., & Chalkley, M. A. Some empirical studies in the acquisition of transformational relations: Passives, negatives, and the past tense. *In* W. A. Collins (Ed.), *Minnesota Symposia in Child Psychology* (Vol. 12). New York: Crowell, in press.

Medin, D. L. & Schaffer, M. M. Context theory of classification learning. *Psychological Review* 1978, 85, 207–238.

Mervis, C. B. Acquisition of object categories. Unpublished doctoral dissertation, Cornell University, 1976.

Mulford, R. Prototypicality and the development of categorization. Paper presented at the second annual Boston University conference on child language, October 1977.

Nelson, K. Concept, word and sentence: Interrelations in acquisition and development. *Psychological Review,* 1974, 81(4), 267–285.

Nelson, K. E. Facilitating syntax acquisition. *Developmental Psychology,* 1977, 13, 101–107.

Posner, M. I. Abstraction and the process of recognition. *In* G. M. Bower & J. T. Spence (Eds.), *The psychology of learning and motivation* (Vol. 3). New York: Academic Press, 1969.

Posner, M. I., & Keele, S. W. On the genesis of abstract ideas. *Journal of Experimental Psychology* 1968, 77, 353–363.

Premack, D. *Intelligence in ape and man.* Hillsdale, N. J.: Lawrence Erlbaum, 1976.

Reed, S. K. Pattern recognition and categorization. *Cognitive Psychology,* 1972, 3, 382–407.

Rips, L. J. Inductive judgements about natural categories. *Journal of Verbal Learning and Verbal Behavior,* 1976, 14, 665–681.

Rosch, E. On the internal structure of perceptual and semantic categories. *In* T. M. Moore (Ed.), *Cognitive development and the acquisition of language.* New York: Academic Press, 1973.

Rosch, E. Universals and cultural specifics in human categorization. In R. Brislin, S. Bochner, & W. Lonner (Eds.), *Cross-cultural perspectives on learning.* New York: Halsted Press, 1975.

Rosch, E., & Mervis, C. B. Family resemblances: Studies in the internal structure of categories. *Cognitive Psychology,* 1975, 7, 573–605.

Ross, J. R. Act. *In* D. Davidson & G. Harman (Eds.), *Semantics of natural languages.* Dordrecht: Reidel, 1972.

Ross, J. R. Three batons for cognitive psychology. *In* W. B. Weimer & D S. Palermo (Eds.), *Cognitive and the symbolic processes.* Hillsdale, N. J.: Lawrence Erlbaum, 1974a.

Ross, J. R. The Center. Paper presented at the Harvard Bilingualism seminar, Cambridge, Mass., March, 1974b.

Schlesinger, I. M. Relational concepts underlying language. *In* R. L. Schiefelbusch & L. L. Lloyd (Eds.), *Language perspectives: Acquisition, retardation and intervention.* Baltimore, Md.: University Park Press, 1974.

Sinclair, A., Sinclair, H., & De Marcellus, O. Young children's comprehension and production of passive sentences. *Archives de psychologie,* 1971, 41, 1–22.

Turner, E. A., & Rommetveit, R. Experimental manipulation of the production of active and passive voice in children. *Language and Speech,* 1968, 169–180.

Whitehurst, G., Ironsmith, E., & Goldfein, M. Selective imitation of the passive construction through modeling. *Journal of Experimental Child Psychology,* 1974, 17, 288–302.

Vygotsky, L. S. *Thought and language.* New York: Wiley, 1962.

# 2

# APPRENTICESHIP IN MEANING

**GORDON WELLS**

In what way should we conceptualise the task of the child learning his native language and the part that the environment plays in facilitating this task? These are questions that have constantly recurred over the last ten years as we have moved through the various stages of planning and carrying out a longitudinal study of the language development of a group of children from shortly after their first birthday until the end of their second year in school.[1] During this period, other researchers have proposed a variety of answers to these questions but, while we have found many of them to be helpful on specific issues, we have also found a tendency to narrowness of focus, stemming from individuals' disciplinal affiliations and the particular biases that these have introduced into their conception of language. Our own observations, on the other hand, have convinced us of the interrelatedness of the various aspects of the child's development, linguistic, cognitive and affective, and of the central place, in all these aspects of development, of interaction with other, more mature, members of the culture.

In this chapter I shall attempt to develop this perspective and to indicate where I think answers are likely to be found. Clearly a multidisciplinary approach to language and its development will be called for, with an emphasis on language as a form of social behaviour. I shall reject as inadequate, therefore, both the nativist position that argues for an autonomous and innate language acquisition device, which merely requires to be triggered by the speech of others (Lenneberg, 1967), and equally the behaviourist position, with its emphasis on imitation, shaping and reinforcement (Staats, 1971). What both these approaches ignore, in their different ways, is the socially situated context in which the child develops control of language through the exchange of meanings in the pursuance of shared, purposeful activities. Innate structures in the child and "training" by more mature language users are both, no doubt, necessary for successful development but these can only be adequately understood, I shall argue, within a framework of interaction, in which the child learns by sharing with another in the intersubjective construction of meaning. It is in this sense that I propose to consider the development of language as an "Apprenticeship in Meaning."

The chapter will be divided into five major sections. In the first, I shall review contributions from workers in a number of disciplines, in an attempt to indicate how they might be integrated in an interactionist position. I shall then consider (sections two and three) some of the empirical evidence that bears upon this argument, including some of the results of the Bristol longitudinal programme. The fourth section will consider a number of examples of adult-child interaction as a basis for the fifth section, which will present the beginnings of a more formal model of interaction. The chapter will conclude with a consideration of some of the implications of the perspective that has been developed.

## THE ARGUMENT FOR AN INTERACTIONIST VIEW OF LANGUAGE ACQUISITION

"An adequate theory of acquisition must start with an adequate account of what has to be learned," wrote Chomsky in 1964, and research on language acquisition in the 1960s had clearly taken this message to heart, for the theories that were developed at that time provide a very clear reflection of the dominant, transformational linguistic theory of that decade—but with a time lag of five or six years. Both were almost exclusively concerned with syntax, and the complexity and abstractness of the grammars that were proposed seemed, to some, to leave no alternative but to attribute the child's remarkable feat of learning to innate knowledge of linguistic universals (Chomsky, 1965; McNeill, 1966). Since then, linguistic theory has broadened in its area of coverage, and developmental psycholinguistics has provided some alternative hypotheses. The claim that human infants have an innate predisposition to learn to communicate through language now seems relatively uncontroversial, but the specification of that predisposition has become less syntax-specific.

Writing on the same subject again in 1976, Chomsky still argues for an innate language faculty endowed with knowledge of linguistic universals, but significantly he adds:

Alongside of the language faculty and interacting with it in the most intimate way is the faculty of mind that constructs what might be called "common-sense understanding," a system of beliefs, expectation and knowledge concerning the nature and behaviour of objects, their place in the system of "natural kinds," the organisation of these categories, and the properties that determine the categorisation of objects and analysis of events. A general "innateness hypothesis" will also include principles that bear on the place and role of people in a social world, the nature and conditions of work, the structure of human action, will and choice, and so on. (Chomsky, 1976; p. 35)

The first step away from the preoccupation with syntax was probably taken as a result of the recognition that even the child's simplest two-word utterances might be semantically ambiguous. Bloom's (1970) well-known example of a single surface structure being uttered in different contexts with two quite distinct meanings demonstrated the inadequacy of purely syntactic descriptions, and there have now been a number of studies of the acquisition of languages as different as Finnish, Luo and English which have used Case Grammar (Fillmore, 1968), or some adaptation of it, to show that the earliest stage of structured utterances can be more adequately described in terms of a small but universal set of semantic relations (Slobin, 1973). In the same paper, Slobin goes on to argue that it is this cognitive-semantic knowledge which forms a prerequisite basis for the acquisition of grammar, and similar arguments have been advanced by Macnamara (1972). In a lengthy review of the arguments for what he calls the "cognition hypothesis," Cromer concludes that "we are able to understand and productively to use particular linguistic structures only when our cognitive abilities enable us to do so" (1974, p. 246), though he does go on to add that the syntactic complexity of a structure must also be taken into account: even with the necessary cognitive ability to cope with the meaning of a particular structure, the meaning/structure unit may still not be acquired if the structure itself is formally too complex.

Probably because of the similarity between the cases of Case Grammar and the categories employed by the Genevan School in their account of cognitive development, the antecedents for the semantic relations expressed in early utterances have been sought in Piaget's developmental theory. After his very detailed analysis of his own and other data from this point of view, Brown concludes that "the first meanings are an extension of the kind of intelligence that Jean Piaget calls sensori-motor" (1973, p. 198) and Wells (1974) has found that there is a clear order of emergence of semantic distinctions in early structured utterances which corresponds to a considerable extent with the order that can be predicted from Piaget's theory.

The ability to produce utterances which are both grammatically struc-

the social nature of knowledge and the interorganismic context in which it is acquired. But such statements leave unexplored the manner in which the individual constructs the internal representations he puts upon the speech and action of others and the options he chooses to deploy in the situations that he encounters. It also leaves unexplored the characteristics of the speech addressed to the child by adults that facilitate his task and how these change over time (Berko Gleason & Weintraub, 1978).

To take part in, and learn from, social interaction, requires the child to develop quite sophisticated communication skills very early in life, and this in turn implies the early development of conceptual schemes about himself and others, and about the way in which people and objects can be related in an intersubjective field of attention. As Shields (1978) points out, it is an essential presupposition of any communication that sender and receiver share a roughly similar scheme of a person, which includes the belief that speaker and hearer are alike in being able to see, hear, and manipulate the same things; they must also believe their communications will be interpreted as expressing intentionality with respect to this shared world.

Although the skills for interpersonal communication are not fully developed until well on into childhood (Flavell, Botkin, Fry, Wright, & Jarvis, 1968), recent research has shown that the infant displays certain behaviours that are important for communication at a very early age. These include a preference for faces (Schaffer, 1971), attention to speechlike sounds (Eimas, Siqueland, Jusezyk, & Vigorito, 1971), the ability, by about six weeks, to modify adult interactive behaviour by change of gaze (Stern, 1974) and, by four to six months, to follow an adult's line of regard when the adult looks away from the infant to another place (Scaife & Bruner, 1975). Stern (1977) notes that the child's interests in objects follows his interest in people, and in this he supports observations by Trevarthen, Hubley, & Sheeran (1975) which showed that some of the child's earliest spontaneous behaviour is directed towards communication with persons. This, together with their observation that at two months, a baby's activity towards people is more elaborate than any acts that he directs towards the physical or impersonal world, leads them to conclude that human infants are preadapted towards interpersonal communication.

More recently, on the basis of continuing observations of the development of the child's interaction with both people and objects, Travarthen and Hubley have identified three main stages. In the first, which they call primary intersubjectivity, the infant is capable of interactive communication with its mother and of both accommodating and assimilating action with respect to objects, but not of engaging in both types of activity simultaneously. The second stage is characterised by games, either person-person games or object-person games, as, for example, when the infant moves an object and the mother tracks it while the infant watches the mother and is amused. But it is only in the third stage, which they label secondary intersubjectivity, that full person-person-object fluency is reached, as when, for example, the mother shows the infant how to do a task, the infant accepts, then looks at mother and both are pleased (Trevarthen & Hubley, 1978). The evidence from this and the other studies mentioned above clearly shows, therefore, that before the end of the first year, the child is well able to communicate with his parents and other familiar adults about the objects and events in his environment. Such is the importance that they attach to the sequence of development they have observed, that both Richards and Trevarthen have suggested that "human intelligence develops from the start as an interpersonal process and that the maturation of consciousness and the ability to act with voluntary control in the physical world is a product rather than an ingredient of this process." (Trevarthen, 1974, p. 230)

Taking all these arguments into account, therefore, we can reasonably conclude that the child's cognitive development is indeed a prerequisite for his acquisition of the language system, but that this cognitive development is itself as much dependent on social interaction with other human beings as on perception and manipulation of a purely physical world. Furthermore, while the mastery of recognizable linguistic form may not begin until the second year, we can recognise the roots of the functional use of language in the preverbal communication between the infant and his parents in the early months of life, in which the exchange of interpersonal "meanings" forms the basis for the intersubjective construction of meanings concerning the world of objects.

However, although the infant may himself be preverbal until almost the end of his first year, language enters into his earliest social encounters with others in a variety of ways. From the beginning, the infant's environment is one in which speech is associated with many of those routine transactions such as feeding and dressing, which provide the basis for some of his earliest meaning structures (Ferrier, 1978). As Bruner (1975) reports, such transactions are often used by the mother in the later part of the first year to set up standard action frames in which vocal, and then verbal, signals are used to mark transition points in a joint activity. At the same time, much adult speech occurs as a commentary on ongoing shared activity (Wells, 1975) and as an expansion and elaboration of his own communications, and is thus, at one and the same time one of the ways in which culturally significant aspects of the child's experience are made salient (Holzman, 1974), and a model of the way in which culturally significant meanings are given linguistic realisation (Brown, Cazden, & Bellugi, 1969, Schlesinger, 1977). Thus when the child begins to produce his own spontaneous utterances, these emerge, as Bruner succinctly puts it, "as a procedural acquisition to deal with events that the child already understands conceptually and to achieve communicative objectives that the child, at least partially, can already realize by other means" (Bruner, 1977, p. 8).

If we now consider the role of the mother or other caretaker in the child's communicative development, it can be seen to be both crucial and complex. First, she must be sensitive to the child's contribution, both synchronizing her behaviour with his rhythms and signals (Stern, 1977) and being prepared to follow the direction set by his attention and interests. From the beginning, and well on into childhood, it is the child who tends to take the initiative in communicating, one of the main tasks of the adult being to sustain the interaction (Schaffer, Collis, & Parsons, 1975). Secondly, in recognising and attributing meaning to the infant's cries and smiles, and later to his actions and utterances, she acts as the "agent of the culture," reflecting back to the child a cultural interpretation of his behaviour and leading him to organize his experience along the lines that the culture treats as meaningful.

Such behaviour seems to come quite naturally, for most mothers and other caretakers—even older siblings (Blount, 1977; Shatz & Gelman, 1973) —quite intuitively treat infants as if their behaviour was intended to communicate. When these communications occur in well-defined and familiar contexts they will normally be treated as potentially meaningful and interpreted according to the mother's culturally-based expectations about the child's intentions in that particular situation. Her interpretations will not always be correct, of course, but they will be close enough on a sufficient number of occasions for successful interaction to occur. But even when they are not, this may be useful for the child, as he is able to discover what interpretation his utterances evoke and to modify them until he achieves his intended result. As Nelson (1973) points out, if the child is to make progress in communicating successfully through the conventional code of language, he must ultimately discover how to give linguistic realisation to his meaning intentions in ways that match the interpretive categories of those with whom he wishes to communicate.

However, if the child is to build up his control of the adult language, he also requires a model from which to learn: this is the third main function that the mother performs, and the one that has been most fully studied in recent years. In the following section we shall consider some of the empirical evidence on the linguistic input to children and on the relationship between this input and the child's linguistic development. Before doing so, however, we must take stock of the argument developed so far.

We have seen that a child does not have to wait until he has acquired language in order to be able to communicate with those around him. On the contrary, the evidence from studies of early infant development suggests that the infant comes into the world innately equipped to produce behaviours that are treated as communicative and that from a very early age he is able to initiate and respond to nonverbal communications. It is at this stage that the foundation of intersubjectivity and reciprocity is laid on which linguistic communication will later be built. We have also seen that this same preverbal communication provides an important context for the child's growing conceptual organisation of experience, as the recurring objects and events in his environment are brought into the arena of intersubjective attention and action. When language begins to develop, it is in this context of interaction and, at least in part, as a means to achieving more effective and mutually satisfying communication.

The stages through which this development passes have already received considerable attention, and a fairly clear picture is beginning to emerge of the sequence of development at the levels of phonology, syntax, and even semantics and pragmatics, although the range of languages studied is still severely limited. However, until very recently the focus has been almost exclusively on the child, and on his production and comprehension of utterances removed from their context of interaction. Yet linguistic interaction provides both the opportunity and the material for language learning as well as the evidence for what has been learned. It is therefore in dialogue —the child's apprenticeship is meaning—that we should look for answers to questions about development.

Before embarking on a consideration of dialogue, however, it will be helpful to consider some of the recent empirical studies of adult input to children. For although they still fail, in the main, to grasp the nettle of interaction as a dynamic process, they have provided an important step along the path towards an understanding of the relationship between linguistic experience and language development.

## ADULT INPUT AND LANGUAGE DEVELOPMENT

There is now ample evidence that adults adopt a specific register when talking to young children. Summarising the results of studies involving a wide variety of languages and cultures, Snow identifies the following features as characteristic: "that it is simple and redundant, that it contains many questions, many imperatives, few past tenses, few co- or sub-ordinations and few disfluencies, and that it is pitched higher and has an exaggerated intonation" (Snow, 1977, p. 36).

But to have identified a specific register for "talking to children" is not sufficient. As Roger Brown points out in his introduction to the collection of papers with that title (Snow & Ferguson, 1977), we must also ask why baby talk is used, and what it accomplishes, and recognise that these two questions may have different answers.

The answer to the first question may well be that the use of baby talk is not always a deliberate choice by adults, but that it is elicited by characteristics of the child's communicative behaviour in much the same way as, Stern (1977) suggests, adult social behaviours to babies are elicited by their distinctive physical appearance and expressive movements. However, when asked to reflect upon their manner of speaking to young children, adults typically are aware of having modified their speech and of having a deliberate purpose in doing so, as Garnica's (1977) study demonstrates.

In this investigation, three tasks—telling a story from a series of pictures, reading a short descriptive passage, and giving instructions on how to solve a puzzle—were administered to a group of mothers under two conditions. In the first condition, the subjects directed their speech to the adult investigator, while in the second, their speech was directed to their own children, half of whom were about 2; 3 years old and the other half 5; 4. Following the administration of the tasks, the mothers were questioned in order to discover how far they were aware of adjusting their speech when addressing young children, and what techniques they used in maintaining verbal interaction with the child. Analysis of the speech samples, which focussed specifically on prosodic features, showed that speech to two-year-olds differed from speech to adults on all six of the features investigated and from speech to five-year-olds on only some:

1. The average fundamental pitch of the speaker's voice was higher when addressing two-year-olds than five-year-olds.
2. The frequency range was greater in speech to both two- and five-year-olds than to adults, with the expansion at the high end of the range.
3. Speech to two-year-olds, but not to five-year-olds or adults, contained instances of a rising tone at the end of utterances, where the grammatical form of the utterance would predict falling tone.
4. Some utterances, or parts of utterances, directed to two-year-olds were whispered, whereas this feature was absent from speech to adults or five-year-olds.
5. The duration of certain key content words was prolonged in speech to two-year-olds, and to a lesser extent to five-year-olds.
6. Speech directed to two-year-olds contained many instances of utterances spoken with two tone units, where one tone unit, and thus only one primary stress, was the norm in speech to adults.

Interpreting her results, Garnica argues that the prosodic modifications may be seen to serve two functions. First, the higher pitch and extended pitch range, and perhaps also the use of whispering, have a predominantly social function: to identify the utterance as intended for a young child and, by giving it salience with respect to speech addressed to others, to gain the child's attention. Young children have a shorter attention span than adults and seem to "tune out" much of the speech going on around them. Prosodic marking of speech intended for a young child thus serves the prerequisite function for any communication, of securing and sustaining the child's attention. Secondly, some of these features, together with those that give prominence to salient parts of utterances such as rising tone at the end of an utterance, are seen as serving an analytic function. All these features direct attention to critical parts of the utterance and may help the child to perceive the structure and key content words in the utterance. Here, one is reminded of Operating Principle A in Slobin's discussion of universal strategies of acquisition: "Pay attention to the ends of words" (Slobin, 1973, p. 191). The rising tone has an additional function, as we shall see in a later section: it signals that the utterance is "referring" to information that is in some sense taken as given, and is calling for some sort of response. In the case of speech to young children, the response called for seems to be no more than some indication that the information has been received. In this respect it is perhaps significant that the first major functional distinction made by Halliday's child Nigel was between rising and falling tone, falling being used to signal a "proclaiming" or "mathetic" function, as Halliday calls it, to which no response was required; while rising tone was used for utterances with what Halliday calls a "pragmatic" function, to which some response was required (Halliday, 1975). However, recent work in Bristol (Montgomery, 1979) suggests that it may be pitch height rather than direction of pitch movement that serves to distinguish between these two basic discourse functions in early speech.

Attention getting and information focussing are thus the functions that Garnica sees as being the probable explanation of the prosodic features that characterised the speech to two-year-olds in her study. It is interesting, therefore, to find that in answer to the questions posed to them on completion of the tasks, the mothers reported being aware of modifying their speech in terms of raised pitch, increased pitch range, reduced volume, and slower pace, and they admitted using these features in almost all interactions, but most of all when trying to gain the child's attention. They also believed that they modified their speech in these ways because this continued to make their communication with the child more effective once attention had been secured.

Some of these features that characterize talk to young children such as higher pitch, exaggerated intonation, and short tone units, are also to be found in the speech of the children themselves. It could be, therefore, that adults adopt a style of speech which approximates that of the child in order to reduce the psychological distance between them, in the belief that this will facilitate communication. Certainly this seems more probable than the explanation given by adults in some studies for using baby talk—that of "teaching the child to speak" (Ferguson, 1977). When adults do deliberately set out to teach young children, they tend to use a narrow and stereotyped range of eliciting utterances which are by no means typical of their normal spontaneous interaction with children of this age. Direct teaching does not seem, therefore, to be the real motivation for adult use of baby talk, so much as the wish to communicate: "to understand and be understood, to keep two minds focussed on the same topic," as Brown puts it (1977, p. 12).

However, it is one thing to argue, with supporting evidence, that adults adopt a specific register in order to facilitate their linguistic interaction with young children, but quite another to demonstrate that the interaction that results makes a significant contribution to the child's linguistic development. The first attempts to show such a relationship were not notably convincing. From an examination of the data from their three subjects, Brown and his colleagues (1969) were able to demonstrate conclusively that simple positive and negative reinforcement, in the form of approval and disapproval, had no accelerating effect on the acquisition of syntax or morphology, nor did they find evidence that a communication pressure to be better understood provided the impetus towards the acquisition by the child of more mature structures (Brown & Hanlon, 1970). Mothers' habit of offering "expansions" of their children's incomplete utterances, on the other hand, seemed a more promising candidate, since the occurrence of a grammatically well-formed model uttered in close juxtaposition to the child's incomplete attempt might seem to provide an optimum opportunity for grammatical learning. To test this hypothesis, Cazden (1965) carried out an experiment in which a treatment consisting of intensive and deliberate expansions was contrasted with a treatment in which the children's utterances were responded to by a semantically appropriate "model." Contrary to expectation, however, the expansion group made no more progress than a control group which received no treatment; on the other hand, children who had received the modelling treatment made significantly greater progress.

A number of alternative explanations of the ineffectiveness of the expansion treatment were considered by Brown et al. (1969), including the possibility that a regime consisting only of expansions would be bound to include some adult utterances that confused the child by providing expansions that did not match with the child's original, incompletely-expressed intention. However, in an experiment by Feldman (1971), in which three treatments—expanding all utterances, expanding only utterances in which the meaning was clear to the experimenter, and not expanding any utterances but replying with a new sentence—were contrasted with a control group that received no treatment, no significant difference between the groups was found when they were given a test of sentence imitation at the end of the study.

Two further experiments have been carried out by Nelson (Nelson, Carskaddon, & Bonvillian, 1973; Nelson, 1977a) to try to resolve this issue. Nelson (1977b) reasons that the child's developing mastery of syntax is based on what he calls "cognitive comparison": discrepancies between the structures perceived in sentences addressed to him and those already in his repertoire lead him, over a period of time, to change his own structures in the direction of those in the language of the more mature speakers he hears. On this argument, systematically to "recast" the child's utterances into new syntactic forms while retaining their essential meaning should give the child abundant evidence to perform cognitive comparisons and thus should facilitate his development. Such a procedure was adopted in both studies (e.g., in response to the child's utterance, "The bunny chased fireflies," the adult might produce the recast sentence "The bunny did chase fireflies, didn't he?"), but the aspects of syntactic structure emphasised varied: the structure of the verb-phrase was emphasised in the first study and tag questions as well as verbs in the second. In both cases, the "recast" treatment was contrasted with a "new-sentence" group and also with a control group. On the basis of gains in complexity of verb construction and on a test of imitation (in the first study) and of change from no use to use of tag-questions (in the second study), Nelson was able to conclude that children receiving the recast sentence treatment made significantly greater progress than the control group children, who received no particular treatment. Comparison with the "new-sentence" treatment was, however, more equivocal: while differences on the measures related to the focus of the "recast" treatment approached significance, other differences were not significant.

Nelson and Nelson (1978) interpret these results as evidence in favour of the "cognitive comparison" theory of development, for which they also provide many other kinds of evidence. In general terms, they are probably right to do so, for this indeed seems to be the most plausible explanation of the child's gradual assimilation of the structure of the language to which he is exposed. But to argue that the "recast sentence" treatment, in particular, facilitates development (Nelson, 1977b) is to go beyond the evidence provided by the experiments. A more conservative interpretation would be that the positive effect of systematic intervention was established, but not the superiority of either of the two treatments. The higher scores of the "recast" groups on the subtests relevant to those aspects of sentence structure emphasized in the "recast" treatments supports their conclusion that specific treatments can facilitate acquisition of specific structures, but it does not allow the conclusion to be drawn that a treatment consisting of responding to the child with semantically and pragmatically relevant "new sentences" is not equally effective in a more general way. Certainly other authors who have experimentally compared "modelling" with "expanding" (McNeill, 1970; Menyuk, 1971) have claimed that the modelling treatment is effective.

Whatever the outcome of this dispute about the relative effectiveness of different experimental treatments, children in everyday life situations, as Brown et al., (1969) pointed out in their original discussion of Cazden's experiment, do not receive an undiluted diet of expansions (or even of "recast" or "model" sentences). Since the expansion is usually a device for checking that the child's meaning has been correctly understood, once this immediate objective has been achieved, the adult is likely to move the conversation on by introducing new but related semantic content. The same argument applies to the "recast" sentence, for in itself it is a rather unproductive contribution to conversation (Compare with the next section, "evidence from the Bristol Longitudinal Study," for further discussion of this issue). Expansions and recasts are thus not likely to occur in normal adult-child interaction with the same frequency as under experimental conditions, although, even at low frequencies, they may still have the important role that Nelson (1977b) attributes to them, of providing opportunities for making cognitive comparisons between alternative syntactic structures. For other aspects of language learning, on the other hand, such as the referential function, or the realisation of interpersonal purposes, different features of interaction may provide more effective opportunities for the appropriate types of cognitive comparison. Nor should the importance of sustaining a general motivation to engage in linguistic interaction be forgotten. To insist, unnecessarily, on expanding or recasting a child's every utterance would seem likely to lead eventually to a withdrawal by the child from engaging in conversation at all.

However, the difficulty of deciding, at this global level, between the relative effectiveness of different forms of adult response, all of which occur in spontaneous adult-child interaction, is just one instance of a more general problem. If the specific characteristics of adult speech to children occur universally throughout childhood, how does the child progress beyond the limits set by the speech addressed to him? And if all parents behave uniformly, how can one discover whether the use of this specialised register is necessary, or at least helpful, to the child?

Fortunately for those interested in finding answers to these questions, neither of these propositions is true. Considering the first of these issues in relation to the question of why adults use this register, Brown writes:

> . . . if parents were really primarily concerned with teaching the language, they ought to limit themselves to forms more advanced than baby's own. If they are really exclusively concerned with communication, with keeping two minds on target, they ought to restrict themselves to what baby knows, to BT [baby talk] and nothing else. I do think parents are exclusively concerned with communication. I do think they continuously monitor the child for signs of distraction or incomprehension and, when they see them, promptly act to correct the situation. Parents seek to communicate, I am sure, but they are not content to communicate always the same limited set of messages. A study of detailed mother-child interaction shows that successful communication on one level is always the launching platform for attempts at communication on a more adult level. (1977, p. 15)

Baby talk is thus a kind of lowest common denominator, providing a level at which communication with very young children is most assured, and to which a return can be made with slightly older children, as and when necessary. If this is correct, a global hypothesis about the use of baby talk will be too coarse; a more appropriate hypothesis will be framed in a more interactional way, with frequency of features of the baby talk register being contingent upon the child's stage of development, and more specifically on his receptive ability and on the moment-by-moment success of the ongoing interaction. Such fine tuning on the part of the adult would require sensitive attention to the child's behaviour—a skill which one might expect some adults to be more able, or more willing, to supply than others. A second hypothesis, therefore, is that children who receive speech that is more finely tuned to their receptive abilities will make more rapid progress than those who receive a less finely-tuned input, with the corollary that those who make more rapid progress will cease to receive baby talk altogether at an earlier age than those who make slower progress.

A recent study by Cross (1977) goes some way towards testing the first of these hypotheses. Working with a sample of 16 children aged between 19 and 32 months, who were selected because they showed signs of rapid language development, she collected samples of spontaneous mother-child interaction from three visits to the child's home, and on the same occasions asked the mothers to intersperse 100 items from a test of comprehension. In addition to a receptive ability score derived from observation of the child's response to these comprehension items, scores were calculated for the child variables of Mean Length of Utterance (MLU), Mean Length of 50 Longest Utterances, comprehensibility of the child's speech and vocabulary type-token ratio, while the mother's speech was scored for discourse features (semantic relatedness of mother's to child's utterances), referential characteristics (whether the utterance referred to immediately present or to displaced objects and events) and syntactic features such as complexity and proportional frequency of interrogatives, imperatives, and the like. Cross found that there was, in general, a quite high correlation between the characteristics of mothers' speech and the children's age and language maturity. Most of the discourse features of mothers' speech—i.e., expansion, self-repetitions, stock phrases—were highly negatively correlated with all measures of the child's language skill, but particularly with the child's receptive ability. On the other hand, semantically new utterances, and utterances referring to nonimmediate events were positively correlated with age and linguistic maturity, again particularly with receptive ability.

Summarising these findings, Cross considers that they provide evidence of a well-tailored input, and she concludes that "the input to rapidly developing children is graded quite continuously in tune with their linguistic and communicative abilities" (1977, p. 163). What is particularly interesting about these results is the much stronger association of features of mothers' speech with the child's receptive ability, rather than with his age or his productive ability, as measured by MLU or conversational vocabulary. On the basis of this evidence, it seems that these mothers do not simply respond in a global way to the fact that they are speaking to young children, nor are they simply modifying their speech in response to a general estimate of the child's linguistic maturity based on his output. Rather it is communication that seems to be the most important single determinant of tuning: the more the child gives evidence of understanding, the closer the mother approaches the norms of adult speech.

A second study which bears on the effectiveness of baby talk for language-learning children in that of Newport, Gleitman, & Gleitman (1977), who focussed on a range of syntactic variables in what they call Basic Motherese. Two samples of spontaneous speech were collected from 15 pairs of mothers and daughters, with the children falling into three age groups (12–15 months, 18–21 months, and 24–27 months) at the time of the first recording. The second recording was made after an interval of six months and the developmental gain made by the children over this period was related to the use of selected syntactic variables by the mothers on the first occasion of recording. As far as the characteristics of the mothers' speech are concerned, Newport and her colleagues, employing a trans-formational-generative grammatical model, argue that in many respects the mothers' speech to the children was syntactically more complex than that addressed to the adult investigator, although average utterance length was significantly shorter (MLU 4.24 compared with 11.94, $p < .001$.) They propose, therefore, that "this language style arises primarily in response to the pressures of communicating with a cognitively and linguistically naive child in the here-and-now, not from the exigencies of the language classroom" (p. 124). However, unlike Cross, they failed to find evidence that mothers tuned their speech to the growing language competence of the children, at least not as far as syntactic complexity is concerned.

Then, having partialled out the effect of the different ages and absolute levels of achievement of the children, and of the differences between mothers that were attributable to differences in the level of achievement of their children, they went on to investigate the relationship between individual differences in mothers' speech styles and children's rate of development. The results of their analyses led them to conclude that

> a broad range of language skills develops under diffuse environmental conditions. These skills, so far as we can see, are just those that reflect universal properties of human communication systems. In contrast, certain structures that are uniquely rendered in the surface forms of English (elements of the auxiliary, the inflection of the noun-phrases) are sensitive to delicate variations in mothers' style. (Newport et al., 1977,. 135)

Taken together, these two studies provide further evidence of the modification of mothers' speech to young children and give greater precision to the notion of fine-tuning. In both cases, the investigators concluded that the modifications that had been observed in the mothers' speech occurred in order to facilitate communication with the children, rather than, as Snow (1972) suggests, to provide lessons in language structure. This conclusion is also reached by de Villiers & de Villiers (1978), who have carried out an extensive review of research on this issue. However, this distinction may be more apparent than real. Information about linguistic form may be of most help to the child when it occurs embedded in the context of successful communication. This is not to argue that to focus on form would never be appropriate, however: drawing attention to causes of communication breakdown may well have an important role to play in facilitating development (Robinson, 1980), and we have already reviewed evidence that demonstrates that providing children with syntactically "recast" sentences can experimentally facilitate learning (Nelson et al., 1973; Nelson, 1977a).

In each of the studies just considered, evidence was found of tuning of mother's speech to the language behaviour of the child, but in neither case is it possible to argue that this evidence unequivocally supports the hypothesis of a facilitating effect on development of such modifications in mothers' speech as were considered in the two studies. Cross's study concerned only children showing signs of rapid linguistic development; it leaves unanswered, therefore, the question as to whether such fine tuning is universal, or whether—as is more likely—there is considerable variation between mothers. Nor, given its design, does her study tackle directly the question of a causal relationship between fine tuning and rate of development.

Newport and her colleagues' study, on the other hand, while concluding that modifications occur in the interests of communication, was concerned chiefly with an investigation of the purely syntactic characteristics of their subjects' speech, taken out of their context of communicative interaction. However, as they themselves argue, the selection of syntactic structures by adults speaking to children is influenced by other factors in addition to their relative complexity. Equally, the processing difficulty of particular structures for the child is dependent on the context in which they occur, as well as on their abstract derivational complexity. In sum, the frequency with which particular syntactic forms occur in mothers' speech may be partly the result of their selection of those which are, in some abstract terms, less complex, but to a much greater extent it results from the pragmatic intentions which are realised in their communications (Gelman & Shatz, 1977), and these in turn are influenced by their assessments of what behaviour, both linguistic and nonlinguistic, their children are capable of at different stages of development (Berko Gleason & Weintraub, 1978).

The second limitation is one that Newport, Gleitman, & Gleitman themselves recognize: it concerns the interpretation of correlational data from parent-child interaction. They argue as follows:

Suppose we were able to discover certain speech forms that could rightly be called Basic Motherese. And suppose we found that some mothers of our subject children use these forms more than other mothers. Suppose, finally, that the children of precisely those mothers who used Basic Motherese most consistently were the children who showed the greatest language growth during the six-month interval. Can we now assume that the use of Basic Motherese was responsible for this accelerated growth? No, on many grounds. One cause for skepticism is that Basic Motherese may be used more when the child is least sophisticated linguistically, but also the child may grow the fastest the less his linguistic sophistication, i.e. the more he has left to learn . . . For many reasons of this sort, any assessment of the influence of maternal speech on child language growth requires analyses more complex than simple correlations. (Newport et al., 1977, p. 113)

Consequently, as reported above, they proceeded to use partial correlational techniques to remove the effect of differences between the children in age and stage of development. However, given the size of the sample ($N = 15$) and the nonnormal distribution of scores on the measures of acquisition over the age range 12 to 27 months, their final partial correlations can only be very approximate and hardly such as to justify such specific conclusions as those that they report.

In order to overcome these problems and to address the question of the possible determining influence on language development of the "tuning" of adult speech to children, it will be necessary to make a longitudinal study of a broadly-based sample of children which spans the full spectrum of rate development. Under such conditions it should be possible to ascertain the extent to which all mothers produce finely-tuned speech and whether whatever variation naturally occurs is significantly related to differences between children in rate of development. Ideally, similar investigations would also have to be carried out across a range of cultures in which child-rearing practices were widely different before any definitive conclusions could be drawn. Although not set up with such an intention in view, the Bristol longitudinal study goes some way towards meeting the first of these requirements and, in the following section, some of the results that are beginning to emerge from this study will be discussed in relation to the question of the facilitating effect of "Motherese."

## EVIDENCE FROM THE BRISTOL LONGITUDINAL STUDY

The Bristol Longitudinal Study was begun in 1972 with the aim of describing the language development of a relatively large and representative sample of children. Two separate groups, each composed of 64 children, were selected at ages 15 months and 39 months to give equal representation to sex, four classes of family background, and all four seasons of the year for date of birth. Observations were made on each child at three monthly intervals over a period of two and a quarter years, thus providing two age points of overlap between the two groups. At each observation, a recording was made in the child's home by means of a radio-microphone worn by the child and, during the course of the day, from 9 A.M. to 6 P.M., 24 samples, each 90 seconds in duration, were taken at approximately 20-minute intervals. No researcher was present during the recording, contextual information being obtained the same evening by replaying the recording to the mother and asking her to recall, in as much detail as possible, the events taking place during each sample. This methodology obviously had disadvantages in terms of the detail and reliability of the contextualisation, but it has the enormous advantage of providing samples, comparable for each child, of the interaction which typically occurs in the normal home setting and which can reasonably be assumed to be the language environment in which development takes place.

The quantity of data obtained on each child-occasion is inevitably but deliberately limited—on average, 123 utterances for the younger children and a rather smaller number of adult utterances. But each child utterance has been comprehensively coded in terms of its pragmatic function, semantic content and syntactic form; preceding and following utterances addressed to the child have also been coded, but in a more summary form (Wells, 1973). Analysis is still in progress, so the following discussion is limited to those results, chiefly those concerning summarising indices such as Mean Length of Utterance (MLU), which are currently available.

MLU was calculated for each child-occasion using the criteria set out by Brown (1973), and a similar index was calculated on all utterances addressed to the child by adult speakers. In both cases, three measures of MLU were calculated: one based on all complete utterances, the second excluding "unstructured" utterances such as "Yes," "Hello," "Please," etc., and the third based on the five longest utterances. In general we are using the second measure, MLU (structured), for comparisons between individuals as it is much less sensitive, as an index of development, to variations in the specific purpose of the interaction, with resulting variation in the number of one-word utterances lacking internal or external grammatical structure. Figure 2-1 shows the mean MLU for both children and adults for the age range 15 to 60 months.

As would have been predicted on the basis of previous studies of adult-child interaction, the increase in the mean MLU(s) of the children is matched by a steady, although smaller, increase in the mean MLU(s) of the adults. The relationship between the two curves, which is very close to linear, yields a correlation of $r = .99$ (N = 64). (As will be seen, there are two data points at the ages of 39 and 42 months; these represent the overlap between the two age cohorts. The differences are not significant.)

When this relationship is explored further with the younger cohort

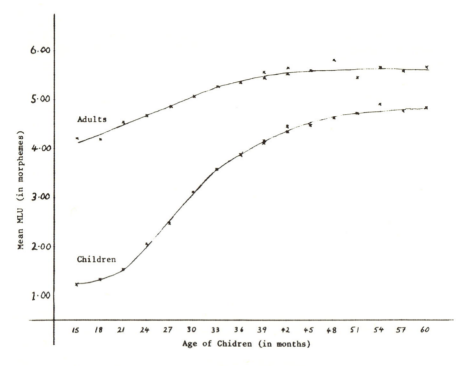

*Figure 2-1.* Mean MLU × Age of Children (N = 64).

alone, two interesting points emerge. The first concerns the relationship between child MLU and adult MLU, when all adult-child pairs are compared at particular age-points. (The term "adult" will be used throughout, as the particular adults interacting with a single child during the course of a recorded day could, and in many cases did, include the father, other relatives, and family friends, as well as the mother; however, the mother was the most frequent conversational partner on the vast majority of occasions.) When correlations between child MLU and adult MLU were calculated within occasions, these were found to be extremely low, ranging from $r = -.17$ to $+.41$, with a mean value of $r = .16$. This hardly accords with the value of $r = .56$ which Cross (1977) found, but is very close to that reported by Newport *et al.* (1977), $r = .14$.

Furthermore, the differences between child MLU and adult MLU differed very considerably from one adult-child pair to another. When the children had an MLU of approximately 1.8 morphemes, for example, the differences between child MLU and adult MLU ranged from 0.67 to 5.52 morphemes, with a mean difference of 2.82 morphemes; similarly, when the mean child MLU was 3.47, the differences ranged from $-0.68$ to $+5.19$

morphemes, with a mean difference of 1.83 morphemes. Thus, although there is a general tendency for higher child MLU to be matched by higher adult MLU, with the difference gradually decreasing, there are very large individual differences between pairs, such that any particular age, the correlation between child and adult MLU is very small.

The second point of interest arises from looking longitudinally rather than cross-sectionally at the relationship between child MLU and adult MLU. Although the number of pairs of data points is small for any adult-child pair (10 age-occasions), the resulting correlations may be taken as a rough index of the degree to which adults matched the increase in the length of their childrens' utterances over time by an increase in the length of their own utterances, irrespective of the size of the difference between adult and child MLU. These correlation coefficients for individual pairs ranged from $r = -0.43$ to $r = +0.91$, with a mean of $r = .44$. This result can be taken to indicate that there is very considerable variation in the extent to which children receive speech which is progressively adjusted to match the increasing length of their own utterances.

The sample of children Cross studied were selected because they were fast developers, and it may be a characteristic of such children that the adults who converse with them match the increase in child MLU quite closely. On the other hand, within a more heterogeneous sample, the degree of match is much more variable. Taking the results of the cross-sectional and longitudinal correlations together, therefore, it appears that while there is a general tendency for adults to match the length of their own utterances to the length of those of their children, there is variation among adults both in the extent to which they modify their speech to produce such a match and also in the size of the MLU gap that they see as appropriate.

Before going on to consider how matching of MLU is related to the children's development, another parameter of potential importance must first be considered. Because the speech data were obtained by means of a time-based sampling procedure, it is possible to compare the actual amount of speech that occurred. Since some 90-second samples were lost because the child, with his radio-microphone, was out of range of the receiver, only 18 of the 24 potential samples were used in calculating Amount of Speech. These were selected in the first instance by randomly selecting 3 out of each block of 4 samples recorded in successive one-and-a-half-hour periods from 9 A.M. to 6 P.M. Where one of these samples was out of range, the remaining sample of the 4 was used as a replacement; only in a small number of cases was it necessary to replace an out-of-range sample with one recorded in a different one-and-a-half-hour period.

Clearly, to some extent, the amount a child speaks is related to his stage of development: younger children tend to speak rather less than older children (though the amount of adult speech to the child *decreases* with the age of the child; see Figure 2-2). In order to control for this source of variation, and for random fluctuations resulting from unknown variations in the "stimulation" provided by the environment, the total number of utterances produced on three consecutive occasions was taken, with the three being selected to centre, as nearly as possible on the point at which the child's MLU (structured) reached 1.5 morphemes. The mean number of child utterances for these three occasions was 402 (S.D. 145, Range 125–697) and the mean number of adult utterances addressed to the child on these occasions was 319 (S.D. 164, Range 45–782). As is to be expected, there was a positive correlation between the amount of speech produced by the child and the amount produced by the adult, $r - .61$ ($p < .001$). For this and all subsequent analyses N = 60: 4 children dropped out of the study before the last observation, so they have been excluded from all longitudinal analyses.

In order to test the hypothesised facilitating effect of fine tuning in adult speech, some measure of development is required on which the children can be compared. One of the aims of the study is to derive a number of such measures and to investigate their interrelationships with a view to selecting the most reliable and informative, but at the time of writing MLU is the only measure that is available for all child occasions. However, since on any one occasion the standard deviation of MLU is in excess of .34 mor-

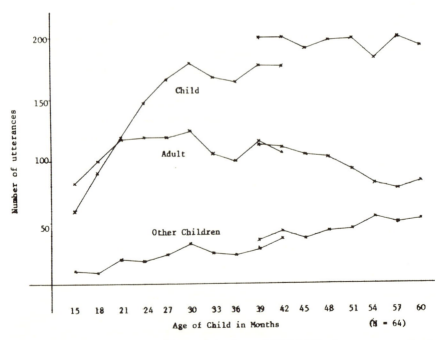

*Figure 2-2.* Mean Amount of Speech by Age of Child (27 mins. per occasion).

phemes and at 33 months is as great as .95 morphemes, it would be inappropriate to use gain in MLU between two age points as the measure of progress. Instead, the measure selected was time taken to increase MLU by a certain amount. Given the size of the interval between observations (3 months), this is inevitably a crude way of measuring progress, but it has the advantage of keeping development independent of age. The two MLU (structured) values selected were 1.5 and 3.0 morphemes. For 70 percent of the sample this interval included the period during which the auxiliary verb system was mastered (see below): only one child produced his first token of an auxiliary verb before reaching MLU = 1.5 and only one child failed to reach the auxiliary-verb criterion within three months after reaching MLU = 3.0. This interval thus corresponds quite closely to Brown's (1973) Stages II and III.

The measure of progress was thus the number of months (occasions × 3) taken to increase MLU from 1.5 to 3.0 morphemes. The shortest time in which this development could occur was 3 months (the interval between successive observations), and the longest actually observed was 18 months. Two slow-developing children still had not reached the upper point by the time of the last observation, although both were close to doing so. The mean number of months for the sample as a whole was 8.8 (S.D. 4.5). It must be stressed, however, that these values are only approximations: although the requirement that the child had to "cross the line" in order to qualify for both the initial and final values will have reduced the error in the estimate for the sample as a whole, the time taken by individuals may be over- or under-estimated by up to 3 months. Nevertheless, for the purposes of relating input to progress for the sample as a whole, it appears to be a reasonably satisfactory measure.

Ideally, an estimate of the strength of the hypothesized relationship would be obtained by carrying out a straightforward correlation of the two sets of scores. Unfortunately, neither the measure of Match in MLU nor that of Rate of progress meets the assumptions necessary for the use of product-moment correlation to be appropriate. The measure of Rate is not a continuous scale and the distribution of obtained scores is truncated, while the values on the measure of Match in MLU are themselves coefficients of correlation obtained from pairs of MLU scores. Furthermore, a scatter diagram shows that the relationship between the two variables is not obviously linear. An estimate of correlation for such data may be obtained however, by casting the data in a contingency table and computing $X^2$ and from that the coefficient of correlation $r_\phi$, by the formula $r_\phi = X^2/N$ (Guilford, 1978; p. 316). The disadvantage of this method is that the correlation values obtained are likely to underestimate the strength of the true relationships; on the other hand, where significant values are obtained, they can be accepted with greater confidence.

Using the above procedure, intercorrelations were obtained for the four variables, Amount of Child Speech, Amount of Adult Speech, Match in MLU, and Rate of Development. The results are given in Table I.

From this table it can be seen that, while Match in MLU is unrelated to Amount of Speech by either child or adult, both the Amount of Speech variables are associated with Rate of Development. The strongest relationship, however, is between Rate of Development and Match in MLU.

In order to explore these relationships further, the method of partial correlation was employed, although with some reservations, for the reasons previously discussed. First-order partial correlations were calculated between Match in MLU and Rate of Development with first Amount of Child Speech, and then Amount of Adult Speech held constant. The results were respectively $r34.1 = .42$ and $r34.2 = .39$. Partialling out the effect of Amounts of both Child and Adult Speech yields the second-order partial correlation $r34.12 = .41$ ($p < .01$). What this suggests is that, while Amount of Speech, particularly Amount of Child Speech, is significantly related to Rate of Development, this is independent of the relationship between Rate and the degree of Match in MLU.

Before discussing the implications of these findings, let us first consider the results of another aspect of the longitudinal study, an investigation of the development of the auxiliary verb system (Wells, 1979). Every instance of an anxiliary verb in the (younger sample) children's speech and in the adult speech addressed to them was classified according to form and meaning, and frequencies of both forms and meanings counted for both individuals and for the sample as a whole. Taking production by 50 percent of the sample of children as the criterion, the order in which the auxiliaries were mastered was also determined, but since a large proportion of auxiliary meanings had not reached criterion by the last observation, an alternative index of acquisition was calculated in the form of proportion of the sample having produced each auxiliary by the time of the last observation at 42 months. A similar index of use was also calculated for the corpus of adult speech. The data on auxiliary meanings are presented in Table II.

**Table I**
**Correlation Matrix: Rate of Development***

| | 1 | 2 | 3 | 4 |
|---|---|---|---|---|
| 1. Amount of Child Speech | - | | | |
| 2. Amount of Adult Speech | .42** | - | | |
| 3. Match in MLU | .05 | .13 | - | |
| 4. Rate of Development | .40 | .30 | .40 | - |

*Significance Levels. .253 $p = .05$; .333 $p = .01$; 424 $p = .001$; (N = 60).
**This correlation has been recomputed as r ∅ for purposes of comparison.

## Table II
## Development and Use of Auxiliary Verb Meanings (from Wells, 1979)

| | Total Child Frequency | Age at Criterion | Percent Children Using | Total Adult Frequency | Percent Adult Using |
|---|---|---|---|---|---|
| "Do" support | 1418 | 27 | 100 | 3374 | 100 |
| Continuous Aspect | 930 | 30 | 97 | 1569 | 100 |
| "Have got" (Possession) | 774 | 27 | 100 | 959 | 100 |
| "Can" (Ability) | 638 | 30 | 98 | 730 | 98 |
| "Will" (Intend) | 542 | 30 | 98 | 781 | 100 |
| Perfect Aspect | 540 | 30 | 98 | 1145 | 100 |
| "Be going to" | 512 | 33 | 92 | 881 | 98 |
| "Can" (Permission) | 509 | 33 | 97 | 414 | 95 |
| Continuous Aspect (Intended) | 219 | 36 | 83 | 469 | 98 |
| "Have got go" (Constraint) | 231 | 36 | 72 | 383 | 98 |
| "Will" (Predict) | 212 | 36 | 82 | 986 | 100 |
| "Shall" (Suggest Action) | 97 | 42 | 52 | 95 | 60 |
| "Will" (Request Action) | 87 | 36 | 65 | 101 | 63 |
| "Have to" (Constraint) | 55 | | 42 | 144 | 65 |
| "Must" (Constraint) | 50 | | 37 | 152 | 82 |
| "Can" (Request Action) | 37 | | 32 | 50 | 45 |
| "Could" (Lack of Constraint) | 33 | | 33 | 17 | 18 |
| "Might" (Likelihood) | 32 | | 32 | 79 | 60 |
| "Can" (Lack of Constraint) | 26 | | 33 | 31 | 33 |
| "Shall" (Intend) | 26 | | 28 | 207 | 87 |
| "Should" (Constraint) | 24 | | 25 | 53 | 53 |
| "Had better" (Constraint) | 23 | | 23 | 124 | 75 |
| "Be" + Passive | 20 | | 20 | 150 | 75 |
| "Would like to" (Request/Offer Action) | 20 | | 17 | 95 | 52 |
| "May" (Permission) | 19 | | 15 | 56 | 8 |
| "Could" (Ability) | 15 | | 20 | 29 | 28 |
| "Could" (Request Action) | 14 | | 12 | 14 | 23 |
| "Would" (Conditional) | 13 | | 17 | 53 | 53 |
| "Must" (Inference) | 7 | | 10 | 22 | 30 |
| "Would" (Intend) | 7 | | 7 | 59 | 47 |
| "May" (Likelihood) | 6 | | 3 | 3 | 5 |
| "Would" (Request Action) | 5 | | 2 | 16 | 17 |
| "Could" (Conditional) | 4 | | 7 | 7 | 7 |
| "Be able to" (Lack of Constraint) | 3 | | 5 | 41 | 43 |
| "Ought" (Constraint) | 2 | | 3 | 21 | 27 |
| "Should" (Inference) | 2 | | 2 | 7 | 8 |
| Others | | | | 11 | |

As will be seen, although the absolute frequencies from the corpus of adult speech are considerably greater than those in the children's corpus, the relative distributions in the two corpora are remarkably similar ($r_s = .88$, $p < .001$), as are the proportions of the two samples who have given evidence of use of each meaning by the time of the last observation ($r_s = .88$, $p < .001$). These similarities are rather surprising considering that, while the frequencies in the children's corpus might be partly determined by the order in which they first emerge, the adults must be presumed to have mastered all the forms before the investigation began and to have all meanings equally available for use. Even more surprising is the number of auxiliary meanings that are never used by a sizeable number of the adults. Of course these data do not allow us to infer that these meanings never occur in the speech addressed to their children by these adults, only that they are used less than once in a sample of approximately one thousand utterances.

The most obvious interpretation of these findings is that the order in which children acquire this particular subsystem of the language, and the frequency with which they use the members of the system, is accounted for by the differential frequency of the auxiliary forms and meanings in the speech addressed to them by adults. This might then be explained in terms of simple modelling or in some more interactional terms (cf. Van der Geest, Gerstel, Appel, & Tervoort, 1973). However, such an explanation assumes, first, that there is an equally close match between individual adult-child pairs and secondly that the model forms and meanings are presented with the same relative frequency throughout the period of development. Both of these assumptions are, in fact, incorrect.

Let us take the second assumption first. Just as adult speech progressively increases in length with that of the child, so does the proportion of utterances containing auxiliary verbs of any kind (from 14.1 percent at 15 months to 29.1 percent at 42 months); adults seem increasingly to use auxiliary verbs in proportion to their children's developing mastery. In addition, however, there is also a tendency for the absolutely less frequent types to be also proportionally less frequent in the early stages.

As far as the match between individual adult-child pairs is concerned, the correlations between relative frequencies in child and adult are considerably lower than for the sample as a whole and range from $r = .28$ to $r = .76$. Similarly, when the degree of match between adult and child in the proportion of utterances containing an auxiliary verb on successive occasions is calculated, as for MLU, the scores obtained range from a negative value of $r = -.44$ to a positive value of $r = +.95$.

In order to test the degree of relationship between the child's acquisition of the auxiliary verb system and variation in input in terms of either absolute frequency of utterances containing auxiliaries or matching in proportional frequency over the period of development, an index of acquisition had to be selected. In fact two such indices were used: first, the total number of auxiliary meanings that the child showed evidence of having mastered by the age of 42 months, and secondly, the amount of time that he took to progress from the first recorded occurrence of any auxiliary verb (excluding imperative "Don't") to the criterion of using 5 different auxiliary forms and of producing auxiliaries in negative and interrogative as well as positive declarative utterances. On the first index, scores ranged from 4 to 29 (Mean 17.9 S.D. 4.79), and on the second from less than 3 months to more than 12 months (Mean 5.6 S.D. 3.22). Scores on these two indices were then related to the two indices of adult input, deriving $r_\phi$ from a 2 × 2 $X^2$ table. The results are set out in Table III.

As might be expected, there is a significant positive correlation between rate of auxiliary acquisition and number of auxiliary meanings at 42 months $(r_\phi = .37, p < .01)$. This can be largely accounted for by the negative correlation between the age at reaching the criterion of 5 auxiliary forms and the number of auxiliary meanings at 42 months $(r = -.61, p < .001)$: the earlier a child reached the criterion, the greater the number of different meanings he was likely to have mastered by 42 months. The relative sizes of the remaining correlations are less easy to explain, however. Matching in proportional frequency between child and adult is not significantly related to rate of acquisition, but it is related to number of auxiliary meanings at 42 months $(r_\phi = .27, p < .05)$; however, the absolute frequency of utterances containing auxiliaries in adult speech is related to both rate of acquisition $(r_\phi = .27, p < .05)$ and, even more significantly, to number of auxiliary meanings at 42 months $(r_\phi = .40, p < .01)$. The relationship between absolute frequency and matching in proportional frequency is not significant. Computing partial correlations does not help to resolve the pattern: all the original correlation between pairs of variables are reduced by

## Table III
### Correlation Matrix: Development of Auxiliary Verb*

| | 1 | 2 | 3 | 4 |
|---|---|---|---|---|
| 1. Frequency of aux. in adult speech | - | | | |
| 2. Match in proportional frequency of aux. | .22 | - | | |
| 3. No. of aux. meanings at 42 months | .40 | .27 | - | |
| 4. Rate of aux. acquis. | .27 | .19 | .37 | - |

*Significance Levels. .253 $p = .05$; .333 $p = .01$; (N = 60).

approximately .05, indicating that the relationships are largely independent of each other.

Taking the results of the two analyses—rate of development and auxiliary verb development—together, however, does tend to confirm the picture that each separately suggests. Both quantity of speech by adult and by child, and matching of adult and child speech, are related to the various indices of development at a level that reaches significance in almost every case, but the relationships are largely independent of each other.

However, to bring these results to bear on the hypothesised facilitating effect of fine-tuning of adult speech is not at all straightforward. The finding that quantity of speech is related to rate of progress is not in itself surprising. Presumably sheer frequency of modelling of what has to be learned is of significance in accounting for development. However, to complicate the issue further, as Cross (1978) suggests, there may be some features of adult speech where sheer quantity is significant and others for which it would be more appropriate to think of a necessary threshold frequency. Nevertheless some chidren manage to make greater than average progress in spite of a relatively reduced experience of adult speech; and conversely some children apparently fail to benefit from receiving a well-above-average amount of adult input. Furthermore, the cause of this variation in amount is difficult to determine. The high correlation ($r = .61$) between amount of child and amount of adult speech suggests that, in most cases, it is a product of the particular child-adult interaction, but there are still a substantial number of cases where one partner is significantly more talkative than the other. The more talkative partner is usually the child, but this is not always the case.

The relationship between the indices of progress and the matching of MLU and of proportional use of auxiliary verbs is prima facie evidence in favour of the fine-tuning hypothesis. But once again the evidence is not unequivocal, as there are children who make more than average progress without the benefit of such fine tuning, just as there are those who fail to make average progress even though they experience a well-tuned input, as defined by the measures investigated. However, even if the relationship between fine tuning and progress is accepted, these data still fail to substantiate a causal connection. The differential progress made by children may be the result of other factors, either differences of personality that are reflected in talkativeness or in innate differences in language-learning ability, or in other differences in the environment which covary with the fine tuning of adult speech. A further problem is that the indices of fine tuning considered so far tend to be extremely gross in their ability to discriminate between the input to different children and also to ignore the ongoing context of the interaction in which specific utterances occur.

As a first attempt at overcoming some of these limitations, a different approach to the problem was adopted in an analysis of data from a subsample of the children in the older age-group, who were the subject of a follow-up study: Children Learning to Read (Wells & Raban, 1978). Instead of focussing on the form of adult speech, as in the investigation just described, attention was directed specifically to the discourse functions of adult utterances.

## Predicting Later Language Levels from Early Discourse Measures

With the gradual mastery of the adult language system, the child also develops an increasing range of topics and interpersonal purposes which he attempts to communicate through language. The role of the adult in promoting successful interaction now becomes that of seeking to understand the child's intended message and of replying in such a way that the dialogue is able to develop a stage further, this process extending over a number of turns. Since adults vary in their ability, or at least in their willingness, to help the child sustain his conversational initiatives, we hypothesized that children who receive adult feedback of this sustaining and developing kind will, compared with children who receive less such feedback, be more highly motivated to engage in conversation and, as a result, will more rapidly develop skills in linguistic communication.

To test this hypothesis, we examined the spontaneous conversation between the 20 children and their adult conversational partners (in most cases, mothers) recorded when the children were 3¼ and 3½ years old (Evans, 1977). Only sequences of conversation initiated by the children were examined, and each adult utterance was classified according to the manner in which, and the extent to which, it functioned to sustain and develop the conversation. Where the adult produced more than one utterance in a turn, each utterance was separately classified. As this was intended as no more than a preliminary investigation it was decided to operate with a limited number of rather gross categories, with the intention of refining and subdividing the categories if this proved appropriate.

The four categories were: (1) *Inappropriate:* in which the adult either ignored the child's intention and talked about something unrelated (i.e., a response showing no form of cohesion with the child's utterance [Halliday and Hasan, 1976], including pragmatic cohesion), or failed to reply altogether; (2) *Procedural:* utterances which requested a repetition or reformulation, or checked, expanded, or corrected the child's utterance, attending to the form or content of his contribution, but without responding to the intention (e.g., C: "I can see a bird"; A: "A what, love?"; C: "Its/a/fire"; A: "It's on fire"; C: "Cat comes"; A: "Yes, the cat is coming."); (3) *Plateau:* utterances responding to the content and/or intention of the child's contribution by acknowledging, confirming, rejecting, or evaluating it, but making no addition to the conversational material (e.g., C: "That will make me big"; A: "That's right"; C: "Look, it's a house"; A: "Is it?"; C: "A seal"; A: "Good boy."); (4) *Developing:* utterances which added new material and either built on the child's utterance or invited him to develop his initial message further (e.g., C: "Here's a square"; A: "Well, stick it on"; C: "I've got one of them"; A: "Yes, Aunty Dorothy gave you that"; C: "Toby lives over the road"; A: Which house does he live in?"). The distinction between this and the procedural category lies in the stance that the adult adopts to the child's contribution. In the case of a procedural response the adult is concerned to establish the well-formedness/accuracy of the child's utterance and assure her own comprehension of it, whereas in a developing response these are taken for granted and the conversation is taken a stage further, with the adult presenting either new content for the child to assimilate and respond to, or a demand for him to make such a contribution himself.

Responses of these four kinds obviously function differentially in promoting conversation. There can be no question that developing responses are more effective than those classified as inappropriate. A case could be made for the long-term effectiveness of procedural responses (cf. the earlier discussion of "recast sentences" [Nelson, 1977b] and recent work on communication breakdown [Robinson, 1980]), but in terms of the immediate conversation they introduce a hiatus in the flow and so, in this context, they are considered to be nondeveloping. Plateau responses, too, do not contribute very positively to the further development of conversation, but because they give positive recognition to the child's communicative intention, they are rated more highly than procedural responses. It is developing utterances, however, which are considered to have the most positive function, and so in assigning a weighting to each category, utterances in this category were given the heaviest weighting.

There do not seem to be any a priori grounds for deciding on a particular system of weighting, and so, as a first step, a somewhat arbitrary weighting scale was applied as follows: Inappropriate: 0; Procedural: 1; Plateau: 2. Within Developing, further distinctions were made and weighted as follows: Commands and Suggestions: 2; Polar Questions: 3; Statements and Explanations: 4; Content (wh-) Questions: 5. This last subcategory was given the heaviest weighting on the grounds that, not only does it introduce new material, but it also provides a focussed request to guide the child's further contribution (e.g., C: "One of them is called George"; A: "Is he? How do you know that?"). Clearly, other systems of weighting could be proposed with equally strong justification; it is intended to explore some of the alternatives in further investigations.

After we had classified each adult utterance, a Mean Feedback Score (MFS) was calculated for each child from the combined occasions. A second index was also computed, which took length of sequence into account, as well as the "quality" of feedback. We argued that it would be possible for a child to receive a large number of developing responses which, because they were inappropriate to his level of comprehension, still failed to encourage him to continue the conversation; in this case, the conversation would either stop, or there would be a procedual hiatus while the difficulty was sorted out. Length of sequence, with procedual exchanges omitted, might thus be an indication of the communicative effectiveness of the adult contribution. Accordingly, a score for mean length of sequence was calculated, omitting procedual exchanges, and this was used to weight the feedback score to yield an index of Conversational Richness (CRS).

In order to test the hypothesis of the facilitating effect on development of experience of sustaining and developing adult feedback, as measured by MFS and CRS, these two indices were correlated with a number of indices of oral language obtained from the spontaneous speech data recorded at 4¾ and 5 years, just prior to the child's entry into school. Since these children were the subjects in an investigation of the development of reading, test scores were also available from the final assessment of their reading attainment at age 7, and from interview schedules administered to their parents at the time of the child's entry to school. Factor analysis of the various measures of reading at 7 years yielded a first factor clearly identifiable as "reading attainment." Scores on this factor were then taken as a broad-based measure of reading attainment. The pattern of intercorrelations among these variables can be seen in Table IV.

In considering these results, let us first examine the relationship between the two indices of adult feedback and the indices of oral language at 5 years. All correlations are positive and most are statistically significant at the 5 percent level or better. In every case the correlations are greater with Mean Feedback. However, since there are substantial positive correlations between the two indices of feedback and the children's MLU at the same age (3½ years), it is possible that the feedback as such is not directly associated with later oral language scores, but is only associated with them by virtue of the relationship between earlier and later oral language measures.

Partial correlations were therefore calculated, holding the effect of MLU at 3½ years constant. The result is that all the correlations between the indices of adult feedback and oral language at age 5 are substantially reduced: all remain positive, but only those between feedback and Semantic Range and Syntactic Complexity now reach the 5 percent significance level. Clearly this must qualify the interpretation of the initial correlations, but it can still be argued that there is evidence of a positive association between quality of adult feedback and children's subsequent rate of oral language development.

The correlations between the adult feedback indices and the measure of

**Table IV**
**Correlation Matrix: Adult Feedback and Language Development***

| | 1 | 2 | 3 | 4 | 5 | 6 | 7 | 8 | 9 | 10 | 11 |
|---|---|---|---|---|---|---|---|---|---|---|---|
| 1. Mean Feedback Score (at age 3½) | - | | | | | | | | | | |
| 2. Conversational Richness (at age 3½) | .92 | - | | | | | | | | | |
| 3. MLU (Structured) (at age 3½) | 46 | .40 | - | | | | | | | | |
| 4. MLU (Structured) (at age 5) | .51 | .41 | .66 | - | | | | | | | |
| 5. MLU (Longest) (at age 5) | .55 | .42 | .62 | .86 | - | | | | | | |
| 6. Semantic Range (at age 5) | .63 | .58 | .43 | .67 | .72 | - | | | | | |
| 7. Semantic Modification (at age 5) | .57 | .49 | .58 | .73 | .77 | .69 | - | | | | |
| 8. Pragmatic Range (at age 5) | .51 | .40 | .52 | .55 | .48 | .56 | .54 | - | | | |
| 9. Syntactic Complexity (at age 5) | .61 | .57 | .86 | .75 | .70 | .64 | .74 | .63 | - | | |
| 10. Parental Interest in Child's Literacy | .60 | .58 | .25 | .45 | .39 | .46 | .47 | .56 | .41 | - | |
| 11. Reading Attainment (at age 7) | .63 | .66 | .22 | .33 | .32 | .39 | .53 | .43 | .32 | .73 | - |

*Significance Levels: .433 $p$ = .05; .549 $p$ = .01; (N = 20).

reading attainment strongly reinforce such an interpretation, and in this case the correlations are not substantially reduced when the effect of MLU at 3½ years is partialled out. Compared with these feedback indices, the indices of oral language on entry to school are much less significantly related to reading, although it is these that might have been expected to be more strongly associated with reading, all the more since they are closer in time. In discussing these latter results, Wells and Raban (1978) suggest that they should not be taken to indicate that oral language ability is not an important prerequisite for making progress in learning to read, but rather that once a certain threshold of oral language ability is reached, it is other factors that account for variation in attainment at this early stage, notably the knowledge the child has on entry to school about the purposes and conventions associated with written language, and the general level of interest in books and reading that has been transmitted to him by his parents' involvement with him in such activities in the preschool years. This interpretation is supported by the strong correlation between Reading Attainment and Parental Interest in Literacy ($r$ = .73 $p$ < .01) and by a similar strong correlation with scores on a test of knowledge of literacy (Clay, 1972) administered on entry to school ($r = .74\, p < .01$).

From these latter results it is clear that the quality of adult feedback is not the only influence that the home exerts on reading attainment in the early years of school. It seems probable, however, that these other influences act in combination with quality of feedback in promoting reading progress. In order to gain some estimate of the relative independence of the two aspects of home influence, a partial correlation between Mean Feedback and Reading Attainment was calculated with Parental Interest in Literacy held constant. As anticipated, the result ($r_{12.3} = .35$) shows that there is a substantial area of overlap between these two influencing factors, with Mean Feedback alone not achieving a statistically significant relationship with reading attainment. (A similar partial correlation for Conversational Richness yields a higher value [$r = .43$] but this too just fails to reach statistical significance.)

The final picture that emerges from this investigation is not straightforward, therefore. Although simple correlations between the indices of feedback and later indices of language development are all positive and in most cases statistically significant, the conclusion that adult feedback exerts a direct facilitating effect must be qualified in a number of ways. First, the measures of feedback were obtained from two occasions of recording only, both at the beginning of the study. But it is very probable that an analysis of subsequent recordings would show a continuation of approximately the same differences between children in the quality of feedback received. The feedback measures are better thought of, therefore, as indices of the general level of the adult contribution to the conversation that the child experiences throughout the period under investigation. Secondly, the positive association between feedback and parental interest in literacy suggests that quality of adult conversational feedback is just one index of a more general difference between parents in the extent to which they encourage their children to use the resources of language, both spoken and written, to extend their understanding and control of the world in which they live.

However, the most important reason for exercising caution in interpreting the results as evidence of a simple causative relationship between adult feedback and children's subsequent language development is to be found in the concept of feedback itself. For adult behaviour to be described as feedback, it must be contingent upon the behaviour of the child. And this immediately implies that the relationship between adult speech at one point in time and child speech at the same or a later time cannot be unidirectional. The correlations between adult feedback and child MLU at 3½ years can be seen as one kind of evidence of just such responsiveness on the part of adults to the children's level of linguistic development, as indeed can most of the results discussed above. On the other hand, the fact that, even with the effect of differences between children in MLU at 3½ partialled out, there is still a strong tendency for differences between children in their rate of language development to be associated with quality of adult feedback suggests that there are important differences between adults in the way in which they take up the opportunities for conversational interaction provided by their children's initiations.

In summary, therefore, the investigations reported in this section provide evidence that variation in some features of adult speech to children is associated with the children's rate of language development. It is tempting to interpret this evidence as providing support for the hypothesis that this relationship is one of facilitation, but there are problems associated with such an argument which cannot be resolved by correlational studies of summary data. If the child learns language through linguistic interaction, which was the argument put forward in the first section of this chapter, "The Argument for an Interactionist View of Language Acquisition," investigations based on an input-output model will never provide an adequate explanation of the processes involved, for these processes are essentially reciprocal. It is to a consideration of linguistic interaction, therefore, and of some of the problems raised by the attempt to study interaction, that we shall turn in the following section.

## LINGUISTIC INTERACTION AND SOME INFLUENCING FACTORS

The evidence reviewed so far convincingly shows that there is a relationship between modifications in adult speech to children and development by children in their control of the language system, but it still leaves unanswered the questions as to whether it is a causal relationship and, if so, the direction of causality, and whether variation in the fine tuning of the modification is responsible for variation in rate of development. In this section I wish to consider some of the problems—all of them to do with the way in which we conceptualise interaction—which have to be resolved before anwers to these questions can be reached. However, before posing the problems, it may be helpful to look at some typical examples of conversation taken from the Bristol longitudinal study and to attempt to describe, in a relatively informal way, what seem to be some of the salient features of the interaction.

The first two examples feature Mark, the eldest child of parents with an intermediate level of education. At the time of the first recording, Mark was 23 months old and had been "talking" for several months, although he was still at what Brown (1973) labels Stage I. On the first occasion Mark had been playing for some time in the kitchen, where his mother was occupied with domestic tasks. His younger sister was sitting in her high chair and

Mark was looking into a mirror. (The conventions of transcription are given in Appendix 1.)

The first thing that strikes one on listening to this snatch of conversation is how many of the features characteristic of mature conversation are already present: turn taking is well established and there is continuity of

## Mark (23 months) is in the kitchen
## with his mother and sister Helen (9 months)

| | | | |
|---|---|---|---|
| 1 | 232 'Mummy (v) | | [Mark is looking in a mirror |
| 2 | 13 'Mummy | | and sees reflections of him- |
| 3 | | M: 23 'What? | self and his mother] |
| 4 | 24 'There / there 34 'Mark | | |
| 5 | | M: Is that 232 'Mark? | |
| 6 | 231 'Mummy | | |
| 7 | | M: 231 'Mm | |
| 8 | 231 'Mummy | | |
| 9 | | M: 231 'Yes / that's 231 'Mummy | |
| 10 | 453* | | |
| 11 | 24 'Mummy | | |
| 12 | 232 'Mummy (v) | | |
| 13 | | M: 231 'Mm | |
| 14 | 24 'There / 231 'Mummy | | |
| | | . . . | |
| 15 | 232 'Mummy (v) | | |
| 16 | 13 'There / Mark 24 'there | | |
| 17 | | M: 2 'Look at 24 'Helen | |
| 18 | | M: She's going to 13 'sleep (30 seconds interruption) | |
| 19 | 13 '/ɛæt/ (=look at that) | | [Mark can see birds in the garden] |
| 20 | 23 'Birds / 34 'Mummy (v) | | |
| 21 | | M: 213 'Mm | |
| 22 | 23 'Jubs (=birds) | | |
| 23 | | M: What are they 34 'doing? | |
| 24 | Jubs 13 'bread | | |
| 25 | | M: Oh 213 'look | |
| 26 | | M: They're 343 'eating / the 12 'berries / 14 'aren't they? | |
| 27 | 24 'Yeh | | |
| 28 | | M: 2 'That's their 213 'food | |
| 29 | | M: They have 343 'berries / for 23 'dinner | |
| 30 | 24 'Oh | | |

topic over several turns; both participants introduce new information, and responses are given which signal that the information has been received. On further examination, however, it becomes apparent that the appearance of normality owes a great deal to the mother's skill, both in interpreting Mark's contributions and in responding in such a way that those contributions are woven into a coherent conversational fabric.

In this passage, Mark performs three different communicative acts: he attempts to initiate interaction (1, 12, 19), he draws his mother's attention to what is currently interesting him (4, 6, 8, 14, 16, 20, 25) and he acknowledges his mother's communications (27, 30). His mother's acts are more varied, but they too can be divided into three matching groups: those that signal willingness to interact (3, 13), those that acknowledge and confirm Mark's contributions (5, 7, 9, 21), and those that introduce new material into the conversation (17, 18, 23, 26, 28, 29). It is noticeable, however, that it is only when Mark has initiated the topic that the mother's attempts to introduce new material are acknowledged. It appears to be easier, in this case at least, for successful communication to take place when the topic for discussion has been proposed by the child.

There are, however, two other features of the mother's contributions that may be significant for the sustaining of the interaction. The first is that, as well as simply acknowledging Mark's ostensive-informing utterances, she responds with utterances which elicit further contributions from Mark (5, 23, 26). These utterances thus have a "prospective" as well as a "retrospective" function in managing the discourse. The second feature is the liberal use of cohesive devices (Halliday & Hasan, 1976) to maintain the linguistic as well as the situational intersubjectivity of the topic. These devices range from direct lexical repetition (5, 9), through anaphoric reference ("they" and "their" in 23-29), to lexical collocation ("berries" - "food" - "dinner" in 26-29). In these latter utterances in particular, the child is being given the opportunity to learn both the referential links between lexical items and the objects and events to which they refer, and the intralinguistic meaning-relations that hold between these words.

Intonation provides yet another dimension that is drawn upon to facilitate collaboration. Perhaps the most striking feature of this example is the unusually high proportion of utterances at the higher end of the pitch range. This, as Garnica has shown (1977), is characteristic of early mother-child interaction: the use of higher than normal pitch by the mother probably serves the function of attracting and retaining the child's attention. But it is interesting to note that the child also makes considerable use of the higher end of his pitch range. Is this because he too is trying to secure his mother's attention and to do so he makes use of the same device, or is there some further explanation?

A careful inspection of the direction of pitch movement and of pitch height in relation to the function of particular utterances suggests that intonation is serving a variety of purposes in this interaction. Looking at Mark's utterances first, we see that he makes systematic use of at least three tones: tone 4 (fall-rise): (1, 12, 15); tone 1 (fall): (2, 4, 16, 19, 20); and tone 2 (high rise): (6, 8). These seem to serve the functions of, respectively, initiating interaction, announcing new information, and seeking agreement about what is announced. The mother also uses the same three tones and with approximately the same functions, with tone 2 being characteristically a response tone which is selected when she confirms Mark's intonationally expressed assumption that his meanings are already shared information (7, 9, 13). She also uses a further tone (tone 5: rise-fall) which occurs twice as the first part of a three-tone-unit contribution containing new information (25, 28). These utterances are particularly interesting as they also show unusually high pitch within the pitch movement of the tone, in what is an exaggerated version of the information-giving tone (tone 1). In both contributions the mother seems to be trying to make Mark aware of both an observable event and the linguistic representation of the event.

If the most salient characteristic of this first example of interaction is the willingness of the mother to allow the child to propose the topics for joint attention, this is seen in an even clearer form in the second example, taken from a recording made just over two months later (page 82).

This extract has even more of the appearance of "conversation" than the first. What is more, it consists of talk about something that is not actually physically present. Mark notices that a man he had seen working in his garden earlier that morning is no longer there, and he asks his mother where the man has gone. However, not satisfied with her rather mundane answer, he offers an alternative possibility which, with his mother's help and encouragement, develops into a fantasized shopping expedition in which he himself takes over the role of principal actor.

The development in Mark's control of linguistic form is quite apparent: the particular characteristic use of tone 4 to signal a question in the absence of syntactic marking (note the mother's use of the same tone with a questioning function in the previous example [5]); the attempt to manage past time reference (1, 35–38); the appearance of subject-verb-object construction (28, 35) but with division of the utterance into more than one tone unit.

What is noticeable about his mother's part in this conversation is her immediate willingness to follow Mark's lead when he suggests that the man has gone to the shop. Having checked that she has correctly understood Mark's suggestion as to where the man has gone, she extends the idea by calling forth a catalogue of purchases, without too much regard to the plausibility of the particular items on the shopping list. The result of this encouragement is that Mark produces his first example of a "story" in the

## Mark (25 months) is in the dining room with his mother.
## He is looking out of the window.

---

| | | |
|---|---|---|
| 1 | Where 232 'man gone? | [Mark has seen a man work- |
| 2 | Where 232 'man gone? | ing in his garden] |
| 3 | | M: I don't 13 'know |
| 4 | | M: I 2 ex'pect he's gone 23 in'side / because it's 34 'snowing . . . |
| 5 | Where man 231 'gone? | |
| 6 | | M: In the 113'⅓house |
| 7 | 32 'Uh? | |
| 8 | | M: Into his 34 'house |
| 9 | 232 'No | |
| 10 | 121 'No | |
| 11 | Gone to 23 'shop / 33 'Mummy(v) | [The local shop is close to |
| 12 | | M: Gone 342 'where? | Mark's house] |
| 13 | Gone 24 'shop | |
| 14 | | M: To the 231 'shop? |
| 15 | 23 'Yeh | |
| 16 | | M: 2 'What's he going to 34 'buy? |
| 17 | 44 er - / 231 'biscuits | |
| 18 | | M: 232 'Biscuits / 343 'mm |
| 19 | 32 'Uh? | |
| 20 | | M: 343 'Mm |
| 21 | | M: What 34 'else? |
| 22 | 44 er - / 231 'meat | |
| 23 | | M: 33 'Mm |
| 24 | 342 'Meat | |
| 25 | 33 er - / 231 'sweeties | |
| 26 | Buy a 23 'big / 34 'bag / 45 'sweets | |
| 27 | | M: Buy 232 'sweets? |
| 28 | 24 'Yeh | |
| 29 | M - er - buy - man / the 23 'man / 23 'buy / 34 'sweets | |
| 30 | | M: 32 'Will he? |
| 31 | 23 'Yeh | |
| 32 | Daddy buy 232 'sweets | |
| 33 | Daddy buy 342 'sweets | |
| 34 | | M: 24 'Why? |
| 35 | 23 'Oh / er - / ə / 23 'shop | |
| 36 | Mark do buy 32 'some - / 32 'sweet - / 43 'sweeties | |
| 37 | Mark buy 32 'some - / 32 'um - | |
| 38 | Mark buy 32 'some - / 32 'um - | |
| 39 | I 342 'did | |

recorded data and, at the same time, some of the most complex utterances that occurred in this recording.

The strategy employed by Mark's mother on this occasion contrasts quite strongly with that of the mother of another boy of identical age. This mother is quick to seize an opportunity to exploit her child's opening to continue the conversation, but the shape she gives to it through her contributions is very different.

Firstly, Thomas's mother treats his initiating utterances as an opportunity to relate the present situation to a previous event, which she believes he will be able to recall. But when Thomas either confuses, or fails to understand, the time reference, and gives answers that fail to match visitors with weekends, his mother insists on "correcting" him. This she does by shifting her own temporal frame of reference to one within which his answer would be factually correct. (Later in this recording, talking about friends Thomas has

---

**Thomas (25 months) is in the living room with his mother.***

| | | |
|---|---|---|
| 1 | 13 'Biscuits | |
| 2 | | M: Those were got 23 'specially / we had 14'⅓visitors at the weekend |
| 3 | | M: Who came to 23 'see / 32 'Tommy (v)? |
| 4 | | M: Who 3 'came in a 34 'car? |
| 5 | See Grannie 24 'Irene / / ə / 33 'car | |
| 6 | | M: Grannie 24 'Irene's coming / 34 'next weekend |
| 7 | | M: But who came 24 'last weekend? |
| 8 | Auntie 23 'Gail / in / ə / 24 'train | |
| 9 | | M: <u>Auntie</u> 3 'Gail's 43 'coming |
| 10 | | M: They're coming on the 35 'train / 34 'yes |
| 11 | Colin in / ə / 24 'train | |
| 12 | | M: 24 'Colin - / Colin er and 24 'Anne came in the <car> / 35 'didn't they? |
| 13 | Colin / ə / 24 'Anne | |
| 14 | Colin / ə / 24 'Anne | |
| 15 | | M: 24 'Yes |
| 16 | Colin / ə / 24 'Anne | |
| 17 | Colin / ə / 24 'Anne | |
| 18 | | M: Colin and 24 'Anne came in the train |
| 19 | In / ə / 33 'train | |
| 20 | Auntie 33 'train | |
| 21 | | M: No 2 'not 34 'Auntie train / 45 'darling(v) |
| 22 | | M: Auntie 23 'Gail / and Grannie 23 'Irene / are coming on the 34 'train / on 24 'Friday |
| 23 | Auntie 232 'Gail / in / ə / 24 'train | |

seen at a party, she adopts the same strategy of changing the frame of reference, in order to be able to impose relevance on his response.)

The second important difference between the two examples lies in the stance she adopts to the information which forms the content of the conversation. Whereas Mark's mother enters into the topics that Mark proposes and makes them shared topics, Thomas's mother adopts the position of arbiter: she is in possession of the information, and Thomas's task is to match his answers to what she already knows. In this way, her style of interaction is very reminiscent of much classroom interaction between teachers and pupils.

However, what the mothers of both Mark and Thomas attempt to do is to find a way of treating their children's utterances as relevant to an agreed topic of discourse and hence as potential material for further conversation. If the utterances fail to fit the "facts" as the adult perceives them, two possible options are open, short of outright rejection: either to change the perception of the facts by moving into a "possible" as opposed to the "actual" world, or to bring utterances and world into a better fit by accepting the utterance and finding some related part of the actual world to which it can be seen to apply. Where Mark's mother takes the first course, Thomas's mother takes the second.

The child's problem is that he is attempting to master three different systems simultaneously: real-world knowledge about events taking place in time, the linguistic representation of those same events, and the rules or maxims that make it possible for two separate centres of individual experience to collaborate in the negotiated construction of a joint edifice of meaning (Shields, 1978). It can hardly be a surprise, therefore, if the child fails to manage all three simultaneously, and that the mother has to deploy strategies of various kinds to maintain the coherence and continuity of the conversation.

The next example again concerns Mark, at the age of nearly 28 months. By now he is quite skilful at using language to negotiate his intentions. In this episode he wants his mother to play, and is willing to "help" her in exchange for her undivided attention.

Completing the task the mother gives him causes Mark problems in converting verbal instructions into action and, in order to guide him in completing the task, she has to use a particular strategy of dividing the instruction into smaller parts (17), and pointing up the key terms by marking them with tonic stress (17, 21–22, 27).

In the previous extracts, it will be recalled, Mark was able to play a full part in conversation if he was the initiator of the topic. Here it is the mother who initiates the sequence concerning the basket lid, and Mark, because he has an interest in satisfying his mother's request, goes on trying to comprehend and carry out the instruction until success permits him to

## Mark (28 months) and his mother are in the kitchen.
## She has just finished washing up.

| | | |
|---|---|---|
| 1 | 13 'Play mummy(v) | |
| 2 | | M: All 232 'right |
| 3 | 1 '/∫i∫/ wash 32 'up /21 'mummy(v)? (= have you finished washing up?) | |
| 4 | | M: 21 'Pardon? |
| 5 | 1 '/∫i∫/ wash 31 'up? | |
| 6 | | M: 44 'Yes |
| 7 | 34 'Oh | |
| 8 | | M: Let me just 24 'dry my hands |
| 9 | 343 'Alright | |
| 10 | 23' In there | [Mark looks for towel] |
| 11 | | M: <24 'Here> |
| 12 | 34 '/i ə α/ (=here you are) | [Mark gives towel to Mother] |
| 13 | | M: 2 'Just a 343 'minute |
| 14 | | M: Will you put the 2 'top back on the 23 'washing basket / 32 'please |
| 15 | 32 'Uh? | |
| 16 | 31 'Uh? | |
| 17 | | M: 3 'Put the 32 'top / back on the 14 'washing basket |
| 18 | ↑On 13 'there /32 'mummy(v)? | |
| 19 | On 232 'there? | |
| 20 | | M: 32 'Yes |
| 21 | | M: No not the 2 'towel in 43 'there |
| 22 | | M: The 2 'top of the 24 'basket on it |
| 23 | 343 'Alright | |
| 24 | On 24 'there | |
| 25 | ↑31 'Uh? | |
| 26 | 32 'Uh? | |
| 27 | | M: 2 'Put the 32 'lid / . . on 2 'top of the 24 'basket |
| 28 | Oh er- on 232 'there? | |
| 29 | | M: Yes 33 'please |
| 30 | 232 'Alright | |
| 31 | 32 'You / 32 'dry / 42 'hands | |
| 32 | | M: I've 23 'dried my hands now |
| 33 | Put towel in 34' there | |
| 34 | | M: 13' No / it's 2 'not 32 'dirty |

**Mark (28 months) and his mother are in the kitchen.**
**She has just finished washing up.**

| | | |
|---|---|---|
| 35 | 342 'Tis | |
| 36 | | M: No it 32 'isn't |
| 37 | 342 'Tis | |
| 38 | 32 'Mummy(v) / 24 'play | |
| 39 | 23 'Play mummy(v) | |
| 40 | | M: Well I 13 'will play / if you put the 2 'top on the 32 'basket |
| 41 | 342 'Alright | [Mark puts top on basket] |
| 42 | 24 'There | |
| 43 | 34 'There | |
| 44 | 14 'Play mummy(v) | |

return to his original demand: "Play, Mummy" (44). A particularly striking feature of his conversational style is the way in which he oscillates between initiating subsequences in the interaction (3, 12, 31) and acknowledging and checking that he is carrying out his mother's request correctly (9, 18, 28). He makes considerable use of "place-holding" vocalisation, "Oh" (7), "alright" (9, 23, 30, 41) "uh" (15, 16, 25, 26), said with appropriate intonation, to maintain the flow of the conversation. As a result, his mother no longer has to work so hard to ensure continuity, and can concentrate more on using speech to control their shared activities.

My final example again concerns a scene in the kitchen, but this time one of potential conflict. While her mother is at the sink washing the dishes, Jacqueline (27 months) is exercising her skill in putting back into the laundry bag the dirty clothes that her mother had taken out in preparation for the weekly wash.

Jacqueline begins by commenting on her activity for her own benefit and then in (5) repeats her utterance in order to share her interest with her mother. Mother's immediate reaction on seeing what Jacqueline is doing is to prohibit the activity (6—7), being more concerned with her own plans than with those of her daughter. However, Jacqueline has equally firm intentions and she attempts to ward off her mother's interference using exactly the same rising pitch and accelerating pace as her mother had just used to her. Her mother, seeming to recognise the validity of Jacqueline's intention, accedes with deferred permission, coupling this (11–12) with a statement of the conditions under which the action will be appropriate.

Later within the same extract there is another potential conflict, this time over what meaning is intended. Jacqueline has seen a pair of her socks in the washing and tries to bring them to her mother's attention, while at the same time focussing on the fact that they had been given to her by her

**Jacqueline (27 months), Jane (13 months) and Mother are in the kitchen. Jacqueline is playing with the laundry and Mother is washing up.**

| | | |
|---|---|---|
| 1 | "24 ˈLaundry bag" (sing-song) | [J picks up laundry bag] |
| 2 | "35 ˈLaundry bag" | |
| 3 | "In 14 ˈthere" | |
| 4 | "↑Put all . 24 ˈthing in" | [J is putting washing in the bag] |
| 5 | ↓I'm putting 35 ˈthings <u>in</u> | |
| 6 | | M: 24 'N<u>o</u> / 53 ˈdarling(v) |
| 7 | | M: No ↑no ↑↑no 15 ˈno (accel.) |
| | | . . . . |
| 8 | ↑I want to ↑↑↑ ˈput those 12 ˈthings (accel.) | |
| 9 | | M: 33 ˈYes |
| 10 | | M: 2 ˈWhen they're 243 ˈwashed you can |
| 11 | | M: 2 ˈNot 243 beˈfore |
| | | . . . |
| 12 | What's 24 ˈthat / 54 ˈMum(v)? | |
| | | M: NR |
| | | . . . . |
| 13 | 3 ˈYou: dirty 45 ˈcat (to Jane) | |
| 14 | | M: ↓34 ˈOh: / she's 24 ˈnot: (softly) |
| | (laughs) | |
| 15 | | M: She's 3 ˈnot a dirty 43 ˈcat |
| 16 | | M: 24 ˈAre you / 34 ˈdar-ling(v)? (to Jane) |
| | | . . . . |
| 17 | | M: 323 ˈNo (command to Jacq.) |
| 18 | | M: 2 ˈLeave Mummy's wash-ing 343 aˈlone / 43 ˈplease |
| 19 | | M: Mummy's got to 354 ˈwash all that (firmly) |
| 20 | Wash 243 ˈLinda's - | [Auntie Linda has given J some socks which she refers to as Linda's socks] |
| 21 | 3 ˈThere's *24 ˈsocks | |
| 22 | | M: *** |
| 23 | 14 ˈLinda / 3 ˈbought you 34 ˈsocks / 54 ˈMum(v) (you = me) | |
| 24 | | M: 34 ˈYes / there's 24 ˈyour socks |
| 25 | Lin- | |
| 26 | | M: Mummy's 24 ˈwashing them |

**Jacqueline (27 months), Jane (13 months) and Mother are in the kitchen. Jacqueline is playing with the laundry and Mother is washing up.**

| | | |
|---|---|---|
| 27 | | M: I've got to 243 'do all that now |
| 28 | 24 'Linda / 3 'bought you 45 'socks / 54 'Mum(v) | |
| 29 | | M: 34 'Yes |
| 30 | | M: Linda bought you 45 'socks (softly) . . 5 . . |
| 31 | | M: They're 24 'dirty |
| 32 | | M: They've 3 'got to be 24 'washed |
| 33 | Did . Linda bought <you> - me got . washed (false starts) ( = ? have the socks that Linda brought me got to be washed?) | |
| 34 | | M: 31 'Pardon? |
| 35 | 24 'Linda wa - / 324 'wash them | |
| 36 | | M: 23 'No |
| 37 | | M: 23 'Mummy's going to / 35 'wash them |
| 38 | 15 'Linda wash them | |
| 39 | | M: 24'No / Linda's 34 'not going to / 45 'wash them |
| 40 | 24 'Linda not going to / 54'wash them | |
| 41 | | M: 35 'No |
| 42 | | M: 35 'Mummy wash them . . . |
| 43 | 12 'This is 13 'Daddy's socks / 43 'Mum(v) | |
| 44 | | M: 32 'Pardon? |
| 45 | This is 24 'Daddy's sock | |

Auntie Linda (23). Her mother is rather slow to pick up this aspect of the message and instead, develops the topic of the second tone-unit: "socks" (26–27, 29–32). Jacqueline then seems to try to incorporate all the information so far mentioned in one utterance (33), but has difficulty in organising the form of her utterance to encode her meaning intention with the designed information focus. A second attempt (35) clearly does not conform to the reality of the situation, nor even, as far as one can judge, to her own meaning intention. The problem seems to result from a conflict between two intentions: the first is to ask for confirmation of the proposition that the socks have to be washed, and the second is still to focus attention on the fact that it was Linda who had given her the socks. However, her control of syntax is inadequate for the task and her mother, not surprisingly, rejects Jacqueline's statement as inaccurate and, using marked tonic placement, offers a constrasting true statement (37). Jacqueline rejects her mother's version, presumably because there is no mention of Linda, and reaffirms her original statement, whereupon her mother tries an alternative strategy and explicitly negates Jacqueline's statement. In reply (40), Jacqueline uses marked tonic placement to indicate her acceptance of the fact that it is not *Linda* who is going to wash the socks, and Mother, picking up the constrastive implication of the tonic placement in Jacqueline's utterance, returns with a positive statement in which "Mummy" is the Agent. Jacqueline's silence is to be taken as agreement with this negotiated description of the situation which, it will be noticed, represents a compromise between what seem to have been the separate meanings contributed by the two participants.

## Some Issues in the Study of Adult-Child Interaction

With these specific examples of mother-child interaction to refer to, we are now in a better position to consider some of the issues which I see as still in need of systematic attention. The first of these concerns the range of influences that are recognised as having an effect on the type of interaction that takes place. The level of the child's linguistic development, particularly his comprehension, has already been singled out for attention, as has the sensitivity of the adult which influences the extent of the "fine tuning" in her response to the child's comprehension. Both these are evident in the examples just considered. But there are clearly other factors that are of importance. The first of these is the situational context, and in particular the purposes of the participants within that situation.

A second, and more enduring, source of variation in style of interaction concerns the effect of temperament or personality (Escalona, 1969). Clearly, differences between children in such traits as activity level, curiosity, and responsiveness are likely to lead to different forms of interaction over and above those related to level of development. Similar tempermental differences between adults are likely to be equally influential, as are more short-term influences such as depression or ill health. There are also likely to be important consequences of temperamental match and mismatch between children and their caretakers. Perhaps here lies part of the explanation of the reports we received from many of the parents in our study that the child we were actually observing had a very different starting age and rate of development from an immediately preceding or following sibling, in spite of the family environment having apparently remained unchanged.

Similarly important in their effect on the interaction are differences between adults in their beliefs and values concerning appropriate methods of child rearing. This is a subject which has been treated both theoretically and empirically by sociologists and social psychologists (Bernstein, 1971, Hess & Shipman, 1965; Newson & Newson, 1970), but which has not yet been systematically attended to in the work on early adult-child interaction, except by Katherine Nelson, in a study to be discussed below (Nelson, 1973). We can, I think, see differences between the mother-child pairs quoted above which are attributable to differences of these kinds. Jacqueline, for example, has a rather more forceful personality than Mark, and this is matched by her mother's brisk, no-nonsense approach to discipline; Mark's mother, on the other hand, is less energetic herself and rather more easygoing in controlling her children. In comparison with both these mothers, Thomas's mother seems much more preoccupied with maintaining adult standards of factual and linguistic "correctness" in their conversation.

While variations of these kinds and resulting from these sources are not going to be as easy to study as the relationship between semantic and syntactic complexity in adult speech and variation in the children's level of receptive or productive control, I believe it is important to take them into account from the beginning. To ignore them is to work with a seriously impoverished model of linguistic interaction.

The second issue that I wish to consider is the imbalance in the way in which the subject of adult-child interaction has generally been treated. Modifications in adult speech to young children, it is true, are hypothesized to be contingent upon the level of the child's linguistic development, but the child himself is usually conceived of as playing a relatively passive role, providing little more than corrective feedback, which allows the adult to "tune" her speech on a variety of dimensions. Why should this be so? One obvious reason is the gap in expertise between adult and child. If fine adjustments are called for, it is obviously the adult who is better equipped to make them. A second reason is that the adult may be thought of as having, whether consciously or not, the aim of providing situations in which the child can learn about the world in which he lives and about his language in particular. In another paper, I suggested that the ideal learning situation would be "a shared activity with an adult in which the adult gave linguistic expression to just those meanings in the situation which the child was already capable of intending and to which he was, at that particular moment, paying attention" (Wells, 1974, p. 267). In the study already discussed,

Cross found a substantial proportion of adult utterances that seemed to fit this description, particularly for the younger children in her study. But she rightly points out:

> . . . the child will not be advanced in these situations if the adult expressions are either too complex for the child to comprehend or already within his con--trol. Thus the level of psycholinguistic complexity is a crucial factor. What the child may require is at least two levels of complexity when he verbally in teracts with adults in Wells' ideal situation: one level pitched very close to his own so that he can process it and comprehend the meaning, and the other slightly in advance of his own syntactic abilities. The child should then be able to comprehend the meaning and also see the relationship between his characteristic mode of expressing it and the more sophisticated version. (Cross, 1977, pp. 180–181)

And this is precisely what one finds in much interaction between adults and linguistically immature children. Adults do frequently provide well-organized learning situations, therefore, though probably, as Brown suggests, more in the interest of maintaining communication than with a deliberately tutorial purpose.

Clearly, then, there are good reasons for giving close attention to the adult side of the interaction. But what about the child? What does he contribute? From a very early age, he is capable of initiating interaction and, as we saw in the examples quoted earlier, he frequently selects the topic and indicates his communicative intent with respect to it, even in some cases in opposition to his adult interlocutor. It also seems possible that to a certain extent he effectively shapes the language behaviour of the adults who interact with him—just as his is shaped by theirs—through the feedback he provides, or fails to provide, to their contribution to the interaction (Berko Gleason & Weintraub, 1978). In many respects, therefore, he is an equal partner in the interaction, albeit a less competent one. Why is it, therefore, that the study of adult-child interaction has tended to focus one-sidedly on the effect of the adult on the child?

The answer, I suspect, is as Schaffer (1974) suggests, that we lack theoretical models for talking about interactions *as* interaction. The continuing reciprocal effect of two people's behaviour on each other is extremely difficult to conceptualise and, because each action is partly contingent on the previous action and that is partly contingent on the one before . . . etc., the identification of causal relationships becomes extremely complex. Nevertheless, such a theoretical model is what is required in order to give an account of language development which attaches importance to the mutual learning that takes place through interaction.

## TOWARD A MODEL OF THE DEVELOPMENT
## OF LINGUISTIC INTERACTION

We shall now attempt to develop such a model, starting with a formalisation of the processes involved in interaction and of the influences that bear on these processes. For purposes of convenience we will distinguish between a macro-level and a micro-level on the time dimension, whilst recognizing that such a distinction is no more than a heuristic device to assist in exposition.

It is at the macro-level that the developmental consequences of interaction are most simply conceptualised. Making the necessary simplifying assumption that a static synchronic description of the communicative systems and strategies of the participants adequately represents reality at any particular point in time, development for the child can be defined in terms of the incremental additions to the system between successive points in time, and learning as the means whereby the participants modify their systems and strategies as a result of their experience of interaction at each point. Katherine Nelson (1973), has developed just such a model (Figure 2–3).

In this model, both the child's and the adult's strategies are interpretative: of his own cognitive structure in the case of the child, and of the real world in the case of the adult. Nelson considers the parents' theory of socialisation and education to be a part of the real world, varying from one parent to another, but characteristic and invariant, at least in the short

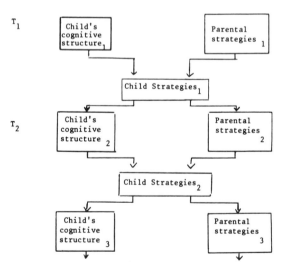

*Figure 2-3.* Schematic model of the interactive language-learning process.

term, for any particular child. In this model, both the child's current cognitive structure and the current parental strategies act on, and are interpreted by, the child strategies available at that time. The child strategies, which include communicative acts, then act as feedback to cognitive structures and parental strategies, leading to the reorganized structures and strategies at $T_2$. Normally a development towards a more mature, or adultlike, state would be expected as the interactants moved from Tn to Tn $^5$ 1, but Nelson recognizes that this may not always be the case. The child's initial cognitive structures may be such that they fail to match with parental interpretative strategies, or the parental strategies may be poorly adjusted to the child's structures, or insensitive to his communicative acts. In either case, this may impede development in the child's cognitive structures or in the strategies he deploys, or may even lead to actual regression in the short term.

Using this model, Nelson investigates the early stages of language development, with particular reference to vocabulary. Three major influences on the interaction process are identified: the degree to which the child's dominant cognitive structures, or "constructs," match the categories that are linguistically coded in the language of his environment (Match/Mismatch); the organizing hypothesis that the child has developed as to the dominant function of language—whether it is basically a social-expressive tool or a tool for naming and describing (Expressive/Referential)—which may conform or not to the dominant function of parental language to him; and the degree to which the mother accepts or rejects the child's communicative, and particularly his linguistic, acts (Acceptance/Rejection). Combinations of these dichotomized factors are then described and illustrated by reference to particular children in the sample that she studied, and she concludes that, in the early stages at least, the Cognitive Match dimension is the most powerful in accounting for progress, while the Expressive/Referential dimension is predictive only of size and type of vocabulary acquired in the second year. However, it is the Acceptance/Rejection dimension which probably has the greatest long-term effects.

These findings, which underline the arguments for attending to the influence of variation in personality and in child rearing, suggest that the initial model should include an explicit distinction between the strategies that parents deploy and the longer-term structures of personality and relevant beliefs and values that motivate these strategies. Similarly, the child's strategies should be seen as the outcome of personality structure as well as of cognitive structure. With these additions, this macro-level model has the considerable merit of allowing predictions to be made and tested with respect to the learning outcomes of interaction between different configurations of adult and child structures and strategies.

However, what any macro-level model lacks is an account of the communicative interaction itself, from experience of which the child is hypothesized to learn. For this we need a micro-level model, which will draw upon the finer-grained linguistic analysis of discourse as well as the psychological analysis of structures and strategies.

## Language in Interaction

Any communicative interaction involves a triangular relationship between the two participants, who alternate in the roles of sender and receiver, and the experienced world, which forms the subject matter of their interaction (Moffett, 1968). The experienced world may be found in the situation that the participants physically share at the time of interacting, or it may be located in the past or expected future experience or in the secondarily acquired knowledge, or even in the imagination, of one or both of the participants. What is essential for successful communication is that the participants should come to attend to the same area of experience which has, for this reason, been called the "field of intersubjective attention."

In adult conversation, of course, there is no restriction on what may be brought into the field of intersubjective attention, but in early adult-child communication it is most frequently to be found in the more-or less-immediately perceptible environment. The earliest form of communication, it is true, seems to be a purely person-to-person exchange, without any semantic content but, well before the end of the first year, the full triangular relationship has appeared—at the stage that Trevarthen and Hubley (1978) call "secondary intersubjectivity"—in the form of adult and child shared attention to, and action upon, some aspect of their common environment. Although the child may not yet realise his role linguistically, the basic patterns of turn taking, and the roles of giver and receiver, demander and supplier, are becoming firmly established in relation to object and events within the intersubjective field of attention. When the child does begin to develop language, it emerges within this established framework as a new form of realisation for meanings that were previously communicated nonlinguistically. As Slobin puts it, with reference to a rather later stage of development, "new forms first express old functions, and new functions are first expressed by old forms" (Slobin, 1973; p. 184).

For this to happen, however, there has to be continuity of potential topics for communication, and this is provided by those aspects of the immediate environment which can, through joint enterprises of various kinds, be made the repeated focus of intersubjective attention. Bruner and his colleagues (Bruner, 1975, 1978; Ratner & Bruner, 1978) have clearly demonstrated how certain specific and highly routinised situations, such as bath time, playing with a mechanical toy, or looking at a picture book, can provide a highly relevant context for language learning. But, to a greater or lesser extent, the same applies to the majority of communication situations which arise from the whole variety of events that make up the child's everyday life.

Although the description of this field of attention as "intersubjective" implies some degree of commonality, it cannot be supposed that both adult and child interpret it in the same way. Whereas the adult's interpretation is strongly influenced by the wider culture and arrived at through the flexible use of mature interpretative strategies, the child at any point in time, as Katherine Nelson points out, has immature interpretative strategies. Nevertheless, there is usually sufficient overlap for communication to take place, and it is precisely one of the aims of communication to bring about a greater degree of isomorphism of interpretation between the participants.

In almost all these situations, then, the intersubjective field of attention is both brought into focus by, and provides the content of, the communicative acts that child and adult exchange. As a sender, the child uses the strategies available to him to interpret the intersubjective field in terms of his cognitive structure and current purpose, and then selects from his linguistic repertoire to produce the conversational act that realises his meaning intention (accompanied perhaps by nonlinguistic, but potentially communicative, actions). Similarly, the receiver interprets the communicative acts of his coparticipant by means of strategies which draw upon his own linguistic repertoire and cognitive structure and upon his interpretation of the intersubjective field (see Figure 2-4).

In the case of the early communication between child and adult, there is obviously a very considerable discrepancy between the participants in the extent and complexity of their cognitive structures and of their linguistic repertoires, and in the range and flexibility of the strategies of action and interpretation that can be deployed in the interaction. Under these conditions, we might expect the more skilled participant to modify his or her behaviour in order to facilitate communication: first, by restricting the topics of communication to aspects of the field of intersubjective attention which are immediately perceptible to the child and which thus allow him to make parallel use of his nonlinguistic strategies of interpretation and secondly, by modifying the form of her communicative acts so that they are better adjusted to the child's linguistic repertoire and to his interpretative strategies. In addition, we might expect the adult, when acting as receiver, to make considerable use of strategies of matching the child's utterance against her interpretation of the shared field in order to arrive at the contextually plausible interpretation of the child's intended meaning. In this way the adult, with his or her greater experience and facility, is able strategically to assist the child towards increasing mastery of the language system and of its use in encoding meaning intentions with respect to that part of the world of his experi-

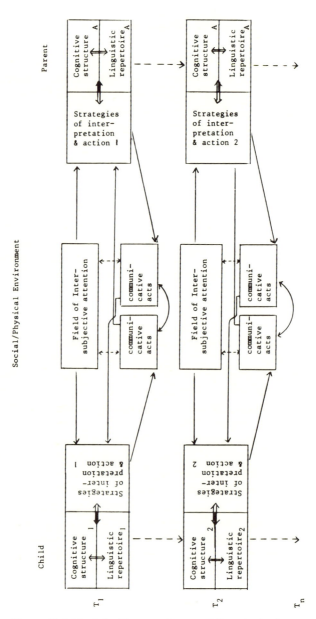

*Figure 2-4:* Model of interaction and linguistic development.

ence which is currently the focus of intersubjective attention. In such exchanges the child both receives feedback to his own communicative acts in the form of checks, expansions and corrections on the one hand, and expressions of interest and understanding allied with actions or "developing" communications on the other; he also encounters, in the communicative acts of his conversational partner, "model" linguistic encodings, at a variety of levels and in a variety of forms, which correspond to, and help to define, aspects of the field of intersubjective attention that he has already begun to interpret nonlinguistically. Under these circumstances he is well placed to make what Nelson (1977b) calls "cognitive comparisons," and over time, gradually to move towards mastery of the linguistic repertoire and cognitive structures of those with whom he interacts.

## Linguistic Repertoires and the Structure of Conversation

The micro-level model of interaction just outlined, while perhaps reasonably convincing in rather general terms, still fails to connect with the actual sequences of communicative acts which constitute observable interaction. It is thus still incapable of systematically identifying the particular features in an adult's communicative behaviour that enable the child to learn from the interaction that occurs on any particular occasion, and equally incapable of identifying how the adult behaviour is communicatively contingent upon, and responsive to, that of the child. To achieve these goals we need a way of describing the dynamic, sequential construction of conversation by participants. That is to say, we need a theory of discourse.

Needless to say, no such fully-developed theory exists, although considerable progress has been made in the last few years in a number of interesting directions. One strong impetus to work in this field has come from sociolinguistics and from those concerned with the "Ethnography of Speaking" (Hymes, 1962). Hymes's insistence that to be a successful speaker/listener in a language requires more than a knowledge of the rules of grammar (Hymes, 1972), has led to a growing interest in "communicative competence" and such investigations into its development as Garvey's (1975) study of requests and Wooton's (1978) of adult refusals, Ervin-Tripp's work on directives (1976, 1977), and Keenan and Schieffelin's (1976) study of how children learn to establish a discourse topic. From a closely-related direction, and following earlier work on conversation opening and closing (Schegloff, 1968; Schegloff & Sacks, 1973) and turn taking (Sacks, Schegloff, & Jefferson, 1974), McTear (1977, 1978) has studied how children learn to get into conversations and Keenan (1977), how they keep them going. Much of this work is reviewed in their editorial introduction by Ervin-Tripp and Mitchell-Kernan (1977). A further dimension to work in this tradition is to be found in Labov and Fanshel's (1977) study of the way in which participants construct and interpret contributions in therapeutic interviews.

On the whole, however, the sociolinguists have tended to tackle discourse one step at a time, seeking to provide a structural description of one particular type of speech event or exchange in terms of what they take to be its constitutive rules or contraints. In contrast, and in a very different tradition, discourse has become the focus of attention for a number of philosophers, who have attempted, on a very broad front, to clarify the maxims and logic that govern and make possible intelligible conversation (Grice, 1975) and the conditions under which utterances effectively perform "speech acts" of various kinds (Austin, 1962; Searle, 1969). This approach, and its implication for the study of the development of communicative competence, is fully reviewed by Dore (1978) in the first volume of this series.

In yet another tradition, Sinclair and Coulthard have applied the methodology of structural linguistics to the description of discourse structure in such formal contexts as the classroom (Sinclair & Coulthard, 1975) and the doctor's consulting room (Coulthard & Ashby, 1973), establishing a hierarchy of units of discourse from transaction down to act, with constituents in the structure of one unit being realised by complete units from the next level below. As a first attempt to capture what might be called the syntax of discourse, this is a very useful framework, which has been applied in a number of further investigations (e.g., Stubbs, 1973; Burton & Stubbs, 1976); but its very tightness makes it less satisfactory for the description of the more loosely-organised conversation that takes place between parents and children. Furthermore, its emphasis on the syntactic dimension of discourse is at the expense of the management of topic.

Early work by both Dore (1975) and Wells (1973) proposed sets of speech act, or function, categories which attempted to cover the much wider range of acts that speakers perform in adult-child conversation and to take account of the purposes for which they speak; but, as both authors realised, their taxonomies were open-ended and required some more theoretical principles of organisation if they were to be capable of casting light on the structure and development of discourse. Dore's more recent work on Nursery School Conversation (1978) situates the analysis of conversation within the framework provided by Searle's (1969) account of illocutionary acts and the rules for performing them, and relates conversational acts to the elements of the task in which they occur.

The approach to be adopted here, however, differs from Dore's, and from most of the work in the speech act tradition, in wishing to avoid making a distinction in descriptive level between the interpersonal function and the propositional content of utterances. One might caricature workers in the speech act tradition as believing that a speaker has one set of rules which enable him to construct semantically and syntactically well-formed sentences and another, quite distinct, set of rules for deploying these sentences appropriately in conversational encounters. Such a belief, I would wish to argue, is a legacy from the almost exclusively syntactic preoccupations of early transformational grammarians. Such a separation has never been central in what might be called European linguistics, however, and is quite explicitly avoided in Systemic Grammar (Halliday, 1967, 1970). Evidence from the earliest stages of language development also tends to refute such a distinction or, if anything, to give precedence to the functional, as opposed to the propositional, dimension of meaning as the root from which the organisation of language springs. But, as argued in the previous section, linguistic communication from the very beginning emerges out of a triangular relationship between speaker, hearer, and situation, in which the child learns to encode both interpersonal and ideational meanings simultaneously (Halliday, 1975).

In developing the notion of a speaker's "linguistic repertoire," therefore, I shall follow Halliday (1977) in seeing this as the sum total of what he "can mean"—his meaning potential. This repertoire consists of networks of meaning options relating to the purposes and topics which he is able to communicate, together with the lexico-grammatical and phonological systems through which they are realised. In contributing a communicative act (CA) to a conversation, a speaker constructs an utterance from the various systems of options that are available in his repertoire under the constraints imposed by the immediate conversational, and wider social, contexts. A CA can thus be described from two complementary points of view; either paradigmatically in terms of its relation to the systems of options in the speaker's repertoire, or syntagmatically in terms of its relation to the preceding and following utterances in the sequence of conversation.

In order to illustrate the form such a description might take, I shall attempt to develop an account of the two extracts from Mark and the one from Thomas (discussed earlier in this chapter). However, in order to keep the description within manageable proportions, I shall concentrate on the options most centrally concerned in the joint construction of the discourse, and on the most closely associated lexico-grammatical and intonational realisation systems; I shall take for granted the semantic systems and the lexico-grammatical realisation systems which are more specifically concerned with the experiential content of the interaction.[3]

In commenting earlier on the first extract from Mark, I claimed that he performs three types of CA: initiating interaction, indicating to his mother what interests him, and responding to some of his mother's CAs. In the second extract, he performs a number of additional CAs: asking questions and responding to his mother's questions and proffering unsolicited information. All these CAs can be thought of as combining options from two major systems. The first system concerns the reciprocal roles that the participants in any conversational exchange take on as they *Initiate* and *Respond.* As Initiator, a participant may either take on the role of *Giver* or *Demander,* while the roles reciprocally assigned to the Responder are those of *Receiver* and *Supplier.* The roles are reciprocal in the sense that the selection of one role by the Initiator of an exchange automatically sets up the expectation that the other participant will accept the matching respondent role. Thus, to take on the role of Giver is to expect the other participant to take on the responding role of Receiver, while to take on the role of Demander is to expect the other to accept the role of Supplier. The basic options of the system can be represented thus:

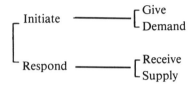

The second system concerns the type of commodity that is exchanged —whether *Goods and Services* or *Information.* Here again the major options are subdivided: Goods/Services may concern either an *Object* or an *Event,* while Information may be concerned with *Identification or Naming* or making some *Comment* about an object or event. Even at this early stage, the commodity of Goods/Services: Event requires further differentiation: the event may involve either *Attention* or *Action* and, in either case, the object may be either *Self* or *Other.* Using the symbol { to indicate simultaneous selection, the complete Commodity system can be shown:

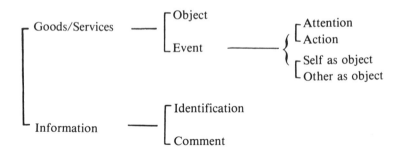

Mark's repertoire of CAs, as manifested in the first extract, can be described in terms of simultaneous selection of options from the two systems, as follows:

Initiate : Demand : Goods/Service : Attention : Self as object (1, 12, 15)
Initiate : Demand : Goods/Service : Attention : Other as object (13)

Initiate : Give : Information : Identification (4, 14, 16, 22)
Respond : Supply : Information : Comment (24
Respond : Receive : Information : Comment (27, 30)

By the time we get to the extract two months later, it is clear that a number of new options have entered the repertoire. As a Receiver of Information, Mark can now exercise the options to *Accept* or *Reject,* and if accepting he can either simply *Acknowledge* (as in utterances 27 and 30 in the first extract) or he can offer positive *Agreement* (as in the present extract: 27). He can also Give and Demand Information: *Comment.*

Another addition is the third type of commodity: *Metalinguistic.* Goods and Services are typically exchanged nonlinguistically as well as linguistically, while Information is exchanged almost exclusively through language. However, there are occasions when the linguistic means being used to carry out the exchanges themselves become the commodity of the exchange, particularly where there has been some breakdown in communication. Such *Procedural* instances of Metalinguistic exchange occur several times in this extract. In the first (7–8) Mark Demands a *Repetition,* and in the second (12–13) he responds to his mother's demand for *Clarification* (although the distinction between the two types is not very clear in this instance). In addition, Mark now has a system for relating his present utterance retrospectively to a previous utterance by himself or by the other speaker: the link may be either *Extending* (some aspect of) the previous utterance or *Contrasting* with it. The first of these options is selected in (26) and the latter in (11).

Amongst the lexico-grammatical systems available to realise these discourse options is a fairly well-developed *Mood* system. Although no example of an *Imperative* occurs in this extract, all other options occur (although often in an incomplete form), and *Ellipsis* is used in Responding as the realisation of the *Incorporation* of the matter of the previous utterance (as in [17]). As far as *Intonation* is concerned, Mark has a system of four contrasting tones, with Tone 4 strongly associated with the Demand options, although not exclusively. Mark makes quite considerable use of rising tone (Tones 2 and 4), but it is not clear from this extract whether he is yet using the distinction between *Rising* and *Falling* tone to realise the distinction between "Referring" and "Proclaiming," described in more detail below.

By 25 months, then, Mark's repertoire has developed to include at least the systems shown in Figure 2-5. However, it must be stressed that no claim is being made that Figure 2-5 gives an exhaustive account of Mark's repertoire at this stage: it is based only on the evidence available in the two extracts considered. The same comments apply equally to the other repertoire descriptions.

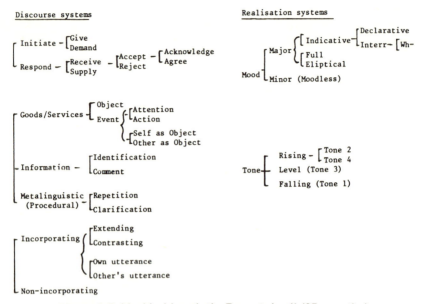

*Figure 2-5.* Mark's Linguistic Repertoire II (25 months).

If we now look at Thomas's repertoire (Figure 2-6), as manifested by his contribution to the conversation contained in his extract at the same age, we can see that it is much less developed, and is closer to that of Mark I. Thomas appears to have only one option in Receiving Information, that of repeating (part of) the previous utterance (13, 19, 23), and there is no call made on him to produce or respond to a Procedural Demand. As far as realisation systems are concerned, he does not yet seem to have developed a Mood system: even the occurrence of ellipsis (13, 19) does not seem to have contrastive value. Neither is there any evidence of a system of contrasting Tones.

One of the results of the lack of differentiation is that Thomas's utterances are more difficult than Mark's to interpret. The first utterance, "Bis-

```
┌ Initiate  ─  ┌Give
│              └Demand
│
└ Respond   ─  ┌Receive
               └Supply

┌ Goods/Services ─ ┌Object
│                  └Event
│
└ Information  ─   ┌Identification
                   └Comment
```

*Figure 2-6.* Thomas's Linguistic Repertoire (25 months).

cuits,'' could be either a Demand: Goods/Services: Object, or Give: Information : Identification. His mother chooses to take it as the latter, but the cues for this interpretation must have been derived from the context, for there is nothing in the form of the utterance that permits disambiguation.

Describing the two mothers' repertoires on the basis of these three short extracts is even more difficult. Clearly, they are not limited to the particular range of options that they choose to deploy on these occasions. On the other hand, to display a full adult system would produce a description of unwieldly proportions and in any case many subsystems remain to be fully described. The solution that will be adopted, therefore, is to assume a full adult repertoire, but to display only those systems that are necessary to account for the options selected within the extracts being compared.

One considerable modification that is required for the description developed for the children's repertoires concerns the basic distinction between Initiate and Respond. Many adult turns that follow an Initiation by the child are not straightforward Responds. Utterance 12 in the Thomas extract, "Colin and Anne came in the car, didn't they?" for example, does not directly respond to Thomas's previous utterance, "Colin in ʃə ʃ train," but rather indirectly rejects it by offering a contrasting piece of information. Similarly, utterance 6, "Grannie Irene's coming next weekend," indirectly rejects Thomas's answer to the previous question (4) "Who came in the car?" These two examples suggest that the simple contrast between Initiate and Respond develops into a more complex system in which a medial utterance in an exchange may be both a *Retrospective* response, albeit indirect, to the previous utterance and, simultaneously, function like an initiating utterance in its *Prospective* expectation of a further response. This modification to the system can be shown by the introduction of the option *Continue,* shown by the following convention, in which the brace symbol {
indicates simultaneity.

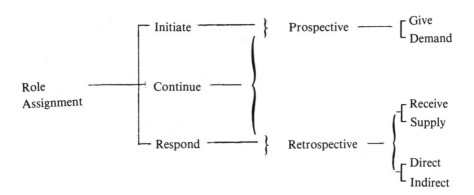

In the case of *Continuing* utterances, the retrospective function will often be *Indirect,* as in the case of the two examples considered above. However, it must be pointed out that all responses that themselves contain new "matter" are potentially prospective, in that the hearer may choose to treat them as such and make a further response. This is what happens in Mark II (9) when Mark rejects his mother's account of where the man has gone.

Further additions are also required to the Metalinguistic (Procedural) subsystem to account for the various ways in which an adult may draw attention to the previous child utterance. The first distinction is between *Form* and *Content.* Utterance 21 in the Thomas extract, for example, *Corrects* the Formal juxtaposition of "Auntie" and "train" in Thomas's utterance, and this is followed by a *Model* Form, which Thomas duly repeats. Mark's mother (Mark II, 12) on the other hand, focusses on the Content of Mark's utterance "Gone where?" though in this particular case it is difficult to decide whether she is Demanding a *Repetition* or a *Clarification.* Mark treats it as a Demand for Repetition, perhaps because no other option is available in his own system. In (14), on the other hand, she selects a Content *Check* to ensure that she has understood correctly. The options for the Metalinguistic (Procedural) system are thus the following:

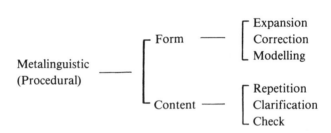

Early in this section, considerable emphasis was placed on the importance, in early adult-child interaction, of the triangular relationship between the participants and the intersubjective field of attention. When the "matter" of the conversation is physically present, nonverbal cues can play an important part in maintaining agreement as to what constitutes the intersubjective field. When the exchange concerns Information about an object or event that is displaced in time or space, as in the Mark II and Thomas extracts, much more emphasis is necessarily thrown on the linguistic means for maintaining agreement about the intersubjective field. This feature of discourse has so far received little attention, but it seems likely to be of importance in characterising differences in linguistic interaction between adult-child pairs.

One aspect of this is the recognition that the current speaker affords to the contribution of the previous speaker. We have already seen that most utterances that are not simply initiations have a retrospective dimension in that they recognise, either directly or indirectly, the prospective expectation of a response that was part of the meaning of the previous utterance. In addition to being retrospective on the speech role dimension, such utterances may also be retrospective along the dimension of the status of the "matter" of the previous utterance—whether it is taken up and *Incorporated,* and if so whether this is by *Repetition* or by *Referring.* In the latter case, the incorporation may have the function of either *Extending* the matter or *Contrasting* it with an alternative. The matter that is incorporated may, of course, be that of the speaker's *Own* utterance or that of the *Other's* utterance. The system of options for Incorporation is thus the following:

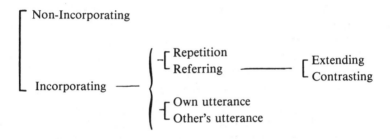

Associated with the maintenance of Intersubjectivity are a number of realisation systems, including *Cohesion* and the choice of *Ellipsis* in the *Mood* system, together with the *Intonation* systems of *Tone* and *Tonic Placement.* However, although closely associated, there is no simple one-to-one correspondence between discourse options and options in the realisation systems, as recent work in Birmingham (Brazil, 1975) and Bristol (Wells, et al., 1978) has demonstrated. Nevertheless the choice of Ellipsis, Cohesion options other than Lexical Repetition, Rising as opposed to Falling Tones, and Marked Tonic Placement all seem to be associated with discourse options that afford substantial recognition to the matter of previous utterances. (In this context it is worth noting that we have found substantial counter-evidence to the generally held view that in children's early utterances there is a simple one-to-one relationship between Rising Tone and the function of "requesting an answer" (Dore, 1975) or "demanding a response" (Halliday, 1975; cf. Montgomery, 1979).

As the system of Cohesion operates at various levels within the clause, all the options may occur, although at each point within the utterance at which a choice is made only one (or none) of the options is selected. A primary distinction may be made between *Lexical* and *Syntactic* exponents of cohesion, the former having more delicate options of *Conjunction* ("so," "however," etc.) *Substitution* ("do," "so," etc.) and *Reference* (Pronouns, demonstratives, etc.) (Halliday and Hasan, 1976).

The important distinction in the Tone system is between *Rising* and *Falling* tones. According to Brazil (1975, 1978), the selection of rising tone marks the matter of the tone unit as considered by the speaker to be within the shared knowledge of speaker and hearer ("referring tone") and falling tone conversely as marking the matter to be considered as not necessarily part of shared knowledge ("proclaiming tone"). It might be expected, therefore, that where an adult was concerned to establish and maintain intersubjectivity, a considerable proportion of her utterances would take referring (rising) tone.

All the systems so far described are set out in the form of a composite adult repertoire that accounts for the utterances produced by both of the mothers (Figure 2-7). As in the case of the children's repertoires, the remainder of the semantic and lexico-grammatical systems are assumed.

The linguistic repertoires, parts of which have just been outlined, describe the paradigmatic systems of options at various levels that are available to a speaker when contributing to an ongoing sequence of interaction. At each turn he constructs his utterance(s) by simultaneously selecting an option from each of his major systems. However, each turn can equally appropriately be described as a move in the sequential organization of a particular conversation and, looked at from this point of view, it is subject to a number of constraints imposed by the syntagmatic and situational context in which it occurs.

These constraints are not absolute, but rather a matter of expectation. The prospective force of a Demand for Information, for example, does not compel the person addressed to Supply the Information, but this is the option that he is expected to select and which he will select unless he has "good reason" to do otherwise (Halliday, 1970); failure to do so will produce a "notable absence" for which he may be held accountable (Sacks et al., 1974). This type of constraint is the necessary consequence of the fact that linguistic interaction involves the collaborative negotiation of meaning between participants who are, nevertheless, autonomous individuals. Perfect reciprocity may be the ideal to which conversation—or at least the description of conversation—aspires, but in practice such perfect reciprocity is rarely achieved. However, just as in music or verse, perfect regularity of rhythm is less interesting than departures from an underlying "norm," so actual conversations are based upon underlying norms or constraints which allow the participants to collaborate effectively while still permitting departures appropriate to the needs of the moment.

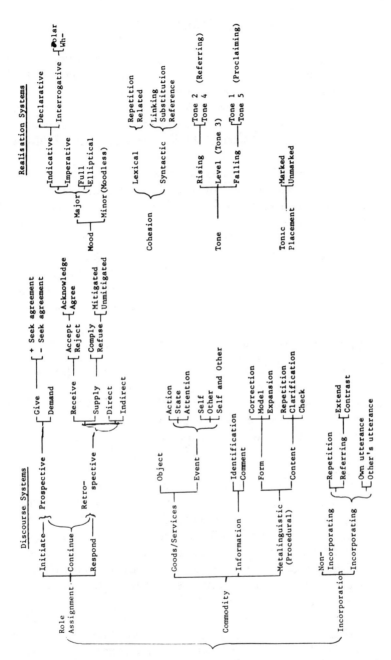

*Figure 2-7.* Generalised Adult Repertoire (selected systems). This should not be treated as the definitive version: development is still in progress.

Although speakers normally conform to at least some of the maxims of conversational cooperativeness which Grice (1975) has described, because the constraints are not absolute, there is considerable variation between individuals in the options they choose from those that are available to them. As a result, "strategies" can be inferred from the sequential patterns of options selected by individuals over whole sequences of interaction and, ultimately, relative frequencies of different strategies in particular contexts can be related to differences between children in rate and pattern of development.

In order to facilitate this type of analysis it is convenient to have a visual means of representing the sequence of turns that make up the temporal dimension of discourse. Each turn itself consists of simultaneous selection from the various systems of options that make up the speaker's repertoire. The "Discourse Record" thus attempts to present this syntagmatic structure of discourse, while at the same time retaining information about the paradigmatic choice of options. As an illustration of the method that is being adopted, let us contrast the two extracts from Mark and Thomas at 25 months. (The key to the conventions of coding is given in Appendix 2.)

## Interpreting the Interactions

In Figures 2-8a, 2-8b, 2-8c, and 2-9a and 2-9b, the horizontal axis represents sequential progression: the coded contributions of the two participants are set out above and below parallel "rows" in which the Prospective/Retrospective status of each contribution to the interaction is indicated respectively by a forward- or backward-pointing arrow. Contributions that are Continuing (i.e., both prospective and retrospective) have arrows pointing in both directions. Where this status is only Indirect, this is shown by a broken arrow. Vertical lines mark boundaries between turns and double vertical lines between sequences (e.g., a new sequence begins after turn 4 in Figure 2-8a). A further set of diagrammatic conventions indicate when the "matter" of a previous utterance is incorporated in the present utterance: an arc connects the arrows representing the utterances concerned. Where the incorporation is of the kind that, either directly or indirectly, rejects the matter of a previous utterance, this is shown by a cross through the arc (e.g., turn 6 in Figure 2-9a).

Several kinds of information relevant to the strategies adopted by the two mothers are made salient by these visual representations of the interaction. While Mark's account of where the man has gone, as discussed earlier, is both implausible and in contradiction to his mother's suggestion, she adopts a supportive role, encouraging him to develop his "story" by means of continuing utterances which serve the functions both of maintaining intersubjectivity with respect to the information that he is giving, and of eliciting further "specific" information. This "mediating" strategy is indicated by the high proportion of double-headed arrows for the mother's contributions. Thomas's mother, on the other hand, adopts a "tutorial" strategy, asking questions to which she already knows the answer and correcting the content (indirectly) and the form (directly) of Thomas's contributions. Her dominating strategy is indicated by the combination of a high proportion of forward-pointing arrows and the high frequency of crosses on those arcs that connect her utterances to previous utterances from the child.

Similarly, with respect to the recognition that is afforded to the "matter" of the child's contributions, Mark's mother typically incorporates and emphasises intersubjectivity through the use of ellipsis, and the selection of anaphoric pronouns and related lexical items. This strategy can be seen in the high proportion of her utterances that have arcs connecting them to preceding utterances by Mark. Thomas's mother, on the other hand, adopts a much less reciprocal strategy. Her frequent selection, when responding to his contributions, of full declarative mood with lexical repetition produced in conjunction with a "proclaiming" tone, has the effect of indirectly denying the matter of his contribution, since she chooses not to refer to it as if it had been brought into the field of intersubjective attention; neither does she treat it intonationally as assumed shared knowledge. This can be seen in the far smaller proportion of her utterances that show Incorporation, which do not, at the same time, reject his previous contribution. In contrast to Thomas's mother, who selects a "proclaiming" tone throughout, Mark's mother makes use of both "referring" and "proclaiming" tones.

In trying to account for the very different strategies employed by the two mothers, considerable weight must be given to the differences in the children's contributions, which result quite largely from the difference in their level of linguistic development. Mark clearly produces utterances that are far more differentiated with respect to their discourse function and more easily interpreted with respect to their "matter." His opening contribution, for example, is clearly to be interpreted as a question about the whereabouts of a particular man, whereas Thomas's opening contribution is ambiguous between Give: Information: Identification and Demand: Goods/Services: Object, and his mother chooses to interpret it as the former. Compared with Mark, Thomas also subsequently contributes less matter to the conversation, although this is as much a function of the opportunities he is offered as of his own lack of resources. However, even when the effect of the general level of the children's ability to contribute to the conversation has been taken into account, there remain important differences between the mothers in the strategies of interaction that they adopt.

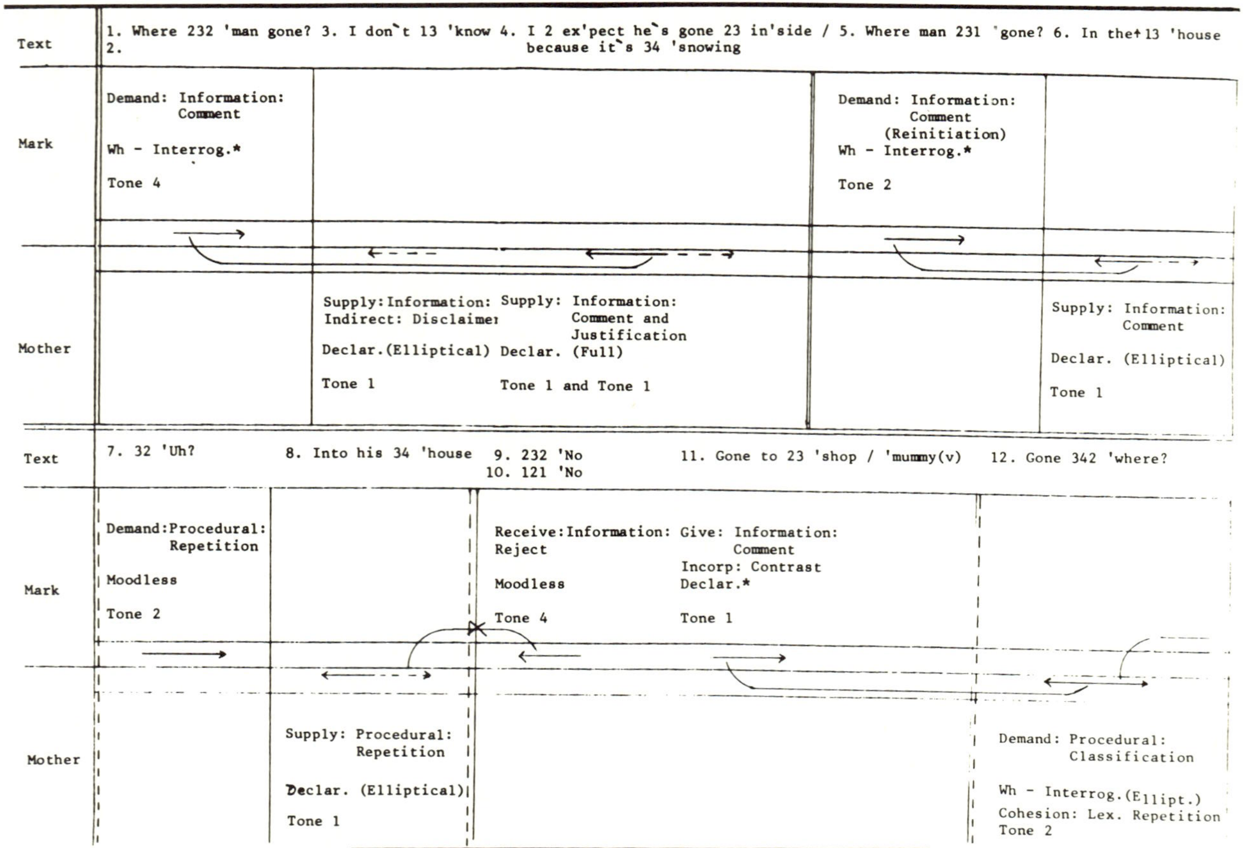

**Text**

1. Where 232 'man gone? 3. I don't 13 'know 4. I 2 ex'pect he's gone 23 in'side / 5. Where man 231 'gone? 6. In the↑13 'house
2. because it's 34 'snowing

**Mark**

Demand: Information:
Comment
Wh – Interrog.*
Tone 4

Demand: Information:
Comment
(Reinitiation)
Wh – Interrog.*
Tone 2

**Mother**

Supply:Information: Supply: Information:
Indirect: Disclaimer Comment and Justification
Declar.(Elliptical) Declar. (Full)
Tone 1  Tone 1 and Tone 1

Supply: Information:
Comment
Declar. (Elliptical)
Tone 1

**Text**

7. 32 'Uh?  8. Into his 34 'house  9. 232 'No 10. 121 'No  11. Gone to 23 'shop / 'mummy(v)  12. Gone 342 'where?

**Mark**

Demand:Procedural:
Repetition
Moodless
Tone 2

Receive:Information: Give: Information:
Reject Comment
Incorp: Contrast
Moodless Declar.*
Tone 4 Tone 1

**Mother**

Supply: Procedural:
Repetition
Declar. (Elliptical)
Tone 1

Demand: Procedural:
Classification
Wh – Interrog.(Ellipt.)
Cohesion: Lex. Repetition
Tone 2

*Figure 2-8a.* Analysis of Mark's Conversation (Extract II).

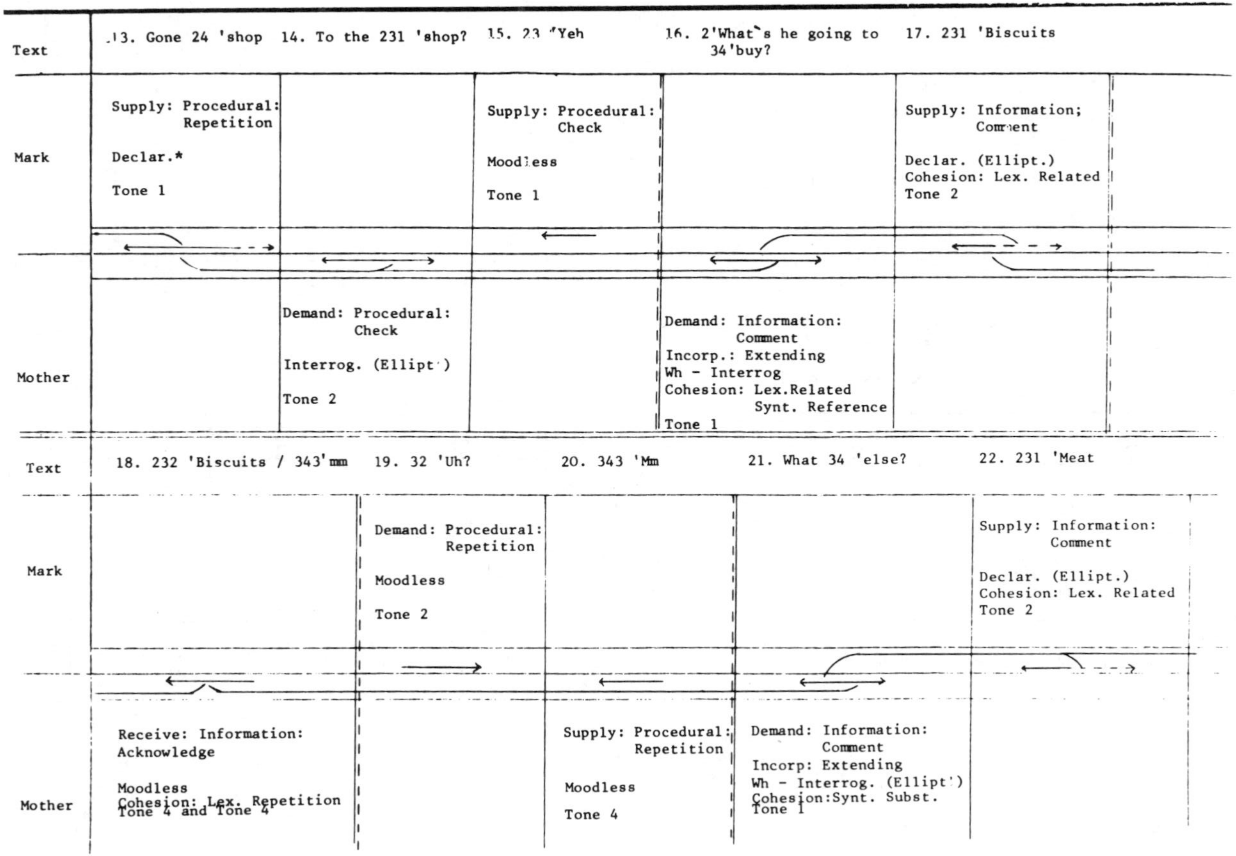

**Text:** .13. Gone 24 'shop   14. To the 231 'shop?   15. 23 "Yeh   16. 2'What's he going to 34'buy?   17. 231 'Biscuits

**Mark:**
- Supply: Procedural: Repetition / Declar.* / Tone 1
- Supply: Procedural: Check / Moodless / Tone 1
- Supply: Information: Comment / Declar. (Ellipt.) / Cohesion: Lex. Related / Tone 2

**Mother:**
- Demand: Procedural: Check / Interrog. (Ellipt.) / Tone 2
- Demand: Information: Comment / Incorp.: Extending / Wh - Interrog. / Cohesion: Lex.Related / Synt. Reference / Tone 1

**Text:** 18. 232 'Biscuits / 343'mm   19. 32 'Uh?   20. 343 'Mm   21. What 34 'else?   22. 231 'Meat

**Mark:**
- Demand: Procedural: Repetition / Moodless / Tone 2
- Supply: Procedural: Repetition / Moodless / Tone 4
- Supply: Information: Comment / Declar. (Ellipt.) / Cohesion: Lex. Related / Tone 2

**Mother:**
- Receive: Information: Acknowledge / Moodless / Cohesion: Lex. Repetition / Tone 4 and Tone 4
- Demand: Information: Comment / Incorp: Extending / Wh - Interrog. (Ellipt') / Cohesion:Synt. Subst.

*Figure 2-8b.* Analysis of Mark's Conversation (cont.).

| Text | 23. 33 'Mm | 24. 342 'Meat | 25. 231 'Sweeties | 26. Buy a 23 'big / 34 'bag / 45 'sweets | 27. Buy 232 'sweets? | 28. 24 'Yeh |
|---|---|---|---|---|---|---|
| Mark | | ? | Supply: Information: Comment<br>Declar. (Ellipt.)<br>Cohesion: Lex. Related.<br>Tone 2 | Give: Information: Comment<br>Incorp: Extend (own utt.)<br>Declar.*<br>Tone 1 | | Supply: Procedural: Check<br>Moodless<br>Tone 1 |
| Mother | ? | | | | Demand: Procedural: Check<br>Interrog. (Ellipt.)<br>Cohesion: Lex. Repetition<br>Tone 4 | |

*Figure 2-8c.* Analysis of Mark's Conversation (cont.).

## CONCLUSION

In this chapter I have tried to develop the case for adopting an interactional approach to the study of language development, basing my arguments on a cross-disciplinary review of theoretical and empirical investigations into the development of the child's ability as a linguistic communicator. From this review, it has become clear that the specific form of the moment-by-moment conversational experience, which provides both the opportunity and the information necessary for the child's development, is best seen as the result of a complex interaction between the communicative intentions and abilities of both child and adult, which are in turn the outcome of their past experiences, both as individuals and as members of particular social groups.

Central to this approach is the conviction that no clear boundary can be drawn between communication and learning through language, and learning language as the means of communication. From the earliest stage of prelinguistic interaction through to the years of formal schooling, there is continuity of development: at each stage the child uses whatever communicative resources are available to him to achieve his purposes in interacting with those who make up his social world. At each stage, too, these interactions provide evidence which contributes both to his learning of the means of communication and to his developing understanding of the socially-structured world in which and about which he communicates. Form and function are thus indissolubly linked in the child's experience of the triangle of linguistic interaction.

This is not to deny that there may be occasions when it is helpful for the child to have his attention focussed on the code itself. Such occasions arise quite naturally when there is a breakdown in communication or when some feature of the code—or its relation to the world of nonlinguistic experience—is called into question by one of the participants. The development of "metalinguistic awareness"—that is to say, of the awareness of the arbitrary but conventional relationship between code and content—has been proposed as a necessary precursor of formal thinking, intimately connected with the development of literacy (Donaldson, 1978; Olson, 1977); it has also been shown to be related to the emergence of awareness of the speaker's obligation to take account of the information needs of the listener, if successful communication is to be achieved (Robinson, in press). Nevertheless, learning how to communicate is, for the most part, a byproduct of communicating for some purpose: it is through the attempt to understand and be understood, as he engages in interaction with those around him about the many and varied events that make up his life, that the child discovers and masters the rules that govern the social structuring of reality, the internal organisation of language, and the relationship between these two systems of representation.

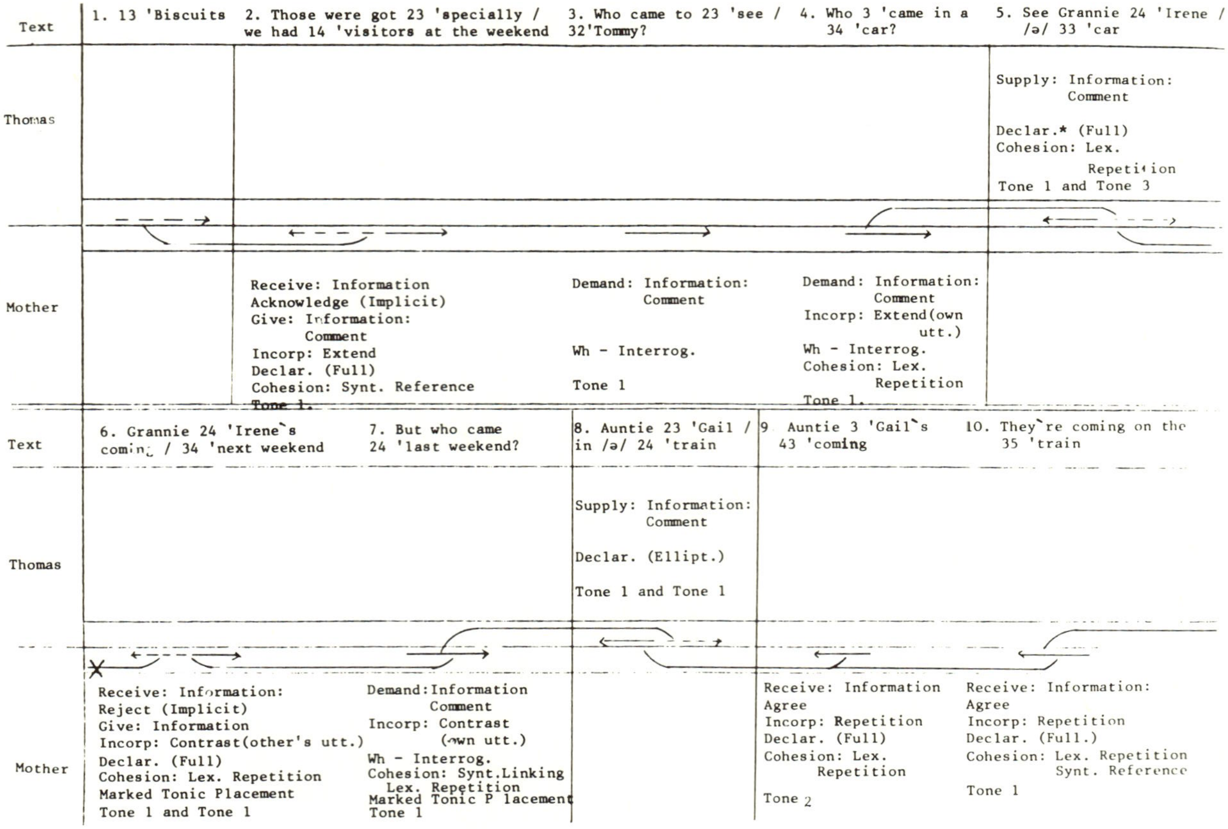

Text

1. 13 'Biscuits   2. Those were got 23 'specially / 3. Who came to 23 'see / 4. Who came in a   5. See Grannie 24 'Irene /
                     we had 14 'visitors at the weekend    32'Tommy?            34 'car?                    /ə/ 33 'car

Thomas

Supply: Information:
Comment

Declar.* (Full)
Cohesion: Lex.
Repetition
Tone 1 and Tone 3

Mother

Receive: Information            Demand: Information:
Acknowledge (Implicit)         Comment
Give: Information:             Incorp: Extend(own
Comment                              utt.)
Incorp: Extend               Wh – Interrog.
Declar. (Full)               Cohesion: Lex.
Cohesion: Synt. Reference        Repetition
Tone 1                       Tone 1

Text

6. Grannie 24 'Irene's   7. But who came   8. Auntie 23 'Gail /   9. Auntie 3 'Gail's   10. They're coming on the
comin_ / 34 'next weekend   24 'last weekend?   in /ə/ 24 'train   43 'coming          35 'train

Thomas

Supply: Information:            Receive: Information
Comment                        Agree
                               Incorp: Repetition
Declar. (Ellipt.)              Declar. (Full)
Tone 1 and Tone 1             Cohesion: Lex.
                               Repetition
                               Tone 2

Mother

Receive: Information:          Demand:Information          Receive: Information:
Reject (Implicit)             Comment                     Agree
Give: Information             Incorp: Contrast            Incorp: Repetition
Incorp: Contrast(other's utt.)   (own utt.)               Declar. (Full.)
Declar. (Full)                Wh – Interrog.              Cohesion: Lex. Repetition
Cohesion: Lex. Repetition     Cohesion: Synt.Linking        Synt. Reference
Marked Tonic Placement        Lex. Repetition            Tone 1
Tone 1 and Tone 1             Marked Tonic Placement
                              Tone 1 and Tone 1

*Figure 2-9a. Analysis of Thomas's Conversation.*

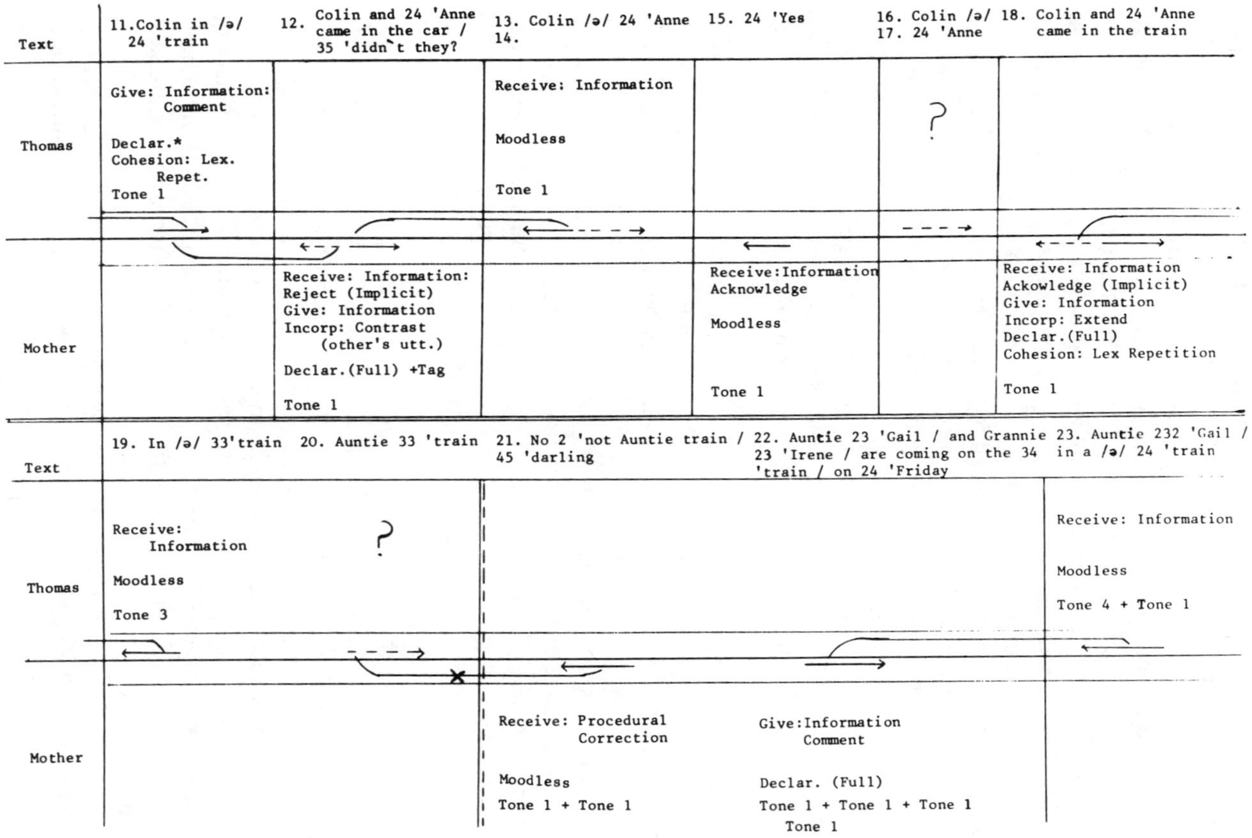

**Text**

11. Colin in /ə/ 24 'train
12. Colin and 24 'Anne came in the car / 35 'didn't they?
13. Colin /ə/ 24 'Anne 14.
15. 24 'Yes
16. Colin /ə/ 18. Colin and 24 'Anne
17. 24 'Anne came in the train

**Thomas**

Give: Information: Comment
Declar.*
Cohesion: Lex. Repet.
Tone 1

Receive: Information
Moodless
Tone 1

Receive: Information
Acknowledge (Implicit)
Give: Information
Incorp: Extend
Declar.(Full)
Cohesion: Lex Repetition
Tone 1

**Mother**

Receive: Information:
Reject (Implicit)
Give: Information
Incorp: Contrast (other's utt.)
Declar.(Full) +Tag
Tone 1

Receive: Information:
Acknowledge
Moodless
Tone 1

**Text**

19. In /ə/ 33'train
20. Auntie 33 'train
21. No 2 'not Auntie train / 45 'darling
22. Auntie 23 'Gail / and Grannie 23. Auntie 232 'Gail /
23 'Irene / are coming on the 34 in a /ə/ 24 'train
'train / on 24 'Friday

**Thomas**

Receive: Information
Moodless
Tone 3

Receive: Information
Moodless
Tone 4 + Tone 1

**Mother**

Receive: Procedural Correction
Moodless
Tone 1 + Tone 1

Give:Information Comment
Declar. (Full)
Tone 1 + Tone 1 + Tone 1
Tone 1

*Figure 2-9b.* Analysis of Thomas's Conversation (cont.).

In all his interactions with the social and physical world, the child's aim above all others is to "make meaning"—to create a coherent inner representation of experience that is at one and the same time a storehouse of past events and a framework of expectations about events which may be encountered in the future. In this way he gains some measure of control over experience and can begin to direct and plan his behaviour instead of remaining entirely at the mercy of the particular events that impinge on him. To a considerable extent the meanings that are given to events are found outside the individual in the structure of institutions, relationships, and practices which constitute the culture into which he is born, and which are given their fullest expression in its language. In learning language, therefore, the child is "learning how to mean" (Halliday, 1975). Initially, he develops his own individual fabric of meaning within the framework provided by the language he learns from those around him but, since language and meaning are generative systems, he may eventually go beyond what has already been achieved, creatively adding to the meaning potential available to members of his linguistic and cultural group by building upon what they have made available to him.

We thus return to the central role of the adults in the child's environment, since it is through interaction that the child most fully develops his skills as a meaning-maker. Although eventually our most rewarding and effective attempts to create new meanings may be carried out in solitude with the aid of pen and paper, this solitary internal dialogue has its roots in the social interchange of meanings that constitute every individual's earliest experience of language. We may eventually learn to communicate with an internalisation of a "generalised other" (Mead, 1934), but we first learn to communicate in face-to-face interaction with particular individuals: parents, teachers, siblings, and friends.

In this chapter we have seen how adults, and particularly parents, modify their speech to young children in a largely unconscious effort to facilitate this exchange of meanings. We have also reviewed evidence that certain types of adult behaviour have a facilitating effect on the child's progress towards effective mastery of the means and purposes of communication, and in the final section we systematically contrasted two instances of interaction which seemed to provide the children with quite different opportunities for the development of skills in the construction and communication of meaning.

The title of this chapter portrays the child as an apprentice in meaning-making: his task being first to learn the skills which are already embodied in the culture, and then to go on to develop and refine them in the creation of new, and personal, artifacts of meaning. The adults' role in facilitating this development is, in terms of this analogy, to act as the already skilled craftsman, engaging with the apprentice in the shared construction of meaning and providing a model of the craft on which the apprentice can base his own attempts. Just as the skilled craftsman selects tasks that are appropriate to the level of skill already acquired by the apprentice, while at the same time encouraging him to attempt new and more complex undertakings, so the ideal adult communicator tailors the interaction to the abilities of the child, while constantly attempting to develop it in ways which will challenge the child to extend his meanings and their linguistic means of realisation.

In describing the development that takes place during the school years, Vygotsky (1934) describes the role of the teacher in very similar terms, pointing out that the teacher's task is to work within the child's "zone of next development," since "the child proves to be stronger and cleverer in cooperation than when he is working on his own; he raises himself up higher in terms of the level of intellectual obstacles that he is able to overcome." Although perhaps less systematically, the ideal parent performs a very similar function, supporting and extending the child's meaning-making through collaboration in the linguistic construction and manipulation of a shared reality.

Such is the very general picture which has so far emerged of the role that the adult performs in facilitating the child's development. How this is realized in practice at successive stages and in response to the demands of different situations and activities has still to be studied in detail, as has the variation that is attributable to group and individual differences. It has been the contention of this chapter that progress along these lines can best be achieved through the careful and systematic study of actual instances of linguistic interaction informed by insights derived from all the relevant disciplines.

## NOTES

[1]This research is supported by grants from the Social Science Research Council of the United Kingdom and from the Nuffield Foundation.

[2]I am grateful to Margaret MacLure for providing me with this example.

[3]This descriptive scheme is further developed in Wells, Montgomery and MacLure (1979) and Wells, MacLure and Montgomery (in press).

## APPENDIX 1

### Language Development Project

#### Conventions and Layout for Transcription

The speech of the child being studied is set out in the left-hand column. The speech of all other participants is set out in the centre column, with identifying initials where necessary. Each new utterance starts on a new line.

Contextual information is enclosed in brackets [ ] and set out in the right-hand column.

Interpretations of utterances and descriptions of tone of voice, where applicable, are enclosed in parentheses ( ) and included immediately after the utterance to which they apply.

Utterances, or parts of utterances, about which there is doubt are enclosed in angular brackets < >; where two interpretations are possible they are both given, separated by an oblique stroke.

Symbols of the International Phonetic Alphabet are used for utterances, or parts of utterances, which cannot be interpreted with certainty. Phonetic symbols are always enclosed by oblique strokes. Except where there is doubt about the speaker's intended meaning, the speech is transcribed in Standard English Orthography.

The following is a list of additional symbols used, with an explanation of their significance. (Stops and commas are not used as in normal punctuation.)

?    used at end of any utterance where an interrogative meaning is considered to have been intended

!    used at the end of an utterance considered to have exclamatory intention

'    apostrophe: used as normal for contractions and elision of syllables

*    used to indicate unintelligibility, for whatever reason. The number of asterisks corresponds as nearly as possible to the number of words judged to have been uttered

. . .  stops are used to indicate pauses. One stop is used for a very short pause. Thereafter, the number of stops used corresponds to the estimated length of the pause in seconds. Pauses over 5 seconds in length are shown with the figure for the length of the pause; e.g., . . 8 . .

_____.underlining. Where utterances overlap because both speakers speak at once, the overlapping portions are underlined.

" "  quotation marks are used to enclose utterances considered to be "speech for self"

⁺    plus mark indicates unbroken intonation contour where a pause or clause boundary might otherwise indicate the end of an utterance

-    hyphen indicates a hiatus, either because the utterance is incomplete or because the speaker makes a fresh start at the word or utterance

(v)  used to indicate that the preceding word was used as a vocative, to call or hold the attention of the addressee

## Intonation

Some of the transcripts include a representation of intonation, in which case the following additional conventions apply[1]:

/    Tone unit boundary. Where an utterance consists of only one tone unit, no boundaries are marked

ı    This symbol immediately precedes both prominent and tonic syllables,

Prominent syllables [2] take a single digit before the symbol to indicate their relative pitch height,

Tonic syllables [3] take two or more digits before the symbol to indicate the onset level, range, and direction of significant pitch movement (see Pitch Height, below)

↑↓   Shift of pitch range relatively higher or lower than that normal for the speaker

↑↑↓↓ Shift to extra high or extra low pitch

:     Lengthened syllable. The symbol follows the syllable to which it applies

Pitch
Height The height, direction and range of significant pitch movement is represented by a set of digits corresponding to points on a scale. The pitch range of a speaker is divided into five notional bands, numbered 1–5 from high to low, thus:

```
1  _____
        _____
   2  
        _____
      3  
        _____
        4  
        _____
          5  
        _____
```

The following information is retrievable from this coding:

| *Direction of Movement* | *Halliday (1967) Tones* |
|---|---|
| Falling: (e.g., 13, 25) | Tone 1 |
| Rising: (e.g., 31, 43) | Tone 2 |
| Level: (e.g., 33) | Tone 3 |
| Fall-Rise: (e.g., 343) or (e.g., 342) | Tone 4 or Tone 2[4] |
| Rise-Fall: (e.g., 324) | Tone 5 |

## Notes

[1]We are grateful to Sandy Hutcheson for advice on this form of representation.

[2]Prominent syllables are salient with respect to combinations of pitch, duration and intensity.

[3]Tonic syllables carry at least the onset of significant pitch movement. Significant pitch movement in its entirety may, of course, occur on a single syllable or be spread over a number of syllables.

[4]Fall-Rise movements may be of two types, corresponding to Halliday's Tone 2 and Tone 4. They are conventionally denoted in the transcripts as follows: Tone 2 is represented with a higher terminal pitch than its onset (e.g., 342), whereas Tone 4 is represented as having a terminal pitch no higher than its onset (e.g., 232, 354).

## APPENDIX 2

### Key to Coded Sequences of Interaction

Utterances are referred to by the index numbers used in the text. A vertical line is drawn at turn boundaries and two vertical lines at sequence boundaries. Broken vertical lines indicate the boundaries of intervening Procedural Exchanges. Options selected in each utterance are set out above and below the diagrammatic representation of the interaction, using abbreviations of the systems and categories presented in the "Linguistic Repertoires." Numbers refer to Tone options selected. Incomplete realisations are indicated by an asterisk.

## Diagrammatic representation

Two parallel rows represent the separate contributions of the two participants, each utterance being represented by an arrow. The direction of the arrow indicates the status of the utterance within the interaction:

→ Prospective; i.e., expecting a response

← Retrospective; i.e., making a response

−− Status is implicit

⌒ Indicates that the "matter" of a previous utterance is acknowledged in the present utterance

⩘ Indicates that the "matter" of a previous utterance is rejected in the present utterance

## REFERENCES

Adlam, D. S. *Code in context.* London: Routledge & Kegan Paul, 1977.

Austin, J. L. *How to do things with words.* London: Oxford University Press, 1962.

Berger, P. L. and Luckman, T. *The social construction of reality.* Harmondsworth: Penguin, 1967.

Berko Gleason, J. and Weintraub, S. Input language and the acquisition of communicative competence. *In* K. Nelson (Ed.), *Children's language,* Vol. 1. New York: Gardner Press, 1978.

Bernstein, B. *Class, codes and control* (Vol. 1). London: Routledge & Kegan Paul, 1976.

Bloom, L. M. *Language development: Form and function in emerging grammars.* Cambridge, Mass: M.I.T. Press, 1970.

Blount, B. G. Ethnography and caretaker-child interaction. *In* C. E. Snow and C. Ferguson (Eds.), *Talking to children: Language input and acquisition.* Cambridge: Cambridge University Press, 1977.

Brazil, D. *Discourse intonation.* Birmingham: English Language Research, University of Birmingham, 1975.

Brazil, D. *Discourse intonation II.* Birmingham: English Language Research, University of Birmingham, 1978.

Brown, R. *A first language: the early stages.* London: Allen and Unwin, 1973.

Brown, R. Introduction. *In* C. E. Snow and C. Ferguson (Eds.), *Talking to children: Language input and acquisition.* Cambridge: Cambridge University Press, 1977.

Brown, R., Cazden, C., and Bellugi, U. The child's grammar from I to III. *In* J. P. Hill (Ed.), *The Second Annual Minnesota Symposium on Child Psychology.* University of Minnesota, 1969.

Brown, R. and Hanlon, C. Derivational complexity and order of acquisition in child speech. *In* R. Brown (Ed.), *Psycholinguistics.* New York: Free Press, 1970.

Bruner, J. S. The ontogenesis of speech acts. *Journal of Child Language,* 1975, 2(1), 1–20.

Bruner, J. S. The role of dialogue in language acquisition. Paper presented at the Conference on the Child's Conception of Language at Nijmegen, Holland. May 1977.

Bruner, J. S. Learning how to do things with words. *In* J. S. Bruner and A. Garton (Eds.), *Human growth and development.* London: Oxford University Press, 1978.

Burton, D. and Stubbs, M. On speaking terms: Analysing conversational data. *Journal of the Midlands Association for Linguistic Studies,* 1976, 2(2), 22–44.

Cazden, C. Environmental assistance to the child's acquisition of grammar. Unpublished doctoral Dissertaion, Harvard University, 1965.

Chomsky, N. A. Discussion of Miller and Ervin's paper. *In* U. Bellugi and R. Brown (Eds.), The Acquisition of Language. *Monographs of the Society for Research in Child Development,* 1964, 29 (1).

Chomsky, N. A. *Aspects of the theory of syntax.* Cambridge, Mass.: M.I.T. Press, 1965.

Chomsky, N. A. *Reflections on language.* London: Fontana Books, 1976.

Clay, M. M. *The early detection of reading difficulties: a diagonostic survey.* London: Heinemann Educational, 1972.

Coulthard, R. M. and Ashby, M. Doctor-patient interviews. *Working Papers in Discourse Analysis, 1.* Birmingham: University of Birmingham, 1973.

Cromer, R. The development of language and cognition: The cognition hypothesis. In B. M. Foss (Ed.), *New perspectives in child development.* Harmondsworth: Penguin, 1974.

Cross, T. G. Mother's speech adjustments: the contribution of selected child listener variables. *In* C. E. Snow and C. Ferguson (Eds.), *Talking to children. Language input and acquisition.* Cambridge University Press, 1977.

Cross, T. G. Mother's speech and its association with rate of linguistic development in young children. *In* N. Waterson and C. Snow (Eds.), *The Development of Communication.* New York: Wiley, 1978.

De Villiers, J. G. and De Villiers, P. A. Semantics and syntax in the first two years: the output of form and function and the form and function of the input. *In* F. D. Minifie and L. L. Lloyd (Eds.), *Communicative and cognitive abilities: Early behavioral assessment.* Baltimore: University Park Press, 1978.

Donaldson, M. *Children's Minds.* London: Croom Helm, 1978.

Dore, J. Holophrases, Speech acts and language universals. *Journal of Child Language,* 1975, 2(1), 21–40.

Dore, J. The structure of nursery school conversation. *In* K. E. Nelson (Ed.), *Children's language,* Vol. 1. New York: Gardner Press, 1978.

Edwards, A. D. *Language in culture and class.* London: Heinemann, 1976.

Eimas, P. D., Siqueland, E. R., Jusczyk, P., and Vigorito, J. Speech perception in infants. *Science,* 1971, 171, 303–306.

Ervin-Tripp, S. M. *Language acquisition and communicative choice.* Palo Alto: Stanford University Press, 1973.

Ervin-Tripp, S. M. Is Sybil There? The structure of some American English directives. *Language in Society,* 1976, 5, 25–66.

Ervin-Tripp, S. M. Wait for me, roller skate! *In* S. M. Ervin-Tripp and C. Mitchell-Kernan (Eds.), *Child discourse.* New York: Academic Press, 1977.

Ervin-Tripp, S. M. and Mitchell-Kernan, C. (Eds.), *Child discourse.* New York: Academic Press, 1977.

Escalona, S. K. *The roots of individuality.* London: Travistock Publications, 1969.

Evans, J. V. The significance of adult feedback on child language development. Unpublished M.Ed. dissertation, University of Bristol, 1977.

Feldman, C. The effects of various types of adult responses in the syntactic acquisition of two to three year olds. Unpublished paper, University of Chicago, 1971.

Ferguson, C. A. Baby talk as a simplified register. *In* C. E. Snow and C. Ferguson (Eds.), *Talking to Children: Language input and acquisition.* Cambridge: Cambridge University Press, 1977.

Ferrier, L. Some observations of error in context. In N. Waterson and C. Snow, (Eds.), *The development of communication.* New York: Wiley, 1978.

Fillmore, C. J. The case for case. *In* E. Bach and R. T. Harms (Eds.), *Universals in linguistic theory.* New York: Holt, Rinehart & Winston, 1968.

Flavell, J. H., Botkins, B. T., Fry, C. L., Wright, J. W., and Jarvis, P. E. *The development of role-taking and communication skills in children.* New York: Wiley, 1968.

Garnica, O. K. Some prosodic and paralinguistic features of speech to young children. *In* C. E. Snow and C. Ferguson (Eds.), *Talking to children: Language input and acquisition.* Cambridge: Cambridge University Press, 1977.

Garvey, C. Requests and responses in children's speech. *Journal of Child Language,* 1975, 2(1), 41–63.

Gelman, R. and Shatz, M. Appropriate speech adjustments: The operation of conversational constraints on talk to two-year-olds. *In* M. Lewis and M. Rosenblum (Eds.), *Interaction, conversation and the development of language.* New York: Wiley, 1977.

Grice, H. P. Logic and conversation. *In* P. Cole and J. L. Morgan (Eds.), *Syntax and semantics* (Vol. 3). New York: Academic Press, 1975.

Guilford, J. P. and Fruchter, B. *Fundamental statistics in psychology and education* (6th Ed.). New York: McGraw Hill, 1978.

Halliday, M. A. K. *Intonation and grammar in British English.* The Hague: Mouton, 1967.

Halliday, M. A. K. Notes on transitivity and theme in English, Parts I–III. *Journal of Linguistics,* 1967–1968 3(1 & 2); 4(2).

Halliday, M. A. K. Language structure and language function. *In* J. Lyons (Ed.), *New horizons in linguistics.* Harmondsworth: Penguin, 1970.

Halliday, M. A. K. *Learning how to mean.* London: Arnold, 1975.

Halliday, M. A. K. Language as code and language as behaviour: a systemic-functional interpretation of the nature and ontogenesis of dialogue. *In* S. M. Lamb and A. Makkai (Eds.), *Semiotics of culture and language,* in press.

Halliday, M. A. K. and Hasan, R. *Cohesion in english.* London: Longmans, 1976.

Hess, R. D. and Shipman, V. C. Early experience and the socialisation of cognitive modes in children. *Child Development* 1965, 36, 869–886.

Holzman, M. (1974) The Verbal environment provided by mothers for their very young children. *Merrill-Palmer Quarterly of Behaviour and Development,* 1974, 20(1).

Hymes, D. The ethnography of speaking. *In* T. Gladwin and W. C. Sturtevant (Eds.), *Anthropology and human behavior,* 1962, Anthropological Society of Washington, D. C.

Hymes, D. *Towards communicative competence.* Philadelphia: University of Pennsylvania Press, 1972.

Keenan, E. O. Making it last: Repetition in children's discourse. In S. M. Ervin-Tripp and C. Mitchell-Kernan, (Eds.), *Child discourse.* New York: Academic Press, 1977.

Keenan, E. O. and Shieffelin, B. B. Topic as a discourse notion: A study of topic in the conversations of children and adults. *In* C. Li (Ed.), *Subject and topic.* New York: Academic Press, 1976.

Labov, W. *Sociolinguistics patterns.* Philadelphia: University of Pennsylvania Pres, 1972.

Labov, W. and Fanshel, D. *Therapeutic discourse: Psychotherapy as conversation.* New York: Academic Press, 1977.

Lenneberg, E. H. *Biological foundations of language.* New York: Wiley, 1967.

Macnamara, J. Cognitive basis of language learning in infants. *Psychological Review,* 1972, 79(1), 1–13.

McNeill, D. The creation of language by children. In J. Lyons, and R. Wales (Eds.), *Psycholinguistics papers.* Edinburgh: University of Edinburgh Press, 1966.

McNeill, D. *The Acquisition of language: The study of developmental psycholinguistics.* New York: Harper & Row, 1970.

McTear, M. F. Starting to talk: How preschool children initiate conversational exchanges. *Belfast Working Papers in Language and Linguistics,* 1977, 2(2).

McTear, M. F. Hey! I've got something to tell you: a study of the initiation of conversational exchanges by preschool children. Paper presented at 5th International Congress of Applied Linguistics, Montreal, Canada, August 1978.

Mead, G. H. *Mind, self and society.* Chicago: University of Chicago Press, 1934.

Menyuk, P. *The acquisition and development of language.* Englewood Cliffs, N. J.: Prentice-Hall, 1971.

Moffett, J. *Teaching the universe of discourse.* Boston: Houghton Mifflin, 1968.

Montgomery, M. M. The values of rising and falling tones in the intonation of one child. *Bristol Working Papers in Language,* 1979, 1, 87–105.

Nelson, Katherine. The relation of form recognition to concept development. *Child Development,* 1972, 43, 67–74.

Nelson, Katherine. Structure and Strategy in Learning to Talk. *Monographs of the*

*Society for Research in Child Development.*1973, 38 (1-2 Ser. No. 149)

Nelson, K. E. Facilitating children's syntax acquisition. *Developmental Psychology,* 1977a, 13, 101–107.

Nelson, K. E. Aspects of language acquisition and use from age two to age twenty. *Journal of American Academy of Child Psychiatry,* 1977b, 16, 584–607.

Nelson, K. E., Carskaddon, G., and Bonvillian, J. D. Syntax acquisition: impact of experimental variation in adult verbal interaction with the child. *Child Development,* 1973, 44, 497–504.

Nelson, K. E. and Nelson, Katherine. Cognitive pendulums and their linguistic Realisation. *In* K. E. Nelson (Ed.), *Children's Language,* Vol. 1. New York: Gardner Press, 1978.

Newport, E. L., Gleitman, H., and Gleitman, L. R. Mother, I'd rather do it myself: some effects and non-effects of maternal speech style. *In* C. E. Snow and C. Ferguson (Eds.), *Talking to children: Language input and acquisition.* Cambridge: Cambridge University Press, 1977.

Newson, J. and Newson, E. *Patterns of infant care.* Harmondsworth: Penguin Books, 1970.

Olson, D. From Utterance to Text: The Bias of Language in Speech and Writing. *Harvard Educational Review,* 1977, 47(3), 257–281.

Ratner, N. and Bruner, J. S. Games, social exchange and the acquisition of language. *Journal of Child Language,* 1978, 5(3).

Robinson, E. J. The child's understanding of inadequate messages in communication failure: a problem of ignorance or egocentrism. *In* W. P. Dickson (Ed.), *Children's oral communication skills,* New York: Academic Press, In press.

Robinson, W. P. *Language management in education: The Australian context.* Sydney: George Allen and Urwin, 1978.

Sacks, H., Schegloff, E. A., and Jefferson, G. A simplest systematics for the organization of turn-taking for conversation. *Language.* 1974, 50, 696–735.

Scaife, M. and Bruner, J. S. The capacity for joint visual attention in the infant. *Nature,* 1975, 253 (5489), 265–266.

Schaffer, H. R. *The growth of sociability.* London: Penguin, 1971.

Schaffer, H. R. Early social behaviour and the study of reciprocity. *Bulletin of the British Psychological Society,* 1974, 27, 209–216.

Schaffer, H. R., Collis, G. M., and Parsons, G. Vocal interchange and visual regard in verbal and pre-verbal children. Paper presented at the Loch Lomond Symposium, University of Strathclyde, September 1975.

Schegloff, E. A. Sequencing in conversational openings. *American Anthropologist,* 1968, 70, 1075–1095.

Schegloff, E. A. and Sacks, H. Opening up closings. *Semiotica,* 1973, 8(4), 289–327.

Schlesinger, I. M. The role of cognitive development and linguistic input in language acquisition. *Journal of Child Language,* 1977, 4(2), 153–170.

Searle, J. R. *Speech acts: An essay in the philosophy of language.* Cambridge: Cambridge University Press, 1969.

Shatz, M. and Gelman, R. Development of communication skills. *Monographs of the Society for Research in Child Development.* 1973, 152.

Shields, M. The child as psychologist: Construing the social world. *In* A. Lock (Ed.), *Action, gesture, symbol: The emergence of language.* New York: Academic Press, 1978.

Sinclair, J. McH. and Coulthard, R. M. *Towards an analysis of discourse: the English used by teachers and pupils.* London: Oxford University Press, 1975.

Slobin, D. I. Cognitive prerequisites for the development of grammar. *In* C. A. Ferguson and D. I. Slobin (Eds.), *Studies in child language development.* New York: Holt Rinehart & Winston, 1973.

Snow, C. E. Mother's speech to children learning language. *Child Development,* 1972,43, 549–565.

Snow, C. E. Mother's speech research: from input to acquisition. *In* C. E. Snow and C. Ferguson (Eds.), *Talking to children.* (Language input and acquisition.) Cambridge: Cambridge University Press, 1977.

Snow, C. E. and Ferguson, C. (Eds.), *Talking to children: Language input and acquisition.* London: Cambridge University Press, 1977.

Staats, A. W. Integrated-Functional learning theory and language development. *In* D. I. Slobin (Ed.), *The ontogenesis of grammar.* New York: Academic Press, 1971.

Stern, D. N. Mother and infant at play: The dyadic interaction involving facial, vocal and gaze behaviors. *In* M. Lewis and L. A. Rosenblum (Eds.), *The Effect of the infant on its caregiver.* New York: Wiley, 1974.

Stern, D. *The first relationship: Infant and mother.* London: Open Books, 1977.

Stubbs, M. Some structural complexities of talk in meetings. *Working Papers in Discourse Analysis 5,* University of Birmingham, 1973.

Trevarthen, C. Conversations with a two-month-old. *New Scientist,* 1974, 2, 230.

Trevarthen, C. and Hubley, P. Secondary intersubjectivity: Confidence, confiding and acts of meaning in the first year. *In* A. Lock (Ed.), *Action, gesture and symbol: The emergence of language.* New York: Academic Press, 1978.

Trevarthen, C., Hubley, P., and Sheeran, L. Les activités innées du nourrissant (Psychological Actions in Early Infancy). *La Recherche,* 1975, 6(56) 447–458.

Turner, G. J. Social class and children's language of control at age 5 and age 7. *In* B. Bernstein (Ed.), *Class, codes & control Vol 2: Applied studies in the sociology of language.* London: Routledge & Kegan Paul, 1973.

van der Geest, T., Gerstel, R., Appel, R., and Tervoort, B. *The child's communicative competence.* The Hague: Mouton, 1973.

Vygotsky, L. S. *Myshlenie i Rech (Thinking and Speech)* (1934). Selected passages translated by A. Sutton. Centre for Child Study, University of Birmingham, 1977.

Wells, C. G. *Coding manual for the description of child speech.* University of Bristol, School of Education, 1973, (rev. ed., 1975).

Wells, C. G. Learning to code experience through language. *Journal of Child Language,* 1974, 1(2), 243–269.

Wells, C. G. The contexts of children's early language experience. *Educational Review,* 1975, 27(2), 114–125.

Wells, C. G. Language use and educational success: an empirical response to Joan Tough's "The Development of Meaning" *Research in Education,* 1977, 18, 9–34.

Wells, C. G. What makes for successful language development? *In* R. Campbell and P. Smith (Eds.), *Advances in the psychology of language.* New York: Plenum, 1978.

Wells, C. G. Learning and using the auxiliary verb in English *In* V. Lee (Ed.), *Language development*. London: Croom Helm, 1979.

Wells, C. G., MacLure, M. and Montgomery, M. M. Some strategies for sustaining conversation. *In* P. Werth (Ed.), *Conversation, speech and discourse*. London: Croom Helm, In press.

Wells, C. G., Montgomery, M. M., and MacLure, M. *Discourse and the development of language*. Paper presented at the Fifth International Congress of Applied Linguistics, Montreal, Canada, August 1978.

Wells, C. G., Montgomery, M. M. and MacLure, M. Adult-child discourse: Outline of a model of analysis. *Journal of Pragmatics,* 1979, 3, 337–380.

Wells, C. G. and Raban, E. B. *Children learning to read*. Final Report to the Social Science Research Council, University of Bristol, School of Education, 1978.

Wooton, A. Conversation in request sequences. Paper presented at the Child Language Seminar, University of York, April 1978.

# 3

# THE INTERNAL LANGUAGE OF CHILDREN'S SYNTAX: THE ONTOGENESIS AND REPRESENTATION OF SYNTACTIC CATEGORIES

## MICHAEL P. MARATSOS
## MARY ANNE CHALKLEY

The task of a child in acquiring the grammar of a language is to formulate a productive system for combining morphemes in such a way that he can produce and comprehend appropriately formed utterances in novel situations. Such an acquisition requires the child to formulate, from hearing terms used one at a time in individual utterances, generalizations about how *classes* of terms combine with each other to express meanings and form acceptable sequences.

The child must thus have a means for representing to himself the analytic properties of individual utterances he hears, and means of analyzing such representations in order to be able to discern and use the more general patterns of grammatical combination of a language. The child must both initially have and further devise languages for the representation of language itself.

An important part of the linguist's representation of grammatical generalization lies in the use of syntactic categories, categories represented by symbols such as noun, verb, adjective, noun phrase, grammatical subject, or various noun gender subclasses such as masculine, feminine, and neuter. Such symbols stand for and guide the general combinatorial properties of individual morphemes; the child must in some way also capture in use and representation some of the general properties of language.

The investigation of this question—what do such symbols represent, how does the child acquire this knowledge, what is the form of the child's own representations—comprises the central issue of this chapter. In particular, we shall propose an hypothesis that such symbols, though used of particular terms or constituents, do not denote semantic or phonological prop-

erties of the terms or constituents themselves. Rather they refer to the correlated uses of those terms or constituents in different semantic-distribu-
tional-phonological sequences. We shall contrast this view to two others: (1)
the nativist view that such grammatical categories are innate givens in the
child's vocabulary for representing syntax, and (2) a view that attempts to
tie the definition of syntactic categories such as verb, subject, or gender subclass to inherent semantic characteristics of the relevant terms or constituents. In the course of the chapter, we shall both exposit the nature of our
view for a number of syntactic categories (form classes, gender classes,
grammatical subject) and attempt to show through the use of the available
empirical evidence that the view provides insight into the course of
children's acquisition. We conclude with a brief, hypothetical sketch, in the
mode of description attempted here, of how the child might formulate an
appropriate representational system. There must remain, however, a number of important problems we shall *not* outline in detail; these include hierarchical structure and transformational relations.

## SPECIFIC AND GENERAL REFERENCES
## IN GRAMMATICAL RULES

Our eventual goal is the delineation of how the child forms descriptions
of grammatical structure which include specifications of general operations
on general classes of morphemes. But what do we mean by this? In fact, not
all grammatical rules of a language are highly general; many rules of a language that a child formulates must refer to highly idiosyncratic semantic-
combinatorial patterns of individual morphemes. For example, one rule of
English is that the word *over* may appear with the term *think* (or its morphological variants; e. g., *thinks, thought, thinking*) in sequences of the
form *think over NP* or *think NP over* to express the notion of considering
or having thoughts about the NP argument. The rule *is* productive within its
limits. A wide (infinite) range of NP arguments may be fit into this schema.
But other aspects of the rule are quite specific and idiosyncratic. There is
nothing about the meaning "consider" which requires the use of a grammatical particle such as *over* with *think*. Nor is there anything about the
meanings of *over* and *think* to make their cooccurrence to express this
meaning any more reasonable than the use with *think* of other particles or
prepositions such as *in, under, up,* and so on.

But the *think* + *over* rule, though highly specific, shares many characteristics with other grammatical rules, particularly in its mixture of primitives from many levels of description. It is the particular terms *think* and
*over* which can be so combined, rather than other sometimes semantically
close terms such as *believe, consider,* or *above;* the rule thus makes reference to particular phonological sequences. The full predicate-argument

rendering of *think over* gives a correspondence of a grammatical sequence with a semantic characterization: $NP_1$ *think over* $NP_2$ = "the referent of $NP_1$ considers the referent of $NP_2$." The rule also makes reference to the general structural entities NP; NP is both grammatically limited and makes reference to a wide, unrealistic range of possible referents. The rule stating the semantic-combinatorial cooccurrence properties of *think* and *over* and its NP arguments is a grammatical rule; it is simply one that is highly specific in some aspects, and is not strongly entailed by the general grammatical or semantic characteristics of its key terms.

Other rules regulating the relations between combinatorial sequence and meaning make crucial reference to more general classes of entities; they have a feeling of greater productivity and more central status in the language. One such rule in English is the rule of expression of generic present tense by use of the morpheme we commonly spell *-s,* in sequences such as *he barks at the moon a lot* or *he likes his food (bark-barks, like-likes).* Of course, knowledge of the relation between *-s* and the term to which it is attached could be like knowledge of the meaning that results from attaching *over* to *think.* The child could encode that adding *-s* to *bark* encodes a present generic disposition to *bark,* separately encode that adding *-s* to *like* denotes a present generic disposition to *like,* and so on through a very long list of terms. Each application could be as specific as the *think + over* rule.

The rule applies, however, to a large number of terms, and the child somehow analyzes and encodes this fact. It is not a *list* of terms; rather there is something general about the nature of V such that the child can apply the rule in a novel and productive manner (Berko, 1958; Brown, 1973). The child must analyze incoming speech so as to be able to formulate this general property or set of properties. But the broadest designation of the rule is insufficient. For example, all Vs are *relational terms,* and the rule might be specified as *relational term + s* = "generic present disposition of the relation." But terms such as *fond (of), nice (to),* or *obnoxious* are all relational terms just as much as *like, help,* or *act,* yet the structural-semantic correspondence only applies to the latter terms, not the former. We do not say that \**John nices to people,* or that \**Mary obnoxiouses all the time.* Relational terms such as *nice* or *obnoxious* instead take the form *is* to denote present generic disposition in the same grammatical context. We say that the rule of *-s* attachment applies only to verbs, symbolized here as V, and not to adjectives. Furthermore, like most such rules, the rule only applies in certain contexts. Using the rule $V + s$ = "generic present disposition of the V relation," one would also produce sentences such as \**does it rolls, \*it doesn't rolls, \*for it to rolls is likely.* That the difficulty with these is not purely semantic is easy to see from the acceptability of *I want to know if it rolls, it's not the case that it rolls,* and *it's likely that it rolls.* The rule can only be used of V relational terms in certain structural contexts, roughly, in the contexts ## (= sentence boundary) + NP + _____ . . . (What occurs after the *V* + *s*—for example, whether there is a grammatical object or not —seems to be irrelevant).

Like the rule for *think, over,* and NP, the entities mentioned in the rule again include semantic (effect of adding *-s*), phonological (list of morphemes that are *-s*), and structural specifications (##, NP, V). But the *-s* rule is more highly generalizable, applying to any *V* in the proper grammatical environment; it is also used frequently and in fact obligatorily. It is the learning of fairly general rules such as the *-s* attachment rule which observers generally contemplate when speaking of the child's learning of grammar. Even though the *think* + *over* coocurrence rule is itself productive, its core (the semantic effect of combining *think* + *over*) is highly specific, its formulation is not impressive, and it is less easy to think of as a rule (though it is one).

The child, of course, is faced with individual uses of morphemes used only in utterances in specific nonlinguistic contexts. No one tells him that certain phonological-sequential-semantic correspondences are highly specific and some are highly general. He must somehow notice which ones are and which ones are not. Furthermore—and it is here that we take our first beginning point—he must eventually find a system of representation to encode these generalizations about classes of individual terms: a form of representation to encode the conditions for their use, and to represent the class of terms to which they apply. For example, our rule for adding *-s* to certain relational terms mentions the entity V to mark off those relational terms. But we already know that V does not include *all* relational terms. What can the child notice about what is similar among all these terms so that he will know which of them to apply the operation to? What is the nature of V as a psycholinguistic entity at all? Some morphemes that figure in general grammatical operations can be specified abstractly, such as Pres in *kicks = V + Pres,* but in fact they can be given as a list, in this case /-z/, /-s/, or /-iz/ depending on the phonological shape of the V. But V, clearly, is not a shorthand for a list of the terms to which the operation applies. What we write as V must refer to something about the individual members of the set of terms which the child can analyze and summarize in his representation.

What is this similarity among the members of the set? When asked about classes of single terms, such as V, Adj, or N, the question is one of *form class* definition. In the next section, we take up a consideration of what the child formulates when he formulates the linguistic properties we summarize by terms such as V. We also include, as clearer in some respects about the same points and as important to later discussions, a discussion of a type of formal subdivision of one of these classes, the system of German noun genders.

## FORM AND GENDER CLASSES

## A Preliminary Theoretical Description

### Form class

One answer which has been given about what form class categories are, and how the child comes to formulate them, is that they are innate syntactic categories. The child does not formulate them: they are essential primitive names of classes of terms with which the child is innately endowed, and thus part of the innate vocabulary of syntactic elements with which the child begins the task of analyzing grammatical sequences. In such a view, they are *substantive universals* of language, and need no further explanation (McNeill, 1966; Chomsky, 1965).

In another view, their definition, or at least basis, lies in semantic analyses (e.g., Slobin, 1966; Bates & MacWhinney, 1978) of the terms themselves. Nouns are terms which denote concrete objects; verbs, terms which denote actions, and adjectives terms which denote states. They thus do not arise from innate abstract syntactic knowledge, but arise instead from the use of natural conceptual formulations to classify words.

The difference between the two views is clearly sharp. But they are similar in at least one respect. Different form classes characteristically undergo different sets of grammatical operations to express similar semantic notions. For example, both adjectives and verbs in English express relations which may be marked for tense in various ways, depending on the surrounding grammatical context. In a simple active affirmative declarative, English verbs characteristically add the morpheme *-ed* to express pastness (*kick-kicked*). Adjectives, contrastively, cannot be marked for tense, but instead take a form of *be* (*was happy, were happy*). In both of the views described above, the child's description of such form class operations can rest on the presupposed availability of general categories such as verb and adjective, either given by innate knowledge or by semantic categorization. The child equipped with an innate vocabulary may be viewed as setting out to see how verbs act in his particular language. The English-speaking child, for example, will find that verbs may add *-ed* to express past, and adjectives may take forms of *be (was, were)* for the same function. Or, if the child's representation of form class is in semantic terms, he may classify major relational terms as expressing action or states, and then analyze the way in which action or state terms participate in, for example, tense-marking operations.

It seems to us that neither of these analyses is correct. We shall show both that general semantic definitions of form class are inadequate and that they do not seem to have overly strong appeal to the child in the process of acquisition. We do not assume, however, that the child begins the task of acquisition with such abstract syntactic categories available to him for the formulation of grammatical sequences. Rather, we believe it is possible to develop an account in which the regularities of the behaviors of terms which we summarize by reference to form classes such as verb and adjective are the outcome of the analyses which begin with the phonological, sequential, and semantic analysis of individual utterances and their correspondence to the nonlinguistic context in which they occur. Thus in this view, form class and other syntactic classes such as gender class are not, at least for a while, primitives on which the child bases further analyses, but an *outcome* of the analysis of more primitive sequential and semantic properties.

We do not offer direct arguments against the nativist hypothesis in this paper, for a variety of reasons. It is not disaprovable, though it can be shown to lead to certain unlikely conclusions. In the end it seems the only certain manner of disproving it is to show it to be unnecessary by proposing an alternative account. We attempt to begin to outline such an account in this paper. The semantics-alone account of form and other grammatical classes, however, can be directly challenged.

Statistically it is true that nouns are more likely to denote concrete referents, verbs, to denote often voluntary actions or processes such as change of state (e.g., *break, melt*), and adjectives, to denote more or less enduring often involuntary states and dispositions. But verbs also include nonactional state terms such as *know, believe, like, have, contain,* and *consist.* Adjectives include actional terms such as *active, reckless, naughty, helpful,* and *obnoxious,* all of which refer to how one does things. They also include terms referring to nonpermanent characteristics such as *hot, wet, nearby,* and others. Often very nearly the same concept is expressed with different form class terms. Examples include *know, (be) aware (of); like, (be) fond (of); treat (well), (be) nice (to); make (noise), (be) noisy.*

Why do we call such semantically dissimilar terms as *like* and *push* verbs, or group together *hot, fond,* and *obnoxious* as adjectives? What members of a form class do share, in varying degree, which motivates our classifying them together, is a common set of diverse combinatorial-semantic properties. For example, both verbs and adjectives are relational terms, and as such express meanings which may be imagined as having obtained in either past or present contexts. Relational terms we call verbs, however, can be marked directly for tense, in the appropriate syntactic-semantic contexts, either by an internal change (*sing-sang*) or more commonly with morphemes such as *-ed* (*kick-kicked*) or *-s* (*kick-kicks*). Or when negated, the negative element and tense may appear on a form of *do* (kick-didn't kick). Questions are also formed with forms of *do* (*did he kick? does he know?*). Adjectives, contrastively, cannot be directly marked for tense. Rather, tense, negation, and interrogation are marked in simple sentences with forms of *be: is busy, wasn't busy, was he busy?*

Thus we say that relational terms which take a certain set of semantic-combinatorial operations are verbs; those which take another set are adjectives. (We are leaving prepositions out of the discussion, though they could easily be included, especially considering uses such as *he is against us, he is with us.*) Rather than verbs and adjectives defining the use of such operations, we can say that being operated on by a certain set of operations comprises being a verb.

This system is clearly circular. For example, knowing that a relational term appears in the context ##NP + _____ + ed . . . (*John kicked*), entailing a past meaning of the relation, we can classify it as a verb. Knowing it is a verb, we know it can appear in the context ##NP + _____ + ed to denote past occurrence. How can such a system lead to productivity?

The productivity of such uses arises from the fact that members of a large form class are used in a highly overlapping set of many *different* combinatorial-semantic operations. These operations are thus correlated to each other through their usage of common terms. By hearing a novel term used in one of the contexts, we can predict its occurrence and accordant change of meaning and structure in still others. For example, suppose we hear the nonsense term *glix* for the first time in the context *Today John glixes.* This corresponds to the frame ##NP + *Relational Term* + s## = occurrence of the relation in the present (signaled by *Today*). From this single occurrence, we can predict other uses such as *John glixed* ( = occurrence of *glix* in the past), *did John glix? John doesn't glix, John will glix, John's glixing is absurd, to glix is fun,* and so on, each with its respective semantic entailments. If we further hear the sentence *John glixed Mary,* we can predict the possibility of a semantically equivalent sentence *Mary was glixed by John,* and other sentences such as *Mary's having been glixed by John was sad, for John to glix Mary is absurd, the glixing of Mary by John is commendable,* and so on. We also know some contingent possibilities. For example, if *glix* denotes a controllable activity, it could be used in sentences such as the progressive *John is glixing Mary,* or imperative *glix Mary!*

In contrast, should we hear *glix* in a context like *John is glix today,* we could predict utterances such as *John isn't glix, was John glix, for John to be glix is sad,* and so on, for many of the same basic semantic functions. If *glix* denotes a controllable activity, utterances such as *John is being glix* or *be glix!* are possible.

Our tendency is to say that hearing *Today John glixes,* we know it is a verb, and thus that it can appear in the related combinatorial-semantic frames of verbs. In a sense this is backwards. It is rather because *glix* can enter into these correlated semantic-sequential patterns that we call it a verb. We should say instead that one semantic-sequential usage implies the others. Veiwed this way, it is not that children learn how verbs act, as though they begin with the notion of verbs. Rather, they come to learn that a certain set of terms may appear in correlated uses. Thus, what we call the productive use of verb vs. adjective privileges corresponds to learning how different operations, contexts, and semantic entailments center on a common set of terms.

## Terminology: Semantic-distributional patterns

One of the types of analysis that figures in this account is sequential analysis: verbs are classes of relational terms that can appear, for example, before the small set of morphemes *-ed, -s,* and often *-ing,* and appear directly after *do*-forms (*didn't go, doesn't see, don't know*). Adjectives are relational terms which appear, unmarked, with forms of *be* to mark many of the same functions (*was busy, is busy, wasn't busy,* and so on). The analysis of terms into formal classes purely on the basis of what other morphemes they can combine with sequentially, without regard for semantic analysis, is a form of *distributional analysis* (Gleason, 1961; Harris, 1951).

We are not, however, attempting a formulation of the child's analysis of form class and other syntactic categories on purely distributional bases. The semantic entailments of such combinations of morphemes also form an essential part of the account. Verbs are thus not just terms that combine with *-ed, -s,* and so on. They are terms which combine with *-ed,* for example, in certain environments to mean past occurrence of the relation, or with *-s* in certain environments to mean generic present occurrence. The kind of analysis of grammatical patterns we have in mind is thus best called distributional-semantic analysis. That this kind of analysis is necessary is shown by the great possible confusion the child would encounter in attempting to analyze grammatical sequences without reference to their meaningful entailments (Miller, 1976). For example, the sound we often write *-s,* aside from often comprising the end of many morpheme stems, is attached variously to both nouns and verbs. With nouns, in certain environments, it designates plurality (*boy-boys*), possession (*boy's*), or in fact sometimes is a contracted form of *be* (*the boy's not nice*). On verbs it designates generic present (*he kick + s*). Reliance on sequential phonological analysis alone would probably lead to confusion. When, however, semantic analyses are included, these emerge as different morphemes, essentially homonyms. Thus, verbs are not simply terms which among other things take *-s;* they are terms which among other things take *-s* to denote generic present. The combination of semantic analyses with distributional analyses is thus essential to our account.

In a sense, then, we mean the various combinations of distributional, phonological, and semantic analyses we discuss here to be taken as units. It is not simply ##NP + Relational Term + *s* . . ., but the equivalence as well of this sequence to the meaning of generic present of the relation. We shall refer to such combinations of analyses *as semantic-distributional patterns* throughout, or sometimes simply as patterns. This usage we mean not as analogous to visual patterns so much as to "pattern of behavior," which often denotes both an analysis of the sequence of overt activities and the underlying interpretations, causes, and motivations associated with those sequences.

So, in this interpretation, a form class such as verb designates a set of terms which can appear in a highly overlapping set of semantic-distributional patterns. Adjectives denote terms which can appear in another set of such patterns. It is not that the formal classification of the term defines its appearance in these correlated patterns. Rather, it is the correlation of term uses in the sets of semantic-distributional patterns that constitutes form class definition.

A problem which may suggest itself is whether there really is a reliable correlation among different uses of different terms that is sufficient to form a clear basis for the child's analysis. For example, not all the terms that take *do*-forms (*doesn't run, does he run?*) takes past tense *-ed* (*\*runned*), or progressive *-ing* (*\*he is knowing it*). Only terms which take *do*-forms can take NP arguments directly following a post-subject finite form in a main clause (*they kiss dogs, \*they nasty dogs, \*they be dogs*), but not all do (*\*they rely dogs*).

However, for the major syntactic categories, there are considerable numbers of perfect or nearly perfect correlations of use. For example, every relational term which takes *did* to mark past occurrence of the relation (*did he run?*) takes the other set of *do*-uses. Every form which takes *-ed* takes the *do*-forms. All these take third-person singular generic present *-s* (even irregular *does* and *has* includes *-s* as third person).

Furthermore, although some irregularities are completely arbitrary, such as irregular past forms, and form a difficulty for any theory of acquisition, others are not true irregularities at all. They follow from the semantic entailment of the pattern and the meaning of the particular term. For example, *-ing* progressive tends to denote a nonsteady, repeatable activity. Terms such as *know* do not fail to take the progressive because of arbitrary subcategorization, but because their meaning, properly understood, is incompatible with the meaning denoted by progressive *-ing*. No doubt initial term-by-term memorization helps fix the meanings which the child eventually attributes to endings such as *-ing* (see later sections); but after a certain point such memorization is not necessary, and the application of the pattern is highly predictable. Thus the presence and the reliability of the clusters of implicational relations among semantic-distributional patterns for sets of terms is extensive enough to, we believe, afford the child the opportunity for adequate analysis.

*Gender classes.* The case we have made for form class consisting of the use of a term in a related set of semantic-distributional patterns can be made even more strongly for formal noun classes such as German masculine, feminine, and neuter genders.[1] The German system of gender is realized through differences in the forms of determiners (English articles, demonstratives), pronouns, and prenominal adjectives. Where the English speaker uses simply *the,* whether saying *the fork, the spoon,* or *the knife is here,* the German speaker must say, respectively, *der Löffel (spoon), die Gabel (fork),* or *das Messer (knife) ist hier.* Where the English speaker can use the pronoun *it* to say of any of these, *it is blue,* the German speaker must say *er, sie,* or *es* respectively to refer to the spoon, fork, and knife.

Furthermore, whereas English has just a rudimentary case system (nominative, genitive, accusative) in some pronouns and determiners (*he, his, him; she, her(s), her; they, their(s), them*), German has four cases: nominative, accusative, genitive, and dative, which combined with gender class govern choice of determiner or pronoun. Thus, for the masculine gender noun *spoon,* the following uses are typical: Nominative case: *der Löffel ist hier; er ist hier* ("the spoon is here;" "(he) is here"). Accusative case: *Er diskutiert den Löffel; er diskutiert ihn* ("he discussed the spoon"; he discussed it (him)"). Dative: *Er spricht von dem Löffel; er spricht von ihm* ("he is speaking about the spoon"; "he is speaking about it (him)"). For a feminine gender noun such as fork, conversely, the same contexts afford *die Gabel ist hier, sie ist hier; er diskutiert die Gabel, er diskutiert sie; er spircht von der Gabel, er spricht von ihr.*

Gender thus corresponds to a largely arbitrary assignment of a noun such that it governs selection from different sets of coreferential pronouns or surrounding determiners and adjectives contingent upon the grammatical case contexts. The paradigm for the three classes, the definite determiners and pronouns, is the following (singular nouns only):

|  | *Masculine* | *Feminine* | *Neuter* |
|---|---|---|---|
| Nominative | der + Noun; er | die + Noun; sie | das + Noun; es |
| Accusative | den + Noun; ihm | die + Noun; sie | das + Noun; es |
| Dative | dem+ Noun; ihm | der + Noun; ihr | dem+ Noun; ihm |
| Genitive | des + Noun; — | der + Noun; — | des + Noun; — |

Such grammatical case distinctions themselves are not transparently based. For example, in English we may say either *he kissed her* (*he* = nominative, *her* = objective case) or *she was kissed by him* (*she* = nominative, *him* = objective). Similarly, the corresponding German sentences are *Er [a nominative] hat sie geküsst* and *Sie wurde von ihm [dative] geküsst.* If one helps *(helfen)* someone, "someone" is dative; but if one does something *(für)* for someone, "someone" is in the accusative. One discusses *(diskutiert)* someone in the accusative, but talks about him *(spricht von)* in the dative. No clear underlying semantic principles always apply, though some do in some grammatical contexts. Case depends on complex mixtures of grammatical context, semantic criteria, the case usages of particular verbs and prepositions, and other criteria. For our discussion, however, we shall assume case as a given context, and concentrate attention on modulations afforded by—or rather corresponding to—gender.

There do exist some weak correspondences between gender class and the phonological and semantic characteristics of terms, but only for a small number of German nouns. Actually masculine referents such as "man," "boy," take the masculine gender determiner, pronoun, and adjective forms. Most feminine nouns take female gender sets. A few phonological characteristics of stems are also correlated with gender; e.g., nouns ending in the diminutive *-chen* are neuter. But even here, the word for "maiden" is neuter, as is the word for "child." A reference to *cat* is always in the feminine, whether the actual cat is male or female. Most nouns are quite arbitrarily assigned. There is no reason *knife, spoon,* and *fork* should be grouped with neuter, masculine, and feminine forms respectively. No semantic or other widely utilizable criterion reliably determines whether a noun takes masculine, feminine, or neuter determiners, adjectives, and pronouns. One must simply memorize its gender.

Despite its arbitrariness, the system is productive. As in the case of form classes, often knowledge of one of the contexts of a term is sufficient to give knowledge of the others. For gender systems also form systems of *correlated* patterns. Knowing a noun can appear in nominative from *der X,* a speaker can predict its other appropriate case-determiner, adjectival, and prenominal correspondents. Thus gender consists of the set of correlated uses centered around nouns. The analogy to distinctions such as those between verbs versus adjectives is actually quite close. In each case, the classification is determined by the correlated set of distributional-semantic uses rather than, for example, an internal semantic defining characteristic of the term, or some phonological characteristic. At the same time, as was shown before, it is not the case that whether a term is a verb or an adjective, for example, governs whether it takes verb or adjective tensing, negation, question, and other characteristic operations. Rather, it is the appearance with the correlated operations that defines the form class. Similarly, especially for German nouns, gender is analytically not a characteristic of the term that governs sets of determiners, pronouns, and adjectives. Instead it is the appearance of the noun in the related patterns (or having a related set of pronouns refer to the noun) that we call having gender in a noun. It is not that terms which we call masculine nouns take *der* in the nominative and *den* in the accusative, and so forth; instead, it is the taking of these determiners that partly *constitutes* what we call masculine gender. Gender is thus not a characteristic of the noun, but a characteristic of how it fits into related semantic-distributional patterns.

Consequences of the preliminary theoretical description

The significance of the theoretical description presented for an account of acquisition is striking. In order to more clearly highlight some of the implications of this system for acquisition, we will contrast two points of view: the one presented here in which the usage of terms is controlled by their uses in other correlated semantic-distributional patterns versus one in which the grammatical behaviors of terms are controlled solely by their semantic analysis (e.g., "action terms take *-ed* to denote past occurrence"). Using such a technique will, we hope, clarify some of the problems facing the child who must master the appropriate regularities found in the language in order to produce grammatical utterances. Before exploring the issues further, however, we need to introduce some analytic terminology and concepts. For if we propose that notions such as V, N, and NP do not themselves comprise analytic primitives for the representation of grammar, then there must be a more primitive system of representation upon which these can be built.

*Analytic primitives for analysis.* At the most abstract level, linguistic utterances can be described as expressing attributes of entities, or relations among them. Such expression can be described at two levels: the conceptual level, from which semantics draws its content, and the linguistic, the level of expression of meaning in phonological form.

At the conceptual level, it is not clear that there truly are single-attribute concepts. Even a classic attribute such as redness or hotness, for example, refers to the relation of a quality of an entity to other points on a continuum of visual frequencies, or temperature. In general, we shall refer either to attributes or obvious relations as *Relations,* and to those things related to each other as *Relational Entities.* We shall call those morphemes or groups of morphemes which refer to the spoken of relational entities as *Arguments.* Terms which refer to the relations or clusters of relations among the described or related entities will be called *Relational Terms.* (We will abbreviate these as *Arg* and *Rel* in discussion.)

As an example, the relation expressed by the relational term *see* relates two entities: the one that sees, and something that is seen. In the utterance *I see Mary, I* is the argument term denoting the entity that sees, and *Mary* denotes the entity that is seen. In the utterance *they disappear, they* denotes the single argument of the relational term *disappear,* which denotes a complex set of relations between states of existence or appearance of its single argument.

Arguments are clearly not limited to single morphemic descriptions. *See* is also a two argument term in the expression *I-see-the girl laugh.* In this instance, the relational entity denoting what is seen is expressed by the argument phrase *the girl laugh* which itself contains a relational term and argument.

Nor are arguments or even relational terms always continuous arrays of morphemes. For example, consider the utterance, *he kicked her*. In the terms we are using here, there is a two-argument relational term *kick,* taking as arguments a kicker (*he*) and something kicked (*her*). Now consider the past tense morpheme *-ed*. It itself is a relational term and takes as its single argument the entire relational term-argument set (*he-kick-her*). It denotes that the entity-relation meaning denoted by these morphemes took place at a time past relative to the time of the utterance. Thus, we would describe *-ed* as a relational term with a single, discontinuous argument, *he kick . . . her*. The fact that such relational terms are often expressed as bound morphemes or other noncentral grammatical forms is not relevant to this classification.

We do not claim great exactness or originality for these notions, which are commonly found in related forms in many linguistic and psycholinguistic descriptions (e.g., Lakoff, 1971; Antinucci & Parisi, 1973). But a thoroughgoing use of this analytic apparatus will aid in our discussion.

Relation, relational entity, relational term, and argument, are naturally very general primitives. They either subsume, presuppose, or must be supplemented by a number of other analytic primitives. In particular, we must assume the child has available whatever conceptual primitives are necessary for the analysis of semantic and pragmatic elements in utterances. This obviously comprises an enormously complex problem for study of itself. But we can for our purposes only assume whatever is needed, including notions such as activity, temporal and aspectual relations, animacy, shape, communication value, emotional state, number, and so on. We must also obviously assume that the child can interpret groups of morphemes, continuous or discontinuous, and the semantic relations to each other of the entities denoted by the morphemes.

These may seem like very complex primitives to assume. But in fact we know of no recent discussions of language acquisition, including those based purely on semantics, that do not presuppose them, in one form or another. It should be clarified that by calling these primitives for our discussion, we do not presuppose that they are necessarily innately given, though we would guess many are. Rather, they are simply assumed as primitives relative to the representations to be constructed from them. Nor do we think it crucial that the primitives proposed here be perfectly accurate. Most of our discussion should hold true with other basic systems of representation.

Finally, we hope it will not be confusing that we shall often refer to some arguments or relational terms by particular phonological descriptions, such as *-ed* for the relational term which denotes pastness in certain contexts. For example, we can describe one level of analysis of the sequence, *the girl disappeared* as being ##Arg + Rel + ed##. That is, *the girl* = Arg (of Rel), *disappear* = Rel, and *-ed* = itself. This is just the level of analysis that happens to be crucial for part of the specification of the past tensing rule for verbs: if a certain kind of relational term is preceded by one of its arguments which follows directly upon a sentence boundary,[2] a past occurrence of the relation may be denoted by adding *-ed* to the relational term. Specifying "certain kind" is equivalent to specifying what verbs are.

Having introduced the necessary primitives, we now turn to the issue of acquisition of form class privileges. In particular, we are interested in how the child achieves novel production: how does he know from one exposure to a given term in a given context what the other patterns are in which that term can participate? We will highlight two accounts, the one presented here in which the analysis of correlated semantic-distributional patterns is critical versus one which focuses on the analysis of the inherent semantics of the terms. We then will consider briefly their implications for the problem of how a system may be acquired which makes productive use possible.

## An Account Based on Correlated Patterns
## Versus A Semantic-Based Account

### Form class analysis

As described earlier, for our account it is the correlation among patterns through their application to common sets of terms which establishes the basis for productivity. Once the child knows one use, one pattern in which a term can appear, that provides information about what other patterns are also acceptable. How, then, does the child represent this information and how does he acquire that representation?

Initially, of course, the child must hear terms happening in certain patterns. For example, he could hear *the cup dropped,* and this would provide the basis for analyzing *drop* as one of the relational terms which can appear in an hypothesized pattern ##Arg[3] + Rel + ed . . . = 'past occurrence of the relation.' Encountering *the ball didn't drop* would provide a basis for the child to analyze *drop* as one of the relational terms which can appear in another pattern, ##Arg + didn't + Rel . . . = 'past nonoccurrence of the relation.' Thus, the child could gradually build a network of patterns and the terms which can appear in them. This network can partially, and only very roughly, be schematized as in Figure 3-1. Although this particular network may not be precisely accurate in schematizing the child's representational system, it is networks similar to the foregoing which allow the child to encode and to make use of the correlations among the patterns. The interconnections among the various patterns through the same set of terms come to constitute the basis for accurate specification of which relational terms can enter into a given semantic-distributional pattern. In short, the patterns come to incorporate one another in the specifications which detail what set of relational terms can apply. Knowing that a term can appear in the pattern ##Arg + Rel + ed . . . = 'past . . .' makes it possible to predict that it can also appear in

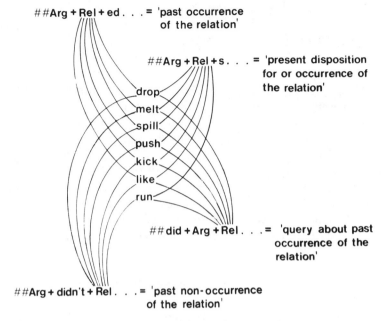

##Arg + Rel + ed . . . = 'past occurrence of the relation'

##Arg + Rel + s . . . = 'present disposition for or occurrence of the relation'

drop
melt
spill
push
kick
like
run

##did + Arg + Rel . . . = 'query about past occurrence of the relation'

##Arg + didn't + Rel . . . = 'past non-occurrence of the relation'

*Figure 3-1*

patterns using various *do*-forms, the pattern including Rel + *s* for third person singular present tense, and so on. Thus the child provided with a single exposure to a new relational term can generate other appropriate uses because knowing one pattern in which the term appears is the key to knowing in which other patterns it may also appear.

The importance of this interconnection or correlation among the various patterns is perhaps best highlighted by contrasting it to a system in which all patterns could be quite independent in their functioning. Suppose one accepted a semantic-based hypothesis in order to account for form class privileges and further suppose that form class boundaries were defined by the inherent semantics of terms; then such as hypothesis would allow the child to acquire each semantic-distributional pattern without connecting it to any other pattern. For example, to parallel the case presented above, suppose the child encountered *the cup dropped.* He could analyze that utterance as fitting the pattern ##Arg + Rel      + ed . . . = 'past occurrence of the action.'
          [+ action]
For the case of *the ball didn't drop,* the analysis could be ##Arg + Rel
                                                              [+ action]
+ didn't . . . = 'past nonoccurrence of the action.' There would be no reason for the child to establish links between these two patterns as productivity should arise from encountering a term, analyzing its semantics, and then using that semantic analysis (in this case, +action), to select the appropriate

patterns to express tensing, negation, and so on. The child's representation of what we call verb privileges would then consist of a list of independent patterns partially exemplified by something like the following:

Arg + Rel        + ed . . .     =   'past occurrence of action'
   [+ action]
Arg + Rel        + s . . .      =   'present generic disposition for ac-
[3 Sg] [+ action]                   tion to occur'
Arg + will + Rel      . . .     =   'future occurrence of action'
   [+ action]
did + Arg + Rel       . . .     =   'query about possible past occur-
   [+ action]                       rence of the action'

Similarly, if adjectives could be defined as denoting states, then for productivity to occur all the child would have to know was that a new relational term denoted a state and that certain patterns were acceptable for terms marked + state. Thus, his knowledge regarding what we call adjective privileges could be captured by a list of independent patterns like (although more complete than) the following:

Arg + was + Rel      . . .      =   'past occurrence of the state'
   [+ state]
Arg + is + Rel       . . .      =   'present occurrence of the state'
[3 S]        [+ state]
Arg + will + be + Rel     . . . =   'future occurrence of the state'
   [+ state]
was + Arg + Rel      . . .      =   'query about possible past occur-
   [+ state]                        rence of the state'

In this system, knowing the inherent semantics of the terms would completely predict the appropriate patterns; there would thus be no necessity to correlate the patterns with each other by representing their common use of overlapping sets of terms.

However, as we discussed earlier, form class boundaries are not actually defined by inherent semantics. In fact, there is so much overlap in semantics across the boundaries that + action and + state simply cannot be used to capture the regularities of the system. Both *push* and *want* take "verb" patterns, though one denotes a + action term, and the other a + mental state term. So, the only semantic categorization which might be broad enough to encompass the class which we call verbs would be + relation. This would result in the child generating a pattern of the form ##Arg + Rel + ed . . . = 'past occurrence of the relation.' Unfortunately, however, the child would also have to represent the pattern ##Arg + was + Rel . . . = 'past occurrence of the relation' in order to deal with terms like *happy* and *active*. Confronted with these two alternative forms for denoting past occurrence, and not being able to resort to using the inherent semantics of a new term in order to make an appropriate choice between the two, the child relying solely on an analysis of inherent semantics of terms to define appropriate privileges would never be able to achieve accurate productivity. Knowing that a term denoted a state relation would not allow the child to predict how to encode its past occurrence. Of course, if he did not maintain his representations of patterns independently of one another but encoded the fact that terms which take the ##Arg + Rel + ed = 'past . . .' pattern appear in certain other patterns, then he could achieve productivity. Knowing the pattern in which a new relational term appeared would provide him with the key to know which other patterns were also appropriate. He could then choose accurately between alternatives. Clearly it is the correlations among the semantic-distributional patterns in which a set of terms appear which determines the definition of form class privileges. The child must encode and represent the necessary interconnections among patterns in order to achieve productivity.

Therefore, the essential information a child needs about a new relational term in order to predict appropriate grammatical usage is not the meaning of the term but at least one semantic-distributional pattern in which it can occur. Given that new terms are generally introduced in the context of ongoing speech, this does not seem to be a particularly peculiar requirement. However, that is not the only analysis the child must make in order to build up this system. The child must be able to encode the semantic-distributional patterns and the connections among them which are a function of their application to overlapping sets of relational terms. Only with such information can the relational term specification for a given semantic-distributional pattern be accurately formulated to reflect the fact that the key for appropriate productive usage of a term is the appearance of the term in other correlated patterns.

## German noun gender classes

The appropriateness of such an account for the acquisition of other grammatical systems of privileges like the German gender system is even clearer. As we discussed earlier, the German speaker must use the information that, for example, for the masculine gender nouns (e.g., *spoon*), definite reference in nominative contexts is denoted by *der* preceding the noun (e.g., *der Löffel [spoon],)* the appropriate pronoun selection for such a context is *er,* definite reference in dative contexts is denoted by *dem* preceding the noun, and so forth. In contrast, for feminine gender nouns (e.g., *fork*) the same case contexts require the selection of *die* (definite reference in the nominative), *sie* (nominative pronoun), *der* (definite reference in the dative), and so on. A third set of appropriate patterns applies for those terms which we call neuter gender nouns (e.g., *knife*). In essence, what we call German gender usage corresponds to three sets of semantic-distributional patterns which represent mutually exclusive alternatives for determining appropriate pronoun and determiner selection in various grammatical case contexts. The semantic-distributional patterns within each gender set are connected to each other by their linkage to a common set of argument terms (i.e., a common subject of what we call noun); specifically, those arguments for which the given subset of patterns constitutes accurate usage. The fact that a term can participate in a particular cluster of patterns (e.g., *der* + *Arg* = "definite reference to entity denoted by the argument" in nominative contexts, *dem* + *Arg* = "definite reference . . ." in dative contexts, etc.) is precisely what we are summarizing when we assign that term a gender designation (in this case, masculine). Unfortunately, for only a small subset of the argument terms we call nouns is it possible to determine which set of patterns is appropriate on the basis of the inherent semantics of the term alone. Thus, for the child learning the German gender system it is not generally possible to achieve accurate usage *solely* by analyzing the inherent semantics of the terms. The child must somehow encode the fact that it is just those terms which take *die* in nominative contexts which are the ones that are replaced by the single term argument (pronoun) *sie* in those same contexts; and furthermore, that those same terms take *der* in the dative and are replaced by pronominal *ihr* in dative contexts, and so forth. It is this correlation through a common set of terms of the various semantic-distributional patterns which make productivity possible. Knowing the interconnections among the patterns in the preceding example is what we mean by labeling the term as one of feminine gender. The child therefore can predict on the basis of knowing one pattern in which the term appears which are the other patterns in which it can also appear. Given the complexity of case contexts themselves, this may seem to be an enormous task, but, as we shall discuss in the following section, children do make the necessary analyses to allow them to accurately produce those patterns which constitute appropriate gender usage; and they make these analyses during the preschool years without the benefit of direct instruction. Once again, the important aspect for the child learning the system is the fact that encoding and representing the correspondence of the uses of terms in *different* patterns is crucial; the child cannot just analyze the individual patterns.

Thus we may say that individual morphemes are nouns, verbs or adjectives or masculine, feminine, or neuter gender; but these categories do not refer to the inherent semantic or phonological characteristics of the terms themselves. Rather, they are summary references to the correlation among the semantic-distributional patterns in which the term can appear.

## Empirical Findings about Form and Gender Class Acquisition

Our major intent in this section is to compare available empirical data for its relevance to the question of what kinds of formulations children make about such syntactic categories. Clearly, as we have already discussed, we do not think that a purely semantic-based approach can ever lead to acquisition of the final adult state. However, we are willing to entertain hypotheses regarding what types of analyses the child may initially attempt to employ. It may be that the child does initially entertain a semantic-based hypothesis. But, once the child begins to encounter terms such as *want, like,* etc., he would have to begin to expand his semantic-based representations and would thus encounter all of the difficulties regarding selection among alternative patterns which we have already discussed with regard to adult performance. Therefore, even if the child attempted to begin with purely semantic analyses, he would eventually have to shift to encoding and making use of the correlations among various semantic-distributional patterns; that is, representing the links among the various patterns— links which are a function of their connections to a common set of terms.

Furthermore, it is not at all apparent from the empirical data that children do strongly attempt early general formulations of form class operations in terms of purely semantic analyses. Nor do the empirical data seem to us at all to support the hypothesis, implied in Bates and McWhinney (1978), that children find somehow "unnatural" the analysis of correlated semantic-distributional uses of terms as a means of governing the application of grammatical patterns. We begin the relevant discussion with data concerning the acquisition of form class uses, and continue with data from the study of children's acquisition of gender-case systems in German and Slavic languages.

## Form class acquisition

The first important general finding is that form class errors—using a member of one grammatical class as though it were a member of another— are extremely rare (Miller & Ervin, 1964; Cazden, 1968; Smith, 1933), although occasional errors do occur (Smith, 1933; Bowerman, 1974, personal communication; Kuczaj, 1978b). Strikingly, given that there is so much semantic overlap between the members of the different sets, few of the reported errors consist of treating adjectives as verbs, or vice versa. The most frequent type of form class error (Smith, 1933) seems to consist of the use of verbs in noun contexts, such as *give me the rub* (meaning "eraser"), or *where's the shoot?* (meaning "gun"). From the examples Smith gives, the difference often seems to be a phonological memory problem (*rub* vs. *rubber, shoot* vs. *shooter*), and in fact the adult language contains instances of phonologically and semantically similar words acting both as nouns and verbs, such as *erase-eraser, push* (*don't push him*) = *push* (*give me a push*). Kuczaj (1978b) also reports a few cases of children's using nouns as verbs, examples such as *you're gunning him*(*gunning* = *'shooting'*) or *I'm shirting my man* (*shirting* = *'putting a shirt on'*) or *our house is firing* (= *'on fire'*). Again there are some similar adult uses of noun-verb pairs, such as *hammer,* or even other means of *firing* (*fire-fire up*). The presence of some adult language models give rise to surprisingly few incorrect analogous uses; where adult models are largely absent, as in verb-adjective or, for example, possible preposition-verb correspondences, errors are markedly infrequent.[4]

Slobin (1973) attributed children's failure to make form class errors to the child's defining form class boundaries along semantic boundaries, and their finding this natural to do. Slobin's analysis presupposed that form classes could be clearly distinguished by semantic criteria, at least in children's lexicons. As we have seen, this is not the case for adult form classes. A use of purely semantic criteria for defining the behavior of terms in grammatical sequences would give rise to frequent errors such as *she naughtied* or *he is niceing to them* for actionlike adjectives, or *he is know it* or *was he love her* for state verbs.

If preschool children's vocabularies contained no semantic overlap among what adults call verbs, adjectives, prepositions, adverbs, and so on, attributing their lack of form class errors to semantic definitions of form class would be appropriate. But such lack of mixture is not the case. Actional adjectives such as *naughty* or *snoopy* appear in their transcripts. So do state verbs such as *know, like,* and *think* (in the sense of having an opinion). Furthermore, many terms could easily be analyzed as multiple-term actional expressions, such as *call up* or *fall down.* The semantic similarity of *fall down* to *fall* is clear, yet children commonly say *falled,* but not *falled downed.* The tendency of children to use directional adverbs and prepositions such as *away, off,* and *out* as action terms without accompanying verbs is in fact common in children's earlier speech. For example, Bloom, Lightbown, & Hood (1975) analyzed children's early sentences about changes of locations, for children of MLUs of about 1.50 through 3.30. Along with locational change verbs such as *go* or *put,* they also placed, on grounds of semantic-structural similarity, terms such as *away* (*away hat*), *out,* and *bye-bye.* Yet when morphological operations appear, errors with such nonverb actional terms are rare.

More subtly, Nelson (1976) finds that children's earlier adjectives in particular denote many brief nonenduring qualities as denoted by *hot,* or *wet;* brevity is a semantic factor also characteristic of many verbs. Conversely, steadiness of disposition towards a relation tends to be an adjective usage. Yet some of children's verbs denote dispositions of such steadiness, as in *like* or *know.* In fact, all actional verbs can be used dispositionally (*it goes here* can mean a general locational possibility; *he barks too much* implies a steady disposition).

In short, even though children probably display more of a statistical tendency than do adults for form class uses to be correlated to modal semantic characteristics of the different form classes, the tendency is not at all perfect enough to account for children's preponderant lack of errors in usage.

Perhaps, however, they somehow memorize individually all the uses of those terms which form exceptions to semantic-based patterns, such as the morphology of nonprocess or nonactional verbs like *know* or *like.* For the adult this hypothesis seems unlikely, since the number of such verbs and uses is so many, but it might be considered for children. This does not seem likely either, however. One of the strongest indications that a child has formulated a process in a generalizable fashion consists of overregularizations —the production of incorrect generalizations. Derived forms like *breaked, runned, ated,* and *goed* are some of the most frequent and best-known errors of children learning English (Ervin, 1964; Brown, 1973). Children's first productions of regular past tense are in fact all appropriate ones, indicating individual memorization of the terms to which the *-ed* past tense morpheme can be applied (Cazden, 1968). But eventually errors such as the above appear. They are not confined only to actional terms, however. Errors also appear such as *knowed, seed, heared, thoughted, sawed,* and *thinked* (Slobin, 1971; Maratsos, Kuczaj, Fox, and Chalkley, 1979). These share little meaning with *-ed* terms such as *spilled* or *kicked;* but they share many semantic-distributional patterns, such as ##Arg + Rel + s . . . = 'present

$$[3 \ S]$$

disposition for or occurrence of the relation.' Maratsos et al. (1979) furthermore give some evidence that such nonstative verb overregularizations appear about as soon as could be expected: that is they appear when children show some ability to encode these complex stative meanings in the past at all, by the use of terms such as *saw* and *thought,* and when other overregularizations such as *breaked* and *runned* appear. Children thus appear to be actively using correspondences such as relational terms which take *do-*forms, *-s* present, and so on, also take *-ed* past tensing.

It might be the case, however, that children do not semantically view these stative terms as denoting states, but instead believe them to denote processes and actions. This argument does not seem very strong. First of all, there are a number of verb uses which are confined to that subgroup of verbs which do denote agentive or process activities. These include the progressive—one can say *I am running,* but not *\*I am knowing it*—and the imperative—one can say *go away!* but not *\*think that he will come!*[5] Children do not use these stative verbs in these process-action uses (Brown, 1973; Kuczaj, 1978b). They thus do not appear to view these terms as process or actional terms (or as agentive relations). Second, if children began with incorrect semantic understanding, eventually they would have to come to some appropriate appreciation of the nonactional meanings of such terms, as well as the actional meanings of actional adjectives. They know a great deal, for example, about the complex semantics of the mental verbs *think* and *know* by the age of four (Johnson & Maratsos, 1977; Hopmann & Maratsos, 1978). Yet no flourishing of form class violations of the hypothesized type occurs, and one would expect such errors to happen in great number when children began to understand the semantics of the terms properly at the same time they were using a semantically-defined system of form class uses.

The evidence from lack of form class errors, and presence of form class appropriate overregularizations, then, opposes an account of children's form class privileges being strongly or actively defined by the semantic characteristics of the major form classes. The evidence instead supports children's actively using the participation of terms in shared grammatical patterns to regulate the grammatical usage of these terms, and to make reasonable novel generalizations such as *runned* and *knowed.*

## The acquisition of noun gender class

Our previous descriptive exposition dealt with some of the structure of correlated grammatical uses of determiners and pronouns that make up the German system of masculine, feminine, and neuter gender. Surprisingly, the productive acquisition of the complex case-gender system of German does not seem to give German-speaking children very much difficulty. Diary reports of Stern (1931), Leopold (1949), and others note that determiners appear productively by the fourth year, about the same as in English. When they do, gender errors are largely absent. These may initially represent individually memorized lexical patterns, like the initially memorized uses of past tense *-ed.* But they eventually must turn productive. MacWhinney (1978), who reports these results, employed a more severe test of children's productive understanding, a Berko-like nonsense word test. In one question, for example, the children were shown a nonsense object and told "Gann. I give you [*ihn,* or *sie,* or *es*]. How do you say, Where is _____?" In this task, a child must use the form of the accusative pronoun to generate correctly the form of the nominative determiner: *ihn* implies *der Gann, sie* implies *die Gann, es* implies *des Gann.* Children as young as three years of age could sometimes perform this task, with proficiency increasing through the preshool years. Productive understanding of the German pronominal-determiner gender system thus arises not very late, and with surprisingly little difficulty. If anything, observers of German-speaking children have reported more difficulty with *case* errors, sometimes a confusion of nominative and accusative uses, but always *within* the appropriate gender class. Such case errors seem analogous to English-speaking children's common use of objective *me* in nominative contexts, such as *me want that; why me can't dance?* (Brown, 1973; Bellugi, 1971; Tanz, 1975).

Such success with the complex case-gender system of German, in which only correlated grammatical environments can give an appropriate analysis, indicates that children under some circumstances do not have extensive difficulty in devising accounts of arbitrary form class subdivisions such as German gender. This picture, however, apparently does not match that found in another important discussion of gender and case, the discussion found in Slobin (1973).

Slobin summarized data from a variety of sources about children's acquisition of Slavic (Russian, Serbo-Croatian, Latvian, and others) case and gender systems, in support of an hypothesized tendency by the child to prefer to formulate grammatical markers as having clear semantic denotation. The major findings Slobin reports are these: children learn to mark noun case before learning to mark gender subdivisions within case markings. Correlative with this, they make errors of using one gender ending rather than another, but not of using one case ending rather than another.

Slobin took children's very early correct marking of case distinctions to be evidence of an easy apprehension of semantic-based distinctions among markers. This interpretation rests on the apparent presupposition that case uses are in fact clearly semantically defined. As we have seen, this is not the case for German. Nor is it so for Russian. Slobin writes elsewhere (1973, p. 268), in a description of the Russian case system, that there are six grammatical cases (nominative, accuative, dative, genitive, prepositional, instrumental) which are determined, variously,

> by semantic criteria (for example, dative of indirect object), and by a variety of arbitrary and semiarbitrary criteria, such as the case requirements of particular verbs, prepositions, or sentence forms. For example, one *learns* something (*uchit'sya*) in the dative, but *masters* something in the instrumental (*ovladivet'*) or the accusative (*usvaivay'*) depending on the verb. One . . . does something with (*s*) him in the instrumental, brings something for (*dlay*) him in the genitive, talks about (*o*) him in the prepositional, and so on.

That case errors are reportedly even fewer than in the acquisition of German is thus remarkable, but does not show children's active preference for clearly semantic-based markers; at least this cannot be claimed without a more extensive analysis of the data.

Nevertheless, Russian investigators do report that case distinctions are observed earlier than gender distinctions (contrary to the German data), and that gender errors continue to be made throughout the preschool years, which in Russia means through the age of seven. The contradiction to the German data thus appears to be a sharp one.

Thorough examination of the evidence here is not possible because of space limitations. But it seems to us that inspection of some of the original sources (e.g., Zakharova, 1973) shows that Russian-speaking children do master the major differentiations among the gender classes productively by the age of three or four for all but a few understandably unclear cases. Briefly, Russian has three gender classes, expressed by endings (or the lack of them) on the noun stems themselves, as well as endings on prenominal adjective modifiers. The major difference between Russian and German lies in the clarity of the nominative case marking as a key to other uses. Some such markings are relatively clear. For example, should a noun end in stressed /a/ in the nominative, it takes /oy/ endings in the genitive, dative, instrumental, and prepositional cases, and /u/ in the accusative (this is called feminine noun gender). If a noun ends in stressed /o/ in the nominative, it takes another corresponding set of endings called the neuter set. A third set, called masculine, takes no ending in the nominative or accusative, and usually the stem ends in hard consonants in these two cases.

For other nouns, however, even knowing the nominative form gives no clue to the other uses. Nouns which end in palatalized consonants in the nominative, for example, are assigned individually and arbitrarily to either masculine or feminine sets of endings. Nouns ending in the unstressed vowel /ə/ in the nominative are still arbitrarily assigned as either neuter or feminine. Compare this to German, in which knowledge of the nominative definite marker or commonly used pronoun gives a completely reliable cue to the other case uses.

Zakharova (1973) studied 200 Russian children aged 3 through 7, using both observational and experimental Berko-type evidence. Though she found children know case distinctions earlier than gender distinctions, she also noted that productive use of the masculine-feminine-neuter correlated uses is "quickly established" for the clear sets, those in which the nominative forms end in stressed /a/ (feminine), stressed /o/ (neuter), or hard consonants (masculine). It is just the sets *not* cued reliably by the nominative use, those ending in palatalized consonants or unstressed /ə/, which continue to cause errors for years.

Thus, it seems to us that Russian-speaking children acquire the essentials of the Russian gender uses early in the preschool years, in those instances in which the correlations among nominative and other uses are roughly comparable to German. It is just those instances in which even a knowledge of most of the system still does not allow clear prediction from the nominative use that errors persist for years. We thus find that Russian and German children acquire complex correlated uses that comprise arbitrary gender systems by about three or four. Investigators of English-speaking children's acquisition of form class morphology and syntax in fact report stable acquisition of such systems by roughly four years of age. We thus find the comparable ages of acquisition of superficially quite different form class and gender uses to offer further support for our hypothesis that children master such complex patterns of correlated uses of terms with surprising skill.

## Summary of Form and Gender Class Acquisition Data

To summarize, our inspection of the available empirical data shows the following:

(1) Children make few form class errors. This cannot be interpreted as their actively formulating the correlated systems of usage (e.g., verb morphology vs. adjective morphology vs. particle and preposition usage) according to a semantic basis, for then many errors would occur in form class boundary crossing instances. Children also overregularize grammatical uses within form classes, *across* semantic boundaries, instances such as *knowed* and *thoughted* and *heared.* Such acquisition seems best accounted for by attributing to children a good ability to analyze the interaction of a class of terms with related grammatical sequences; for instance, the appearance of many terms in the contexts: *don't* + _____ for negation, _____ + *ed* for simple past, _____ + *s* for present generic, and so on (i.e., verb form class privileges).

(2) Children show great skill in formulating systems such as German gender and much of Russian gender systems, in which correlated differences in expressing case determine (comprise) usage. That is, German children easily learn that nouns that take *der* + _____ in the nominative take *den* + _____ in the accusative, while *das* + _____ in the nominative goes with *das* + _____ in the accusative. Similarly, they do comparably well at formulations such as correlating the privilege *Noun* + *a* in the nominative with *Noun* + *oy* in the instrumental in Russian.

(3) That children display a largely error-free acquisition (at least Russian children—and the reported amount of German acquisition errors is low, though not as low) of grammatical case divisions is also surprising, given that case differences correspond to a variety of appearances of nouns in different grammatical contexts, such that the same or similar semantic notion takes different case expressions, and so on. Nor do their errors seem to follow from systematically overextended semantic analyses.

From these data, we conclude that children find it natural to define the formal units for a semantic-distributional pattern according partly to the appearance of terms in other distributional-semantic patterns. Such abilities suit them well for formulating the generalizations implicit in human languages.

## GRAMMATICAL SUBJECT AND DEFINITION BY CORRELATION OF GRAMMATICAL PATTERNS

Our arguments so far have centered on formal syntactic categories for single-morpheme units, such as denoted by the symbols V, Adjective, or different noun gender classes. Because of space limitations, the analysis of hierarchical structures such as NP, VP, or S will not be treated here. Presupposing such analyses, we would like instead to discuss both theoretically and empirically those grammatical properties denoted by the notion of grammatical subject. We proceed first to a discussion of a fragment of the adult system, and then give a discussion of problems of acquisition. In this discussion, we shall attempt to show that the discussion of children's "acquisition" of grammatical subject has suffered from a reification of what are in fact correlated uses of terms in semantic-distributional patterns, rather than a single unitary entity. This problem appears particularly in discussions of the child's earliest efforts at formulating grammar. We shall also show that a clear explication of what the term "subject" actually means gives an easier interpretation of the child's earliest acquisitions, and makes clear how subject properties would be expected to be acquired over a long period of development.

## Grammatical Subject in Adult Grammar

In the following discussion, we shall for convenience write as though there were an isolable unitary construct "grammatical subject." It should be clear, however, that this is a matter of terminological convenience. In general, we think that "subject" is essentially, like form class category, a possibly reified abstraction from the general coordination of uses of terms in related semantic-distributional patterns. In particular, the view taken here is somewhat like Fillmore (1968), in that grammatical subject properties are essentially part of the related semantic-distributional pattern uses of certain kinds of relational terms, rather than being an analytic primitive. Our use of the terminology of "grammatical subject" in the following discussion, then, is merely a device to make quick reference to a group of grammatical phenomena.

In discussing grammatical subject, writers have noted that in fact "subjects" vary from language to language in the properties they take. It is often puzzling to determine whether or not different languages really use the same notion of subject, or whether the notion of subject is necessary at all in some languages (Lyons, 1968; Li, 1976). Some languages, for example, do not have the passive-active relationship which plays a key role in defining English "underlying" or "logical" subject. Still other languages do not correlate the usual marking of agenthood, nominative case, and treatment of intransitive sentence NPs in the same way as Indo-European languages (Lyons, 1968).

As before, there seem to be two kinds of account of grammatical subject, a nativist account (Chomsky, 1965; McNeill, 1966), and a semantic-based account (called "notional" by Lyons [1968]). As before, we do not argue here directly against the nativist account, though we shall begin an outline of an account in which grammatical subject is not a primitive of analysis. We shall also describe, in a later section, empirical data that fail to support the nativist account of the acquisition of grammatical relations.

### The inadequacy of semantic-based accounts

It is, however, again possible to criticize directly various forms of the notional, or semantic-based account. This we proceed to do before outlining aspects of a more positive account.

In a semantic-based account, the grammatical privileges of relational terms and their NP arguments are predictable from their semantic analysis alone. In English, for example, important grammatical subject properties include initial placement before the main verb or copula verb in nonpassive declarative sentences, number agreement with this NP argument, nominative pronoun use (*he, she, they*), and other properties. A semantic-based account should accordingly be able to state which kinds of relational terms can take subject initial NP arguments in terms of the semantics of the terms only. It should also be able to predict which NP arguments of a given relational term will comprise that NP argument which takes grammatical subject properties on the basis of the semantic analyses of the terms.

Neither of these proposed relations between semantic and grammatical structure in fact holds. The semantic analysis of a relational term and its NP arguments does not predict securely which NP argument will take on grammatical subject properties. Nor does the semantic analysis of a relational term predict with sureness whether or not it will take NP arguments with grammatical subject properties at all.

We consider initially the first of these points, that the semantic analysis of a relational term and its NP arguments does not predict which NP argument will take grammatical subject properties. To facilitate the discussion, we need first to refer to the notion of the semantic roles denoted by the NP arguments of relational terms. Consider a particular relational term such as *murder*. At the most specific level of description, *murder* takes two major arguments, an NP denoting the one who commits the murder, and an NP denoting the one murdered. Such roles are unique to the term *murder*. At a more superordinate level, the one that carries out the murder may be viewed as an *agent* (Fillmore, 1968)—one who instigates the activity or state referred to by the relational term. *Agent* is a role common to the arguments of many terms, such as *run,* the pusher of *push,* and so on. The one who undergoes the murder may similarly be seen as a *patient,* the undergoer of the force of an action. Other commonly proposed NP semantic roles include *experiencer,* the experiencer of a mental sensation, *stimulus,* the experienced entity, *possessor, location,* and others. A claim that the semantic analyses of terms may predict which NP argument takes grammatical subject properties, then, may be viewed as a claim that knowledge of the semantic role of the NP arguments predicts, for example, which NP will be initial in declarative, active sentences. In English generally, for example, agents are placed initially in nonpassives. If there is no agent, the experiencer NP generally takes grammatical subject properties.

While there are some statistical generalizations which can be made, and even more exact generalizations if structural specifications are considered, over all it is not possible to predict grammatical form in this fashion, even if the domain considered is that of simple active declarative sentences. The examples below provide some examples of this:

(1) John - likes - tables       = experiencer - experience - stimulus
    Tables - please - John       = stimulus - experience - experiencer
(2) John - is angry - at Mary     = experiencer - experience - stimulus
    Mary - is infuriating - to John   = stimulus - experience - experiencer
(3) John - owns - this house      = possessor - possession - possessed object
    This house - belongs - to John   = possessed object - possession - possessor
(4) This box - contains, has - forty   = location - containment - located object
    marbles
    Forty marbles - are in - this      = located object - containment - location
    box
(5) Mary - kissed - John        = agent - action - patient
    Mary - received a kiss - from   = patient - activity - agent
    John

It is obvious that, frequently, knowledge of which semantic-structural pattern is to be used is dictated by the particular pattern controlled by the relational term. *Own* places the possessor NP initially, *belong (to)* places the possessed object initially. *Like* takes experiencers first, as does *angry; please* and *infuriating* place the stimulus NP in initial position.

We do not wish to claim that there are no semantic-structural generalizations available at all. It is statistically overwhelmingly likely that an agentive argument NP will be placed initially in a nonpassive sentence. More specifically, in a nonpassive of the form $NP_1 \ldots V \ldots NP_2$, if no NP argument intervenes between $NP_2$ and V, only the first NP argument can denote an agent. Other semantic-structural generalizations, sometimes depending on the identity of particular lexical items in the construction, are also present in English. Such analyses must, however, be combined with knowledge of the governance of structural-semantic patterns by particular terms, or by complex contingencies based on a combination of the structural sequences in which a relational term appears and the semantic roles of its

NP arguments. From semantic analysis alone of the relational term and its NP arguments, it is not possible to predict which NP argument will have grammatical subject properties such as initial appearance in simple declaratives.

Furthermore, as noted above, whether or not a relational term takes NP arguments, or subject NP arguments, cannot really be predicted generally and reliably from its semantic analysis. As outlined earlier, *relational term* denotes any morpheme which expresses a relation between, or property of, relational entities denoted by another morpheme or group of morphemes. Using these definitions, we find that many relational terms may be found which have similar basic semantic argument-relational term analyses, yet do not take grammatically similar relational term-argument structures. For example, consider the meanings denoted by the terms *possible, might, could, maybe,* and *possibly.* Very clearly these have quite similar meanings. *Possible* in particular is semantically more similar to these than it is to relational terms such as *true* or *nice.* Yet *possible, true,* and *nice* are grammatically more similar, in that each takes initial NP arguments or sentential arguments as grammatical subjects, in utterances such as *that's possible, it's true,* or *that he will come - is possible. Possible* is a single argument relational term; its single argument denotes the event or state which is judged possible, and typically takes grammatical subject reflexes.

Constrastively, consider *maybe.* It clearly cannot take the subject-predicate uses that *possible* can. Sentences such as *\*it's maybe* or *\*that he will come is maybe* are unacceptable. Yet consider the semantic relation of *maybe* to *he will come* in a sentence such as *maybe he will come.* The relation is obviously similar to that of *possible* to *he will come* in *that he will come is possible. Maybe* and *possible* denote possibility of the meaning denoted by *(that) he will come.* That is, *maybe* takes *he will come* as an argument just as *possible* does, semantically. Yet it does not do so in a manner that is described as naving subject-predicate form. The case is similar for terms such as *might* or *could.* Their grammatical privileges class them as still another category of term, as modal auxiliaries. Semantically, however, they are relational terms taking as arguments the relational term-argument set of the relational term which they precede, in sentences such as *he might come.*

Even highly characteristic main verb kinds of meanings show similar disjunction between taking and not taking grammatical subjects. A central verb meaning, for example, is that of casuality, instantiated in fact in the verb *cause.* Yet like *cause,* the preposition *because of* takes as semantic arguments a cause and an outcome; but unlike *cause,* it does not do so in the manner we call taking a grammatical subject. In sentences such as *Mary cried because of her mother, Mary cried* is the outcome argument of *because of,* and *her mother* denotes a causer; but neither has grammatical subject properties.

Generative semanticists (e.g., Lakoff, 1971; McCawley, 1970) have long pointed out such facts, which show that grammatical subject properties of arguments and relational terms do not correspond to the semantic analysis of such terms. They have used such facts, along with other kinds of arguments, to argue for "deeper" underlying representations in which the relations of terms such as *might* and *possible* to their arguments are more uniformly represented, given that the level of representation exemplified by the use of grammatical relations cannot do so properly. These facts about the lack of relation between grammatical relations and semantic analyses do argue for more than one level of representation of grammar and semantics, though we do not agree that the facts show that such a level should be a deeper "syntactic" level of description. We are working with more obvious regularities in semantic-distributional structure that the child must analyze; and we find that grammatical subject as more traditionally used does denote part of a system which has some consistent internal organization. But the point is, in any case, that whether or not a relational term even takes NP arguments, or takes NP arguments with grammatical subject properties, cannot be reliably predicted from semantic analysis.

## Some grammatical subject properties outlined

Grammatical subject thus cannot be defined as a group of properties governed by the semantic analysis of relational terms and their NP argument roles. What is "grammatical subject" then? Keenan (1976) notes 34 properties that have been associated with the notion of subject across different languages. We shall confine our initial discussion to a fragment of the system of English grammatical subject properties. In particular, we shall first discuss some properties of English *surface* grammatical subject in simple active declarative sentences.

Essentially, grammatical subject is the name we give to a section of the semantic-distributional properties of certain relational terms. In English in particular, the following properties appear to be central parts of this system:

(1) Certain relational terms, called main verbs, can either be marked directly for tense or aspect (e.g., *push-pushed-pushes-pushing*) or under other circumstances take *do*-forms to mark tense and negation relations (e.g., *he didn't push it*).

(2) Other relational terms are such that under various circumstances they may take a form of the morpheme set we call copula *be* to mark tense or aspect, as in *he is happy,* or *he's in the house.* These *be*-taking relational terms are generally differentiated among themselves by other semantic-distributional pattern uses; they include the form classes called prepositions and adjectives.[6]

(3) Among other pragmatic circumstances, if an utterance serves to make a declaration of fact or opinion, and does not comprise an answer to a question, the utterance must contain such a relational term as defined in (1) or (2) above. This relational term must appear with a pre-relational term NP argument. There are other complex contingencies governing these conditions. For example, if a copula-taking relational term comprises the initial argument-taking term, it must take a form of *be,* at least in standard English. (Of course, in black English, the use of the copula is optional in these circumstances; *he big* is acceptable.)

(4) The semantic relation of this initial NP argument to the rest of the relational term-argument set comprising the sentence is fixed by the particular semantic-distributional structure governed by the obligatory relational term. The initial NP argument of *like,* for example, denotes an experiencer; the initial NP argument of *please* denotes a stimulus.

These four properties comprise the central definitional segment of grammatical subject properties for English. Many other properties are governed by parts of this relational term-argument set. For example:

(1) As Lyons (1968) points out, in Indo-European languages it is overwhelmingly the case that if a relational term has an agentive NP argument, and that NP argument is included in a declaration, it appears as the initial argument (except in passive form sentences).

(2) If the marking of the relational term or one of its dependent verbal elements (e.g., perfective *have,* auxiliary *do,* progressive *be,* copula *be*) can be marked for singular or plural number of one of the NP arguments, the number marking is done in concordance with the number of the initial NP argument (e.g., one says *he likes them,* not *\*he like them*).

(3) This initial NP argument may be denoted by *he, she,* or *they* (nominative pronouns). Only these pronouns may be used for the corresponding referents in this position (*\*him likes the dog*), and they are only used in this position (*\*the girl likes he*).

While the above generalizations hold largely for declarative sentences, or sentences with declarative form, these particular generalizations actually form just a small part of the system of correlated semantic-distributional patterns of such relational terms. For example, if a relational term has correlated main verb semantic-distributional properties, and its declarative form includes an initial NP argument, the semantic role of which is agentive (e.g., *he drinks coca cola*), then this term may also be used in an utterance which begins with the relational term, uninflected, and which has no initial argument; the utterance denotes a command to the listener (e.g., *drink coca cola*). Such utterances are called imperative sentences. This is not to say that one pattern is in some way derived from the other. Rather, the correspondence of semantic-distributional patterns reflects a true correlation. One could just as well say, for example, that relational terms which may begin, in uninflected form, an utterance which denotes a command, may fill the role of the obligatory initial-NP argument taking relational term of a declarative. That is, hearing a new term in the usage *grutch coca cola!* and knowing that *grutch coca cola* denotes a command, we know that *grutch* has other main verb properties, such as appearing in utterances like *he grutches coca cola.*[7]

Thus, the usage of sentence initial NP arguments, number agreement, pronominal usage, and so on, are all part of a larger system of correlated patterns largely centered around the uses of relational terms. Isolation of the subject argument as a particular, unitary analytic unit is artificial.

*Logical subject.* One part of the correlated pattern usage of the English relational term system, however, observes all of the restrictions and properties previously noted except for one. In this class of sentences, marked often by a form of *be* preceding the past participial form of the central relational term, the usual initial placement of agentive NP roles is not found; in declarative forms of such sentences, in fact, if there is an agentive argument, it is always *non*initial. This class is generally called the passive. It includes long passives such as *he was pushed by the old men* or *he was liked by most people,* and short passives such as *he was liked.* These sentences show most of the same basic properties of surface grammatical subject as displayed in active sentences. There is a member of one of the class of obligatory relational terms. This relational term is, however, always a main verb. Even though there are actional adjectives, such as *nice (to),* there are no adjectival passives such as *\*he was niced to by everyone.* In passives as in actives, the main verb always takes an obligatory initial NP argument. The first auxiliary marker agrees in number with this initial NP argument, which is encoded by nominative pronouns (*he, she,* and *they*). Again, the semantic role of the initial NP depends on the semantic-distributional structure of the individual relational term, aside from never being an agent. For *this table was liked by Mary* the initial NP argument denotes a stimulus; for *she was pleased by this table,* it denotes an experiencer. Thus, the major deviance lies in the consistent failure of agentive NPs to appear in initial position.

In fact, however, this failure follows from the fact that agentives never appear in postverbal position in active form sentences, for there is a complex but systematic semantic-distributional relation among the relational term-argument sets of passive and nonpassive forms of sentences. Essentially, the relation is something like the following: if there is a sentence of the form $NP_{Argument_1} \ldots V \ldots NP_{Argument_2}$, in which V does not have the surrounding syntax BE + V + *ed,* there is a correspondent sentence of the form $NP_{Argument_1} + \ldots$ BE + V + *ed,* or optionally, $NP_{Argument_1} \ldots$ BE + V + *ed* by $NP_{Argument_2}$. The initial $NP_{Argument_1}$ of the BE + V + *ed* sentence has the same semantic relation to the rest of the sentence as the postverbal $NP_{Argument_2}$ of the active. The $NP_{Argument_2}$ of the *by* + NP phrase of the passive conversely has the same relation to the rest of the sentence as the initial $NP_{Argument_1}$ of the active.[8]

For a given verb, the role played by the initial NP argument of the active, and by the *by* + NP argument of the passive, is generally described as denoting the *logical subject* or *underlying subject* of the verb. Similarly, the postverbal NP argument of the active and the initial NP argument of the passive are often described (for two-argument verbs) as the *logical or underlying object*. As Bowerman (1973) has noted, the passive-active relationship seems to provide the chief motivation in English for the use of terminology of logical subject and object.

But if this is so, rather than speaking of logical subject and object being underlying primitives which *govern* the passive-action relation, it is sufficient to speak of logical subject as being our name for aspects of the complex semantic-distributional relations which obtain, verb by verb, between these two semantically and distributionally definable patterns of main verb relational term-argument sets. Rather than saying that the child learns that the logical subject is the initial NP argument of actives and the post-*by* NP argument of passives, we can simply describe him or her as analyzing the passive-active relationship, which is what has to be done in any case. It is a complex task to do so, but a combination of semantic and distributional analyses made properly can achieve the appropriate knowledge.

*Ergatives.* In this analysis, then, surface grammatical subject and logical subject are not unanalyzable abstract primitives which somehow govern grammatical properties of argument-relational term uses. Instead they are the name we give to those various complex relations among semantic-distributional analyses of the correlated properties of relational terms, their NP arguments, and other semantic-distributional phenomena. Such correlated properties can be analyzed, and presumably acquired, somewhat independently. Perhaps the best way to see this potential independence of the correlated properties is to consider an instance in which the properties that typically fall together for Indo-European languages fail to do so in other languages. Lyons (1968) discusses such an instance, that of ergative languages. These include a good number of languages, all of which are outside the Indo-European family; Eskimo, Basque, and Georgian are all ergative languages.

Where ergative languages differ from languages such as English or other Indo-European languages is in the different correlation of NP argument inflectional properties with agentivity. In Indo-European languages, as already discussed, agents NPs, if present, overwhelmingly carry nominative inflection or position, and take number agreement, at least in nonpassive sentences. The association of properties for ergatives is quite different. Lyons (1968) gives an example of the operation of Eskimo.

Suppose *-q* to be the marker of the sole NP argument of an intransitive sentence. Thus, Eskimo sentences observe the pattern *John-q died, John-q ran away.* In transitive sentences, the two NP arguments are marked *-p* and *-q*. In an Indo-European language, if there is an agent and a patient, the agent would receive the *-q* marking of the single NP of an intransitive. Thus an Indo-European pattern for "John killed Mary" would be *John-q Mary-p killed.* In an ergative language, however, it is the *patient* that is consistently given the intransitive NP argument marking. Thus the pattern is *John-q ran away,* but *John-p Mary-q killed* "John killed Mary." Ergative languages do not observe the same correlation between the usual marking of agency and the marking of the only NP of an intransitive sentence that nonergative languages such as Indo-European languages do. Suppose we decided every sentence must have a subject NP; this seems, after all, to be part of the definition of subject. Then it is reasonable to say that the single NP of an intransitive sentence must be its subject; the *-q* inflection of such NP arguments thus marks the subject NP. Then in transitive sentences with agents, such as *John-p Mary-q hit,* we must conclude that the patient is always marked as the subject, and the agent as the object.

Or we might decide that the agent of a transitive sentence must comprise the subject. In this case, *-p* becomes the subject marker, *-q* the object marker, and intransitive sentences only take grammatical object NP arguments, not subjects.

Neither of these arguments generally feels satisfactory to speakers of nonergative languages, and ergatives often seem peculiar to them. Yet ergatives are not uncommon languages, and so it is difficult to justify labeling them as atypical or somehow deviant.

What this example perhaps shows is that properties that we often assume must go together because they seem to be indissolubly part of the notion of "subject," are indeed separable. The marking of the single NP argument of an intransitive is not necessarily identical with the marking of the agent of a transitive. If we think of our grammatical subject as comprising the name for a clustering of potentially separable relational term-NP argument correlated grammatical analyses, such cross-linguistic differences are far less puzzling. Rather than speaking of children as acquiring "subject," we can speak of them as acquiring the correlations among various semantic-distributional patterns of relational terms, including how they take NP arguments, how those are marked, how they affect the surrounding environment (number agreement), and agentive meaning for those relational terms which take agents.

In fact, other languages may differ in still other ways that are striking if we hold to the central importance of the notions of grammatical subject or logical subject. Many languages are difficult to describe at all as true subject-taking languages (Li, 1976). Still other languages, such as Finnish, which appear to be subject-predicate in nature, lack the passive-active relationship, and hence lack justification for the positing of underlying, or logical, subject and object. Rather than describing such languages as basically different from English, however, it seems more reasonable simply to describe them as not sharing all the same semantic-distributional relationships among relational terms and arguments as are found in more familiar tongues.

## Children's Acquisition of Grammatical Subject

It should be clear that in the view offered here, there is no unitary notion of subject which the child acquires that somehow is necessarily a magical step in acquisition. Rather, children acquire knowledge or correlations among relational term patterns, including the manner in which they take various kinds of NP arguments, relations among pronominal usage and position or inflection, and relations of knowledge of number agreement and NP position or inflection, and so on. Children might somehow internally "name" part of this set of properties with an internal designation such as subject, but that is a (difficult to investigate) theoretical and empirical question. In the case of logical subject, at least, this is an hypothesis for which it is difficult to find compelling evidence (Maratsos, Kuczaj, Fox & Chalkley, 1979).

We would thus describe acquisition differently than is commonly done. The type of rephrasing and rethinking we have in mind may be easiest illustrated by the following example. Bates and MacWhinney (1978) describe the acquisition of grammatical subject for two Italian children studied longitudinally:

> Soon thereafter, both children pass into a brief period of preserving SVO order in fairly rigid fashion, and lexicalizing the subject in situations where adults would delete it. Given this pattern, Bates concludes that the surface notion of subject emerges between MLU 2.0 and 3.0, coordinating the surface mechanisms: word order, subject pronouns, and noun-verb agreement. (p. 35)

Rather than saying that the "surface notion of subject" emerges to coordinate the surface mechanisms (except in the mind of the investigator), we would claim that the Italian children Bates studied gave a definite word order position to the same NP argument with which the verb[9] agreed in number, and that pronoun arguments which appeared in the same relation to the verb, had a nominative form (in English, for example, *he* and *she* vs. *him* and *her; he* and *she* are nominative). That is, we would simply say these surface mechanisms were coordinated, without positing some notion of "subject" that coordinates them. This seems to us more descriptively accurate in that it does not involve the reified use of subject as is found in the original form. Its usefulness is perhaps further illustrated by the following passage, in which Bates and MacWhinney describe data from a study by Fava and Tirondola (1977):

> Unlike the children studied by Bates, Fava and Tirondola's six subjects continue to use pragmatically-based ordering beyond the point at which subject-verb agreement and subject pronouns are acquired. Hence the acquisition of the surface category of subject does not necessarily result in ordering tendencies based on syntactic relations. (Bates & MacWhinney, 1978, p. 35)

It might be tempting to some to argue about whether Fava and Tirondola's six subjects really "had" the notion of subject as "strongly," or in "the same" way as Bates's.[10] But we think it is more accurate simply to say that at this developmental point, Fava and Tirondola's subjects used nominative form pronouns for those uses where the pronoun had the same relation to the verb as that of the NP arguments with which the verb agreed in number. But the NP arguments with which the verb agreed in number, and for which pronominal forms with the same semantic relation to the verb were nominative, were not ordered in a uniform fashion relative to the verb or to other NP arguments of the verb.

This position of not talking about "subjects" as separate from the correlated properties to which it *refers* is in many ways difficult. The phrasing is often clumsy. It is natural to want clear breaking points, to be able to say, for example, that "at this point, this child has acquired The Notion of Grammatical Subject." But on the other hand, we also know that properties which we analyze as being correlated aspects of operations in the adult system frequently do not emerge together in the child in a quick and convergent fashion; often this leads to what seem like somewhat arbitrary arguments over which properties or uses or correlations are really "critical" so that the child can be said to "have" the notion once he has acquired them.

Describing the child as acquiring and correlating various relational term-argument uses obviates this problem. For acquistion is seen as the growth of the child's formulation of these theoretically partly separable correlated semantic-distributional uses of morphemes. The investigator may still hold some acquisitional formulations more crucial for various purposes than others, but what it is that is seen as important can be seen more clearly disentangled from the far too global, and probably reified, question of when the child really "acquires" grammatical subject.

Unfortunately for our purposes, very little literature or extant analyzed data bear in detail on the child's acquisition of these patterns and their relation to each other. Investigators have given much effort to particular problems, such as the question of whether grammatical subjects exist in children's earliest utterances, or various aspects of children's knowledge of the passive-active relationship, or particular facts about the acquisition of copula and inflectional morphemes. But, for example, we do not know of any investigator who has clearly described the developmental point at which a particular child always supplied obligatory subject arguments in appropriate contexts, despite the centrality of this obligatoriness condition among grammatical subject properties. Enough literature exists, however, for a critique of nativist and purely semantic-based views of grammatical subject. In the following sections, we exposit various aspects of children's early, later, and relatively late (late preschool) utterances to substantiate this claim. We also attempt to outline some properties of a positive account.

### The early word combinations

It is clear that the semantic-distributional knowledge that we summarize as comprising knowledge of English grammatical subject properties is quite complex. It includes knowledge of criteria for judging which relational terms must take obligatory NP arguments, knowledge of a diversity of lexical-semantic patterns, proper knowledge of at least the passive-active relation, and in the complete system, still more. It thus seems surprising that investigators have seriously discussed whether early children's utterances such as *want ball, mommy sock, all cleaned, wet shoe,* or *more cereal* show consistent usage of relations such as grammatical subject and object, inclusive even of logical grammatical subject.

The reason for this interest probably arose from a development of the nativist position stated by Chomsky (1965) and McNeill (1966). In this position, it was held that abstract grammatical relations such as underlying grammatical subject and object were not tied in any clear way to surface structural or semantic analysis; they thus had to be analyzed as primitives available to the child as he attempted to formulate a grammar of his language. McNeill (1966) further attempted arguments that even children's earliest utterances displayed use of grammatical subject and predicate. Usage in such early formulations, he argued, would clearly show innate analytic tendencies at work. Other authors since that time have argued that the best underlying description of early speech is in terms of general semantic-based patterns, such as Agent + Action, Attribute + Object, Action + Patient (e.g., Schlesinger, 1971), or they have offered other descriptions.

What are the facts? It seems to us that the best early analyses of the earliest productive combinations have been made by Braine (1976) and, with some elegant methodological additions to Braine's method, Bowerman (1976). Basically Braine's method consisted of analyzing early two-word combinations that did and did not show stable and productive word order patterns in a variety of children in order to clarify what the appropriate level of analysis was of their speech. Bowerman, analyzing one- and two-word speech from her two children, was able to further see which terms of those available in the one-word repertoire became used productively in combinations afterwards (see those sources for further details). The types of patterns children used often showed considerable individual variation (Bowerman, 1976). But there were a number of common pattern types, which we now summarize.

*Individual word patterns.* Often children first analyze the semantic-distributional behaviors of single relational terms, apparently without analyzing them as part of a larger possible category. For example, a child studied by Bowerman used the formula *more + X* = 'recurrence of X,' without using productively any of seven other words that might be called modifiers or attribute terms in adult grammar, such as *wet.* Over the succeeding weeks, each of the other terms became productively used at different times. She also had related single words such as *again, allgone,* and *no more.* These also entered into combinations later, at separate times. Bowerman concluded that the child learned each combinatorial pattern as a single-word lexical pattern, rather than necessarily apprehending a larger formula such as *Attribute + X.* She similarly found, for the same child, individual words that for adult speakers comprised verbs, entering productivity one by one. Braine similarly found evidence for many single-word productive formulas such as *no + X* or *more + X.*

*Semantic category patterns.* In another kind of pattern, both positional possibilities were defined by semantic categories of varying size. For example, in studying one child, Braine found that while not all terms denoting properties fell into a productive formula *Property + X,* the child nearly simultaneously used *small + X* and *big + X* productively. He concluded the child had a formula *Size-word + X* = 'size of X.' Braine did find a broad pattern roughly corresponding to Actor + Action to be productive in many children. Bowerman similarly found that one of the two children she studied seemed to suddenly elaborate, for example, a pattern that might be called Mover + Movement; the child practically simultaneously used patterns such as *X + away, X + off, X + on,* and other movement relational terms in productive combinations.

A third kind of pattern was like the foregoing, except that in both the single-word formulas and narrow semantic category formulas above, the relational term is overtly encoded. In this third pattern, only the relational entities of a relation are given an order, and the underlying relation is not encoded. For example, a commonly found pattern is the formula *X = Possessor + Y = Possessed;* for example, *mommy sock* said of a sock of mommy's. The underlying relation of possession is not encoded by a relational term such as the possessive marker (*mommy's sock*) or another term (*mommy have sock*). Braine also analyzed some children as encoding just the relational entites of relations such as containment (*in*) or support (*on*). Like Bloom (1970), he found uses such as *sweater chair* ("chair supporting sweater," "sweater on chair") in which the arguments are apparently given a stable order to encode an underlying locative relation without overt mention of the relation itself.

Note that in all these cases, children are given credit for using systematic linguistic knowledge on the basis of their ordering patterns matching *common* orders. For example, possession may actually be denoted in English either with the order possessor first (*mommy's sock; mommy owns this sock*) or possessor second (*this sock of mommy's; this sock belongs to mommy*). The fact of the children settling on what investigators guess to be the commonest orders, or their showing stable order tendencies, are taken to argue for the reasonableness of attributing children's ordering tendencies to some partly appropriate underlying structure.

*"Grammatical subject" absent from early speech.* What questions can we ask of this early speech? Clearly sentences often completely lack relational terms which might comprise subject-taking relational terms. The copula *be*-form so central in the definition of adult grammar grammatical subject is missing completely. There is in fact no good semantic-distributional evidence for separating early single-argument relational terms that will later become verbs, such as *want* in the formula *want* + *X*, or *go* in the usage *X* + *go*, from other single-argument relational terms such as *more* or *away* in *more* + *X* or *X* + *away*.

Nevertheless investigators have frequently asked of this data whether or not they show children's direct or indirect observance of important properties of adult speech that constitute the use of grammatical subject (McNeill, 1966; Bloom, 1970; Bowerman, 1973; Bloom, Lightbown, & Hood, 1975). If we consider the question literally, the answer must be that adult grammatical subject is absent. Just one property is really present at all; terms denoting agentive arguments reliably occur initially, when they occur.

Suppose we try instead to find from analogical question which might be asked earlier. A central characteristic of English grammar, for example, is that sentences contain central relational terms which take at least one initial argument. The semantic relations of this argument to the rest of the sentence are furthermore quite diverse, including agency, possession, experiencer, located object (*it is in here*), and so on. Perhaps these questions could be asked: do early speech samples show use of a general fixed order for relational terms which denote meanings like those of relational terms which take subject arguments in adult grammar? Do they show the same order (initial position) for comparable arguments? Do they also show a semantic diversity in the roles of the arguments?

If we are generous about which relational terms to include, the answer to the first two questions is clearly "no." For example, two very common early formulas are ones such as *no* + *X* = 'disappearance or nonexistences of X,' and *more* + *X* = 'recurrence of X' (Brown, 1973; Bloom et al. 1975). *More* and *no* in this usage are clearly one-argument relational terms. Furthermore, the meanings they encode are quite similar to relational terms of adult English which are actually verbs or adjectives. *No* + *X,* for example, often encodes nonexistence or disappearance. Both *nonexistent* and *disappear* are terms which have the correlated properties that correspond to taking their single arguments as grammatical subjects (*X disappeared; X is nonexistent*). Obviously *no* and *more,* however, do not encode this grammatical-subject-like argument in initial position. A similar argument may be made about the relations of *more* and *recur: recur* takes an initial argument as grammatical subject, and *more* takes a semantically similar argument in post-relational term position.

It is really not clear that there is any good reason for separating *no* and *more* and similar terms from consideration for the early period. But suppose one arbitrarily does so, and only considers those relational terms which will acquire surface properties in development such that they are described as taking grammatical subjects; that is, terms such as *hot, go, sleep, wet, red,* and so on, all of which can take grammatical subjects in adult grammar.

We then find that the semantic diversity of early speech is still marked. But there is still no uniform ordering tendency. Sometimes such relational terms take their future subject arguments in initial position in this early speech (*X* + *sleep, X* + *write, X* + *go*). But they also take them in second position as well (*red* + *X, wet* + *X, big* + *X*).

Is this analysis too undiscriminating? Some investigators, for example, have analyzed utterance types such as *red* + *X* or *big* + *X* as denoting modifier + head relations, as they would in adult uses such as *I like red hats.* The claim would be that for young children, these patterns do not really express subject + predicate relations, but modifier + head or determiner + head, another grammatical relation (McNeill, 1966). The evidence for this alternative claim, however, is essentially that children are not observing subject + predicate order in using these terms. There is, in fact, no evidence that young children who use these orders *think* of them as semantically different from adult uses such as *X is big.* Their grammar completely lacks hierarchical NPs in which relational terms can be described as appearing prenominally, so there is no reason to analyze these patterns as though they were adult structural uses different from subject-predicate.

Finally, an investigator might wish to argue that only terms that will become main verbs should be counted in these early analyses. For the other relational-argument expressions depend on use of copula *be* to be counted as relevant for subject-predicate tabulations, and copula *be* is absent. Main verbs, however, are a critical element which is at least sometimes present in these utterances.

This arguement again seems far too adult-centered. As already discussed, the *is* form in sentences such as *it is hot* contributes no more real meaning than does *-s* to the utterance *he sleeps*. Yet few would exclude uninflected *sleep* from such discussion because it is missing tense, number, and person marking in utterances like *he sleep*.

On the whole, the best description of the early data seems to be one that eschews attempts to impose complex properties of grammatical subject or object uses upon it by the use of adult-centered descriptions. Children's earliest speech seems to be best described as a collection of different types of semantic-distributional formulas, varying in breadth from single-word formulas (e.g., *more + X =* 'recurrence of X') to semantically-based categories of varying breadth, from *size + X* to Actor + Action. This conclusion is very much like that given in Braine (1976). There is thus little evidence from children's early speech that they are actively attempting to analyze language in terms of underlying well-developed notions of grammatical subject and predicate properties. Many expected regularities of expression simply do not arise.

## "Grammatical subject" and later developments

Nor are later developments particularly impressive in supporting a nativist position. General discussions of acquisition sometimes give the impression that because the major semantic relations found in subject-verb-object sequences can be found by the time a child's mean length of utterance is about 2.0 morphemes, the development of the child's knowledge of major sentential constituent structure is in a highly advanced state by this point (e.g., deVilliers and deVilliers, 1978). This is clearly not at all so. As we shall see, children still leave out obligatory initial constituents in acquiring English at least until a mean length of utterance of about 3.30 (Bloom, Lightbown, & Hood, 1975), if not later. It seems to us that given the very strong claims to prior knowledge made by the nativist view, a more rapid apprehension of one of the key properties of English grammatical subject might be expected earlier. That is, if children were born with knowledge of the importance of certain types of relational term arguments and their central role in many languages, they might be expected to actively hypothesize and seek corresponding regularities concerning obligatory argument usage. This does not occur.

*"Logical subject" and the passive-active relation.* Most of our preceding discussion has been centered on the construct of surface grammatical subject. What of underlying, or logical, grammatical subject? As discussed, the passive-active relation provides the central justification for proposing such a construct. Some evidence against children's formulating such subject constructs uniformly during the preschool years comes from studies reported in Maratsos, Kuczaj, Fox, and Chalkley (1979). The basic premise of

these studies was as follows: early on, the passives to which children are ex-posed and themselves produce do not have the full semantic range of the adult passive. They instead seem all to be actional passives such as *he got knocked over by someone,* or *it was busted by those boys.* Such passives do not require a knowledge of the passive-active relation. Instead they could be adequately analyzed by the child as corresponding to a semantic-structural pattern such as the following: if Rel is an action-denoting term of the V type (that is, has correlated main verb properties), then a sequence of the form $Arg_{NP}(-) \ldots BE + Rel + ed (-) by Arg_{NP}$ has the semantic reading "acted on -action - agent of action." Use of such a formula requires no discreet gener-alized knowledge of the *relations* between active and passive sentence pat-terns; it requires only the formulation of a phrase structure-semantic cor-respondence, much like $Arg_{NP} + BE + being +$ Adjective $=$ "agent[11] + process" (e.g., *John is being obnoxious*). The "acted on - action - agent" pas-sive formula could not, however, allow reliable interpretation of passives such as *John was liked by Mary,* or *Frank was seen by John,* for these do not involve actions and agents, and so do not fit a formula $Arg_{NP}(-) \ldots BE + V + ed (-) by$ NP $=$ "acted on - action - agent."

A strong nativist theory, however, might predict that if children sys-tematically understand the passive relation for a large class of sentences, they should understand it for all; in fact, so would a theory in which the child had actively derived a notion of subject and object relations from pre-vious experience. For then passives, especially in the strong nativist view, should be interpreted for each verb in underlying representations in which the deep structure order of constitutents was identical for active and passive forms. That is, the child should produce and understand a sentence such as *John was kicked by Mary* by giving it an underlying representation quite similar to that for *Mary kicked John.* This rule for formulating actives and passives having been devised, it should be available for nonactional experi-ence passives such as *John was liked by Mary.*

Maratsos, Kuczaj, Fox, and Chalkley (1979) report a pair of studies in which preschool chidlren were asked questions about sentences they heard, and were thus tested for their comprehension of agentive and experiencer active and passive sentences. The children comprehended agentive and ex-periencer active sentences equally well in the task. But their comprehension of experiencer passives was random, while that of actual passives was reli-ably above chance. Using an easier picture comprehension procedure, Becker and Maratsos (1979) have found even stronger results; they find further that experiencer passives are not understood as well as agentive pas-sives until near the end of the grammar-school years in their sample. The data thus fail to support a strong nativist view; they also contradict a view that children form in the preschool years a notion of underlying subject which is reliably uscd to analyze grammatical constructions.

In general, then, the available data tend to oppose a nativist view of the child's innate knowledge and use of underlying grammatical relations such as logical subject. Chomsky (1975) has in fact recently argued that such innate knowledge may not be available to the child until it is triggered by earlier developments, or until it is made maturationally available. Such an argument is not at all theoretically impossible, given what is known of development in general. The argument protects, however, the strong nativist view from searching empirical inspection. In particular, such an argument seems to leave as the only available means of proof of the nativist theory a proof that it is impossible to describe the child's formulation of an adult grammar in any other fashion. This proposition we of course disagree with.

## Semantic-Based Accounts of the Formulation of Grammatical Subject Properties

We have seen that at present, various derivatives of strong nativist views regarding the notion of grammatical subject command little compelling support. What of attempts to base knowledge of grammatical subject properties on the purely semantic analyses of terms? It should be clear we do *not* wish to argue that semantic analyses of terms and their grammatical configurations are not relevant to formulations of how relational term and argument patterns are modulated and correlated. They clearly are. But analyses based on semantic formulations alone are clearly not *sufficient*. In this section, then, we do not take up the question of whether an adequate purely semantic-based account of grammatical subject properties can be acquired by the child, for it cannot. The question is more one of the degree to which children actively *attempt* to analyze their language in such a form, without using analyses of correlated semantic-distributional patterns of terms, or without analyzing the manner in which different lexical items govern the use of different patterns. We shall examine two hypothesis, and conclude the evidence does not favor them strongly.

### Early semantic-distributional patterns

The first of these hypotheses is that children initially attempt to analyze *all* relational term + argument sequencing patterns in terms of general or semigeneral semantic category formulas, such as actor + action, or action + patient. Early studies of acquisition, even with rigorous analytic criteria (e.g., Braine, 1976) do show children make use of such rules in varying degree. For example, Braine (1976), as discussed above, found evidence for the productivity of actor + action and possessor + possessed formulas in many children. He also found evidence that some children observed a regularity roughly of the form Located object + Location in the production of such utterances as *sweater chair* ( = "sweater located on chair").

But his (and others') analyses also show children failing to make semantic formulas as general as possible, and in fact show them often apparently formulating single-word formulas such as *more* + *X* = 'recurrence of X,' *wet* + *X* = 'wetness of X,' and so on, a tendency very marked in some children (Braine, 1976; Bowerman, 1976). It is worth further stressing that even relatively early on, there is evidence that children not only encode productive patterns based on single-word semantic-distributional formulas; they may also appropriately encode highly similar semantic relations with different semantic category orderings for different terms, just as adult competence requires for the mastery of such structures as *X pleases Y* vs. *Y likes X*. For example, Braine (1976) noted that a couple of children who seemed to have a general formula Located object + Location also seemed to analyze, correctly, that the locational terms *here* and *there* may appear either initially or finally (e.g., *here dog, dog here*); examples cited in Bloom et al (1975) also show this pattern. Many authors have noted that all children seem to properly encode that the locational interrogative *where* appears initially, even if other locational terms appear finally.

Other impressive examples appear soon afterward in the course of acquisition. For example, the term *belong* denotes a possessive relation. But unlike the ususal order of Possessor + Possessed, *belong* takes the possessed object reference in initial position. We have seen such uses of *belong,* without *to,* in children's transcripts around an MLU of 2.5, accurately used in not following the more common possessor-first order.

Bloom et al. (1975) studied the relational terms which refer to the change of location of an object. The proper use of some of these terms requires that the argument denoting the moved object is placed after the relational term, as in *put it, take it.* Other relational terms take the argument denoting the moved object in initial position; for instance, *it go here,* said as the child moves the object. Bloom et al would perhaps give a different interpretation, but it seems impressive to us that although the initial argument for terms such as *put* and *take* was usually missing throughout a long period in the children's speech, and these relational terms denoted change of position as did *go,* children apparently did not produce sentences of the form *it put there,* or *go it there.* That is, they properly sorted out the way in which the individual lexical items controlled the placement of the argument denoting the moved object.

These, along with other examples, show children properly sensitive to the manner in which different lexical items, often semantically quite similar in nature, may control the use of different semantic-structural patterns, a necessary sensitivity for attainment of the final adult system.

An agent-centered account

But such mixtures of lexical and semantic analyses, though generically appropriate as beginnings, are still a long way from the analysis of the conditions of obligatory NP argument usage, number agreement and pronominal use paterns, and other characteristics of the pattern of English grammatical subject usage. Could strongly semantic-based formulations still form some key part of children's developing analyses of these properties?

There is no single hypothesis to be considered in this area. But we can consider a particularly likely candidate, one in fact similar to that proposed in Bates and MacWhinney (1978) for English. Their proposal is that the "prototypical" English sentence pattern includes an agent in initial position, followed by an actual relational term and a patient of the action. Roughly, they further propose that English-speaking children will acquire patterns of subject usage such as number agreement and pronominal usage earlier for sentences which fit this semantic pattern. Other semantic patterns for subject-verb-object sentences, such as experiencer-experience-stimulus (*I like dogs*) may be expected to acquire grammatical subject patterns with a quickness proportional to their greater or lesser semantic similarity to the basic agent-action-patient pattern. In the end, of course, children cannot hope to link the relevant relational term-argument properties of the system only to semantic analyses, as we have shown. But again, perhaps they at first actively attempt to do so.

Evidence relevant to this hypothesis such as consideration of skill in number agreement, or skill in the use of obligatory initial arguments, has not really been presented this way in the published literature. Yet there are some hints that it is not a fruitful hypothesis, despite the important correlation of agentivity to grammatical subject uses in English (as opposed to ergative languages). For example, Bloom et al. (1975) investigated, for other purposes, children's use of constituents in three kinds of locative action constructions. These were as follows: (1) Agent - Locative action - Patient, in which the initial argument causes the movement of the postrelational term patient (*Gia away a lamb;* or *put this down,* in which an initial agent *should* be present); (2) Patient - Locative action, in which the initial argument denoted an entity which moves, but by the agency of some other entity; for instances, *it goes here* uttered as the child moves the object; (3) Mover - Locative action, in which the initial argument is both the thing moved (patient) and the agent of movement; for example, *I sit down there* (child moves, and is the causer of movement).

Bloom et al. (1975) list, for four children at various MLU levels, how often each constitutent was actually realized. For example, in *I put here,* the initial agent is realized; in *put it here,* it is not. We might expect that if agent were an important organizer of grammatical subject privileges in English, it would appear earlier and more reliably in agent-locative action sequences than would the patient argument in patient-locative action sequences. In fact, however, Bloom et al.'s tables (Bloom, 1978, p. 186) show the opposite. Each child's usage was analyzed at three or four different levels of MLU. For all four children, at MLU levels varying from 1.42 to a maximum of 3.30, patient was more frequently supplied. One child, Gia, once supplied patient 100 percent of the time when agent was supplied just 60 percent.

Bloom et al. (1975) also supply similar frequencies for agentive constructions for nonlocative actional terms (e.g., *my open that*). For all four children at all MLU levels, the frequency of supplying obligatory agent was generally lower than the proportion with which patient was supplied for patient-locative action sequences, again sometimes very much lower.

Are other data available? For example, *be* appears in English grammar, marked for person-number agreement, as both progressive *be* (*the boy's singing*) and copula *be* (*the boy's happy*). Although not all progressive uses require initial Agents (e.g., *the rock's falling*), surely more do than is the case for sentences with copula *be*. Yet uses of *be* attain stable 90 percent correct use at least simultaneously and perhaps earlier as copula forms than as progressive forms (Brown, 1973).

As we can see, no decisive data are available, for these are not detailed reports of the complete acquisition of the system. But agent does not seem to serve as a dramatic or central organizer for grammatical subject privileges. We now proceed to a consideration of a more positive account.

## Grammatical Subject as Part of the System of Correlated Patterns

It is clear that in fact very little of the patterns of use that include grammatical subject properties are known by the child in the early period of word combinations. What are major developments after this period?

Part of the development, a major part, must consist of learning the correlated patterns of usage which define major form classes such as main verb, adjective, and preposition, and differentiating them from nonsubject-taking relational terms which are present early or appear later on. Some early-appearing relational terms never take arguments in the manner we call taking a grammatical subject. *More* and *another,* for example, despite their complex meanings of recurrence of different members of a given class in a context, will only appear before their arguments in larger argument structures called hierarchical NPs. An example of such a structure is

$$\underline{1} \;\; \{\text{Arg}_1 \text{ of } \underline{see}\;\} \;\; \underline{see}\;\; \{\underline{more}\;\; [\underline{(dog)}\;\;\; (\text{Arg of } \underline{-s})\;\underline{s}]\;\; [\text{Arg of } \underline{more}]\}$$

$$\{\text{Arg}_2 \text{ of } \underline{see}\;\} \;\; ; \text{ that is, } \underline{(I)\; see}\;\; \{\underline{more}\;\;\;\; [\underline{(dog)s}]\} \;.$$

Often subjects of later-developing relational terms will form intricate systems of their own, such as the English auxiliary verb system or various kinds of adverbials.

Some of the early- or later-appearing relational terms will conversely acquire correlated patterns such as use of *do*-forms for tensing and negation, *-s* for present generic disposition, *-ed* for past occurrence, and so on. Among their patterns of usage will be the requirement of an initial NP argument in various semantic-pragmatic contexts, various number agreement properties, and so on: this is the class of main verbs. Still others, the classes of prepositions and adjectives, will acquire another set of uses revolving around the uses of copula *be,* including knowledge of the circumstances under which obligatory initial arguments of noun phrase form are also used. The child will have to learn generally when such potentially obligatory uses of initial NP arguments are not to be used. For example, in various uses of inifinitival clauses, the surface subject cannot be specified—one cannot say, for example, *\*the boy wants the boy to have some* if both references are to the same individual; instead it must be, *the boy wants to have some.* The child will have to learn when obligatory argument uses are not necessary, as in answers to questions (Q.: *what was he doing?* Ans.: *eating flowers*), or when they are optional (choice between *go away!* or *you go away!*). During this time, the child must also be making analyses of the ways in which some relational term pattern uses are sometimes governed by semantic analyses. The most conspicuous example of this, of course, is the almost invariant appearance of agentive arguments, should they be used, in initial argument positions in English nonpassive declaratives. Others involve more complex interactions of semantic, correlated pattern, and individual lexical analyses which cannot be discussed here (see Bowerman [1977] for relevant discussion of a class of such cases). It would be surprising if the children's formulation of this vast network of correlated uses were extremely rapid, and it in fact is not.

Beyond this very general outline, however, little more can be said, for in fact little systematic study has been made of the manner in which such properties of NP argument usage, the development of correlated relational term uses, number agreement, pronominal usage, related sentence forms, and so on are all correlated. We can easily imagine many alternatives: some children might know that certain kinds of relational terms require initial NP arguments without knowing that others do; some children might know when initial NP arguments are required in utterances in general, but lack complete knowledge of what kinds of relational terms take such arguments obligatorily; some children might master some properties of the system but fail to know when important uses are obligatory, and so on. We will here briefly describe one type of analysis which shows how the child might be expected to master the system only in parts, rather than as a whole.

There is an apparent great division, often observed in linguistic descriptions (e.g., Chomsky, 1965) between subject-predicate forms involving main verbs versus those involving copula verb structures. In fact, we might expect the developmental course of these systems to be separate for some period for many reasons. Main verbs, for example, typically denote relational material of great semantic importance; they are usually phonologically relatively distinct; and they are associated with a number of relatively conspicuous semantic-distributional patterns, such as the use of *do-* forms, progressive *-ing*, and so on. On the other hand, consider those relations and relational terms bound up with the copula verb system, itself a major part of the subject-predicate structure of English. The copula itself is semantically not very important, mostly denoting tense and aspect relations rather than more salient relational material. Its phonological forms are diverse, and often negligible; the forms include *am, are, were, was, be, is, 's* (on nouns) and *'re* (on nouns). They fall into three main uses: taking prepositional phrases, taking adjectival phrases, and taking attributive noun phrases. It is well known that early in development they show many peculiar limitations of usage, including instantiation only with prenominal subjects for a long period (Brown, 1973; Bellugi, 1967).

In fact, the copula system itself contains subsystems of considerable intricacy, which are often tied to superficial rather than profound semantic aspects of sentences. Let us consider one such system the child must master, the system of usage with prepositional relational terms and various adverbs such as *here, there,* and so on. We shall analyze, as exemplary of the larger class, the uses of the prepositional relational term *in*. Semantically, *in* takes two arguments. Its general form is $X = Contained - in = Containment - Y = Container$. When the first argument has the grammatical form of a simple NP, *in* takes a supporting form of *be,* and the entire sentence is said to have subject-predicate grammatical form. For example:

(1) The king - was in - the cathedral $= X - in - Y =$ contained - containment - container. But the initial argument of *in* can in fact denote a whole event. If the initial argument is still in simple NP form, *in* still takes a supporting form of *be,* as in

(2) The explosion - was in - the cathedral $= X - in - Y$. Suppose, however, that the initial argument of *in* does not have the grammatical reflexes of a simple NP; suppose this initial event is instead denoted by the phrase *it exploded* instead of *the explosion.* Then no supporting form of *be* appears:

(3) It exploded - in - the cathedral $= X - in - Y$. The resulting structure is thus not an example of a subject-predicate construction, despite its semantic similarity to (1) and (2). The case is similar if the initial argument of *in* appears after a relational term denoting the movement of the entity causing it to be in a position of being contained. For example:

(4) He threw (it - in - the wastebasket): *it - in - the wastebasket = X - in*

- $Y$ = Contained - containment - container. Again no supporting form of *be* appears, and the contained-containment-container relation fails to be classified as a grammatical subject-predicate construction, because of the failure of *be* to appear.

The examples show two facets of usage: (1) they show the combination of complexity and superficiality of conditions which determine the use of copula *be,* and (2) they thus show the complexity and partial superficiality, in semantic terms, of the subject-predicate relation, dependent here partly on superficial structural conditions.

But these semantic-distributional facts about *in,* properly analyzed, are not isolated ones. They apply to the whole set of locative prepositions and adverbs. They apply, for example, to uses of locative adverbs such as *here* (*he threw it here; it exploded here; the explosion was here*).

Interestingly, children do not seem to produce overgeneralizations that might follow from these patterns. They do not produce sentences such as *I threw it to be in there,* which are not unreasonable extensions. It is probable that they accumulate considerable information about the manner in which the individual terms participate in such semantic-distributional patterns before actively extending possibilities. (However, see Bowerman [1974] for a discussion of errors regarding causatives.)

This system of copula uses with locative prepositions and adverts comprises but a subsystem of the system of copula uses that in turn constitute just a part of the system of complete knowledge of relational term and argument uses which we call the English system of grammatical subject uses. It seems clear that while such a system clearly presents many interesting semantic-distributional problems for investigators to study and for the child to analyze, we should not expect that its acquisition would be closely or completely tied, for example, to the developing system of main verb - NP argument uses that constitute another aspect of English grammatical subject properties.

Clearly, then, the growth of the systems and subsystems implicated in what we describe as "grammatical subject" uses provides a rich possible source of problems and complex grammatical systems for detailed and insightful study. But at the same time, we think it important to summarize: through some aspects of acquisition are no doubt more interesting or crucial than others, "grammatical subject" does not comprise a single notion or insight which the child somehow suddenly acquires and can use to direct and control other grammatical constructions. "Grammatical subject" is our summary for a complex of correlated relational term-argument uses of remarkable intricacy and complexity. These can only be assumed analytically and psychologically to be a single "thing" or "idea" at the cost of impairing our study and understanding of the course of children's formulation of grammar.

## SEMANTIC ACCOUNTS OF ACQUISITION
## AND REPRESENTATION RECONSIDERED

### A Semantic-Based Prototype Theory of Acquisition

The heart of our claim about the formulation of syntactic categories is that such formulations rest on the analysis of the use of sets of terms in correlated semantic-distributional patterns. Form class distinctions rest upon the differences in the sets of semantic-distributional patterns in which terms may appear. The inherent or situationally-given semantic analyses of terms do not distinguish them reliably for the purposes of grammatical usage, although such analyses play important parts in regulating the uses of terms.

We have in the previous sections listed both theoretical and empirical reasons to support this point of view. The arguments listed before, we think, serve to show that the adult system cannot be described as being regulated by the semantic analysis of terms. Nor does the developmental evidence support such an account. Although such a strictly semantic-based theory fails to account for the adult system for children's acquisition of it, there is an alternative semantic hypothesis which nevertheless suggests itself: an hypothesis founded in prototype theory (Rosch, 1973; Rosch & Mervis, 1975). Prototype theory provides an especially interesting framework because it is more flexible in its application, at least apparently, than the semantic-based accounts we have mostly considered so far. Such systems can tolerate "good" and "bad" members of a set. Thus, for example, perhaps verbs could be basically represented and analyzed as actional terms, with stative verbs being represented as "bad" members of the verb set. We ought to consider whether this additional flexibility will allow an essentially semantic-based prototype theory of syntactic categories to account for the correlations among the grammatical uses of terms, and yet circumvent the difficulties which were insoluble for a stricter semantic-based account.

To fulfill this objective, a detailed discussion of how a particular prototype theory might work will be considered here. This account will be followed by a demonstration that such a theory still fails to account for adult usage adequately, and still fails to provide an adequate framework for the description of the course of children's acquisition of syntactic category uses.[12]

### An hypothesized semantic-based prototype

In the general prototype theory, category or class membership is defined along a gradient from "best" to "worst." The more central or "best" members of the category are those which best exemplify the most typical (or most common) attributes which define the class. By virtue of thus comprising the "best" examples of the overall category, they participate in all or most of the operations which are available on the basis of category membership. When an item is considered to be a more peripheral or "worse" member of the category (in that it less accurately embodies the "essence" of the defining class characteristics), it is also more restricted as to which class operations it can participate in. Thus a "better" member of a prototypical class generally participates in all the operations that a peripheral member does, and more besides.

In the particular form of prototype theory to be considered here, the hypothesized basic assumption is that people both analyze and permanently represent major categories which we call verb, adjective, noun, subject, and soon, according to the statistically modal or "core" semantic analysis of their members. Representations of grammatical operations are individually attached to these semantically defined categories. Representations thus have forms like "action terms take -*ed* in simple active affirmative declaratives to denote past occurrence; action terms take -*s* after a singular agent to denote present disposition; an action term takes *didn't* between itself and the agent to denote past nonoccurrence." Similarly, "core" adjectives are state terms, and representations might include "a state term takes *was* between itself and the entity described to denote past occurrence of the state; a state term takes *n't* or *not* between itself and *was, were . . .* to denote negation; and so on." Grammatical patterns are controlled by the semantic characteristics common to the central members (those exemplfying the modal semantic analysis) of the set; the semantic-distributional patterns are not correlated to each other through their connections to common terms.

In addition to these general representations, each lexical item must presumably be labeled as to how good a member it is of its category. Thus *break, run, kiss,* and *push* may all be labeled as "good" exemplars of the action term set in that they represent brief, physical, often agentive actions. "Bad" members include terms such as *like* or *know,* which have less of an actional meaning, and in fact fail to participate in some characteristic verb operations, such as the imperative or progressive constructions. Similarly, *red, tall,* and *soft,* by virtue of referring to steady, nonagentive, nonprocess states, would be examples of "good" state terms. *Careful, obnoxious,* and *nice* would conversely comprise worse members of the state term category.

The question is whether this apparently more flexible system can escape in insoluble problems encountered by a stricter semantic-based account such as was presented earlier. We begin the answer with an examination of the ability of this semantic-based prototype theory to describe adult competence accurately.

## Adult competence and prototype theory

As soon as one begins seriously to attempt to devise a prototypical semantic representation of sets of terms that could possibly account for an adult speaker's competence, it becomes obvious that the theory is inadequate. The major difficulties are three: (1) the extreme semantic overlap of the form class categories; (2) the inherently self-contradictory nature of some of the resulting general representations; and (3) the inherent problems involved in *selecting* some appropriate prototype (i.e., the "best" example).

First, as we have discussed before, the semantics of the verb and adjective form classes overlap considerably. Yet a semantic-based prototypical representation, through allowing "bad" members of different categories, still requires that terms be able to be sorted into different categories on a semantic basis. Although this may not be too awkward when considering "best" exemplars of the prototype, it immediately becomes enormously difficult and ultimately impossible to do when one considers peripheral members of given categories, and their similarity to the "best" members of other categories. For example, the verb *like* and the prototypical adjective *fond (of)* have nearly identical meanings and yet, according to semantic prototype theory, one would have to be able to differentiate them semantically in order to assign them to the appropriate category. *Consist* similarly functions grammatically as a verb, but semantically it more closely resembles a prototypical state term (i.e., there is no necessary animate entity involved; there is no process or change of state involved; it refers to a steady state). Conversely, the term *careful* functions gramatically as an adjective but semantically it very closely resembles the "best" examples of an action term prototype (i.e., physical contact can be involved, an animate entity intentionally controls the activity; it can refer to a brief event). There exists, simply, no semantic boundary which can adequately deal with the profligate crossover of meanings of terms of different syntactic categories. Thus, the hypothesized semantic-based prototype should result in errors such as incorrectly labeling *consist* as a semantically "good" state term and *careful* as a "good" action term; and lead to errors of use like *\*This toy is consist of three parts* and *\*He carefuls the toy*. If one uses only semantic criteria (even in the form of a prototype) for determining how to cluster grammatical privileges to terms, one would never be able to achieve adult linguistic competence.

The second and even more striking problem with applying a semantic-based prototype theory to define English form classes is that at a general level the representation would sometimes become inherently self-contradictory. For English sometimes offers *general* ways for members of one form class to be involved in constructions which mark some of the prototypical meanings characteristic of the best members of *another* form class. In particular, adjectives have associated with them regular and general means of participating in progressive (linked to process semantics) and imperative (linked to agentivity) constructions. Agentive-process adjectives can take the progressive by marking it on the copula *be* marker: *he's being noisy.* Similarly, imperatives with adjectives as the central relational term can be marked with finite *be: be careful! don't be obnoxious!*

General representations for these phenomena would have to be something like the following:

*(1)   To form the imperative,*

$$\underline{Be} + \left[ \begin{array}{l} \text{member of state category} \\ + \text{ process} \end{array} \right] = \begin{array}{l} \text{speaker commands listener to carry out} \\ \text{the appropriate activity} \end{array}$$

(2)   To form the progressive,

$$\text{Arg}_{NP} + \text{form of BE} + \underline{be} + \underline{ing} + \left[ \begin{array}{l} \text{member of state of category} \\ + \text{ process} \end{array} \right] =$$

temporary ongoing process of the state relation

The labeling must refer to membership in the state grouping because verbs (the putative action terms category) do *not* form the progressive and the imperative in this fashion. Yet, the general representation of the relevant subset of relational terms must also be labeled [+ process], because *true* stative adjectives cannot participate in these constructions (*\*he is being tall, \*be red*). Thus at a general level of representation, the relevant category of relational terms is represented as having both + state and + process characteristics; the representations are therefore self-contradictory.

Quite simply, the semantics of the adjectival terms which can appear in the progressive and the imperative constructions disagree with the "core" semantics of the adjective class. Defining the general representation of adjectives in terms of the prototypical stative meaning of adjectives leads to internally self-contradictory general representations of the imperative and progressive uses, such that various adjectives must be represented as stative and nonstative.[13]

There is not really any self-contradiction in the actual situation, of course. Adjectives are not defined as stative terms, though they do denote state relations more often than verbs. Some denote state relations, and some do not. Those adjectives which are process terms may take the progressive and imperative in certain ways characteristic of adjectives, just as those verbs which are process terms may take progressive and imperative in ways characteristic of verbs. The self-contradiction arises only if one attempts to represent adjectives at a general level as "state" terms, while simultaneously trying to represent the *general* manner in which adjectives may be implicated in nonstative (process) meanings such as are entailed by the progressive and imperative constructions.[14]

Finally, the problems involved in considering process adjectives touch upon some facts which we think give some difficulty even to other related prototypical theories of form class. By definition, prototypically defined "best" exemplars of a set should be the very terms which participate in all or most legitimate privileges of the set. But process adjectives are semantically *peripheral* members of their set; yet they, not the "best" members, participate in more privileges than many semantically "better" members, such as the adjectival progressive and imperative constructions. It is furthermore not only the imperative and progressive constructions which involve this difficulty. Many adjectives can be changed into adverbs by the addition of -*ly* to the adjective form (*happy - happily; sad - sadly- quiet -quietly*). *All* of the agentive-process adjectives seem to take this grammatical privilege. Some other adjectives also take the privilege (e.g., *happy*). But many of the central or *"best"* members of the class do not, or only do so under limited circumstances (*tall - \*tally; red - \*redly*). Thus, if semantic characteristics are implicated in defining the "best" adjectives, a major tenet of prototype theory is contradicted, the tenet that the "best" members of the class have more of the privileges which are characteristic of the class, while the more peripheral members have fewer.

In summary, we find that the hypothetical semantic-based prototypic account of form class groupings and privileges fails to account for adult usage. It cannot overcome the problems presented by the extensive semantic overlap of the members of different form classes. It leads to inherently self-contradictory representations of various constructions, and, ultimately, a concept of prototype or "best" exemplar in which semantic definition plays any key role encounters at least some empirical difficulties. Strongly semantic-based prototypical representations of syntactic categories cannot account for the general structure and actual use of adult linguistic systems.

## Childhood data

Despite the fact that a prototypical semantic account cannot account for adult linguistic performance, there is a temptation to consider the possibility that children begin forming form classes this way and only later abandon the strategy. Is there any evidence that children actually do try to do this?

As we have discussed before, the difficulty with any semantic account of form class membership is a function of its inability to deal with the semantic overlap among categories. There are terms which are process adjectives (e.g., *active, noisy*); there are verbs which are very stative (e.g., *see, remember, miss*). If the child did attempt to develop a semantic prototype for form classes, the net result should be an enormous number of errors which would occur for two reasons: (1) During the acquisition phase, the child should encounter terms like *active, noisy, see, remember,* which semantically fit the incorrect prototype. If the child is already employing a semantic prototypical description, he should commonly assign these terms to the *wrong* form class group. This would result in his producing errors like *the boy actives, *they noisied, *he is see the book, *he isn't remember the movie.* (2) Even if the child could on some grounds assign deviant terms to the form class which appropriately defines their grammatical privileges, given that the definition of these categories is hypothesized to be semantically prototypically based, there should be a contradiction between the actual semantics of the terms and the prototypical semantics of the classes. This contradiction should lead to a very confusing situation for the child. If he pays attention to the semantic nature of the deviant item (e.g., *see*), then he is apt to confuse it with the prototypical semantic of the *opposing* form class (e.g., nonprocess, nonagentive state), and allow it to incorrectly participate in some of the privileges of that form class (e.g *I am see it*). If the child were to attempt to use a semantically defined prototype to cluster correlated grammatical privileges, he should produce many, many form class errors—both during early acquisition and later production. As we have already pointed out, errors of this type are extremely rare. The absence of these errors lends support to the premise that they probably do not actively attempt to analyze their language world this way.

Furthermore, the theory predicts that "anomalous" or "bad" members of classes should fail to take on characteristic privileges of the class at all as readily as "better" members. Yet, as discussed before, semantically "anomalous" stative verbs such as *think, know, see,* and *hear,* do take on appropriate overregularizations such as *thinked* and *knowed* in a systematic and reasonable fashion. Similarly, nonagentive initial NP arguments seem to acquire properties such as obligatory appearance or number agreement as well as, or better than, agentive arguments (cf. earlier discussion). Perhaps data could still be said to be small in extent. But it seems that children do not show, in their patterns of acquisition, strong active attempts to analyze language in a semantic-based prototype fashion, any more than they attempt to do so on a stricter semantic basis.

## The Inherent Semantics of Terms and Grammatical Usage

In the previous pages, we have outlined an account in which grammatical categories such as verb, adjective, gender class, or grammatical subject stand for the convergence of a number of correlated semantic-distributional patterns on a set of terms or constituents. We find that such categories cannot be defined by the inherent semantic characteristics of their members; they are instead defined by, and participate in, productive processes because of the speaker's knowledge (somehow encoded) of the correlation to one another of different semantic-distributional frames: knowing one often arbitrarily assigned pattern use of a term or constituent, we know other possible uses. We have also made arguments that such analyses do not appear to be unnatural to children. They acquire form and gender class uses with surprisingly little error, for example, and do not seem actively to seek to extend semantic-structural correspondences for grammatical subject privileges at the expense of the semantic-structural patterns appropriate for individual terms.

There is some possibility, however, of misunderstanding the general nature of the implied claims being made here about the nature of language and language acquisition. Our account stresses term-by-term assignment to correlated grammatical semantic-distributional patterns in a way that makes less important the inherent semantic characteristics of those terms. Does such an account give no part to general semantic analyses of terms or constituents in the nature, formation, and acquisition of languages?

This is not our intent. We think that analyses of language suffer when they attempt to show that grammar is all one thing or another. It is probable that what are called *syntactic* categories, such as verb, adjective, or gender class, are so called because they rest on differentiation among themselves by partly distributional distinctions among the sets of correlated semantic-distributional patterns in which their members may appear. Since it is these syntactic categories that we have chosen to discuss and elaborate, it is natural that semantic analysis alone would not serve to describe and define them. As will be seen, there are probably reasons why the sequential properties of language rely so heavily on the use of partly distributional definition rather than relying only on the inherent semantic characteristics of terms to govern sequential privileges.

But it is worth clarifying how general semantic analyses of terms also interact with such analyses of their correlated semantic-distributional patterns, for such general semantic characteristics commonly play a role in modulating grammatical expression. In a sense, all grammatical operations depend on the semantic nature of the term. For example, whether or not a term denotes something that can be meaningfully spoken of as having tense or aspect depends on the nature of the term. Such a category of eligible terms is quite broad. But in other cases, the inherent semantic nature of the term plays a sharp and distinctive role. For example, among the terms that share in verb-correlated semantic-distributional patterns, some denote a process meaning and some denote a stative meaning. Verbs take -*ing* as one of their privileges, and can appear in finite form at the beginning of imperatives. But these partly distributionally regulated privileges also depend on the semantic nature of the verb, since just process verbs enter into them (Fillmore, 1968).

For adjectives, the inherent semantic conditions on the term interact even more sharply. Adjectives may also take progressive -*ing* and the imperative, but in a characteristically different way from verbs: -*ing* appears on supporting copula *be,* and it is copula *be* that is untensed in imperatives. Thus, that appropriate usage is *he is being careful* rather than \**he is carefuling* follows from the distributionally differentiated form class nature of *careful,* not its inherent meaning. But that *careful* takes the progressive and imperative at all is fixed by its inherent meaning: it denotes a controllable, agentive process meaning. In fact, adjectives must be agentive to take the progressive, while verbs need not be. Compare *the rock is changing in temperature all the time* to \**the rock is being variable in temperature all the time.* Any sequence of the form *NP is being Adj,* if it is semantically acceptable, denotes an agentive relation: NP - BE + *being* + Adj = Agent -ongoing process. Clearly, general semantic analyses of terms play a role in directing their sequential uses, generally in interaction with their correlated semantic-distributional uses; this is certainly so for process versus stative adjectives and verbs. In sum, as these instances and many others discussed above show, children must also be able to analyze how the inherent semantic nature of terms may participate in the formulation of grammatical sequences, when this is relevant.

Agentivity also figured importantly in other English constructions, or in children's interpretations of them. In declarations of nonpassive form, for example, an agentive argument is overwhelmingly placed as initial argument. We also saw earlier how children, by hypothesis exposed nearly always to agentive-actional passives, reasonably derived an analysis in which the passive structure NP - . . . BE + V + *ed* - by NP corresponds to a semantic categorial sequence Patient - Action - Causative Agent, rather than deriving the active-passive relationship of adult competence.

Furthermore, sometimes relevant examples may be even more clearly found in languages other than English. In Navajo, for example, NPs denoting a nonhuman entity may not precede those denoting a human. A Navajo speaker cannot say the equivalent of *the rock crushed the boy,* though the equivalent of *the boy was crushed by the rock* is acceptable (Navajo has a passive construction similar to English).

As another kind of example, in languages in which relational-term arg-

ument relations are clarified by devices such as case markings on nouns or
determiners, pragmatic-semantic functions of constituents, such as their
conversational information value, often assumes a greater role in regulating
the ordering of terms than in English. German main clauses, for example,
have an overall structure corresponding to the formula, initial constituent
-first verbal element - other nonverbal constitutents - rest of verb. The nonverbal elements are arranged from beginning to end, with a few formal-
based exceptions, in terms of increasing information value. For example,
answers to questions generally introduce new information. In answer to the
question translatable as, "when have you the dog petted?" a German might
naturally answer, "the dog have I today petted," or "I have the dog today
petted," but not "today have I the dog petted." For *today,* providing new
information, should be placed near the end of the clause. Either *the dog,* or
*I,* referring to old information, may be placed initially (Lohnes & Strothmann, 1967, p. 52).

It must not be forgotten how such semantic specifications interact with
the syntactic categorial pattern uses of terms. Children may at first believe
all passives denote patient-action-causative agent sequences. But they restrict such constructions just to main verb actional terms; they do not produce patient-action-agent sequences such as *he was niced (to) by his
mother,* even as they produce *he got knocked over by someone.* In German,
not all term placements are determined by pragmatic value. For example,
prepositions and determiners must appear in front with their head noun.
One could not say, "this person have I everything for done" instead of,
"for this person have I everything done," even if pragmatic function suggested such a use. How an English process relational term participates in
imperative and progressive constructions is determined by whether it takes
main verb or adjectival semantic-distributional patterns. The complexities
of the interactions of semantic analysis of terms with their appearance in
correlated semantic-distributional patterns is, unfortunately for the analyst
of children's language acquisition, very great. This means that we cannot
look for a "standard" answer to the question of how children acquire
grammatical constructions, through there will be recurring patterns among
the answers we find which have great interest and theoretical importance.
Children are not always amazingly quick in making their analyses, relative
to some criteria. Stable use of morphological and syntactic properties of
form class and gender systems may not come about until the age of four.
But they are quite skillful and accurate given the complexities of the task.
We can only conclude that analyses of the semantic nature of terms, and of
the combination of such analyses with their appearances in related semantic-distributional patterns, are both analyses which they find natural enough
to do.

## Why Are Syntactic Categories
## Not Equivalent to Semantic Categories?

The claim that grammatical constructions draw flexibly and easily from all kinds of analyses—distributional (sequential), semantic, pragmatic, and phonological—is thus central to our thesis. The facts of how languages are actually constructed, and of how children learn them, seem to support such a claim. We would guess that grammar draws from all these domains because all are implicated in human natural languages in a basic way: such languages consist of auditory sequences, the purpose of which is to convey meaning in a conversational situation.

Other theorists, however, take a contrary view about the reasonable ways in which languages might and should be constructed, and further posit that the manner in which children acquire language should reflect similar tendencies. Bates and MacWhinney (1978), for example, make a series of reasonable and related claims. They note that language is, after all, a system devised for the *purpose* of communication; therefore, semantic and pragmatic concerns should be preeminent in its structure. They also assume that in the construction and use of languages, there are only limited processing capabilities available to speakers, and limited linguistic resources, too; that is, there are only a small set of devices available, such as word order, morphology, stress patterns, and so on. As a corollary, they infer that these limitations require that the grammatical features of the language reflect the more essential concern of pragmatics; they thus hold that semantic-based grammar will predominate over more "formal" analyses, such as those presented here.

It is very clear that we disagree with this claim, not on any a priori grounds, but simply because of what we actually find both in adult language structure and in the course of language acquisition. The species seems to be quite capable, for example, of maintaining and acquiring largely arbitrary and "formal" distinctions among sets of semantic-distributional patterns as reflected in systems such as noun gender class, verb conjugational classes, or even form class distinctions.

But there is an underlying problem to be dealt with. For there are some striking *tendencies* towards clustering around various semantic poles in form class categories, or, within languages, in subject versus object NP uses. If agency is not somehow a central organizer for NP argument grammatical properties, why does it predict as well as it does the clustering of grammatical privileges such as case marking, NP argument position, pronominal usage, and number agreement in Indo-European languages? Why do the major form class categories of adjective, verb, and noun cluster as strongly as they do around the poles of action, state, and object reference, if not because of a correspondence to a basic conceptual division among actions, qualities, and objects which is being marked by the grammatical system?

Again, it must be stated that although there do seem to be semantic clustering tendencies, these tendencies are not reliable. It is true, for example, that in many languages a number of clustered properties are assigned to agents in a fairly uniform fashion. But, as described above, the tendency to mark agents uniformly in transitive and intransitive sentences is *not* universal. In ergative languages (Lyons, 1968), it is the patient (*the cup broke, he broke the cup*) which is generally marked the same in transitive and intransitive sentences. We simply do not see as much uniformity of constraint by central semantic notions of agentivity or degree of agentivity as it seems natural for speakers of Indo-European languages to claim. Furthermore, we should note that in our consideration of Bloom, et al.'s (1975) data, we found little support for the notion that children use agents to organize their usage of the correlated privileges which we call grammatical subject.

A similar problem has already been discussed regarding form class semantic boundaries. Not only do the semantics of certain verbs, adjectives, adverbs, and prepositions overlap with one another and actually ultimately resemble, in some uses, the modal semantics of a different form class; but there are even systematic ways for some terms in one form class to mark some of the characteristic semantics of another form class (for instance, agentive adjectives can participate in agentive-progressive and agentive-imperative constructions). The system simply cannot be viewed as reliably semantic-based or encoded, even if the statistical tendencies are present.

But again, why *not* create form class boundaries (for example) on a clear semantic basis, so that differences in morphology and syntax corresponded to semantic differences among the classes of terms? That is, why not have verb morphology and syntax go with actual semantics, and adjective morphology and syntax go with stative semantics? And whatever reasons account for this failure to do so, how can they account for the presence of the statistical semantic tendencies?

Although speculations of this sort are quite mythic in nature, our guess is that the present state results from two tendencies which run contrary to differentiating syntactic uses on purely semantic grounds: (1) it is difficult to classify all terms and concepts in a clear fashion semantically; (2) another system of interpretation is available and natural enough to be actively constructed and adopted, the system of correlated semantic-distributional uses of terms.

The potential weakness of semantic-based differentiations lies in the indefinite boundaries between, and the shifting analyses of, individual concepts. For example, the prototypical action concept may be said to involve a number of qualities: instantaneousness, change of state of some referent, physical contact or force, perpetration by an intentional animate agent upon an inanimate object. Such terms might include agentive uses of *break, throw, hit, push,* and *kick.* Contrastively, qualities of prototypic-state terms might include a steady characteristic or quality of some object, involuntariness, and absence of physical contact, force, or definition. But many of the concepts which humans have found useful to encode include mixtures of these characteristics. One may seek voluntarily to bring about nonphysical mental states (*look for, learn, watch*). One may intentionally bring about or control physical states in a manner involving little phyical exertion or activity (*quiet, sleep[ing]*). An entity may display constant characteristic tendencies towards certain types of change or activity (*changeable, unstable, labile, evanescent, obnoxious, aggressive, nasty, helpful*). A relation may involve a causative force, but one which is steady and nonagentive (*attract, attractive*). Some terms provide no clear interpretation one way or the other (*resemble, clever, dumb*).

Furthermore, people can think differently even about the "same" concept. The same general characteristic of an entity can be thought of as an involuntary though active characteristic (*John is [unintentionally] quite obnoxious*) or as a voluntary active one (*John is being obnoxious*). Activities may be viewed as true of an actor just once or temporarily (*the dog barked at the girl*) or as an enduring quality or characteristic of the actor (*this dog barks at the moon; he is noisy*).

Thus, consistently organizing sequential (grammatical) properties of terms on the basis of the semantic characteristics may not be as simple as it seems, though it might provide the beginning point for a system of grammatical organization. The complexity and variety of human conceptual thought sets the stage for a certain instability and vagueness of classification of concepts.

To continue with our hypothetical account, let us assume that furthermore, an ability to notice and encode the correlations of uses of terms in sets of semantic-distributional patterns is a type of analytic ability also available to speakers. Perhaps it is more easily available to some more than others, but it is present in all. Certainly some children appear even early on to eschew general semantic-based analyses of grammatical patterns in favor of analyzing small-pattern lexical-semantic patterns at first, a naturally allied form of analysis (Braine, 1976). Even if various ways in which terms act were originally formed on the basis of conceptual divisions, speakers could obviously have disagreed on which conceptual elements were critical in introducing new terms into the language. A concept which incorporated semantic elements of two different form class domains (e.g., *watch,* which refers to a voluntary, nonphysical state) would have been apt to be assigned to different systems of grammatical usage by different speakers, or at least to have been assigned in conflict with some speakers' natural intuitions. As a result, the semantic basis of term usage would become more and more diffuse. Either a speaker of the language or the child encountering the language for the first time might thus tend to rely more heavily on an analysis employing the correlations of semantic-distributional patterns in which terms appeared. Ultimately this shift, which allows the syntactic properties of terms to be somewhat self-governing, may have even had some value in permitting the semantics of the major classes of terms to vary more and more freely within and across categories, thus allowing a more variegated and finely tuned set of semantic concepts to be represented. Some modal clustering of terms in a category around certain semantic poles would furthermore still persist for two reasons: (1) the original state of the language would result in such a tendency, and (2) new terms which are introduced probably are sometimes assigned to a category partly to the degree the individual speaker judges they fit the semantics of the category. The clearer the fit to the "prototypical" semantics, the more likely the term will be assigned to that category. Though the semantic variety of terms in categories shows such a tendency not to be completely dominant, it is almost certainly present.

This speculation may help to make it reasonable that modal semantic clustering might occur within the syntactic categories of a language, even though a more comprehensive and reliable system of syntactic category definition is based on correlated sets of semantic-distributional pattern uses of terms. It of course presupposes that the analysis of correlated semantic-distributional uses of terms in a natural system of analysis for speakers, but we see no alternative to doing so.

Nor do we find much serious support in the structure of the world's languages for the claim that there are heavy channel and processing constraints within the system which naturally favor semantic-pragmatic analyses. There is, for example, very little disagreement that by and large, arbitrary gender subclass systems such as those found in Russian and German have virtually no communicative value. Occasionally a pronominal reference may be disambiguated because of its gender reference. But otherwise such systems are without known communicative value. They certainly do not reward graciously the effort to learn them by a child acquiring French, Italian, German, or Russian.

Yet such systems are generally rather common, as are systems such as arbitrary verb conjugations or arbitrary noun declensions in various languages. Again, it might be that these systems sometimes originally arose from systematic markings of different semantic categories such as masculinity versus femininity versus nonsexedness objects (though what the six noun genders of Sanskrit might have arisen from is difficult to determine). But their present state does not allow a semantic-based analysis except in small parts of the system. Gender systems, verb conjugation systems, and similar systems thus in many ways comprise systems of luxurious waste. They serve little function, probably require some effort to acquire and use, yet are very common. Such systems seem to be the sign of a species that has more than limited resources available. At any rate, such systems do not display a linguistic system molded by the constraints of a fierce and well-directed competition for channel resources for the expression of important meanings.[15]

In short, we find that it is natural for speakers to use both semantic and correlated distributional analyses. However, in current languages and perhaps increasingly so during the evolution of language, semantic-based definitions are not reliable because the semantics of the category members have become too diffuse. This diffusion of meaning results in the speaker being left with only one reliably accurate system of analysis: the use of the correlated sets of grammatical privileges to define grammatical categories. The continued use of this type of analysis also indicates that the language system itself does not seem to be highly restricted either in terms of processing or channel capacity. Rather, its structure appears to be a very rich though complicated phenomenon.

We have thus argued that the use of all kinds of analyses—semantic, pragmatic, distributional, phonological—find their way into the structure of grammar. Syntactic categories such as verb or adjective, or gender class, are actually summaries of the productive systems of correlated sets of distributional-semantic-phonological contexts into which such classes of terms fit. In the final sections, we consider some models of how children might begin with analyses of terms in individual utterances, and come to represent their properties in a manner amenable to the complex nature of the adult system.

## MODELS OF ACQUISITION AND REPRESENTATION

In the previous pages, we have argued that whether a term may be used in a semantic-distributional pattern is determined in large part by the possibility of its being used in other semantic-distributional patterns. Indeed, the crucial elements of what is meant by syntactic category specification for use of a term in a given pattern involve the encoding and representing of other patterns in which the term may also appear.

A large number of representational scheme are consonant with these constraints, however. In the succeeding sections we shall not attempt any exhaustive consideration of various possible models. Instead we shall offer a limited consideration of one representational and acquisitional possibility. This we do with the sense that a discussion of some of the central issues affecting that system will better highlight those considerations which would be essential to any adequate characterization of the adult speaker's knowledge.

Following a brief sketch of a relatively simple system of general representation, we shall take up two bodies of related issues. The first of these is whether general representations are necessary at all, or whether a very detailed lexicon supplemented by various processes of analogical extension might not be adequate. We shall give reasons that such generalized representations can be shown to be necessary even for relatively simple rules. We shall then conclude with a discussion of mechanisms necessary in an acquisitional device to deal with the fact that languages are not simple or perfect generalizing systems.

## Acquisition of a Simplified Generalization System

We shall initially develop an acquisitional model appropriate to a system in which the overlap among semantic-distributional pattern occurrences of terms is very high, symmetrical, and freely predictive.

### Terminology

In the next pages, we shall be speaking of some general properties of category formation. We shall thus also need a general terminology, one more general than that which has been employed in past sections.

First, let us refer to semantic-distributional patterns in general by the designation P ( . . . . . ), making general reference to different patterns by subscripts such as $P_i$ ( . . . ), $P_j$ ( . . . ), and so on.

We also need a convention for referring to any general category specification in any semantic-distributional pattern $P_i$ ( . . . ). In the previous pages, we have posited entities such as Argument and Relational Term as basic representational primitives. Although these prove to be useful in many discussions, there is no need to take so committed a position about the particular form to be employed for describing the basic elements of primitive distributional-semantic encodings. Nor are such representations germane to all general representations of grammatical properties. Let us instead introduce a more general and noncommital mode of reference to any category specification of a class of terms in any pattern $P_i$ ( . . . ), by referring to such categories as $X_m$, $X_n$, and so on.

Then generally we may say that a child must learn, for a given category specification $X_m$ in a pattern $P_i$ ( . . . $X_m$ . . . ) which general properties distinguish terms which may play the role of $X_m$ in $P_i$ ( . . . $X_m$ . . . ). In the terms of this chapter, part of the specification of characteristics of the terms that may be $X_m$ in $P_i$ ( . . . $X_m$ . . . ) is the specification of other category appearances of such terms — that is, that they may also appear as $X_n$ in $P_j$ ( . . . $X_n$ . . . ), $X_p$ in $P_k$ ( . . . $X_p$ . . . ), and so on. For example, there is a pattern $P_i$

which denotes generic present tense of the meaning encoded by any given term in the class of terms $X_m$ by adding -*s* to the terms, in certain semantic-distributional contexts (this is in reference to uses such as *he barks* + *s*). Part of the specification of the characteristics of which terms can be $X_m$ in $P_i$ ( . . . $X_m$ . . . ) turns out to be that they can take the role of $X_n$ in the pattern $P_j$ ( . . . $X_n$ . . . ). (For example, *didn't* + $X_n$ . . . + 'past nonoccurrence of the meaning denoted by $X_n$'.)

Finally, we shall refer to individual terms as $W_a$, $W_b$, . . . $W_n$. When we say that a particular term $W_a$ appears in $P_i$ ( . . . $X_m$ . . . ), it will mean that $W_a$ can act as $X_m$ in $P_i$ ( . . . $X_m$ . . . ). Then perfect cospecification and co-prediction of two category descriptions occurs if every term $W_a$ . . . $W_n$ which can appear as $X_m$ in $P_i$ ( . . . $X_m$ . . . ) and only those terms $W_a$ . . . $W_n$ which can appear as $X_m$ in $P_i$ ( . . . $X_m$ . . . ) can also appear as $X_n$ in $P_j$ ( . . . $X_n$ . . . ).

Further identification of the nature of the representation of such systems of perfect coprediction is better articulated in the context of the model of acquisition to which we now turn.

## An acquisitional model

Let us assume, following Braine (1971), there exists a scanner of incoming speech which analyzes sequential properties of morpheme strings. We shall also assume that this scanner simultaneously can register accompanying semantic analyses of the meanings of terms used in context. We shall simply have to presuppose here that various mechanisms exist for generating semantic-distributional hypotheses which form the basis for future rule growth. For example, the child, hearing a term such as *spilled,* must by some combination of semantic, phonological, and lexical analysis from the hypothesis that *spilled* is not an indissoluble unit. Rather, it may be broken into two parts, one of which denotes the relations encoded by *spill,* the other of which, -*ed,* denotes a past occurrence of this relation.

Again partly following Braine (1971), we may hypothesize the child to store at some point a more general specification of such individual analyses —one which encompasses more general pattern possibilities. This more general analysis in the particular case might be something like ... X + *ed* ... = "past occurrence of meaning denoted by X." This means, roughly, "you can add -*ed* to a term to denote past occurrence of the relation denoted by the term." Simultaneously, however, this general specification is connected to the particular phonological-semantic analysis that comprises the lexical item *spill*. Let us schematize such a simultaneously general yet specific entry in the following fashion:

$$\ldots \underset{spill}{X} + ed \ldots = \textit{``past occurrence of the meaning denoted by X''}$$

Such an entry translates into something like, "you can add -ed to a term to denote past occurrence of the meaning denoted by the term if the term = *spill.*" More generally, we can symbolize the case for any semantic-distributional pattern $P_i$ ( . . . $X_m$ . . . ) and any word $W_a$ as $P_i$ ( . . . $\underset{W_a}{X_m}$ . . . )

Such initially formed semantic-distributional patterns clearly do not immediately generalize. Instead, they apply only to those specific terms to which they are "directly connected." Braine (1971) makes the ultimate generalizability of such rules dependent, apparently, upon strict frequency of analysis. If a rule is analyzed as occurring frequently enough, it goes into permanent storage; it then becomes productive.

It is not our purpose here to develop a general critique of Braine's model. Let us, however, begin a continuation of our own account by noting one important difficulty. The analysis gives no means of encoding the general characteristics of the terms to which the operation can apply. For example, clearly the past tensing operation . . . X + *ed* . . . = 'past . . .' becomes analyzed frequently enough to become productive. But without any further specification of the characteristics of which terms can undergo the operation, there is no way of selecting just the proper group of terms and thus preventing the operation of -*ed* past tensing from applying to *any* term which denotes something capable of past occurrence. Many terms, including *happy,* or *in,* or even many nouns (for instance, *life,* as in *John's past life*), could potentially be so marked, but obviously they do not take -*ed* past tensing. In general, the problem of this chapter is to consider how an $X_m$ for a pattern $P_i$ ( . . . $X_m$ . . . ) becomes properly specified at a general level of representation.

Suppose such semantic-distributional patterns as the primitive past-tensing operation are stored and compared against incoming speech. If a term is recognized as appearing in a given pattern, and if that term is identical to one which has previously appeared in the same semantic-distributional pattern, the bond between the pattern and the term is, in some abstract way, strengthened. If a term appears for the first time in a pattern, the representation of that term and the primitive category description now become connected. At the same time, the more frequently $P_i$ ( . . . $X_m$ . . . ) is analyzed, the more likely its probability of being analyzed in future comprehension situations, and the more easily it becomes "alerted" for possible uses in speech production.

Thus, over time, an increasingly strongly represented pattern $P_i$ ( . . . $X_m$ . . . ) becomes linked with greater strength to a larger number of specific lexical items:

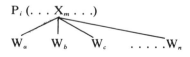

More or less simultaneously, many of these same lexical items are also becoming linked with increasingly strong bonds to other semantic-distributional patterns. So, our general brief sketch above should be expanded (see Figure 3-2 below).

Given this brief sketch, let us suppose, as a first approximation, that productivity takes place in the following fashion. With time, pathways between category specifications in patterns become, via intervening lexical connections, stronger and more numerous. Also suppose the child has encoded a new lexical item $W_x$ which is linked to $P_j ( \dots X_n \dots )$, $P_k ( \dots X_p \dots )$, and $P_1 ( \dots X_q \dots )$, but not to $P_i ( \dots X_m \dots )$. For example, $P_j$, $P_k$, and $P_1$ might represent various verb operations, such as *-s* tensing, and *do-*form uses, while $P_i ( \dots X_m \dots )$ corresponds to *-ed* past tensing. If we wish to represent the course of the clearest example of productivity—an over-regularization—we may let $W_x = $ *know*. Then the situation might be represented roughly as in Figure 3-3 below).

Now further suppose that the child wishes to use *know* in a distributional-semantic context which corresponds to that context in which the *-ed* past-tensing pattern often applies. That is, *know* would occur directly after its initial argument, that argument occurring directly at the sentence boundary, and the relation encoded by the term *know* has occurred in the past. In some sense this situation "alerts" or activiates the *-ed* past-tensing operation as it is a possible occasion for its application, and such semantic-distributional patterns continually seek for occasions for application, depending on their own proportional frequency of use. The likelihood of $P_i ( \dots X_m \dots )$ actually applying in this circumstance depends on the strength, number, and directness of intervening individual pattern-lexical item pathways between *know* and *-ed* tensing. At a certain period of development, both the frequency and strength of such bonds has increased to the point where in fact generalization occurs. The result is the novel production of the term *knowed*.

Although we will turn later to a consideration of how cases of inappropriate generalization—that is, overregularization—eventually come to be adequately curtailed, it is important to note here that our above sketch of generalization is actually too restrictive. In discussing the child's encoded

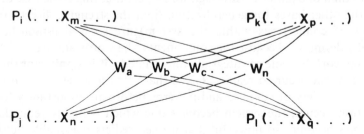

*Figure 3-2*

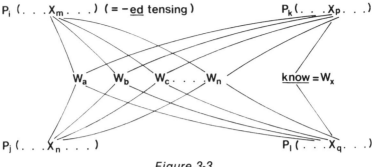

*Figure 3-3*

information regarding the term *know,* we assumed that *know* was linked to patterns $P_k ( \ldots X_p \ldots )$, $P_j ( \ldots X_n \ldots )$, and $P_l ( \ldots X_q \ldots )$. In essence our remarks regarding the number (or frequency) of connections between the new word $W_x$ and the activated pattern $P_i ( \ldots X_m \ldots )$ subsumed two different types of variety. Not only is variety represented by the fact that there is a large set of terms $W_a$, $W_b$, $W_c$, $\ldots W_n$ such that each term is linked to all four patterns, but variety is also encompassed by the fact that the novel term $W_x$ is connected to three *different* patterns in the network. Thus there exist at least three completely separable sets of pattern-lexical item connections between $W_x$ and the pattern $P_i ( \ldots X_m \ldots )$. Let us call this latter type of variety the number of connections into the system and the former, the number of connections within the system. It turns out that ultimately, even one set of pattern-lexical connections into the system may become numerous and strong enough to allow a novel use. For adult and many child speakers can often predict accurate pattern usage for a nonsense term on the basis of the appearance of that term in a *single* correlated pattern. Hearing *today John glixes,* they can generate *yesterday John glixed, did John glix,* and so on. Clearly, in this circumstance, there is only one completely unique set of pathways between the novel term $W_x$ and any activated pattern. A single connection into the system becomes sufficient for generalization to occur.

Thus productivity eventually can arise without a new term being linked to more than one pattern. Although we suspect that this is the case only because the other bases for generalization (i.e., the strength, directness, and number of connections within the system) are so well established and mutually defining—because the components (the words and patterns) within the network become so integrally interrelated—it is significant that generalization can occur so readily. Given that often new terms are probably heard in a variety of contexts and patterns before an opportunity for generalization occurs, the system becomes one which is highly redundant. It sometimes becomes so powerful that it overpredicts reasonable but incorrect generalizations.

In sum, in the account we have given here, categories come to be defined as a result of semantic-distributional patterns coming to specify their appropriate general scope of application. Because of the frequent overlap in terms to which various sets of patterns apply (such as verb tensing and negation uses), category specifications of certain large sets of semantic-distributional patterns come to be connected to, and thus predict, each other. Participation in such a network of mutually predicting category specifications we then call being a verb, or an adjective, or a member of an arbitrary gender class—that is, being a member of a syntactic category.

## Are General Rules Necessary?

We have presupposed throughout this chapter, as is commonly assumed throughout the language acquisition literature, that novel and appropriate productivity in and of itself demonstrates the presence of a generalized representation of a regularity in the language. Such an assumption, however, is not warranted. Productivity is theoretically possible *without* the use of generalized rule representations (MacWhinney, 1978; Maratsos, 1979). How this might be so becomes apparent when such an alternative system is considered. In the end, it will become clear that this alternative is inadequate, but only because other aspects of rule usage—not productivity per se—must be considered in justifying the proposal of generalized representations.

### Implicit versus explicit rules (analogy versus rule use)

It is evident that the speaker of any natural language must memorize many individual semantic-distributional facts about lexical items. Such a fact, for example, is that the combinatorial rule *think + over =* "consider" is restricted to just those terms. That *like* takes an experiencer argument in initial position (*John likes . . .* ), while *please* takes an experiencer argument in second position ( *. . . pleases John*) constitute further examples of the nature of these facts about individual lexical items. Even in a system presupposing generalized rules, considerable individual lexical memorization of various types of facts is required.

It turns out that given an extremely rich storage of facts about individual lexical entries, combined with an on-the-spot process of analogical generalization, it is possible to obtain a productive system without appealing to permanently represented generalized rules. Suppose a child has memorized highly detailed facts about individual lexical entries. For the word *spill,* for example, he would have entered that it takes the following operations, among others: Arg + *spill* + *s* . . . = 'generic present of spilling . . .,' Arg + *spill* + *ed* . . . = 'past occurrence of spilling . . .,' Arg + *didn't* + *spill* . . . = 'past nonoccurrence of spilling . . .,' Arg + *will* +

*spill* . . . = 'future occurrence of spilling . . .,' and so on. The child would also have representations for *kick* such as Arg + *kick* + *s* . . . = 'generic present . . .,' Arg + *kick* + *ed* . . . = 'past . . .,' Arg + *didn't* + *kick* . . . = 'past nonoccurrence . . .,' and so on through a number of uses. Suppose the child has formed a number of such rich individual lexical entries. Then facts such as terms which take -*s* tensing also take *do*-forms, -*ed* tensing, and so on, would be *implicit* in the lexicon. But they would *not* be explicitly stated in permanent generalized representations. That the child commands many related uses does not by itself justify positing that the child has either general rules or general category representations.

Such a system would give the child the ability to encode many situations. But how could productivity come about? Suppose the child wishes to express that someone who may be referred to as *Mary* has allowed an object to fall from her hands at some past time. Suppose this object to be denotable by *it*. The child finds in his lexicon the term *drop,* which takes a first argument and a second argument. The first argument denotes that entity which allowed the entity denoted by the second argument to fall. The child can thus construct *Mary drop it.* Suppose, however, that the child does not have entered for *drop* a way of indicating past occurrence. The child may then proceed as follows: he scans his lexicon for terms which have associated with them ways of indicating past occurrence. Some such terms take *was* or *were* (Arg *was hot*), while others take -*ed* (Arg *liked* . . . ). Further suppose the child has other semantic-distributional properties stored for *drop,* such as Arg + *drop* + *s* = 'present generic ...,' Arg + *didn't drop* . . . = 'past nonoccurrence . . . .' Using the on-the-spot analysis the child finds that *drop* shares more characteristics of this type with terms which take -*ed* to denote past occurrence than it does with other terms which can be marked for past occurrences. He thus analogically infers that one may say *dropped,* and produces *Mary dropped it.*


## Obligatory rules

Such analogical systems are thus capable of grammatical productivity. It turns out, however, that careful analysis shows them to be inadequate for dealing with various common phenomena of language and rule use. We shall present here only one such argument, which is based on the *obligatory* nature of many linguistic rules. Note that in the example above, the child conveniently *wished* to express the past occurrence of the situation. Suppose he had not been interested in expressing the past occurrence of the activity? Then the result would have been *Mary drop it.* Or suppose the child communicated the past occurrence specifically with *yesterday,* and produced *Mary drop it yesterday.* Either of these might communicate perfectly adequately, but neither is an acceptable sentence of standard English.

The difficulty is that in every known human language, certain rules *must* apply in certain grammatical-semantic circumstances. It is not a matter of whether the speaker is interested in expressing the meaning or structure which use of the rules conveys. Nor do languages conveniently happen to make obligatory the expressions of just those meanings which people always wish to express. For example, many languages or dialects do not obligatorily require the encoding of temporal relations with verbs. Nor can a speaker capture the essence of obligatory requirements by the use of simple semantic conditions. For example, a speaker of standard English could not simply realize that expression of temporal relations is always necessary. For then *Mary drop it yesterday* would suffice, and it does not.

The problem is that there must be a means for stating in more general terms the conditions about when something must be expressed. If we choose to try to remain within an analogy framework, we would have to say that something in what the speaker has formulated tells him that he has to make certain analogies under certain conditions. But it would quickly turn out to be the case that the specification of which analogies have to be made, under which conditions, would be equivalent to the very general representations which analogical systems are supposed to provide means of doing without. Therefore, general representations of semantic-distributional patterns and the types of terms to which they apply are necessary. The rule must be able, so to speak, to lay in wait, searching for its opportunity to apply, always recognizing it, and always applying when it arises.[16]

The problems of obligatory usage also make it clear that linguistic rules must acquire a certain autonomy vis-à-vis the intentions or desires of the speaker. Although the speaker may draw upon a system of rules and stored information partly to generate expressions of his focally intended meaning, it is also necessary for his utterances to satisfy general conditions placed upon them by the system of rules. Thus, he may have to encode meanings which do not necessarily form part of his focal intentions. In essence, such rules must become virtually automatic in application.

This chapter has concentrated on discovering what the general definitional nature of syntactic categories is. We have found it to be a system in which related uses of terms predict each other. But it turns out that in considering how such knowledge may be acquired and represented, these properties by themselves do not even justify the positing of general representations. We instead needed to recruit another property of the use of grammatical systems, the obligatory usage of some rules, to provide an adequate justification for such a proposal. In effect, a proposal about part of a system can never be judged for generic correctness except as measured against the requirements of the total working system. Clearly we cannot attempt to sketch here a complete system of representation and use of the entire system of English grammatical rules. Given that whole classes of proposals may ultimately be dispensed with by careful consideration of just one or two particular phenomena, the vulnerability of any temporarily surviving proposals should be self-evident. Having stated this caution, we return to a consideration of aspects of a possible model of acquisition.

## Negative Induction Systems

Above we described the definition of category representations for grammatical rules as essentially as abstraction process. Those characteristics which appeared consistently linked to those terms which can appear as $X_m$ in $P_i ( \ldots X_m \ldots )$ come to predict novel uses of terms as $X_m$. For example, all terms which take various *do*-tensing and negation operations also take *-s* generic present tensing. Hearing a term in contexts such as *today John glixes,* we may predict uses such as *they didn't glix, I don't glix,* and so on. Even a single distinguishing characteristic may form a good predictor for a related use.

What has been so far developed is a model of positive induction. In this model, the important hypothetical variables determining whether or not one use predicts another are *frequency, variety,* and *directness* of connection. *Variety* corresponds to how many different direct pathways through individual terms and patterns the two categorical specifications $X_m$ and $X_n$ share in common; *frequency* corresponds to how often individual terms are used in both $P_i ( \ldots X_m \ldots )$ and $P_j ( \ldots X_n \ldots )$; and *directness* correspnds to how directly the uses are connected—that is, category specifications connected to the same lexical item are the most directly connected. The probability of prediction of one use from another is hypothesized to represent some joint function of these variables.

A system of positive prediction alone, however, leads quickly to a large number of incorrect predictions. In general, we can say that the problem for specifying an $X_m$ of $P_i ( \ldots X_m \ldots )$ is to abstract those characteristics $C_j$, whether semantic-distributional uses or other properties, such as semantic or phonological ones, which individually or jointly predict usage as $X_m$. Thus we might say, if all or most terms to which $X_m$ is attached have a characteristic property $C_j$, if a new term $W_x$ has $C_j$, $W_x$ may be safely predicted to be able to appear as $X_m$ in $P_i ( \ldots X_m \ldots )$.

The difficulty with this reasonable-sounding formulation is that it is wrong. Let us illustrate this problem, using the prediction of the category of terms which can take the past tensing *-ed* operation as an example. We chose this example because it is well known that this rule becomes productive. Actually, as has been discussed, it is also one of the most irregularly applied rules, since many terms which could be predicted to take it in fact do not do so. What we should like to do is to presuppose, for the sake of discussion, that the rule is essentially regular and highly predictable. Later we shall deal with the irregularities.

Now consider the following problem. There are various properties of the terms which take -*ed* tensing which are, essentially, good predictors. For example, all terms which take -*ed* tensing also take the use of *don't* or *didn't* or -*s* tensing, and usage in these patterns predict -*ed* tensing as well as any positive predictors can. But in fact, all terms which take -*ed* tensing have the property of denoting a relation. Furthermore, in children's early lexicons, most terms which take -*ed* do seem to denote some kind of actional relation. Yet denoting a relation or denoting an actional relation is not a particularly good predictor of -*ed* tensing, in the sense that they also seem to predict uses such as *\*he call upped his mother,* or *he noisied.* We may put the problem this way: in a positive induction system, a possible specification for a category will be confirmed by every positive instance of use. Moreover, a poor overall predictor for a category will sometimes be *positively confirmed* just as often as a good predictor. For example, a child may record uses such as *spilled, kicked, pushed,* and so on. Since each of these takes -*s* tensing, each of these uses confirms the prediction of -*ed* tensing from -*s* tensing. But since each of these terms denotes a relation, each such -*ed* use also positively confirms the prediction of use of -*ed* from use of a term to denote a relation.

Why, then, do children not assume that if a term denotes a relation for an action, for that matter, which is a reasonably good positive predictor, in this sense), it may also take -*ed* tensing, thus producing outlandish uses such as *\*he noisied,* or *\*he inned the house,* or *\*he threw awayed the ball?* In all of these -*ed* has been applied to terms which denote relations, and all terms which take -*ed* tensing denote relations, or actions.

The heart of the problem, and the solution, should be clear. The problem is that a characteristic such as 'denotes a relation' or 'denotes an action' is true of many terms which do *not* take -*ed* tensing. It predicts all the appropriate -*ed* uses, but it also predicts, inaccurately, many nonoccurring -*ed* uses. Though linked to -*ed*-taking terms in great variety and frequency, it fails in accuracy, in that it predicts many possible occurrences which do not occur. In contrast, -*s* tensing is a far more accurate predictor. For large numbers of terms which do not take -*ed* tensing are not inaccurately predicted to do so by -*s* tensing. *Noisy, in,* and *away* do not take -*s* tensing, and so if -*s* tensing is part of the category specification for -*ed* tensing, it will not falsely predict them, even as it accurately predicts *pushed, kicked,* and *liked.*

This problem is a highly general one. For positive predictors, such as variety and frequency of correlation, by themselves ultimately confirm any overly general specification just as often as they confirm appropriate ones. When one begins to consider the number of erroneous positive predictors the child might encounter, it is clear that children's abilities to filter out such false predictors must be very great. Let us now examine some general means by which category specifications might not erroneously be influenced by false positive predictors.

Implicit mechanisms: Failures to reach generalization criterion

As always, a variety of mechanisms may be invoked to explain the workings of the system, and again, for reasons of space, we shall only posit here a bare outline of the characteristics of one such possible system. Let us schematize (Figure 3-4) the basic incorrect prediction situation which we have been describing. In this situation, $C_j$ is linked to all or most of the terms which actually appear as $X_m$ in $P_i ( \ldots X_m \ldots )$; but it is also linked to a very large number of terms which do not appear in $P_i ( \ldots X_m \ldots )$. (Although the actual number of terms involved would be much larger, as throughout, we simplify our representations by representing far too few lexical items.)

Now suppose a term $W_x$, which has characteristic $C_j$, is to be used in an utterance. Further suppose that it appears in a semantic-distributional context such that $P_i ( \ldots X_m \ldots )$ is a potential use of $W_x$. For example, suppose $P_i ( \ldots X_m \ldots )$ = the *-ed* tensing pattern, $C_j$ = denoting a relational term, and suppose the speaker wishes to produce an utterance to denote a past occurrence of the relation denoted by $W_x$. $P_i ( \ldots X_m \ldots )$ may thus be "alerted" for possible use, as is $W_x$ in the lexicon. In the preceding sketch, there are in fact many pathways from $W_x$ through $C_j$ to $X_m$; there are exactly as many as there would be for a more accurate predictor which was linked to far fewer terms which do not take $P_i ( \ldots X_m \ldots )$. Thus, by the criterion for generalization considered in our initial section, use of $W_x$ in $P_i ( \ldots X_m \ldots )$ might be rather likely.

Suppose, however, that we build into our condition for generalization another criterion. In the foregoing sketch, there are also many pathways from $W_x$ through $C_j$ and on through lexical nodes $W_f \ldots W_n$ which do *not* lead to $X_m$ in $P_i ( \ldots X_m \ldots )$. To use a metaphor derived from physics, suppose we think of the impulse (or charge or energy) from $W_x$ through $C_j$ to $P_i ( \ldots X_m \ldots )$ being dissipated in the many pathways which do not lead to $X_m$ in $P_i ( \ldots X_m \ldots )$. Or less metaphorically, we may simply say that by some mechanism, the probability of use of $W_x$ in $P_i ( \ldots X_m \ldots )$ is reduced

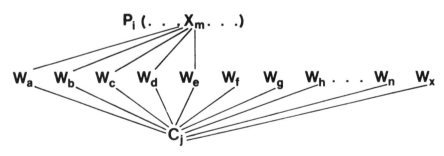

*Figure 3-4*

as a function of the presence of pathways which do not lead to $X_m$. Then probability of prediction of a generalized use becomes not only positively predicted by the joint function of the frequency and variety of connections between $W_x$ and $X_m$ through $C_j$; it also becomes an inverse probability according to the number of connections that do not lead from $W_x$ to $X_m$ through $C_j$. In such a fashion, we can build *accuracy* into the system as well as frequency and variety. Thus, by adjustment of the inherent criteria in the system for generalization, it may be frequently possible to prevent false predictions without having recourse to any explicitly stated inhibitions upon such predictions.

## Explicit inhibitory mechanisms

In such a system as we have just described, no explicit blocks are ever put in the pattern-lexical system against false predictors. Instead, false predictors consistently fail to have an effect.

But self-monitoring devices could also place explicit blocks upon such predictors. As connections between $C_j$ and lexical items which did *not* lead to $X_m$ in $P_j$ ( . . . $X_m$ . . . ) became both sufficiently strong and numerous, some automatic reverberation mechanism, constantly testing the probability of $C_j$ leading through lexical nodes to $P_i$ ( . . . $X_m$ . . . ), could put some kind of explicitly represented condition on $X_m$ that $C_j$ could not be trusted as a predictor of $X_m$. Such representations might consist of some modification of network connections, or some other representational device more powerful than those we have discussed so far.

For many cases, of course, it is simply impossible to tell apart such implicit and explicit inhibitory systems. Languages are in fact full of possible correspondences which are not productive for adult speakers, as will later be illustrated. But how can we tell whether these result from active, explicitly stated inhibitory mechanisms, or more passive, implicit inhibitory systems?

The question is not a simple one, but we think it is likely that such active explicit inhibitory mechanisms do exist. Let us turn to a few examples of these.

*The past-tensing operation.* The clearest indication that inhibition may require some active mechanism occurs when we have evidence that in fact an incorrect prediction reaches generalization strength sufficient for productive use, and then it is later inhibited. Such a well-known case is found in children's use of overregularized forms such as *breaked, runned,* and *knowed.* These forms, of course, are predicted by all of the characteristic semantic-distributional uses we call main verb uses, such as *-s* tensing, use of *do*-forms, and many others. In fact, it is more peculiar that irregular terms do not take *-ed* tensing than that children sometimes assume they do. Eventually, of course, such overregularized uses are inhibited.

Is incorrect *-ed* actively suppressed by a generally stated inhibition, however, or is it more simply prevented on a word-by-word basis? The answer to this question may imply quite different inhibitory mechanisms, and we should consider why this is so.

Let us first discuss a possible generalized inhibition. It is easy to think that in the end, whether or not a term takes *-ed* tensing is completely a matter of unpredictable lexical specification. But there is in fact a highly general additional condition which can be put on the applicability of the *-ed* rule to make its predictive power essentially perfect. That is, it can be applied to any term with main verb characteristics if that term is not specified as taking a non-*ed* form in the same semantic-distributional context in which the *-ed* applies. This means that the rule can be applied to a term unless it is known to have a non-*ed* past form. If a term is not recorded as having such a competing form, it may take the *-ed* rule freely.

There are simpler word-by-word mechanisms which work quite differently. For each word, essentially, the irregular form might finally come to predominate because it is finally heard so much that it simply is the more successful competitor for that word in the past usage context. For *break,* for example, generalized predictors strongly predict *breaked;* specific lexical information predicts *broke.* With time, as the child hears only *broke* in his environment, *broke* will acquire sufficient response strength to always be chosen over the *-ed* form. In short, the *-ed* form will simply fail to generalize. No specific inhibition against its use, either general, of specific to *break,* would be needed. Each irregular verb would undergo its own period of the irregular form coming to dominate.

This simple, in effect purely positive, account has much appeal. But we believe it to be inadequate for a variety of reasons. First, there is really no reason the two forms of past tensing cannot coexist. Many children say forms such as *broked* and *thoughted.* Before overregularizations finally generally vanish and become judged deviant, such doubly tensed forms tend even to grow in frequency and in judged acceptability relative to simpler overregularized forms such as *breaked* and *thinked* (Kuczaj, 1977, 1978a).

Second, we find the explanation unimpressive for another reason. Children may vary in use between regular and irregular forms of various verbs for periods of months—for example, sometimes using *falled,* sometimes using *fell,* (Kuczaj, 1977; Maratsos, 1979). If simple positive strength of the irregular form were sufficient to inhibit overregularization, it should gain such strength without variation persisting for months.

Third, we think it is likely that children do eventually learn the more general prohibition: if a verb has an irregular past form, the regular past marker should not be used. In effect, for example, we claim that if we teach an advanced enough child (or adult) a new verb, and teach him an irregular past form, he will rather automatically not use the regular past form, yet will not require long practice in use of the irregular. This would be because he had a general condition that if a verb takes an irregular, it should automatically not have the *-ed* operation apply to it.

How can we describe such a condition as coming about? The process cannot begin simply because of the absence of linkages between the past tense rule and a number of terms. For overgeneralization has already proceeded for months under these conditions.

The first step we would propose is a new pattern-item mechanism: explicit inhibitory blocks. Essentially, such an inhibitory link would be an explicit specification that lexical item $W_x$ definitely does *not* appear as $X_m$ in $P_i$ $( \ldots X_m \ldots )$. It is not simply the absence of a positive linkage, but the presence of a specified pattern-item block; it might be viewed as a negatively valenced link.

We think there is evidence for such blocks in other parts of the adult grammar. For example, the passive-active correspondence holds for a wide number of terms which have main verb properties and take two arguments. Such terms include not only actional verbs, but also practically all experiencer verbs. Typical passives include *John was liked by most people, this outcome was desired by all citizens, Harriet wasn't seen in the yard,* and so on. Let us assume that the passive *is* productive for experiencer verbs. But then there is a puzzle. The verb *want* certainly denotes an experience, and is semantically and structurally extremely similar to *desire,* which takes the passive. Yet for many speakers, passives with *want* are unacceptable, as, for instance, *\*this coat was wanted by Mary.* One cannot say simply that *want* is unlinked with the passive, since presumably speakers can use terms with constructions they have not heard them linked with. Instead there seems to be a definite individual lexical item-pattern prohibition against using *want* in this way.

How might such prohibitions arise? Suppose speakers keep track of whether a lexical item has been heard to appear in a particular construction, and that novel, generalized uses which the speaker produces do not cause a lexical item-pattern link to be formed. Only hearing someone else use a term in a construction adds linkages in the network. Then *want* is never heard as taking the passive, and never linked with it. On the other hand, *want* is a frequently used term, and many occasions arise in which a speaker might, implicitly, predict its use. This would be so any time the speaker encoded someone's wanting something or someone, which could be encoded by a passive. We will then suppose that some mechanism exists such that if a term constantly encounters situations in which a construction might be used with it, and yet remains unlinked to the construction, some kind of lexical item-pattern tabulator constructs a positive inhibitory block between the term and the pattern. This seems to be as plausible an explanation as any for the failure of *want* to be usable in passives for many speakers.

Let us now suppose that the same process occurs eventually for some irregular verbs and the past tense construction: many terms individually eventually acquire such pattern-term explicit blocks. The next step, we theorize, is that if a pattern has a certain number or proportion of such explicitly specified blocks, distinct from a simple lack of linkage, a special analytic procedure is brought to bear. The point of this procedure is to see whether there is any widespread commonality to explain these pervasive failures. That is, do blocked terms share any common property or properties? If there is, productive generalization is blocked for those terms which have the common characteristic. For irregulars, this commonality is the presence of a competing form in the distributional-semantic environment appropriate for use of the past form. The -ed tensing operation then acquires a general condition upon its use: it cannot apply to terms which have a competitor. But it can remain otherwise unconstrained, and thus productive.

Therefore the past-tense operation may comprise a semantic-distributional pattern, the productivity of which is saved by the possibility of specifying the conditions for its nonapplication in a systematic fashion. To make this claim stronger, we should show evidence of what happens when in fact no systematic commonality can be found to explain a large number of positive exceptions. We believe that a number of cases, both from children's literature and from adult linguistic structures, show that when such a situation is encountered, the productivity of the construction is generally shut down, for either all or a definable subset of the terms to which it might apply. Let us discuss a few of these cases briefly.

*The causative.* Bowerman (1974) has discussed interesting, though very infrequent, errors of the following sort: *\*I falled it down, \*I'm gonna stay it here,* and so on. The implicit regularity from which these follows may be seen in the following pairs: *it opened—John opened it; it moved—John moved it; it spilled—John spilled it; it broke—John broke it.* The regularity may be something like this. Suppose a process verb has an intransitive form denoting a relation of the single NP argument. Then there may also be a transitive, in which the same argument for the verb is put in postverbal position, and an initial argument denotes a causer of the relation. Thus, in *it falled, fall* denotes a change of location of *it;* in *John falled it,* the relation of change of location of *it* still takes place, *it* is an postverbal position, and *John,* the initial argument, denotes the causer.

Certainly many verbs in English show this relation. It may be instantiated as often as the passive-active relation, though not on as wide a variety of verbs. Furthermore, the overgeneralizations shown by Bowerman's examples demonstrate that it may actually reach the positive implicit criteria for generalization. But in the end, adults do not produce such incorrect causatives as *\*I fell it;* the construction is not productive. Why not?

We believe the problem is not that there are not enough verbs which exemplify the possible relation. There are many. Instead, we think what happens is that an internal system of pattern-term connections which predicts the generalized use develops. But after a while, so many individual term-pattern blocks build up that the procedure to search for a commonality among the blockages is signaled. Here, however, none can be found. There really seems to be no good commonality among the many exceptions. The result is a general shutdown of the productive predictive power of the relation.

In the preceding cases, we have been able to depend on reports of children's actually making overgeneralizations as positive evidence that a pattern-term correspondence was at one time predictive, and then positively inhibited. In some of the most interesting adult cases, such strong evidence is not really available. But we think it probable that in many such cases, part of a pattern-term-pattern predictive system remains productive, while other subsets are systematically inhibited from novel prediction to old terms. Such cases have provided great general difficulties in linguistics (as has the causative, in fact [Chomsky, 1965, 1970; Lakoff, 1970]), and at least one or two are quite surprising.

*The passive.* We have heretofore treated the passive-active relation as generally and completely productive. It is clear, however, that it is really not quite so. Many passives are structurally identical with acceptable passives, yet are either unacceptable or, in fact, nearly unintelligible. The following provide examples of some of these: *John was resembled by those old men; *four houses were had by these owners; *Harry was seemed like by Mary; *this problem is entered into by three considerations; *three parts were consisted of by Harry's device.* Structurally, all of these examples are parallel to acceptable passives such as *this conclusion was supported by three considerations,* or *many topics were spoken about by John.*

There is apparently no completely reliable, generally statable condition which predicts such exceptions. For example, *want* fails to passivize freely, despite the fact that nearly all experiencer verbs do so. Possessive *have* fails to take the passive, but possessive *own* does take it (*three houses were owned by those people*). Such facts might lead one to propose that although speakers may be aware of relations between actives and passives, the two constructions do not predict each other productively. Instead, whether a particular verb-argument configuration appears in the passive must have to be marked for each verb individually.

We think such a description would fail to capture what are probably some general productive properties of the relation, however. For certain classes of active sentences, the corresponding passive is freely predictable. For example, there is hardly a single possible passive failing to be acceptable in which the verb denotes an agentive relation, and the *by*-phrase denotes an agent (for instance, *John was talked about by many people; Harry was kissed by a little girl*).[17] Experiencer verb configurations are almost always acceptable, with the apparent single exception of *want*. It is when the passive departs more and more significantly from such structural-semantic configurations that whether or not a verb takes the passive seems to depend on whether it is positively specified as doing so. We would guess that the predictability or suppression of the passive depends on a number of complex factors. Essentially, a certain subset is shut off from productivity systematically. If a verb is not known to take the passive, and falls into this semantic-argument subset, it is not predicted. For other subsets—for example, an agentive or experiencer verb-argument configurations—productivity is essentially free except for very infrequent individual lexical blocks. In effect we are claiming that subsets of the active-passive predictive system are saved for productivity because the problem of nonproductivity is partly isolable in a general way. The passive is thus at least partly productive, unlike the causative, which appears to be completely suppressed.

*Un- adjectives.* The case is similar for many grammatical rules involving *derivational morphology:* the derivation of one word from another. One such rule, for example, is the rule of prefixing *un-* in front of adjectival terms. For past participles related to passives such as *known* or *broken* (*this solution is known, the known solution; the vase has been broken [for years]; the broken vase*) the relation seems to be essentially perfect (*unbroken; unknown; unthought-of*). But for simple adjectives, while many take *un-* (*unsympathetic, unhappy, unintelligent*), many do not (*\*unnice; \*unsad; \*unridiculous*). Interestingly, speakers probably can be shown to know much about the grammar of such unproductive uses. All the deviant cases are interpretable. Furthermore, it is clear that they sound much better than nonterms which result from prefixing *un-* inappropriately to nonadjectivals, such as *\*an unfriend, \*an unsympathy,* or the atrocious *\*he was un-in the house.*

We would guess the complex situation is that for adjectivals which are participles derived from verbs, the use of *un-* is essentially productive. For simple adjectives, what speakers have, in essence, is a rule that "*un-* may be prefixed to a term to denote the negative of the term, if the term is an adjective, and if the term is known to take *un-*." That is, speakers have a nonproductive but generally encoded rule. We also guess that there is a "waiting period" for determination of such nonproductive subsets of a predictive system. One can readily learn to place *un-* before a newly learned adjective. After a period, however, a positive inhibition occurs if the new term is repeatedly encountered but no use of *un-* + term is recorded. This ultimately results in the absolute unacceptability of forms such as *\*unsad, \*unridiculous,* and so on.

Such "generalizations" as the above may hardly seem like general knowledge at all. They imply a form of nonproductive general rules that seem peculiar. Yet if we analyze the situation properly, such rules constitute a surprisingly large amount of the knowledge of an adult speaker. For example, English phrase structure rules specify that verbs may take simple NP complements (*he discussed Mary*), prepositional phrase complements (*he talked about Mary*), or no complement (*he died*). Yet, as is well known, just because a term actually has main verb properties does not mean it will freely take such generally available configurations at all. Many verbs do not take transitive direct objects freely. One cannot say, *he will speak the problem* or *he will think the problem,* even though one can say, *he will discuss the problem* or *he will consider the problem.* Other verbs cannot take prepositional phrase complements (*he blamed for the accident; *he will discuss over the problem*), and so on. In effect, the relation between the regularities captured by the phrase structure rules and the actual state of lexical usage is that the rules say that a term may take these complement configurations, if it has verb properties and furthermore is marked as taking these configurations. Again, we would guess that for the adult speaker, a newly learned verb may be freely learned to take such patterns, though not freely predicted to do so. After a while, if it is not heard in such patterns, the usage is suppressed. The gain afforded by such knowledge is thus not free productivity. The gains might be something such as easier learnability of new usage for new terms compared to what the situation would be if every instance were completely unique. There is also probably greater ease in setting up comprehension and production systems if the general possibilities are limited.

Our discussion of this vast problem must necessarily be inconclusive. There is really little empirical evidence available, and the problem has not been considered seriously enough in the psychological literature, though it has had continuing and deep effects upon formulations in linguistics (Chomsky, 1965, 1970; Lakoff, 1970; Bresnan, 1978). Thus any attempts at beginning to derive psychological developmental accounts must be primitive.

To conclude, however, we have discussed the likely role in controlling overproductivity of the following mechanisms: (1) implicit control through failures to reach generalization criteria in the grammatical system; (2) individual lexical item-pattern blocks; (3) searches for commonalities among blocked connections; (4) general pattern-item blocks applying to a whole construction (the causative) or to subsets of constructions (uses of the passive, uses of *un-*). It seems to us that acquisitional mechanisms must include analytic and representational means for capturing all of these: an account which describes mechanisms only for capturing productive generalization is so seriously incomplete as to be useless, for in the end it must predict that nearly everything generalizes to everything.

## SOME CLOSING REMARKS

Our central point in this chapter could be lost in the detailed and partly inconclusive negative considerations of the preceding pages. That point is the following: part of the specification of the characteristics that define which terms may appear in generalized semantic-distributional patterns include specifications of what other semantic-distributional patterns the same terms may appear in. It may be natural to wish to describe generalized rules as operations upon already available units. But in the case of linguistic rules, we find it to be pervasively true that the developing definitions of the units depends upon which operations on the units are possible. Linguistic rules thus come to be partly self-defining, even though they depend initially for their formulation upon a primitive "language" derived from auditory, conceptual, and sequential analyses available from other areas of cognition.

But even if this primitive language is available from general cognitive capabilities, we have been forced to imply a tremendously complex system of organization, self-definition by mutual uses, and complex inhibitory and analytic systems, simply to account for some no doubt relatively simple linguistic regularities (and irregularities). The necessity of proposing such complex organizations in the child to account for linguistic acquisition may seem to demonstrate the nativist point, that language truly is a system involving organizational principles unique to itself.

As we have proceeded, however, we have become impressed by the profound similarities in the nature of processes to be found in linguistic structure and its acquisition, and other kinds of cognitive structures. The notion of categories as essentially being comprised of the coprediction of a potentially vast number of properties and cooccurrences in the world seems to us a basic tenet of descriptions of general cognitive structure (Rosch, Mervis, Gray, Johnson, & Boyes-Braem, 1976) and of perceptual knowledge such as cross-modal transfer (Bushnell, 1978) as well. Linguistic category specifications seem to involve a partly self-defining system of how uses in the whole system predict other uses in the system. But again one may find profound analogies in the realm of concept formation (Nelson, 1974; Rosch, et al., 1976), and, we think, in social role systems as well. In general, for societal concepts and social roles such as president, or mother and child, or proletariet, it is not the "inherent characteristics" of the person per se that define what we mean by social role. It is rather the whole structure of how social elements function in relation to one another that defines social roles. The notion of "president," for example, seems to us to be essentially a definition by a correlation of social functions, rather than some inherent physical or other property of the person himself or herself. Again, such social notions must build upon primitive analyses. But in the end, we think they come to define each other much as linguistic category uses come to define each other. Language is wonderful for the evident compexities of its combination of primitive defining elements and self-defining characteristics. Yet we believe that appropriate analyses of complex social, cognitive, and perceptual systems would show much of the same analytic structure as linguistic structures. If this were so, language would indeed provide a particularly fertile example for studying the general analytic properties of the mind.

Finally, though this is perhaps a less serious and weighty-sounding consideration, it appears contrary to the ambiance of most strong linguistic nativist accounts that languages are far less well-devised than it seems to us a nativist formulation implies they would be. Linguistic systems do display remarkable characteristics of systematicity and abstractness. But they also contain arbitrary exceptions, idiosyncracies, semigeneralizations, defeated generalizations, and cases such as gender systems, and other large self-defined organizational structures which really have little important function. (We are maintaining, clearly, that arbitrary gender and verb conjugation and noun declension systems are essentially the results of diachronic confusion combined with extreme systematizing tendencies.) These remind us very much of all naturally evolved human cultural systems, such as government bureaucracies, schools of art, and any number of other characteristically human activities. These all likewise display surprising mixtures of impressive generality, rational function, formal beauty, semiregularities, needless self-defined organizations, arbitrary exceptions, and individual idiosyncracies. The case is perhaps best stated by another:

> Grammar, with its mixture of logical rule and arbitrary usage, proposes to a young mind a foretaste of what will be offered to him later on by law and ethics, those sciences of human conduct, and by all the systems wherein man has codified his instinctive experience. (Yourcenar, 1961)

Perhaps the best argument of all for the uniqueness of language would be that language turned out to be a perfectly rational and predictive system. For then language would indeed resemble no other human system of which we know.

## ACKNOWLEDGEMENTS

The preparation of this manuscript was aided by Grant HD 091212 and support from the Center for Research in Human Learning to the senior author, and by Grant NIH 5 TO1 MH 06668 to the second author. We wish to acknowledge helpful comments on preliminary forms of this paper by Melissa Bowerman, Brian MacWhinney, George Miller, Elissa Newport,

Thomas Roeper, and Igzchak Schlesinger, along with helpful comments by many others to verbal presentations of this material.

## NOTES

[1]We use German because of our greater familiarity with it, and because of its particularly clear application to our exposition. Similar arguments obtain in varying degrees for many noun classes, noun declensional classes, and verb conjugations in a wide variety of languages.

[2]We are treating sentence boundary here as a primitive only for descriptive convenience. Though we shall not do so in this chapter, it is in fact possible eventually to describe it in terms of other underlying analytic primitives.

[3]We are implicitly using a terminological abbreviation here. *Arg* refers to the argument of the relational term specified in the description.

[4]Bowerman (1974) reports a few adjective-verb errors, such as *I fulled it up.* Again, these may arise from some adult causative examples, such as *it's open - I'm gonna open it.* She also has noted, typically as *late* occurrences, a very occasional error such as *he terribled me,* an example which will require later discussion.

[5]Some adjectives can also be used in this way, but only with forms of *be* carrying the progressive or imperative markings: *he is being obnoxious, don't be so obnoxious.*

[6]Generally we are viewing copula *be* as a supporting tense morpheme. As Fillmore (1968) and Lyons (1968) note, it has little meaning of its own. For example, it is clear that *is* has much the same function in the sentence *he is aware of it* as does *-s* in *he knows it.* There is, however, one underlying relation which has no relational term involved in its expression, unless copula *be* is considered as such: the relation of attribution of NP characteristics to the initial NP argument. Examples include *this dog - is - a dachshund, John - is - a fool,* and so on.

[7]This particular analysis rests on the assumption that *grutch* is not a peculiar pronunciation of *be,* which can also be the first relational term of an imperative, and does not take main verb properties in general. Note that if one hears a *be*-imperative, one can draw conclusions about the nature of the main relational term. For example, hearing *##be grat!* one can predict uses such as *##he is grat, ##that is a grat person,* and so on.

[8]Two details: (1) we use *-ed* to symbolize the past participle, because that is in fact the most generally used form; (2) the *by*-phrase might actually denote a location for a short passive, as in *he was shot by the O.K. corral.* We are also ignoring the interaction of the passive-active correspondence with many other grammatical constructions, such as *wh*-questioning (e.g., *who was he pushed by,* in which the initial NP argument denotes an agent because *wh*-questioning brought the argument to the front).

[9]We are actually simplifying our description in a perhaps misleading way by use of the terminology *verb* here. Actually, such uses as number agreement, for example, are part of what define what we mean by "verb." The actual description we would give of these data is more complex, and would use more basic primitives than those we use here for convenience.

[10]It should be noted that in adult Italian, pragmatic variables do play a more important role in the ordering of constituents than in English, so that Bates's subjects' fixed order was not necessarily more advanced.

[11]All adjectives which take the progressive are agentive, process-denoting adjectives.

[12]Prototype theories do not dictate a single mode of description of a given conceptual realm. In particular, the purely semantic-based prototypical theory considered here is not isomorphic with the prototypical possibilities discussed by deVilliers in this volume for the representation of syntactic categories. In her account, participation in semantic-distributional patterns such as tensing and negation patterns may comprise part of the basic prototypical

description of a particular grammatical category. It is likely that the manner in which such a clustering of category characteristics comes about is essentially the same as that proposed in this chapter for syntactic category representation. The prototype theory hypothetically considered here is a far more radically semantically based one than deVilliers presents, in that grammatical operations are controlled and in general represented by the semantic qualities of terms and phrases. Bates and MacWhinney (1978), for example, appear to propose such a theory.

[13]Proponents of such a hypothetical prototype theory might wish to try to circumvent this problem by claiming that these terms are so peripheral or deviant—are such "bad" members of the class—that actually the label of state term membership really only means "treat this deviant member as if it were a state term for grammatical purposes." This, however, will not eliminate the contradiction. For what does it mean to treat the term "as if it were a state term"? Taken literally such a direction could immediately prevent its participation in the imperative and progressive constructions. Thus the role would instead have to be repeatedly qualified, until it ultimately was reduced to a restatement of the situation as it actually occurs. Such a definition could ultimately rely only on correlated grammatical privileges and any hope of a semantic definition of form class membership would have to be abandoned.

[14]Proponents of this hypothetical prototypical view might attempt one last argument. Suppose *adjective* really = 'state,' and it is the verb *be* which is marked as + process or + agentive. Thus *be* would be represented as semantically transparent, becoming + agentive and + process according to the meaning of the relational term which it precedes. Such an argument entails the following difficulty: *be* only shows such semantic "transparency," resulting in the *-ing* and imperative constructions when it appears in front of *certain* relational terms (adjectives). One would have to be able to represent the appropriate class of terms with which it could so cooccur. This category of relational terms would have to be represented, generally, as the + state category. But it is only the + agentive, + process members of this class which would confer upon *be* the + agentive, + process meaning—a fact which would have to be represented in the general representation of the rules. Therefore the relevant category of relational terms would have to be represented as + state, + process, and + agentive all at once just as before.

Essentially, we cannot list all such possible prototypical "solutions" and their difficulties here, but every one we can devise eventually becomes incoherent or unworkable in its attempts to preserve the representation of form class according to the statistically most common semantic characteristics of the class alone, if one seriously tries to see how such rules would work.

[15]Similarly, in Japanese, there is a morphology for the marking of the different kinds of shapes of objects. It is used *only* on *numbers*. One must mark number expressions such as "one," "two" for the shape of the thing counted; nothing else is marked. Again, there results some disambiguation in a few situations. But such systems strike us mostly as cheerfully undirected waste of channel resources; from this we once more draw the conclusion that the system is not one of dearth, but wealth.

[16]Elsewhere the senoir author (Maratsos, 1979) indicated a preference for implicit-analogical schemes of rule representation and use, because of their greater theoretical parsimony. At that time, he mentioned briefly problems with such systems in handling a few complex constructions such as sentence embedding and *wh*-question preposing. What was not understood was the inability of such analogical systems to cope with basic phenomena such as obligatory usage even for relatively simple rules such as tensing, along with many other problems not exposited here.

[17]Actually, we have encountered one active verb which so fails: *get.* Unacceptable examples include **many pets were gotten by parents for their children.* *Get* is a very frequently used verb; this we claim will be the case for any simple lexical exception to a generally productive construction.

# REFERENCES

Antinucci, F. & Parisi, D. Early language acquisition: A model and some data. *In* C. A. Ferguson & D. I. Slobin (Eds.), *Studies of child language development.* New York: Holt, Rinehart & Winston, 1973.

Bates, E. & MacWhinney, B. Functionalism and grammatical categories. Paper presented at the conference, Language Acquisition—The State of the Art, University of Pennsylvania, Philadelphia, May 1978.

Becker, J. & Maratsos, M. Development of comprehension of the passive. Paper presented at the biennial meeting of the Society for Research in Child Development, San Francisco, March 1979.

Bellugi. U. The acquisition of negation. Unpublished doctoral dissertation, Harvard University, 1967.

Bellugi, U. Simplification in children's language. *In* R. Huxley & E. Ingram (Eds.), *Language acquisition: Models and methods.* New York: Academic Press, 1971.

Berko, J. The child's learning of English morphology. *Word,* 1958, 14, 150–177.

Bloom, L. *Language development: Form and function in emerging grammars.* Cambridge, Mass.: M.I.T. Press, 1970.

Bloom, L. (Ed.). *Readings in language development.* New York: John Wiley & Sons, 1978.

Bloom, L., Lightbown, P., & Hood, L. Structure and variation in child language. *Monographs of the Society for Research in Child Development,* 1975, 40 (2, Serial No. 160).

Bowerman, M. *Early syntactic development: A cross-linguistic study with special reference to Finnish.* London: Cambridge University Press, 1973.

Bowerman, M. Learning the structure of causative verbs: A study in the relationship of cognitive, semantic and syntactic development. Committee on Linguistics, Stanford University, *Papers and Reports on Child Language Development,* April 1974, 142–178.

Bowerman, M. Semantic factors in the acquisition of rules for word use and sentence construction. *In* D. M. Morehead & A. E. Morehead (Eds.), *Normal and deficient child language.* Baltimore: University Park Press, 1976.

Bowerman, M. The acquisition of rules governing "possible lexical items": Evidence from spontaneous speech errors. Stanford University Department of Linguistics, *Papers and Reports on Child Language Development,* 1977, 13, 148–156.

Braine, M. D. S. On two types of models of the internalization of grammars. *In* D. I. Slobin (Ed.), *The ontogenesis of grammar.* New York: Academic Press, 1971.

Braine, M. D. S. Children's first word combinations. *Monographs of the Society for Research in Child Development,* 1976, 41 (1, Serial No. 164).

Bresnan, J. A realistic transformational grammar. *In* M. Halle, G. A. Miller, & J. Bresnan (Eds.), *Linguistic theory and psychological reality.* Cambridge, Mass.: M.I.T. Press, 1978.

Brown, R. *A first language: The early stages.* Cambridge, Mass.: Harvard University Press, 1973.

Bushnell, E. The ontogeny of intermodal relations: Vision and touch in infancy. Unpublished manuscript, 1978.

Cazden, Courtney, B. The acquisition of noun and verb inflections. *Child Development,* 1968, 39, 433–448.

Chomsky, N. *Aspects of the theory of syntax.* Cambridge, Mass.: M.I.T. Press, 1965.

Chomsky, N. Remarks on nominalization. *In* R. A. Jacobs & P. S. Rosenbaum (Eds.), *Readings in English transformational grammar.* Waltham, Mass.: Ginn & Co., 1970.

Chomsky, N. *Reflecting on language.* New York: Pantheon, 1975.

deVilliers, J. G. & deVilliers, P. A. *Language acquisition.* Cambridge, Mass.: Harvard University Press, 1978.

Ervin, S. M. Imitation and structural change in children's language. *In* E. H. Lenneberg (Ed.). *New directions in the study of language.* Cambridge, Mass.: M.I.T. Press, 1964.

Fava, E., & Tirondola, G. *Syntactic and pragmatic regularities in Italian child discourse: Grammatical relations and word order.* Institute d: Glottologia, Italy. Unpublished manuscript, 1977.

Fillmore, C. J. The case for case. *In* E. Bach & R. Harms (Eds.), *Universals in linguistic theory.* New York: Holt, Rinehart & Winston, 1968.

Gleason, Henry A. *An introduction to descriptive linguistics* (rev. ed.). New York: Holt, Rinehart & Winston, 1961.

Harris, Z. S. *Methods in structural linguistics.* Chicago: University of Chicago Press, 1951.

Hopmann, M. R. & Maratsos, M. A developmental study of factivity and negation in complex syntax. *Journal of Child Language,* 1978, 5, 295–309.

Johnson, C. N. & Maratsos, M. P. Early comprehension of mental verbs: *Think* and *know. Child Development,* 1977, 48, 1747–1751.

Keenan, E. Remarkable subjects in Malagasy. *In* C. Li (Ed.), *Subject and Topic.* New York: Academic Press, 1976.

Kuczaj, S. A. The acquisition of regular and irregular past tense forms. *Journal of Verbal Learning and Verbal Behavior,* 1977, 16, 589–600.

Kuczaj, S. A. Children's judgments of grammatical and ungrammatical irregular past-tense verbs. *Child Development,* 1978a, 49, 319–328.

Kuczaj, S. A. Why do children fail to overgeneralize the progressive inflection? *Journal of Child Language,* 1978b, 5, 167–171.

Lakoff, G. *Irregularity in syntax.* New York: Holt, Rinehart & Winston, 1970.

Lakoff, G. On generative semantics. *In* D. D. Steinberg & L. A. Jakobovits (Eds.), *Semantics: An interdisciplinary reader in philosophy, linguistics and psychology.* London: Cambridge University Press, 1971.

Leopold, W. F. *Speech development of a bilingual child: A linguist's record. Vol. 4, Diary from age 2.* Evanston, Ill.: Northwestern University Press, 1949.

Li, C. N. (Ed.) *Subject and topic.* New York: Academic Press, 1976.

Lohnes, F. W. F., & Strothmann, W. F. *German: A structural approach.* New York: Norton, 1967.

Lyons, J. *Introduction to theoretical linguistics.* London: Cambridge University Press, 1968.

Maratsos, M. P. How to get from words to sentences. *In* D. Aaronson & R. J. Rieber (Eds.), *Psycholinguistic research: Implications and applications.* Hillsdale, N. J.: Lawrence Erlbaum Assoc., 1979.

Maratsos, M., Kuczaj, S. A., Fox, D. E. C., & Chalkley, M. A. Some empirical studies in the acquisition of transformational relations. *In* W. A. Collins (Ed.), *The Minnesota Symposium on Child Psychology* (Vol. 12). Hillsdale, N. J.: Lawrence Erlbaum Assoc., 1979.

McCawley, J. D. Semantic representation. *In* P. L. Garvin (Ed.), *Cognition: A multiple view.* New York: Spartan Books, 1970.

McNeill, D. Developmental psycholinguistics. *In* F. Smith & G. A. Miller (Eds.), *The genesis of language.* Cambridge, Mass.: M.I.T. Press, 1966.

MacWhinney, B. The acquisition of morphonology. *Monographs of the Society for Research in Child Development,* 1978 (Serial No. 174).

Miller, G. A. Paper presented at the Lenneberg Symposium, Cornell University, Ithaca, 1976.

Miller, W. R. & Ervin, S. M. The development of grammar in child language. *In* U. Bellugi & R. Brown (Eds.), *The acquisition of language.* Chicago: University of Chicago Press, 1964.

Nelson, K. Concept, word, and sentence: Interrelations in acquisition and development. *Psychological Review,* 1974, 81, 267–285.

Nelson, K. Some attributes of adjectives used by young children. *Cognition,* 1976, 4, 13–30.

Rosch, E. H. On the internal structure of perceptual and semantic categories. *In* T. E. Moore (Ed.), *Cognitive development and the acquisition of language.* New York: Academic Press, 1973.

Rosch, E. H. & Mervis, C. B. Family resemblances: Studies in the internal structure of categories. *Cognitive Psychology,* 1975, 7, 573–605.

Rosch, E., Mervis, C. B., Gray, W. D., Johnson, D. M., & Boyes-Braem, P. Basic objects in natural categories. *Cognitive Psychology,* 1976, 8, 382–439.

Schlesinger, I. M. Production of utterances and language acquisition. *In* D. I. Slobin (Ed.), *The ontogenesis of grammar.* New York: Academic Press, 1971.

Slobin, D. I. Developmental psycholinguistics. *In* F. Smith & G. A. Miller (Eds.), *The genesis of language.* Cambridge, Mass.: M.I.T. Press, 1966.

Slobin, D. I. On the learning of morphological rules: A reply to Palermo and Eberhardt. *In* D. I. Slobin (Ed.), *The ontogenesis of grammar.* New York: Academic Press, 1971.

Slobin, D. I. Cognitive prerequisites for the development of grammar. *In* C. A. Ferguson & D. I. Slobin (Eds.), *Studies of child language development.* New York: Holt, Rinehart & Winston, 1973.

Smith, M. E. Grammatical errors in the speech of preschool children. *Child Development,* 1933, 4, 183–190.

Stern, G. *Meaning and change of meaning.* Bloomington: Indiana University Press, 1964. (Originally published in German, 1931).

Tanz, C. Learning how *it* works. Department of Linguistics, Stanford University, *Papers and Reports on Child Language Development,* September 1975, 10.

Yourcenar, M. *The memoirs of Hadrian.* New York: Farrar, Strauss, 1961.

Zakharova, A. V. Acquisition of forms of grammatical case by preschool children. *In* C. A. Ferguson & D. I. Slobin (Eds.), *Studies of child language development.* New York: Holt, Rinehart & Winston, 1973.

# 4

# BILINGUAL CHILDREN: SOME INTERPRETATIONS OF COGNITIVE AND LINGUISTIC DEVELOPMENT[1]

## KATHRYN J. LINDHOLM

Bilingualism is a worldwide phenomenon. Since only six of the more than three thousand languages in the world are spoken by 100 million people (Williams, 1978), millions of individuals must learn more than one language. In the United States, one-tenth of the population over four years of age reports knowing a second language (U.S. Bureau of the Census, 1975). In spite of the fact that bilingualism is a universal phenomenon, little is known about the sociolinguistic, linguistic, cognitive, or social variables that are important in bilingualism. Nor do we have a clear conception of the developmental process underlying bilingual language development or the effects of child bilingualism on cognitive development.

The purpose of this chapter is to provide more insight into the process of duo-language acquisition in children. In order to accomplish this goal, we must first define what we mean by bilingualism. Proceeding the definition will be a review of the literature on bilingual language acquisition. This review will introduce the major issues involved in child bilingualism and integrate the findings of all available studies on bilingual children. Finally, the methodologies and results from a program of research which has investigated each of the major issues in child bilingualism will be presented. It is hoped that these results will provide a clearer understanding of the process of bilingual language acquisition.

## Bilingualism Defined

The term bilingual is derived from the medieval Latin adjective *lingualis,* which was a derivative of the Latin word *lingua,* meaning tongue. Although bilingual literally means two tongues, or the speaking of two languages, it is often used to refer to people who, although they do not speak two languages, are able to speak one and understand a second. Haugen (1956) offers a definition of bilingualism based on its literal meaning: a bilingual must be able to produce utterances in another language which are complete and meaningful. A less restrictive definition has been suggested by Macnamara (1967), who interprets a bilingual as someone who possesses one or more of the following skills in a second language: ability to speak, listen, read, or write. Each of these skills requires either encoding or decoding semantic, syntactic, and lexical information. Furthermore, the bilingual must be familiar with the phonemic system for the purposes of listening and speaking, and the graphemic system for reading and writing. To accommodate children into a definition of bilingualism, we can combine and adapt Haugen's and Macnamara's definitions; that is, to consider bilingual any child who is able to understand and/or produce meaningful utterances which contain semantic, syntactic, lexical, and phonemic components in a second language.[2]

Two types of childhood bilingual acquisition processes can be distinguished: simultaneous and successive. In simultaneous acquisition, the child is exposed to two languages from birth, usually with the mother speaking one language and the father speaking a different one. Successive acquisition involves the child's acquisition of one language from birth and at some later point in time, a second one. The age at which the second language is acquired is important because preschool children who acquire a second language are usually considered to be simultaneous bilinguals.

## OVERVIEW OF RESEARCH ON CHILD BILINGUALISM

In a compilation of the child bilingualism literature only 250 articles or books were located which dealt with the topic (Padilla, Romero, & Lindholm, 1978). Of the 79 reports which were empirical investigations of children's language development, only 47 articles discussed infant or preschool children's simultaneous acquisition of their two languages. In the only remaining materials which were even tangentially related empirical studies, the authors looked at the relationship of bilingualism to cognition, intelligence, language attitudes, personality, and acculturation, or they presented tests which can be used to assess bilingual language acquisition. The rest of the literature consists of essays or reviews of literature on some aspect of bilingualism sans data.

Three main issues emerge from the child bilingualism literature. The first one concerns the process of duo-language acquisition. To study this process, corpora of bilingual children's naturalistic speech samples are collected over a lengthy period of time and then examined for either phonological, lexical, syntactic, and/or semantic development. The analysis of the children's speech usually raises the second issue, that of "linguistic interference." There are a number of articles which discuss the interference between the two languages at the phonological, lexical, or syntactic level. Several of these articles are impressionistic and anecdotal, relying on personal observations. Rarely is "linguistic interference" the focus of study in naturalistic studies, but it is usually discussed. The third issue pertains to the relationship of bilingualism to cognitive development. A relatively new issue, cognitive development is experimentally studied in an attempt to determine whether the process of cognitive development is influenced by a child's acquisition of two languages. This issue has in part emanated from the studies which found that the IQ of bilingual children was lower than monolingual children's IQ. In the 1960s, Lambert and his coworkers began to study cognitive flexibility in Canadian French-English bilingual children. Several other researchers have followed the lead with empirical inquiry into the cognitive processes of bilingual children (e.g., Ben-Zeev, 1975, 1977a, 1977b; Worrall, 1970, 1972).

Since the process and interference issues are studied naturalistically and the cognitive development issue is investigated experimentally, the literature will be reviewed in terms of the type of methodology that was used to collect the data; that is, naturalistic or experimental.

## NATURALISTIC STUDIES

The naturalistic studies are usually of three types: (1) intensive longitudinal case studies of one child, usually by a linguist parent, (2) studies of several children over some shorter period of time, and (3) informative but somewhat impressionistic studies of chidren with the limited data gathered by the parents or friends.

The earliest studies of child bilingualism were carried out in Europe (Emlich, 1938; Pavlovitch, 1920; Ronjat, 1913). Ronjat studied his French- and German-speaking child from birth to five years. He reported that the child was essentially unilingual in both languages. That is, there was very little interference and the acquisition of syntax, morphology, and phonemics was similar in both languages. Ronjat noted that his child was able to speak both languages quite fluently, a finding he attributed to the strategy used by Ronjat and his wife, *une personne-une langue* ("one person-one language").

Pavlovitch recorded his son's acquisition of French and Serbian from infancy to two years of age. Using the same strategy, one person-one language, enabled the child to acquire the phonemic systems of both languages without confusion. There was an initial period of lexical confusion, but by two years of age, Pavlovitch reported that his child was aware that he was bilingual. This study suffers from being terminated too soon, leaving unanswered questions regarding the child's further development in the two languages.

Geissler (1938) reported on the linguistic development of several bilingual children in Belgrade. Although his data were gathered unsystematically and his results impressionistic, it is interesting that he found bilingual children who could master up to four languages without apparent confusion and interference.

At the same time, Emlich (1938) was studying her German- and Bulgarian-speaking child. The child acquired the phonemic, lexical, and syntactic components of each language and spoke both languages with ease.

The most exhaustive study on the linguistic aspects of bilingual language acquisition continues to be that of Leopold (1939, 1947, 1949a, 1949b). In his detailed diary study, Leopold collected language samples from his German- and English-speaking infant daughter, Hildegard, over a four-year period. Not only did Leopold include precise notes on context, phonological, lexical, syntactic, and semantic development, but he also added comments on any problems he felt Hildegard had in acquiring two languages simultaneously. After careful analysis of Hildegard's speech, Leopold found "very few effects of bilingualism" (p. 187, 1949a).

Like Leopold, Burling (1959) recorded language samples from his English- and Garo-speaking infant over a two-year period. From his analysis of the child's use of phonemes, morphology, syntax, and semantics in the two languages, Burling found vowel but not consonant differentiation. In addition, he observed that the morphological development was more extensive in Garo than in English. Moreover, the child used Garo morphology and syntax with English lexical items and vice versa. The child's language input was not totally differentiated since adults in the child's environment appeared to mix their languages frequently. Nevertheless, Burling found that once his son did have two linguistic systems, they "never appeared to interfere with each other" (p. 68).

In another study where the parents did not employ the strategy "one person-one language" but instead mixed their presentations of French and German, the child was reported to mix the two languages (Tabouret-Keller, 1962). In fact, Tabouret-Keller noted that this child mixed 60 percent of her utterances and produced 20 percent French utterances and 20 percent of German ones. Although the child's parents spoke French two-thirds of the time and German one-third, her playmates spoke German, accounting for the equivalent amount of German output. This study was terminated prior to the child's third birthday, and thus further development is unknown.

In each of these studies, the children were able to differentiate the phonemic systems of both languages easily. Several other researches have documented this result with many different language combinations (Engel, 1965; Mazeika, 1971; Metraux, 1965; Murrell, 1966; Oksaar, 1970; Totten, 1960). However, Rūķe-Draviņa (1965) Zaręba (1953) reported that their bilingual children assimilated a sound from the subordinate language similar to a sound in the dominant language. This result led Rūķe-Draviņa to conclude that the closer two languages are phonologically, the more interference there will be between the two languages.

At the morphological and syntactic levels there have also been reports of interference. Oksaar (1970) and Engel (1965) found that their children attached the inflections of one language onto stems in the second language. Grammatical as well as semantic relations appear to emerge earlier in the language in which the structure is less complex. Imedadze (1967) reported that the genitive and instrumental cases appeared at the same time. The equivalent development was attributed to the fact that these cases express the same semantic notion in both languages and have the same level of difficulty in acquisition. On the other hand, the linguistically more complex subject-to-object relation in Georgian was acquired after the simpler Russian form. Similarily, Mikés (1967) found that the Serbo-Croatian locative terms were acquired after the Hungarian terms as a result of the greater complexity of the surface features required for expressing locative concepts in Serbo-Croatian.

In a psycholinguistic study of four French/English bilingual children, Swain (1972) found that the process of interrogative acquisition was similar in the two languages but that the bilingual children's acquisition was about four to five months behind the monolingual children's acquisition of interrogatives. Swain attributed her results to the fact that the bilingual children had twice as much to learn as the monolingual children.

Volterra and Taeschner (1978) employed a "stage" approach to describe the development of their two Italian/German bilingual children. In stage one, the children had one undifferentiated system which included words from both languages. By stage two, the children distinguished two lexical systems but possessed only one syntactic system for both languages. In the third stage, the children were able to differentiate their two languages at the lexical and syntactic levels. Both Leopold (1949a) and Imedadze (1967) have reported similar conclusions. That is, the bilingual child first speaks a nondifferentiated language composed of both language systems and only gradually differentiates the two languages. The age at which this differentiation occurs varies from 1;8 (Imedadze, 1967) to 2;9 (Volterra & Taeschner, 1978). Bergman (1976) has provided a very convincing argument against this hypothesis suggesting initial nondifferentiation followed by gradual distinction. She posits three hypotheses which could account for the overextension of the structure of one language on the structure of the second language. The Mish Mash Hypothesis states that the children only have one undifferentiated system as Imedadze, Leopold, and Volterra and Taeschner claim. The Interference Hypothesis indicates that the child will impose the system of one language on the system of the other. This case usually is related to second language learning where the child already has established one language system. The rules of the first language system serve as a foundation for the second language until the rules of the second language are learned. Finally, the Independent Development Hypothesis (IDH), which was found to explain her data of overextension, can be summarized as follows:

> In cases of simultaneous language acquisition, each language will develop independently of the other, reflecting the acquisition of that language by monolingual children, unless it is the case that the lines between the two languages are not clearly drawn in the linguistic environment of the child. In such a case, which may be caused by code-switching patterns in the bilingual community or by deviations in the adult language of the child's environment from the norm in the monolingual community, the child will sort out the two systems according to the input that he receives.
>
> The resulting grammar developed under these conditions may have interference-like features, but in each case the cause may be traced to the linguistic input and not the child's inability to keep the two languages separate. (p. 94)

For example, Bergman discusses the acquisition of the possessive in English and Spanish. On the surface it would appear that the child has only one possessive system because she overextended the English's construction into Spanish (e.g., *"Es Ani's libro"*) where the sentence should be *"Es el libro de Ani."* In addition, she would use English sentences such as, "That's the book of Annie," which corresponded to the Spanish sentence. Bergman draws on Slobin's (1973) language universals to show how the child is overgeneralizing a construction within Spanish rather than across languages from English to Spanish. Further, she attributes the structures with interference-like properties to language input and the child's linguistic environment.

The role of language input can be assessed to some extent by noting the amount of mixing in the above studies. The smallest amount of mixing was observed in a language environment in which the parents used the strategy of one person-one language, while the largest amount of mixing appears to occur in language environments in which there is no language differentiation (Tabouret-Keller, 1962). Smith's (1935) study of Chinese/English bilinguals confirms the importance of separate input in the two languages. Smith studied eight children from the same family. These children did not appear to have received differentiated input since the mother spoke mostly English. However, she increased her use of Chinese at times for two of the younger children. Also, two of the older children spent a great deal of time in the United States and received largely English input while the younger children heard more Chinese. All of the children reportedly mixed their languages frequently, but the younger children appeared to confuse the two languages. Thus, the one person-one language strategy seems to produce bilingual children who are able to distinguish their two languages very early.

Sociolinguistic reports of how children use their two languages also provide evidence that children are able from an early age to separate their two linguistic systems. Ronjat (1913), Oksaar (1970), Fantini (1974), and Bergman (1976, 1977) have each reported that the children learn the sociolinguistic rules which require them to respond in the correct language according to interlocutor and setting. Fantini describes his son's sociolinguistic distinctions of language use as follows:

> The first signs of switching occurred within a few days of Mario's first production of English utterances. At this time he was visiting relatives with his parents and nursemaid in Philadelphia. This visit was previously described wherein Mario acquired many new lexical items and almost immediately began to sort them into sets—one for use with his parents and caretaker, the other with his grandparents and other relatives. The circumstances were quite clear—of the ten to twelve people with whom the child interacted, some used one code, some used another. Appropriate code choice depended entirely upon the interlocutor. During the next two months, Mario's world consisted primarily of home and the nursery. At home, Spanish was the medium; at the nursery, it was English. Again the division of language use was clear, marked this time by place (or setting) in addition to interlocutors. Since this was a time of rapid acquisition, some mixing of codes occurred. However, interference occurred in only one direction—from English to Spanish. At home, Mario was prone to use the new words and expressions he learned at the nursery; on the other hand the nursery attendant reported that he used no Spanish with the other children. The utterances which Mario carried into the home were primarily commands, salutations, a demonstrative, and various expressive interjections common to children this age, such as "unhuh," "yuk," and "ouch". . . . During this period of limited language, Mario apparently drew upon all of the linguistic resources available to him, knowing his parents understood both languages. However, when necessary, he also demonstrated ability to use only one language without borrowings. This was illustrated in the earlier account of his conduct with the little girl he met at the shopping center. On this occasion at age 2;8 he spoke only English. The account is also important because it was the first time in which two variables (interlocutor *and* setting) had potential influence on the choice of code, by contrast with the incident in Philadelphia where only the interlocutor was a factor to consider, the setting being constant. (pp. 81–82)

Thus, the child must acquire the sociolinguistic as well as linguistic rules of each language. Experimental studies have begun to provide some interesting information on the process of linguistic rule acquisition as well as the cognitive dimensions of bilingual acquisition.

## EXPERIMENTAL STUDIES

Most of the experimental studies which deal with bilingual children are merely tests of their language development (e.g., Carrow, 1971; Van Metre, 1972) or of their intelligence (e.g., Peal & Lambert, 1962). Few of the studies actually contain an experimental manipulation. Those that do contain a manipulation of independent variables are usually studies of teaching techniques (Lim, 1968; Perinpanayagam, 1973; Spolsky & Holm, 1971; Stockfelt-Hoatson, 1977; Titone, 1975; Woods, 1971) or of the language development of children learning a second language in school (e.g., Lambert, Just, & Segalowitz, 1970; Lambert & Macnamara, 1969).

The majority of experimental studies of bilingual children's language development focus on phonological or syntactic development. For the most part, the phonological studies concentrate on assessing grade school children who are learning a second language, usually English. When compared with monolingual children, these successive bilinguals are described as having articulation problems or language handicaps (Axelrod, 1974; McCarthy, 1946, 1954; Riley, 1972; Travis, Johnson, & Shover, 1937; Troike, 1972). However, if these children are bilingually instructed, they develop a distinctive sensitivity for second language sound sequences by the third grade (Davine, Tucker, & Lambert, 1971). Cuban children who were simultaneous and early successive bilinguals (between one and six years of age) and who lived in the United States for five to eight years had a high probability of achieving a nativelike pronounciation of English (Asher & Garcia, 1969).

Carrow (1957, 1971) developed the Test for Auditory Comprehension of Language (TACL) in English and Spanish to assess Mexican-American bilingual children's language acquisition. She found that these children had delayed language development in specific areas but that their language skills increased with age. Rueda and Perozzi (1977) administered the Spanish version of the TACL and the receptive portion of the Screening Test of Spanish Grammar to Spanish/English bilingual children to determine the correlation between these two assessment instruments. The correlation obtained between the 24 syntactic items that were common to both tests was not significant. Rueda and Perozzi attributed the nonsignificance to problems inherent in the tests and they offered a critique of the TACL.

Several studies have assessed the acquisition of syntactic elements in bilingual children (Brisk, 1972, 1976; Hamayan, Markman, Pelletier, &

Tucker, 1976; Johnson, 1973; Keller, 1976; Kessler, 1971). The acquisition of Spanish grammatical gender was investigated by Brisk (1976). She gave first-grade Spanish/English bilingual children two tests of gender and found that they had not fully acquired grammatical gender. Brisk reported that the bilingual child has the same kind of difficulties as monolingual Spanish-speaking children. Thus, the development of Spanish grammatical gender appears to be similar in monolingual and bilingual children.

In comparing monolingual English-speaking and Spanish- and English-speaking bilingual children on their performance on reversible actives and reversible passives, Keller (1976) reported that the bilingual children were equally proficient in their active constructions. Furthermore, the bilingual children used the same overgeneralization of active voice strategy, which had the same effect of deteriorating the performance with passives, as the monolingual children. However, the onstart of the deterioration process was later in the bilinguals and there was a slower recovery of passives than with the monolinguals. Keller attributed these differences to possible interference between English and Spanish passives and possibly to the different socioeconomic levels between the monolinguals and the bilinguals.

In Young's (1974) study of syntax acquisition, he found that interlanguage interference caused the persistence of errors with negatives, lack of inversion in questions, and the use of "no" in questions. However, Dulay and Burt (1974a, 1974b) analyzed the error speech of five- to eight-year-old Spanish/English bilingual children and found that the children did not appear to apply their first language habits in the process of learning their second language. Only 4.7 percent of the errors reflected Spanish interference while 87.1 percent of the errors reflected the same developmental structures used by monolingual children learning English.

Ervin-Tripp (1974), Boyd (1974), and Kessler (1971) have found that the developmental process for first and second language acquisition are similar. Ervin-Tripp compared the processes of first and second language acquisition in a group of English-speaking children acquiring French. Results indicated that the comprehension of syntax in the first and second languages followed the same order. Similar results were obtained by Kessler (1971) in her study of Spanish/English bilingual children. She gave the children production and comprehension tests focusing on similar and dissimilar syntactic structures across and between languages. It was found that similar structures in the two languages were acquired in the same order and at the same rate. For divergent structures, the most linguistically complex structures were acquired last.

In sum, it appears that regardless of whether the child is a simultaneous or successive bilingual, the process of acquisition is structurally similar for the two languages. For simultaneous bilinguals, the rate of acquisition will differ depending on the complexity of the structures (Slobin, 1973), a conclusion which was drawn in the previous section on naturalistic studies. Thus, the process of monolingual and bilingual language acquisition is similar, and bilingualism does not appear to entail serious language difficulties for most bilingual children.

Leaving linguistic development aside, several studies have concerned themselves with the question of whether bilingualism affects cognitive or intellectual development. To determine the effect of bilingualism upon intellectual development, bilingual children have been given IQ tests and their scores have been compared with monolingual children's scores.

Although some studies find bilinguals to score significantly lower than monolinguals overall (Jones & Stewart, 1951; Saer, 1923; Smith, 1923; Yoshioka, 1929), other research indicates that bilinguals only score lower in the verbal portions of the intelligence tests (Barke, 1933; Kittell, 1959). Many investigators explain that the results showing superior performance of monolinguals should be interpreted with caution because many environmental factors, such as socioeconomic status or lack of test sophistication, can serve to lower scores (Anastasi & Cordova, 1953; Carlson & Henderson, 1950; Jones, 1960; Yoshika, 1929). A few studies report no difference between bilingual and monolingual functioning (Hill, 1936, Murdoch, Maddon, & Berg, 1928; Pinter & Arsenian, 1937). Barke (1933), Cummins and Gulutsan (1974), and Peal and Lambert (1962) have found bilinguals to excell monolinguals in (portions of) tests of intelligence.

Landry (1974) and Torrance, Gowan, and Aliohi (1970) have reported that bilinguals are more creative and better able to reorganize relations and concepts. In a well-controlled study on a series of intellectual tasks, Peal and Lambert (1962) found that monolingual children possessed a unitary structure of intelligence that they applied to all intellectual tasks. In contrast, bilingual children were more flexible in their approach to the tasks which resulted in superior concept formation and a more heterogeneous pattern of cognitive abilities. Peal and Lambert attributed the enhanced creativity of bilinguals in part to their ability to "conceptualize environmental events in terms of their general properties without reliance on their [being encoded into] linguistic symbols" (p. 14).

Studies of cognitive development (Bruner, 1964; Piaget, 1974) have indicated that early word-object separation is important for further cognitive and intellectual development. Detailed investigations of bilingual children's speech have shown that bilingual children are able to separate the word from its referent at an earlier age than monolingual children (Fantini, 1974; Leopold, 1939). Similar results have been obtained in experimental studies (Feldman & Shen, 1971; Ianco-Worrall, 1972). Feldman and Shen compared monolingual and bilingual children's performance on cognitive tasks such as object constancy, naming, and sentence construction. These tasks required the children to separate the word from its referent. Results indicated that the bilingual children excelled the monolingual children. Feldman and Shen concluded that the presence of two language codes facilitates the shift from the notion of meaning as a referent to the notion of meaning as a function of use, which enables the child to have a more abstract concept of language, or metalanguage.

In order to test whether child bilingualism results in accelerated development in specific areas of cognitive functioning and cognitive flexibility, Ianco-Worrall (1972) compared four- to six- and seven- to nine-year-old bilingual Afrikaans/English- and monolingual Afrikaans- and English-speaking children on various tasks. These tasks included measures of semantic and phonemic preference and the degree of interchangeability of object names when used in isolation and play situations. Results indicated a semantic preference in the four- to six-year-old bilinguals, but not the monolinguals. Also, both age groups of bilinguals were superior at interchanging object names in isolation but no difference was found for play situations. Similarly, there were no significant differences between monolingual and bilingual children on the psychological functioning tasks. It appears that methodological problems may have influenced the results and masked any significant differences. Despite the absence of significant results, the trends demonstrated superior cognitive flexibility in bilingual children.

Other studies have looked at bilingual children's problem-solving strategies (Bain, 1974; Ben-Zeev, 1977a). In tests of mathematical ability, Bain found that French-English and German-English bilinguals were superior in making verbal analogies and in their sensitivity to emotional expression than matched groups of monolinguals aged five years to adult.

Ben-Zeev (1977a) approached the study of cognitive development from a different angle than any of the above studies. She cited Stern's (1919) contention that there are positive and negative aspects to bilingualism; on the negative side it leads to interference, and on the positive side it leads to individual acts of thought. Ben-Zeev maintained that these are not two separate effects but that it is the interference which is the stimulus to the individual acts of thought. Thus, the interference between the two languages causes the child to develop coping strategies which accelerate linguistic and cognitive development. Three major hypotheses were tested: (1) highly bilingual children process syntactic rules with special flexibility, (2) highly bilingual children exhibit precocious development of categorical associations, and (3) the child's knowledge of the systematic basis of linguistic structural features extends to an enhanced ability to analyze nonverbal structures. To assess these hypotheses, Ben-Zeev tested the performance of middle-class Hebrew/English bilingual, Hebrew monolingual, and English monolingual children on a set of tasks. The Wechsler Intelligence Scale for Children was administered to make sure there was no significant difference in intelligence between the monolingual and bilingual children. To assess the syntactic flexibility hypothesis, the children were given a verbal trans-formations test and a symbol substitution test. Both of these tests require the child to reorganize linguistic information. Since the bilingual children performed significantly better than the monolingual children on these tests, the results appear to support the hypothesis of increased flexibility in syntactic processing. Another two tests, the Paradigmatic Associations Test and the Peabody Picture Vocabulary Test, assessed the second hypothesis of precocious development of categorical associations in semantic processing. For both of these tests, the bilinguals did more poorly than the monolinguals. Ben-Zeev explains that the reason the hypothesis failed to hold up was probably because of the poor vocabulary of the bilinguals. The last hypothesis, which specifies that linguistic flexibility can be extended to non-verbal tasks, was assessed via the Matrix Transposition and Naming of Dimensions task and the Ravens Progressive Matrices Test. For the Matrix Transformation Task, the bilinguals performed significantly better than the monolinguals in isolating and specifying underlying dimensions of the matrix. However, there was no difference on the second task. Ben-Zeev concludes that the bilinguals possess two strategies for verbal material: (1) readiness to impute structure, and (2) readiness to reorganize. Furthermore, similar results were obtained, although somewhat attenuated, in a second study of Spanish/English bilingual children (Ben-Zeev, 1977b).

Although much of the research is not definitive, there is a good deal of support for the hypothesis that child bilingualism can positively influence cognitive development in terms of increased mental flexibility, divergent modes of thinking and responding, and enhanced strategies for dealing with language.

Combining information from both naturalistic and experimental studies, it is evident that the language and cognitive development of bilingual children is not handicapped by their acquisition of two languages. The process of acquisition in a child's two languages appears to be similar, since children generally acquire corresponding linguistic structures in the two languages in the same order. The rate of structural development will vary depending on the complexity of the structure. Furthermore, the reported interference between the languages, which mostly seems related to lexical or syntactic development, is not evidence that children cannot separate their two language systems. Data have accumulated from linguistic and sociolinguistic studies which demonstrate that children are able from a very early age to separate their two languages. Additionally, bilingual children may have greater cognitive plasticity than monolingual children because their linguistic experiences have enabled them to see alternative ways of perceiving relations between symbols and signs. As a result, bilingual children often appear to be superior in their concept formation and to possess a more diversified set of mental abilities.

## PURPOSE OF THE RESEARCH PROGRAM

Research in child bilingualism has only begun to attack the major issues concerning the process of duo-language acquisition, linguistic interference, and the effect of bilingualism on cognitive development. There now exist several detailed diary studies of bilingual children acquiring different language combinations. Also, there are a few experimental studies which have looked at children's language acquisition. By studying the results which have emerged from all of these studies, one can have a better idea of the process of language acquisition. However, our understanding is inhibited by the limited amount of analyzed data on the acquisition of linguistic structures in bilingual children's speech. Furthermore, these results are limited in generalizability since the children are from different socioeconomic, cultural, and linguistic backgrounds. Those studies that control for these variables either draw their conclusions on the basis of several minutes' of taped conversation or from conducting language tests. What is lacking are studies to bridge the gaps of information between naturalistic studies which observe one child's natural language and experimental studies which sample a minute portion of several children's speech.

Cross-sectional and longitudinal studies of groups of bilingual children in which fairly extensive corpora of naturalistic speech are gathered and analyzed for the acquisition of linguistic structure are needed. Information from these types of studies would provide a more realistic index of the natural language bilingual children use in their environment, as well as further insight into the process of bilingual language acquisition. To determine whether linguistic interference is really such an important issue in bilingual language acquisition, the corpora of naturalistic speech samples of bilingual children should be examined to determine what percentage of their speech is actually mixed. Furthermore, analyses should concentrate on whether there is some systematic pattern of mixing or whether it is random.

There are a multitude of questions that could be raised regarding the effects of bilingualism on cognitive development. Three important questions concern further exploration of the word-referant separation in monolinguals and bilinguals, the process of acquisition of cognitive concepts in bilinguals and monolinguals, and the performance of bilingual children on reasoning tasks.

Many of the foregoing concerns are addressed in an ongoing program of research on child bilingualism at the University of California, Los Angeles, under the direction of Dr. Amado Padilla. Two naturalistic studies have been conducted: one longitudinal study of 3 children and one cross-sectional study of 19 children, all Spanish/English bilinguals between the ages of one and six years. The children's speech has been analyzed in terms of their development of linguistic structures and linguistic interference.

Also, cognitive development has been investigated in three separate experiments to add to our knowledge of the relationship between bilingualism and cognitive development.

The remainder of this chapter will present the methodologies and results of this research program. First the naturalistic studies will be presented and their results discussed in terms of the process of duo-language acquisition and linguistic interaction. Then the methodologies and results from the experimental studies will be explained. Finally, suggestions and recommendations will be offered for further investigatory efforts into child bilingualism.

## NATURALISTIC STUDY #1: LONGITUDINAL

The purpose of the first study was to conduct a longitudinal research project to begin collecting a corpus of naturalistic speech on three very young (aged 1;5 to 2;2) bilinguals. Two were male and one was female; all three were first-born only children. They were visited weekly by a female experimenter who tape-recorded the Spanish and English interactions between the child and the caretaker, who used both Spanish and English, for approximately six months. The methodology employed was similar to that of Brown (1973), so that comparisons could be made with his English monolingual children and also with Gonzalez's (1970) Spanish monolingual children. It was hoped that such comparisons would shed some light on the process of duo-language acquisition.

Each of the children's linguistic structures in both languages were analyzed and their Mean Length of Utterance (MLU) in Spanish and English were computed. Results indicated that the children's MLUs in each language increased in the course of the study. The youngest child, a female, was 1;5 at the beginning of the study and was at the one-word stage of development. She used nonverbal gestures many times, but would produce questions by adding a rising intonation to her utterance; she also displayed commands and other assorted words. Her formation and use of the imperatives *ten* and *tenga* were correct and they occurred at about the same time as the Spanish monolingual children studied by Gonzalez (1970). Although the other two children, 2;1 and 2;2 at the onset of the study, were still using simple one- and two-word utterances, these were beginning to contain more complexity. The children were producing sentences containing functors, modifiers, subject nouns, negatives, conjunctions, and wh-k/d questions.

At the second stage of development, all three children's structures resembled those of Brown's (1973) children. These structures were telegraphic, consisting of content words. The use of negation was limited to No + sentence in Spanish and English, but negative particles were developing in English as well. Questions were formed by a rising intonation added to a sentence for yes/*sí*-no questions and with a wh-k/d word for wh questions.

The wh-k/d questions were produced much more frequently than the yes/*sí*-no questions. Gonzalez (1970) has also reported the more prevalent use of wh-k/d questions with his monolingual children. The formation of morphemes and verbs was also occurring at this second stage. The verbs *ser* and *estar,* which correspond to the English verb "to be," were developed correctly in that the differential functions of these verbs were maintained.

Analyses indicated that the children had two distinct sets of linguistic rules, one for English construction and one for Spanish construction. Even in mixed utterances, the correct word order was preserved. Thus, there were never any occurrences of a sentence like "raining *está*," "a *es* baby," or "*es un* a baby pony." On the other hand, the children did produce such *structural correct mixings as "está* raining" or "*es un* baby pony." There were never any instances of structural mixing, only lexical insertions. The lexical insertions never produced any redundancy of words. These analyses indicate that the children are able to differentiate their two language systems at the syntactic and lexical levels. The children also distinguished the two phonological systems. When English words were mixed into a Spanish utterance, the English words were pronounced with an English pronunciation. Similarly, Spanish insertions into English utterances were given their correct Spanish pronunciation.

It should be pointed out that the language input was not separated for these children. They received Spanish and English input from both parents. Despite this nondifferentiated language input, the children had mastered the sociolinguistic rules about which language should be used with whom and when.

The importance of language input was illustrated in an analysis of one child's language sessions. When the mother was instructed to speak Spanish to the child for one hour prior to the sessions, the child's use of Spanish during those sessions increased.

In sum, analysis of the language samples of the three children demonstrated two very important points: (1) these three young bilingual children were acquiring their linguistic structures at the same rate as both the Spanish and English monolingual children; and (2) there was no initial stage of confusion where the children could not differentiate their two languages. Although the children did mix utterances, they maintained structural consistency in the utterance. (See Padilla & Leibman, 1975, for a detailed discussion of the language development of the three children.)

## NATURALISTIC STUDY #2: CROSS-SECTIONAL

The purpose of the cross-sectional study was to examine the speech of young bilingual children in greater detail in order to provide a more complete picture of some of the developmental processes that children acquiring two languages go through.

Nineteen bilingual children were selected for observation; three two-year-olds (2;0 to 2;10), four three-year-olds (3;1 to 3;9), six four-year-olds (4;3 to 4;11), three five-year-olds (5;1 to 5;9), and three six-year-olds (6;1 to 6;4). The children were chosen in accordance with the following criteria: (1) that the amount of Spanish and English that the child heard and used be reasonably close to equal; (2) that the parents be of Mexican descent, and (3) that the children be verbal enough to communicate in both languages with strangers. Of the 19 children, 11 were males and 8 females. Within each age group, there was at least one male and one female child.

Although socioeconomic status was not specifically controlled for, all of the children were from working-class families. Eighteen of the fathers and all but 4 of the mothers of the children were born in Mexico. All of the children, however, were born in the United States. No child was the offspring of parents who had both been born in the United States. Thus, all of the children whose language was studied here were second-generation Mexican Americans.

In order to obtain background information on each child's language history, the parents were asked a series of questions concerning the language spoken to the child by each of the parents, siblings, and playmates. Also of interest was the language used by each child in interacting with parents, siblings, and playmates.

In response to questions concerning the language(s) first spoken by the child, the parents of 10 of the children indicated that the children had spoken both Spanish and English from the time their language production began (simultaneous bilinguals). Of the remaining 9 children, the parents indicated that their children had first produced Spanish utterances and then, at some later point, English ones. Seven of the 9 children can be classified as simultaneous, and 2 of the children as successive, bilinguals. Although for more than half the families the parent-child interaction was conducted in Spanish, 6 of the mothers and 2 of the fathers spoke to their children half of the time in English and half in Spanish. Four mothers and 4 fathers used mostly Spanish, but some English as well. Interactions with older siblings and playmates were conducted in both Spanish and English. In those cases where younger siblings were involved, most of the interactions were completely in Spanish. It should be emphasized that the language input of these children was not differentiated. It was definitely not of the one person-one language strategy which Ronjat (1913) recommended and considered important in order for children to be able to distinguish their two languages.

Sony cassette tape recorders (TC-110) with Scotch C60-minute and C90-minute tapes were used to collect the language samples. Experimenters also recorded utterances and context by hand on legal-sized tablets. Toys (e.g., airplanes, boats, doctor and nurse kits, telephones, blocks, drawing materials, picture books) were used to encourage spontaneous speech.

To collect a representative language sample from each child in Spanish and in English, a minimum of 400 utterances were collected in each language. When one language was used more frequently by a child, it was necessary to record more than the minimal requirement of utterances in the more frequently occurring language in order to obtain the minimum of 400 utterances in the language which occurred less frequently.

To standardize the procedure of counting the utterances across children, an utterance was operationally defined as: (1) a child's grammatical phrase which expresses a complete thought; (2) an incomplete phrase resulting from the child's shift in attention; e.g., "the boy was . . ." (child stops talking and becomes interested in something else); (3) a one-word utterance (e.g., dog or *perro*); and (4) a repetition of an utterance, elicited by huh?, ¿cómo? (how?), or ¿qué? (what?) on the part of another individual, which differs from the initially produced utterance.

Four pairs of female experimenters collected the language samples. Each pair consisted of one Spanish/English bilingual and one English monolingual who in most cases had some knowledge of Spanish. The bilingual experimenter spoke only Spanish and the monolingual experimenter, only English during all interactions with the child. Three of the pairs of experimenters collected language samples from 5 children each, while the fourth group of experimenters gathered language samples from 4 children. An entire language sample for each child was collected by the same pair of experimenters.

The language sample for each child was based primarily on interaction between the experimenters and the child. However, since the sample was obtained in the child's home, other people (e.g., mother or siblings) interacted on some occasions with the child during a session.

### Process of Duo-Language Acquisition.

The primary questions addressing the process issue were: (1) Is the development of grammatical structures for children acquiring two languages parallel, or do children first acquire the structure of one language and then transfer the structural rules to the second language? (2) Does there appear to be interference from one language that could result in serious consequences in the linguistic development of the bilingual child?

The first analysis of the language samples was a preliminary analysis which only looked at interrogative, negative, and possessive structures. Children's structrues were analyzed in terms of transformational rules within in a developmental stage framework. Interrogative and negative structures were chosen because an index of monolingual children's acquisition of these structures was available (Klima & Bellugi-Klima, 1966). Possessives were chosen because the English and Spanish possessive structures could be compared and contrasted in a number of ways which would enable determination of whether children were acquiring the structure in one language and transferring it to the other language or whether there was separate development of structures in both languages. Results indicated that equally complex structures were acquired at the same time. When the rules pertaining to a structure in one language were more complex, those rules were developed later than the less complex rules. Comparison with monolingual children's development indicated that the bilingual children were acquiring the English structural rules no later than monolingual English-speaking children. In fact, some of the bilingual children's development was somewhat precocious compared to the monolingual children's development. (For a detailed discussion of the findings, see Padilla & Lindholm, 1976a.)

The purpose of the second analysis was to expand the grammatical structures to incorporate the adverbs (which includes negatives) and adjectives (of which possessives are a subcomponent). Thus, a descriptive analysis will demonstrate how the bilingual child acquires the interrogative, adverb, and adjective structures in the two languages.

The two basic components of the interrogative in Spanish and in English are the interrogative word questions and the yes/no-*sí/no* questions. In the interrogative-word questions, which may be shortened to wh in English and k/d in Spanish, one or more parts of the sentence are questioned, whereas in the yes/no-*sí/no* questions the whole sentence is interrogated. Since the wh and k/d questions interrogate only a part of the sentence, the interrogative word replaces the element that requires information. The substituted interrogative words are for the most part semantically equivalent in Spanish and English; for example, the subject (who/*quién*), object (what/-*qué*), locative (where/*dónde*), and temporal (when/*cuándo*).

Spanish and English interrogative structures are very similar; that is, both languages possess rules to: (1) prepose interrogative words, (2) invert the subject-noun phrase with the verb (phrase), (3) prepose prepositions with the wh and k/d words whenever necessary. However, (4) in English, an auxiliary verb (usually "do") is inserted into the question structure if one is not already present or if an already existent auxiliary verb is only marking the tense of the main verb (e.g., "What do you want?" rather than "What you want?"). In addition, (5) inflections must be added to some k/d words so that there is agreement in gender (*cuál-es, cuánto-s, quién-es*) with the *cuánto-s, quién-es*) with the element of the sentence being questioned.

Table I presents the acquisition of question words and structures in both English and Spanish. Inspection of Table I indicates that in both languages, the preposing rule was the first rule to appear, and it was apparently acquired as soon as the children began utilizing wh and k/d words. For the subject-verb inversion rule, there is a contrast in the children's development in the two languages. In Spanish the children employed the inversion rule almost as soon as the k/d-preposing rule, but in English they did not use the inversion rule for over a year. When the English inversion rule emerged, it occurred simultaneously with the rule for inserting an auxiliary verb. The concurrent acquisition of these two rules is surprising in view of the speech of monolingual English-speaking children, who inserted auxiliary verbs first and then, at a later time, inverted the subject-noun phrase with the verb (Klima & Bellugi-Klima, 1966). It may be that in English the children were concentrating on inserting the auxiliary verb and expanding superficial structures before beginning to invert the subject-noun phrase with the verb. Analyses of the language samples indicate that during this interlude, other more superficial structures were emerging (e.g., modifiers and pronouns). Klima and Bellugi-Klima (1966) have also reported a period of superficial structural expansion similar to that reported here.

Another explanation for the differential rate of development between Spanish and English inversion rules may be the different uses of the verb in English and Spanish. In Spanish a speaker need not specify the subject noun with the verb in many cases (e.g., *¿Qué quieres? ¿Dónde estás?*). But in English the noun must be specified with the verb (e.g., What do you want? Where are you?).

The rule pertaining to the use of prepositions with the wh and k/d words was observed mostly in Spanish. When prepositions did occur with wh words in English (e.g., for what?), they were used inappropriately by the children. The near absence of prepositional preposing in English is consistent with the structure of English, where few prepositions are preposed, especially in conversation.

The first wh and k/d words to appear expressed object (what/*qué*) and location (where/*dónde*). In English the subject wh word (who) also appeared at this time, but in Spanish the comparable k/d word (*quién*) was not observed until a short time later. In contrast, the k/d word *por qué* was acquired much sooner than the corresponding wh word in English (why). Similarly, *cuál* and *cómo* appeared about a year before "which" and "how." A possible explanation for this variance in k/d and wh word acquisition can be found in the different nuances for the k/d and wh words. Although the wh and k/d words are for the most part semantically equivalent, there are some subtle differences in their meanings. For example, the Spanish word *cómo* is used to denote "how," but it is also used as "what" would be in some instances in English. A similar case obtains with the word *cuál*. Neither of the temporal interrogative words (when/*cuándo*) occurred very often, but they did appear more often in Spanish than in English. The relatively infrequent use of "when" and *cuándo* may be partially explained by the children's more persistent use of "what time"/*a qué hora*.

The yes/no-*sí/no* interrogative questions the whole sentence. The rules for forming yes/no and *sí/no* questions in the two languages are: (1) in-

# Table 1
## English Wh- and Spanish K/D-Questions

### Interrogative Words

| Child Age | What | Where | Who | How | Which | When | Why | Whose | |
|---|---|---|---|---|---|---|---|---|---|
| | Qué | Dónde | Quién | Cómo | Cuál | Cuándo | Por que | De quién | Cuánto |
| 2.0 | X* | X | | | | | | | |
| 2.6 | X | X | X | | | | | | |
| 2.10 | X | X | X | | | | | | |
| 3.1 | X | X | X | X | X | | X | | |
| 3.2 | X | X | X | X | | | X | | |
| 3.5 | X | X | X | X | | X | X | | |
| 3.9 | X | X | X | X | X | | X | | |
| 4.3 | X | X | X | X | | | X | X | |
| 4.3 | X | X | X | X | X | | X | | |
| 4.4 | X | X | X | X | X | X | X | | |
| 4.6 | X | X | X | X | X | X | X | | |
| 4.9 | X | X | X | X | X | X | X | | |
| 4.11 | X | X | X | X | X | | X | | |
| 5.1 | X | X | X | X | X | X | X | | |
| 5.8 | X | X | X | X | X | X | X | X | X |
| 5.9 | X | X | X | X | X | | X | X | |
| 6.1 | X | X | X | X | X | | X | | |
| 6.2 | X | X | X | X | | | X | | X |
| 6.4 | X | X | X | X | | | X | | |

# Interrogative Word Rules

| Child Age | Preposing Wh- | K/D | Subject Noun-Verb Inversion | Auxiliary Verb Insertion | Preposition Preposing | Gender | Number |
|---|---|---|---|---|---|---|---|
| 2.0 | X | X | | | | | |
| 2.6 | X | X | | | | | |
| 2.10 | X | X | X | | X | | |
| 3.1 | X | X | X | | X | | |
| 3.2 | X | X | X | | | | |
| 3.5 | X | X | X | | | | |
| 3.9 | X | X | X | | X | | |
| 4.3 | X | X | X | | | | |
| 4.3 | X | X | X | X | | | X |
| 4.4 | X | X | X | X | | | |
| 4.6 | X | X | X | X | X | | |
| 4.9 | X | X | X | X | X | | X |
| 4.11 | X | X | X | X | X | | X |
| 5.1 | X | X | X | X | X | | X |
| 5.8 | X | X | X | X | X | X | X |
| 5.9 | X | X | X | X | X | | X |
| 6.1 | X | X | X | X | X | | X |
| 6.2 | X | X | X | X | X | X | X |
| 6.4 | X | X | X | X | | | X |

*X indicates presence of structure in child's speech.

Adapted from Padilla, A.M. and Lindholm, K.J. Acquisition of bilingualism: An analysis of the linguistic structures of Spanish/English speaking children. *In* G.D. Keller, T. Teschner, & S. Viera (Eds.), *Bilingualism in the bicentennial and beyond*. New York: Bilingual Press/Editorial Bilingue, 1976.

version of the intonation pattern from falling to rising, (2) inversion of the subject-noun phrase with the verb (phrase), and (3) in English, the insertion of an auxiliary verb if there is not one already present or if an already existent auxiliary verb is only marking tense.

The intonation inversion rule was acquired very early. In fact, intonation inversion was the only clue to indicate that the child was forming a question rather than a declarative sentence. Again, some period intervened before the next structure was acquired. During this interval, the children were expanding their superficial structures. In English they began producing questions with inserted auxiliary verbs and inversion of subject-noun phrases and verbs, both of these rules occurring simultaneously (as with the wh question structure). The Spanish rule for inversion of the subject noun phrase with the verb phrase did not appear until approximately age five, and even then it was employed by only 2 children. We do not believe that the absence of the inversion rule accurately reflects the ability of the children to form *si/no* questions since most children produced very few questions of this type. It is probable that inversion was not apparent because when the children used verbs they did not include subject nouns, and without subject nouns there cannot be any subject noun-verb phrase inversion. It might also be pointed out here that in conversational Spanish the inclusion of the subject noun is usually for emphasis, formality, or for clarifying the third-person singular form of the verb.

The various components comprising the grammatical category of adverbs evade easy description because their placement is quite variable, not only in relation to each other but also in relation to other elements of the sentence. To confound this problem even further, it seems that even though both languages appear to function by many of the same rules, Spanish adverb placement is even more elastic than placement in English (Stockwell, Bowen, & Martin 1965). Thus, the adverbs were divided into the subcomponents of simple adverbs (place, time, manner, extent) and negatives.

Comparison of the acquisition of the place and time categories in English and Spanish revealed that by age 2;3 (2;0 for the Spanish place subcomponent), the children were beginning to learn place and time adverbs. It was also noted that the children used semantically equivalent words in the two languages for these categories (e.g., place: here/*aquí;* time: now/*ahora*). Some examples of sentences containing place or time adverbs are: (1) place: "Cause this goes on top like this"; "*Yo voy afuera a pegarlo*" (I'm going outside to hit it); (2) time: "I finished before you did;" "*Ahora yo primero y después tu primero*" (Now me first and then you first).

Manner adverbs were acquired at the same age in both languages, and their placement conformed to adult rules. Additionally, when speaking Spanish, the children inflected the manner adverb. The children used manner adverbs to quantify or to specify measurement. Children constructed comparatives to specify measurement and in both languages the inherent comparative form better/*mejor* was overgeneralized with insertion of the periphrastic more/*más* before the comparative form. Extent adverbs appeared sooner in Spanish than in English. Representative examples of manner and extent adverbs are: (1) Manner: "They go softly"; "*Pues, si me porto mal*" (Well, if I'm bad); (2) Extent: Make it more louder"; "*Este va a brincar más alto*" (This one is going to jump higher).

In terms of the children's English and Spanish negative structures, the "no" construction appeared prior to the structures involving negative indefinite elements (e.g., "kitty no"; "*no que este*" [not this one]). The children produced the equivalent negative indefinites (i.e., nothing/*nada*) at about the same time in the two languages. Insertion of the negative indefinite elements into a negative structure demonstrated the children's ability to differentiate the variant placement in the two languages; in Spanish, insertion is preverbal to the phrase, while in English the negative element is inserted between the auxiliary verb and the main verb (e.g., "I don't like those either"; "*Nadie está manejando*" [No one is driving]). Double negatives appeared in both languages (e.g., "No, snakes don't have none"; "*Ya no falta nada*" [Now there's nothing missing]), but they occurred for only a short period in English. Double negation seems to be a brief intermediate stage before completely achieving the adult structure in English (McNeill, 1970). Spanish structure allows double negation in sentences.

The children's negative structure appeared to be fairly well developed in Spanish by age five, a finding in contrast to earlier research by Brisk (1972), who reported that the negative structure in the speech of her five-year-old Spanish/English bilinguals consisted primarily of "no" constructions. She also noted that in their negative structures, "no" was sometimes produced with an affirmative word rather than the expected negative word (e.g., "*Yo no me acuerdo, también*" [I don't remember, too]; *tampoco* should have been used here instead of *también* for the correct form, "I don't remember either").

Since the simple adverbs correspond to the wh and k/d words "where"/ /*dónde* (place), "when"/*cuándo* (time), "how"/*cómo* (manner), and "how much"/*cuánto* (extent), a few comparisons can be made between these two grammatical categories. Both the English and Spanish place adverbs and the "where"/*dónde* question words appeared by about age 2;0 (English place adverbs occurred by age 2;6). This was not true of the temporal category; time adverbs were acquired by age 2;6 but "when" and *cuándo* were not acquired until much later and appeared in the speech of only a few children. The simple manner adverbs were produced at about the same time as the corresponding question words in each language, but the ages of acquisition in the two languages differed. There seems to be no relationship between the appearance of extent adverbs and the corresponding question words in either language. In English, extent adverbs were produced by only five children, and the wh word "how much" never appeared in the speech samples of the children. The extent adverbs were acquired by age 2;10 in Spanish, but *cuánto* was not produced until age 5;8, and even then it was only used by two children.

Adjectives were separated into determiners (articles, demonstratives), limiters, possessives, descriptives (absolute, comparative, superlative), and intensifiers. The children acquired the English and Spanish determiners simultaneously even though they had to attach both gender and number inflections to all of the Spanish forms. The fact that English only requires number agreement for the indefinite articles and the demonstratives proved problematic for the children until about age 4;9. Some examples of the children's use of determiners are: "All of these clocks are not the same"; "*Aquéllas chiquitas*" (Those little ones). Limiting adjectives also seemed to present difficulties for the children because of the inconsistencies of number agreement in English. Also, there were a few instances where number and/or gender inflections were incorrect in Spanish. The same limiters appeared initially in the two languages (i.e., other, another/*otro;* same/ *mismo*), and they were acquired quite early in both languages.

By age 2;6, descriptive adjectives were produced in the absolute form in both English and Spanish. Generally, there was consistent number and gender agreement in the Spanish speech of the bilingual children. The English comparative and superlative forms appeared by ages 3;5 and 4;9 respectively. In both structures there were some instances of overgeneralizations of the forms (e.g., "more smaller," "bestest," "mostest"). Comparative and superlative forms were nearly absent in the Spanish speech of the children, but this absence was compensated for by the wide use of intensifiers in the form of both words and diminutive and augmentative suffixes. Intensifiers were acquired by age 2;10 in Spanish and did not appear in English until 4;3, when most intensifiers were used for emphasis. Representative examples of the children's descriptives and intensifiers are: (1) Descriptive: "Because you thought it was a for-reals monster"; "I like hers mostest"; "*Un* pajarito chiquito" (A small birdie); "*Ese es más grandote que ese*" (That one is bigger than that one); (2) Intensifier: "He'll have to take his big giant shoe off"; "*Esto es para niñitos chiquitos y para grandotes, ¿verdad?*" (This is for tiny little babies and for big ones, right?).

In both languages the possessive pronouns were the possessives first developed, and they occurred with both number and gender agreement. The structures *de* and *'s* as well as the prepositional phrase form with "of" were acquired next, and the "whose" and *de quién* question words followed. Thus, the possessive structures appeared to be acquired at the same rate in both languages. In drawing this conclusion, it is interesting to point out two complexities in acquiring the possessive form that bilingual children must overcome. First, there is the fact that in Spanish there are two forms of the possessive pronouns—shortened (*mi, tu, su*) and lengthened (*mío, tuyo, suyo*)—which the child bilingual speaker must acquire. Second, the two English possessive forms—"of" and *'s*—are equivalent to the single form *de* in Spanish. These differences, however, do not appear to create problems for the bilingual children learning to form the possessive in Spanish and English.

## Morpheme acquisition order

The purpose of this analysis was to describe the order of acquisition of fourteen English grammatical morphemes. The acquisition of English grammatical morphemes has been investigated by Brown (1973) and de Villiers and de Villiers (1973). Brown describes the order of acquisition of fourteen English grammatical morphemes by 3 monolingual English-speaking children who were involved in a longitudinal language development study. De Villiers and de Villiers, in a cross-sectional study, describe the acquisition by 21 monolingual English-speaking children aged 16–40 months of the same fourteen grammatical morphemes discussed by Brown. Morphemes were scored as present or absent in obligatory contexts (as defined by Brown, 1973). Results showed a high correlation between the youngest group of 6 children of the present study (ages from 2;4 to 3;9) and Brown's subjects ($r = .72$) and the de Villiers' ($r = .72$) children. It is important to note that the youngest group of 6 children in this study more closely approximates the age breakdown of the subjects studied by both Brown and de Villiers'. The two older groups of subjects (ages 4;3 to 4;11 and 5;1 to 6;4, respectively) deviated somewhat in the order of acquisition of morphemes from Brown ($r = .51$ and .39) and the de Villiers' children ($r = .67$ and .39).

The difference in acquisition may be due to the discrepancy in the ages of the bilingual children with the monolingual children or to other factors (e.g., the older bilingual children may have learned English somewhat differently than the younger bilingual children). Nonetheless, the results obtained here indicate that younger bilingual children acquire the fourteen grammatical morphemes in much the same order as do monolingual children. For a more detailed discussion, see Padilla (1978).

Taken together, these three analyses provide information on the acquisition of thirteen linguistic structures in each language by the bilingual children *(morphemes; interrogatives: wh-k/d, yes/no-sí/no*; adverbs: negatives, place, manner, time, extent; adjectives: possessives, determiners, limiters, descriptive intensifiers). The questions asked in the beginning can now be addressed: do children acquiring two languages simultaneously develop their two linguistic structures in a parallel manner or do they first acquire the structural rules of one language and then transfer the structural rules to the second language? Does there appear to be interference from one language to another which could have deleterious effects on how bilingual children acquire either of their two languages?

First, from the comparisons of the bilingual children's acquisition of English interrogative and negative structures and grammatical morphemes to that of English speaking monolingual children, we find that the bilingual children acquire the rules and structures not only in the same order but at about the same time as well. Their acquisition is certainly not behind that of monolingual children and is in fact ahead, at least in their acquisition of the subject-verb inversion rule in interrogative acquisition.

These findings are especially interesting in view of the apparent large differences between our bilingual children and the monolingual children studied by Brown, the de Villiers's, and Klima and Bellugi-Klima (1966). For example, aside from the apparent differences in language histories, the present children differ in sociocultural backgrounds and have lower social economic status.

Second, it was found that the children acquired rules and structures which were equally complex at the same time but when structures differed in complexity, the more complicated structure or rule was typically acquired later. Similar results have been found by other researchers (e.g., Kessler, 1971; Mikés, 1967). However, there were no cases where the children transferred the structure of one language over to the structure of the second language. If the children did not have a certain structure, they simply did not use the structure in that language. Thus, it appears that the children had no problem acquiring the rules and structures for the two languages. Furthermore, they were able to separate which rules and structures belonged to which language. There was no evidence that children transferred rules or structures from one language to the other.

In sum, the results of these three studies on thirteen linguistic structures indicate that bilingual children are able to separate the grammatical rules and structures for each language. Moreover, there is no evidence of interference in terms of acquiring grammatical structures, with the single exception of number agreement in Spanish and English determiners.

In view of the near absence of interference, one might wonder: what is the nature of the interference that is so frequently discussed in the literature? The next section will examine the linguistic interference in the speech of the children in order to elucidate this much misunderstood phenomenon.

## LINGUISTIC INTERFERENCE/INTERACTION

Linguistic interference is a major issue in child bilingualism and has consequently received a substantial amount of attention. Wald (1974) points out that "observers have noted a large degree of intermixture of the vocabulary of the two languages in free utterances" (p. 316). From

Ramirez's (1974) review of the literature it is evident that children's language mixing has been interpreted by most investigators as the failure of bilingual children to separate their two languages. Part of the problem surrounding this issue is the fact that linguistic interference has largely gone without systematic study. As Wald says, "observers" of child language have talked about the phenomenon. Another part of the problem is that, like bilingualism, there are various interpretations of what interference means. Even translations are considered by some to be a form of mixing (Swain & Wesche, 1975). Although translations are usually awarded the status of demonstrating that children can distinguish between their two language systems (Bergman, 1976; Swain & Wesche, 1975), mixing is evidence that a child cannot discriminate the two linguistic systems (Swain & Wesche, 1975).

Weinreich (1953) has defined linguistic interference as "instances of deviation from the norms of either language which occur in the speech of bilinguals as a result of their familiarity with more than one language" (p. 1). At this juncture, I would like to point out that the term "interference" is actually a misnomer when applied to bilingualism. Interference implies considerable opposition or clashing, which does not fit what happens when a bilingual knows two languages. There may be an *interaction* between the two languages, which denotes reciprocal effect and actually defines the bilingual phenomenon more accurately. For this reason, the remainder of the chapter will refer to "linguistic interference" as "linguistic interaction." Further division of linguistic interaction is necessary to distinguish between the various types of linguistic interaction. Language mixes will refer to interactions that occur within a sentence boundary. Three levels of mixing can exist: lexical (e.g., *Yo tengo un* car [I have a car]), morphosyntactic (e.g., She's my sister*ita*), or phrasal (e.g., *Yo voy a ir a* first grade next year [I'm going to go to . . . ]). In contrast, language switches will be defined as an interaction which occurs at the sentence boundary (e.g., *Estoy jugando con mis juguetes.* You wanna play? [I'm playing with my toys . . . .]). Translations will be defined as the conversion of a linguistic unit from one language to another. The linguistic unit may be as small as a word or as large as discourse. There are two types of translations: literal and idiomatic. Literal translations are functional in the sense that they conform to structural requirements of the translated material, whereas idiomatic translations are semantically based and concerned with providing the actual meaning of the material. Further, translations can either be spontaneous or elicited.

The bilingual children produced a total of 17, 864 utterances in English and Spanish. An examination of these utterances indicated that only 538, or 3 percent, contained what has here been defined as a linguistic interaction. The interactions were classified accounting to whether they were language mixes, switches, or translations. Also, the mixes and switches were categorized according to the language environment; that is, the language being spoken at the time of the switch or mix. Table II summarizes the breakdown of linguistic interactions in terms of the level of interaction and the language environment.

Attention to Table II indicates that of the total 17,864 utterances, only 319, or 1.7 percent, of the children's speech were mixed utterances. Lexical mixes occur much more frequently than phrasal ones, and the most common mix involves nouns, especially the insertion of an English noun into a Spanish environment. Much less frequent, although more predominant than other mixes, is the substitution of Spanish nouns for English nouns into English utterances. The few remaining lexical mixes were scattered throughout other linguistic categories. There was no particular pattern to the phrasal mixing; a noun phrase was almost as likely to be mixed as any other combination of words. There were no examples of morphosyntactic mixing.

The majority of English nouns mixed into Spanish sentences consisted of the names for animals, social roles, toys, foods, vehicles, structures, instruments, body articles, and celebrations. Animal names such as "dinosaur," "snake," "bee," and, "horse" occurred most frequently (63 utterances, or 29 percent of Spanish mixed utterances with English nouns), followed by social role labels such as "cowboy," "policeman," "grandma," or "postman" (37, or 17 percent). Toys such as "balloons," "clay," and "bike" appeared in 26 utterances (12 percent), and foods such as "candy," "eggs," or "lollipop" were observed. Celebrations such as "birthday" and "Christmas," vehicles such as "bus," "fire engine," or "rocket," and structures such as "window," "bunk bed," or "swimming pool" were also found. In addition, in Spanish utterances children mixed instrument-type names such as "TV," "telephone," or "stick," and body articles such as "shorts," "pants," or "face."

An examination of the lexically mixed utterances consisting of the insertion of English nouns into Spanish utterances was undertaken to determine what preceded the English noun. It was found that the article was the most predominant precursory linguistic element. Spanish feminine and masculine definite and indefinite articles appeared before English nouns in over two-thirds of the mixes in Spanish utterances; out of these, the masculine form accounted for 80 percent of the articles.

Inherent in Spanish noun phrases are gender and number agreements between the article and the noun. The children's choice of number was always correct: "*Este es un* fireman" (This [one] is a fireman); "*Los* policemen *están allí también*" (The policemen are over there too). However, their choice of the gender of the article did not always coincide with what the gender of the correct Spanish noun would have been. For example,"*¿Dónde está la* worm?" (Where's the worm?) "*¿Y dónde está el* whale *grandote que va aquí*?" (And where is the big whale that goes here?).

## Table II
## Classification of Linguistic Interactions*

| Type of Interaction | Language Environment | | |
|---|---|---|---|
| | Spanish Utterance | English Utterance | Total |
| **Lexical Mixing** | | | |
| Noun | 214 | 33 | |
| Verb | 3 | 3 | |
| Ajective | 7 | 2 | |
| Article | 1 | 5 | |
| Demonstrative | 0 | 2 | |
| Conjunction | 6 | 3 | |
| Salutation | 3 | 0 | |
| **Phrasal Mixing** | | | |
| Adjective + Noun | 5 | 3 | |
| Article + Noun | 4 | 1 | |
| Verb + Object | 0 | 3 | |
| Subject + Verb | 2 | 0 | |
| Subject + Verb + Object | 1 | 0 | |
| Miscellaneous | 10 | 8 | |
| Total Mixing | 256 | 63 | 319 |
| **Translations, Both Languages** | | | |
| Spontaneous | 29 | | 29 |
| Elicited | 46 | | 46 |
| Grand Total | | | 538 |

*Based on a total of 17,864 utterances in English and Spanish.

Adapted from Lindholm, K. J. & Padilla, A. M. Child bilingualism: Report on language mixing, switching and translations. *Linguistics,* 1978, 211, 23–44.

The assignment of gender to the articles generally appeared to follow two criteria: (1) corresponding to the natural gender of the noun (e.g., *la* lady; *un* fireman); and (2) neutral words with ambiguous genders were preceded by masculine articles (e.g., *el* whale, *un* swimming pool).

Cornejo (1975), in his study of the gender selection of mixed utterances in the speech of five-year-old Spanish/English bilinguals, found that the children chose the correct gender. He attributed the cases of correct gender selection to the children's knowledge of the corresponding Spanish word. In drawing such a conclusion, Cornejo failed to point out the examples of incorrect gender choice, and that some words appeared with both genders (e.g., "*un* book," "*una* book," "*la* bottle," "*un* bottle"; p. 170). These examples are contradictory to a conclusion that the children have knowledge of the corresponding Spanish word and are assigning gender accordingly. A closer examination of the mixed utterances revealed that Cornejo's children were assigning gender like the 19 bilingual children reported on here, according to the two criteria listed above. It would appear that in some cases the children did know the corresponding Spanish word, but it was less salient than the English word or else it was just momentarily forgotten. In other cases, the children appeared not to know the Spanish word.

Spanish nouns inserted into English environments also consisted predominately of animal names such as *ballena* (whale), *puercos* (pigs), or *vaca* (cow) (13, or 40 percent). Names for food, *frijoles* (beans), *dulce* (candies), instruments (e.g., *guitarra* [guitar], *paragua* [umbrella]), *vehicles* (e.g., *tren* [train] *carro* [car]), body articles (e.g., *jabón* [soap], *pestaña* [eyelash]), social roles *cartero* (mailman), and toys (e.g., *pelota* [ball]) were also observed.

In English, there is no gender agreement between the article and the noun, nor is there any number agreement between the definite article (the) and the noun. However, the indefinite article "a" requires number agreement since it can only be used singularly and it must be changed to "an" whenever it precedes a word which is initially vocalic (i.e., usually a word beginning with a vowel). The bilingual children adhered to the lack of number and gender agreements for the definite article (e.g., "well, let's get the *árboles*" [trees]) and to the singularity of the indefinite article (e.g., "and a *tambor* [drum] and a guitar").

The remaining lexical mixes were very infrequent and consisted of adjectives, verbs, articles, conjunctions, demonstratives, and salutations. English adjectives and conjunctions were more commonly inserted into Spanish sentences, while Spanish articles, verbs, and conjunctions were more frequently substituted into English sentences. Verbs and demonstratives were inflected correctly in both languages and the salutations were used appropriately (e.g., "*Dice:* Hi, *mira quien vive aquí*" [He says, Hi, look who lives here]).

Phrasal mixing was much less frequent and also less systematic than lexical mixing. Phrasal mixing accounted for only 0.2 percent of the total language samples and 12 percent of the mixed utterances. Again, the majority of mixes occurred in Spanish environments. The most common phrases were the adjective + noun (e.g., "*Quiero el* purple one" [I want the . . . ]) and article + noun (e.g., "*Eso no es* the back, *ésta*" [That's not the back, this is]) phrases. There were also phrases in which the verb and either the object or the subject of the verb, or both, were substituted. In addition, there were phrasal mixes which could not easily be categorized and these were designated as miscellaneous (e.g., "*Se está* brushing his teeth" [He/She is]).

Although several of the mixes occurred at phrase boundaries (e.g., "*Otra vez,* what's your name?" [Again . . . ]), the majority of phrasal mixes appeared within phrases. Since the phrasal mixes accounted for only 0.2 percent of the children's speech, it is possible that many of them were slips in speech, or perhaps they were due to a child's unfamiliarity with one word or concept of the phrasal mix in the appropriate language. Instead of lexically mixing the utterance, the child elaborated the lexical intrusion with one or more words. Other phrasal mixes are accounted for by cases in which children would begin the sentence in English and mix part of the way through while turning to their mother for verification (e.g., "It was walking up, *pero salió, verdad Mami*?" [. . . but it left, right, Mommy?]).

Language switching accounts for less than one percent of the total speech of the bilingual children and for 26 percent of all the linguistic interactions. Twice as many switches were observed in Spanish language environments than when English was being spoken.

Most of the language switches are attributed to six children who produced 10–20 switches in one or the other languages. The remaining children switched an average of four times each. There are several interpretations which can be offered for the switching. One is saliency. There are some topics or words which are more salient to children either because of the language environment in which they learned it or because the word or topic may be used with much greater frequency in one language. Many times children were telling a story from a book which was written in English and perhaps read to them in English. Repetition in English or slipping into English would be much easier in these cases. Also, there were a few occasions when children would switch in order to purposely exclude the experimenter from the conversation. The children appeared to do this when they wanted to talk with the other experimenter or when they wanted to make fun of the experimenter they were talking with. An example of a child (C) switching in order to make fun of an experimenter (E) is:

*C:* Know what's wrong with your teeth?
*E:* What about my teeth?
*C:* Look at this one.
*E:* What about it?
*C: Es chueco.* (It's crooked.) [the child is giggling]
*E:* It's what?
*C: Es chueco.*
*E:* What's that?
*C: Chueco.* [giggles again].
*E:* What's the English for that? I don't understand what you're saying.
*C: Chueco.* [changes subject]

Another motive for switching was to ascertain whether the two monolingual experimenters were really monolingual. Several children were skeptical about whether the experimenters really did not understand them when they mixed or switched languages. Too many times experimenters, who intended to speak monolingually, were reinforcing the children's doubt by replying to a switch or a mixed utterance (e.g., C: "It goes in back over here." E: "*¿Cómo va?*" [Where does it go?] C: "In back, it goes in back.").

Language switching neither directly supports nor refutes the case for language differentiation. In some respects, switching appears to validate the view that children cannot distinguish between the two systems. On the other hand, switching also indicates that children know the sociolinguistic rules of correct language use when they can switch languages to accommodate the other experimenter and when they can use the one language which an experimenter does not understand in order to banter her.

Translations accounted for only 0.4 percent of the children's speech. Children provided more literal than idiomatic translations, and more elicited than spontaneous translations. All of the spontaneous translations were translated correctly regardless of whether they were literal or idiomatic. Most of the children's literal translations of their own words involved saying the word in the one language and then translating it into the other language (e.g., "oh *caricaturas,* cartoons"), a finding that Swain and Wesche (1975) have reported with their French/English bilingual child. Other translations involved utterances which were begun in the appropriate language and, in the same utterance, translated to the other language in order to accommodate the experimenter.

Idiomatic translations occurred more often when the translations were elicited rather than spontaneous. Some examples of children's elicited idiomatic translations are:


E: *¿Qué es esto? No sé que es.*
  (What is that? I don't know what it is!)
C: *Un* spider.
E: *¡Qué es eso*
  (What is that?)
C: *Pues, un* spider. (Well, a spider.)
C: *Araña.* (Spider.)
C: But I don't know what are they.
E: *No te entiendo.*
  (I don't understand you.)
E: *En español, Miguel.*
  (In Spanish, Miguel.)
C: *Yo no sé que son.*
  (I don't know what they are.)

These direct translations are indicative of the children's knowledge of the corresponding word(s) in the other language as well as their ability to translate it (them) correctly. There were only a few examples where a word was translated incorrectly: these words were "see" translated as *mirar* (look at) rather than *ver*, "moon" translated as *sol* (sun) instead of *luna;* *vaca* (cow) translated as bull; and *árboles* (trees) translated as "arrows." The confusion of "see" with "look" is a common conceptual difficulty encountered by many monolingual children as they are learning these two words (Chomsky, 1969). In the example of *arbol* (tree) translated as "arrow," we find that Fantini (1974) has termed "conceptual shift"; that is, two words, one from each language, which sound alike but which are conceptually different. This shift may be due to the phonological similarities. Several English nouns which were mixed into Spanish utterances were phonologically similar. For example the words "banana," "dentist," "rock," "car," "monster," and "guitar" sound very similar to the respective Spanish words *banana, dentista, roca, carro, monstruo,* and *guitarra.*

Perhaps the most interesting translations were those provided by two children. One child was defining to the Spanish speaking experimenter what a "guard" is. She defined guards in terms of their function: *Son los que miran . . . la gente escula algo* (They are the ones that look [watch] . . . the people frisk something.) The other child told a story in Spanish and then proceeded to tell the other experimenter the same story, but changed the character's name from Jarbo in Spanish to Graven in English. This little girl also repeatedly quizzed the experimenters. She would tell me a story one day and the other experimenter a similar story the next day. Then she would proceed to quiz us to determine whether we were really monolinguals. The interesting point is that she knew which details she had changed in the corresponding stories.

Although the design of the experiment did not include eliciting translations, the children's mixing or switching languages within an utterance prompted the experimenter to request that the child repeat the mixed item or the switch in the appropriate language. In the majority of cases, the children gave a correct literal translation. The children also provided descriptive idiomatic translations. The ability of these children to translate demonstrates their competence in distinguishing between the two languages, especially when the experimenter elicits their translations with, "How do you say that in English?" or *¿Cómo se dice eso en español?*

Although the children's utterances contained lexical or phrasal mixes, there was overall maintenance of structural consistency. Phrasal mixes were much less systematic than lexical mixes, but there was no repetition of sentential information. The complexity of the phrasal mixes is compensated for by the simplicity and organization of the lexical mixes. In fact it is possible that the "disorder" of the phrasal mixes results in part from the child's initial intention to produce a lexical mix, but in order to express the concept, the child believes that more elaboration is necessary.

For the lexically mixed utterances, a consistent pattern of mixing emerged. In both Spanish and English, the predominant lexical mixes involved nouns, especially zoological terms. The children's mixing of the nouns follows the *léxico "nomenclador"* discussed by Coseriu (1967) and further elaborated on by Trujillo-Carreño (1974). These authors described two sets of lexical categories in language use, nomenclatural or technical and structural. Trujillo-Carreño explains that one set of terms, those in the technical lexicon, are definable and hence have a universal character. This set consists of nouns which are identical for all linguistic communities so that the technical language can always be easily translated into another language. This is not true of the second set, structural lexicon, whose terms are not definable because their use differs from language to language. This translation becomes a very difficult process.

That the children's mixing is not only internally consistent but follows linguistic theories of language use demonstrates that language mixing is not a random phenomenon caused by nondifferentiation of the two languages. The structural consistency of the mixed utterances corroborates such a conclusion. In Spanish utterances, the functors agreed in number with the substituted English nouns. Where necessary, the English functors also agreed in number with the Spanish inserted nouns. In addition, in the lexically mixed utterances, there was no overlap in meaning; that is, when a word was mixed, the word was not repeated in the appropriate language, even when the two languages differed structurally.

It is also interesting to note that many of the lexical mixes were preceded by silent and/or verbal pauses (e.g., um, uh); for example, *¿En dónde vivían muchos* um babies *de, de animales?* (Where did they live, many, um babies of, of animals?). (A better translation would be, Where did many of the animals' babies live?) Fantini (1974) has noted a similar action in his bilingual child, who would set the mixed word(s) off with "verbal quotation marks"; that is, a slight pause. There were also occurrences when the inserted noun followed functors that were repeated (e.g., *Ese, ese es un, ese es un, un* Christmas. [This, this is a, this is a, a Christmas.]).

These examples suggest that the children are conscious of mixing the two languages, and are reluctant to mix them. This hesitancy to mix utterances has also been reported Swain and Wesche (1975) with their French/English bilingual child.

There are several possible reasons for the children's mixing. First, one word might be more salient to the child in a particular language. The overrepresentation of English nouns mixed into Spanish utterances may be partly due to television and other media where the child is exposed to an English word more frequently than the Spanish word. Second, the child may have simply momentarily forgotten the correct word because of a problem in the retrieval process. The example of elicited translations showed that in many cases the child did have the correct term [e.g., C: "Um, yellow." E: "¿Y cómo es en español?" (And what is it in Spanish?) C: "*Amarillo*"]. Children would have more occasion to hear yellow than *amarillo,* especially from television and older siblings who are in school. Third, the child may not have known the word to begin with. Fantini (1974) found that lexical mixing ceased when his child acquired the corresponding word and in cases where no equivalent existed (structural terms) the mixed term persisted in the child's speech.

Switching appeared to be more sociolinguistically motivated. There were examples which could follow the above three reasons for mixing. However, for the most part they appeared to be determined by social factors. Children would switch languages in order to determine whether the supposedly monolingual speaker actually understood another language. Children picked up several cues that the monolinguals understood more than they let on, by means of exchanges where the experimenter would ask a question pertaining to the mixed word as if the word had not been mixed [e.g., E: "¿Y qué son estos?" (And what are these?) C: "Wings" E: "¿Son alas de quién?" (Whose wings are they?)]. Also, some children switched languages to enable them to banter an experimenter. Furthermore, in most bilingual environments, the communication process involves language mixing. Gumperz (1967) has pointed out that bilinguals switch their languages to have some social impact. Similarly, Fantini (1974) ascribes switching to social factors.

One further point must be made. The process of data collection involved one experimenter speaking in Spanish for 30–45 minutes and the other experimenter speaking in English for 30–45 minutes. One would think that such a situation would have confused the children, yet they seemed to be able to switch from one language to the next quite easily. Also, the children's language input appears to be undifferentiated. That is, in most families parents and siblings spoke both languages to the child. Considering all of these factors, one might expect these children to have mixed their utterances much more frequently than 3 percent. In fact, when one considers that the children mixed less frequently than might be expected of a bilingual, it appears that linguistic interactions may have been inhibited by the monolingual experimenters.

In sum, the small amount of mixing and the systematic lexical mixing and translations taken together with environmental communicative aspects of bilinguals lead us to conclude that the children are able, from an early age, to distinguish between their two language systems. This conclusion is consistent with findings obtained in section one of the research project and from other studies (e.g., Bergman, 1976; Fantini, 1974; Padilla & Lindholm, 1976a, 1976b). The results of this study are elaborated on in Lindholm and Padilla (1978a, 1978b).

## RESEARCH PROGRAM: EXPERIMENTAL STUDIES

### Experimental Study #1: Word-Object Separation

Sandoval (1976) conducted this study to replicate Ianco-Worrall's (1972) study with Spanish/English bilingual children and to test for possible sex differences in language development.

A total of 30 monolingual and 40 bilingual kindergarteners and third graders participated in the study. Socioeconomic status was controlled for, and children were given the Peabody Picture Vocabulary Test to control for intelligence. The first part of the experiment was similar to Ianco-Worrall's (1972) semantic/phonemic preference. The children were verbally presented with two sentences: "I have three words, word 1, word 2, and word 3. Which is more like word 1, word 2 or word 3?" Word 1 was the test word, and words 2 and 3 were target words. One of the target words was semantically similar to the test word and the other target word was phonologically similar. There were eight sets of monosyllabic words. Similarly, the second part was a modified version of Ianco-Worrall's (1972) and Feldman and Shen's (1971) word-objection separation test. The four tasks in the second part of the experiment required the children to demonstrate their ability to use words independent of their denotative referents. Task one tested the children's ability to use verbal labels to name familiar objects. In task two, the children were asked whether or not nonsense names could be substituted for the regular names (e.g., "Can you call a chair 'wug'?"). In tasks three and four, the children were told that this was a game of make-believe and that the names of objects were going to be changed. For task three, the objects were renamed and the children had to point to the object when the experimenter said the new name. In the fourth task, the child was given a relational sentence with two of the renamed objects in task three. The child had to arrange the physical objects to depict the relationship described in the sentence.

Results indicated no statistically significant differences between the monolingual and bilingual children. However, there was a consistent trend in each testing phase suggesting slightly better performance of the bilingual children over the monolingual children. There were a few problems with this study involving sampling procedures and time limitations in conducting studies during school hours. The sampling problem pertained to the fact that the English monolingual group was familiar with Spanish and perhaps familiar enough to confound the results.

Sex differences were found in the kindergarten but not the third-grade samples, with females outperforming males. This finding is consistent with the hypothesis that the language development of younger females is advanced compared to the males' development, but with increasing age the gap in development narrows (Maccoby & Jacklin, 1974).

In sum, the results, while not definitive, do *suggest* that bilingual children have a slight advantage over monolingual children in some language or cognitive tasks.

## Experimental Study #2: Class-Inclusion Reasoning

The development of class-inclusion reasoning has been described by Inhelder and Piaget (1964) as the construction of hierarchical classification and the understanding of the relations among the levels of the hierarchy. To attain this level of intellectual development, Inhelder and Piaget claim that the child must be able to recognize that physically dissimilar objects may be related by virtue of some other observable property (e.g., different types of fruit are subclasses of the superordinate class of fruit).

In studies of class-inclusion reasoning, researchers have found that when questions are asked in a purely verbal format (e.g., "If I had five apples and three oranges, are there more apples or more fruit?"), children make more correct responses than when they are presented with pictorial cues and asked the same question. Wohlwill (1968) attributes this differential responding between the two types of stimulus presentation to the strong perceptual contrast that occurs between numerically unbalanced subclasses of pictorial items when a pictorial format is used to test for class-inclusion reasoning. The perceptual cues create a mental set which causes the child to translate the class-inclusion question into a question involving a comparison of subclasses rather than a comparison of the correct subordinate-superordinate class. On the other hand, Winer (1974) assumes that the development of class-inclusion reasoning is largely dependent on linguistic cues, or encoding abilities, and hypothesizes that questions of the form, "Are there more apples or more fruit?" may lead the child to interpret "fruit" as referring to any fruit, excluding apples. As a result, the child is led to make a comparison between mutually exclusive classes. When the question is asked in the purely verbal format, the mention of both subordinate classes and the superordinate class counteracts the child's tendency to make an erroneous interpretation of the task.

Regardless of which hypothesis is correct, verbal facilitation is contrary to the Piagetian expectation that thinking with respect to concrete material is easier than thinking conducted at a purely abstract level. This would suggest that Piaget's analysis of class-inclusion behavior is probably correct theoretically but that the behavior is modifiable by means of a number of procedural variations (e.g., Ahr & Youniss, 1970).

The purpose of the present study was first to use bilingual children to separate the confounded linguistic and methodological variables inherent in this task, and secondly to test bilingual children's class-inclusion reasoning. Accordingly, the use of bilingual children tested in either their dominant or subordinate language should allow the determination of whether it is the linguistic or the methodological variable that is the more important factor in this class-inclusion task. It was hypothesized that if the interpretation of distracting perceptual cues was accurate, children performing in either their dominant or subordinate language would find the pictorial format more difficult than the verbal format. On the other hand, if Winer's linguistic encoding hypothesis was correct, only children performing in their dominant language should perform better on the verbal format since only these children have the advantage of being tested in a language where their linguistic skills are sufficiently developed to allow for an interpretation of the problem as a subordinate-superordinate comparison. Moreover, the verbal facilitation should be greater for older children than for younger children because encoding skills should be more developed, especially when testing is conducted in the dominant language.

Forty-four male and 44 female third- and fifth-grade Mexican-American children categorized as either English- or Spanish-language dominant were presented both verbal- and pictorial-type class-inclusion questions. Half of the children were tested in their dominant, and the other half in their subordinate, language.

Results indicated that the children produced more correct responses when they were presented questions in the verbal format than when they were presented with the pictorial format questions, regardless of whether the children were tested in their dominant or subordinate language. This finding supports Wohlwill's (1968) hypothesis which claims that the distracting perceptual cues work against the child in translating the question into its proper subordinate-superordinate comparisons. The pictorial cues are so distracting that even when the children are tested in their subordinate language, they find the verbal-format type of class-inclusion problem easier. It is also important to note that the perceptual cues continue to interfere with class-inclusion reasoning at the older age range. Thus, the perceptual difficulties associated with presenting the class-inclusion task pictorially far outweigh the advantages of being tested in the dominant language or the disadvantage of testing in the subordinate language. (For further information on the study, see Padilla & Romero, 1976.)

There was a distinct advantage in using bilingual children in this study. It allowed Padilla and Romero to determine which of the two hypotheses — Winer's or Wohlwill's — could explain the data, since both hypotheses are consistent with data on monolingual children. This advantage has been discussed by Slobin (1971), who suggests that more precise methodologies can be designed by using bilingual children.

The third study capitalized on the methodological advantage of using bilingual children to separate the cognitive and linguistic variables present in language acquisition. Since bilinguals have been discussed as having two linguistic systems and a common "conceptual core" (Kolers, 1966; Preston and Lambert, 1969; Slobin, 1973), bilingual children enable the investigator to compare the two linguistic systems while "controlling" for the cognitive system. The purpose of the next study was to determine whether by using bilingual children one could find out more about language acquisition in general and establish some general operating principles that would apply to a larger model of language acquisition.

## Experimental Study #3: Relational Concepts

Results from several studies have indicated that the development of a certain structure in one language is later than a corresponding structure, as a result of the greater surface feature complexity (e.g., Engel, 1965; Mikés, 1967; Oksaar, 1970; Padilla & Lindholm, 1976a, 1976b). Slobin (1971) has suggested that this greater linguistic complexity influences the bilingual child's rate of acquisition of the structures, while cognitive complexity may influence the order of acquisition.

There were several purposes to the present study: (1) to hypothesize a set of operating principles, two of which included Slobin's assertion; (2) to establish a methodology to differentiate between cognitive and linguistic factors in the comprehensional acquisition of relational concepts; and (3) to test bilingual children's comprehension of relational concepts.

Relational concepts were chosen because they are abstractions which inherently contain meaning and because they have received a large amount of investigative attention. Clark's (1972, 1973) introduction of the Semantic Feature Hypothesis has stimulated a sizable amount of research into the acquisition of relational concepts. The Semantic Feature Hypothesis states that the meaning of words are made up of smaller parts such as features or components of meaning and that children learn the meaning of words by gradually adding features to the terms. As meanings must become differentiated, more and more perceptual features are used until the information is eventually encoded from a bundle or combination of features. Then this bundle of features is employed to attach meaning to lexical items. For relational terms, this bundle of features consists of dimensional and polarity information. Studies have indicated that children do acquire adjective pairs corresponding to the terms' semantic generality (Clark, 1972; Eilers, Oller, & Ellington, 1974; Ehri, 1976). Furthermore, it appears from most investigations that children acquire unmarked terms prior to marked terms (Clark, 1972; Donaldson & Balfour, 1968; Donaldson & Wales, 1970; Ehri, 1976; Townsend, 1976).

From these two bits of information concerning polarity and dimension, we have constructed two operating principles: (1) concepts with positive polarity will be acquired prior to concepts with negative polarity, so that unmarked terms will be acquired before marked terms; and (2) terms will be acquired from the most general to the most specific as more dimensional features become differentiated. Adding Slobin's (1971) assertion provides two more operating principles: (3) the rate of acquisition for the terms in two languages will be a function of linguistic complexity so that the terms will be acquired at the same rate when linguistic complexity is equivalent; and (4) terms will be acquired in identical order in two languages when cognitive complexity is equivalent.

One hundred-twenty Spanish/English bilingual Mexican-American and 24 monolingual Anglo children participated in the study. These preschool, kindergarten, and first-grade children were presented with 10 stimulus cards on which objects were arranged in antonym pairs. The antonym pairs were presented in arrays so that each array had 4 objects designating 2 antonym pairs. The antonym pairs were: (1) up-down/*arriba-abajo*, (2) wide-narrow/*ancho-angosto*, (3) above-beneath/*encima-debajo*, (4) big-little/*grande-pequeño*, (5) tall-short/*alto-corto*, (6) deep-shallow/*hondo-bajo*, (7) more-less/*más-menos*, (8) long-short/*largo-corto*, (9) fat-skinny/*gordo-flaco*, (11) more-less/*más-menos*, (12) high-low/*alto-bajo*, and (13) thick-thin/*grueso-delgado*. "More-less" was used twice with different cards to distinguish between numerical quantity and a conflict between numerical quantity and physical quantity. The children were asked to "point to the one that _____" *apunte al que está* _____, where the investigator filled in the blank with the concept being tested. Grammatical modifications to this form were made where appropriate.

Three analyses of variance were run to test for the effects of preschool experience, grade, ethnicity, and language dominance, and to provide information regarding the first and third operating principles.

All three of the analyses of variance demonstrated that with age, the children provided more correct responses. Furthermore, the children made significantly more correct responses to the unmarked terms than to the marked terms, a result which verifies the first operating principle and corroborates other studies which have found that unmarked terms are acquired before their marked counterparts (Clark, 1972; Ehri, 1976; Townsend, 1976).

Two of the analyses of variance indicated that test language is an important variable with Spanish-dominant and English-dominant groups making significantly more correct responses in Spanish. Language dominance is not a significant main effect but interacts significantly with test language ($p < .001$). The language dominance by test language interaction indicates that Spanish-dominant children tested in Spanish provided more correct responses than English-dominant children tested in English. Furthermore, English-dominant children performed better in Spanish than did the Spanish-dominant children tested in English. If we subscribe to Slobin's (1971) suggestion that linguistic complexity influences the rate of acquisition, and assume that "rate" is depicted in the superior performance of the children when they are tested with Spanish rather than English terms, then the conclusion that Spanish contains less linguistic complexity than English would be justified. The evidence also lends credence to the third operating principle, which posits that the rate of acquisition will be a function of linguistic complexity.

That linguistic structure of the terms differed in the two languages is evident in view of the results of a factor analysis. The factor analysis was employed with six corresponding antonym pairs in English and Spanish to determine whether any underlying pattern or relationships existed so that the data could be reduced to a smaller set of components. Furthermore, it was felt that factor analysis could shed some light on whether there were any linguistic differences between these pairs of terms. The concept pairs (up-down/*arriba-abajo,* wide-narrow/*ancho-angosto,* tall-short/*alto-corto,* deep-shallow/*hondo-bajo,* high-low/*alto-bajo,* thick-thin/*grueso-delgado*) were chosen because it was felt that since up-down, tall-short, and high-low and their corresponding Spanish terms all refer to a vertical dimension (i.e., height) they would all load on one factor. Similarly, wide-narrow, deep-shallow, thick-thin, and the relevant Spanish terms were chosen because they require additional dimensions (i.e., width, depth) for their comprehension and description. Although other terms could also have been chosen, it was thought that this collection would provide information as to whether factor-analytic techniques are feasible to use with relational concepts. Furthermore, only six pairs could be chosen because of the limited number of subjects (Comrey, 1973). In English, the results occurred as hypothesized. That is, Factor 2 was loaded with the vertical dimension terms while Factor 1 was loaded with the width and depth dimensions, with the exception of tall-short also loading on Factor 1. However, in Spanish, Factor 1 contains the vertical dimension as well as the depth dimension. Since *bajo* also means "low" or "below," and is derived from the verb *bajar,* which means "to descend" or "go down," it is not surprising that *hondo/ bajo* (corresponding to deep/shallow) would appear in the vertical dimension. Factor 2 in Spanish can only be interpreted as including all three dimensions. If the complexity and structure of the terms was equivalent in the two languages, then the factors should have been loaded with the same terms in English and Spanish.

To test the fourth operating principle, which concerns cognitive complexity, it was necessary to determine whether the *order* of acquisition of relational terms was the same in Spanish and English. The terms were rank ordered in each language both singly and in antonym pairs. Inspection of the rank orderings demonstrated that the concepts and concept pairs were acquired in approximately the same order. To verify this observation, correlation coefficients were computed between the English and Spanish terms for both single-term orders and antonym-pair orders. The correlation coefficients were significant for both the single-term ($r = .96$) and antonym-pair ($r = .97$) rank orderings. With values of rho this high, it seems safe to conclude that the children acquired the terms in the two languages in the same order, both singly and in antonym pairs.

The order of acquisition of the terms also corresponded to the order of relational concepts reported by other studies (Clark, 1972, 1973; Eilers et al., 1974). Moreover, the terms were acquired from the most general to the most specific, verifying the second operating principle. Clark (1972) specifies that big-small should be acquired prior to tall-short, high-low, and long-short, and that long-short should appear before wide-narrow, thick-thin, and deep-shallow. This order corresponds to each pair's *n*-space and goes from the most general to the most specific. This exact order materialized in both languages.

## SUMMARY AND CONCLUSIONS

Three main issues pertaining to child bilingualism emerged from the literature review. These issues were: 1) process of duo-language acquisition, 2) linguistic interference, and 3) the effects of bilingualism on cognitive development. This chapter presented the results obtained from a research program which has focused on the study of these three issues in both naturalistic and experimental investigations of Spanish/English bilingual children.

The process of bilingual language development was examined by studying the naturalistic speech of 22 bilingual children from 1-1/2 to 6 years of age. Comparison of the three bilingual children studied longitudinally with Brown's (1973) monolingual English-speaking children demonstrated that the English-language development of the bilingual children was similar to that of the monolingual children. That is, the bilingual children's Mean Length of Utterance (MLU) and their development of linguistic structures were approximately equivalent to the MLU and linguistic development of the monolingual children. Similarly, in comparing the bilingual children's Spanish-language development with Gonzalez's (1970) monolingual Spanish-speaking children's acquisition of language, results showed that the bilingual children's acquisition of Spanish linguistic structures was analogous to the monolingual children's linguistic development. The same case obtains in comparing the English-language development of the 19 bilingual children to that of English-speaking monolingual children. Comparison of the bilingual children's English interrogative and negative structures with Klima and Bellugi-Klima's (1966) English monolingual children's interrogative and negative structures indicated that the bilingual and monolingual children were proceeding through the same stages of rule acquisition for these two English structures. Also, the bilingual children's English morphological development was similar to the morphological development of Brown's (1973) and de Villiers and de Villiers' (1973) English monolingual children. Thus it appears that the English language development of the bilingual children follows the same acquisition process as English monolingual children's development. Kessler (1971, 1972) has also reported that comparison of the process of language development is similar for bilingual and monolingual children. Not only do the bilingual children acquire their linguistic structures in a fashion similar to monolinguals, but they also acquire the structures at about the same time. Swain (1972) reached the same conclusion in her comparative study of monolingual and bilingual children as Kessler (1971), who found that her bilingual children acquired the linguistic structures at about the same time as monolinguals. Although Swain reported that there was approximately a three-month lag in the bilingual children's development, this amount of time is rather insignificant and probably reflects individual differences. These results demonstrating the homogeneous language development of monolingual and bilingual children contradict earlier literature suggesting that bilingual children are handicapped in their language development as a consequence of their simultaneous acquisition of two languages (e.g., Axelrod, 1974; Riley, 1972; Troike, 1972). It should be pointed out that not one of these studies, which found bilingual children to be deficient in their language development compared to monolingual children, actually investigated the language structures in bilingual children's conversations. Instead, the results were obtained by either casual observation or formal testing of the bilingual children's language development.

Comparing the bilingual children's acquisition of their two languages, it was found that the children developed the linguistic rules and structures at about the same time. When the rules or structures differed so that they were more complex in one language than another, the rules or structures of the more complex language almost always were acquired later. Kessler (1971), Mikeš (1967), and Slobin (1973) have drawn the same conclusion in their investigations of bilingual children. Furthermore, there were no instances observed of a child trying to transfer the rules or structures of one language to another. Instead, the children appeared to approach the rules and structures of each language as a monolingual speaker.

Turning to the linguistic interference issue, it was suggested that the term "interference" be replaced with the word "interaction" because of the negative meaning associated with the label "linguistic interference." Further, "interaction" is a more accurate descriptive term because the phenomenon of "linguistic interaction" is actually a result of the contact or interaction between the two language systems. Linguistic interaction consists of three components: 1) language mixing, 2) language or code switching, and 3) translation. The speech of the 19 bilingual children was systematically examined to determine whether there was any pattern of linguistic interaction or whether it was a random process. By its very nature, translation must be considered a pattern of linguistic interaction because in translation, one defines the relationship between a referent and its two phonological shapes in the two languages. Several investigators regard translation as evidence that a bilingual child can distinguish between two linguistic systems (Bergman, 1976; Swain & Wesche, 1975). Conversely, language mixing and language switching have been considered as proof that bilingual children cannot separate the two language systems (e.g., Swain & Wesche, 1975; Volterra & Taeschner, 1978). With the exception of Swain and Wesche's (1975) study, there have been no systematic investigations of the mixing and switching observed in natural speech. Thus, the conclusions that simultaneous bilingual language acquisition create confusion because the child cannot sort out the two languages have been based on very limited observation.

The results from the cross-sectional study of 19 bilingual children indicated that linguistic interaction (including translation) was observed in only 3 percent of the children's speech. The speech analyzed was to adults who conversed essentially as monolinguals. In terms of language mixing, not only was there a very low frequency of mixing, but the mixing followed a systematic pattern. Lexical mixing occurred much more frequently than phrasal mixing. A pattern of lexical mixing emerged; animal names were mixed more often than any other category of terms, followed by labels for social roles (e.g., cowboy, mailman). This pattern occurred in both English and Spanish. Thus, language mixing is not a random process caused by undifferentiated language systems; rather it is a systematic process that follows a hierarchical pattern of mixing mostly nouns, and then verbs, adjectives, and adverbs. Further evidence that the linguistic interaction is systematic is obtained by an examination of the structure of a mixed utterance. The mixed utterances were always structurally correct so that there were never any instances of an utterance such as "oh, that is a *un perro*" although we did observe "oh, that is *a perro*." Thus, children did not repeat sentential information inappropriately as a consequence of mixing. This conclusion held also for the three young bilinguals studied longitudinally.

In the case of language switching, which occurred very infrequently, children appeared to change language to accommodate another speaker or to make fun of the monolingual speaker the child was conversing with.

Finally, the children translated words and phrases correctly. Translation was usually elicited by the experimenter, rather than spontaneous, because of a mixing or switching.

The results obtained from the examination of linguistic interaction demonstrate the children's ability to distinguish between their two language systems. In fact, the amount of linguistic interaction observed was very small considering that language switching and mixing occur frequently in bilingual environments (Gumperz, 1967). It was suggested that the children may have inhibited mixing and switching because they were conversing in two "monolingual" environments.

Further investigation must be conducted on bilingual children's use of linguistic interaction. Such a study should collect extensive language samples of several bilingual children interacting naturally with family members and friends and also with speakers who are definitely monolingual. This study would also need an experimental arm consisting of translation tests in order to understand how children translate. Moreover, it would be interesting to assess the children's motives and rules for switching and mixing.

The last issue concerns the effects of bilingualism on cognitive development. Results from the experiment designed to test the separation of referent and sound in bilingual versus monolingual children revealed a trend toward superior performance of bilinguals over monolinguals. It appeared that, as with Worrall's (1970) and Feldman and Shen's (1971) studies, methodological problems masked the expected results. This problem pertaining to methodology is important. As mentioned earlier, there is a continuum of bilingualism in which bilinguals have not only various skills in a second language but also differing proficiencies in those skills. With bilinguals, it is hard to know in a brief investigation what levels of proficiency the speaker has in the two languages. This problem is compounded by the fact that it is difficult to locate the appropriate samples. In California, and more specifically in Los Angeles, there is a large Hispanic population. If this population were arranged along the bilingualism continuum, we would probably see every space filled up. There are many speakers who are for all intents and purposes English monolinguals. However, when these individuals are put in a control group, we find that they may actually have some limited comprehension skills in Spanish which confound the results.

On the other hand, bilinguals also enable the investigator to design more efficient methodologies to untangle variables which may be confounded for monolinguals. The class-inclusion and relational concepts experiments were successful in differentiating between confounded variables. In the class-inclusion experiment, the two distinct hypotheses which account for monolingual children's class-inclusion behavior were pitted against one another. By using children with two languages, it was found that only one of the hypotheses could account for the obtained results. In the relational concepts experiment, the use of bilingual children enabled us to separate some cognitive and linguistic variables inherently confounded in relational concepts.

260 Kathryn J. Lindholm

Finally, more studies must be done with bilingual children. The literature contains a large number of intensive case studies of one (or two) children. However, there are very few intensive and experimental investigations of simultaneous bilingual language acquisition. These intensive studies need an experimental component to not only observe but to rigorously assess the child's development. At this point, only a small amount of information has accumulated on bilingual children's structural development. We know very little about semantic or cognitive development (excluding IQ testing) or linguistic interaction. Furthermore, we have only rarely taken advantage of the information we can obtain about language development in general by using bilingual children.

## NOTES

[1]The research reported in this paper was supported by Research Grant MH24854 from the National Institute of Mental Health to the Spanish Speaking Mental Health Research Center, UCLA, and by Research Grant OHD90C905 from the Administration for Children, Youth and Families. I would like to extend sincere appreciation to Dr. Amado M. Padilla whose encouragement and assistance in the research and manuscript preparation made this chapter and the research program described in it possible.

[2]Reading and writing are excluded in the definition of young bilingual children since the ability to read or write has usually not yet developed.

## REFERENCES

Ahr, P. R. & Youniss, J. Reasons for failure on the class-inclusion problem. Child Development, 1970, 41, 131–143.

Anastasi, A. & Cordova, F. Some effects of bilingualism upon intelligence test performance of Puerto Rican children in New York. Journal of Educational Psychology, 1953, 44(1), 1–19.

Asher, J. & Garcia, R. The optimal age to learn a foreign language. Modern Language Journal, 1969, 53, 334–341.

Axelrod, J. Some pronounciation and linguistic problems of Spanish-speaking children in American classrooms. Elementary English, 1974, 51, 203–206.

Bain, B. Toward an integration of Piaget and Vygotsky: Bilingual considerations. Paper presented at the 18th International Congress of Applied Psychology, Montreal, 1974.

Barke, E. M. A study of the comparative intelligence of children in certain bilingual and monoglot schools in South Wales. British Journal of Education Psychology, 1933, 3, 237–250.

Ben-Zeev, S. The effect of Spanish-English bilingualism in children from less privileged neighborhoods on cognitive development and cognitive strategy. Unpublished research report to National Institute of Child Health and Human Development, 1975.

Ben-Zeev, S. The influence of bilingualism on cognitive strategy and cognitive development. Child Development, 1977a, 48, 1009–1018.

Ben-Zeev, S. The effect of bilingualism in children from Spanish-English low economic neighborhoods on cognitive development and cognitive strategy. *Working papers on Bilingualism,* 1977b, No. 14, 83–122.

Bergman, C. Interference vs. independent development in infant bilingualism. *In* G. D. Keller, R. V. Taeschner, & S. Viera (Eds.), *Bilingualism in the bicentennial and beyond.* New York: Bilingual Press, 1976.

Bergman, C. Problems of developmental psycholinguistics of bilingualism: language acquisition and language use. Unpublished Ph.D. dissertation, University of California, San Diego, 1977.

Boyd, P. A. Second language learning: The grammatical development of anglo children learning through Spanish. Unpublished master's thesis, University of California, Los Angeles, 1974.

Brisk, M.E. The Spanish syntax of the preschool Spanish American: The case of New Mexican five year old children. Unpublished Ph.D. dissertation, University of New Mexico, Albuquerque, 1972.

Brisk, M. E. The acquisition of Spanish gender by first grade Spanish speaking children. *In* G. D. Keller, R. V. Taeschner, & S. Viera (Eds.), *Bilingualism in the bicentennial and beyond.* New York: The Bilingual Press, 1976.

Brown, R. *A first language: The early stages.* Cambridge, Mass.: Harvard University Press, 1973.

Bruner, J. S. The course of cognitive growth. *American Psychologist,* 1964, 19, 1–15.

Burling, R. Language development of a Garo and English-speaking child. *Word,* 1959, 15, 45–68.

Carlson, H. B. & Henderson, N. The intelligence of American children of Mexican parentage. *Journal of Abnormal and Social Psychology,* 1950, 45, 544–551.

Carrow, E. Comprehension of English and Spanish by preschool Mexican-American children. *Modern Language Journal,* 1971, 55, 299–307.

Carrow, M. A. Linguistic functioning of bilingual and monolingual children. *Journal of Speech and Hearing Disorders,* 1957, 22, 371–380.

Chomsky, C. *The acquisition of syntax in children from 5 to 10.* Cambridge, Mass.: M.I.T. Press, 1969.

Clark, E. V. On the child's acquisition of antonyms in two semantic fields. *Journal of Verbal Learning and Verbal Behavior,* 1972, 11, 750–758.

Clark, E. V. What's in a word? On the child's acquisition of semantics in his first language. *In* T. E. Moore (Ed.), *Cognitive development and the acquisition of language.* New York: Academic Press, 1973.

Comrey, A. L. *A first course in factor analysis.* New York: Academic Press, 1973.

Cornejo, R. The acquisition of lexicon in the speech of bilingual children. *In* P. Turner (Ed.), *Bilingualism in the Southwest.* Tucson, Ariz.: University of Arizona Press, 1975.

Coseriu, E. Structure lexicale et enseignement du vocabulaire. *Les Théories Linguistiques et Leurs Applications.* L'Association International d'Editeurs de Linguistique Apliquée (AIDELA), 1967.

Cummins, J. P. & Gulutsun, M. Some effects of bilingualism on cognitive functioning. *In* S. Carey (Ed.), *Bilingualism, biculturalism and education.* Proceedings from the conference at College Universitaire Saint-Jean, The University of Alberta, 1974.

Davine, M. Tucker, G. R., & Lambert, W. E. The perception of phoneme sequences by monolingual and bilingual elementary school children. *Canadian Journal of Behavioral Science,* 1971, 3(1), 72–76.

de Villiers, J. G. & de Villiers, P. A. Development of the use of word order in comprehension. *Journal of Psycholinguistic Research,* 1973, 2, 331–341.

Donaldson, M. & Balfour, G. Less is more: A study of language comprehension in children. *British Journal of Psychology,* 1968, 59, 461–472.

Donaldson, M. & Wales, R. On the acquisition of relational terms. *In* J. R. Hayes (Ed.), *Cognition and the development of knowledge.* New York: Wiley, 1970.

Dulay, H. C. & Burt, M. K. Errors and stategies in child second language acquisition. *TESOL Quarterly,* 1974a, 8, 129–138.

Dulay, H. C. & Burt, M. K. Natural sequence in child second language acquisition. *Language Learning,* 1974b, 24, 37–53.

Ehri, L. C. Comprehension and production of adjectives and seriation. *Journal of Child Language,* 1976, 3, 369–384.

Eilers, R. E., Oller, D. K., & Ellington, J. The acquisition of word-meaning for dimensional adjectives: The long and short of it. *Journal of Child Language,* 1974, 1, 195–204.

Emlich, L. Beobachtungen über Zweisprachigkeit in ihrem Anfangsstadium. *Deutschtum im Ausland,* 1938, 21, 419–424.

Engel, W. von R. Del bilinguismo infantile. *Archivo Glottologico Italiano,* 1965, 50, 175–180.

Ervin-Tripp, S. Is second language learning like the first? *TESOL Quarterly,* 1974, 8, 111–127.

Fantini, A. *Language acquisition of a bilingual child: A sociolinguistic perspective.* Brattleboro, Vt: The Experiment Press, 1974.

Feldman, C. & Shen, M. Some language-related cognitive advantages of bilingual 5-year-olds. *Journal of Genetic Psychology,* 1971, 118, 235–244.

Geissler, H. *Zwiesprachigkeit deutscher Kinder im Ausland.* Stuttgart: Kohlhammer, 1938.

Gonzalez, G. The acquisition of Spanish grammar by native Spanish speakers. Unpublished Ph.D. dissertation, University of Texas, Austin, 1970.

Gumperz, J. J. On the linguistic markers of bilingual communication. *Journal of Social Issues,* 1967, 23, 48–57.

Hamayan, E., Markman, B. R., Pelletier, S., and Tucker, G. R. Differences in performance in elicited imitation between French monolingual and English speaking bilingual children. *Working Papers on Bilingualism, Issue #8.* Toronto. The Ontario Institute for Studies in Education, 1976.

Haugen, E. *Bilingualism in the Americas.* University, Ala.: University of Alabama Press, 1956.

Hill, H. S. The effect of bilingualism on the measurement of intelligence of elementary school children of Italian parentage. *Journal of Experimental Education,* 1936, 5, 75–79.

Ianco-Worrall, A. D. Bilingualism and cognitive development. *Child Development,* 1972, 43, 1390–1400.

Imedadze, N. V. On the psychological nature of child formation under conditions of exposure to two languages. *International Journal of Psychology,* 1967, 2, 129–132.

Inhelder, B. & Piaget, J. *The early growth of logic in the child.* New York: Harper & Row, 1964.

Johnson, N. A psycholinguistic study of bilingual language acquisition. Unpublished doctoral dissertation, University of Texas at Austin, 1973.

Jones, W. R. A critical study of bilingualism and nonverbal intelligence. *British Journal of Educational Psychology,* 1960, 30, 71–77.

Jones, W. R. & Stewart, W. A. C. Bilingualism and verbal intelligence. *British Journal of Psychology,* 1951, 4, 3–8.

Keller, G. D. Acquisition of the English and Spanish passive voices among bilingual children. *In* G. Keller, R. Teschner, & S. Viera (Eds.), *Bilingualism in the bicentennial and beyond.* New York: Bilingual Press/Editorial Bilingüe, 1976.

Kessler, C. *The acquisition of syntax in bilingual children.* Washington, D. C.: Georgetown University Press, 1971.

Kessler, C. Syntactic contrasts in child bilingualism. *Language Learning,* 1972, 22, 221–233.

Kittell, J. E. Bilingualism and language: Non-language intelligence scores of third grade children. *Journal of Educational Research,* 1959, 52, 263–268.

Klima, E. S. & Bellugi-Klima, U. Syntactic regularities in the speech of children. *In* J. Lyons & R. J. Wales (Eds.), *Psycholinguistics papers.* Edinburgh: Edinburgh University Press, 1966.

Kolers, P. A. Bilingualism and information processing. *Scientific American,* 1966, 218(3), 78–86.

Lambert, W., Just, M., & Segalowitz, N. Some cognitive consequences of following the curricula of the early school grades in a foreign language. Report to the Twenty-First Round Table Meeting on *Linguistics and Language Studies,* 1970, 21, 229–279.

Lambert, W. & Macnamara, J. Some cognitive consequences of following a first grade curriculum in a second language. *Journal of Educational Psychology,* 1969, 60, 86–96.

Landry, R. G. A comparison of 2nd-language learners and monolinguals on divergent thinking tasks at the elementary school level. *Modern Language Journal,* 1974, 58, 10–15.

Leopold, W. *Speech development of a bilingual child: A linguist's record.* Vol. 1: *Vocabulary growth in the first two years,* 1939. Vol. 2: *Sound learning in the first two years,* 1974. Vol. 3: *Grammars and general problems in the first two years,* 1949a. Vol. 4: *Diary from age two,* 1949b. Evanston, Ill.: Northwestern University Press.

Lim, K. B. Prompting versus confirmation, pictures versus translations and other variables in children's learning of grammar in a second language. *Dissertation Abstracts,* 1968, 29, 1885A–1886A.

Lindholm, K. J. & Padilla, A. M. Language mixing in bilingual children. *Journal of Child Language,* 1978, 5, 327–335.(a)

Lindholm, K. J. & Padilla, A. M. Child bilingualism: Report on language mixing, switching and translations. *Linguistics,* 1978, 211, 23–44.(b)

Maccoby, E. & Jacklin, C. *The psychology of sex differences.* Stanford: Stanford University Press, 1974.

Macnamara, J. The bilingual's linguistic performance—a psychological overview. *Journal of Social Issues,* 1967, 23, 58–77.

Mazeika, E. A descriptive analysis of the language of a bilingual child. Unpublished doctoral dissertation, University of Rochester, 1971.

McCarthy, D. Language development in children. *In* L. Carmichael (Ed.), *Manual child psychology.* New York: Wiley, 1946.

McCarthy, D. Language disorders and parent-child relationships. *Journal of Speech and Hearing Disorders,* 1954, 19, 514–523.

McNeill, D. *The acquisition of language: The study of developmental psycholinguistics.* New York: Harper & Row, 1970.

Metraux, R. W. Study of bilingualism among children of U.S.-French parents. *French Review,* 1965, 38, 650–665.

Mikes, M. Acquisition des categoires grammaticales dans le language de l'enfant. *Enfance,* 967, 20, 289–298.

Murdoch, K. D., Maddon, D., & Berg, N. L. A study of the relation between intelligence and the acquisition of English. *Nature and Nurture, 27th Yearbook of the National Society for the Study of Education.* Bloomington: Public School Publishing Company, 1928, 343–353.

Murrell, M. Language acquisition in a trilingual environment: Notes from a case study. *Studia Linguistica,* 1966, 20, 9–35.

Oksaar, E. Zum Spracherwerb des Kindes in zweisprachiger Umgebung. *Folia Linguistica,* 1970, 4, 330–358.

Padilla, A. M. Acquisition of fourteen English grammatical morphemes in the speech of bilingual children. *The Bilingual Review/La Revista Bilingüe,* 1978, 5, 163–168.

Padilla, A. M. & Leibman, E. Language acquisition in the bilingual child. *The Bilingual Review/La Revista Bilingüe.* 1975, 2, 34–55.

Padilla, A. M. & Lindholm, K. J. Development of interrogative, negative, and possessive forms in the speech of young Spanish/English bilinguals. *The Bilingual Review/La Revista Bilingüe,* 1976a, 3, 122–152.

Padilla, A. M. & Lindholm, K. J. Acquisition of bilingualism: A descriptive analysis of the linguistic structures of Spanish/English speaking children. *In* G. Keller, R. Teschner, & S. Viera (Eds.), *Bilingualism in the bicentennial and beyond.* New York: Bilingüal Press/Editorial Bilingüe, 1976b.

Padilla, A. M. & Romero, A. Verbal facilitation of class-inclusion reasoning: Children tested in their dominant or subordinate language. *Perceptual and Motor Skills,* 1976, 42, 727–733.

Padilla, A. M., Romero, A., & Lindholm, K. J. Child bilingualism: An annotated bibliography. Unpublished paper, 1978.

Pavlovitch, M. *Le language enfantin: Acquisition du serbe et du français par un enfant serbe.* Paris: Champion, 1920.

Peal, E. & Lambert, W. E. The relation of bilingualism to intelligence. *Psychological Monographs,* 1962, 76, 1–23 (No. 546).

Perinpanayagam, G. T. Towards becoming bilingual: Cognitive and semantic considerations in language acquisition. Unpublished doctoral dissertation, University of New Mexico, 1973.

Piaget, J. *The language and thought of the child* (M. Gabain, trans.). New York: New American Library, 1974.

Pinter, R. & Arsenian, S. The relation of bilingualism to verbal intelligence and school adjustment. *Journal of Educational Research,* 1937, 31, 255–263.

Preston, M. S. & Lambert, W. E. Interlingual interference in a bilingual version of the Stroop color-word task. *Journal of Verbal Learning and Verbal Behavior,* 1969, 8, 295–301.

Ramirez, A. The Spoken English of Spanish Speaking Pupils in a Bilingual and Monolingual School Setting. Unpublished doctoral dissertation, Stanford University, 1974.

Riley, G. D. Language problems of culturally disadvantaged children. *In* M. V. Jones (Ed.), *Language development: The key to learning.* Springfield, Ill.: Charles C Thomas, 1972.

Ronjat, J. *Le développement du language observé chez un enfant bilingue.* Paris: Librairie Ancienne H. Champion, 1913.

Rueda, R. & Perozzi, J. A. A comparison of two Spanish tests of receptive language. *Journal of Speech and Hearing Disorders,* 1977, 42, 210–215.

Rūķe-Draviņa, V. The process of acquisition of apical /r/ and uvular /R/ in the speech of children. *Linguistics,* 1965, 17, 56–68.

Saer, D. J. The effect of bilingualism on intelligence. *British Journal of Psychology,* 1923, 14, 25–38.

Sandoval, J. Aspects of cognitive development in the bilingual: An exploratory study of the word-object separation. Unpublished master's thesis, University of California, Los Angeles, 1976.

Slobin, D. I. Developmental psycholinguistics. *In* W. Dingwall (Ed.), *A survey of linguistic science.* Maryland: University of Maryland, 1971.

Slobin, D. I. Cognitive prerequisites for the development of grammar. *In* C. A. Ferguson and D. I. Slobin (Eds.), *Studies of child language development,* New York: Holt, Rinehart & Winston, 1973.

Smith, F. Bilingualism and mental development. *British Journal of Psychology,* 1923, 13, 270–282.

Smith, M. E. A study of the speech of eight bilingual children of the same family. *Child Development,* 1935, 6, 19–25.

Spolsky, B. & Holm, W. *Bilingualism in the six year old Navajo hild.* Quebec: Centre International de Recherche sur le Bilinguisme, 1971, 225–239, ERIC ED 060747.

Stern, W. *Die Erlernung and Beherrschung fremder Sprachen Zietschrift fuer padagogesche. Psychologie,* 1919, 20, 104–108.

Stockfelt-Hoatson, B. The teaching of bilingual infant immigrants in a Swedish town. *Linguistics,* 1977, 198, 119–125.

Stockwell, R. P., Bowen, J. D., & Martin, J. W. *The grammatical structures of English and Spanish.* Chicago: University of Chicago Press, 1965.

Swain, M. K. Bilingualism as a first language. Unpublished Ph.D. Dissertation University of California, Irvine, 1972.

Swain, M. & Wesche, M. Linguistic interaction: Case study of a bilingual child. *Language Sciences,* 1975, 37, 17–22.

Tabouret-Keller, A. L'acquisition du langage parle chez un petit enfant en milieu bilingue. *Problemes de Psycholinguistique,* 1962, 8, 205–219.

Titone, R. *Bilingües a los tres años.* Buenos Aires: Editorial Kadelusz, 1975.

Torrance, E. P., Gowan, J. W. J., & Aliohi, N. C. Creative functioning of monolingual and bilingual children in Singapore. *Journal of Educational Psychology,* 1970, 61, 72–75.

Totten, G. O. Bringing up children bilingually. *American Scandinavian Review,* 1960, 48, 42–50.

Townsend, D. Do children interpret marked comparative adjectives as their opposites? *Journal of Child Language,* 1976, 3, 385–396.

Travis, L., Johnson, W., & Shover, J. The relation of bilingualism to stuttering. *Journal of Speech Disorders,* 1937, 2, 185–189.

Troike, R. C. English and the bilingual child. *In* D. L. Shores (Ed.), *Contemporary English: Change and variation.* Philadelphia: Lippincott, 1972.

Trujillo-Carreño, R. El lenguaje de la tecnica. *In* C. Castro Cubells (Ed.), *Doce Ensayos sobre el Lenguaje.* Madrid: Foundacion Juan March, 1974.

U.S. Bureau of the Census, Current Population Reports, Series P-23, No. 60 (Revised), "Language Usage in the United States: July 1975." Washington, D.C.: U.S. Government Printing Office, 1975.

Van Metre, P.D. Syntactic characteristics of selected bilingual children. Unpublished doctoral dissertation, University of Arizona, 1972.

Volterra, V. & Taeschner, T. The acquisition and development of language by bilingual children. *Journal of Child Language,* 1978, 5, 311–326.

Wald, B. Bilingualism. *Annual Review of Anthropology,* 1974, 3, 301–321.

Weinreich, U. *Languages in contact.* New York: Linguistic Circle of New York, 1953.

Williams, J. Cited in McLaughlin, B. *Second language acquisition in childhood.* Hillsdale, N.J.: Lawrence Erlbaum Associates, 1978.

Winer, G. A. An analysis of verbal facilitation of class-inclusion reasoning. *Child Development,* 1974, 45, 224–227.

Wohlwill, J. F. Responses to class-inclusion questions for verbally and pictorially presented items. *Child Development,* 1968, 39, 449–465.

Woods, F. M. First language interference with English verbs and personal nouns by Ilocano students. Unpublished Ed.D. dissertation, University of California, Los Angeles, 1971.

Worrall, A. D. Bilingualism and cognitive development. Unpublished Ph.D. dissertation, Cornell University, 1970.

Worrall, A. D., 1972. See Ianco-Worrall, 1972.

Yoshioka, J. G. A study of bilingualism. *Journal of Genetic Psychology,* 1929, 36, 473–479.

Young, D. I. The acquisition of English syntax by three Spanish-speaking children. Unpublished master's thesis, University of California, Los Angeles, 1974.

Zaręba, A. Język polski w szwecji. *Jesyk Polski,* 1953, 33, 29–31, 98–111. Cited in McLaughlin, B. *Second language acquisition in childhood.* Hillsdale, N.J.: Lawrence Erlbaum Associates, 1978.

# 5

# LANGUAGE ANALOGUE PROJECT, PHASE II: THEORY AND TACTICS[1]

## E. SUE SAVAGE-RUMBAUGH
## DUANE M. RUMBAUGH

Research of the past 15 years which bears upon the question of whether or not life forms other than human might be capable of at least the rudiments of language has had a major impact upon perspectives of communication, language, learning, and cognition, and on views of the ape in its relationship to man (Gardner & Gardner, 1971; Premack, 1971; Fouts, 1974; Rumbaugh, 1977a, 1977b; Patterson, 1978). Communication is vital to the adaptation of animal life in general.

In our view, it is not reasonable to consider language apart from communication: language is a subset of communication. Nonverbal and verbal communicative processes overlap, and at times are even interchangeable in their effects.

It also appears that among animal forms apart from man, there is a relationship between the natural complexity of their social behavioral systems and the degree to which we view the members thereof as likely candidates for language-relevant research. It is no chance event, no coincidence, that all of the relatively successful animal-language research projects have employed apes (Pongidae: *Gorilla, Pongo* and *Pan*). The apes are noted for the complexities of their social behaviors and the degree to which they emulate the behaviors of man. One perspective is that apes show complex behaviors because their cognition allows for inferences regarding the social milieu in a way which fosters the generation of behaviors that appear to be as much manlike as they are apelike.

Because the ape is fundamentally a pure preparation for language research in the sense that it has no humanlike language skills except those

267

which it is taught, it is possible for us to gain a better understanding of these basic questions: (1) What are the requisites for the emergence of the initial language skills? (2) What are the optimal steps of training for the hierarchical arrangements of those skills if the goal is the enhancement of productive linguistic output? (3) Can the relationship between language and cognition be more accurately understood through this type of research with apes? (4) Can the ape become a behavioral model for the research of developmental processes? (5) Might the ape come to serve as a meaningful, valid animal model for certain types of linguistic research which cannot be conducted with the human child either because of ethical constraints or because some research questions imply total control over all experiences that relate directly or indirectly to the language world of the developing child?

## The LANA Project

The original Language Analogue Project (LANA) demonstrated that it is possible for a chimpanzee to achieve a sophisticated form of symbolic communication with human beings via an abstract graphic symbol system. In contrast to the work of earlier investigators in this field (Premack, 1971; Gardner & Gardner, 1971), our communication system is interfaced with a PDP8 computer which unequivocally monitors and records the form and sequence of all symbolic exchanges between chimpanzee and human being. The printed symbols or "lexigrams" appear when "spoken" (i.e., depressed) as projected images both inside and outside the animal's room, so that the chimpanzee can employ a sort of visual telephone to communicate with persons not in sight. This capability permits unequivocal, easily instigated blind tests of the animal's performance.

All symbols that the animal has learned are constantly availed to it. To use a symbol, the animal need only recall its meaning and depress a key. Key depression, as an *output modality,* is essentially equivalent to speaking a word or forming a manual sign. (This of course should not imply without proof that "words" expressed via different modalities have a similar semantic base.) Because the motor response required to express any given word is virtually identical for all words, the chimpanzee cannot rely on cues provided by contextual motor memory, memory linked to an iconicity often present between object or action and word in the case of gesture-based systems. This means that the Yerkish system is considerably more abstract for many symbols.

## Problems of Iconicity

While AMESLAN as employed by fluent human beings involves primarily noniconic gestures, this does not appear to be the case when it is employed by chimpanzees. Our review of the form and contextual use of

Washoe's signs, as described by Gardner and Gardner (1975, 1977) reveals that of 132 signs attributed to Washoe, 79, or 60 percent of them, are highly iconic. This inconicity is related to either the object represented by the sign (as in the case of telephone: thumb and little finger extended from compact hand to ear and corner of mouth), or the action typically preformed with the object (comb-curved fingers drawn across the head in a combing motion). Not only are a majority of Washoe's signs iconic; many signs which are translated as different words involve a similar basic pointing, or open hand, indicative form of gesture. You, me, there or that, mine, and the like, all entail simple indicative gesturing. The chimpanzees in our lab have all spontaneously developed similar indicative gestures and we believe that it is more accurate to refer to them as nonverbal contextual indicators. They are communicative, but they are not abstract context-free symbols.

Furthermore, of the 132 signs attributed to Washoe, the Gardners (1971, 1975) have reported controlled tests employing randomly presented exemplars and controls for cueing for only 32 different signs. (For their new subjects, Moja and Pili, *no* controlled vocabulary tests have been reported, though a considerable amount of comparative data analysis between these chimpanzees and children has been attempted [Gardner & Gardner, 1977].) Since the Gardners have not reported which of Washoe's vocabulary items were tested in a controlled manner, it is not possible to determine the degree of iconicity present in those words which Washoe apparently did master well enough to report controlled tests for.

The issue of iconicity is of concern, but not because an iconic gesture *cannot* function adequately as an abstract symbol. It is clear that adult human signers are totally independent of the inherent iconicity in many signs, for they can as readily employ the finger-spelling mode of production as they can the iconic gesture. However, when a chimpanzee sees someone hammering and begins to make a similar swinging motion with its arm, it is unclear whether the animal is symbolically communicating, imitating, or using a type of performative signing (Greenfield & Smith, 1976), in which this motion simply becomes something habitually associated with hammers and their use. This is a critical issue, because the Gardners' (1977) criterion for determining vocabulary does not exempt such contextually dependent usage. Thus for 15 days (the Gardners' criterion is occurrence of a sign for 15 consecutive days), an individual who was hammering might find that a chimpanzee imitated his motion. He might even note that the chimpanzee came to anticipate his motion and evidenced arm-swinging movements as soon as he picked up the hammer. We have, in our chimpanzees, often noted that this type of imitative behavior becomes associated with the use of a wide range of objects (keys, screwdrivers, faucets, door latches, and so on), but we believe it would be misleading to call these actions symbols. The simple association of iconic sign and object, or action, leaves open to question the chimpanzee's semantic and symbolic comprehension of its own motion. With a purely abstract symbol system like Yerkish, it is clear from the outset that symbol production is not cued by iconicity of action or object and lexigram.

While it surely would be incorrect to presume that *all* of Washoe's sign usage can be attributed to iconic associations between sign and action or object, the burden of proof that such is not the case falls upon the Gardners and others who choose to employ a system which permits such a possibility. To date, the only evidence presented to the contrary is anecdotal, and while considered and informed anecdote surely has a place in reports of language usage, critical issues basic to the overall comprehension evidenced by the animal must be settled by more satisfactory and rigorous means.

Iconic gestures and indicative pointing and/or gesturing are surely important precursors of language (Hewes, 1977; Savage & Rumbaugh, 1977). They often precede word usage in children (Bates, Benigni, Bretherton, Camaioni, & Volterra, 1976), and during the one-word stage they continue to accompany speech as clarifiers of otherwise ambiguous one-word referents (Greenfield & Smith, 1976). However, as the hearing human child gains linguistic competency, vocally produced symbols such as "there" *plus* "car" replace the nonverbal form, indicative point *plus* "car." The complication with AMESLAN, as used by the Gardners, is that for certain signs no explicit distinction is made between linguistic precursors, such as pointing, and language-based abstract symbols, such as a spoken "there."

We believe that any system which purports to permit symbolic languagelike communication between chimpanzee and human being must be abstractly based, as indeed is human speech. Otherwise, the close link between gestural precursors of language and language itself can cloud the major issues of concern and make it extremely difficult to determine at any given point in time the level at which the chimpanzee is operating. Furthermore, because the nonverbal system augments the verbal system in a nonredundant manner (Argyle & Cook, 1976) in our own species, it would seem that parallels between chimpanzee and human communication could be drawn more clearly if the chimpanzee employed, as do we, one output system for nonverbal information and another for abstract verbal symbolic information.

## Problems with Problem Solving

If human-chimpanzee parallels are to be drawn, the symbol system employed by the chimpanzee *must also function in a communicative sense.* This means that it is not sufficient to operationalize language into sets of component parts and present them as a series of problem-solving tasks, each with a limited set of alternatives. This approach, as employed by

Premack (1976), bears little functional similarity to language as used by our own species. Human beings use language to communicate desires, intents, and thoughts, and there is no clear relationship between this sort of activity and the series of if-then problem solving tasks attributed to Sarah. Attempts to replicate Premack's (1976) errorless trials approach to word learning in our own lab have produced only simplistic, context-specific, associationistic performance (Savage-Rumbaugh & Rumbaugh, 1978). It is not possible to attribute this poor performance to any lack of capability on the part of the animals, for they have all demonstrated an ability to symbolically encode and sequence lexigrams in other situations. The problem with the errorless trials and limited alternatives approach is that it does not permit communication and thus tends to be meaningless and perfunctory for the chimpanzee.

## THE YERKES COMPUTER-BASED SYSTEM

We believe that any nonspeech communication system which purports to be symbol based to avail to apes an opportunity to engage in two-way nonvocal, languagelike communication must include and/or permit the following attributes:

1. The user should be able to employ any word in his vocabulary at all times.
2. The "verbal" symbol system should be abstract.
3. The "verbal" symbol system should be distinct from the nonverbal communication system.
4. The main focus of use should be upon communication or, more explicitly, the transfer of symbolic information.
5. Its system should provide for the development and testing of both receptive and productive skills.
6. It should permit unbiased tests to be readily conducted

The only nonspeech communication system so far employed with apes which meets all of the above criteria is the computer-based system at Yerkes Regional Primate Research Center. This system also has the following characteristics which are an important aid to the scientific study of languagelike phenomena in apes:

1. unequivocal instantaneous recording of all exchanges between chimpanzees and between chimpanzee and researcher;
2. clear, consistent responses which are uniform in nature and which can easily be evaluated and judged correct or incorrect. (This bene-

fits the chimpanzee who must interpret the researcher as much as the researcher who must interpret the chimpanzee);

3. a permanent printed copy and magnetic tape of each day's exchange;
4. a summary of all word usage at the end of each day which gives the number of different phrases, their content, and all uses of each word;
5. communication with the chimpanzee while the experimenter is out of the room for control tests;
6. the chimpanzee produces utterances through simple motor responses which facilitate word sequencing.

## The Concept of Animal Model in Language

It is these unique capabilities operating in concert in the Yerkes system which make the Animal Model Approach—or Phase II of the LANA Project—a realistic and viable research program. The long-term goal of the Animal Model Approach is to determine whether or not the chimpanzee is a reasonable animal model for the human child, particularly the retarded child, where ethical constraints and/or problems of control make research with such children unfeasible. This does not mean that we view the chimpanzee as a somewhat deficient or retarded human. (Likewise, the researcher who uses the chimpanzee as a medical model does not view the chimpanzee as a sick human being.) Rather, to the degree that (1) training techniques developed with chimpanzees transfer readily to the teaching of similar skills to nonlinguistic retarded children; and (2) retarded children and chimpanzees show similar transfer abilities, encounter similar difficulties, and evidence similar cognitive strategies; and (3) use their language in a similar communicative and social manner; it may be concluded that the chimpanzee is a valuable animal model for language-relevant research.

From its inception, the Animal Model Project has been closely linked methodologically, technically, and philosophically to a keyboard computer-based language program at the Georgia Retardation Center. Because of this, our research goals have been, in a sense, pragmatically based. Procedures, ideas, and findings can be meaningfully translated to the companion project at the Georgia Retardation Center only to the degree that they reflect a sound semantic base for symbol use and comprehension. Neither anecdote nor statistical proof that correct word usage is above chance suffice when a nonspeech system is being taught to alinguistic children. Arguments which focus upon the issue of whether or not the phenomenon is "really language" (Limber, 1977) become unimportant. Functional symbolic communication emerges, as it should, as the issue of concern. Clearly, if time and energy are to be devoted to teaching a nonvocal communication system to retarded alinguistic children, this system must provide them with the ability to express things which they could not otherwise make clear via simpler alternatives like indicative pointing. This means that their comprehension must be concise, and their productive and receptive skills reliable. This union of applied and basic research which the relationship between these two projects fosters has served to sharpen the focus of the chimpanzee work. Primary emphasis now rests upon semantics, communicative function, and methods of expanding cognitive-linguistic comprehension. Problems of syntax and human uniqueness have become secondary. Likewise, just as language must be an around-the-clock social phenomenon for children, so must it be for the chimpanzee if the ape is to be a realistic model. Therefore the Animal Model Project differs from the LANA Project in several distinct ways.

1. The chimpanzees are worked with throughout the day in a social setting consisting of other animals and human companions.
2. Syntax and word usage as originally designed in the Yerkish gramer of von Glasersfeld (1977) are not followed. In their place we have substituted common English grammar and word usage.
3. Communication between animals and joint use of the keyboard is emphasized early in training.

These changes were made in the interest of promoting productive and relevant exchange between the Animal Model Project and the Georgia Retardation Center Project.

It is not possible in a single chapter to cover all aspects of training and findings relevant thereto since the inception of the animal model project. Therefore, we would like to concentrate upon information generated by two aspects of ape language research which to date have been combined only in the Yerkes project: symbolic communication between chimpanzees and the unique aspects of data generated by ubiquitous recording.

## CHIMP-CHIMP COMMUNICATION

Once the younger animals (Austin, 3½ years; Sherman, 4½ years) had learned to accurately request a variety of foods and drinks (Savage-Rumbaugh & Rumbaugh, 1978), we began to look for a way to encourage them to use these symbols to communicate with one another. Asking one another for food was not satisfactory, as chimpanzees, including these, have an extensive repertoire of begging and pointing gestures (Van Lawick-Goodall, 1968) which can easily be employed to communicate such desires. While it is possible to insist that the chimpanzees use the keyboard to communicate in such situations, there is little to be gained from forcing the symbolic communication mode to supercede the nonverbal mode. The value of symbolic-linguistic communication is that it permits exchange of information that would be impossible via other means. It is highly improbable that a cognitive-behavioral system as complex as language would have emerged among early hominids if it did not enhance their communicative ability beyond the degree already made possible by a complex *non*verbal system.

A central element of symbolic communication is that it permits information exchange regarding objects or events which are displaced in space and time. Human children, even at the one-word stage, evidence an ability to employ language in this way. Greenfield and Smith (1976) report that children in the one-word stage (1 to 2 years old) use single words to express, among other things (1) a desired but absent state (such as having a fan or record "on"), (2) the identity of persons who are absent but who can be identified by sounds associated with them (such as an individual walking about upstairs), and (3) an action that has taken place a short time ago (such as "down" to describe a tower of blocks which has just fallen). Interestingly, none of these messages would be clear if the child's only communicative modality was a nonverbal one.

It thus seems appropriate to conclude that the situations which would best promote interanimal communication would be those which would require the animals to transmit a type of information that could not be exchanged nonverbally. Given the small food-oriented vocabulary (20 words) that the animals had initially, their options for transferring such information were limited. Their vocabulary would permit them, however, to inform each to a type of food one of them had seen being hidden in a container—if the exchange of this information were to be made mutually beneficial to both. Such a task would require that the chimpanzees be able to use a food name as a *name qua name,* apart from whether or not they received the named food. It would require that their receptive competence equal their productive competence and that they be able symbolically to negotiate at least a brief delay between the time they saw a food hidden and the time they communicated the specified food to another animal. It would also seem to require that the animals comprehend the basic nature of their communication, that they attend to one another's symbolic output closely and that, as they shift roles from observer to informer, they have some appreciation of both their own temporary role and the role being played by the other animal (Savage-Rumbaugh, Rumbaugh, & Boysen, 1978a).

Training with the end to providing the animals with these skills entailed three phases. First, a retest of the animals' ability to request the foods and drinks previously learned was given. During this retest, all foods were presented on a randomly sequenced basis and the animals' keyboard performance was not visible to the experimenter, who remained out of the room and questioned the animals by operating the projectors. Table I, row 1 across gives the results: errorless performance.

Next, the animals were asked to name, via their keyboards, various foods and drinks in response to the question, *"What this?"* posed through the projectors by the experimenter, who stood outside the animal's room and held up one of two foods (either beancake or banana). The animals could not request or eat the foods during this task, only name them. If they were correct, they received social praise and/or the opportunity to request a different food from the machine by asking, *"Please machine give* (name of food in vendor)." The number of trials required to learn to name foods without ingesting them is shown in Table I, row 2 across. The initial difficulty with this task did not arise because the animals could not accurately assign labels learned in one setting to the same foods in a more abstract setting. In fact, on the first few trials the animals made no errors. The problem stemmed from their apparent assumption that if they were not allowed to eat the food, they must have misnamed it; thus, on later trials they chose a different name. As we began to understand the nature of their difficulty, we assured the animals through copious social praise that they were indeed correct, even though they could not eat the food. Once they learned that there need not be a correspondence between naming and ingesting a food, we tested this naming skill with foods and objects never employed during naming training (Table I, row 3 across). The animals readily transferred this skill immediately to other words in their vocabulary. It was clear that, had

**TABLE I**

| | Sherman | | Austin | |
|---|---|---|---|---|
| | **Trials** | **% correct** | **Trials** | **% correct** |
| Retest of ability to properly request previously learned foods and drinks (beancake, banana, sweet potato, bread, chow, M&M, juice, orange fruit, milk, orange drink, and coke). | 22/22 | 100 | 22/22 | 100 |
| Number of trials required to learn to name foods in an abstract sense, independent of ingestion of named food. | 93/96 | 97 | 88/96 | 92 |
| Performance on first occasion animals were asked to name foods and objects not used during naming training per se. | 20/22 | 91 | 21/22 | 95 |
| Requests hidden food based on information provided by the experimenter. | 35/36 | 98 | 34/36 | 95 |

we understood their initial cause of confusion, they would have learned indicative abstract naming much more rapidly.

Following the acquisition of naming skills, the chimpanzees were encouraged to use food-name information provided by the experimenters regarding the contents of a sealed container. This was done by standing outside the chimpanzee's room and pointing to a sealed container that had been baited with food out of the chimpanzee's view. The experimenter pointed to the container, then via the experimenter's keyboard stated, ''This (name of food item).'' If the chimpanzee understood this information, he could then request that the food in the container be given because he had been informed as to the type of food, even though he had not seen it. (During this particular task, requests for foods which were not in the container were not honored.)

At first, the animals did not attend to the information provided by the experimenter. They wanted to hold, smell, and bite the container. Initially when the experimenter asked, ''Want this?'' (e.g., orange) they ignored the question, saying instead, ''open'' or ''give open.'' However, following a few opportunities to observe the correspondence between the information provided by the experimenter and the contents of the container once it was opened, they began to attend closely to the experimenter's information and to reliably request the food which had been placed in the container. A high level of performance was rapidly reached on this task as can be seen by the performance on a series of randomly sequenced test trials with the experimenter out of the room (Table I, row 4 across).

Following this training, a test of the animals' ability to symbolically communicate with one another began. Both animals initially used a common keyboard. Each chimpanzee, on alternate trials, was led to an adjacent room where it observed the baiting and sealing of a container with one of 11 foods and drinks (beancake, banana, chow, milk, orange drink, juice, coke, orange fruit, sweet potato, bread, or candy). The contents of the container had to be remembered for approximately 1 minute as each chimpanzee was led (with the container) back to the keyboard, where we then asked him about the container's contents. The second (observer) chimpanzee, who had *not* seen the baiting process, was then given access to the keyboard and allowed to request the food. If he correctly decoded the answer provided by the informer and through the use of that information correctly requested the food, the container was opened. Only if both animals were correct were they each given the food or drink. If either the observer or the informer was incorrect, nothing was given to either (Table II, row 1 across).

The roles of the animals were reversed on each trial and the food or drink to be baited was randomly determined. During the first test of interanimal communication, the experimenter who accompanied the animal during the baiting process was also aware of the container's contents during the communication task. However, during all remaining tests, the baiting

## TABLE II

| | Trials correct/total | % correct |
|---|---|---|
| Animals use single keyboard. Experimenter knowledge. (Vocabulary size = 36) | 33/35 | 94 |
| Animals use single keyboard. Experimenters blind. (Vocabulary size = 36) | 60/62 | 97 |
| Animals use single keyboard but view only projected response of informed animal (control for key position). Experimenters blind. (Vocabulary size = 40) | 24/26 | 92 |
| Animals use separate and differently spaced keyboards, observe one another through window. (A further control for key position). Experimenters blind. (Vocabulary size = 40) | 36/40 | 90 |
| Animals use single keyboard, observing animal points to photograph of food following his request. Experimenters blind. (Vocabulary size = 40) | 27/30 | 90 |
| Control condition to assess chance success. Informed animal not allowed to use keyboard to describe contents of sealed container. Experimenters blind. (Vocabulary size = 40) | 4/26 | 15 |

was done by another experimenter so that no person in the test room with the animals had knowledge of the container's contents. This blind was not instigated at the outset because it was expected that the animals would need some tutoring on this task. They did not. *All* trials given under *all* conditions of interanimal communication are reported. It is clear that the animals exploited previously acquired skills in the successful communication achieved here (Table II, rows 1 and 2 across)

Following these initial tests, four additional control conditions were run with *no* further training. The first two control conditions were instigated to eliminate any possibility that the animals were using position of the key, as opposed to the symbol per se, to communicate. Therefore, in the first condition, the animals were *not* allowed to see one another name the contents of the container; rather, they were only allowed to see the informer's answer as it remained on the projectors above the keyboard (Table II, row 3 across). In the second condition, a window was installed between two test rooms and each animal used its own keyboard to inform the other animal of the container's contents. The observer chimpanzee watched the informer through the window, then used his own keyboard to request the food. Since none of the word keys were in the same exact or relative location on the boards, the observer chimpanzee had to ignore the positions of keys used by the informer to find the same words on his keybaord. The higher level of accuracy on all 40 trials of this test indicates that the information was being transferred via symbols, not key position (Table II, row 4 across). The third control condition was designed to determine whether or not the observing animal, on any given trial, understood the information provided by the informer, or whether he was merely matching the symbol provided by the informer. This was accomplished by providing the observer with 3 randomly selected photos of foods after he had requested the food named by the informer. The observing animal was then asked to point to a photograph of the food that he had requested. If the informer's food name, the observer's food request, and the observer's indication of the correct photograph all agreed, the container was opened by the experimenter. If the appropriate food was found, it was shared (Table II, row 5 across). To determine chance success rates, a final control was run in which the animals who saw the container being baited were *not* allowed to use the keyboard to declare its contents. Both animals were, however, allowed to interact and employ any gestural, vocal, or postural cues at their disposal to inform one another, if possible, of the container's contents. After a brief period of interaction, the second animal was encouraged to go to the keyboard and request the contents of the container. Only a few of these trails were run (Table II, row 6 across) because of the high error rate (chance), disinterest, and negative behaviors (e.g., attempts to steal the container or to get us to press the keys).

Clearly, the exchange of specific information between these two chimpanzees was made possible through their use of symbols. Errors were infrequent and were always names of other foods and drinks, never names for the nonedibles also on the keyboard. The chimpanzees were mutually attentive and readily took turns in the task. If one appeared to have difficulty finding a key, the other one often tried to assist, though we restrained them from doing so.

These studies demonstrated that these chimpanzees could use symbols to communicate specific information. To determine whether these subjects might also ask one another for food through use of the keyboards, we gave one of the chimpanzees a variety of foods on a tray. The second animal was allowed to survey it through the window between the rooms. Spontaneously, the observer used the keyboard and asked for the food by name. The animal with the food was encouraged to observe and to comply with the request for food. The roles were then reversed, and once again the observer spontaneously used the keyboard to request food that it saw in the other's possession. As in the first instance, the animal with the food was encouraged to comply with the request. These experiences were sufficient to the end of facilitating the giving of foods requested to one another. From this point on, the animals readily exchanged roles according to which one had the food, and complied by giving the food requested by specific name. The compliance of the "giver" ranged from 70 percent to 100 percent across sessions, with noncompliance being higher when the food requested was a highly preferred piece of chocolate rather than a relatively nonpreferred item such as a piece of monkey chow.

In another series of studies (Savage-Rumbaugh, Rumbaugh, & Boysen, 1978b), we have also demonstrated with these chimpanzees that information requisite to the exchange of goods (tools) can be mediated through the use of a learned symbol system. At the time, Austin and Sherman were 3½ and 4½ years of age respectively. They had learned the names and functions of six simple tools: key (which unlocked boxes and doors), money (small metal washers which activated a vending machine which dispensed food), straw (a length of plastic tubing which could be threaded through holes in walls and lids of containers to obtain liquid incentives), stick (to dip pudding, yogurt, and so forth, from containers otherwise out of reach), sponge (to obtain liquids from a tall, vertically mounted tube), and wrench (to unscrew bolts so as to open doors for access to incentives). The names for these tools had been learned by the chimpanzees through observations of humans using the materials and through their own attempts to request and to use the tools appropriately in response to seeing incentives baited in a variety of situations. To excel on this task, the chimpanzees had to note which food or drink had been placed in which site, to attend to the physical aspects surrounding the food, to determine what sort of tool would be needed, to recall and to request the tool for use.

Initially, their use of words for the tools suggested that each was a combination of something like a noun and something like a verb. "Stickness" for example, was something associated with the act of taking a long, narrow object and inserting it into a hole. Gradually, however, the words became focused upon the tools per se, and the subjects were able both to accurately name them in physical or photographed representations and to select and give them, each in turn, upon request to the experimenter, in addition to asking for them according to the demands of a given trial on which an incentive was to be obtained through their use.

We then wondered whether they might ask one another for tools. If only one of them had a set of tools, but had no food to be obtained through their use, would he be responsive to requests from the other for a specific tool needed to obtain food in adjacent quarters? Would they comply with one another's requests?

One animal was chosen as the requester of the tool. Food or drink was baited in his view in one of the various sites in his room. The other animal, with the set of tools, could not observe the baiting due to the fact that a blind covered the window during the baiting phase. The blind was raised and the chimpanzee in need of the tool could ask for it through the use of his keyboard. Initially, there was an apparent expectancy, clearly based on past experience, that it would be the experimenter, not the other chimpanzee, who would vend the tool requested. However, with a little encourage-

*Figure 5-1.* Tool kit.

*Figure 5-2.* Austin watches as M&Ms are placed in a long, narrow tube. Sherman is in the adjacent room, but the window between the rooms is covered so that he cannot see where the food is being placed. White tape around the tube renders the M&Ms invisible once they are in the tube.

*Figure 5-3.* The window between the two rooms is open and Austin asks for a stick via the keyboard.

*Figure 5-4 and 5-5.* Sherman selects the stick and passes it through the window to Austin.

*Figure 5-6.* Sherman watches as Austin prepares to insert the stick into the tube.

*Figure 5-7 and 5-8.* Austin uses the stick to push the M&Ms out of the tube.

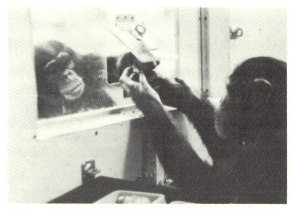

*Figure 5-9.* Austin takes some M&Ms to Sherman.

*Figure 5-10.* Austin and Sherman share use of the stick as a food dipping tool. Austin inserts the stick into a container filled with yogurt outside the room.

*Figure 5-11.* Austin licks yogurt off the end of the stick as Sherman watches closely.

*Figure 5-12.* Austin lets Sherman have a lick also.

ment, the requester soon learned that the experimenter had nothing to give —but the chimpanzee in the adjoining room did. After a few trials on which their respective roles were reversed, the chimpanzees rapidly learned that they had to look to one another for cooperative assistance. With all tool sites baited randomly and with no repeating sequences across trials, performance of the animals improved steadily from the very beginning. Their joint correctness (asking for the correct tool by the first subject, and giving the tool requested by the second subject) across the first four days was 68 percent, 76 percent, 70 percent, and 90 percent. In control tests with the experimenters blind, they were 92 percent correct; with the keyboard *not* available for making the requests, performance was near chance (10 percent; chance correct per trial was 3 percent). Clearly, inadvertent cueing had been ruled out. The rapidity with which their performances increased, together with their previous performance on naming, functional, and receptive skills, serve to support the interpretation that the increase in performance was due to increased ability to communicate and to cooperatively reverse roles.

Observations on certain trials support the conclusion that the animals were not functioning as automatons, but were instead very sensitive to the course of events set into play by a request by one of them. For instance, on one trial Sherman requested ''key'' erroneously when he really had need for a wrench. He watched carefully as Austin searched through his tool kit. When Austin started to pick up the key, Sherman quickly looked over his shoulder to check his request. When he observed the word ''key'' on the projectors, he rushed back to the keyboard and asked for the wrench, then tapped on the newly produced word to draw Austin's attention to it. Austin looked at it, dropped the key, and then picked up the wrench and gave it to Sherman. Both chimpanzees engaged in appropriate correction procedures in apparent response to the other's behavior.

While the foregoing studies do not pretend to simulate the conditions under which early hominids acquired language, their major finding, that chimpanzees can learn to communicate with one another symbolically, suggests that languagelike skills might have been adaptively exploited by even very early hominids. The studies show that a modicum of symbolic ability permits types of information exchange otherwise impossible at the nonverbal level, thereby potentially conferring a considerable advantage on any group of early hominids who possessed a small but shared vocabulary.

## ADVANTAGES OF UBIQUITOUS RECORDING

Recent studies of early language acquisition processes in human children (Greenfield & Smith, 1976; Bates, Benigni, Bretherton, Camaioni, & Volterra, 1976; Nelson, 1973) have shown that previous studies (Braine,

1963; McNeill, 1970) based on a relatively small sample of the corpus of child speech, produced misleading interpretations regarding the nature of early language. Not only were the number of recorded utterances too few to permit generalization regarding the nature of early speech, but the importance of the context, both verbal and nonverbal, surrounding the utterance went virtually unrecognized. Greenfield and Smith's (1976) careful work has revealed that many of the most important aspects of child language had previously been overlooked. Significant aspects of early child language (as emphasized by Greenfield and Smith) include:

1. the parental interpretation, in context, of the child's speech, even at the single-word stage;
2. the use of question-answer dialogue to classify and provide the verbal grammatical base for the early utterances of the child;
3. the development of sequenced one-word utterances toward two- and three-word grammatical phrases;
4. the widening semantic base of a word as its usage moves from a few, narrowly defined, contextually linked situations to a broad comprehension of the word which enables it to be used in response to complex verbal questions, independent of the presence of the referrent.

While we do not yet know whether these same kinds of considerations will prove to be important to chimpanzee language acquisition, it is clear that a powerful and detailed recording system will be necessary if these issues are to be thoroughly investigated. In addition, we submit that to the degree that similarities are found to exist between language as used by children and language as used by chimpanzees, these similarities will be shown to arise from cognitive schemas which permit man and ape to share a common semantic framework underlying all their linguistic exchange. We further agree with Greenfield and Smith (1976) that

> word order is important in establishing the presence of *syntax,* but it is not necessary to establish the presence of underlying *semantic structure* . . . in other words, semantic relations are a more fundamental component of grammar than are syntactic relations. Thus, early semantic relations could *both* lack syntax *and* still be fundamental to the acquisition of grammar. (p. 47)

Premature attempts to compare chimpanzee and child language usage based solely on frequency counts (Gardner & Gardner, 1977) unfortunately only cloud the issue by superficially suggesting that chimpanzees and children are evidencing equivalent language use. Clearly, questions of language acquisition and use are far too complex to be solved in this way. Issues of semantics, changing question-answer dialogues, context-dependent and context-changing usage, can only be adequately addressed if a full account exists of the animals' performance and the training strategies which lead to this performance. This type of record assumes a dual importance when one begins to attempt to translate findings and procedures developed with chimpanzees to mentally retarded children.

It is sometimes difficult to understand, without direct experience, the degree to which the completeness and specificity provided by ubiquitous recording can serve to elucidate numerous aspects of language usage and language-training strategies. For this reason, we present below a day's record. This record is not edited, but is shortened where repetitious so as not to be tedious. It is also annotated so that the reader will be able to understand the context of the exchanges given below. This type of contextual annotation is part of each day's record. The record presented below reflects the performance of Sherman, male *Pan troglodytes* 4½ years old.

Sherman had been actively involved in language training a little over one year at this point. Fifty-six keys were lighted on his board: all were part of his working vocabulary. This day did not differ much from others during this period, except that it was shorter than usual. Contextual notes (inside brackets) appear in regular print, and actual keyboard exchanges, as recorded by the computer, appear beside the "speaker is" name. Proper names besides Sherman, Austin, Columbus, and Ericka, refer to people who are working with the chimpanzees. Implied words are indicated in parentheses.

Janet stands in the lab work area (Figure 5-13) holding Columbus, a 1½ month old infant who is being reared in the language project. Sue brings Sherman into the test room. Sherman looks through the lexan which surrounds the test room, toward Columbus, then approaches the keyboard.

*Time*

| 9:45:50 | *Sherman:* | Give Columbus. |
| 9:45:54 | *Sue:* | Yes, give Columbus. |
| 9:49:58 | *Sue:* | (Go) out room. |

Columbus is outside of the test room. Sherman and Sue walk out of the room. Sue takes Columbus from Janet and returns to the test room with both Sherman and Columbus.

| 9:50:29 | *Sherman:* | Columbus. |
| 9:50:33 | *Sue:* | Yes, give Sherman Columbus. |

Sue transfers Columbus to Sherman and he carries Columbus ventrally and builds a nest of blankets and a tire.

| 9:51:55 | *Sherman:* | Out room. | [Request is implied here by |

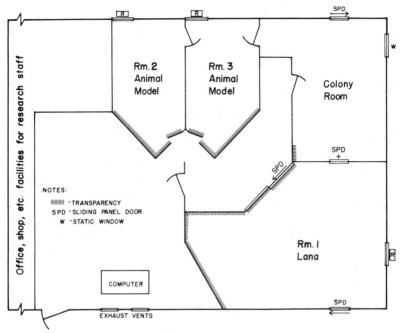

*Figure 5-13.* Floorplan of the laboratory. The work area, which includes kitchen facilities, is in the lower left quadrant.

| | | | |
|---|---|---|---|
| 9:52:00 | *Sue:* | Yes. | |
| 9:52:04 | *Sue:* | What (is) this? | |
| 9:52:19 | *Sherman:* | Wrench. | |
| 9:52:21 | *Sue:* | No. | |
| 9:52:25 | *Sue:* | What (is) this? | |
| 9:52:28 | *Sherman:* | Money. | |
| 9:52:30 | *Sue:* | Yes, money. | |
| 9:52:32 | *Sue:* | Sherman (go) out room. | |

Sherman's hesitant facial expression.]
[This request will be honored.]
[Sue holds up a piece of money and encourages Sherman to name it prior to going out the room. In this way, indicative naming is worked in with spontaneous requests for other things so that it does not become something that the chimpanzee does only during drilling.]

Sherman carries Columbus out into the general lab area. Columbus begins to fuss, so Sue takes Columbus from Sherman and returns him to the nearby incubator. Sherman is then lead back to the test room.

| | | | |
|---|---|---|---|
| 9:55:35 | *Sherman:* | Out room. | [Sue ignores this request.] |
| 9:55:42 | *Sherman:* | Sherman out room. | [Question implied by Sherman's hesitant facial expression.] |

| 9:55:45 | *Sue:* | Yes. | |
|---|---|---|---|
| 9:55:50 | *Sue:* | What (is) this? | [Sue holds up a key] |
| 9:55:52 | *Sherman:* | Key. | |
| 9:55:53 | *Sue:* | Yes. | |
| 9:55:56 | *Sue:* | Sherman (go) out room. | |

Sherman goes out of room, plays in the sink, and with utensils on cabinet. He then tries to take Columbus out of the incubator. Sue prevents this and leads Sherman back to the test room.

| 9:59:49 | *Sherman:* | Give Columbus. | |
|---|---|---|---|
| 9:59:51 | *Sue:* | No. | |
| 10:00:40 | *Sue:* | (Want to) go (to) Austin's room? | [Austin is a 3½ year-old chimpanzee who is being |
| 10:00:41 | *Sherman:* | Room out. | worked with in a room adjacent to Sherman. They can see each other clearly through the window between the two rooms.] |
| 10:00:50 | *Sue:* | What's this? | [Sue holds up stick to be named.] |
| 10:00:52 | *Sherman:* | Stick. | |
| 10:00:54 | *Sue:* | Yes stick. | |
| 10:00:57 | *Sherman:* | Sherman out room. | |

Sherman appears to understand that he has correctly named the stick and can go out of the room. He so states, and walks out of his room toward Austin's room. Sue brings him back in. He looks toward Austin's room.

| 10:01:54 | *Sherman:* | Austin. |
|---|---|---|
| 10:01:58 | *Sue:* | Yes go (to) Austin's room. |

Sherman runs rapidly into Austin's room. These two chimpanzees have a similar vocabulary. For both, the keys are moved regularly and are never in the same position on both keyboards. Once they have learned a word well, they have no problem using it on one location on one keyboard and in another on the other chimpanzee's keyboard. Austin is drinking orange drink and ignores Sherman.

| 10:02:59 | *Sue:* | [using Austin's keyboard] Sherman (want) go out room? |
|---|---|---|
| 10:03:01 | *Sherman:* | Out room. |

Sherman is led back to his own room. Before going into the room, Sue turns on a slide projector. . . . which displays a photograph of the wooded and grassy areas outside of the language building. (There are various slides of food, people, the outdoors, and so on, so that the chimpanzee will not learn simply a specific response to a specific slide.)

| | | | |
|---|---|---|---|
| 10:04:01 | *Sherman:* | Go open. | [Pointing to the slide] |
| 10:04:03 | *Sue:* | No. | |
| 10:04:24 | *Sue:* | Go playroom (or) out-doors? | |
| 10:04:25 | *Sherman:* | Outdoors. | |
| 10:04:29 | *Sue:* | Yes, go outdoors. | |

Sue and Sherman go outdoors and play on the grass. When they come back, Sue picks up some food and places it where one of a number of tools is needed by Sherman in order to obtain the food. Both Sherman and Austin have kits which at this point in training are composed of seven tools: a stick, a key, a magnet, a piece of money, a straw, a wrench, and a sponge. All of these tools can be employed in a number of ways to obtain food placed in various locations. This provides the animals with a functional base for word knowledge and use regarding these tools. Tools are also named, in an indicative sense, and tested in a receptive sense each day, during this phase of training. As Sue and Sherman come inside, food is placed in a token vending device which dispenses food each time a piece of money (a metal washer) is inserted.

| | | | |
|---|---|---|---|
| 10:10:01 | *Sue:* | Sue move money. | [Before Sherman has a chance to ask for money, Sue picks it up and drops it into a three-foot-long narrow tube attached to the wall. The only way metal objects can be retrieved from this tube is through use of a magnet attached to a string.] |
| 10:10:12 | *Sherman:* | Give magnet. | |
| 10:10:16 | *Sue:* | Yes magnet. | |

In addition, Sue then shows Sherman three photographs of tools and he points to the picture of the magnet. He is handed the magnet, which he uses to retrieve the money dropped in the tube. He then uses the money to operate the token vending device to get the food.

| | | | |
|---|---|---|---|
| 10:11:15 | *Sherman:* | Out give room. | [Sherman indicates question by facial expression— he requests that he go out of the test room.] |
| 10:11:20 | *Sue:* | What's this? | [Sue holds up straw.] |
| 10:11:24 | *Sherman:* | Straw. | [The straw is plastic tubing that can be used to drink liquids from containers that have only a small opening in the top.] |
| 10:11:25 | *Sue:* | Yes straw. | |
| 10:11:28 | *Sue:* | Sherman (go) out room. | |

Sherman and Sue go out of the room. Sherman sees Austin drinking orange drink in the adjacent room and goes back to his keyboard.

| | | | |
|---|---|---|---|
| 10:13:47 | *Sherman:* | Want orange drink. | |
| 10:13:52 | *Sue:* | Want orange drink out (of) room? | |
| 10:13:57 | *Sherman:* | Room out. | ["yes, out of room."] |
| | | | |
| 10:23:15 | *Sherman:* | Tickle. | [Sherman looks at Sue with |
| 10:23:16 | *Sue:* | Yes, tickle Sherman. | playful expression.] |
| | | Room out. | ["Yes, out of room."] |
| 10:14:09 | *Sue:* | Yes orange drink out (of) room. | |

Sue and Sherman go out of the room and get a small paper cup and a large container of orange drink. Sherman knows that he is not allowed to drink out of the juice containers.

| | | | |
|---|---|---|---|
| 10:15:57 | *Sherman:* | Pour orange drink. | [Sue attempts to pour orange drink but the lid is tightly screwed on the container and none comes out.] |
| 10:16:01 | *Sue:* | This orange drink (is) shut. | |
| 10:16:05 | *Sherman:* | Give open. | |
| 10:16:10 | *Sue:* | Yes, open this. | [Sue takes the lid off the container and Sherman attempts to stick his hand inside it.] |
| 10:16:18 | *Sue:* | (Want) pour orange drink? | |
| 10:16:28 | *Sherman:* | Pour orange drink. | [Sue pours orange drink into Sherman's cup and as he drinks it, she closes the orange-drink container again.] |
| 10:17:59 | *Sherman:* | Open. | [Sherman points to the orange-drink container and whines.] |
| 10:18:02 | *Sue:* | Yes, open orange drink. | |
| 10:18:13 | *Sherman:* | Pour orange drink. | [Sherman holds his cup |
| 10:18:16 | *Sue:* | Yes, pour orange drink. | toward the orange drink.] |

Exchanges regarding the opening, shutting, and pouring of the orange drink continue until Sherman appears to have had his fill at 10:22:22. He attempts to engage Sue in a tickling bout by pulling on her with a playful expression.

| | | | |
|---|---|---|---|
| 10:22:22 | *Sue:* | (Sue) move orange drink out (of room). | |
| 10:23:12 | *Sue:* | Tickle Sherman? | |
| 10:23:15 | *Sherman:* | Tickle. | [Sherman looks at Sue |
| 10:23:16 | *Sue:* | Yes, tickle Sherman. | with playful expression.] |

Sue tickles Sherman briefly, then stops.

| 10:24:52 | *Sherman:* | Tickle. | [Sherman looks at Sue with |
|          | *Sue:* | Yes, Sue tickle Sher-<br>man. | playful expression.] |

Sherman stops tickling, watches through the window Austin and Janet, who are tickling in the adjacent room.

| 10:26:30 | *Sherman:* | Austin. | |
| 10:26:34 | *Sue:* | (Go) Austin's room? | [Sue indicates "go" |
| 10:26:35 | *Sherman:* | Room. | through use of pointing |
| 10:26:38 | *Sue:* | (Go) Austin's room? | towards Austin's room.] |
| 10:26:41 | *Sherman:* | Austin's room. | |
| 10:26:45 | *Sue:* | Yes, go Austin's room. | |

Sherman runs into Austin's room. The following exchanges take place on Austin's keyboard, with Sherman, Janet, Austin, and Sue.

| 10:29:42 | *Sherman:* | Tickle. |
|---|---|---|

Sherman clearly directs this message, via his gaze toward Janet, who responds, then tickles Sherman.

| 10:29:47 | *Janet:* | Tickle, yes. | |
| 10:29:54 | *Austin:* | Give Austin tickle. | [Austin directs this message to<br>Sue via his gaze.] |
| 10:30:00 | *Sue:* | Yes, tickle Austin. | |

After tickling Austin, Sue points toward the door and asks:

| 10:34:07 | *Sue:* | Sherman (go) out room? |
|---|---|---|

Sherman ignores Sue but looks at Janet.

| 10:34:10 | *Sherman:* | Tickle. |
| 10:34:12 | *Janet:* | Yes, tickle Sherman. |

When Janet stops tickling Sherman, Austin looks at Sherman with a playful face and gambols toward the keyboard.

| 10:39:10 | *Austin:* | Give— | [Before Austin can say any-<br>thing further, Sherman<br>jumps on him and play-<br>bites him.] |
| 10:39:27 | *Austin:* | Give Austin tickle. | [This also appears to be dir-<br>ected toward Sherman, who<br>does continue tickling Austin.] |

Sue holds up a swing which can be attached to the ceiling.

| 10:40:11 | *Sue:* | Want swing? |
| 10:40:54 | *Austin:* | Give swing. |
| 10:41:02 | *Sue:* | Yes, give Austin swing. |

The swing is hooked to the ceiling and Austin immediately begins to play on it. Sue again points to the door and asks:

| 10:44:39 | *Sue:* | Sherman (want) out (of) room? | |
| 10:44:55 | *Sue:* | Sherman (want) out (of) room? | [Sue is pointedly ignored.] |
| 10:45:06 | *Sue:* | Sherman (go) out (of) room. | [Sherman is led out of the the room.] |

When Sherman is led out of the room, Austin runs to the keyboard.

| 10:46:15 | *Austin:* | Give out room. |
| 10:46:28 | *Janet:* | Yes, Austin (go) out room. |

Sherman is led back to his room, but keeps looking toward the lab work area, where Columbus's incubator is located.

| 10:47:44 | *Sherman:* | Give Columbus. |
| 10:47:48 | *Sue:* | No. |
| 10:47:58 | *Sue:* | Sherman go playroom. |

Sherman's room is dirty, so he is taken back to the general play area while it is cleaned. Upon returning to his room, Sherman notes that the orange drink has been left right next to door of the test room.

| 11:23:51 | *Sherman:* | Pour orange drink. |
| 11:23:57 | *Sue:* | Yes, Sue move orange drink. |
| 11:24:02 | *Sue:* | (want to) go out room? |
| 11:24:04 | *Sherman:* | Room out. |
| 11:24:07 | *Sue:* | Yes, Sherman (go) out room. |

Sherman and Sue go out of room. Orange drink is poured in a container outside of the room. To reach it from inside the room, Sherman must use a straw.

| 11:24:52 | *Sherman:* | Give straw. |
| 11:24:56 | *Sue:* | Give straw (to) Sherman. |

Sue hands the straw to Sherman, who tries to thread it through a narrow hole in the lexan to the orange drink outside. He is not successful.

| 11:25:02 | *Sherman:* | Do. | [Sherman whimpers and |
| 11:25:06 | *Sue:* | Yes, Sue do straw. | looks at Sue.] |

Sue helps Sherman thread the straw through the wall.

| 11:26:31 | *Sue:* | (want) M&M out room? | [Sue attempts to get |
| 11:26:34 | *Sherman:* | Out room. | Sherman to specify whether |
| 11:26:39 | *Sue:* | Want M&M? | or not he would like a par- |
| 11:26:41 | *Sherman:* | Give M&M. | ticular food once he goes out |

the room. However, Sherman does not combine here his request to go out of the room and his request for a given food.]

Sherman is given some M&Ms out of the room, and additional M&Ms are placed behind a small door which is bolted shut.

| 11:28:06 | *Sherman:* | Wrench. | [Sherman "asks" for the appropriate tool to open the door.] |
| 11:28:10 | *Sue:* | Yes, wrench. | [Sue takes a wrench out of the tool kit and holds it up so that Sherman can see that he has requested the correct tool.] |
| 11:28:14 | *Sue:* | Open wrench door? | ["Wrench door" is a phrase used to distinguish this door which must be opened with a wrench from others which are latched and can be opened by the chimpanzees without a tool.] |
| 11:29:19 | *Sherman:* | Door. | |
| 11:29:22 | *Sue:* | Yes, open wrench door. | |

Sue helps Sherman use the wrench to loosen the bolt. Once it is loosened Sherman unscrews it by hand, opens the small door, and retrieves the M&Ms. This kind of exchange continues, with Sherman requesting various tools as needed, aid as needed, and identifying a photo or naming a tool if asked to do so until 11:56:31, when he again goes to the playroom with Austin and Ericka (a 4½ year-old female chimpanzee).

The afternoon session began with a review of slides. As each appeared above Sherman's keyboard, he was to identify it. If he was correct he received a token which he could use to operate a nearby vending device and buy a piece of peanut butter and jelly sandwich, one of his favorite foods. The first set of slides includes Austin, Columbus, and Sue. Sherman has just begun to use these names for pictures.

Previously they have been associated with desired activities accompanied by a particular person or chimpanzee. The first slide is of Columbus. Sherman rarely misidentified Columbus, though at this point in training he did experience some difficulty with other chimpanzees and with people.

| | | | |
|---|---|---|---|
| 13:37:48 | *Sue:* | Want slide? | |
| 13:37:50 | *Sherman:* | Slide. | [Sherman points to the |
| 13:37:52 | *Sue:* | Yes, slide. | slide projector screen above his keyboard.] |

Sue hands Sherman the slide advance control and he pushes the button, causing a picture of Columbus to appear on the screen.

| | | |
|---|---|---|
| 13:38:13 | *Sherman:* | Give Columbus. |
| 13:38:17 | *Sue:* | Yes, this Columbus. |

Sue gives Sherman a piece of money, but he ignores it. He climbs onto her back as though he thinks he is going to go out of the room to see Columbus. Sue puts Sherman down and he advances the slide. This time a picture of Austin appears. Sherman hesitates.

| | | |
|---|---|---|
| 13:38:47 | *Sue:* | What's this? |
| 13:38:55 | *Sherman:* | Door Austin. |
| 13:39:02 | *Sue:* | Yes, Austin. |

The "door" key is right above the key for "Austin," and both have similar lexigrams. It appeared that Sherman accidentally depressed "door," realized his error, then depressed Austin.

This naming task continues until 14:03:19. Sherman is correct on 20 out of 27 trials. (Note: this is not a controlled test; it is simply daily practice.) Sherman continues activating the slide projector until the vending device is empty. A slide of the outdoors is then projected above the keyboard.

| | | | |
|---|---|---|---|
| 14:03:13 | *Sherman:* | Outdoors. | |
| 14:03:19 | *Sue:* | Go outdoors? | [Sue tries to encourage the use of the two-word phrase, "go outdoors."] |
| 14:03:20 | *Sherman:* | Outdoors. | |
| 14:03:22 | *Sue:* | Yes. | |
| 14:03:27 | *Sue:* | Go outdoors? | |
| 14:03:29 | *Sherman:* | Out room. | |
| 14:03:36 | *Sue:* | Go outdoors? | |
| 14:13:39 | *Sherman:* | Tickle. | |
| 14:13:43 | *Sue:* | Yes. | [Sherman appears to abandon attempts to get Sue to take him outdoors. Instead of using a two-word phrase, he requests a different activity.] |

After a brief tickling bout, Sue points to the slide.

14:03:58  *Sue:*       Go outdoors?
14:03:59  *Sherman:*   Outdoors.

Sherman is hesitant to sequence these words. Sue directs his attention to the "go" key.

14:04:05  *Sherman:*   Go outdoors.
14:04:10  *Sue:*       Yes, go outdoors.

After a brief outing, Sherman is asked to name slides of tools, food, people, and other chimpanzees. Again Sherman operates the slide projector himself. If he becomes bored during this naming task, his requests to go out of the room or outdoors are honored.

14:14:24  *Sue:*       (Want) slide?
14:14:25  *Sherman:*   Slide.
14:14:58  *Sherman:*   Money.

A picture of money is on the screen.

14:15:08  *Sue:*       Yes (this) money.
14:15:18  *Sherman:*   Orange drink.

A picture of orange drink is on the screen.

14:15:28  *Sue:*       Yes (this) orange drink.
14:15:34  *Sherman:*   Wrench.
14:15:44  *Sue:*       Yes, (this) wrench.

This naming task continues until 14:48:51. It is interrupted by one request to go outdoors. Overall Sherman is correct on 37 out of 41 trials. All errors are on "Sue" and "Austin."

Following the naming task, Sherman's receptive skills are tested. Sue gives Sherman the tool box, stands outside the room, and uses the experimenter's keyboard to request that Sherman hand her a tool.

15:02:29  *Sue:*   Give sponge.
15:02:32  *Sue:*   Yes.          [Sherman gives Sue the sponge.]
15:02:48  *Sue:*   Give wrench.
15:02:59  *Sue:*   Yes.          [Sherman gives Sue the wrench.]

This task continues until 15:17:49. Sherman is correct on 27 out of 30 trials. All errors are on "straw." Following the completion of this task, Sherman looks through the lexan at Columbus.

| 15:18:04 | *Sherman:* | Columbus. |
| 15:18:10 | *Sue:* | Go (to) Columbus. |
| 15:18:12 | *Sherman:* | Give out Columbus. |
| 15:18:17 | *Sue:* | Yes, give Columbus out |
| | | room. |

Sue and Sherman go out of the room and Sherman is allowed to play with Columbus. Sherman starts to eat a peanut butter sandwich that was on the counter. Sue takes the sandwich and leads Sherman back to his room. Sherman does not have a name for peanut butter and jelly sandwich, although he does know "bread."

| 15:19:25 | *Sue:* | Want this? |

She holds out the sandwich.

Sherman looks all over the keyboard, starts to depress "bread," but hesitates, noting that the key is not lighted. (Unlighted keys are inactive. In this case, the microswitch for bread had failed that morning, hence the key was dark.)

| 15:19:38 | *Sherman:* | Austin. |

Sue does not know whether Sherman has called the sandwich "Austin" or if he wants to go to Austin's room.

| 15:19:45 | *Sue:* | Go (to) Austin's room? |
| 15:19:47 | *Sherman:* | Room. |

Sherman looks toward Austin's room.

| 15:19:54 | *Sue:* | Yes, go (to) Austin's |
| | | room. |

Sherman runs to Austin's room, and Sue follows carrying the sandwich. Sherman does not play with Austin, but begins an immediate search of Austin's keyboard.

| 15:20:16 | *Sherman:* | Bread. |

Sherman holds a hand out toward sandwich.

| 15:20:22 | *Sue:* | Yes, (this) bread. |
| 15:20:27 | *Sherman:* | Bread. |
| 15:20:35 | *Sue:* | Give Sherman bread? |
| 15:20:37 | *Sherman:* | Sherman want bread. |

It appears that Sherman had asked to go to Austin's room, not for play and company, but rather to have access to his keyboard so as to be able to use the key for "bread." This conclusion is strengthened by the fact that after Sherman uses

Austin's keyboard to obtain the sandwich, he then asks for another food, the key for which was not working on his own board, but was working on Austin's.

| | | |
|---|---|---|
| 15:20:55 | *Sherman:* | Corn. |
| 15:21:00 | *Sue:* | Yes, corn. |
| 15:21:06 | *Sue:* | (Want) corn out (of) room. |
| 15:21:08 | *Sherman:* | Out room. |
| 15:21:10 | *Sue:* | Yes. |

Sue and Sherman go out of the room and get a package of corn (chips). They go back into Austin's room since this key is not functioning on Sherman's board.

| | | |
|---|---|---|
| 15:22:36 | *Sherman:* | Corn. |
| 15:22:41 | *Sue:* | Yes, this corn. |
| 15:22:45 | *Sue:* | Give Sherman corn? |
| 15:22:47 | *Sherman:* | Sherman corn. |
| 15:22:50 | *Sue:* | Yes, give Sherman corn. |

Sherman then asks for orange drink, that it be opened as he had done in the morning session. After drinking several cups of orange drink and playing with Austin, Sherman asks:

| | | |
|---|---|---|
| 15:26:38 | *Sherman:* | Give scare. |
| 15:26:42 | *Sue:* | Yes, scare Sherman. |
| 15:27:20 | *Sherman:* | No. |

When Sherman asks to be scared, Sue enters the room with a rubber snake, halloween mask, and the like, and chases Sherman. When frightened, Sherman uses the word "no" to terminate the activity. If only mildly scared, Sherman will ask to be scared over and over. If scared so badly that he screams, Sherman does not ask to be scared any more that day. Sherman is taken back to his own room, where he asks for Columbus and again asks to be scared. These requests are honored and the afternoon session continues in a fashion similar to the morning's session. At 15:54:05, a new word, "gone," is introduced. Sue enters Sherman's room with a few M&Ms in a cup. Sherman requests them and when the M&Ms are gone, Sue notes this by pointing to the empty cup and saying, "M&M gone," through the keyboard. After noting the nonexistence of M&Ms twice by using "gone," Sherman spontaneously notes this fact the third time the cup is empty by saying "gone."

| | | |
|---|---|---|
| 15:54:05 | *Sherman:* | M&M. |
| 15:54:08 | *Sue:* | Yes, this M&M. |
| 15:54:11 | *Sherman:* | Give Sherman M&M. |
| 15:54:14 | *Sue:* | Yes, give Sherman M&M. |

Sue gives the M&Ms.

| | | |
|---|---|---|
| 15:54:23 | *Sherman:* | Sherman give M&M? |

Sue hesitates, because Sherman has no M&Ms to give.

| 15:54:28 | *Sue:* | Give Sherman M&M. |
| 15:43:31 | *Sherman:* | Give Sherman M&M |
| 15:54:34 | *Sue:* | Yes, give Sherman M&M. |
| 15:54:41 | *Sue:* | M&M gone. |
| 15:54:45 | *Sherman:* | Gone. |
| 15:54:48 | *Sue:* | M&M gone. |
| 15:54:52 | *Sue:* | (Want) M&M out room? |
| 15:54:54 | *Sherman:* | Out room. |
| 15:54:59 | *Sue:* | Yes, go out room (get) M&M. |

Sherman and Sue go out of the room and put more M&Ms in the cup.

| 15:55:57 | *Sherman:* | M&M. |
| 15:56:00 | *Sue:* | Yes, this M&M. |
| 15:56:02 | *Sherman:* | Give Sherman M&M. |
| 15:56:06 | *Sue:* | Yes, give Sherman M&M. |
| 15:56:18 | *Sue:* | M&M gone. |
| 15:56:20 | *Sherman:* | Gone. |
| 15:56:24 | *Sue:* | Yes, M&M gone. |
| 15:56:30 | *Sue:* | Want M&M out room. |
| 15:56:33 | *Sherman:* | Room out. |
| 15:56:35 | *Sherman:* | Out room. |
| 15:56:38 | *Sue:* | Yes. |

Sue and Sherman go out of the room and put more M&Ms in the cup for the third time.

| 15:57:31 | *Sherman:* | M&M. |
| 15:57:34 | *Sue:* | Yes, this M&M. |
| 15:57:36 | *Sherman:* | Sherman M&M. |
| 15:57:39 | *Sue:* | Yes, give Sherman M&M. |
| 15:57:58 | *Sherman:* | Give Sherman M&M. |
| 15:58:02 | *Sue:* | Yes, give Sherman M&M. |

There are no more M&Ms in the cup. Sue shows Sherman the empty cup.

| 15:58:08 | *Sherman:* | Gone. |
| 15:58:11 | *Sue:* | Yes, M&M gone. |
| 15:58:15 | *Sherman:* | Out room. |
| 15:58:17 | *Sue:* | Yes. |

Then Sherman asks to go into Austin's room once again, where Austin requests that Sherman tickle. At 16:16:15, Sherman returns to his room and requests milk. Sue shares some milk with Sherman and returns him to the playroom at 16:19:43.

The summary made by the computer of all of Sherman's statements for that day, rank-ordered by frequency of occurrence (left column), follows.

```
0029  SHER:  OUT ROOM
0024  SHER:  POUR ORANGE DRINK
0022  SHER:  AUSTIN
0021  SHER:  OPEN
0012  SHER:  SUE
0010  SHER:  M&M
0009  SHER:  GIVE COLUMBUS
0009  SHER:  STICK
0007  SHER:  COLUMBUS
0007  SHER:  ROOM OUT
0006  SHER:  OUTDOORS
0006  SHER:  GONE
0005  SHER:  WRENCH
0004  SHER:  ROOM
0004  SHER:  GIVE OUT ROOM
0004  SHER:  MONEY
0004  SHER:  MILK
0004  SHER:  MAGNET
0004  SHER:  GIVE SHERMAN M&M
0003  SHER:  SHERMAN OUT ROOM
0003  SHER:  WANT ORANGE DRINK
0003  SHER:  GIVE OPEN
0003  SHER:  TICKLE
0003  SHER:  DOOR
0003  SHER:  SHERMAN GIVE M&M
0003  SHER:  SHERMAN M&M
0002  SHER:  SHERMAN ROOM OUT
0002  SHER:  GIVE PUDDING
0002  SHER:  SCARE
0002  SHER:  SWEET POTATO
0002  SHER:  GIVE POUR DRINK
0002  SHER:  SLIDE
0002  SHER:  DOOR AUSTIN
0002  SHER:  YES SUE
0002  SHER:  GO OUTDOORS
0002  SHER:  ORANGE DRINK
0002  SHER:  SPONGE
0002  SHER:  JUICE
0002  SHER:  BLANKET
0002  SHER:  KEY
0002  SHER:  NO
0002  SHER:  GIVE MONEY
0002  SHER:  GIVE MILK
0001  SHER:  YES
```

| 0001 | SHER: | GIVE COLUMBUS GONE |
|------|-------|--------------------|
| 0001 | SHER: | GO OPEN |
| 0001 | SHER: | BREAD MAGNET |
| 0001 | SHER: | OUT GIVE ROOM |
| 0001 | SHER: | OPEN ORANGE DRINK |
| 0001 | SHER: | POUR TICKLE |
| 0001 | SHER: | STICK AUSTIN |
| 0001 | SHER: | GIVE STRAW |
| 0001 | SHER: | DO |
| 0001 | SHER: | GIVE M&M |
| 0001 | SHER: | GIVE STICK |
| 0001 | SHER: | SHERMAN PUDDING |
| 0001 | SHER: | GIVE KEY |
| 0001 | SHER: | GIVE ROOM |
| 0001 | SHER: | OUT ORANGE DRINK POUR |
| 0001 | SHER: | SHUT |
| 0001 | SHER: | POUR GIVE ORANGE DRINK |
| 0001 | SHER: | GIVE SUE |
| 0001 | SHER: | CHOW |
| 0001 | SHER: | CORN |
| 0001 | SHER: | BEANCAKE |
| 0001 | SHER: | COKE |
| 0001 | SHER: | BANANA |
| 0001 | SHER: | PUDDING |
| 0001 | SHER: | GIVE OUTDOORS |
| 0001 | SHER: | MELON |
| 0001 | SHER: | ORANGE |
| 0001 | SHER: | GO SCARE |
| 0001 | SHER: | GIVE OUT COLUMBUS |
| 0001 | SHER: | GIVE AUSTIN WRENCH |
| 0001 | SHER: | GIVE WRENCH |
| 0001 | SHER: | SHERMAN POUR ORANGE DRINK |
| 0001 | SHER: | SUE COLUMBUS |
| 0001 | SHER: | DOOR OUTDOORS |
| 0001 | SHER: | GO OUT ROOM |
| 0001 | SHER: | POUR |
| 0001 | SHER: | PLAYROOM |

This type of summary can be obtained for the experimenter's statements as well. These summaries are collated daily for each animal and are entered into the logs of the research program.

The type of total recording and summary we have presented, when collected regularly from the very beginnings of language acquisition, can provide the appropriate data base for realistic assessment of such questions as (1) the function of question-answer dialogue in later syntactical structures,

(2) the nature and development of word usage and the accompanying widening semantic base, (3) the joint or disjoint development of productive and receptive skills, (4) the changing verbal usage context, (5) the effectiveness of human usage as a model for chimpanzee usage, (6) the importance of utterance expansion, and many others. For example, although we would not draw general conclusions from one day's data, it can be seen in the preceding report of Sherman's performance that (1) he tends, at this point, toward one-word responses—particularly if "give" is not used in the phrase, (2) his word sequence often does not follow that of the experimenter (as in "Room Out" instead of "Out Room"), (3) the majority of his comments reflect specific and immediate desire, (4) in some cases, he models the experimenter's phrase usage (as in "Austin's room"), but in others he stays with a one-word response (as in "outdoors") or shifts to another request, and (5) he often names an object before he specifies the action associated with it. It is also clear that he is able to use his communicative skills in a variety of ways, including receptive tasks, productive tasks, and naming tasks. However, only by careful analysis of these factors across a greater time span, as proficiency is improved, will a proper perspective of the underlying dynamics of language acquisition by a different species become clear.

## On Controlled Tests and Symbol Use

Understanding prelinguistic or linguistic symbols is a complex issue and cannot be demonstrated in chimpanzees by simple sign or symbol occurrence. A lack of control and specificity in testing is evidenced by the Gardners (1975) when they attempt to deal with syntactical questions. In particular, in their relatively recent report (Gardner & Gardner, 1975) of Washoe's performance in response to any array of Wh questions (e.g., Who you? Who go out? Whose that? What that? What want? Where we go? these being limited examples of who, whose, what, and where questions), 7 of the 10 dealt with who and what, and there was no control whatever for the specific Wh sign which had the original position in each question. If, for example, the second sign was "you," the first sign of the Wh frame was always Who, never Whose, Where, or What. If either the second or third sign were "go," the first sign for the Wh question frame was always Who or Where, never any of the other Wh signs. Only in one fortuitous instance can it be concluded that there might have been opportunity for the Wh sign per se to have a determining effect upon Washoe's response, and that entailed the use of a sign for "that" in conjunction with the signs for Whose and What, for composition of the question frames, Whose that? and What that?

A review of their questions as provided in their report (p. 250) reveals, then, a very high degree of confounding of the specific Wh word of a question and the word-signs which followed. Consequently, one cannot conclude, as they do, that Washoe was categorically sensitive to the Wh question per se. Further, Washoe was worked with *en face* by six of Washoe's regular human companions, with no attenuation of visual access to mitigate against possible cueing. The use of regular human companions serving as experimenters, familiar materials, familiar question frames (e.g., Where we go?), and lack of controlled test situations, does not constitute an adequate situation within which to collect data to make a valid assessment of Washoe's ability to respond appropriately to the Wh questions.

The Gardners' defense with regard to controls is that total control is inherent in the fact that Washoe had to *produce* her answers; i.e., to generate her answers through use of signs. According to the Gardners, as this left Washoe free to use any and all signs of her repertoire, "this effectively eliminates the problem of Clever Hans' cueing that haunts the forced choice tests because any hints given in a productive test must contain as much information as the correct replies" (1975, p. 256). Not so. It is quite possible that even a subtle cue might have served to indicate to Washoe the one or two signs which constituted her answer. That problem not withstanding, the main deficiency of the study is that there was no control, no systematic recombination of the specific Wh words, which constituted the ordinal positions in the sentence frames, with other signs that occupied the next ordinal positions; and there was no control for the effects of past experience in training in her response to the familiar exemplars and events used for data acquisition in the course of their study (Rumbaugh & Savage-Rumbaugh, 1978).

## Advantages of the Computer-Based Keyboard System

The acquisition of knowledge through scientific research is clearly a function of methods and equipment employed. The system employed in the Language Analogue Project at the Yerkes Primate Center offers opportunities for control and objectivity in research that bear summary: (1) There is complete objectivity as to the utterances of the subjects and the experimenter, (2) the expression of a word or set of words requires the simple motoric act of depressing keys selected, and a recently introduced keyboard requires only a touch of plates immediately below the lexigrams selected, (3) there is immediate feedback to the subject through the production of lexigrams in the row of projectors and through the increased back illumination of the lexigrams used, (4) all of the subject's words may be made available to him for use by having all of them in a "ready" state, which is the normal practice we employ, or they may be systematically activated and deactivated for specific detailed training, (5) the lexigrams are abstract and noniconic, a point of contrast with many ASL signs, (6) the subject can be totally isolated from another subject or from the experimenter for special projects and for tight experimental control over possible cueing, the risk of which is exceedingly high when humans work with chimpanzees face to face as with ASL, (7) an instant printout of all linguistic events is available for review, along with specific times to the second, (8) all linguistic events are recorded magnetically for future computer summary and analysis, and (9) the approach lends itself to the development of miniaturized keyboards which are portable and inexpensive, for flexible use including out of doors.

The approach has proven powerful for the development of substantial vocabularies (50–130 words) and conversational skills in three out of nine severely and profoundly retarded children in one of our program's projects situated at the Georgia Retardation Center and headed by Dorothy Parkel and Royce White. These children had mastered only token skills through their lifetimes and through other efforts (in two instances) to teach them other symbol systems. ASL may fail with such children, for they too frequently lack the motor skills for facile production of varied signs. Plans for the future include the development of portable, economical keyboards which will facilitate the extension of the children's newly acquired language skills into the workaday world. The keyboard systems will provide automation translation for communication with English-speaking people.

A final advantage offered by the present approach is that it provides for possible performance-contingent linguistic exchanges between subjects and the computer to the end of benefiting some computer-assisted training programs designed to achieve specific skills. Currently we are implementing this new dimension to our research. We are optimistic that in due course, it will enhance the efficiency of language training with children who have acquisition and production problems. The specific programs which will be applied to them will have emerged in basic form from our continued work with the apes as animal models, models with which we can work exhaustively throughout each day and week, and models who know no language skills whatsoever other than those they learn through specific methods which we apply and objectively record.

The use of a computer-based keyboard system suggests to some that our methods and treatment of our chimpanzee subjects must be antithetical with social interaction, both among the chimpanzees and between them and the experimenters. In point of truth, this is not the case. Currently, in our laboratory we are studying 5 chimpanzees, 3 of which are full grown. All 5 are worked with closely by the staff throughout the day. None are "caged" in the traditional sense, though free movement throughout the center is prohibited for their own safety. They can request to go out of the room that they are in, to go for a walk outdoors, to go to the kitchen, and so forth, and these requests are honored by the humans who work with them. Their grouping during the day and for the evening and night-time hours reflects their predilections as expressed to the humans. As the foregoing experiments reveal, current work emphasizes chimp-to-chimp communication, a requisite of which is a healthy social adjustment and a desire to interrelate by all participants. The computer allows us to objectify our research methods, data collection, and data analysis, and it brings the state-of-the-art for ape-language research into the context of modern technology. But it does not mitigate against social factors, which are basic requisites to language itself and to successful research efforts into its antecedents with our close relatives, the great apes.

## CONCLUSIONS

One of the main questions that has come to the fore as a result of work on this project is: what are the attributes which a given response must accrue in order for it to be classified as a word (Rumbaugh & Savage-Rumbaugh, 1978)? Stated more simply, we need to gain a better understanding of what a word is.

A word can be thought of as a response produced by a sender. How is it that that response has come to be differentiated from other responses of the organism so as to draw our attention to it as a word?

It is not sufficient to conclude that something becomes a word when it functions as a word. We must eventualy be able to trace and to define the accrual of meaning to those responses, to those units we term words. We believe that it is through ape-language research that a particularly clear meaning of "wordness" might be achieved, for we work with organisms who know no formal language except that which we teach through our interactions with them in training programs.

We believe it reasonable to conclude that the matter of wordness should be considered as a continuum, with, at one extreme, only an operant, and at the other, a cognition, an understanding of the message which is intended by the sender as that operant is employed in the communicative act.

From this perspective, a sign in AMESLAN, the use of a plastic token, and the depression of a key on a console, quite apart from the first utterances of a child, might initially be thought of as basic operants. Their use becomes increasingly reliable because of reinforcement in the form of incentives and social approval, including attention. Initially it would be presumptuous for us to conclude that any of these "operants" have "meanings" which are understood and under the command of the sender. Thus a pivotal question emerges: what are the criteria whereby we can conclude that various levels of meaning, various levels of wordness, various levels of semanticity have accrued to that intial operant?

This point, which we view as pivotal, might be made clearer through consideration of an array of AMESLAN signs used by chimpanzees. They might be viewed as an array of distinctive responses given reliably in association with various exemplars and situations. Similarly, the selection of plastic word tokens and the selective use of keys on our computer-based keyboard might be viewed as differential responses to an array of exemplars and events. But are these *really* words? A good sheep dog might learn to respond in 20 or 30 different ways to an equal number of specific signals or developments (exemplars?) while it is in the course of doing its job — managing the movement of sheep — but we would be loath to conclude on this evidence alone that the sheep dog has a 20- to 30-word vocabulary. On the other hand, we would not be reluctant to agree that the dog has 20 or 30 responses, acts, or even tricks which it performs upon cue.

All investigators, regardless of approach, in ape-language research (and in child-language research as well) are obliged to demonstrate that the "words" of their subjects are something other than specific responses (operants) to discriminative stimuli (cues). Failure to do so results in confusion and extraordinarily rich interpretations of the apes' abilities. That a chimpanzee uses a sign for "funny' or for "mine" does not mean that it has any semantic understanding of either the sign or its potential for varied use in conjunction with others that we would expect of a human, who uses those signs in the communicative act. Similarly, the same should be said of the subjects who employ plastic word tokens, and *is* said for those who use keys on a computer-based keyboard.

One criterion for helping to assure that words are other than basic operants is, we believe, through the demonstration that the word is used appropriately in a wide variety of contexts, not all of the same type. Thus, within the course of the Animal Model Project, we have taught lexigrams as: (1) names for things; (2) names for things pictured both on prints and in slides; (3) names of things which are vital to the procurement of an incentive otherwise not available; e.g., those things serving as tools; and (4) the symbolic representations of things which are out of sight and concealed in containers—foods and drinks which can be obtained if accurately requested through use of the symbols indicated (Savage-Rumbaugh & Rumbaugh, 1978). We have developed, used, and tested (not merely assumed) receptive skills as well as productive ones. We have differentiated between indicative naming, volitional requesting, and statements of relationship. We have not presumed that complex skills and multidimensional and multicontextual usage of one or two words (such as open or more) means that the animal can use all words with equal facility. We have separated action and word in form, time, and space; and through these varied forms of training sought to decontextualize responses and to both extend and delimit appropriately the meaning and the semantic base for each word. It is this type of varied "training" which facilitates the accurate usage, interanimal communication, and hierarchial integration of symbolic skills so characteristic of language in the human species.

## NOTES

[1]This research was supported by the National Institute of Child Health, and Human Development, Grant #01016, and by Animal Resources, Grant #RR00165, NIH.

## REFERENCES

Argyle, M. & Cook, M. *Gaze and mutual gaze.* London: Cambridge University Press, 1976.

Bates, E., Benigni, L. Bretherton, I., Camaioni, L., & Volterra, V. From gesture to the first word: On cognitive and social prerequisites. *In* M. Lewis and L. Rosenblum (Eds.), *Origins of behavior: Language and communication.* New York: Wiley, 1976.

Braine, M. D. S. The ontogeny of English phrase structure: The first phrase. *Language,* 39, 1963, 1-13. Reprinted in C. A. Ferguson and D. I. Slobin (Eds.), *Studies of child language development.* New York: Holt, Rinehart, & Winton, 1970.

Fouts, R. S. Language: Origins, definition and chimpanzees. *Journal of Human Evolution,* 1974, 3, 475-482.

Gardner, B. T. & Gardner, R. A. Two-way communication with an infant chimpanzee. *In* A. Schrier and F. Stollnitz (Eds.), *Behavior of Nonhuman Primates* (Vol. 4). New York: Academic Press, 1971.

Gardner, B. T. & Gardner, R. A. Evidence for sentence constituents in the early utterances of child and chimpanzee. *Journal of Experimental Psychology: General,* 1975, 104, 244-267.

Gardner, R. A. and Gardner, B. T. Comparative psychology and language acquisition.*In* K. Salzinger and F. Denmark (Eds.), *Psychology the state of the art.* New York: Annals of the New York Academy of Sciences, 1977.

Greenfield, P. M. & Smith, J. H. *The structure of communication in early childhood development.* New York: Academic Press, 1976.

Hewes, G. W. Language Origin Theories. *In* D. M. Rumbaugh (Ed.), *Language learning by a chimpanzee: The LANA Project.* New York: Academic Press, 1977.

Limber, J. Languages in child and chimpanzee. *American Psychologist,* 1977, 32, 280-296.

McNeill, D. The development of language. *In* P. H. Mussan (Ed.), *Carmichael's manual of child psychology* (Vol. 1). New York: Wiley, 1970.

Nelson, K. Structure and strategy in learning to talk. *Monographs of the Society for Research in Child Development,* 1973, 29(1), 9-33.

Patterson, F. The gestures of a Gorilla: Sign language acquisition in another pongid species. *Brain and Language,* 1978, 5, 72–97.

Premack, D. Language in Chimpanzee? *Science,* 1971, 172, 802–822.

Premack, D. *Intelligence in ape and man.* Hillsdale, N. J.: Lawrence Erlbaum Associates, 1976.

Rumbaugh, D. M. (Ed.), *Language learning by a chimpanzee: The LANA Project.* New York: Academic Press, 1977a.

Rumbaugh, D. M. Language Behavior of Apes. *In* A. M. Schrier (Ed.), *Behavioral primatology: Advances in research and theory.* Hillsdale, N.J.: Lawrence Erlbaum Associates, 1977b.

Rumbaugh, D. M. & Savage-Rumbaugh, E. S. Chimpanzee Language Research: Status and Potential. *Behavior Research Methods & Instrumentation,* 1978, 10, 119–131.

Savage, E. S. & Rumbaugh, D. M. Communication and LANA: A Perspective. In D. M. Rumbaugh (Ed.), *Language learning by a chimpanzee: The LANA Project.* New York: Academic Press, 1977.

Savage-Rumbaugh, E. S. & Rumbaugh, D. M. Symbolization, language and chimpanzees: A theoretical Reevaluation based on Initial Language Acquisition Processes in Four Young *Pan troglodytes. Brain and Language,* 1978, 6, 65–300.

Savage-Rumbaugh, E. S., Rumbaugh, D. M., & Boysen, S. Symbolic communication between two chimpanzees (*Pan troglodytes*). *Science,* 1978a, 201, 641–644.

Savage-Rumbaugh, E. S., Rumbaugh, D. M., & Boysen, S. Linguistically mediated tool use and exchange by chimpanzees (*Pan troglodytes*). *Behavioral & Brain Sciences,* 1978b, 4, 539–554.

Van Lawick-Goodall, J. The behavior of free-living chimpanzees in the Gombe Stream Reserve. *Animal Behavior Monographs,* 1968, 1, 161–311.

von Glasersfeld, E. Linguistic Communication: Theory and Definition. In D. M. Rumbaugh (Ed.), *Language learning by a chimpanzee: The LANA project.* New York: Academic Press, 1977.

# 6

# ON ASKING THE QUESTION: CAN APES LEARN LANGUAGE?[1]

## HERBERT F. W. STAHLKE

In a review of Premack (1976), Peters (1977, p. 965) poses one of the central questions of primate language research: "Can we agree on operational criteria for what an organism must do in order to provide evidence of having genuine linguistic capabilities?" So stated, the question is an empirically more acceptable and practicable way of asking the question broached by Plato in the *Cratylus;* namely, what is language? The two questions may differ less in substance than in Weltanschauung, the modern writer seeking an observationally valid typology and the ancient an intensive idealized essence. Modern research teams, combining the interests and methods of both psychologists and linguists, are posing both questions, the linguist asking, "What is language?" and the psychologist, "How can we know whether what we have created in the laboratory is language?"

This chapter examines examples of the empirical and the model-theoretic approaches to asking the questions, "Can apes learn language?" Perhaps the best known and most often cited set of empirical, operational criteria are Hockett's "design features" (Hockett 1958, 1963; Hockett & Altmann, 1968). Hockett's design features are a set of observationally determined systemic and behavioral properties which characterize normal communicative behavior among humans and are descriptive rather than prescriptive in nature. That is, they provide an observationally verifiable description of the set of phenomena called human language and do so with sufficient comprehensiveness to exclude unequivocally forms of communicative behavior which are either nonhuman or nonlinguistic. To the extent that Hockett's design features are a necessary and sufficient observational

description of human language, their success is a product of the total set of
features rather than of any single feature or subset of features. The design
features are in some cases common to many animal communication systems, such as, for example, the feature termed rapid fading of the message.
Others, such as duality of patterning and cultural transmission, are more
exclusively human. One must ask at times whether the absence of one or
another criterion is sufficient to preclude a system from being considered a
language. Is Sumerian, a language preserved almost entirely in dried clay,
not a language since it no longer exhibits rapid decay of signal? Or is it necessary that an otherwise very languagelike system of communication be
passed on from one group to another, as across generations, before it can be
considered a language? These are questions of the sort Hockett (1963)
raises. Hockett's design features offer an interesting set of parameters along
which to assess the degree of similarity a nonhuman communication system
has to human language.

The model-theoretic approach to the question underlying the psychologist's and linguist's queries asks what sort of device would produce the set
of things we normally accept as tokens of a human language. Using the sort
of abstract modeling employed by linguists for especially the last two decades, the goal of this approach is to construct a model of the linguistic
knowledge a speaker/hearer has that makes normal linguistic behavior possible. To be completely successful, the model would also have to define the
nature of the cognitive and intellectual preparedness a child brings to language acquisition that makes possible such accurate mastery of a complex
of phonological, lexical, syntactic, and semantic systems in a period of ten
to twelve years, a task the individual usually finds impossible to repeat with
equal success for any language other than the one learned first.

## A PROPOSED SET OF OPERATIONAL CRITERIA

Hockett's design features have been used a number of times in the literature as the sort of operational criteria Peters (1977) seeks. Linden (1974),
in a popular treatment of research with signing chimpanzees, devotes considerable time to a comparison of human language and chimpanzee signing,
using the earliest version of Hockett's design features (Hockett, 1958). Linden attempts to demonstrate the closeness of the two species in their linguistic behavior, claiming that in both species language exhibits duality of patterning, productivity, interchangeability, specialization, displacement, and
cultural transmission. The feature of arbitrariness of sign is partially
mooted by the highly iconic nature of many Ameslan signs. By Hockett's
(1958) design features, the language of apes that have been taught to communicate in Ameslan and the language of humans communicating through

naturally acquired human language would differ only in degree, not in kind, a claim that will be examined from another perspective later.

In this 1963 paper, Hockett expands his list of design features to sixteen and distinguishes among them those that are " . . . the crucial or nuclear or central properties of human language (1963, pp. 17–18)," those which he considers the " . . . defining set for language (1963, p. 15)," and those that are entailed by defining features or are found in all human languages but do not appear to be necessary. The design features which he considers central are openness, displacement, duality, and cultural transmission. *Openness* refers to the productivity or creativity of language; that is, to the capacity for generating an infinite set of messages from a finite set of elements. *Displacement* refers to the ability of language to refer to and discuss things not immediately perceivable, *duality* to the fact that the message consists of a system of units, phonological segments, which is independent of the system of meaning-bearing units or morphemes, and *cultural transmission* to the fact that language is learned and passed on through cultural institutions rather than genetically. The defining set includes all but the last of the central properties listed above, as well as arbitrariness, discreteness, interchangeability, complete feedback, specialization, rapid fading, and broadcast transmission with directional reception. *Arbitrariness* refers to the physical independence of symbol and referent, and *discreteness* to the fact that "utterances cannot be indefinitely similar to one another," but must differ " . . . by at least a whole phonological feature" (Hockett, 1963, p. 10). By *interchangeability* Hockett means that the language user can produce and perceive utterances with equal facility. *Complete feedback* means that the language user can monitor the transmission. *Specialization* refers to the irrelevance of the physical event to the meaning of a spoken message, and *rapid fading* to the fact that one must be there at the time of speaking to receive the message. *Broadcast transmission* with directional reception is a function of another design feature, the use of a *vocal-auditory channel,* which Hockett does not consider a defining factor (1963, pp. 18–19). The feature of *semanticity* is not considered defining since it is a consequence of the contrast between arbitrariness and iconicity. Hockett notes also that every human language has a capacity for *prevarication* and for *reflexiveness,* the ability to talk about itself. Finally, Hockett cites *learnability,* the ability of a human to learn another language, as a consequence of the fact that language is not passed on entirely through the genes.

Hockett points out that "some of the [features] apply directly to a language as an 'abstract' system . . .; others rather to the organisms that use the system; still others to how the organisms use or acquire the system" (1963, p. 14). Although he does not offer a breakdown into these three categories, Table I is, presumably, not far from his intentions. The three different categories of feature must be weighted differently when one considers

## Table I
## A Classification of Hockett's Design Features

| Features of the System | Features of the Organism | Features of Use and Acquisition |
|---|---|---|
| Specialization | Vocal-auditory channel | Cultural transmission |
| Semanticity | Broadcast transmission with direc- | Prevarication |
| Arbitrariness | tional reception | Reflectiveness |
| Discreteness | Rapid fading | Learnability |
| Displacement | Interchangeability | |
| Openness | Complete feedback | |
| Duality | | |

Peters' (1977) question in their light. The channel properties, for example, may well vary with the species, independently of the systemic properties, and features of use and acquisition may vary along sociological and biological parameters. However, it must be noted that if the features in Table I are taken as a description of human language, no organism that differs from humans in acoustic potential, as apes do, can be capable of behavior fitting Hockett's description. It is necessary, then, to base interspecies comparison on a modified set or even a different set of criteria.

## LINGUISTIC UNIVERSALS

Linguists approach the question of what language is by searching for linguistic universals, which define what is a possible natural language. Some of these universals are substantive, such as most of Hockett's design features, Greenberg's (1963) universals of word order, Keenan's (1972) Hierarchy of Accessibility, and Ross's (1967) constraints on variable movement rules in syntax. Others, on the other hand, are formal, such as the claim that a grammar makes explicit the relationships between meaning and form and to do this a grammar must have at least such formal devices as context-free and context-sensitive phrase structure rules and transformations. The discovery and description of substantive universals requires extensive data from a wide variety of languages and frequently entails argumentation of exceeding subtlety. For reasons which should be obvious, linguistics and comparative psychology are some time away from having the capacity to posit and define substantive universals of ape language analogs—if, indeed, such universals exist. Formal linguistic universals can be developed by modeling the knowledge which makes possible rule-governed linguistic behavior. Given a sufficiently large and varied body of linguistic behavior and the possibility of eliciting further, crucial bits of data, it is possible to construct a formal device which will generate all and only the sentences of an ape language analog. Such a device would be of the same sort as models of human linguistic competence constructed by linguists. Having constructed such models, it is then possible to compare a model of chimpanzee linguistic competence with a model of human linguistic competence. Such a comparison may enable researchers to judge the formal similarity of the models to each other and hence to judge the formal similarity of the competences of the two species to each other.

## FORMAL PROPERTIES OF NATURAL LANGUAGE

Any viable linguistic model must attempt to characterize the duality of language, that is, the fact that the pairing of meaning and form is not isomorphic. Natural language allows meaning-form relationships such as *ambiguity,* where a single form must be assigned more than one meaning, and *paraphrase,* where several distinct forms are assigned the same or very similar meanings. This duality can be represented in a model of natural language by two types of rule. One is a set of *phrase structure rules* which defines the set of possible underlying representations, which may be meanings (Lakoff, 1971) or may be the basis for assigning meaning (Chomsky, 1965). The other is a set of *transformational rules,* each of which represents a factorization of some element in the meaning-form relationship, and some proper subset of which, if one follows the approach of Lakoff (1971), mediates the relationship between meaning and form for a particular sentence.

Various other linguistic models of weaker formal power which have been proposed have been shown to be insufficient for natural language (Postal, 1964). The weakest model one might reasonably propose is one in which sentences are comprised of linear sequences of words such that for any word $w$, the choice of word and $w_{j+1}$ is governed by the transitional probability between $w_j$ and $w_{j+1}$. A model of this sort is a type of *finite state machine,* such as a first-order Markov Process (Chomsky, 1957). A more powerful model would be a *context-free phrase structure grammar* (CFPSG), which generates a linear string, the elements of which are grouped and interrelated hierarchically. This grammar more closely approximates the formal power needed to describe natural language. It is possible in a CFPSG to describe substitutability not merely of words, but of groups of words, such as prepositional phrases or noun clauses. A third model, of somewhat greater formal power, is the *context-sensitive phrase structure grammar* (CSPSG). A CSPSG differs from a CFPSG in that the insertion of some word or string may depend on or be conditioned by words or strings elsewhere in the sentence. Thus, the words "slaughter" and "assassinate," in their basic meanings, are inserted into English sentences by rules which are sensitive to whether the direct object is a quadruped used for food or a human in a position of high public prominence. Thus it is semantically well formed to slaughter a steer or assassinate a king, but not vice versa. A fourth model, of still greater formal power, is a *transformational grammar* (TG), containing a context-sensitive phrase structure grammar. Such a TG can provide an explicit account of relations between noncontiguous elements in sentences, can explain the presence of conditioned markers in sentences which seem not to contain the conditioning element, and can explicate the relationship between sentences of different structure but identical propositional content. Chomsky (1957) demonstrated that natural language requires a grammar with at least the formal power of a TG.

## FORMAL PROPERTIES OF
## A CHIMPANZEE LANGUAGE GRAMMAR

To compare the formal linguistic properties of chimpanzee language grammars with those of human language grammars it is necessary first to construct a model of a chimpanzee language grammar. This construction is based on a computerized concordance of the second year of the LANA Project, approximately 110,000 lines of data produced by Lana, and on the daily print-out of the fourth year, the quantity of which has not been calculated but is quite large. Each line of data is bounded and is listed with its preceding and following lines. Thus each line is effectively treated as a separate utterance and is found in its original linguistic context.

### Finite State Grammars

Two arguments can be used to demonstrate the formal insufficiency of a finite state grammar as a model for the syntax of Lana's language. The first argument draws on the syntax of color names, concrete nouns, and the lexigrams for *this* and *thats*. In Lana's vocabulary the lexigram for *thats* serves to mark a following lexigram or string as modifying the noun preceding it. *Thats* is an apparently nonreferential syntactic marker roughly corresponding to the word "that" as used in English sentences such as, "I know the book that you read" and "I know that you read the book" (Stahlke, 1976). It must be noted that *thats* is at no time used like the English distal demonstrative "that" as in "I read that book." The only demonstrative in LANA's vocabulary is *this*, corresponding for the most part to the English proximal demonstrative "this." Since *thats* can only follow nouns and since all adjectives, such as the color names, must be preceded by *thats* when they modify nouns, it follows that there will be high transitional probability between certain nouns, especially names of inanimates, and *thats*; that there will be a high transitional probability between *thats* and a following color word; and that the transitional probability between a noun and a color word will be very low.

There is, however, one type of string in which a color word may follow a noun immediately. This is a string in which the color of an object is being given, as in the following Year 2 example.

096966211     COLOR OF THIS BOWL RED

If the first word (or the second if the first is *question)* of the string is *color,* then the noun must be followed immediately by a color lexigram. In strings of this type there is an extremely high probability that a noun will be followed immediately by a color word, but the conditioning factor is not the immediately preceding word. Rather it is a word three positions earlier. Only a higher order Markov Process can handle such a distant conditioning. A simple finite state grammar cannot. The distribution of *thats* and color words described above could be handled by a fourth- or fifth-order Markov Process, but such a grammar would approach being simply a list of all four or five word strings possible in Lana's language and would lose virtually all capacity for generalization, a capacity which Lana has clearly demonstrated.

The second argument against a finite state grammar has to do with some fourth-year developments. Lana now uses prepositional phrases to modify nouns, as in the following strings recorded on January 18, 1977.

LANA WANT EAT BANANA IN MACHINE     11:51:23
LANA WANT EAT BREAD IN MACHINE     11:54:25

In this situation, the desired food was in a dispenser and Lana was requesting that particular food. On the other hand, on November 12, 1976, Lana produced the following sentence:

QUESTION YOU PUT CHOW IN MACHINE
THATS BEHIND ROOM     16:31:25

In it, an adnominal prepositional phrase is introduced by *thats*. This construction is decidedly rarer. The important point of these examples is that in a finite state grammar the transitional probability of *thats* after a noun is much lower in strings in which *thats* is followed by a preposition than in strings in which it is followed by an adjective. Finite state grammars are formally incapable of capturing such a generalization, since transitional probabilities are all left-to-right linear and this case involves a right-to-left linear dependency. Thus a finite state grammar is insufficiently powerful to generate Lana's language.

## Phrase Structure Grammars

The next more powerful class of grammars is the phrase structure grammar. Phrase structure grammars involve *rewrite rules* of the form XAY→XBY. If X and Y are both null, then the grammar is context-free. If either X or Y or both are nonnull, then the grammar is context-sensitive. Rewrite rules generate branching diagrams, or phrase markers, which define both linear and hierarchical relationships. Thus the sample grammar given below generates—that is, assigns structural descriptions to—the sentences given in the example. Parenthesized elements are considered optional.

*Sample Grammar I*
    A  →   BC
    B  →   D (E)
    C  →   (F) G

*Figure 6-1.* Sentences generated by Sample Grammar I.

The strings DEFG, DEG, DFG, and DG are the well-formed sentences of this artificial language (see Figure 6-1). D and DE are strings which are constituents of type B, just as G and FG are constituents of type C. BC and the four terminal strings given above are constituents of type A. While each terminal node is a constituent, EF, EG, and DF are not constituents since they are not uniquely and exhaustively dominated by a single node. Sample Grammar I is a CFPSG. If it were revised by the inclusion of a rule like that in Sample Grammar II, then it would be a context-sensitive phrase structure grammar (CSPSG).

*Sample Grammar II*
    All rules as in Sample Grammar I, except
    DEF  →   DBF

Note that since the symbol E is optional and is rewritten as B, if it occurs, the addition of this rule permits such terminal strings as DG, DFG, DEG, DDFG, DDDFG, and DDDDFG (see Figure 6-2). The string DEFG is now permitted as a terminal string since such an occurrence of E will always be rewritten as B. This recursive device makes it possible for Sample Grammar II to generate an infinite set of strings.

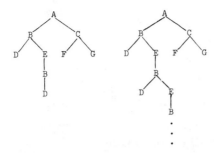

*Figure 6-2.* Sentences of the sort generated by Sample Grammar II, but not by Sample Grammar I.

To demonstrate that Lana's language requires a phrase structure grammar, it is necessary to demonstrate that substrings of lexigrams function as constituents. Prepositional phrases appear to function in this way, as in the sentences below, recorded on December 25, 1976.

| | |
|---|---|
| QUESTION YOU GIVE COKE TO LANA IN CUP | 13:50:36 |
| QUESTION YOU PUT COKE IN CUP | 13:51:13 |
| QUESTION YOU GIVE COKE IN CUP TO LANA | 13:52:54 |

The substring *in cup* occurs in different environments in this sample. In the first sentence, the cup is empty and Lana is making a double request, one she has used in such a situation repeatedly. One part of the request is stated in the second sentence, where *in cup* functions as a directional prepositional phrase. The third sentence is used when Lana sees that the coke is in the cup. She can then use either this string or the string *cup of coke*. In either case, the prepositional phrase modifies the noun *coke* and is a structure analogous to the string MACHINE THATS BEHIND ROOM cited above. That is, these strings are examples of constituents containing a head noun and a prepositional phrase. Such a head noun is normally labelled as a Noun Phrase (NP) and has essentially the structure shown in Figure 6-3, where the labels N, P, and PP mean noun, preposition, and prepositional phrase, respectively. Strings such as QUESTION YOU GIVE COKE TO

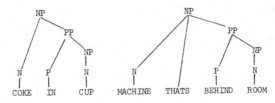

*Figure 6-3.* Phrase markers for NP with adnominal PP.

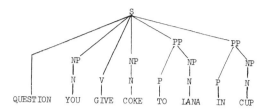

*Figure 6-4.* Phrase marker for QUESTION YOU GIVE COKE TO LANA IN CUP.

LANA IN CUP cited above, would require at least the structure in Figure 6-4. Whether any of the constituents are grouped together as a higher-level constituent, such as a Verb Phrase (VP) containing GIVE . . . CUP, is not clear from the data. The label NP is used on even single-word nominal expressions because of the substitutability of multiword and pronominal expressions in those positions. That is, Lana could ask for *this thats in cup* instead of *coke,* or she could simply use *this,* not naming the item she wants. The referential and deictic functions of *this* are demonstrated in Lana's sentences as reported by Rumbaugh and Gill (1976a, 1976b, 1977). Thus it is clear that a grammar for Lana's language requires at least the power of a CFPSG and contains phrase structure rules like the following.

The following is a partial CFPSG of Lana's language:

$$S \longrightarrow ( \begin{Bmatrix} \text{Question} \\ \text{Please} \end{Bmatrix} ) \quad NP \quad V \quad (NP) \quad (PP) \quad (PP)$$

$$PP \longrightarrow P \quad NP$$
$$NP \longrightarrow (\text{THIS}) \quad N \quad (\text{THATS} \begin{Bmatrix} \text{ADJ} \\ PP \end{Bmatrix} )$$

Other phrase structure rules will ultimately prove necessary but are not illustrated by the types of data presented here.

To show that a context-free phrase structure grammar (CFPSG) is insufficient for Lana's language, all that is necessary is to show that some rule of Yerkish must be context-sensitive. This can be demonstrated from the subject-verb sequences found in the data and from experiments with her ability to recognize and complete well-formed strings and to distinguish them from ill-formed strings (Rumbaugh, Gill, & von Glaserfeld, 1973). Lana systematically avoids such strings as PLEASE MACHINE CARRY CHOW TO LANA or QUESTION LANA GROOM M AND M. That is, Lana selects lexigrams on the basis of the context in which they are to be used. Thus the lexigrams *carry* and *groom* are misused in the strings given above. *Carry* requires an animate subject, and *groom* requires both an animate subject and an animate object. It follows then that Lana's language has constraints on the cooccurrence of lexigrams that are context-sensitive.

If it is possible, as appears likely, to subclassify Lana's nouns by their combinatory possibilities, then we could subclassify them as, for example, [± Animate], [± Ingestible], and [± Concrete] (cf. von Glasersfeld, 1977, for semantic categories used in Yerkish). With such subclassification, we can then state context-sensitive rules for the insertion of verbs, such as the following.

V ⟶ CARRY / [+ ANIMATE] _____ [+ CONCRETE]
V ⟶ GROOM / [+ ANIMATE] _____ [+ ANIMATE]

Other formalisms are possible for lexical insertion (Chomsky, 1965), but they will share the property of being context-sensitive.

## Transformational Grammar

Arguments that transformational power is needed in a grammar are of several types, including arguments from simplicity of formulation and arguments from stylistic variation and paraphrase relations. The earliest arguments advanced in support of the claim that natural language grammars contain grammatical transformations were based on the relatively greater simplicity of formulation such rules permitted (Harris, 1957; Chomsky, 1957; Lees, 1961). These arguments are in the tradition of the scientific principle said to go back to William of Occam, often referred to as Occam's Razor, that of two ways of accounting for a phenomenon the simpler is to be preferred. In addition, a few compelling arguments (McCawley, 1968) have been produced to date that a context-sensitive phrase structure grammar (CSPSG) is not sufficiently powerful to generate all and only the well-formed strings of a natural language. Still central, however, are the cumbersom complexity and redundancy of a CSPSG for a natural language which make the transformational grammar much simpler by comparison and therefore to be preferred. And if a grammar attempts not only to generate well-formed strings, but also to relate these strings to their meanings and to account for such nonunique meaning/form relationships as ambiguity and paraphrase, then some sort of mapping function, of which the grammatical transformation is an example, becomes essential. It is motivated in such grammars not on the basis of simplicity but on the basis of formal, mathematical power. It must be stressed here that the claim that a linguistic model must have rules of a certain form is not equivalent to the claim that the language-user operates such rules in sentence production. The model presented here is a generative grammar describing the knowledge of language which must be presupposed in an account of an individual's ability to use language. A generative grammar is not a model of behavior. Two types of argument for transformational power in the grammar of Lana's language are presented below.

## *Thats* Insertion

The first type of argument that Lana's language requires transformations involves the use of the lexigram for *thats*. In the data illustrated above were two prepositional phrases modifying nouns, one of which was introduced by *thats*. The phrases were COKE IN CUP and MACHINE THATS BEHIND ROOM. Since adjectival modifiers normally use *thats*, as in CUP THATS BLACK, one could account for the use of *thats*, as was done above, with a phrase structural rule. To account for the absence of *thats* in COKE IN CUP, one could revise the rule to express the optionality of *thats*. However, the rule

$$NP \longrightarrow (THIS) \quad N \quad ((THATS) \left\{ \begin{matrix} ADJ \\ PP \end{matrix} \right\} )$$

now says that *thats* is optional before adjectives. The data do not show that *thats* can be omitted before adjectives. Thus a PSG account of the distribution of *thats* makes an incorrect claim. A simpler solution would be to revise the phrase structure rule to exclude *thats* and insert it transformationally, making the transformation obligatory before adjectives and optional before prepositional phrases. The rules needed are as follows:

$$NP \longrightarrow (THIS) \quad N \quad ( \left\{ \begin{matrix} ADJ \\ PP \end{matrix} \right\} )$$

Transformation: *thats*-Insertion

| | Structural Description: | X | N | $\left\{ \begin{matrix} ADJ \\ PP \end{matrix} \right\}$ | Y |
|---|---|---|---|---|---|
| | | 1 | 2 | 3 | 4 |
| | Structural Change: | 1 | 2 | *thats* 3 | 4 |
| | Conditions: | \multicolumn{4}{l}{1) 2 + 3 are dominated by NP} |
| | | \multicolumn{4}{l}{2) rule is optional if 3 = PP} |

The above rule of *thats*-Insertion says that any string consisting of a noun followed by an adjective or a prepositional phrase requires a *thats* before the adjective and permits it before a prepositional phrase.

## *Of* Insertion

Another transformation involves the lexigram for *of*. *Of* is one of a very small set of lexigrams in Lana's vocabulary which seem not to have any semantic content. These lexigrams, including *thats*, function purely as syntactic markers of certain types of semantic relationships. *Of* is found between nouns under three different conditions. First, if $N_1$ is the lexigram for *piece* and $N_2$ is some segmentable item, usually some kind of food, *of* will occur between $N_1$ and $N_2$. Second, if $N_1$ is the lexigram for *color* and $N_2$ is any object, *of* will intervene. Third, if $N_1$ is a container, such as *cup, bowl, box,* or *can,* and $N_2$ is some substance, such as *water* or *milk,* the *of* will be found between the two nouns. *of* is not used after *name,* as in a sentence like QUESTION WHAT NAME THIS. This last is an irregularity built into the language (von Glasersfeld, 1977) as originally taught Lana, and she has not deviated from it.

The lexigram for *of* has the black color matrix common to lexigrams for prepositions, and so strings with *of* look superficially like prepositional phrases. They are, however, unique among prepositional phrases for three reasons. First, the preposition is predictable from the semantic classes of the nouns around it. No other preposition, with the partial exception of *to,* is in any way predictable. Second, prepositional phrases can ordinarily be either adverbial or adnominal in Yerkish. That is, Lana can ask, as she did on December 25, 1976,

QUESTION YOU PUT COKE IN CUP           13:51:13

or

QUESTION YOU GIVE COKE IN CUP TO LANA       13:52:54

using the prepositional phrase to modify *put* in the former example and *coke* in the latter. Prepositional phrases with *of,* on the other hand, can occur only adnominally, never adverbially. Third, any adnominal prepositional phrase can be introduced by *thats,* as in the example containing MACHINE THATS BEHIND ROOM cited above, but prepositional phrases with *of* are never preceded by *thats.* The one apparent counter-example in the entire Year 2 corpus is in line 058260116. The example, with its context, is the following.

| | |
|---|---|
| 058257116 | QUESTION SHELLEY GIVE SHOE THATS RED. |
| 058258116 | SHUT. |
| 058259116 | QUESTION SHELLEY GIVE THATS. |
| 058260116 | THATS OF THIS BLACK. |
| 058261116 | QUESTION SHELLEY GIVE SHOE THATS BLUE. |

The crucial line, line 058260116, is apparently a step in an attempt to ask for a shoe of a particular color. What suggests that this line is not a relevant counter-example is, first, that *thats* is initial. There is no preceding noun and so its use is not clearly adnominal. Second, *thats* seems simply to be out of place. If it were after *this*, giving OF THIS THATS BLACK, the string would be well-formed. There seems little reason at all for *of* to occur in this string. Finally, this is the only case of *thats of* in the approximately 7900 uses of *of* in the second year. Thus, discounting this one anomalous sentence, *of* appears to be unique among prepositions.

The problem for linguistic analysis is accounting for the distribution of *of* and *thats* so that they will never occur together. Both lexigrams are predictable from syntax or from semantic class, which makes them both unique among lexigrams in Yerkish. The fact that the occurrence of these lexigrams in well-formed strings is predictable means that they do not contribute to the propositional content of the string. Thus *of*, like *thats*, must be inserted transformationally. The *of*-Insertion transformation presupposes that *of*, like *thats*, is not found in the phrase structure rules. Rather, the phrase structure grammar will generate NP of the type N ADJ, N PP, and N NP. The rule given above, then, must be revised to read

$$NP \longrightarrow (THIS) \quad N \quad ( \quad \left\{ \begin{array}{c} ADJ \\ PP \\ NP \end{array} \right\} \quad )$$

*Of*-insertion will then insert *of* between two nouns just if they are in the same NP and $N_1$ is not *name*. The rule can be stated as follows.

Transformation: *of*-Insertion

| Structural Description: | X | N | NP | Y |
|---|---|---|---|---|
| | 1 | 2 | 3 | 4 |
| Structural Change: | 1 | 2 | *of* 3 | 4 |

Conditions:  a) 2 + 3 are dominated by the same NP node,

b) 2 is not *name*

However, *of*-insertion clearly generates something that looks very much like a prepositional phrase. In order to block the insertion of *thats* into strings containing N *of*, the grammar must order *thats*-insertion before *of*-insertion, as illustrated below.

| Underlying String | MACHINE BEHIND ROOM | CUP COKE |
|---|---|---|
| *Thats*-insertion | MACHINE THATS BEHIND ROOM | not applicable |
| *Of*-insertion | not applicable | CUP OF COKE |
| Surface String | MACHINE THATS BEHIND ROOM | CUP OF COKE |

In this analysis, *thats*-insertion applies to a set of strings which includes no prepositional phrases with *of*, and so *of* never occurs after *thats*. A transformational analysis of this sort is possible only within a model of language which explicitly treats meaning and form as two separate levels of representation.

## Paraphrase and Ambiguity

Another indication that meaning and form are distinct in Lana's language comes from her use of paraphrase. A fairly typical example of paraphrase—like sentence sets can be found in the December 25, 1976 conversation quoted previously. The conversation is reproduced below.

| | |
|---|---|
| LANA: QUESTION YOU GIVE COKE IN CUP | 13:46:27 |
| LANA: QUESTION GIVE COKE | 13:47:08 |
| LANA: QUESTION YOU GIVE COKE IN CUP | 13:47:15 |
| LANA: QUESTION YOU COKE | 13:47:31 |
| LANA: QUESTION YOU GIVE COKE TO LANA | 13:47:40 |
| LANA: QUESTION YOU GIVE COKE IN CUP | 13:48:09 |
| LANA: QUESTION YOU GIVE COKE TO LANA | 13:48:20 |
| LANA: QUESTION YOU GIVE COKE TO LANA IN CUP | 13:48:37 |
| LANA: QUESTION YOU GIVE COKE TO LANA IN CUP | 13:49:13 |
| LANA: QUESTION YOU YOU GIVE | 13:49:27 |
| LANA: QUESTION YOU GIVE COKE TO LANA IN CUP | 13:49:39 |
| LANA: QUESTION YOU GIVE COKE TO LANA IN CUP | 13:50:00 |
| LANA: QUESTION YOU GIVE COKE TO LANA IN CUP | 13:50:36 |
| TIM:   NO MORE COKE | 13:51:06 |
| LANA: QUESTION YOU PUT COKE IN CUP | 13:51:13 |
| TIM:   NO MORE COKE TO LANA | 13:51:28 |
| LANA: QUESTION YOU GIVE COKE TO LANA IN IN CUP | 13:51:38 |
| LANA: QUESTION YOU GIVE COKE TO LANA IN CUP | 13:51:48 |
| TIM:   NO MORE COKE TO LANA IN CUP | 13:52:16 |
| LANA: YES | 13:52:22 |
| LANA: NO | 13:52:24 |
| LANA: QUESTION YOU GIVE COKE IN CUP TO LANA | 13:52:54 |
| LANA: QUESTION YOU GIVE COKE IN MACHINE | 13:53:42 |
| LANA: QUESTION YOU GIVE COKE IN CUP | 13:54:00 |
| LANA: QUESTION YOU GIVE COKE TO LANA IN MACHINE | 13:54:22 |
| LANA: QUESTION YOU GIVE COKE TO LANA IN CUP | 13:55:11 |
| LANA: PLEASE MACHINE GIVE WATER | 13:55:29 |

Lana's initial question is ambiguous as to whether she wants Tim's cup of coke or wants Tim to pour her a cup of coke. At 13:48:37, she produces a sentence with the phrase *to Lana* beween *coke* and *in cup,* a structure which results in Tim pouring coke into a cup for her. An inviting interpretation of her use of this sentence is that she sought to disambiguate her earlier request. Requests like 13:48:09 QUESTION YOU GIVE COKE IN CUP are ambiguous for syntactic reasons. That is, the grammar can generate the phrase *in cup* either as a constituent of NP or as a constituent of S. The former structure is assigned the meaning that Lana is requesting the coke which is in a cup. The latter allows for the coke to be poured into a cup and given to her. It is not clear from the data that Lana can actually manipulate structure with such subtle semantic purpose. Although she has used each of these structures unambiguously, the data are insufficient here to justify a claim that the disambiguation effected at 13:48:37 is a purposeful linguistic act. A more conservative interpretation allowed by the data is that Lana has a repertoire of syntactic patterns defined by a phrase structure grammar of the sort described above, and that she tries one variant of a structure after another until she finds one that gets her what she wants. It is worth noting, in line with this interpretation, that, having found a structure that worked, she persisted in using that structure. The existence of paraphrase remains in this interpretation, but the issue of her perception and control of ambiguity is mooted. This issue will undoubtedly be more difficult to resolve than that of her control of paraphrase since the evidence necessary must reveal conclusively what she is perceiving rather than what she is producing.

Later, at 13:51:13, after Tim has refused her more coke, she then produces a partial paraphrase in QUESTION YOU PUT COKE IN CUP. This sentence is, in fact, entailed by her sentence at 13:48:37. The sentence at 13:51:13 is also nearly identical in meaning to the sentence at 13:46:27, expressing one of the meanings involved in the later sentence. This conversation illustrates Lana's ability to manipulate syntax for the more efficient attainment of a goal. In the linguistic communication, this skill requires duality, and a grammar of the sort just described is a way of formalizing this concept of duality.

## A Summary Model

It is clear that Lana's linguistic behavior motivates a grammar of a degree of formal power equivalent to a context-sensitive phrase structure grammar (CSPSG) with transformational rules. Even if it should prove to be possible to generate all of the well-formed strings of Lana's language with a CSPSG without using transformations, such a grammar would be inherently incapable of saying that two distinct strings have the same meaning. While this could be done without using derivations, by allowing equivalence conditions on pairs of sentences stating that the two sentences mean the same thing, such equivalence conditions (which is what transformations originally were in the early work of Zellig Harris [1957]) are formally and functionally the same as the transformations posited here in that they make explicit the claim that the meaning/form relationship is not isomorphic. Thus, even if another model of grammar is appealed to, it will have to be equivalent in power to a transformational grammar and will probably be a notational variant of a transformational grammar.

## CAN APES LEARN LANGUAGE?

The question central to this chaper is clearly not fully answered, nor is it clear that it is answerable without much more research. The linguist approaches this question in a way which supplements the work of the experimental psychologist: where the psychologist asks a question similar to that of Peters (1977) on "genuine linguistic capabilities," the linguist asks what sort of formal devices are needed to generate the set of sentences which can be observed and how these formal devices compare with those known to be necessary to generate the set of sentences of a natural language.

It has been demonstrated that the linguistic competenece of at least one ape language grammar requires a set of formal devices including a CFPSG, a CSPSG, and a TG. Precisely these formal devices are among the formal universals of natural language. While both natural language and ape language analogues may yet be shown to require some further formal devices, those presented above suggest that the grammars of natural language and ape language analogues are qualitatively similar.

This is not to say that there are not striking differences between them. Apes, for example, have so far not learned language without extensive overt conditioning, including operant training methods. Apes have so far shown little evidence of using language, of the sort under discussion, among themselves, except under controlled laboratory conditions (Savage-Rumbaugh, Rumbaugh, & Boysen, 1978), and it is not known if they might teach language to their offspring. Also, apes generally do not seem to use language for much beyond achieving immediate gratification of some physical need or in direct response to human-initiated stimuli, although there are on record some marked exceptions to this claim. These are, however, functional differences, not formal differences. The formal differences that exist seem to be quantitative rather than qualitative. The respective grammars do not differ markedly in formal power. However, humans seem to be able to handle sentences of greater structural and perceptual complexity than apes as yet show evidence of handling. Humans are capable of a much larger vocabulary than apes, although the upper limits of apes' lexical storage have hardly been reached. Humans use modalities, tense, and aspect, which seem at best to be rudimentary in ape language. These are not differences which require grammars of different formal power.

Hockett's design feature, semanticity, may also be a dimension along

which humans and apes differ in linguistic abilities. The semanticity of
words in ape language analogues has been amply demonstrated in the literature, but the issue of semanticity extends beyond the simple symbol to complex, syntactically structured symbols such as phrases or sentences. In
human language, sentences are usually intended to have meanings, although
this relationship between these meanings and their forms may be obscure, as
in idiomatic expressions. It could, however, be claimed that not all sentences in human language are intended to have meanings, at least not in a
strictly linguistic sense. Phatic communion is an example of this sort of
form without meaning. Much ritualized language use, including greeting
rituals in many languages, incantations, and perhaps glossolallic speech,
can be regarded as phatic communion. What is important in phatic communion is not the analytic or synthetic meaning of the utterance, but its
situational relevance or appropriateness. The use of structure without
semantic intent may well be evident in other areas of human communication
also.

The structural variation in Lana's language use cannot unequivocally
be ascribed to semantic intent. It is quite possible that some parts of well-
formed sentences she produces may be a sort of syntactic subroutine or
habit. She may, for example, produce the phrase *to Lana* after *give x,* not
because it is necessary semantically but simply because she was trained to do
so. The number of times she has followed *give x to* with a lexigram other
than *Lana* is statistically insignificant, and most of them are ill-formed
strings as well. The function of the verb *give* in her language use seems to assume the speaker as recipient and so the expression of *to Lana* is redundant.
It conveys nothing that is not already implied in the verb. Thus a string like
this, while syntactically well-formed, cannot unequivocally be said to have
semanticity *in her usage.* The ascription of semanticity to this and similar
strings may be an artifact of the interpretation.

If both apes and humans sometimes treat syntactic productivity and
semanticity as separate parameters, then human language behavior and ape
language behavior can be compared on the basis of how pervasive the
semanticity of syntactic structures is. Apes, it would seem, more frequently
use structures with little or no semantic intent than do humans.

## Caveats

The very cautiously hedged affirmative answer which this discussion
suggests to the question of whether apes can learn language must be interpreted even more circumspectly in light of certain limitations inherent in
formal linguistic modelling. First of all, the data upon which such analyses
are based are more restricted than is normally the case in linguistic research.
In working with human language, the linguist can request from a native

speaker sentences and forms which will enable him to test his hypotheses immediately. The native speaker supplies not only sentences, but also judgments as to relative well-formedness of sentences. It is exceedingly difficult to extract this sort of information from an ape. The difference between human and pongid informants in this area is characterized by Hockett's design feature of reflexivization. Mature humans can talk about their language. The languages that apes have learned to date do not exhibit the design feature of reflexivization. By the criterion of reflexivization, then, what the apes learn and use is not language, since it is not reflexive. However, this criterion would also disqualify the language of children below, perhaps, the age of six or eight. As developmental psycholinguists have learned, young children have great difficulty talking about their language.

Grammars of early stages of a child language (Brown, 1973) are based on the same sorts of data as is the fragmentary chimpanzee language grammar presented above. If what the child is using very early in his language development is called language, it can only be because it will under normal circumstances develop into natural language. To the extent that ape language is like child language, a topic which needs further exploration beyond Brown (1970), ape language is on the same developmental continuum as child language. Does the fact that it has not been shown to develop into an adultlike natural language mean that it is not language, or is this a fact about apes rather than about the languages they can learn? If it is a fact about apes, it is not a linguistic fact and does not illuminate us as to the nature of the languages they can learn. In this case, a limit is placed on the affirmative answer given above. What apes are able to learn may, then, be a developmentally early sort of language. Formal grammars of this sort of language are not based on the same type of data as are formal grammars of adult natural language, since the native speaker intuition which supplies crucial bits of data is virtually inaccessible. Because they are not based on fully comparable types of data, the grammars are not fully comparable. It is worth noting at this point that some analogue to native speaker intuition has been shown to exist in apes. Rumbaugh, Gill, and von Glasersfeld (1973) report experiments in sentence completion in which Lana rejected strings presented to her when those strings contained an ungrammatical sequence of lexigrams. Her accuracy in detecting ill-formed strings was above 90 percent.

A further caveat to the acceptance of an affirmative answer grows out of the nature of the formal devices employed in grammars. Phrase structure rules and transformations are ultimately formalisms of certain abstract algebras and have no inherent relevance to language, human or pongid. While it has been demonstrated in this chapter that formal grammars of languages learnable by apes require the power of these devices, as do grammars of natural languages, it should also be apparent that the formal devices used may be far too powerful, as they are for human language (Chomsky, 1965). One of the chief preoccupations of linguistic theorists is the matter of limiting the power of the grammar. To be a theory of language, the theory should account for all of language, but it should not also account for phenomena that are not linguistic. If these devices are too powerful for human language, it is no surprise that they are also too powerful for ape language grammars and must be limited. Constraints must be placed on what transformations can be used to explain, on what sorts of relations may exist within the sentence, and on how meaning may be related to form. The degree to which these constraints reflect the constraints on formal devices in natural language grammars will be a further measure of the similarities, or disparities, between the linguistic abilities of members of the two species.

The application of formal linguistic analysis to the linguistic output of ape language projects offers to researchers in comparative psychology and psycholinguistics an additional tool for evaluating the results of their experiments. While Peters's (1977) request for operational criteria may not be met by this line of inquiry, a distinct and fruitful area of comparative psycholinguistics is opened which will help to provide answers to the ancient question, "What is language?"

## NOTES

[1]While the linguistic analysis and writing of this chapter was the responsibility of the author, a work of this sort would have been impossible without the basic theoretical and experimental background and contributions of the talented investigators on the LANA Project, many stimulating discussions with Duane Rumbaugh, and the experimental work of Timothy Gill directly underlying many parts of this chapter. This research was supported by NIH Grants HD-06016 and RR-00155.

## REFERENCES

Brown, R. The first sentences of child and chimpanzee. *In:* R. Brown (Ed.), *Psycholinguistics.* New York: The Free Press, 1970.

Brown, R. *A First language: the early stages.* Cambridge, Mass.: Harvard University Press, 1973.

Chomsky, N. A. *Syntactic structures.* The Hague: Mouton, 1957.

Chomsky, N. A. *Aspects of the theory of syntax.* Cambridge, Mass.: M.I.T. Press, 1965.

Greenberg, J. H. Some universals of word order with particular reference to the order of meaningful elements. *In* J. H. Greenberg, (Ed.), *Universals of language* (2nd ed.). Cambridge, Mass.: M.I.T. Press, 1963.

Greenberg, J. H. (Ed.). *Universals of language* (2nd ed.). Cambridge, Mass.: M.I.T. Press, 1963.

Harris, Z. S. Co-occurrence and transformation in linguistic structure. *Language,* 1957, 33, 283–340.

Hockett, C. F. *A course in modern linguistics.* New York: Macmillan, 1958.

Hockett, C. F. The problem of universals in language. *In* J. H. Greenberg, (Ed.), *Universals of language* (2nd ed.). Cambridge, Mass.: M.I.T. Press, 1963.

Hockett, C. F. & Altmann, S. A. A note on design features. *In* T. A. Sebeok (Ed.), *Animal communication: techniques of study and results of research.* Bloomington, Indiana: Indiana University Press, 1968.

Keenan, E. L. On semantically based grammar. *Linguistic Inquiry,* 1973, 3, 414–461.

Lakoff, G. On generative semantics. *In* D. D. Steinberg & L. A. Jakobovitz (Eds.), *Semantics: an interdisciplinary reader in philosophy, linguistics and psychology.* London: Cambridge University Press, 1971.

Lees, R. B. What are transformations? *In* J. D. McCawley, (Ed.), *Syntax and semantics.* Vol. 7: *Notes from the linguistic underground.* New York: Academic Press, 1976. Originally published as *Cto takoje transformatsija?* (What are transformations?). *Voprosy Jazykoznanija,* 1961, 10(3), 69–77.

Linden, E. *Apes, men, and language.* New York: Penguin Books, 1974.

McCawley, J. D. The role of semantics in a grammar. *In:* E. Bach & R. T. Harms (Eds.), *Universals in linguistic theory.* New York: Holt, Rinehart & Winston, 1968.

Peters, C. R. Review of Premack 1976. *Language,* 1977, 53, 963–965.

Postal, P. M. *Constituent structure.* Bloomington, Indiana: Indiana University Press, 1964.

Premack, A. J. *Why chimps can read.* New York: Harper & Row, 1976.

Ross, J. R. Constraints on variables in syntax. Unpublished doctoral dissertation, M.I.T., Cambridge, Massachusetts, 1967.

Rumbaugh, D. M. (Ed.). *Language learning by a chimpanzee.* New York: Academic Press, 1977.

Rumbaugh, D. M. & Gill, T. V., Language and the acquisition of language-type skills by a chimpanzee *(Pan). In* K. Salzinger (Ed.), *Psychology in progress. Annals of the New York Academy of Sciences,* 1976a.

Rumbaugh, D. M. & Gill, T. V. Lana's mastery of language skills. *In* H. Steklis, S. Harnad, & J. Lancaster (Eds.), *Origins and evolution of language and speech.* New York: Annals of the New York Academy of Sciences, 1976b.

Rumbaugh, D. M. & Gill, T. V. Lana's acquisition of language skills. *In* Rumbaugh, D. M. (Ed.), *Language learning by a chimpanzee.* New York: Academic Press, 1977.

Rumbaugh, D. M., Gill, T. V., & von Glasersfeld, E. C. Reading and sentence completion by a chimpanzee (*Pan*). *Science,* 1973, 182, 731–733.

Savage-Rumbaugh, E. S., Rumbaugh, D. M., & Boysen, S. Symbolic communication between two chimpanzees (Pan Troglaydtes). *Science,* 1978, 201, 641–644.

Stahlke, H. F. W. Which that. *Language,* 1976, 52, 584–610.

von Glasersfeld, E. C. The Yerkish language for nonhuman primates. *American Journal of Computational Linguistics,* Microfiche 12, 1975.

von Glasersfeld, E. C. The Yerkish language and its automatic parser. *In* Rumbaugh, D. M. (Ed.), 1977, *Language learning by a chimpanzee.* New York: Academic Press, 1977.

# 7

# TWO COMPARATIVE
# PSYCHOLOGISTS LOOK AT
# LANGUAGE ACQUISITION

BEATRICE T. GARDNER
R. ALLEN GARDNER[1]

In reviewing the literature on language acquisition in apes, Kellogg (1968) noted:

> Apes as household pets are not uncommon and several books by lay authors attest to the problems involved. Such ventures have never given any indication of the development of human language. But pet behavior is not child behavior, and pet treatment is not child treatment. It is quite another story, therefore, for trained and qualified psychobiologists to observe and measure the reactions of a home-raised pongid amid controlled experimental home surroundings. Such research is difficult, confining, and time-consuming . . . Although often misunderstood, the scientific rationale for rearing an anthropoid ape in a human household is to find out just how far the ape can go in absorbing the civilizing influences of the environment. To what degree is it capable of responding like a child and to what degree will genetic factors limit its development? (p. 423)

By Kellogg's criteria there were only three cases before Project Washoe in which professional psychobiologists had obtained comparative data for chimpanzees and children. In all three cases, early development was indeed comparable, with one striking exception: the chimpanzees failed to acquire the most rudimentary elements of human language. This failure of the chimpanzee subjects set severe limits on their intellectual development. Because the evaluation of human intellectual development is so intimately related to the acquisition of language, the chimpanzee subjects were soon outdistanced by normal human children.

For many years this evidence, particularly the thorough, professional seven-year effort of Hayes and Hayes (1951), was cited to bolster the traditional doctrine of absolute, unbridgeable discontinuity between human and nonhuman intelligence—a discontinuity defined by the acquisition of productive language. Nevertheless, many comparative psychologists remained convinced that this negative conclusion was premature, and that new techniques might yet reveal a much greater degree of continuity. The results of Project Washoe and the research that it has stimulated demonstrated that this was indeed the case. The volume of commentary devoted to the interprctation of the new data attests to the fact that the new line of research has reopened a central question.

Those of us who argue for continuity tend to stress similarities in the linguistic development of ape and child; those who argue for discontinuity tend to stress differences. In this atmosphere of controversy, the linguistic achievements of the chimpanzee subjects are often treated as positive results and the linguistic failures as negative results. But this is a basic misunderstanding of the continuity position. The notion of identity in the behavior of ape and man is as foreign to Darwinism as the notion of absolute discontinuity. For the same reasons that we expect significant similarities we also expect significant differences. The objective of this line of research is to measure the degree of overlap as precisely as possible. To the extent that the methods of investigation provide the chimpanzee subjects with comparable learning tasks and comparable learning conditions, their linguistic failures are as significant as their linguistic successes.

Before Project Washoe, questions about the ability of a nonhuman primate to acquire a human language had always been raised in a yes-or-no, can-they-or-can't-they fashion, and the answer was always a categorical negative. As an alternative, animal intelligence was studied by analyzing general functions into specific paradigmatic tasks such as matching to sample, or dimensional transfer. In and of itself, this has been a fruitful line of attack on the problem of human and nonhuman intelligence and will undoubtedly continue to yield valuable insights into the nature of intelligence. In Project Washoe, Gardner and Gardner (1969) asked the direct comparative question that had originally been asked by Kellogg and Kellogg (1933) and Hayes and Hayes (1951); except that we used American Sign Language (Ameslan), a natural language which does not require speech (Bellugi and Klima, 1975).

Washoe's progress in sign language was evaluated by making direct comparisons between her utterances and the early utterances of human children. Washoe's early utterances compared closely with those of young children both in general patterns and in specific details (Brown, 1970, 1973; Gardner & Gardner, 1969, 1971, 1973, 1974a, 1975a). In many respects the progress of her linguistic development was indistinguishable from that of human children, particularly if one allowed for the fact that the grammatical structure of Ameslan depends more upon inflection and less upon word order than does English. But the success of Project Washoe lay not so much in answering the original question, can a nonhuman being learn to use a human language, as in discovering a technique whereby the categorical question could be replaced by quantitative questions such as which aspects of human language, how soon, and how far can they go?

Those who study the acquisition of language by human children have not found and do not expect to find a litmus paper test that can reveal just when this or that child has acquired its native language. What they do find is a pattern of development extending over a period of years. If the earliest utterances can be described as language, then they are best described as a primitive, childish language. Gradually and piecemeal, but in an orderly sequence, the language of the child evolves into the language spoken by the adult. This orderly sequence of development can be used as a yardstick to measure the achievements of nonhuman subjects. Because it is based on normative data it avoids some of the murkier definitional lacunae of linguistics and psycholinguistics. Morever, to the extent that the child and the chimpanzee exhibit similar patterns of development in the utterances that we can record, then a theory that accounts for the pattern found in the child must also be applicable to the pattern found in the chimpanzee.

To be sure, it seems safe to assume that most of the normal children that we study today will grow up to be linguistically normal adults. It does not seem safe to make such an assumption about the young chimpanzees we have studied so far. On the contrary, it seems safe to assume that the adult patterns will be distinctly different. But how different, and in what ways? This remains an empirical question.

In Gardner and Gardner (1969), we reported some of the results of Project Washoe for the period that ended when Washoe's estimated age was three years. These first results were considered to be major achievements at the time, but it was also clear that Washoe's linguistic development was behind that of most three-year-old children. Many of the early commentators concluded that Washoe must have reached the limits of her linguistic capacity, and some thought they could identify the particular functions that would never be mastered by a chimpanzee. In Gardner and Gardner (1971), we reported results for the period that ended when Washoe's estimated age was four; there had been dramatic progress. Reviewing these results in detail, Roger Brown (1973) concluded, "the evidence that Washoe has Stage 1 language is about the same as it is for children . . ." (p. 43). Nevertheless, at age four, Washoe was further behind children of her age than she had been at three. This prompted still more commentators to conclude that the limits had been reached and to list the particular functions that must forever remain beyond the capacity of the chimpanzee.

But Washoe's linguistic development persisted (Gardner & Gardner 1974a, 1975a), and the pattern of development continued to resemble the pattern found in human children until the project ended. At that time, her estimated age was five and she was further behind children of her age than she had been when she was four. She had still progressed, but most children do so at an even greater rate. Our current project includes major improvements over Project Washoe such as: starting subjects when they are newborn; and providing adult models who are fluent in Ameslan, including research assistants who are deaf themselves and others who were raised by deaf parents. As expected, the rate of progress has been greater at each level of development (Gardner & Gardner 1975b, 1978).

From the most gifted down to the most retarded, human intellectual development continues until sexual maturity, at least (Mussen, 1970). We predict that chimpanzees who are maintained under stimulating conditions will also continue to develop all of their intellectual functions, including linguistic functions, until sexual maturity. It is not that we believe there are no limits or that a chimpanzee, however favorable its environment, will ever become the intellectual or linguistic equal of a human being of the same age. It is only that it seems reasonable to expect the psychological development of all species to continue until maturity (Riopelle & Rogers, 1965).

Because we expect further gains during the next phase of the project, we plan to continue to keep our subjects under conditions which are as comparable as possible to those of human children. Only in this way does it seem likely that maximum gains can be realized. But if we took the opposite point of view, if we believed that the limits had already been reached or that they would soon be reached, then we could make an even stronger case for insisting on keeping our subjects under the most favorable conditions. The evidence that a chimpanzee cannot achieve a function that is normally achieved by human children is only as good as the evidence that the methods of procedure have provided the chimpanzee with equal opportunities.

## APPROPRIATE LABORATORY CONDITIONS

In some areas of research it may be reasonable to compare caged chimpanzees with caged members of other species, but in the case of language acquisition, human beings are the only standard of comparison. Only the most devout nativist would expect language to unfold normally in human children who were kept in cages with infrequent, sporadic exposure to their native language. Most psychologists are convinced that there is an intimate relationship between language acquisition and every other aspect of behavioral development, and many of us believe that language acquisition may be especially sensitive to the quality of the behavioral environment.

Our procedure can be distinguished from the procedures of other ape projects which have sprung up since Project Washoe on the basis of our emphasis on the quality of the behavioral environment throughout the waking day. This aspect of procedure has a twofold purpose: the best language acquisition is to be expected under the best conditions, and the best comparisons between child and chimpanzee are those that are made under the most comparable conditions. It is feasible to provide comparable conditions because of the high degree of similarity between human and chimpanzee childhoods.

Morphological and behavioral similarities between chimpanzees and humans have long been recognized, but recent research indicates that there is an even closer relationship between chimpanzees and men than most authorities would have conceded twenty, or even ten, years ago. In blood chemistry, for example, relationships between species have been quantified, and the chimpanzee is not only the closest animal to man by this measure, but it is also closer to man than the chimpanzee itself is to any other species (Goodman, Tashian, & Tashian, 1976). Where reliable information is available, the sensory systems of the chimpanzee and human are found to be highly similar in structure and function (Prestrude, 1970). Under natural conditions infant chimpanzees are weaned at about five and continue to live with their mothers until they are seven or eight, often ten years old. The youngest chimpanzee mother that Jane Goodall observed at the Gombe Stream was twelve years old (Goodall, 1974). All of these discoveries, but most particularly the discovery of the prolonged childhood and adolescence of the chimpanzee, indicate a close relationship between the two species.

Because of this close relationship, the chimpanzee subjects can be maintained in an environment that is very similar to that of a human child (see Appendix 1). In such a laboratory their waking hours follow a schedule of meals, naps, baths, play, and schooling, much like that of a young child. Living quarters are well stocked with furniture, tools, and toys of all kinds, and frequent excursions are made to other interesting places—a pond or a meadow, the home of a human or chimpanzee friend. Whenever a subject is awake, one or more human companions are present. The companions use Ameslan to communicate with the subjects, and with each other, so that linguistic training is an integral part of daily life, and not an activity restricted to special training sessions. These human companions are to see that the environment is as stimulating as possible and as much associated with Ameslan as can be. They demonstrate the uses and extol the virtues of the many interesting objects around them. They anticipate the routine activities of the day and describe these with appropriate signs. They invent games, introduce novel objects, show pictures in books and magazines, and make special scrapbooks of favorite pictures, all to demonstrate the use of Ameslan.

The model for this laboratory is the normal linguistic interaction of human parents with their children. We sign to the chimpanzees about ongoing events, or about objects that have come to their attention, as mothers do in the case of the child. We ask questions, back and forth, to probe the effectiveness of communication. We modify our signing to become an especially simple and repetitous register of Ameslan, which makes the form of signs and the structure of phrases particularly clear. And we use devices to capture attention, such as signing on the chimpanzee's body, which are also used by parents of deaf children (Schlesinger & Meadow, 1972).

At the time of our early reports of Project Washoe much more than today, psycholinguistics was dominated by Chomsky's doctrines of innateness and antibehaviorism. A common response to our detailed descriptions of teaching procedures was the assertion that no teaching procedures are involved in the language acquisition of human children. This assertion always seemed to us to contradict our informal observations of parents and young children. The Chomskian child absorbing language from the air seemed more remote from normal human children than did our chimpanzee subjects exposed to a continual patter of simple declaratives interspersed with probing questions.

On this point as on many others, empirical studies of human children have provided observations which agree with ours. A large body of recent research indicates that parents throughout the world speak to their children as if they had very similar notions of the best way to teach language to a young primate. In a volume devoted to this new evidence and entitled *Talking to Children,* Snow (1977) remarks,

> The first descriptions of mothers' speech to young children were undertaken in the late sixties in order to refute the prevailing view that language acquisition was largely innate and occurred almost independently of the language environment. The results of those mothers' speech studies may have contributed to the widespread abandonment of this hypothesis about language acquisition, but a general shift from syntactic to semantic-cognitive aspects of language acquisition would probably have caused it to lose its central place as a tenet of research in any case (p. 31) . . . all language learning children have access to this simplified speech register. No one has to learn to talk from a confused, error-ridden garble of opaque structure. Many of the characteristics of mothers' speech have been seen as ways of making grammatical structure transparent, and others have been seen as attention-getters and probes to the effectiveness of the communication. (p. 38)

## WASHOE AND THE SEQUEL TO PROJECT WASHOE

The human language, the homelike environment, and the continual exposure to language were also used in the case of our first subject, Washoe. But for the next subjects—Moja, Pili, Tatu, and Dar (Gardner & Gardner, 1978)—we improved the procedure in two significant ways. We started to expose the subjects to language at birth. A newborn chimpanzee is tiny and helpless and requires the same care, such as round-the-clock feedings, as do human infants (Figure 7-1). When they are 1 month old, infant chimpanzees are attentive and alert, and quite responsive to simple social games: tickling, for example, elicits a playface (Figure 7-2). By 3 months of age, the chimpanzees show interest in pictures (Figure 7-3), which we utilize extensively to increase the abundance of exemplars of signs which the subjects can use or understand (Figure 7-4). Also by three months, the first signs start to appear (Gardner & Gardner, 1975b).[2]

The second improvement in procedure was to use fluent signers as adult models. A fluent native signer finds it easy to provide a running commentary on objects and events as these engage the chimpanzee's interest (Figure 7-5). Moreover, these fluent native signers find it much easier to recognize the immature variants of signs that infants produce, as indeed would be the case for a native speaker of English listening to early utterances of English-speaking and French-speaking babies. The conditions of the second project, then, are closer to those of human language acquisition, and provide more valid comparisons (cf Bonvillian & Nelson, 1978).

## RESULTS

Our procedures for recording the use of signs by chimpanzees are fashioned on those that have been developed for young children. They include diary records, inventories of phrases, repeated samples of all verbal in-

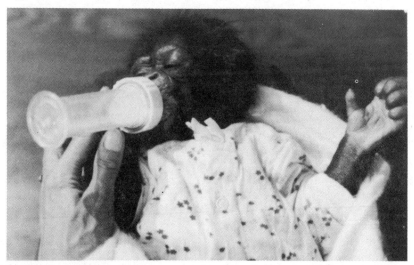

*Figure 7-1.* Newborn chimpanzee, Pili, being fed from a preemie bottle. The exposure of Moja, Pili, Tatu, and Dar to sign language began within a few days of birth.

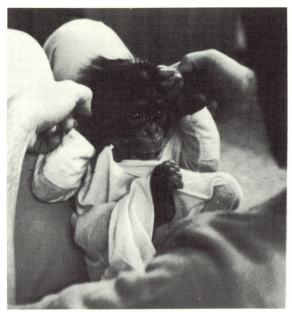

*Figure 7-2.* Tatu at 1 month, showing a playface during tickling. At this age the infant chimpanzees can also grasp toys and differentiate familiar companions from strangers.

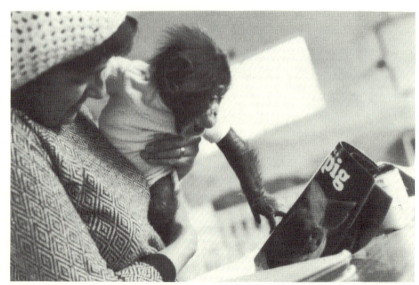

*Figure 7-3.* Tatu at 3 months, responding to a magazine picture. In this laboratory, illustrations in books and magazines multiply the number of exemplars for signs.

*Figure 7-4.* Pili at 1½ years, looking through his picture book. Special scrapbooks of favorite pictures are made for the subjects, and these are used to teach and test the use of Ameslan.

*Figure 7-5.* As Moja, age 2, looks at a flower, Ted Supalla, a native signer, names it. Fluent signers find it easy to chat about ongoing events, and about objects which have captured the attention of the infant chimpanzee.

put and output occurring during a brief period of time, and formal tests, with pictures and questions. The essential control group of children provides us with norms, with patterns of language development, and with developmental stages. For example, in terms of vocabulary, there are age norms for attaining a given vocabulary size, and we speak of patterns because it is not a matter of adding more and more words: different types of words—nouns, adjectives, functors—are added at different rates. Developmental stages have been described for various forms of negation and various forms of questions, which replace each other as the child develops. And beyond providing the data which makes it possible to evaluate what the chimpanzees have accomplished at each stage, the children provide us with expectations about further developments which might occur as the research continues.

Our finding on the use of sign language by chimpanzees can be characterized very broadly in terms of three networks of connections that develop concurrently. The first of these networks develops between signs and their referents; the second, among the signs themselves, governing the ways in which they can be combined; and the third between the signing of participants in discourse, which makes possible conversational interchanges.

## Early Vocabulary Development

We count a gesture produced by the chimpanzee as an item of vocabulary when it has been identified as a sign by at least three of the fluent adult companions of the chimpanzee. For this to be so, there must be consistency in the form of the gesture, and consistency in its usage, and both must be recognizably similar to the form and usage of this sign in Ameslan. Of course we accept baby-talk variants, which have been described for the form of signs, and for the concepts that these express when used by human infants (McIntire, 1977; Schlesinger & Meadow, 1972). In order to refer to the sign we use its nearest word equivalent in adult English, a single English word which is entered as a gloss for this particular sign in one of the standard manuals of sign language (Fant, 1972; Watson 1973), or in the *Dictionary of American Sign Language* (Stokoe, Casterline, & Croneberg, 1965). And aside from the fact that we are talking about manual gestures rather than spoken words, there is little difference between our procedures and what mothers or psycholinguistic investigators do when they report on children's early words. "The first stage of communication [is] . . . when parents feel that their children have really begun to speak. Individual words are being pronounced intelligibly—that is, so that parents can match them with words in their own speech—and are being related to things and events" (Bollinger, 1975). When three independent observers report that the subject has used a sign, we count it as an item that has entered the vocabulary. We do not count it as a reliable item of vocabulary, however, until there are reports for a period of 15 consecutive days of appropriate and spontaneous usage (Gardner & Gardner, 1971).

As an illustration, here are the form and context descriptions for three early vocabulary items: *cat, hear,* and *no.* The form of the sign that we glossed by the English word *cat* was described in terms of the place at which the gesture was made—the side of the mouth; the hand configuration that was used—a grasping fist, or, sometimes, a spread hand with thumb and index touching; and the movement—pinching or pulling. For early signs, the place is usually constant, but there are variants in configuration and in movement. Another immature variant was to repeat the sign, or to double it by forming the sign with both hands. This is baby talk, but not for chimpanzees alone; these are the immature variants of children also (Schlesinger & Meadow, 1972). The context descriptions show that the sign *cat* was used both in the presence of live cats and for cats in picture books, and that in the second situation, which was the most common, an associated sound often occurred. This is usual when human adults introduce animal names to children; they say, "This is a cat, it says, 'meow.' " The sounds are attention-getters, and make the referent more intriguing (Nelson, 1973). In the case of *hear,* the form description was simple: the place was the ear with the extended index finger moving to contact it. Again there were baby-talk variants: the index finger might be extended from a fist or from a relaxed hand. The contexts described for early usage of *hear* were rather complex since *hear* was reported both for sounds the subject produced, as when drawing a fingernail down a grating, and for sounds from an outside source, as when a fire-truck came by with sirens blazing, or when the human companion blew on a blade of grass. Moreover, the sign was reported both at the onset of the sound and when ongoing sounds stopped: a power saw in the next room was turned off, and Tatu signed, *hear.* The last of the early signs that we want to describe in detail is *no.* The form was the simplest: a slow, side-to-side turning of the head. But the context descriptions showed a most interesting and abstract usage of *no.* The earliest context notes described opposition or rejection to what the adult proposed, either by action or by signing. *No* was reported as the adult started to put the infant chimpanzee down, and also when another adult, who was departing, requested a good-bye kiss in signs, and in another context involving signing, when the adult asked whether the infant was *Ready for milk now?* Several descriptions of early contexts for *no* showed that negation was applied to the infant's own actions: in one example, the chimpanzee Tatu crawled to the edge of a couch, looked down, signed *no,* and backed away.

## The 50-Item Vocabulary of Child and Chimpanzee

In earlier publications (Gardner & Gardner, 1975a, 1978), we described in detail the criteria that we have used in our laboratory for reports of spontaneous (i.e., unprompted) and appropriate usage; for determining that a sign has become a reliable item in the vocabulary of a chimpanzee subject; for dating the initial appearance of a particular item; and for reassessment, to determine whether and in what form a particular sign did indeed remain a reliable item in the vocabulary of a particular chimpanzee subject. Similarly stringent criteria, or even similarly detailed descriptions of criteria, are absent from the literature of child language acquisition. Nevertheless, in the most thorough analysis of the early vocabulary of human children that has appeared so far, Nelson (1973) has provided us with a useable basis for comparison.

Of the several comparisons that can be made (cf. Gardner & Gardner, 1978), we would like to discuss here the striking similarity in the referents of the first 50 words for Nelson's sample of children and the first 50 signs for the sample of chimpanzees in our laboratory. Nelson's subjects were just under 2 years of age when they reached the 50-item level of vocabulary, as was also the case for Moja, Pili, and Tatu, the chimpanzees reared in a signing environment from birth (Nelson, 1973; Gardner & Gardner, 1978).

We can classify the vocabulary of our chimpanzee subjects into the six categories which Nelson devised for the vocabularies of her child subjects: General Nominals, Specific Nominals, Action terms, Modifiers, Personal-Social terms, and Function terms. For both child and chimpanzee, General Nominals were by far the most numerous, accounting for half the vocabulary, and the proportion of items falling into each of the five remaining categories was very similar (see Table I). Specific nominals include the proper names for the children and parents, as well as the words *Mommy* and *Daddy;* in the case of the chimpanzees, the category included the name signs for some of the human companions and their own name signs. The Action terms *go, hurry, hug* describe and accompany action and were in the early vocabulary of both children and chimpanzees. Locative terms, when used for locative action, as they often were by infants of both species, belong among Action terms in Nelson's classification: *Up* for "Pick me up" and *Out* for "Let's go out." Modifiers used by both children and chimpanzees included states such as *dirty, hot,* and *all-done,* and the possessive *mine.* In the Personal-Social category, the social expressive terms *please* and *good-bye,* the assertion *yes,* and several signs for negation, *no, can't, won't,* were used both by children and by chimpanzees. The Function terms used by both species included the question word *What?* and the questioning form of *That.* In the case of spoken language, *That?* is conveyed by rising intonation, and in the case of sign language it is carried by a facial gesture and by maintaining the sign for longer than usual. In this questioning form, *That?* has inevitably been interpreted as a request for a name.

Nelson also presented a semantic analysis for General Nominals. She listed ten categories such as food, clothing, outdoor objects, animals, and

## TABLE I
## PARALLEL GRAMMATICAL CATEGORIZATION FOR
## THE EARLY VOCABULARY OF CHILDREN AND CHIMPANZEES

| Categories used by Nelson | Nelson's data for children (N = 18) | | The data for chimpanzees (N = 4) | |
| | Examples | Mean Percentage of 50-item vocabulary | Examples | Mean Percentage of 50-item vocabulary |
| --- | --- | --- | --- | --- |
| Nominals | | | | |
| Specific | *Mommy, Daddy, Dizzy* | 14 | *Betty, Pili, Susan* | 8 |
| General | *ball, doggie, milk* | 51 | *dog, milk, shoe* | 42 |
| Actions | *go, look, up* | 13 | *go, see, up* | 28 |
| Modifiers | *all done, hot, mine* | 9 | *finished, hot, mine* | 13 |
| Personal-Social | *no, please, want* | 8 | *no, please, refusal* | 8 |
| Functions | *for, tha?, where* | 4 | *that?—what* | 1 |

so on, which described the range of General Nominals that the children were using. This descriptive system fitted the range of chimpanzee nominals also, and there were exemplars from the early vocabulary of our subjects for seven of the categories. Within a semantic class, Nelson noted that frequent exposure to the referents does not guarantee that they will be named; the referents commonly named by children were changeable, movable, and manipulable. Within the category of clothing, hats and shoes, which the children take off and put on, were named, but coats were not. Among household items, lights, which the children switch on and off, were named, but not sofas and tables. The same principle governed the popularity of General Nominals in the vocabularies of our signing chimpanzees: they also named hats, shoes, lights, watches, keys, and so on. The English glosses that Nelson assigned to items in the vocabularies of her children were chosen to identify the referent categories rather than the speech of the children. A dog, for example, was called a *doggie* by one child, a *woof-woof* by a second, and a *puppy* by a third. Thus the popularity of items is governed by their relevance to the world of the child rather than by pronounceability. This principle of classification permits us to make precise comparisons between vocabularies, even when the languages are as different as English and Amelsan.

We can quantify specific item overlap because Nelson provided a complete listing of vocabulary for eight of her subjects. While there were eight 50-word vocabularies, there were not 400 different words, but only 188. The children showed considerable agreement in what they would name. The extent of overlap between our subjects and Nelson's can be evaluated by counting the number of items that any one child had in common with the other seven. For the 8 children, the number of shared items ranged from 24 to 32 (see Table II). We then counted the number of items that each of the

## TABLE II
## OVERLAP IN THE EARLY VOCABULARY
## OF 8 CHILDREN (NELSON, 1973)

| Subject | Basis of Early Vocabulary | Number of Matching Items |
|---|---|---|
| Paul | | 24 |
| Beth | | 27 |
| Robert | Remaining | 28 |
| Jane | 7 child | 29 |
| Mark | Ss | 29 |
| Ellen | | 31 |
| Lisa | | 31 |
| Leslie | | 32 |
| Median for Child$_i$ | | 29 |

chimpanzees shared with the 8 sets of 7 children, and found that the median ranged from 24.5 to 28.5 (see Table III). Thus, the 50-sign vocabulary of any one of our chimpanzees could be substituted for the 50-word vocabulary of any one of Nelson's children without changing the degree of overlap. By this measure, the first 50-word vocabularies of a sample of human children are indistinguishable from the first 50-sign vocabularies of our signing chimpanzees.

The items of vocabulary that the young chimpanzees and the young children adopted have evident ecological validity in a nursery world, both in the case of objects—*apple, blanket, shoe*—and in the case of states, actions and so on—*all-done, hot, mine, no, up.* These are the objects, properties, and actions that figure prominently in the daily lives of the young subjects and in their interactions with adult caretakers. Note that the similarity in vocabulary was present even though the medium of expressive vocabulary was not the same. The similarity, then, was in a set of meanings that young children and young chimpanzees expressed when reared similarly and given similar access to a natural language.

### Early Sign Combinations

The network of connections between signs is made manifest in phrases. Our chimpanzee subjects commonly use signs in combination, and they begin to do so before they are one year old. During this early period, we recorded all combinations or phrase tokens, although we report development in terms of the number of different combinations, or phrase types, that have been recorded. The age at which the first 10 different phrases had been recorded was 6 months for Tatu, and 7 months for Moja, Pili, and Dar. On this measure of linguistic achievement the current subjects were ahead of English-speaking children, where the age at 10 phrases ranges from 16 to 24 months (Nelson, 1973). Children who sign are more comparable to our subjects, for recent information indicates that they start to form phrases at 9 or 10 months (McIntire, 1977; Williams, 1976).

Just as with individual words and signs, combinations of items in multiword or multisign utterances express meanings. This is the basis of Brown's system of classifying the early sentences of children into a small set of relations between two terms, such as Agent and Action, Action and Object, and so on (Brown, 1973). Because these are types of construction, the particular terms can assume many values, and the name of a given referent can play one role in one utterance and a different role in another. However, children do not, at first, use a construction over the full semantic range to which it applies. Bloom (1970) remarked that "the isolated or occasional occurrence of a structure is not sufficient evidence for crediting the child with the pertinent rule" (p. 18). She defined a structure as productive when it occurred five or more times, with different formatives, in a given speech sample. Bloom was concerned with writing grammars for consecutive samples of child speech, and for this purpose she excluded structures that were not productive.

During the first two years of development, it was feasible to maintain nearly complete inventories of the subject's phrases, together with notes on context. The early phrases were grouped according to the signs that they contained, to reveal productive construction patterns. For example during the first 12 months Tatu followed the sign, *There,* with object names to produce the set of phrases, *There milk, There drink, There eat, There diaper,* and *There hat,* which all expressed the same basic relation, Demonstrative and Entity. Moja in her first year combined name signs and pronouns with signs for action, to produce a set of Agent-Action phrases which included *Susan hug, Susan brush, Naomi hug, Me drink,* and *You go.*

## TABLE III
## OVERLAP IN THE EARLY VOCABULARY
## OF 8 CHILDREN AND 4 CHIMPANZEES

| Subject | Basis of Early Vocabulary | Number of Matching Items | |
|---------|---------------------------|--------|-------|
| | | Median | Range |
| Child$_i$ | | 29 | 24–32 |
| Washoe | All | 28.5 | 27–30 |
| Moja | 8 sets | 24.5 | 22–25 |
| Pili | of 7 | 28.5 | 27–30 |
| Tatu | child Ss | 26.8 | 25–28 |

For all four infants, Moja, Pili, Tatu, and Dar, the phrases recorded in the first 12 months exhibited the basic sentence relations which children express in their early two-word utterances: Agent and Action (*Susan brush, Pili potty*), Action and Object (*Chase me, Gimme drink*), Demonstrative and Entity (*There drink, There diaper*), and Action and Location (*Tickle there, Up go*). We found that from 74 to 90 percent of the chimpanzee's two-term constructions expressed the sentence relations characteristic of Stage-one child speech (Brown, 1973) and child signing (Fischer, 1974; Klima & Bellugi, 1972), and Brown reports that 75 percent of the two-word utterances that he classified did so.

Within Brown's system of classification, combinations involving negative terms are regarded as the most advanced. All four chimpanzee infants occasionally used negative terms in phrases. These included phrases such as *Gum no,* a comment on the nonexistence of gum at a customary location, and refusals such as *Hug no.* As in the early negative constructions of children who speak (Bloom, 1970; Bowerman, 1973), and those who sign (Collins-Ahlgren, 1975), notes about context showed that the negative term was sometimes combined with an element being negated, as in *Hug no* when refusing to hug, and sometimes with a positive alternative, as in *No, drink* when refusing solids. This is significant because Bloom (1970) considers the semantic paradoxes created by sentence-initial negatives to be evidence for the integration of the negative into the structure of the sentence. According to Bloom, when young children express negation, this adds structural complexity to their sentence and requires that the remainder of the sentence be reduced before it can be uttered.

As the subjects develop, and the frequency of signing increases, maintaining a complete inventory of phrases and context descriptions becomes impractical. Often the brisk pace of an extended conversational interchange precludes verbatim recording. From the end of the subject's second year, it becomes necessary to rely on a different method of recording. During a specified period of time, usually 20 minutes, we record everything signed by the chimpanzee and a description of context, which includes all signing addressed to the chimpanzee. These comprehensive signing records require a team of two persons, both of whom remain near the subject throughout the recording period. One member of the team whispers an immediate spoken transcription of signing, together with notes about context, into the microphone of a miniature cassette recorder. The other person performs the usual role of teacher, caretaker, playmate, and interlocutor. The technique is based on that used by Brown and his coworkers for the study of language development in Adam, Eve, and Sarah (Brown, 1973) and by Bloom in her extensive study with three other English-speaking children (Bloom, 1970). In terms of quantitative characteristics such as rate of utterances and proportion of phrases, the technique yields material for young chimpanzees that is well within the range of language samples for the young English-speaking children, and of language samples obtained by videotaping young children who sign (Gardner & Gardner, 1978; Hoffmeister, Moores, & Ellenberger, 1975).

We have refined this technique by designating the events that are to be sampled in the recording sessions. Each session consists of a series of 5 events, such as sharing food or drink, looking through a picture book, and preparing to go outdoors. The person interacting with the chimpanzee chooses the particular treat, book, or outdoor destination, and determines how long to remain on each of the 5 topics of conversation. The object of the new technique is to manipulate context in ways which vary the roles—agent, object, possessor—the chimpanzee subject and the human companion assume in the interaction.

The procedure with predesignated contexts was first used in records of signing with Moja when she was 42 months old. The total time for the set of recording sessions was 5 hours; this yielded 1,096 utterances, of which 424 were phrases. Because Moja used signs appropriately, the substantive vocabulary (nouns, verbs) changed as the context was changed. Thus for phrases recorded during food-sharing, the most frequently used substantive was *drink;* for preparing to go outdoors, it was *out;* while for toileting it was *potty.* Each of these signs was rare or absent in the other contexts. Unlike nouns and verbs, signs such as *me, hurry,* and *there* were recorded in phrases in each of the 5 contexts, and were used frequently ($>20$ percent of phrases) in more than one context.

Since the role of self, other person, and object of action changed with context, we expected that the types of construction that Moja used would also change with context. A comparison of the first 25 phrases recorded in each of the 5 contexts showed that this was indeed the case. Thus, Possessor—Possession (*My drink, Your drink*) was the most frequent construction type in the food-sharing context, constructions with negatives (*Me can't, Me please potty can't*) in the toileting context, and the question, *What that* together with Demonstrative-Entity constructions (*That boy, That me*) in the context of looking through picture books. In each case, these constructions were much less frequent or absent in the other contexts.

Names and pronouns both preceded and followed verbs in the phrases of this sample, and a plausible interpretation could be assigned to the contrasting word order that the chimpanzee used in phrases such as *Moja help* and *Jump Moja.* Such interpretative data are often cited to support the claim that children use word order correctly (Brown, 1973). But with the predesignated context procedure, contextual evidence can be used to evaluate the use of grammatical devices such as sign order, by the chimpanzee. Thus the pronoun *me* or the name *Moja* should be in subject position when the chimpanzee is in control of an event (or experience), in terms of being able to affect action as agent, but in object position when the ad-dressee is in control. The latter is by far the most frequent case, given that the participants in the interactions are a very young chimpanzee and its adult caretaker. Phrases containing *me* occurred frequently in two situa-tions which contrast the role of the chimpanzee and the human compan-ions. In going outdoors, the human was in full control: he chose the time, dressed the chimpanzee, and opened the door. In almost all recorded phrases containing both *me* and *out, me* followed *out.* The reverse was true for phrases recorded in the toileting context. Here Moja was in control of events, and she used *me* as the subject of phrases, as in *Me can't, Me finish,* and *Me potty.*

### Early Discourse

The question-and-answer process exhibits a basic coordination between participants in discourse. Questions call for replies, and different types of questions, with different interrogative forms, call for different types of replies. We have been interested in the chimpanzees' replies to questions be-cause there are extensive data on the developments that occur for children acquiring spoken language (Brown, 1968; Ervin-Tripp, 1970; Ervin-Tripp & Miller, 1977) as well as a report on a child who signs (Fischer, 1974). Chil-dren answer questions readily at age 21 months, and there is a definite order in which different types of questions come to be answered appropriately. In terms of major interrogatives, the types of questions that children answer early contain *What* and *Where* and *Who;* replies to *Whose* and *What do* are later developments, and replies to *Why, How,* and *When* are much later still.

With the new subjects, we have traced the development of the ability to answer questions. Following methods developed for testing Washoe at age 5 (Gardner & Gardner, 1975a), we began sampling replies to questions with much younger chimpanzees, and have repeated the sampling at intervals of 6 to 12 months. From the onset of testing (at 30 months for Moja and at 18 months for Pili, Tatu, and Dar), the subjects replied to over half the ques-tions addressed to them.

As with Washoe, we tested with question types that were common in everyday conversation with the subjects, and we have thus been able to add new types of questions on successive tests (see Table IV). Using the same cri-terion for mastery as has been used with children (Brown, 1968; Ervin-Tripp, 1970), Pili & Tatu at 18 months were replying appropriately to questions containing *What* and *Where,* but not yet to those containing *Who* (cf. Table IV). Between 2 and 3 years of age, both Moja and Tatu were us-ing proper names and pronouns in over half their replies to *Who nominal* questions. Between 3 and 4, Moja was using *mine* and *yours* in most of her replies to questions containing *Whose,* and was using these possessives al-

## TABLE IV
## RELATIONS BETWEEN QUESTIONS AND REPLIES
## FOR YOUNG CHIMPANZEES

| Question form | Target category | Example of question and appropriate reply | | % Appropriate replies |
|---|---|---|---|---|
| **Pili, 20 months old** | | | | |
| Who demonstrative | Proper Name | RL: *Who that?* | P: *Susan* | 12 |
| Who subject/object | Proper Name or Pronoun | HP: *Who chase you or me?* | P: *Chase Pili.* | 25 |
| What demonstrative | Noun | HP: *What that?* | P: *Bib.* | 100* |
| What want | Noun or Verb | NR: *What you want?* | P: *Gum.* | 88* |
| Where nominal or action | Locative | NR: *Where you want tickle?* | P: *Tickle there.* | 50* |
| **Tatu, 18 months old** | | | | |
| Who subject/object | Proper name or Pronoun | CM: *Who I tickle?* | T: *Tickle me.* | 30 |
| What demonstrative | Noun | KW: *What name that?* | T: *Diaper.* | 70* |
| What want | Noun or Verb | NR: *What you want?* | T: *Toothbrush gimme.* | 90* |
| Where nominal or action | Locative | KW: *Where your bib?* | T: *There.* | 60* |
| **Moja, 37 months old** | | | | |
| Who demonstrative | Proper Name | RL: *Who you?* | M: *Moja.* | 58* |
| Who subject/object | Proper Name or Pronoun | BTG: *Who drink?* | M: *Drink me drink.* | 25 |
| Who trait | Proper Name or Pronoun | HP: *Who good girl?* | M: *Harold.* | 25 |
| Whose | Possessive | NR: *Whose shirt?* | M: *Mine please.* | 25 |
| What demonstrative | Noun | SN: *What that?* | M: *Bug.* | 92* |
| What want | Noun or Verb | HP: *What you want?* | M: *Tickle.* | 75* |
| What predicate | Verb | NR: *What we play?* | M: *Me chase.* | 92* |
| What color | Color adjective | SN: *Dog color what?* | M: *Black.* | 83* |
| Where nominal | Locative | SN: *Where Susan?* | M: *Out.* | 33 |
| Where action | Locative | NR: *Where you want go?* | M: *Out go.* | 75* |
| **Tatu, 34 months old** | | | | |
| Who demonstrative | Proper Name | BH: *Who me?* | T: *Bart.* | 90* |
| Who subject/object | Proper Name or Pronoun | NR: *Who I chase?* | T: *Me.* | 60* |

**TABLE IV (Continued)**

| Question form | Target category | Example of question and appropriate reply | | % Appropriate replies |
|---|---|---|---|---|
| Who trait | Proper Name or Pronoun | BH: *Who good?* | T: *Me Tatu good.* | 50* |
| Whose | Possessive | NR: *Whose bib?* | T: *Mine.* | 20 |
| What demonstrative | Noun | BP: *What that?* | T: *Cow.* | 80* |
| What want | Noun or Verb | NR: *What Tatu want?* | T: *Sweet berry there.* | 100* |
| What predicate | Verb | NR: *What me play?* | T: *Chase Tatu.* | 90* |
| What complement | Noun | BP: *What you drink?* | T: *Milk drink.* | 50* |
| Where nominal | Locative | BP: *Where your blanket?* | T: *Blanket there.* | 60* |
| Where action | Locative | BP: *Tickle where?* | T: *There tickle.* | 70* |

*The appearance of words from the appropriate category in half the replies is the criterion used to attribute mastery of a question form to children (Brown, 1968; Ervin-Tripp, 1970).

most exclusively for this question type. In the sample taken when she was 5 years old, Moja was replying appropriately to *Who, What, Where,* and *Whose,* as before. In addition, she was replying with number signs to most of the questions containing *How many,* and with action signs, when asked causal questions, *What for that?* of an object. Thus, a *nut* she had requested was for *eat,* a whistle was for *blow,* and the shoes and hat the questioner indicated were for *Go out.*

## WHAT IS A SIGN?

### Recording Output

Is the output that we have recorded for the chimpanzee subjects in our laboratory comparable to the output of human children? The principal data of this study are transcriptions, in English words, of the signing of young chimpanzees in conversation with adult human caretakers. For the speech of very young children, we must tolerate reductions due to poor intelligibility, but a considerable amount of successful transcription has been accomplished. The situation is similar for transcriptions of signing. Yet, while the speech and signing of human beings, even of young children, have been adequately transcribed, one could still doubt that we can accurately transcribe the signing of the chimpanzee subjects. Without additional evidence, it could be contended that we are observing some vague gesturing behavior and reading different appropriate meanings into it, depending upon context.

Each time that we have published an article that included new vocabulary material, we have published with it a list of all the signs that we credited to the subject (Gardner & Gardner 1969, 1971, 1972, 1975a). Each list included a detailed description of form that we used to identify each sign: place, hand configuration, and movement. For descriptions of usage, we followed Lois Bloom's codification scheme for noting contexts of child utterances (Bloom, 1970, pp. 18–21). Bloom's scheme included both aspects of the referent (e.g., for an object, is it visible? accessible? novel?) and aspects of the linguistic context (e.g., is the utterance an initiating one, or is it a response to a question or comment by the adult?). The procedures that we have used to confirm and reconfirm the observations are also described in these publications. They insured that each sign in the vocabulary was observed on many occasions by many different observers, and that there was agreement among all of the observers. The lists are keyed to two well-known dictionaries of American Sign Language (Stokoe et al., 1965; Watson, 1973) so that anyone can compare them to standard descriptions of human signing. After we had five different subjects with overlapping but different vocabularies, and some variation in diction and reference, it was no longer practical to publish such lists for every increase in vocabulary. The lists are still kept for each item of vocabulary for each subject, and are always available for inspection.

These procedures of codification are in the best tradition of all observational research. But we have gone further than that. From the early days of Project Washoe, professional scientists and members of the deaf community have been encouraged to visit our laboratory. By now a considerable number of competent judges have had the opportunity to observe and to comment on the signing behavior of our subjects under typical conditions. Some have observed through one-way glass, others have had direct encounters in which they could carry on conversations with the chimpanzee subjects. In addition we have made 16mm film and videotapes of a generous sample and many more observers have had the opportunity to view this material.

The informal utterances of our chimpanzee subjects (they do not recite either for the visitors or for the camera) are not perfectly intelligible and are more intelligible to some of the observers than to others. It is what would be expected if equally young children were observed under similar conditions by strangers. By now, so many different outside observers have agreed that it can no longer be doubted that there is a significant degree of intelligibility.

Not satisfied with this type of confirmation, we devised tests in which a subject can sign to an observer about a stimulus that is visible to the subject but not to the observer. Different versions of these tests are described in detail in Gardner and Gardner (1971, 1973, 1974a, and 1978). The tests insure that the signs made by the subject are the *only* information available to the observer. When the test stimuli are projected from 35mm slides onto a screen, a second observer can view the subject through one-way glass. Elsewhere, we have stressed the performance of the subject in terms of percent of correct responses. But for the moment we would like to stress the performance of the observers in terms of their agreement with each other. Agreement between the two independent observers under these context-free conditions has ranged from 79 percent to nearly 100 percent, when correct and incorrect responses are combined. Much of the disagreement occurs on trials in which errors are made—as if signing is less clear when the signer is in doubt. We were able to get, among other outside observers, two deaf graduates of Gallaudet College, who were fluent in Ameslan but had had neglible contact with Washoe, to serve as second observers of some of her tests. For one of the outside observers, the agreement with the first observer was 67 percent during the first test session that he observed, and 89 percent during the second. For the other, agreement with the first observer was 71 percent during the first test, also rising to 89 percent for the second test. (The outside observers were familiarized with the lists before each test, as is the customary procedure in our laboratory for all observers. Note that the measured intelligibility of adult speech declines when single words are presented randomly in a context-free situation as opposed to the intelligibility of connected discourse in a full-cue situation.)

## Development of Reference

The question "Are the chimpanzee subjects using the signs of Ameslan or are we reading meaning into some vague gesturing?" is only partly answered by the evidence discussed in the preceding section. There is evidence that the subjects have extensive repertoires of gestures that are intelligible under blind conditions, and evidence that independent outside observers agree that the form of these gestures and the contexts in which they occur are reasonably close to the signs of Ameslan. But are the chimpanzees expressing what human beings express with signs?

The meanings intended by our immature chimpanzee subjects should not be confused with the meanings intended by adult signers or adult speakers, when the latter use English words that are the equivalents of the signs (we assume that the problems of translation need not be discussed here). There is considerable confusion on this point because of a widespread belief that understanding comes before production. If this were true, it would follow that children understand all of the expressions that they produce. But children commonly use expessions that they do not understand the way adults do. The literature abounds with good examples. A favorite of ours can be found in Berko (1958) who asked children questions such as "Why is Thanksgiving Day called Thanksgiving Day?" and got answers such as "Because we eat lots of turkey." Closer to home, we have tested a few English-speaking children with Washoe's vocabulary test material. As exemplars for *drink* we showed photographs of a variety of liquids in glasses, cups, bottles, and cans. One two-year-old boy called most of these either *Seven-Up* or *Booze.* His parents explained that the child used these words to differentiate liquids that he was allowed to drink from those he was forbidden to drink.

Much of the confusion on this point stems from the eagerness of many writers to claim that children are linguistic prodigies from a very early age. In a similar way, most of the investigators who have undertaken to teach language to apes, and particularly most of the commentators, have failed to distinguish between the usage of the subjects and the usage of fluent adults when speaking the English words used as glosses for the vocabulary items. We Gardners have maintained this distinction explicitly throughout our articles: each vocabulary list that we have published has included a careful description of the usage of each item. Our writings on vocabulary have included an extended discussion of the difference between early and later usage, with emphasis on the dynamic relationship between semantic range and the growth of vocabulary, of communicative skill, and of sophistication. We have emphasized this relationship because we believe that the patterns of growth that emerge are one of the strongest lines of evidence that our subjects are developing semantic meaning in a way that resembles the development of children. Commentators who are thoroughly familiar with the child data, such as Roger Brown (1970, 1973), have agreed that there is evidence that chimpanzees can "use signs with some degree of appropriate semanticity" (1970, p. 213) and that the "semantic generalization of each sign is quite astonishingly childlike" (1970, p. 214).

## Obligatory Contexts

The study of conversational usage is essential for two reasons. First, spontaneity is a critical aspect of the demonstration of linguistic ability in chimpanzees. The fact that the subjects initiate most of the interchanges by themselves, with their own questions, requests, and comments, is one of the most significant findings of this whole line of research (Gardner & Gardner, 1973; Fouts et al., 1978). Commenting on the contrast between the results of our procedures and the results of other procedures, Roger Brown (1973) states, "An interest in initiating communication does not appear on any list

of linguistic universals I know of, but when it is absent we notice how un-
human the performance is" (p. 44). The other and closely related reason is
that the bulk of the evidence used in the analysis and discussion of the development of extended utterances in human children is based on observations
of conversational usage. Our strategy in this regard has been to look at
measures existing for children—size of vocabulary, proportions of phrase
types, patterns of phrase construction, etc.—and to demonstrate that the
same sort of measures show similar results for our chimpanzee subjects, except that progress of the chimpanzees is slower.

We have obtained extensive documentation of parallels with human development both in terms of particular examples and in terms of such quanti-
fiable characteristics of multisign utterances as length, frequency, variety
(type/token ratio), and the proportion of different construction patterns
(Gardner & Gardner, 1971, 1978). So far, the comparative analysis of construction patterns has concentrated on two-term relations, as have the
analyses of early grammar in children. Since combinations of four, five, or
more signs are now commonly recorded both for Moja and for Tatu (*You
give gum Moja, Tatu please drink coffee, Open that key out*), we can under-
take a comparison with children in terms of the constituents of the main
verb paradigm, agent-action-dative-object-location, as utterances increase
in length (cf. Brown, 1973).

When utterances occur under subject-determined conditions, the
meaning of the speaker or signer must be inferred from the correlation of
certain kinds of utterances with certain kinds of contexts. Most of the research on child language depends upon correlations of this kind, as does a
great deal of field observation in animal communication. Because the spontaneous utterances that we have reported are the most dramatically languagelike, and also the most parallel to utterances observed in children,
these are the results that are most widely cited in secondary sources. Nevertheless, from the earliest days of Project Washoe we have devoted a large
amount of research effort to utterances that occur under *obligatory* contexts. By obligatory contexts we mean an experimenter-determined situation, in which context plus a particular question determine the correct response. In an obligatory context, we score whether the subject produces the
correct response or fails to do so together with the relation between correct
and incorrect responses. As we have described in detail in several publications (Gardner & Gardner 1971, 1972, 1975, 1978), once observed in the
repertoire of a given subject, a sign must pass a stringent criterion of continuous daily occurrence for 15 days in either obligatory or other appropriate contexts before it is entered as a reliable item of vocabulary for that subject. After that, a check on each item of vocabulary is made periodically
to see whether the sign continues to occur in obligatory contexts. In addition, we record incorrect signs produced in the obligatory context.

In general, we make use of obligatory contexts for systematic verification of developments that occur first in spontaneous utterances. A good example of this is the use of the sign *orange* as an adjective as well as a noun. When Moja was 31 months old, the sign *orange* reached the criterion of reliability as a name for the fruit. One day, when she was 54 months old, Moja drew the attention of her human companion to a brilliant orange reflection and signed *orange.* Later in the same month, she signed *orange* for some orange-colored medicine. (Other colors in Moja's vocabulary at that time were *red, white,* and *black.*) Once this spontaneous use of *orange* was noted, we systematically asked her for the color of orange objects. Eventually the adjectival use of *orange* met our criterion of reliability.

A similar point is illustrated in the observation of the twenty-second month of Project Washoe, when for the first time Washoe was asked *Who that?* of her image in a mirror. She replied, *Me.* (Fortunately, this "first" was recorded on motion picture film, so that there have been many, many observers to verify the fact that such observations can be made reliably.) As in the case of Moja's spontaneous transfer of *orange,* it is only the first observation that is significant here. Because it is impossible to preclude the possibility that human companions may reinforce the subject in some way for such responses, replication of spontaneous and appropriate usage with the same subject might rest primarily on the effect of the reinforcement. In the case of Washoe's identification of her mirror image, we used the method of obligatory contexts to replicate this observation with each of the four subjects of the current project. Not all of the first observations are as dramatic or as pertinent to classical problems in cognitive psychology, but many are. Replications of earlier findings tend to seem less exciting: in some ways Washoe stole most of the thunder, and Moja seems to be stealing most of the rest. Nevertheless, the extent of replication will determine the lasting scientific value of this line of research.

The use of obligatory contexts permits us to test our subjects while preserving the openness of the signing medium. While correct replies are defined by the obligatory context, the subjects are still free to reply with any item of vocabulary and to respond with an utterance of any length. The vocabulary test that we described earlier (Gardner & Gardner 1971, 1974a, 1978) was originally designed to test intelligibility of signing by the subjects in a situation in which there was no information available to the observer apart from the sign made by the subjects. As a vocabulary test for the subjects, the test is a good illustration of the use of obligatory contexts: the situational context is the picture shown to the subject, and the linguistic context is the question *What that?* or *What name that?* With photographic slides we can present a range of exemplars as wide as the conceptual category of any vocabulary item. Our library of exemplars is extensive, including, for *bug,* photographs of a large sample of the entomological collection of the Biology Department. With such slides, any test can consist entirely of new exemplars so that every trial of the test is a first trial. The range of items that can be tested is as wide as the number of picturable nouns in the vocabulary, and the range of responses that the subject can make is as wide as the subject's vocabulary at the time of testing.

In our current project, the expanded vocabularies of the subjects have altered the method of obligatory contexts. In project Washoe, we avoided synonyms, and we restricted the vocabulary that we used with Washoe in various ways to simplify the system. In our current project we try not to introduce any artificial restrictions. The presence of native signers together with a generally higher level of fluency among the human companions results in exposure to a more normal vocabulary. When nearly five years old, Washoe had only one sign, *drink,* for all potable liquids, and it was fairly easy to present her with a wide range of obligatory contexts for this sign. By three years of age, subjects in the current project have different signs for *milk, water, orange juice, sodapop,* and *coffee* so that it is not possible to present an obligatory context for the sign *drink.* In fact, the sign *drink* which is very popular when it is first acquired is observed less and less often as a noun as the vocabulary grows. You might think that we could get an obligatory context by presenting an unfamilar exemplar. When we do so, as when we presented an advertising photograph for a "Blue Hawaiian" cocktail, Moja guessed that it was *sodapop* (much like the child who divided novel exemplars of drinks into *Seven-Up* and *Booze*).

Most discussions of language emphasize the use of new combinations of elements to express new meanings. The signing chimpanzees often use two or more signs in combination, to describe an object that is not represented by a sign in their vocabulary. The subjects form such compounds spontaneously as when Washoe referred to a swan as a *water bird* and Moja referred to Alka Seltzer in a glass as a *listen drink.* We can also use the method of obligatory contexts and ask the subjects about familiar objects for which there is no single sign in their vocabulary or for which there may be no single sign in Ameslan, as when we questioned Washoe about her potty chair and she called it a *dirty good,* or when Moja called a cigarette lighter a *metal hot* and a thermos bottle a *metal cup drink coffee.* The use of such compounds has been studied systematically by Fouts and Mellgren (Fouts, 1975).

For children, the two-word stage is seen as a great advance over the single-word or holophrastic stage of language acquisition, but utterances are still highly telegraphic, that is, functors and inflectional morphemes are virtually absent. The obvious lack of other grammatical devices in these "first sentences" forced many early writers to overstate the case for word order as a grammatical device in young children's speech. Some were ready to claim that two- and three-year-old children are nearly perfect in their grammatical use of word order, and these extravagant claims have often been contrasted with our rather conservative statements about chimpanzees and sign order.

From the beginning of Project Washoe, we observed and reported variable sign order whether we tabulated multisign utterances in terms of specific pairs (e.g., *drink more* and *more drink*) or distributional categories (e.g., for Attributes, *comb black,* and *good Washoe).* Gradually we came to understand the discrepancy between our reports and those of early writers on child language: they were using a method that Brown (1973) has called "the method of rich interpretation" and is attributed to Schlesinger and Bloom. Thus, both *Adam sit chair* and *sit Adam chair* were observed by Brown in the Stage 1 speech of Adam. They both are examples of correct English word order because *Adam sit chair* is a case of subject-verb-object, while *sit Adam chair* is a case of an "action-object relation" in which the object, *Adam chair,* is a "noun-phrase expansion" of the "possessor-possessed" type. Where we were thinking and writing in terms of statistical analyses, the students of child language were thinking and writing in terms of utterance by utterance interpretations with careful attention to the verbal and nonverbal context of each utterance.

What no student of child language has yet done, or even suggested that anyone else do, is the sort of statistical analysis that Terrace et al. (Chapter 8, this volume) have done with their observations of utterances by the chimpanzee Nim: that is, lump together 4 years' worth of recorded utterances, remove all verbal and nonverbal context, and grind the result through a computer to look for statistical regularities. Since examples such as *Adam sit chair* and *sit Adam chair* are common in samples of child speech (cf. Gardner & Gardner, 1974), the results of a similarly mechanical analysis of child speech is apt to yield similarly negative results: in any event, the results of the Terrace et al. analysis cannot be placed in relation to children's language without a parallel analysis of child speech or sign. It is neither fixed nor variable order that provides the critical evidence that subjects are using order effectively; rather, it is the use of different orders to signal contrasts as in *dog bites man* and *man bites dog* (Gardner & Gardner 1974). To obtain data on this, we have analyzed systematically recurring obligatory contexts which require contrasts in the use of sign order: and, where there has been child data also, we have shown that the proportion of ordered phrases was comparable (Gardner & Gardner, 1971, 1978).

The method of obligatory contexts uses particular questions and particular contexts to elicit particular replies. We have demonstrated that this is the case for different types of questions about the same type of object (see table 2, Gardner & Gardner, 1974), and there is a good illustration of this material in our film (Gardner & Gardner, 1973). Gregory Gaustad shows Washoe a red boot, asks *What that?,* and Washoe replies, *Shoe;* next he asks *Whose that?* and she replies *Mine;* and then he asks *What color that?* and she replies *Red.* Even in the case of factual errors, replies are usually selected from the category that is specified by the question. Similarly, when asked *Who that?* of Gregory Gaustad, all semantically correct replies by Washoe have to include the name sign, *Greg* (e.g., *You Greg*), but incorrect name signs such as *Jim* or *Ken* are still correct in ways that such answers as *Hat, Black,* or *Tickle me* are not. That our subjects usually answer *Who that, Who action* and *Who trait* questions with name-signs or pronouns is in some respects more significant than their ability to associate particular name-signs with particular individuals. Of course, the power of this evidence depends on the free access of the subject to the items in his vocabulary, as in the case of signing chimpanzees and signing or speaking children.

The restriction of replies to a correct category is also a more general characteristic of replies to questions because there is an important group of questions such as *Who good?* and *What you want?* that refer to matters of opinion and preference, rather than to matters of fact. Strictly speaking, the only objective judgment that an observer can make about the correctness of a reply to such a question is a judgment about the correctness of its grammatical category. Hence, as elsewhere, (Gardner & Gardner 1974, 1975, 1978), we have followed Brown (1968) and Ervin-Tripp (1970) in referring to these as Wh-questions, not Wh-signs. This is because a Wh-sign, like a Wh-word, cannot specify a category of reply unless it is part of a longer utterance.

The productive use of Wh-questions is a rather late development in the speech of children. In his seminal article on this subject, Brown discusses in great detail the grammatical relationship between questions and answers to show how replies to Wh-questions can be used to reveal grammatical competence in the early stages of development: "The derivation rules we have described for Wh-questions presupposes the establishment of the major sentence constituents. The best evidence in the child's spontaneous speech that he has such constituents is his ability to make the right sort of answers to the various Wh-questions addressed him, giving noun phrases in response to *Who* and *What* questions, locatives to *Where* questions, predicates to *What do* questions, etc." (Brown, 1968, p. 268). Brown's own analyses and much of the later work on Wh-questions (e.g., Ervin-Tripp, 1970; Ervin-Tripp & Miller, 1977) was based on samples of spontaneous discourse; hence the analyses depended heavily on the adventitious occurrence of question types and replies. In our work with chimpanzees, we have used the method of obligatory contexts to present questions belonging to specified types in a systematic and balanced fashion, while at the same time embedding these questions in the normal course of daily conversation.

## SUMMARY: FIRST STEPS

In this chapter, we have described a comparative project on the acquisition of sign language by chimpanzees. The long-term plan of this research is to develop and describe verbal communication in chimpanzees from birth to maturity, in order to determine the extent and limits of their linguistic capacity.

The basic research method is to foster the acquisition of sign language by maintaining the chimpanzees in a socially and intellectually stimulating environment in which this system of verbal communication is constantly used. The progress of the subjects is recorded as comprehensively as possible, and documented by tests and assessment procedures fashioned on those that have been used with human children. The data on children learning their first language provide norms and an orderly sequence of developments which we use to evaluate the achievements of nonhuman subjects. The data on children also provide expectations about future linguistic advances in our subjects. If these chimpanzees continue to follow the pattern of development of human children, they should be showing further development of questioning and negation, longer and more complex sentences, and sentences which involve quantifiers, embedding, and the description of events in time.

Up to this point, the pattern of chimpanzee development has been comparable to the human pattern, but the rate of development has been much slower. Our subjects are still very immature, so that it will be several years before we can make definitive statements about the highest level of achievement, or establish a pattern of failures that could reveal qualitative differences between chimpanzee and human intelligence.

At a symposium on linguistics, or when reading a linguistic paper, it is easy to be overwhelmed by everything that we know about proper English usage. We can distinguish myriads of sentences from nonsentences about midgets that are only two feet tall but not two feet short, and about a two-week-old infant who is not two weeks young. As we make such distinctions, we realize that they touch a trivially small aspect of what we know about our language. But judgments such as these are made by adults, and perhaps only highly educated adults can make them. Clearly, our research deals with first steps, and first steps are at the same time tiny and gigantic. But steps, whether ordinal or interval, are the start of a scale. In our research, and in the research on sign language and on child development that has been taking place at the same time, the road to language has become longer and more believable.

## NOTES

[1]Research for this chapter was supported by NSF grants GB-35586 and BNS 75-17290, by NIMH research development grant MH-34953 (to Beatrice T. Gardner), and by The Grant Foundation, New York.

[2]The age at which these infant chimpanzees produce their first signs may seem early when compared to the age at which hearing children produce their first words, but it is not so different from the age at which deaf children produce their first signs. There are parental reports of first signs appearing at age 5 and 6 months for children exposed to sign language from birth. It may be that the human infant finds it easier to form signs than to form words. Also, it may be easier for human adults to recognize and then encourage the infant's first approximation at a sign that to recognize the earliest attempts at a word.

[3]The reasons that copyrights on the films *The First Signs of Washoe* and *Teaching Sign Language to the Chimpanzee: Washoe* were not released to Terrace et al. (Chapter 8, this volume) are that selected single frames misrepresent and distort the film material on Washoe's participation in discourse in three areas. First, motion is one of the basic aspects of a sign; presented in single frames, with the characteristic movement eliminated, many signs become indistinguishable (Terrace et al. misread Washoe's *mine* and an adult human's *please*). Second, the average duration of a sign is 8 frames and the final sign of a question is held for at least 12 to 16 frames (Baker, 1977). Thus widely spaced frames (for example, the 12 that Terrace selected out of nearly 400 in the originally filmed sequences of the conversation about *Time eat*) distort the temporal relations of the signing of participants in discourse by failing to show the start and finish of the signs. Third, without special positioning of the speaker and addressee, or a two-camera setup, many of the acts that are regulators of turn-taking in American Sign Language discourse—direction of gaze, facial and brow activity, learning forward and the like—will not be recorded. Terrace et al. ignore the literature on turn-taking in American Sign Language both in omitting the acts that are important as regulators and in treating overlapping utterances as failures of turn-taking. (These failures are all ascribed to Washoe, even when the human adult interrupts the chimpanzee.) As a matter of fact, Baker's (1977) analysis of videotaped conversations between native signers shows that "approximately 30 percent of discourse involved overlap of one interactant's signs with the other's" (p. 228). The addressee's short repetitions of some of the speaker's signs is a continuation regulator, a "listening noise," indicating that the speaker may continue. When questions are being signed, "the smooth exchange of roles is facilitated by calling devices . . . the final sign is raised slightly and held longer, and the addressee becomes speaker (begins signing) before the old speaker returns his/her hands to rest position" (p. 229). Now this is exactly the "interruption" that Terrace found when Washoe replied to *"What now?"* The interruptions that Terrace et al. reported are evidence that our subjects and their teachers are indeed acting as partners in conversation! We would like to recommend these films to interested readers, who may be surprised and delighted by the conversational give-and-take between Washoe and her companions. It is of a quite different order from that which Terrace et al. have described.

## APPENDIX 1. THE DAILY ROUTINE OF THE SUBJECTS
## AT AGE 18–36 MONTHS

| Time | Activity | Detailed Notes *on activities* |
|------|----------|--------------------------------|
| 7:00 A.M. | *Morning HC* (Human Companion) *arrives.*<br><br>Turn intercom off.<br><br>Pick up C; hug, *potty*<br><br>Wash C's bottom.<br><br>Unplug humidifier, put it away.<br><br>Check Sign of Day and any special samples for signs to work on today. | *Potty:* Stay in physical contact with C (Chimpanzee) while C sits on potty. Do not force C to stay if C becomes upset. Potty C at least every 45 mins., and before meals, before and after naps. Use diapers only when necessary; e.g., on car rides. Clean up accidents immediately with Lysol. |
| 7:10 A.M. | *Breakfast meal.* The menu posted on the cupboard lists types and amounts of food for each meal. After meal, wipe hands and face. *Brush teeth.* Wash, dry, put away dishes. | *Meals:* Put C in plastic dishpan on counter so that C can watch food preparations, but do not force C to stay there if C fusses. Smell or taste all food and drink before preparing it; if it smells funny throw it out. All food should be served warm. When meal is ready, leave milk on counter and invite C to feeding table. Encourage C to put on bib and feed himself. Then offer cup of warm milk. Date all containers when you open them; use already opened foods first. Throw out any food that is over a week old. At breakfast only, give C one full dropper of vitamins.<br><br>*Toothbrushing:* Encourage C to brush own teeth while on potty or in feeding table. Provide a cup of water in which C may dip the brush. |
| 7:30 A.M. | *Oil and brush.* Clean ears and nose with oiled Q-tip, | *Oiling and brushing:* Warm Lubriderm by placing con- |

## APPENDIX 1 (Continued)

| Time | Activity | Detailed Notes *on activities* |
|------|----------|-------------------------------|
| 7:30 A.M. | no deeper than you can see. Dress C according to the weather; no clothes in very warm weather. | tainer in hot water, or by rubbing the lotion between your palms. The bed or the couch are good locations for oiling and brushing. Rub lotion all over C, and brush well. |
| 7:45 A.M. | Remove curtains now, or after Signing Practice. Store them in cupboard. | |
| 8:00 A.M. | *Signing Practice.* Keep up record sheets; do not let more than one hour lapse before making entries in the log and on data sheets. See Recording Instructions for details. | *Signing Practice:* Work on signs for Sign of Day, special samples, also any new signs that we are teaching. Use picture books, stories, objects, or activities related to these signs. Ask questions, use the signs yourself, and mold signs. Check Sign Description file for current description of C's form and contexts. |
| 8:30 A.M. | *Do chores.* Those for the day are listed on the Weekly Chores and Tests sheet. | *Chores:* C's can and will help with routines and chores. For example, they will wipe up spills, help with washing and drying dishes, and fetch and carry objects, both indoors and outdoors. There are two reasons to encourage help with chores, even though this does take effort and patience, and the HC's can usually do the task more quickly and better without the C's help. First, more signing, and signing in a more natural fashion about the individuals and the activities, will occur. Second, we do not want a spoiled C, and a C that has everything done for it will become spoiled. |
| 9:00 A.M. | *Active Play,* outdoors if | *Active Play* suggestions: Chase, |

## APPENDIX 1 (Continued)

| Time | Activity | Detailed Notes *on activities* |
|------|----------|-------------------------------|
| 9:30 A.M. | weather permits. Use outdoor potty chairs. | keepaway, swinging and tossing C. The C's prefer to be chased but will reverse roles in chase, so be sure to sign about who does what. Tickle is a favorite activity; C's can be tickled in a variety of ways, and in a variety of places on their body, and will tickle HC's. Sign about who, where, and how between bouts of tickling. The C's will search for objects that you hide indoors, and play hide and seek outdoors. The game requires two HC's, one of whom hides with the C while the other searches. Plan the game by signing before a bout of hide; while hiding, the C's like to be hushed by the HC, and viceversa. Additional activities that C's enjoy: indoors—marking on steamed up windows, play with the soap bubbles, and play with the clothing in the dressup kit, before a mirror, outdoors —feeding the ducks, making nests in the tall grass, marking the ground with sticks and breaking sticks. |
| 9:30 A.M. | Offer water, plain soda, or fruit juice. You may also offer a noncaloric snack (celery, carrot, 1 or 2 nuts, cottage cheese). | |
| 10:00 A.M. | C must be in his room. *Dayshift HC arrives,* checks logs and records, and takes over with C.<br><br>Morning HC finishes notes, chores, and tidies up. After this, both HC's play and sign with C. | *10:00–11:00 overlap:* HCs may plan an interaction between two C's during the overlap. Only two interactions are permitted per day. These must take place outdoors, in the playroom, or on a car ride. Plan active games; bring toys or ideas for games. One HC |
| 11:00 A.M. | Morning HC departs. | plays with the C's while the |

## APPENDIX 1 (Continued)

| Time | Activity | Detailed Notes on activities |
|------|----------|------------------------------|
| 11:00 A.M. | *Lunch* (check menu). Wash hands and face before meal; wipe after meal. *Brush teeth.* Wash dishes. | other records notes on the Interaction Form, with special attention to notes on signing. Suggestions for games that two HCs can play with a C: tickling, ball-rolling, tug-of-war, hide-and-seek. It is also good for C's to see HC's conversing with each other in Ameslan. But remember to chose topics of conversation that are likely to interest young C's, or else C will claim the attention of HC's by getting into mischief. |
| 11:30 A.M. | *Nap,* following *oil and brush, potty.* | *Naps:* Before nap, oil C's face, hands and feet well. Comb and brush C; this will help to calm C for nap. Provide a blanket for C, and remain in physical contact until he is asleep. |
| 12:30 P.M. | *Potty,* when C awakens.<br><br>Quiet play, *Educational Activity,* or *Signing Practice.* Tests are usually scheduled after the nap, when C is very calm. | *Educational Activities:* HC may bring books, magazines or educational toys from the cupboard in conference room, or use those in C's room. HC may want to seat C in the feeding table for activities such as scribbling, block stacking, sorting, lacing, etc. Check index cards in cupboard for ideas. Activities with the longest span of attention are often those initiated by the C, so capitalize on them when you can.<br>If C starts to mark up your log notes, follow up on this by producing materials for drawing; if C plays with your shoelaces, sewing could carry on his activity. |

## APPENDIX 1 (Continued)

| Time | Activity | Detailed Notes *on activities* |
|------|----------|-------------------------------|
| 1:00 P.M. | *Visitor* arrives. | *Visits:* HC's may plan an interaction between C's, two-HC games, a car ride, or active play. |
| 1:30 P.M. | Offer water, plain soda, or juice. HC may also offer a snack. | |
| 2:00 P.M. | Visitor departs. | Day-shift HC may finish notes, chores, etc., while visitor takes over C. |
| | Day-shift HC plans *active play*, outdoors if weather permits. | |
| 2:50 P.M. | *Sponge bath.* | *Sponge Bath:* Wipe C all over with warm, damp cloth; dry thoroughly |
| 3:00 P.M. | *Tea Meal*, check menu. Wipe hands and face after meal. *Brush teeth.* Wash dishes. | |
| 3:30 P.M. | *Nap,* following *oil* and *brush, potty.* | |
| 4:30 P.M. | *Potty,* when C awakens. | *4:30–5:00 overlap:* See 10:00–11:00 A.M. overlap for ideas. |
| | Evening-shift HC arrives, reads log and records, takes over with C. | |
| | Day-shift HC finishes notes, chores, empties outdoor potties, tidies up generally. | |
| 5:00 P.M. | Day-shift HC departs. | 5:00–6:30: HC should plan alternate indoor/outdoor, quiet/active play, as suggested above, under *Signing Practice, Active Play,* and *Educational Activities.* |
| | Offer water, plain soda or juice. HC may also offer a snack. | |
| 6:30 P.M. | *Bath.* Put up curtains. | *Bath:* Make sure that room is warm and free of drafts. Use dishpan placed on floor or counter, or bathe yourself with C in the shower or bathtub. Have soap, towels, and bath toys close at hand. Offer C toys or a washcloth to play |
| 7:00 P.M. | *Dinner,* check menu. Wipe hands and face after meal. | |
| | *Brush teeth.* | |
| | Wash dishes. | |
| 7:30 P.M. | *Oil* and *brush. Potty.* | |

## APPENDIX 1 (Continued)

| Time | Activity | Detailed Notes *on activities* |
|------|----------|--------------------------------|
| 7:45 P.M. | Change to night clothes, diaper and plastic pants. Evening routines: 1. Tidy up generally. 2. Set up fresh trash bags. 3. Fill and plug in humidifier. 4. Lock all cupboards. 5. Check thermostat (68 degrees). *Put C to bed.* Turn on intercom. Take log, clipboard and trash; turn out lights. | with. C may resist bath; wash as much as possible without unduly upsetting C. Dissuade C from eating soap, which causes diarrhea. Using soap or shampoo sparingly, rinse thoroughly, and wash thoroughly to prevent a rash. Dress in towel robe or loose sweatshirt until bedtime, to complete drying. *Bedtime:* Cover C with blankets. Remain in physical contact with C until he is asleep. |
| 8:00 P.M. | Evening HC departs: 1. Deposit trash in barrel. 2. Bring log and clipboard to front office. Put next day's forms on clipboard, today's records in log. 3. Check with chimpsitter in front office. 4. Do not leave until you are sure that your chimp is asleep and that someone is monitoring the intercoms. | For D, the youngest chimpanzee: When D is asleep, place pillows at side of bed so that he won't roll out of bed. Lock the bathroom and bedroom doors. If you want to request help after 8:00, signal the chimpsitter by whistling over the intercom. |
| 10:30 P.M. | Chimpsitter returns log to C's room. Check the temperature (68 degrees). The humidifier should be filled and running. *Potty C, put C back to bed.* | |
| 11:00 P.M. | Overnight HC takes over intercom. Chimpsitter departs. | |

## APPENDIX 2. SIGNING SUGGESTIONS FOR RESEARCH ASSISTANTS

Whatever you are doing, encourage conversation by signing about what you do. Ask questions and make comments; these are more effective together than either is alone. Comments can provide a topic of conversation and suggest that you are ready to converse; then the questions encourage the C to sign back to you on the same topic.

Reply to the C with signing before responding with an action. For example, when C signs, *Drink,* ask, *What kind of drink?* before running to get the C a glass of water.

A few of the many topics of conversation that are possible with the C's are listed below:

1. *Games.* Discuss the participants and their respective activities; e.g., who hides, seeks, chases, etc.? Where will the activity occur? Comment on whether the activity is good, bad, fun, tiring, etc.

2. *Routines.* The Cs participate in and anticipate many of the daily routines. They will request these if you pause during the routine, and will reply to questions about what is to happen next. For some routines, questions about places can be asked: where are things kept, where will the activity occur, where would C like to be brushed, oiled, etc. Requests can be made to the C to get or to put away objects.

3. *Meals.* Describe what you do as you prepare food. Sign about sharing food, since Cs are very willing to do this, and intrigued by HC's eating, chewing, and swallowing. Ask *What want?* and *What now?* questions.

4. *Arrivals and departures.* Discuss who has been with C, and who is to come, who is working with the other C's, who is working in the shop. Sign about where people and C's are headed, when they are seen walking by the windows.

5. *Excursions.* Discuss the various destinations (barns, pond, etc.) and modes of travel (in wagon, walking, by car), and what will happen on arrival at the destination (picnic, tree climbing, etc.). Sign about the preparations for going outdoors: clothing, need for potty, who is to go.

6. *Review of the day.* Has C been good? Sign about important or interesting events in the day: who did C see, and what did C do?

## REFERENCES

Baker, C. Regulators and turn-taking in American Sign Language. In L. A. Friedman (Ed.), *On the other hand.* New York, Academic Press, 1977.

Bellugi, U. & Klima, E. S. Aspects of sign language and its structure. *In* J. F. Kavanagh & J. E. Cutting (Eds.), *The role of speech in language.* Cambridge, Mass.: M.I.T. Press, 1975.

Berko, J. The child's learning of English Morphology. *Word,* 1958, **14**, 150–177.

Bloom, L. *Language development.* Cambridge, Mass.: M.I.T. Press, 1970.

Bollinger, D. *Aspects of language.* New York: Harcourt, Brace, Jovanovich, 1975.

Bonvillian, J. D. & Nelson, K. E. Development of sign language in language-handicapped individuals. *In* P. Siple (Ed.), *Understanding language through sign language research.* New York: Academic Press, 1978.

Bowerman, M. *Early syntactic development.* London: Cambridge University Press, 1973.

Brown, R. The development of wh questions in child speech. *Journal of Verbal Learning and Verbal Behavior,* 1968, 7, 277–290.

Brown, R. The first sentences of child and chimpanzee. *In* R. Brown, (Ed.), *Selected Psycholinguistic papers.* New York: Macmillan, 1970.

Brown, R. *A first language.* Cambridge, Mass.: Harvard University Press, 1973.

Collins-Ahlgren, M. Language development of two deaf children. *American Annals of the Deaf,* 1975, 120, 524–539.

Ervin-Tripp, S. Discourse agreement: how children answer questions. *In* J. R. Hayes (Ed.), *Cognition and the development of language.* New York: Wiley, 1970.

Ervin-Tripp, S. & Miller, W. Early discourse: some questions about questions. *In* M. Lewis & L. A. Rosenblum (Eds.), *Interaction, conversation and the development of language.* New York: Wiley, 1977.

Fant, L. J., Jr. *Ameslan: an introduction to American Sign Language.* Silver Spring, Md.: National Association of the Deaf, 1972.

Fischer, S. D. The ontogenetic development of language. *In* E. W. Straus (Ed.) *Language and language disturbances: The fifth Lexington Conference on phenomenology.* Pittsburgh: Duquesne University Press, 1974.

Fouts, R. S. Communication with chimpanzees. In I. Eibl–Eibesfeldt & G. Kurth (Eds.) *Hominisation and behavior.* Stuttgart: Fisher Verlag, 1975.

Fouts, R. S., Shapiro, G., & O'Neil, C. Studies of linguistic behavior in apes and children. In P. Siple (Ed.) *Understanding language through sign language research.* New York: Academic Press, 1978.

Gardner, B. T. & Gardner, R. A. Two-way communication with an infant chimpanzee. *In* A. Schrier & F. Stollnitz (Eds.), *Behavior of nonhuman primates* (Vol. 4), New York: Academic Press, 1971.

Gardner, B. T. & Gardner, R. A. Comparing the early utterances of child and chimpanzee. *In* A. Pick (Ed.), *Minnesota symposium on child psychology* (Vol. 8). Minneappolis: University of Minnesota Press, 1974a.

Gardner, B. T. & Gardner, R. A. Evidence for sentence constituents in the early utterances of child and chimpanzee. *Journal of Experimental Psychology: General,* 1975a, 104, 244–267.

Gardner, R. A. & Gardner, B. T. Teaching sign language to a chimpanzee. *Science,* 1969, 165, 664–672.

Gardner, R. A. & Gardner, B. T. Communications with a young chimpanzee: Washoe's vocabulary. In R. Chauvin (Ed.), *Modeles animaux du comportement humain.* Paris: Centre National de la Recherche Scientifique, 1972.

Gardner, R. A. & Gardner, B. T. Teaching sign language to the chimpanzee, Washoie (16mm. sound film). State College, Pa.: Psychological Cinema Register, 1973.

Gardner, R. A. and Gardner, B. T. Review of Roger Brown's *A first language: The early stages. American Journal of Psychology,* 1974b, 87, 729–736.

Gardner, R. A. & Gardner, B. T. Early signs of language in child and chimpanzee. *Science,* 1975b, 187, 752–753.

Gardner, R. A. & Gardner, B. T. Comparative psychology and language acquisition. *In* K. Salzinger & F. Denmark (Eds.), *Psychology the state of the art. Annals of the New York Academy of Sciences,* 1978, 309, 37–76.

Goodall, J. Behavior of male and female chimpanzees. Paper presented at the L. S. B. Leakey Memorial Lectures, Philadelphia, October 1974.

Goodman, M., Tashian, R. E., & Tashian, J. H. *Molecular anthropology.* New York: Plenum, 1976.

Hayes, K. J. & Hayes, C. The intellectual development of a home-raised chimpanzee. *Proceedings of the American Philosophical Society,* 1951, 95, 105–109.

Hoffmeister, R. J., Moores, D. F., & Ellenberger, R. L. Some procedural guidelines for the study of the acquisition of sign languages. *Sign Language Studies,* 1975, 7, 121–137.

Kellogg, W. N. & Kellogg, L. A. *The ape and the child.* New York: McGraw-Hill, 1933.

Kellogg, W. N. Communication and language in the home-raised chimpanzee. *Science,* 1968, 162, 423–427.

Klima, E. S. & Bellugi, U. The signs of language in child and chimpanzee. *In* T. Alloway (Ed.), *Communication and affect.* New York: Academic Press, 1972.

McIntire, M. L. The acquisition of American Sign Language hand configuration. *Sign Language Studies,* 1977, 16, 247–266.

Mussen, P. H. (Ed.). *Carmichael's manual of child psychology* (3rd ed., Vols. I & II). New York: Wiley, 1970.

Nelson, K. Structure and strategy in learning to talk. *Monograph of the Society for Research in Child Development,* 1973, 38, (1–2, Serial No. 149), 1–137.

Prestrude, A. M. Sensory capacities of the chimpanzee: A review. *Psychological Bulletin,* 1970, 74, 47–67.

Riopelle, A. J. & Rogers, C. M. Age changes in chimpanzees. In A. M. Schrier, H. F. Harlow, & F. Stollnitz (Eds.), *Behavior of nonhuman primates.* New York: Academic Press, 1965.

Schlesinger, H. S. & Meadow, K. P. *Sound and sign: Childhood deafness and mental health.* Berkeley: University of California Press, 1972.

Snow, C. Mothers' speech research: from input to interaction. In C. Snow and C. Ferguson (Eds.), *Talking to children.* Cambridge University Press, 1977.

Stokoe, W. C., Casterline, D., & Croneberg, C. G. *A dictionary of American Sign Language.* Washington, D. C.: Gallaudet College Press, 1965.

Watson, D. O. *Talk with your hands* (Vols. I & II). Winnecone, Wisconsin: Author, 1973.

Williams, J. S. Bilingual experiences of a deaf child. *Sign Language Studies.* 1976, 10, 37–41.

# 8

# ON THE GRAMMATICAL CAPACITY OF APES[1]

H. S. TERRACE
L. A. PETITTO
R. J. SANDERS
T. G. BEVER

## INTRODUCTION

The innovative studies of the Gardners (1969, 1975a, 1975b) and Premack (1970, 1971, 1976) show that a chimpanzee (*Pan troglodytes*) can learn substantial vocabularies of visually differentiated "words." The Gardners taught Washoe, an infant female chimpanzee, American Sign Language[2]. Premack taught Sarah, a juvenile female, an "artificial" language of plastic chips of different colors and shapes. In a related study, Rumbaugh (1977) taught Lana, also a juvenile chimpanzee, to use an artificial visual language called "Yerkish." These and other studies show that the shift from vocal to visual symbols can compensate effectively for the chimpanzee's inability to articulate many sounds. That inability alone might account for earlier failures to teach chimpanzees to communicate via a spoken language (cf. Hayes, 1951; Hayes & Hayes, 1951; Kellogg, 1968; Kellogg & Kellogg, 1933; Khouts, 1935).

Washoe, Sarah, and Lana each acquired vocabularies of more than 100 symbols in their respective languages. The psychologists who trained these chimpanzees interpreted the words of their subjects' vocabularies just as they would the corresponding words of human languages: as names of people and objects, actions, attributes, and various relationships. In subsequent studies, other chimpanzees acquired similar vocabularies, although of smaller size (Fouts, 1972; Gardner & Gardner, 1975b; Premack, 1976; Temerlin, 1975). A current study reports that an infant female gorilla (Koko) has acquired a vocabulary of more than 400 signs in American Sign Language (Patterson, 1978).

The words taught to each of these apes were symbolically arbitrary in the sense that it was not generally possible to infer their referents from their form. In Sarah's language, for example, the word *apple* was a triangular piece of blue plastic. In Yerkish, the word *apple* is a nonsense geometric form on a red background[3]. In American Sign Language (ASL), *apple* is made by pressing the knuckle of the index finger into the cheek and twisting forward. The signs of ASL may not be as arbitrary in form as spoken words. It is nevertheless difficult and usually impossible for a naive observer to guess the meanings of signs (cf. Bellugi & Klima, 1976; Hoemann, 1975b).

Human language makes use of two easily isolable levels of structure: the *word* and the *sentence*. The meaning of a word is flexible and arbitrary across languages and dialects. This characteristic of words stands in contrast to the immutability of signals in animal communication. Many bird species, for example, sing one song when in distress, another song when courting a mate, and still another when asserting their territory. As far as we know, birds are unable to produce other songs in these situations. Such rigidity is true of other genera; for example, bees communicating about the location and quality of food and sticklebacks engaging in courtship behavior (cf. Thorpe, 1961; Frisch, 1954; Tinbergen, 1951).

Human language is most obviously distinctive because of a structural level which subsumes the word: the sentence. It suffices here to note that a sentence characteristically expresses a complete semantic proposition through a set of words and phrases, each bearing particular grammatical relations to one another such as actor, action, and object (see Bever, Katz, & Langenden, 1975; Burt, 1971; Chomsky, 1965; Gross, Halle, & Schutzenberger, 1973; Katz & Postal, 1964; Lakoff, 1972; and McCawley, 1968, for additional discussion). Unlike words, whose meanings can be learned one by one, most sentences are not learned individually. Instead, children master grammatical rules that allow new meanings to be created by arranging, rearranging or inflecting a set of words or by substituting other appropriate words (for example, *John hit Bill* vs. *Bill hit John; the owner's cat* vs. *the cat's owner, John ate the apple; Bill chased the cat; John, who ate the apple, chased the cat's owner*).

Psychologists, psycholinguists, and linguists are in general agreement that knowing a human language entails knowing a grammar. How else can one account for the child's ultimate ability to create an indeterminately large number of meaningful sentences from a finite number of words? There less agreement, however, on the nature of the grammatical systems that humans use to speak and understand sequences of words. It is still unclear to what extent grammars are learned (cf. Jenkins & Palermo, 1964; Skinner, 1957; Staats, 1968) and to what extent they are the specific expression of an "innate language acquisition device" (Chomsky, 1965). It is also unclear whether a child's first sentences are best characterized by semantic (Bowerman, 1973b) or by syntactic rules (Bloom, 1970, 1973; Brown, 1973). These controversies provide the background for a simpler but equally controversial question about human language. Is the ability to create and understand sentences uniquely human? Chimpanzees and gorillas can communicate with humans via arbitrary "words," an ability denied them prior to the studies of the Gardners and Premack (e.g., Lenneberg, 1971; Bronowski & Bellugi, 1970). It is therefore natural to ask whether apes can produce and understand *sequences* of words whose structure is governed by a grammar.

The Gardners (1975b), Premack (1976), Rumbaugh (1977), and Patterson (1978) have each claimed that the symbol sequences produced and understood by their pongid subjects were governed by grammatical rules. The evidence consists of the production of different sequences of words (for example, *Washoe more eat, Mary give Sarah apple*) and specific behaviors which follow an instruction presented as a sequence of words (for example, putting an apple in a pail following the instruction: *Sarah apple pail insert*). In each case, these sequences of words were regarded as sentences.

If an ape can truly create a sentence, there would be a strong basis for asserting, as Patterson (1978, p. 95) has, that "language is no longer the exclusive domain of man." The purpose of this chapter is to summarize a large body of data we have collected concerning a chimpanzee's ability to create sentences in ASL. A major segment of these data is a corpus of multi-sign utterances, the first such corpus to be obtained from an ape. Superficially, many of these utterances seem like sentences. However, careful analyses of our data, as well as of those extracted from other studies, yielded no evidence of an ape's ability to use a grammar. Each instance of presumed grammatical competence could be explained adequately by simpler nonlinguistic processes.

After presenting the results of our study, we will review briefly the results of other recent studies that claim to demonstrate that an ape has the ability to create sentences. At this point we simply note an important limitation of the Gardners' analyses of Washoe's sign combinations which makes it impossible to examine their structure. That limitation is symptomatic of much research in this area and serves as the point of departure of our study.

With but a few exceptions, the Gardners' publications do not distinguish explicitly between Washoe's multisign combinations which contained the same signs in different orders (Gardner & Gardner, 1974a, 1974b, 1978). For example, the relative frequencies of *more tickle* and *tickle more* were not reported. Thus, the Gardners' published data provide an quate basis for deciding whether Washoe's multisign combinations obeyed rules of sign order. Nor in our view do the Gardners provide compelling evidence that Washoe understood how the signs of her sequences were related to one another. One could conclude that Washoe had learned that both *more* and *tickle* were appropriate ways of requesting another bout of tickling and that she signed both signs because of her prior training to sign each sign separately.

A widely cited example of Washoe's ability to create new meanings through novel combinations of her signs is her utterance, *water bird*. Fouts (1975) reported that Washoe signed *water bird* in the presence of a swan when she was asked *what that?* Washoe's answer may seem creative in that it names a new referent by juxtaposing two signs from her vocabulary. English word order notwithstanding, it is risky to conclude that Washoe was characterizing the swan as a "bird that inhabits water." Washoe had a long history of being asked *what that?* in the presence of objects such as birds and bodies of water. In this instance, Washoe may have simply been answering the question, *what that?* by identifying correctly a body of water and a bird, in that order. Before concluding that Washoe was relating the sign *water* to the sign *bird,* one must know whether she regularly placed an adjective before or after a noun. Accessible, systematic observations are needed rather than anecdotes, no matter how compelling those anecdotes may seem to an English-speaking observer. The same qualification applies to other acts of creativity attributed to Washoe (e.g., *cry hurt food* for radish) and to Koko (e.g., *cookie rock* for a stale sweet roll and *eye hat* for a mask).

Word order is but one of a number of ways in which sentences can encode different meanings. In a language of specific hand configurations, body movements, and facial expressions such as ASL, spatial organization and nuances of movement provide additional devices for encoding meaning[4]. Thus sign order per se is not the only way to demonstrate that sequences of signs were generated by a grammatical rule. When, however, regularities of sign order can be demonstrated, it does provide strong evidence for the existence of grammatical structure. (Even regularities of sign order would not be a conclusive demonstration unless evidence of appropriate semantic structure were provided. Given the difficulty of documenting other aspects of an ape's signing, regularities of sign order may provide the simplest way of demonstrating that an ape's utterances are grammatical.)

## PROJECT NIM

The purpose of the present study is to analyze the multisign sequences of a chimpanzee from an objective point of view. A basic goal was to amass a large enough corpus of a chimpanzee's utterances to determine if its multisign utterances are regularly ordered. Our subject was a male chimpanzee, Neam Chimpsky ("Nim" for short). From the age of two weeks, Nim was raised in a home environment by human surrogate parents and teachers who communicated with him and among themselves in ASL (see note 2). During his waking hours, Nim was always in the company of at least one project member.

Some observers have claimed that natural languages are "ill-defined" (Premack, 1976). We nevertheless chose to teach our chimpanzee ASL because ordinarily, language is a concommitant of an infant's socialization—as "ill-defined" as such socialization may be. More so than an artificial language, a natural language makes it possible to interact with an infant chimpanzee the way that parents interact with a child. Clearly, the complex nature of socializing an infant makes it difficult to specify all of the variables that bear on language development. It is also difficult to say just how different Nim's socialization was from that experienced by children. Our purpose, however, was not to delineate *how* Nim learned sign language, but to see what features of a natural language he could master. It was also our belief that intensive socialization would increase Nim's motivation to please. If Nim tried to please by signing, his motivation for using language would be considerably more diverse than the motivation of cage-reared subjects whose only obvious reason to use language is to acquire objects they can ingest or play with.

## History and Socialization

Nim was born on November 21, 1973, at the Institute for Primate Studies in Norman, Oklahoma[5].

On December 3, 1972, Nim was flown to New York accompanied by Mrs. Staphanie LaFarge who, along with her family, raised Nim in their home on New York's West Side[6]. Between August 15, 1975, and September 25, 1977, Nim lived in a large house (Delafield) with private grounds in Riverdale, N.Y. At Delafield, Nim was cared for by four undergraduate students who had spent long periods of time with Nim at the LaFarge house. As a result, the move from the LaFarge house to Delafield occurred smoothly and without any sign of emotional stress on Nim's part. At Delafield, the living space was separated into two areas which overlapped only in the kitchen. In Nim's area, there were rooms for sleeping, eating, and recreation. The remainder of the living area at Delafield was used by the human residents and was off limits to Nim.

Nim formed particularly close attachments with certain members of the project. The first author was the only project member who maintained a strong and a continuous bond with Nim throughout the project. During the first 18 months of the project, Stephanie LaFarge was the most central person in Nim's life. Following his move to Delafield, Nim became closely attached to the second author, who supervised his care both at Delafield and in a special classroom built for Nim in the psychology department of Columbia University. After the second author left the project (when Nim was 34 months old), Nim became closely attached to two resident teachers at Delafield, Bill Tynan and Joyce Butler. An extensive account of Nim's socialization is provided elsewhere (Terrace, 1979b).

From the time Nim was two months old, he was visited regularly by volunteers recruited mainly from Columbia University and Barnard College. These volunteers, all of whom had some training in ASL, tried to teach Nim to sign through various activities such as looking at pictures, playing with dolls and mirrors, preparing meals, and so on. The volunteers also signed to Nim and tried to mold (cf. Fouts & Goodin, 1974; Gardner & Gardner, 1969) his hands into the configurations of different signs. From September 1974 until August 1977, Nim was driven to his classroom at Columbia three to five times a week. The classroom was a small, bare room approximately eight feet square. One wall of the classroom contained a large one-way mirror which allowed observers in an adjacent room to observe Nim without being seen. Beneath the one-way mirror was a portal which could house various cameras used to photograph Nim's signing. Across from the classroom and the observation room was another small area in which Nim was allowed to recreate during breaks from the classroom.

During a typical day, Nim was taught by a number of different teachers. All teachers were encouraged to emphasize those activities and objects which were conducive to signing and which maintained Nim's attention. At Delafield, Nim's caretakers (who also taught in the Columbia classroom) involved him regularly in such everyday activities as food preparation, eating, laundry, and cleaning. Nim also ate all of his meals with one or more of his companions. These activities provided opportunities for lengthy exchanges in ASL.

In the classroom Nim was given intensive instruction in both the expression and the comprehension of signs. Nim was also taught regularly at Delafield, albeit in a less formal manner. Extensive analyses of his signing at Delafield and in the Columbia classroom revealed no systematic differences in any of the aspects of Nim's signing reported below.

During the 46 months in which he lived in New York, Nim was taught by 60 nonpermanent volunteer teachers. As he grew older, it became increasingly difficult to arrange for the kind of overlap between new and old personnel which had been possible when the responsibility for supervising Nim's day-to-day existence transferred from Stephanie LaFarge's family to the resident teachers at Delafield. Because of Nim's emotional reactions to some of those changes it also became increasingly difficult for new teachers to command Nim's attention (Terrace, 1979b). By September 1977, it was clear that we did not have the resources necessary to hire a staff of qualified permanent teachers who could advance the scientific aspects of the project.

Our choice was to provide "babysitters" who could look after Nim, but who were not uniformly qualified to further Nim's understanding of sign language, or to terminate the project. With great reluctance, we decided on the latter course of action. On September 25, 1977, Nim was flown back to his birthplace in Oklahoma.

## Training Methods

Nim was trained to sign by an eclectic method. His teachers were familiarized with a small number of techniques and then encouraged to use whatever technique(s) they found most comfortable to work with. Our basic method was modeled after the "molding" and "guidance" techniques developed on other projects (cf. Gardner & Gardner, 1969; Fouts & Goodin, 1974); the trainer physically molded Nim's hands into the appropriate configuration. In most instances, we molded the sign in an appropriate context. Some signs, especially those which required fine and complex movements, were taught by first molding the new sign out of context. Teaching the sign out of context was especially important in situations in which Nim's attempt to reach for the desired referent interfered with our efforts to mold his hands (for example, the signs *book, shoe,* and *apple*).

Typically, Nim reached for something he might want to play with, eat, or inspect. The teacher withheld the item, molded the object's name sign, and then asked Nim to sign for the object. Signs such as *give, me,* and *Nim,* while appropriate, were deemed unacceptable when we were trying to teach Nim a new sign. Since the age of 18 months, Nim often offered his hands to his teacher in an apparent request for the teacher to mold the new sign that the teacher wanted him to use.

Nim's signs were classified in three mutually exclusive categories. An *imitative* sign is one which repeated the teacher's immediately prior utterance. A *spontaneous* sign is one which did not occur in the teacher's immediately prior utterance. A *prompted* sign was a sign of the teacher's immediately prior utterance that used only part of the sign's configuration, movement, or location. For example the sign *Nim* (first and second fingers drawn down the temple) might be prompted by the teacher's extending those two fingers from a fist held in front of the signer or by touching the signer's temple with a finger. By age 30 months, Nim began to learn new signs by imitation. In the context of the desired object, such as a baby doll, the teacher withheld the object, pointed to it, and then signed *baby*. Nim responded by imitating the teachers sign; often Nim made the new sign spontaneously.

Nim was given food and drink objects only when he was being taught a sign about a particular food or drink. Other signs were rewarded by praise (for example, the teacher signed *good* or *correct*), by social reinforcers (such as a smile or a hug from the teacher), by access to an object (such as a book or a cat), or by the opportunity to carry out an action (such as running or jumping). Even when Nim signed about a particular food or drink, he was not necessarily rewarded with a sample of what he signed about. Often Nim was asked only about the color of a food or a drink or about its similarity to other food and drink objects which the teacher presented. After noting Nim's response, the teacher simply shifted to another activity. During picture-labeling sessions, Nim signed regularly about pictures of food and drink objects, with little apparent interest in obtaining these objects. His only reward for signing about such pictures was occasional praise from his teacher. Nim was also observed to sign about pictures when looking at them on his own, without attempting to involve the teacher.

## Data Collection

In many respects our methods of data collection paralleled those used in studies of the development of language in children (cf. Brown, 1973). The main goal was to obtain an extensive corpus of Nim's utterances that would allow one to go beyond anecdotal examples of an ape's apparent linguistic ability.

During each session, Nim's teacher whispered into a miniature cassette recorder the pertinent details of Nim's signing. As soon as possible after their sessions, Nim's teachers transcribed their tapes and wrote detailed reports about the signs Nim made, the context in which they occurred, and other aspects of Nim's behavior. Our transcription forms included sections covering developmental data, unusual sign exchanges or sign configurations, and a record of dialogues between Nim and his teacher. The sign record was supplemented by notations on context, references, and so on to aid in subsequent interpretation.

In recording Nim's signs, his teachers distinguished among signs which were spontaneous, imitated, prompted, molded, or approximations of the correct sign. Occasional reliability checks were made by comparing teachers' reports with those of independent observers who watched Nim and his teacher through the one-way window of the classroom. The reliability of teachers' reports was also assessed by comparing transcripts of videotapes with a teacher's transcript of the same session. In some instances, transcripts were prepared by professional interpreters of ASL who had never seen Nim sign prior to their viewing of the videotapes.

Agreement between a teacher's report and the transcript of independent observers and videotapes ranged between 77 percent and 94 percent. There was almost perfect agreement between the teacher's and the independent observers' interpretation of each recorded sign. Typically disagreements between a teacher's report and the independent assessments occurred when the teacher failed to record a sign. This often happened when the teacher was busy preparing an activity, when Nim was signing too quickly, or when the teacher was signing to Nim. At worst, the teachers' reports underestimated the extent to which Nim signed. There was, however, no evidence that the omissions of the teacher were systematic. Thus, teachers' reports appear to provide an objective sample of Nim's signing, with the qualification that they underestimate slightly the frequency of his signs[7].

## Vocabulary

### Expressive vocabulary

As of September 25, 1977, Nim had acquired 125 signs. Nim satisfied our criterion of acquiring a sign when, (a) on different occasions, three independent observers reported its spontaneous occurrence, and (b) it occurred spontaneously on each of five successive days.

The sequence and the rate at which he learned these signs are shown in Figure 8-1[8]. Nim acquired his first sign, *drink,* on March 2, 1974, at which time he was four months old. During the next four months, Nim acquired five other signs (*up, sweet, give, more,* and *eat*).

Between the ages of 19 and 34 months, Nim learned new signs at a rate of 1.4 signs per week. If Nim continued to learn new signs at that rate, he would have had a vocabulary of 250 words by the time he was 5 years old. Nevertheless, it seems probable that Nim could acquire signs at an even faster rate. Until Nim's last year in New York, most of his teachers were not highly fluent in sign language[9]. A more serious problem was the large number of teachers (60 in all) with whom Nim had to contend.

How Nim's rate of sign acquisition can be influenced by the teachers who worked with him can be seen by comparing two time periods (June 1975–September 1976, age 19–34 months; and September 1976–February 1977, age 34–39 months). During the first period, Nim was taught by a relatively stable group of teachers (Walter Benesch, Andrea Liebert, Laura Petitto, and Amy Schacter). When they had to be replaced, Nim's rate of acquisition decreased from 1.4 to 0.3 signs per week. Once Nim adapted to his new teachers, he acquired signs at a rate of 1.0 signs per week. During Nim's last two months in New York, he learned new signs at the rate of 2.0 signs a week. The rate at which Nim acquired new signs seems to reveal as much about his teachers as it does about his actual ability to master new signs.

### Usage

Nim's day-to-day usage of signs was determined by his needs, the demands of his teachers, and the situations to which he was exposed. As far as we could tell, the main (and perhaps only) reason for a sign to drop out

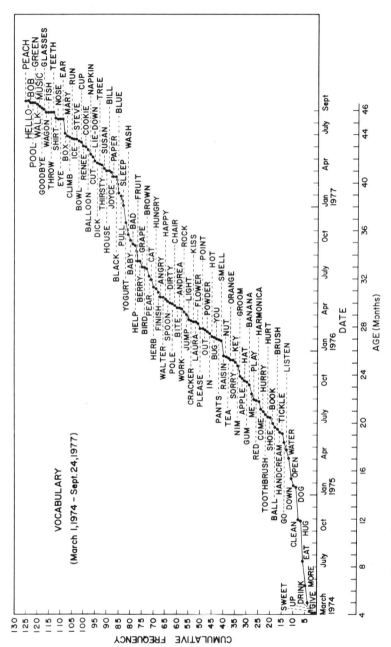

*Figure 8-1.* Rate and sequence of the acquisition of signs of Nim's expressive vocabulary.

of Nim's day-to-day vocabulary was that a situation was not set up in which the sign was likely to occur. For example, once Nim learned to sign *dog,* he would regularly make the sign when he saw a dog or a picture of a dog. If Nim did not come in contact with a dog for several days, the sign did not occur. However, in this and in other instances, it was relatively easy to reestablish the sign simply by restoring the appropriate circumstances that occasioned its occurence.

Figure 8-2 shows the number of days on which each sign of his vocabulary was observed to occur during an early phase of the project[10]. Generally, once a sign was acquired, it occurred each day. The few exceptions can be attributed to the absence of a demand that a sign be used (for example, *clean, hurt, ball, harmonica, up*). *Harmonica* was prevalent during the tenure of a volunteer teacher who worked with Nim for only three months. After that teacher left, the frequency of *harmonica* decreased sharply. *Hurt* was used only when Nim hurt himself or when he noticed a scratch or scar on someone else. As Nim became more mobile, he signed *up* (and *down*) less frequently[11]. During the phase of the project shown in Figure 8-2, *ball* and *clean* were rarely called for in the classroom and only sporadically at home.

As Nim's vocabulary grew, it became increasingly difficult to maintain all of the signs on a daily basis. Accordingly, the relative frequency with which particular words were signed did not remain constant. Table I shows the rank and the absolute frequencies of Nim's most frequent 25 signs during five periods between June 1, 1975 and February 7, 1977. Also shown in Table I are the number of different signs Nim was observed to make during each period.

## Comprehension of signs

The task of evaluating what words a child or chimpanzee understands poses problems which, in practice, are seldom encountered in evaluating what words they express. When evaluating expressive ability, it is usually only necessary to observe whether a particular sign occurred and in what context. In evaluating comprehension, however, it is essential to devise behaviorial tasks which show that comprehension is specific to the sign, and not to some other cue that the teacher may be transmitting (cf. Bever, 1970; Brown, 1973; Fodor, Bever, & Garrett, 1974; Macnamara, 1972). If, for example, the teacher signed *book,* Nim may pick up the book, not because he understands *book,* but because the teacher was looking at the book.

In most instances our basis for concluding that Nim could comprehend a sign came from tests performed in the classroom. For example, his teacher would arrange Nim's brush, a bottle of hand cream, a mirror, and other grooming articles on the floor. Nim was positioned beside his teacher,

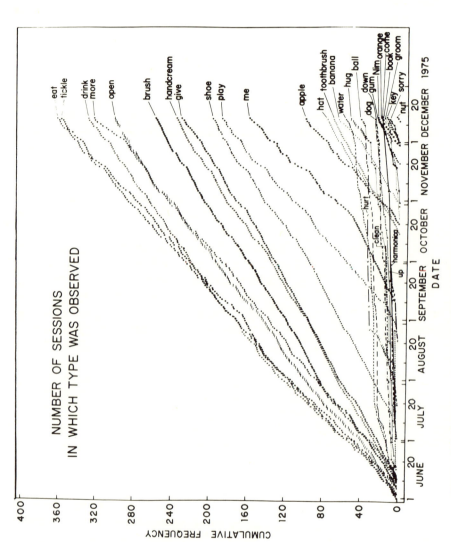

*Figure 8-2.* The cumulative number of days on which a sign occurred spontaneously at least once a day between June 1 and December 20, 1975.

equidistant from each item. The teacher signed, *Nim give me hand cream,* deliberately not looking at or pointing at the object in question. Nim reliably walked across the room, got the hand cream, and brought it to the teacher. If the teacher signed, *Nim give me brush,* Nim walked over, picked up the brush, and placed it next to the teacher.

Another variation of this procedure was to present Nim with a closed but familiar book. The teacher then signed, *Nim where banana?* or *show me banana.* Nim often responded by looking through the book, finding the picture of the banana, and placing the book with he page open to the banana in front of his teacher. He then signed *banana* and pointed to it.

### Table I
### Twenty-five Most Frequent Signs During Each Period

| Period I (6/1/75– 12/20/75) | | | Period II (1/5– 2/29/76) | | | Period III (3/1– 3/29/75) | | | Period IV (4/5– 7/4/76) | | | Period V (7/5/76– 2/7/77) | | |
|---|---|---|---|---|---|---|---|---|---|---|---|---|---|---|
| Rank | Sign | Freq. | Rank | Sign | Freq. | Rank | Sign | Freq. | Rank | Sign | Freq. | Rank | Sign | Freq. |
| 1 | eat | 360 | 1 | me | 169 | 1 | play | 219 | 1 | play | 767 | 1 | hug | 1650 |
| 2 | tickle | 356 | 2 | play | 156 | 2 | hug | 174 | 2 | eat | 515 | 2 | play | 1545 |
| 3 | drink | 327 | 3 | hug | 138 | 3 | me | 169 | 3 | hug | 440 | 3 | finish | 1103 |
| 4 | more | 320 | 4 | tea | 99 | 4 | eat | 137 | 4 | drink | 321 | 4 | eat | 951 |
| 5 | open | 299 | 5 | more | 75 | 5 | give | 101 | 5 | Nim | 273 | 5 | dirty | 788 |
| 6 | brush | 256 | 6 | drink | 73 | 6 | banana | 99 | 6 | me | 267 | 6 | drink | 712 |
| 7 | hand cream | 234 | 7 | eat | 65 | 7 | tickle | 94 | 7 | open | 211 | 7 | out | 615 |
| 8 | give | 229 | 8 | tickle | 62 | 8 | drink | 87 | 8 | angry | 205 | 8 | Nim | 613 |
| 9 | shoe | 196 | 9 | Nim | 56 | 9 | more | 85 | 9 | tickle | 186 | 9 | open | 554 |
| 10 | play | 186 | 10 | banana | 50 | 10 | Nim | 81 | 10 | toothbrush | 166 | 10 | tickle | 414 |
| 11 | me | 157 | 11 | nut | 39 | 11 | tea | 73 | 11 | bite | 165 | 11 | bite | 407 |
| 12 | apple | 98 | 12 | sorry | 38 | 12 | water | 58 | 12 | gum | 162 | 12 | shoe | 405 |
| 13 | hat | 75 | 13 | open | 37 | 13 | apple | 51 | 13 | banana | 145 | 13 | pants | 377 |
| 14 | toothbrush | 68 | 14 | give | 36 | 14 | hot | 50 | 14 | chair | 144 | 14 | red | 380 |
| 15 | banana | 63 | 15 | water | 35 | 15 | jump | 41 | 15 | sorry | 140 | 15 | sorry | 366 |
| 16 | water | 56 | 16 | you | 33 | 16 | cracker | 38 | 16 | groom | 139 | 16 | angry | 354 |
| 17 | hug | 50 | 17 | smell | 32 | 17 | listen | 35 | 17 | red | 138 | 17 | me | 351 |
| 18 | ball | 40 | 18 | toothbrush | 28 | 19 | brush | 33 | 18 | book | 136 | 18 | banana | 348 |
| 19 | hurt | 33 | 19 | brush | 77 | 19 | gum | 33 | 19 | water | 133 | 19 | nut | 323 |
| 20 | dog | 26 | 20.5 | hat | 26 | 19 | open | 33 | 20 | nut | 127 | 20 | down | 316 |
| 21 | down | 24 | 20.5 | shoe | 26 | 21 | hat | 30 | 21 | jump | 120 | 21 | toothbrush | 302 |
| 22 | gum | 22 | 22 | apple | 24 | 22.5 | you | 29 | 22 | give | 118 | 22 | change | 301 |
| 23 | Nim | 22 | 23 | hand cream | 23 | 22.5 | orange | 29 | 23 | hand cream | 115 | 23 | grape | 239 |
| 24 | orange | 20 | 24 | groom | 19 | 24 | toothbrush | 28 | 24 | tea | 111 | 24 | sweet | 236 |
| | | | 25.5 | in | 15 | | | | | | | | | |
| 25 | come | 18 | 25.5 | sweet | 15 | 25 | dog | 25 | 25 | Andrea | 106 | 25 | apple | 228 |

| Total Number of Different Signs Observed in Period | 33 | 49 | 60 | 106 | 157 |
|---|---|---|---|---|---|

While there is no limit to the fineness of tests of comprehension, we felt that our tests adequately demonstrate Nim's responsiveness to specific signs. In each case, his behavior was both appropriate and immediate. In many of our tests, it was possible for alternative modes of behavior to have taken place as, for example, looking for a picture of an object in a picture book. A list of signs that Nim comprehended, as determined by tests administered independently by at least two of his teachers, appears in Table II.

## Some anecdotal observations of Nim's use of sign language

The main goal of Project Nim was to collect a corpus of sign combinations which would allow us to assess their structure. While collecting our basic data, we also observed a number of interesting usages of sign language. Some have not been reported in other studies of an ape's ability to learn a language; others have been given a different interpretation. In considering our observations the reader should keep in mind their anecdotal nature. Even though each usage we will describe was reported independently by at least four of Nim's teachers, these observations were not subjected to experimental manipulation.

*Emotional expression.* The study of private events in humans poses an obvious problem: how can one establish that a verbal report about an internal state is an expression of that state and not a device to manipulate the listener's behavior (cf. Skinner, 1945)? Through language, one can often query the speaker and thereby obtain additional clues as to the veracity of the speaker's description of an internal state. The listener can also judge from the speaker's bodily expressions and overall behavior whether the speaker's statements about a bodily state are credible.

In attempting to communicate with nonhuman species, a human listener has few options for evaluating utterances about a bodily state. The main source of information is the subject's overall behavior. There's little basis for expecting the subject to reply to queries about its feelings (cf. Terrace & Bever, 1976). With these qualifications in mind let us consider a number of instances in which Nim appeared to use sign language as a means of emotional expression and some instances in which he appeared to misrepresent certain bodily states.

Nim learned the signs for *bite* and *angry* with the aid of photographs showing an actor making an angry face, and, in a different scene, attempting to bite someone's hand. Without any specific training to do so, Nim began to sign *bite* and *angry* during confrontations with his teachers. In many instances Nim signed *bite* or *angry* while on the verge of attacking his teacher. Before signing *bite* or *angry* he appeared ready to bite or attack: his lips were pulled back over his bare teeth, he ran toward the target of aggression, and his hair was often erect. After signing *bite* Nim appeared to relax and showed no further interest in attacking the target of his anger. On

# Table II
## Signs Nim Comprehends

| | | | |
|---|---|---|---|
| afraid | door | light | shoe |
| airplane | down | listen | sign |
| alone | draw | little | sit |
| Andrea | drink | look | sleep |
| angry | ear | make | smell |
| apple | easy | Mary | smile |
| attention | eat | match | sock |
| baby | egg | me | sorry |
| bad | eye | mine | spaghetti |
| ball | fall | mirror | spoon |
| balloon | false | more | squirrel |
| banana | finish | mouse | stand up |
| belt | first | mouth | stay |
| berry | fish | music | Steve |
| big | flower | napkin | stop |
| Bill | fruit | Nim | Susan |
| bird | give | no | sweet |
| bite | go | nose | swing |
| black | good | now | table |
| blue | goodbye | nut | take out |
| Bob | grape | on | taste |
| book | green | one | tea |
| bowl | groom | open | teeth |
| box | gum | orange | telephone |
| bring | gym | out | thirsty |
| brown | hand cream | paint | throw |
| brush | handkerchief | pants | tickle |
| bug | happy | paper | time |
| butterfly | harmonica | peach | toilet |
| camera | harness | pear | toothbrush |
| car | hat | peekaboo | toys |
| cat | hello | plant | train |
| chair | help | play | tree |
| change | Herb | play key | under |
| clean | here | point | up |
| climb | hot | pole | wagon |
| close | house | pool | wait |
| coat | hug | pour | walk |
| color | hungry | powder | Walter |
| come | hurry | pull | want |
| cookie | hurt | put-in | wash |
| crayon | ice | quiet | water |
| cup | in | raisin | what |
| cut | Joyce | red | where |
| diaper | jump | Renee | who |
| Dick | key | right | window |
| dirty | kiss | rock | with |
| dog | later | run | work |
| don't | Laura | shirt | yellow |
| | lie down | | yes |
| | | | you |

some occasions, Nim was observed to sign both *bite* and *angry* as a warning. Such warnings were not followed by a full display of aggression or anger.

These observations suggest that the signs *bite* and *angry* may have functioned as substitutes for the chimpanzee's natural expression of aggression. Unfortunately, the evidence that is needed to demonstrate this function of language is not complete. We do know that, unless he was restrained from doing so, Nim would often bite or attack someone when he exhibited an aggressive posture. After signing *bite* or *angry,* Nim's tendency to inflict physical damage seemed greatly reduced. But we have no way of knowing to what extent Nim would have actually attacked someone he threatened when he didn't sign *bite* and *angry.* Often when a teacher responded to Nim's physical threat by signing *stop* or *careful,* Nim backed down and became quite docile. It may also be the case that *bite* and *angry* were signed during weak states of arousal and that Nim was able to inhibit his impulse to attack without actually signing *bite* or *angry.* Further clarification of this issue requires an experiment which would pose both practical and ethical difficulties. One would want to create a situation in which Nim reliably attacked a person or an object. If Nim refrained from attacking after signing *bite* or *angry* (either spontaneously, or in response to questions such as *what you feel*?), one could conclude that an arbitrary symbol functioned as a substitute for physical impulse.

*Sorry* was another "emotional state" that Nim signed about, particularly after misbehaving (e.g., nipping someone's hand, jumping around too much in the classroom, or breaking a toy). Nim was often observed to sign *sorry* before his teacher reacted to his transgression. From Nim's troubled expression (a protruding lower lip and fear vocalizations), it was apparent that Nim's use of *sorry* was motivated by his anticipation of being reprimanded. (*Sorry* also appears in the expressive vocabularies of Washoe and Koko [Gardner & Gardner, 1975b; Patterson, 1978].)

Two of Nim's signs were used to misrepresent bodily states. Once he was toilet trained, Nim learned to sign *dirty* when he wanted to use the toilet (Terrace, 1979b). Nim also learned the sign *sleep* when he wanted to go to bed. Normally, Nim was taken to the bathroom after having signed *dirty*, and allowed to take a nap or go to his bedroom, having signed *sleep*. Having learned to sign *dirty* and *sleep* when appropriate, Nim began to make these signs when they were clearly inappropriate. For example, within minutes of having urinated and/or defecated, Nim often signed *dirty*. Likewise Nim signed *sleep* while showing every sign of being fully alert.

The misuse of *dirty* and *sleep* seemed motivated by a desire to change the situation. For example, when Nim looked bored he was prone to sign *dirty* or *sleep*. Symptoms of Nim's boredom included his looking away from his teacher, running around the classroom, and otherwise resisting his teacher's efforts to focus his attention. The inappropriate use of *dirty* also occurred when Nim wanted to delay his transfer to a new teacher. At first he resisted the transfer physically. If that effort failed, he signed *dirty* even though he had just used the toilet.

In instances in which Nim may have been misrepresenting his condition, his teachers often signed *you not dirty* or *you not sleepy,* or otherwise indicated that they were not fooled by Nim's sign. Nim's response to this teacher's signing provided additional evidence that Nim was not using *dirty* or *sleepy* appropriately. When challenged by his teacher after signing *dirty* or *sleep* inappropriately, he often backed down and abandoned his effort to be taken to the toilet or to be allowed to lie down. When Nim's expression of his need was genuine, he persisted in his signing even when challenged by his teacher. For example, he might sign *me out, dirty hug, Nim point, me sleep,* and so on. In addition, his nonlinguistic behavior also revealed a strong motivation to satisfy his needs. Often he would stick out his lips and begin to pout. Following a genuine *dirty* or *sleep* sign that was not honored by his teacher, Nim took his teacher's hand and led the teacher to the potty or his bedroom respectively. Figure 8-3 shows Nim underscoring his need to use the toilet while signing *dirty*. In this instance, he removed his pants after his first *dirty* sign was ignored. In Figure 8-4 Nim is emphasizing his need to use the toilet by signing *dirty* with both hands. (Nim signed with two hands a sign which he normally signed with one hand, in order to emphasize other requests as well. A similar phenomenon has been reported by observers of sign language in deaf children [Klima & Bellugi, 1972]. Figure 8-5 shows Nim signing *apple* with one hand; Figure 8-6 shows him making the same sign with two hands.)

*Development of sign topography from "baby" to "mature" form.* In the case of some signs we accepted approximations of standard ASL signs which were referred to as "baby signs." Through the concerted efforts of his teachers, Nim was slowly weaned away from the baby configuration toward the adult version of the sign. A similar development has been observed in children who learned sign language as a first language (Schlesinger & Meadow, 1972). Figure 8-7 through 8-9 show Nim signing *more* when he was 2, 2 1/2, and 3 1/2 years old. At first Nim touched only the index fingers of each hand (Figure 8-7). Later he touched the index fingers and the remaining fingers but in separate groups (Figure 8-8). Eventually he learned to sign the standard form of *more* (Figure 8-9). Other signs which went through a similar evolution were *eat, open, come, me, tea, smell* (see Terrace, 1979b, Appendix C for additional detils).

*Topographical vs. semantic errors.* Another interesting example of systematic variation in Nim's signing can be seen in errors of topography. Our meager data on such errors also point to some interesting similarities between sign language as practiced by humans and by Nim. The nature of these errors is most easily appreciated by considering how humans re-

Figure 8-3. Nim underscoring his need to go to the bathroom by signing *dirty.*

*Figure 8-4.* Nim signs *dirty* with both hands (Photos by H.S. Terrace).

*Figure 8-5. Apple* produced with one hand.

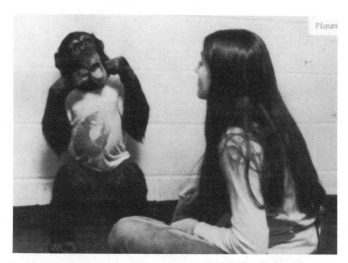

*Figure 8-6. Apple* produced using both hands.

*Figure 8-7.* 2 years; *more.*

*Figure 8-8.* 2½ years; *more.*

*Figure 8-9.* 3½ years; *more* (photos by H.S. Terrace).

member a list of unrelated words (e.g, *bad, cat, big* and so on). Typically, the errors that occur in this process are phonetic and not semantic (Conrad, 1964). Words like *pad* are substituted for *bad* instead of words like *rotten* or *wicked; cap* might be substituted for *cat* instead of *pet* or *feline; pig* might be substituted for *big* rather than *large* or *huge,* and so on. Phonetic errors in list learning of spoken words have an analog in the list learning of signs (Bellugi & Klima, 1976, 1979). Signs which are made in a similar fashion are often substituted for one another; for instance, *potato* for *time,* and *vote* for *tea.*

In learning to make the name sign of the senior author, Nim often signed variations of *cat,* a sign which is topographically similar to *Herb.* Having learned to sign *Herb,* Nim signed *Herb* while trying to sign *cat* and *cat* while trying to sign *Herb.* Figure 8-13 shows Nim signing *Herb* correctly. A mixture of the signs *cat* and *Herb,* where Nim is trying to sign *cat,* can be seen in Figure 8-10. Figure 8-11 shows Nim signing a one-handed *cat* sign while trying to sign *Herb.* Figure 8-12 shows Nim signing *cat* with one hand and *Herb* with the other, when it would have been appropriate to sign only *Herb.* Other pairs of topographically related signs whose components occurred in inappropriate situations were *rock-work, hot-drink, run-berry,* and *Bill-Andrea* (see Terrace, 1979b, Appendix C, for additional details).

## Combinations of Signs

The major goal of this study was to determine whether a chimpanzee could create a sentence. To answer that question, we analyzed Nim's multi-sign utterances with an eye toward distributional and semantic regularities.

*Figure 8-10.* Nim signing a mixture of *Herb* and *cat* (photo by H.S. Terrace).

*Figure 8-11.* Nim incorrectly signing *cat while trying to sign Herb* (photo by S. Kuklin).

*Figure 8-12.* Nim signing *Herb* with one hand and incorrectly signing *cat* with the other (photo by S. Kuklin).

*Figure 8-13.* Nim signing *Herb* correctly (photo by S. Kuklin).

Before we could argue that one or more structural rules account for Nim's multisign utterances, it was necessary to demonstrate that regularities of sign order and semantic usage could not be explained by simpler processes such as sampling artifacts, rote learning, or imitation.

A combination of signs was defined as the occurrence of two or more different signs which were not interrupted by the occurence of other behavior or by the return of the hands to a relaxed position (see Stokoe, Casterline, and Croneberg [1965] for a discussion of constituent boundaries in ASL). In ASL, the segmentation of signs into combinations has a function similar to that of the segmentation of speech into clauses in spoken language. Segmentation delineates word sequences which are immediately related to one another (Brown & Miron, 1971; Lane & Grosjean, 1973).

The corpus of combinations we analyzed consisted entirely of sequences of distinct signs which occurred successively. Such sequences accounted for approximately 95 percent of Nim's combinations. It is of interest to consider first two kinds of combinations which were *not* included in the corpus. These were contractions of two or more signs and simultaneous combinations in which two distinct signs occurred at the same time. Even though contractions and simultaneous combinations occur normally in ASL, they were excluded from our corpus because it was impossible to specify the temporal order of the signs they contained.

An example of a contraction can be seen in Figures 8-14 and 8-15,

*Figure 8-14.* Nim contracting the signs *more* and *drink* (photo by H.S. Terrace).

*Figure 8-15.* Nim signing *drink* (photo by H.S. Terrace).

which show Nim contracting the signs *more* and *drink*. In Figure 8-14, Nim's right hand forms the sign *drink* while his left hand makes a movement similar to the conventional *more* sign. Figure 8-9 above show a conventional *more* sign. In the contraction of *more* and *drink, more* is articulated at the mouth rather than in opposition to the other hand. In Figure 8-16, Nim is shown contracting the elements of two signs: *Nim* and *hug*. These signs are shown as they would occur separately in Figures 8-17 (*Nim*) and 8-18 (*hug*).

Examples of simultaneous signing can be seen in Figures 8-19 and 8-20. Figure 8-19 shows Nim signing *me* and *hat* simultaneously. Both *me* and *hat* were signed as they would be signed if signed separately. Figure 8-20 shows Nim signing three signs, *me, point,* and *hug. Me* and *point,* however, were signed simultaneously. In signing two distinct signs simultaneously, Nim has also been observed to maintain a particular sign with one hand while signing other signs with his other hand. Consider the following example from a video transcript made while Nim was asking for a grape and a sip of tea on January 17, 1977 (adapted from a transcript prepared by W. J. Tynan).

time (sec):  0  1  2  3  4  5  6  7  8  9  10  11

|—|—|—|—|—|—|—|—|—|—| |—|

left hand:  *drink    Nim Nim eat   ⟶ grape*

right hand:  *me    drink Nim tea*

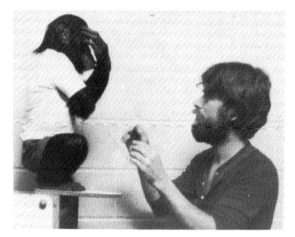

*Figure 8-16.* Nim contracting the signs *Nim* and *hug* (teacher: Bill Tynan).

*Figure 8-17.* Nim signed in its normal form (teacher: Susan Quinby).

*Figure 8-18. Hug* signed in its normal form (Teacher: Bill Tynan). (Figures 8-16, 8-17, and 8-18 photographed in the Columbia classroom by H.S. Terrace.)

*Figure 8-19.* Nim signed *me* and *hat* simultaneously in the classroom with the first author (photo by L.A. Petitto).

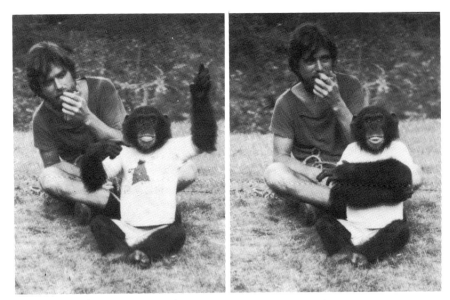

*Figure 8-20.* Left-hand panel: Nim signing *me* and *point* simultaneously. Right-hand panel: Nim completes utterance by signing *hug*. (Not visible is the cat Nim was trying to obtain.) Bill Tynan, the teacher, is dictating what Nim is signing. (Photographed at Delafield by H.S. Terrace.)

In this relatively simple example of simultaneous signing, Nim maintained the sign *eat* with his left hand while signing *me drink* with his right hand.

In each of the foregoing examples it should be clear that there is no basis for referring to the sequential nature of a particular combination. The contraction *more* and *drink,* and *Nim* and *hug,* could just as well have been referred to as *drink* and *more,* or *hug* and *Nim.* Likewise, there is nothing in Figures 8-10 through 8-15 which suggests that *me hat* or *me point* are more appropriate descriptions of what Nim is signing than *hat me* or *point me.*

*Figure 8-21 shows a combination, me hug cat,* in which there is no temporal overlap between any of the signs. This is the typical manner in which Nim combined signs. The corpus we will describe below consists exclusively of such linear combinations.

Nim's first documented combinations (*more drink* and *more eat*) occurred on March 3, 1975, at age 16 months. Since that time, he has made numerous combinations, some containing as many as 16 signs. In no instance were specific sequences, contractions, or simultaneous combinations reinforced differentially. Indeed, Nim was never required to make a combination of signs as opposed to a single sign. We must, of course, recognize that Nim's teachers exerted some influence on Nim's combinations.

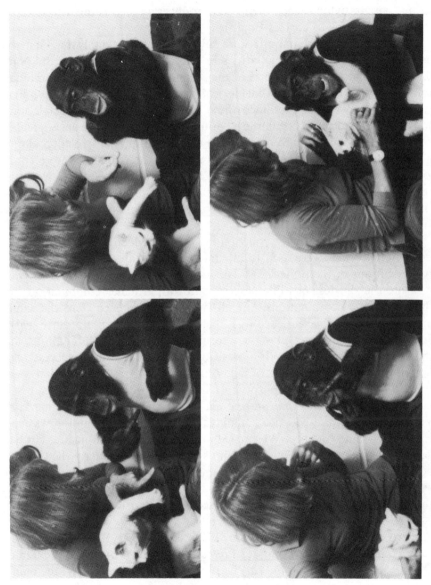

*Figure 8-21.* Nim signing the linear combination, *me hug cat* to his teacher, Susan Quinby. (Photographed in classroom by H.S. Terrace.)

Typically, they signed to him in stereotyped orders that were modeled after English usage. It may also be the case that some of Nim's teachers unwittingly gave him special praise when he signed an interesting combination. Such unintentional reactions do not, however, appear to differ from the reactions parents exhibit when their child produces an interesting utterance or one that conforms to correct English.

Nim's linear combinations were subjected to three analyses. First we looked for distributional regularities in Nim's 2-sign utterances: did Nim place particular signs in the first or the second position of 2-sign combinations? Having established that lexical regularities did exist in 2-sign combinations, we then examined these regularities for semantic relationships. The existence of semantic relationships was explored in a smaller corpus of 2-sign combinations for which we had comprehensive notes about the context of each combination. The results of these analyses were equivocal. Our final analysis, a "discourse" analysis, sought to relate Nim's signing to his teachers' signing. For that purpose we assembled a third corpus from video-transcripts which provided reliable records of both Nim's and his teachers' signing.

In order to minimize the contribution of signs which were repeated successively, two rules were used to tabulate combinations containing successive repetitions of the same signs. The motivation for using these rules was to insure the shortest possible description of a particular combination. In "homogeneous combinations," if all signs in a sequence were the same (e.g., *eat eat eat*), the sequence was treated as a single sign utterance (*eat*). Homogeneous sequences of signs were not tabulated as combinations. In "heterogeneous sequences," if a particular sign repeated itself successively in a heterogeneous sequence of signs, immediate repetitions of that sign were not counted. For the purpose of tabulation within the corpus, a sequence such as *banana me me me eat* was reduced to *banana me eat.* Whereas the original sequence contained 5 signs, this combination was entered as a 3-sign sequence. We carried out this procedure to insure that we did not overestimate the length of Nim's utterances. In general the sign $Y$, repeated in succession $n$ times, was counted as a single occurrence of $Y$, independently of the value of $n$. This same rule was applied in deciding whether a sequence was a new type of sequence. Consider the sequence $X$, $(Y)n$, $Z$. This would be reduced to $X$, $Y$, $Z$. Accordingly $X$, $Y$, $Z$ would be tallied as a new type of sequence only if the sequence $X$, $Y$, $Z$ had not been observed previously. For example, if *banana me me me eat* (which is entered into the corpus as *banana me eat*) had been observed previously, the combination *banana me me me me eat* would not be considered as an instance of a new *type* of combination. In tabulating *tokens* of multisign sequences, *banana (me)n eat* would be counted as an instance of a 3-sign sequence[13].

## Corpus and distributional regularities

A corpus of linear combinations assembled through the application of the above rules consisted of 5,235 types of 19213 tokens of combinations of 2, 3, 4, 5, or more signs. This corpus included all linear combinations entered in teachers' reports between June 1, 1975, and February 7, 1977 (ages 18–38 months). An overall view of Nim's production of combinations during this period is shown in Figures 8-22 and 8-23. These figures show the cumulative frequencies of tokens (Figure 8-22) and types (Figure 8-23) of combinations of 2, 3, 4, 5, or more signs. Different sequences of the same sign were regarded as different types (for example, *banana eat* vs. *eat banana*). The functions shown in Figures 8-22 and 8-23 are based upon the number of types and tokens of Nim's linear combinations we observed before using the reduction rules employed to minimize the contribution of repeated signs. The appendix shows a complete listing of all combinations of 2, 3, 4, 5, or more signs *following* application of the reduction rules.

The length of an utterance was related inversely to its frequency. This was true both in the case of types and tokens. As of April 1976, the frequency of new types of 3-sign combinations exceeded that of 2-sign combinations, and as of June 1976, the frequency of combinations of 5 or more signs exceeded that of 4-sign combinations. The reasons for the crossing of these functions was, however, different in each case. The frequency of 5-sign combinations per se was consistently lower than that of 4-sign combinations, but Nim began to make combinations longer than 5 signs with increased frequency. In the case of the 2- and 3-sign functions, the frequency of 3-sign types did in fact exceed that of 2-sign types. This could be a consequence of Nim's elaborating what he learned to say with two signs by adding a third sign; for example, *Joyce tickle me* rather than *tickle me,* or a consequence of adding a relevant, but redundant, sign for emphasis (see the later section, "Relationship between Nim's 2-, 3-, and 4-sign combinations").

The sheer variety of Nim's combinations and the fact that he was not required to combine signs suffices to show that Nim's combinations were not learned by rote. Considering only Nim's 2- and 3-sign combinations, the occurrence of more than 2,700 types of combinations would strain the capacity of any known estimate of a chimpanzee's memory. As mentioned earlier, however, a large variety of combinations is not sufficient to demonstrate that such combinations are sentences; that is, that they express a semantic proposition in a rule-governed sequence of signs. In the absence of additional evidence, the most parsimonious explanation of Nim's utterances is that they are unstructured combinations of signs, in which each sign is appropriate to the situation at hand.

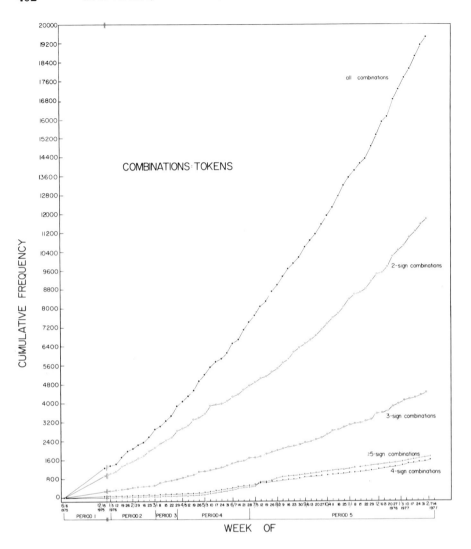

COMBINATIONS: TOKENS

all combinations

2-sign combinations

3-sign combinations

≥5-sign combinations

4-sign combinations

CUMULATIVE FREQUENCY

PERIOD I     PERIOD 2     PERIOD 3     PERIOD 4     PERIOD 5

WEEK   OF

*Figure 8-22.* Cumulative number of tokens of linear combinations during the period June 16, 1975–February 7, 1977.

Nevertheless, the regularity and the variety of Nim's 2-sign combinations suggest that some structural rules may be needed to account for their construction. Table III shows all 2-sign combinations of the corpus containing *more*. There were considerably more types and tokens containing *more* in the first position than in the second position, irrespective of whether *more* was combined with signs designating objects (e.g., *banana*) or actions (e.g., *tickle*). A similar state of affairs can be seen in Table IV, which shows all 2-sign combinations containing *give*. Here again there is a strong tendency for *give* to occur in the first position. The regularities shown in Tables III and IV (as well as in Tables V-VII below) were apparent through each of the five time-periods during which these data were obtained.

In the case of combinations containing *more,* it might be argued that Nim modeled the construction *more + X* after his teachers' utterances. Often a teacher would sign to Nim, *more + X?,* to see if Nim would sign *more* or *X* in reply. On this view, Nim learned to sign *more + X* by first imitating a few instances of *more + X* and then generalizing this construction to new

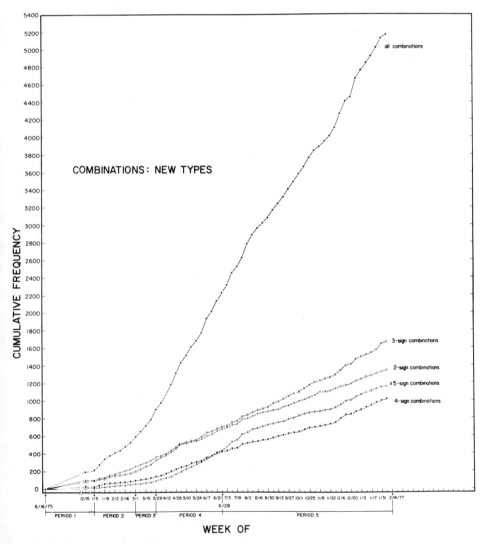

*Figure 8-23.* Cumulative number of types of linear combinations during the period June 16, 1975–February 7, 1977.

## Table III
## Two-Sign Combinations Containing *more*

| | *more* +X | | | *X* +*more* | |
|---|---|---|---|---|---|
| **Types** | | **Tokens** | **Types** | | **Tokens** |
| more | apple | 12 | apple | more | 5 |
| | | | baby | more | 1 |
| more | ball | 2 | | | |
| more | banana | 62 | banana | more | 5 |
| more | berry | 2 | | | |
| more | bill | 1 | | | |
| more | bite | 2 | | | |
| more | brush | 5 | | | |
| more | chair | 19 | chair | more | 3 |
| more | drink | 99 | drink | more | 14 |
| more | eat | 287 | eat | more | 58 |
| more | fruit | 2 | | | |
| more | give | 1 | give | more | 1 |
| more | go | 7 | go | more | 2 |
| more | grape | 11 | grape | more | 2 |
| more | groom | 4 | | | |
| more | gum | 29 | gum | more | 1 |
| more | hand cream | 23 | hand cream | more | 5 |
| | | | hat | more | 2 |
| more | hug | 16 | hug | more | 3 |
| more | hurry | 1 | hurry | more | 2 |
| more | in | 1 | | | |
| more | jump | 1 | | | |
| more | key | 1 | | | |
| more | listen | 1 | | | |
| more | me | 42 | me | more | 12 |
| more | Nim | 24 | Nim | more | 7 |
| more | nut | 11 | nut | more | 3 |
| more | open | 1 | | | |
| more | orange | 6 | | | |
| more | paint | 1 | | | |
| more | peach | 2 | | | |
| more | pair | 13 | | | |
| more | play | 41 | play | more | 7 |
| more | pole | 9 | pole | more | 1 |
| more | raisin | 1 | raisin | more | 1 |
| | | | red | more | 1 |
| more | shoe | 2 | shoe | more | 1 |
| more | smell | 3 | | | |
| more | spoon | 2 | | | |
| more | sweet | 14 | sweet | more | 5 |
| more | swing | 1 | | | |
| more | tea | 23 | tea | more | 8 |
| more | tickle | 136 | tickle | more | 23 |
| more | toothbrush | 3 | toothbrush | more | 23 |
| more | up | 1 | | | |
| more | water | 10 | water | more | 1 |
| more | what | 6 | | | |
| more | yogurt | 5 | yogurt | more | 2 |
| **Totals:** | 47 | 974 | 27 | | 174 |

## Table IV
## Two-Sign Combinations Containing *give*

| give +X | | | X +give | | |
|---|---|---|---|---|---|
| Types | | Tokens | Types | | Tokens |
| give + | apple | 9 | apple +give | | 3 |
| | baby | 1 | baby | | 1 |
| | ball | 14 | ball | | 1 |
| | bananna | 7 | | | |
| | black | 1 | | | |
| | blue | 2 | | | |
| | brown | 1 | | | |
| | brush | 3 | brush | | 2 |
| | bug | 2 | | | |
| | clean | 1 | | | |
| | | | come | | 3 |
| | | | cracker | | 2 |
| | crayon | 2 | | | |
| | dog | 1 | | | |
| | drink | 15 | drink | | 7 |
| | eat | 54 | eat | | 12 |
| | finish | 1 | finish | | 3 |
| | flower | 2 | | | |
| | grape | 3 | grape | | 1 |
| | gum | 4 | gum | | 3 |
| | hand cream | 14 | hand cream | | 3 |
| | harmonica | 2 | | | |
| | here | 1 | | | |
| | hug | 3 | hug | | 1 |
| | hungry | 2 | | | |
| | hurry | 2 | | | |
| | jump | 2 | | | |
| | key | 1 | | | |
| | kiss | 1 | | | |
| | light | 2 | light | | 2 |
| | listen | 1 | | | |
| | point | 6 | point | | 2 |
| | me | 41 | me | | 11 |
| | more | 3 | | | |
| | Nim | 23 | Nim | | 4 |
| | nut | 2 | nut | | 2 |
| | open | 2 | open | | 2 |
| | orange | 3 | | | |
| | out | 1 | | | |
| | pear | 2 | pear | | 2 |
| | play | 1 | play | | 3 |
| | raisin | 2 | raisin | | 2 |
| | red | 2 | | | |
| | rock | 1 | | | |

*(continued)*

**Table IV (Continued)**
**Two-Sign Combinations Containing** *give*

| give + X | | X + give | |
|---|---|---|---|
| **Types** | **Tokens** | **Types** | **Tokens** |
| | | shoe | 1 |
| smell | 1 | | |
| spoon | 1 | | |
| sweet | 6 | | |
| tea | 1 | | |
| that | 4 | | |
| tickle | 1 | | |
| toothbrush | 4 | | |
| water | 9 | water | 4 |
| what | 1 | | |
| Totals:   51 | 271 | 24 | 77 |

objects and actions. Such generalization would be necessary because Nim produced most of the first tokens of each type of *more + X* combination without any modeling by the teacher. This type of explanation seems less cogent in the case of *give + X*. Nim began signing *give + X* reliably long before his teachers asked Nim to give them objects by signing *give + X*.

Two other interesting examples of regularities in Nim's 2-sign combinations can be seen in his use of transitive verbs and in his reference to himself as *me* or *Nim*. Table V shows Nim's 2-sign sequences in which transitive verbs such as *hug, open,* or *tickle* were combined either with *me* or *Nim*. The number of tokens with the verb in the first position far exceeds the reverse construction.

On some occasions, Nim's teachers queried Nim with questions such as *tickle you*? in order to prompt him to sign before tickling him. In these instances simple imitation of the teacher's signing could explain Nim's preference for signing the verb in the first position of the sequence types shown in Table V. Nim, however, was signing *tickle me* quite regularly, long before his teachers asked Nim to tickle them by signing *tickle + teacher's-name-sign*. Furthermore, the argument that Nim was imitating his teachers' questions does not apply in the case of other transitive verbs shown in Table V (e.g., *finish*). Nim was not asked questions in which these signs could have served as models.

Table V also shows that Nim combined transitive verbs as readily with *Nim* as with *me*. The number of types of sequences containing *Nim* and *me* are essentially the same. That there are more tokens of 2-sign combinations containing *me* than *Nim* is perhaps best explained by the fact that Nim learned the sign *me* before he learned the sign Nim. During Period V (July 5, 1976–February 7, 1977 ages 33–39 months), the frequencies with which *Nim* and *me* were combined with transitive verbs was essentially the same.

Nim's preference for using *me* and *Nim* in the second position of 2-sign combinations can also be seen in requests for items of food and drink. Table VI shows all 2-sign combinations containing *me* and *Nim* as combined with either food or drink nouns. The signs *me* and *Nim* tend to follow food and drink nouns in 2-sign combinations. A somewhat smaller preference for the location of the signs *me* and *Nim* is apparent in the case of 2-sign combinations in which these signs were combined with nonfood/-drink nouns (cf. Table VII).

The proportion of tokens in which *me* and *Nim* appears in the second position was highest when those signs were combined with transitive verbs (0.83), next highest when combined with food and drink nouns (0.75), and lowest when combined with nonfood and nondrink nouns (0.65). Why the different frequencies of combining the signs *me* and *Nim* with these categories of signs? One explanation is that when Nim combined transitive

### Table V
### Two-Sign Combinations Containing *me* or *Nim* and Transitive Verbs (V[t])

| V(t) +me | | V(t) +Nim | | me +V(t) | | Nim +V(t) | |
|---|---|---|---|---|---|---|---|
| **Types** | **Tokens** | **Types** | **Tokens** | **Types** | **Tokens** | **Types** | **Tokens** |
| bite me | 3 | bite Nim | 2 | me bite | 2 | | |
| break me | 2 | | | | | | |
| brush me | 35 | brush Nim | 13 | me brush | 9 | Nim brush | 4 |
| clean me | 2 | clean Nim | 1 | me clean | 2 | | |
| | | | | me cook | 1 | | |
| | | draw Nim | 1 | | | | |
| finish me | 1 | finish Nim | 7 | | | Nim finish | 1 |
| give me | 41 | give Nim | 23 | me give | 11 | Nim give | 4 |
| | | | | | | Nim go | 4 |
| groom me | 21 | groom Nim | 6 | | | Nim groom | 1 |
| help me | 6 | help Nim | 4 | me help | 2 | | |
| hug me | 74 | hug Nim | 106 | me hug | 40 | Nim hug | 23 |
| kiss me | 1 | kiss Nim | 6 | me kiss | 1 | Nim kiss | 2 |
| open me | 13 | open Nim | 6 | me open | 10 | Nim open | 5 |
| | | pull Nim | 1 | | | | |
| tickle me | 316 | tickle Nim | 107 | me tickle | 20 | Nim tickle | 16 |
| Totals: 12 | 515 | 13 | 283 | 10 | 98 | 9 | 60 |

Total Types: 25
Total Tokens: 788

Total Types: 19
Total Tokens: 158

## Table VI
## Two-Sign Combinations of Nim +Noun or Me +Noun (food/drink)

| Noun +Nim | | | Noun +me | | | Nim + Noun | | | me +Noun | | |
|---|---|---|---|---|---|---|---|---|---|---|---|
| Types | | Tokens | Types | | Tokens | Types | | Tokens | Types | | Tokens |
| apple | Nim | 65 | apple | me | 27 | Nim | apple | 25 | me | apple | 17 |
| banana | Nim | 73 | banana | me | 97 | Nim | banana | 18 | me | banana | 34 |
| berry | Nim | 1 | berry | me | 2 | | | | | | |
| cracker | Nim | 21 | cracker | me | 3 | Nim | cracker | 3 | me | cracker | 1 |
| egg | Nim | 2 | egg | me | 2 | | | | | | |
| fruit | Nim | 11 | fruit | me | 1 | Nim | fruit | 6 | | | |
| grape | Nim | 21 | grape | me | 12 | Nim | grape | 5 | me | grape | 2 |
| gum | Nim | 47 | gum | me | 19 | Nim | gum | 21 | me | gum | 43 |
| nut | Nim | 71 | nut | me | 16 | Nim | nut | 9 | me | nut | 4 |
| orange | Nim | 4 | | | | | | | | | |
| pancake | Nim | 2 | pancake | me | 2 | | | | | | |
| peach | Nim | 3 | | | | Nim | peach | 1 | me | peach | 1 |
| pear | Nim | 20 | pear | me | 4 | Nim | pear | 4 | | | |
| raisin | Nim | 23 | raisin | me | 5 | Nim | raisin | 6 | me | raisin | 4 |
| sweet | Nim | 85 | sweet | me | 23 | Nim | sweet | 13 | me | sweet | 8 |
| tea | Nim | 14 | tea | me | 17 | Nim | tea | 7 | me | tea | 13 |
| water | Nim | 10 | water | me | 13 | Nim | water | 2 | me | water | 5 |
| yogurt | Nim | 57 | yogurt | me | 2 | Nim | yogurt | 8 | me | yogurt | 1 |
| Totals: 18 | | 530 | 14 | | 245 | 14 | | 28 | 12 | | 133 |

Total Types: 34  
Total Tokens: 775

Total Types: 26  
Total Tokens: 261

verbs with food or drink nouns, he was using the signs *me* and *Nim* mainly as what would be an indirect object in a sentence. However, when Nim signed about objects that were neither edible nor drinkable, he may have signed *me* and *Nim* to indicate possession on some occasions, and to refer to himself as an indirect object on other occasions. For example, when Nim signed *hat me,* he may have been asking his teacher to give him the hat. But when he signed *me hat,* he may have been saying that he regarded the hat as his. These and other interpretations of Nim's signing will be considered below in our semantic analysis of Nim's 2-sign combinations.

The fact that certain categories tend to appear more frequently in the first position (for instance, transitive verbs and *more*) and certain ones in the second position (for example, *me* and *Nim*) indicates that Nim differentiated between the first and the second positions of 2-sign sequences. Further, the absence of a universal pattern with which *me* or *Nim* is combined with other types of signs suggests that Nim was not using simple position habits to form combinations. However, different frequency patterns, such as those shown in Tables III–VII, are not sufficient to demonstrate

**Table VII**
**Two-Sign Combination of Nim +Noun or me +Noun (nonfood/drink)**

| Noun +Nim | | | Noun +me | | | Nim +Noun | | | me +Noun | | |
|---|---|---|---|---|---|---|---|---|---|---|---|
| Types | | Tokens | Types | | Tokens | Types | | Tokens | Types | | Tokens |
| baby | Nim | 20 | baby | me | 2 | Nim | baby | 6 | | | |
| ball | Nim | 6 | ball | me | 7 | | | | me | ball | 10 |
| | | | | | | Nim | bird | 1 | | | |
| book | Nim | 2 | | | | Nim | book | 1 | me | book | 3 |
| brush | Nim | 13 | brush | me | 35 | Nim | brush | 4 | me | brush | 9 |
| bug | Nim | 1 | | | | Nim | bug | 1 | | | |
| | | | cat | me | 1 | | | | | | |
| chair | Nim | 2 | chair | me | 1 | Nim | chair | 2 | | | |
| | | | | | | Nim | color | 2 | | | |
| | | | dog | me | 2 | | | | | | |
| | | | | | | | | | me | flower | 1 |
| hand- | Nim | 6 | hand- | me | 4 | Nim | hand- | 7 | me | hand- | 3 |
| cream | | | cream | | | | cream | | | cream | |
| harmon- | Nim | 1 | harmon- | me | 1 | | | | | | |
| ica | | | ica | | | | | | | | |
| hat | Nim | 3 | hat | me | 20 | Nim | hat | 8 | me | hat | 26 |
| ice | Nim | 2 | | | | | | | | | |
| key | Nim | 1 | key | me | 3 | Nim | key | 1 | | | |
| | | | | | | Nim | music | 1 | | | |
| pants | Nim | 2 | pants | me | 4 | Nim | pants | 1 | me | pants | 2 |
| | | | | | | Nim | paper | 1 | | | |
| pole | Nim | 1 | pole | me | 2 | | | | me | pole | 1 |
| shoe | Nim | 3 | shoe | me | 4 | Nim | shoe | 1 | me | shoe | 1 |
| smell | Nim | 2 | smell | me | 1 | | | | me | smell | 1 |
| socks | Nim | 1 | | | | | | | | | |
| spoon | Nim | 3 | spoon | me | 1 | | | | | | |
| | | | time | me | 1 | | | | | | |
| tooth- | Nim | 17 | tooth- | me | 6 | Nim | tooth- | 4 | me | tooth- | 1 |
| brush | Nim | 17 | brush | | | | brush | | | brush | |
| Totals: 18 | | 86 | 17 | | 95 | 15 | | 41 | 11 | | 58 |
| | | | Total Types: 35 | | | | | | Total Types: 26 | | |
| | | | Total Tokens: 181 | | | | | | Total Types: 99 | | |

that Nim's sequences are constrained structurally. Nim could have a set of independent first- and second-position "habits" that generated the distributional regularities we observed. A conservative interpretation of these regularities which does not require the postulation of syntactic rules would hold that Nim used certain categories as relatively "initial" or "final," irrespective of the context in which they occur. If this were true, it should be possible to predict the observed frequency of different constructions, such as *verb + me* or *verb + Nim,* from the relative frequency of their constituents in the initial and final positions.

The accuracy of such predictions was tested as follows. First, each sign of a 2-sign sequence was assigned to a lexical category. These categories, and the relative frequency of their occurrence in the first and second positions, are shown in Table VIII. In some instances, specific signs were given as lexical types because they were the only examples of a particular kind of sign (for example, *me* was the only personal pronoun) or because their status as a particular lexical type was ambiguous (for instance, it was not always clear when *eat* and *drink* were used as nouns or verbs).

The relative frequencies shown in Table VIII were used to predict the probabilities of 2-sign lexical types which occurred at least 10 times. The predicted value of the probability of a particular sequence was calculated by multiplying the probabilities of the relevant lexical types appearing in the

## Table VIII
### Frequencies of Lexical Types by Position in 2-Sign Combinations (types whose frequencies ≥ 10)

| Lexical Type | First Position Frequency | | Second Position Frequency | |
|---|---|---|---|---|
| | Absolute | Relative | Absolute | Relative |
| Noun (animate—human) | 59 | 0.0066 | 149 | 0.0164 |
| Noun (animate—nonhuman) | 33 | 0.0037 | 29 | 0.0032 |
| Noun (inanimate—food) | 1453 | 0.1616 | 999 | 0.1100 |
| Noun (inanimate—nonfood) | 430 | 0.0478 | 477 | 0.0525 |
| Adjective (personal) | 353 | 0.0393 | 160 | 0.0176 |
| Adjective (nonpersonal) | 89 | 0.0099 | 100 | 0.0110 |
| Verb (transitive) | 1371 | 0.1525 | 1243 | 0.1368 |
| Verb (intransitive) | 729 | 0.0811 | 269 | 0.0296 |
| point | 283 | 0.0315 | 368 | 0.0405 |
| drink | 376 | 0.0418 | 461 | 0.0508 |
| eat | 924 | 0.1028 | 1358 | 0.1495 |
| give | 238 | 0.0265 | 42 | 0.0046 |
| me | 1088 | 0.1210 | 1530 | 0.1684 |
| more | 931 | 0.1036 | 156 | 0.0171 |
| Nim | 634 | 0.0705 | 1743 | 0.1919 |

first and second positions respectively. In predicting the probability of *me eat,* for example, the probability of *me* in the first position (0.121) was multiplied by the probability of *eat* in the second position (0.149). This yielded a predicted relative frequency of 0.016. The observed relative frequency of *me eat* was 0.024. In the case of some lexical types, the agreement between the observed and predicted probabilities is quite good; as, for example, noun (animate, food) + *me.* There were, however, many discrepancies between predicted and observed probabilities.

A comparison of the predicted and observed probabilities of the lexical sequences generated by combining the lexical categories shown in Table VIII does not provide strong support for an independent position model. The correlation between 124 pairs of predicted and observed probabilities was 0.0036. The average predicted probability was 0.015; the average value of the absolute deviation between predicted and observed relative frequencies was 0.007. Since the average predicted probability did not differ substantially from the average value of the absolute deviation between predicted and observed relative frequencies, and since the correlation between these probabilities was essentially zero, it seems reasonable to conclude that overall, Nim's 2-sign sequences are not formed by independent position habits for each item. The same conclusion would follow if we relaxed our conservative rule of considering only reliable two-sign lexical types.

A similar analysis was performed on reliable 3-sign utterances (frequency $\geq$ 5). Table IX shows the probability of a particular lexical category appearing in each position of a 3-sign sequence. The average value of the predicted relative frequencies of the 66 lexical types we considered was 0.0011; the average value of the absolute deviation between observed and predicted values was 0.0012. The correlation between the 66 pairs of predicted and observed probabilities was 0.05. Similar results obtained when all 3-sign combinations were considered. As in the case of 2-sign combinations, it is not possible to predict the observed relative frequencies of lexical types of 3-sign combinations from the relative frequencies of their constituents in a particular serial position.

## Relationship between Nim's 2-, 3-, and 4-sign combinations

As children's utterances grow in length, it is possible to discern how their initially short utterances are elaborated so as to provide additional information about some topic (Bloom, 1973; Brown, 1973). For example, instead of saying *sit chair,* the child might say *sit daddy chair.* In general it is possible to characterize long utterances as a composite of shorter constituents which were mastered separately. Longer utterances are not, however, unstructured concatenations of short utterances. In making longer utterances, the child combines words in short utterances in just one order; he deletes repeated elements and he treats shorter utterances as units when they are used to expand what was expressed previously by a single word.

Our corpus of Nim's combinations allowed us to evaluate the lexical similarity between Nim's 2- and 3-sign combinations. The 25 most frequent 2- and 3-sign combination types and their absolute frequencies are shown in Table X. A comparison of these combinations reveals that, from a lexical point of view, the topic of Nim's 3-sign combinations overlapped considerably with the topic of his 2-sign combinations. Eighteen of Nim's 25 most frequent 2-sign combination types can be seen in his 25 most frequent 3-sign combination types, in virtually the same order in which they appear in his 2-sign combinations. A striking similarity emerges between Nim's 2- and 3-sign combinations if one considers only the signs that appeared in 2-sign combinations (and not their order of occurrence). All but 5 signs which appear in Nim's 25 most frequent 2-sign combinations appear in his 25 most frequent 3-sign combinations. The 5 exceptions are *gum, tea, sorry, in,* and *pants.* (The combination *in pants* was the least frequent 2-sign combination shown in Table X. It occurred mainly during dressing and after trips to the toilet.)

With the few exceptions noted, it appears as if the topic of Nim's signing remained the same whether he produced a 3-sign or a 2-sign combination. We did not have enough contextual information to perform a semantic analysis of all of Nim's 2- and 3-sign combinations. However, Nim's teach-

**Table IX**

**Frequency of Lexical Types by Position in 3-sign Combinations**
**(types whose frequency ≥ 10)**

| Lexical Type | First Position Abs. | Rel. | Second Position Abs. | Rel. | Third Position Abs. | Rel. | Total |
|---|---|---|---|---|---|---|---|
| Adjective | 91 | 0.3105 | 70 | 0.0239 | 84 | 0.0287 | 245 |
| Noun (inanimate) | 780 | 0.2662 | 342 | 0.1167 | 494 | 0.1686 | 1616 |
| Noun (animate) | 60 | 0.0205 | 50 | 0.0171 | 73 | 0.0249 | 183 |
| verb | 504 | 0.1720 | 257 | 0.0877 | 363 | 0.1239 | 1124 |
| drink | 13 | 0.0471 | 127 | 0.0433 | 133 | 0.0454 | 398 |
| eat | 363 | 0.1239 | 499 | 0.1703 | 559 | 0.1908 | 1421 |
| me | 297 | 0.1014 | 735 | 0.2509 | 267 | 0.0911 | 1299 |
| more | 178 | 0.0608 | 108 | 0.0386 | 65 | 0.0222 | 351 |
| Nim | 225 | 0.0768 | 623 | 0.2126 | 718 | 0.2451 | 1566 |
| wh- | 13 | 0.0044 | 6 | 0.0020 | 7 | 0.0024 | 26 |
| you | 36 | 0.0123 | 6 | 0.0020 | 28 | 0.0096 | 70 |
| give | 147 | 0.0502 | 37 | 0.0126 | 33 | 0.0113 | 217 |
| other | 16 | 0.0055 | 11 | 0.0038 | 7 | 0.0024 | 34 |
| point | 45 | 0.1534 | 44 | 0.0150 | 80 | 0.0273 | 169 |

## Table X
### Twenty-five Most Frequent 2- and 3-sign Combination Types

| 2-Sign Comb. | | Frequency | 3-Sign Comb. | | | Frequency |
|---|---|---|---|---|---|---|
| play | me | 375 | play | me | Nim | 81 |
| me | Nim | 328 | eat | me | Nim | 48 |
| tickle | me | 316 | eat | Nim | eat | 46 |
| eat | Nim | 302 | tickle | me | Nim | 44 |
| more | eat | 287 | grape | eat | Nim | 37 |
| me | eat | 237 | banana | Nim | eat | 33 |
| Nim | eat | 209 | Nim | me | eat | 27 |
| finish | hug | 187 | banana | eat | Nim | 26 |
| drink | Nim | 143 | eat | me | eat | 22 |
| more | tickle | 136 | me | Nim | eat | 21 |
| sorry | hug | 123 | hug | me | Nim | 20 |
| tickle | Nim | 107 | yogurt | Nim | eat | 20 |
| hug | Nim | 106 | me | more | eat | 19 |
| more | drink | 99 | more | eat | Nim | 19 |
| eat | drink | 98 | finish | hug | Nim | 18 |
| banana | me | 97 | banana | me | eat | 17 |
| Nim | me | 89 | Nim | eat | Nim | 17 |
| sweet | Nim | 85 | tickle | me | tickle | 17 |
| me | play | 81 | apple | me | eat | 15 |
| gum | eat | 79 | eat | Nim | me | 15 |
| tea | drink | 77 | give | me | eat | 15 |
| grape | eat | 74 | nut | Nim | nut | 15 |
| hug | me | 74 | drink | me | Nim | 14 |
| banana | Nim | 73 | hug | Nim | hug | 14 |
| in | pants | 70 | play | me | play | 14 |
| | | | sweet | Nim | sweet | 14 |

ers' reports indicate that the individual signs of his combinations were appropriate to their context and that equivalent 2- and 3-sign combinations occurred in the same context.

Though lexically related to 2-sign combinations, the 3-sign combinations shown in Table X do not appear to be informative elaborations of 2-sign combinations. Rather they seem to be redundant with 2-sign utterances. Consider, for example, Nim's most frequent 2- and 3-sign combinations: *play me* and *play me Nim.* Adding *Nim* to *play me* to produce the 3-sign combination *play me Nim,* adds a redundant proper noun to a personal pronoun. A further complication is revealed when one considers an alternative derivation of the 3-sign combination *play me Nim.* It could have occurred by adding the single sign, *play,* to Nim's second most frequent 2-sign combination, *me Nim.* Even when one takes into account the relative frequencies of single signs (cf. Table I), there is no obvious way to choose between the two derivations of *play me Nim* suggested by Table X: *play me + Nim* and *play + me Nim*. Similar alternatives present themselves when trying to derive the other 3-sign combinations shown in Table X.

Another aspect of Nim's 3-sign combinations which suggests that they are not informative elaborations of 2-sign combinations is the occurrence of combinations in which the same sign is repeated; for example, *eat Nim eat, nut Nim nut,* and so on. Ten of the most frequent combination types contain *me* and *Nim;* 8 contain a repetition of the same sign. Of the 2,925 tokens of 3-sign combinations, 460 (16 percent) contain *Nim* and *me,* and 591 (20 percent) contain the repetition of a sign (cf. Appendix). In producing a 3-sign combination, it appears as if Nim is adding emphasis rather than new information.

Nim's 4-sign combinations reveal a similar picture. Table XI shows all 4-sign combinations whose frequency is equal to or greater than three. Fifteen of the 21 types of signs shown in Table XI contain repetitions of some signs; for example, *eat banana Nim eat* and *grape eat Nim eat.* If *me* and *Nim* are equated on the grounds that they have the same referent, 20 of the 21 combinations shown in Table XI repeat the same sign. That leaves but one combination type, *me eat drink more,* which contains 4 distinctly different signs. Seven of the 21 combinations shown in Table XI repeat 2-sign combinations in the same order; for example, *drink Nim drink Nim* and *me gum me gum.* Similar generalizations hold for the remainder of all of Nim's combinations containing 4, 5, or more signs (cf. Appendix). Of the 708 tokens of 4-sign combinations, 123 (17 percent) contain *Nim* and *me,* and 379 (54 percent) contain a repetition of the same sign. Of the 309 tokens of combinations containing 5 or more signs, 116 (37 percent) contain *Nim* and *me,* and 165 (54 percent) contain a repetition of the same sign. If combinations containing *Nim* and *me* and repetitions of the same sign are considered redundant, there is a clear increase in redundancy as Nim's combinations grow in length: 35 percent of 3-sign combinations, 71 percent of 4-sign combinations, and 91 percent of combinations containing 5 or more signs were redundant.

## Differences Between Nim's and a Child's Utterances

Instead of adding new information when producing combinations of 3, 4, or 5 or more signs, Nim seems to be simply repeating or emphasizing what he signed in shorter combinations. The absence of a difference between the semantic and syntactic complexities of Nim's short and long utterances is but one of a number of differences between the initial multiword utterances of Nim and a child. As far as we can tell from published reports describing children's utterances, the repetition in an utterance of a word or

**Table XI**
**Twenty-one Most Frequent 4-Sign Combination Types**

| 4-Sign Comb. | Frequency |
| --- | --- |
| eat drink eat drink | 15 |
| eat Nim eat Nim | 7 |
| banana Nim banana Nim | 5 |
| drink Nim drink Nim | 5 |
| banana eat me Nim | 4 |
| banana me eat banana | 4 |
| banana me Nim me | 4 |
| grape eat Nim eat | 4 |
| Nim eat Nim eat | 4 |
| play me Nim play | 4 |
| drink eat drink eat | 3 |
| drink eat me Nim | 3 |
| eat grape eat Nim | 3 |
| eat me Nim drink | 3 |
| grape eat me Nim | 3 |
| me eat drink more | 3 |
| me eat me eat | 3 |
| me gum me gum | 3 |
| me Nim eat me | 3 |
| Nim me Nim me | 3 |
| tickle me Nim play | 3 |

sequence of words that were not considered to be examples of stuttering, is a rather rare event (Colburn, 1979). It is rather the case that each additional word of a child's utterance tends to provide information which is integrated semantically and syntactically into existing structures.

Other differences between Nim's signing and that of a child are elaborated below. The many differences indicate that Nim's general use of combinations bears only a superficial similarity to the early utterances of children. Most of the comparisons we will make draw upon data obtained from studies of the acquisition of spoken language by hearing children of hearing parents. Nim was taught by hearing teachers who were not uniformly fluent signers. Accordingly, studies describing the acquisition of sign language by deaf children of hearing parents would provide the most relevant point of reference for evaluating the data we obtained from Nim. However, to the extent that data are available from deaf children (of either deaf or hearing parents) there is no evidence that any major differences exist between the general features of language acquisition by deaf and hearing children (Newport & Ashbrook, 1977; Hoffmeister, 1972; Klima & Bellugi, 1972).

## The mean length of Nim's utterances

Recent studies of language acquisition in children suggest certain universal patterns of language development. One important observation is the orderly increase in the mean length of a child's utterances (MLU) which is accompanied by a progressive increase in their complexity (Bloom, 1973; Brown, 1973). In English, for example, subject-verb and verb-object construction merge into subject-verb-object constructions. As evidenced by Nim's longer utterances, length per se does not imply an increase in grammatical complexity. An increase in MLU is, however, a necessary condition for the production of the many types of construction that demonstrate a knowledge of grammar.

In calculating a child's MLU, certain conventions are followed which cannot be applied directly to sequences of signs. A spoken utterance, for example, is broken down into morphemes rather than words: *running* and *run there* would each be regarded as a 2-morpheme utterance. In sign language, the utterance *run there* can be expressed by a single sign[13]. Despite these and other difficulties in measuring MLU in a sign language, it serves as a rough measure of a child's linguistic development.

Figure 8-24 shows Nim's MLU (the mean number of signs in each utterance) between the ages of 26 and 45 months. The method used to calculate Nim's MLU differed somewhat from the one that is generally followed in child language studies (Brown, 1973). Nim's MLU was calculated as follows: (1) All intelligible single sign utterances were counted. Excluded were ambiguous single-sign utterances or movements that were approximations of signs. (2) Repetitions of signs in multisign utterances were first collapsed; i.e., wherever the same sign occurred successively, only one occurrence of that sign was counted. Thus an utterance such as *Nim eat eat apple apple,* which contains 5 signs with 2 successive repetitions, was counted as a 3-sign utterance. Approximations were included in combinations. (3) Instances of nonlinear signing, such as contractions and simultaneous signs, were not included. (4) An utterance was not adjusted in any way to account for its relationship to the teacher's prior utterance. This is in contrast to Bloom (1973), who does not count words in a child's utterance which have appeared in any of the adults' 5 prior utterances. (5) The entire sign record from beginning to end was used regardless of the length of the transcript. (6) The total number of signs in the utterances that were counted was divided by the number of utterances to yield the MLU.

The functions showing Nim's MLU between January 1976 and February 1977 (age 26-39 months) are based on data obtained from teachers reports; the function showing Nim's MLU between February 1976 and August 1977 (ages 27–45 months) is based upon video-transcript data. The most striking aspect of these functions is the lack of growth of Nim's MLU during a 19-month period.

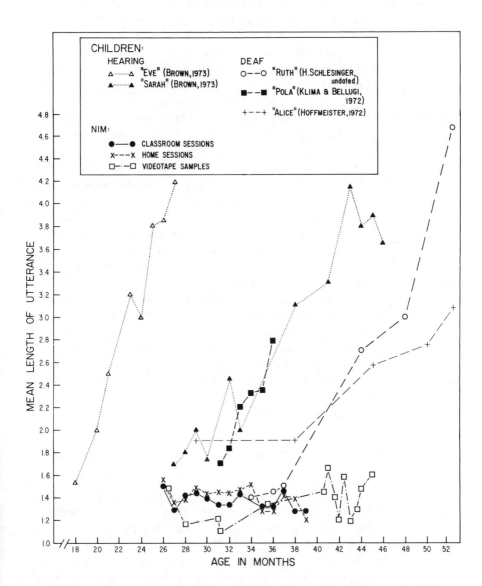

*Figure 8-24.* Mean length of signed utterances of Nim and three deaf children, and mean length of spoken utterances of two hearing children. See note 68 regarding the calculation of MLU's for signed utterances.

Figure 8-24 also shows comparable MLU functions obtained from hearing (speaking) and deaf (signing) children. The function based upon Sarah's utterances shows the longest delay in the growth of MLU that we could locate in the literature on language development in speaking children; the MLU function from the other speaking child (Eve) begins to rise at a much younger age. The 3 remaining functions (based upon Ruth's, Pola's, and Alice's utterances) show the MLU of deaf children learning sign language (Klima & Bellugi, 1972; Schlesinger, personal communication 1975; Hoffmeister, 1972). All children start at an MLU similar to Nim's at 26 months. But unlike Nim's flat MLU functions, the functions obtained from children all show increases in MLU.

The lack of growth of Nim's MLU defines a major difference between the development of language in young apes and children. Another difference has to do with the value of the MLU and its upper bound. According to Brown, "the upper bound of the (MLU) distribution is very reliably related to the mean . . . At MLU = 2.0 the upper bound will be, most liberally, $5 + 2$" (Brown, personal communication, 1978). Nim, however, made utterances containing as many as 16 signs (e.g., *give orange me give eat orange me eat orange give me eat orange give me you*) with an MLU that never exceeded 1.6. This is at variance with the relationship between the upper bound of the MLU distribution and a child's MLU. We have already noted that Nim's longer utterances were neither semantic or syntactic elaborations of his shorter utterances. In our discourse analyses of Nim's and Washoe's signing (see the following sections, "Discourse Analysis" and "Comparisons of Nim's Discourse With That of Other Signing Apes"), we will suggest other mechanisms which lengthen an ape's utterance but do not presuppose an increase in semantic or syntactic competence.

## Semantic relationships expressed in Nim's 2-sign combinations

The regularities we observed in our distributional analysis of Nim's 2-sign combinations are lexical: certain lexical categories occur in the initial or in the final position when combined with other signs. These regularities provide no direct information about the intended meaning of Nim's combinations, nor do they reveal whether they express a limited set of semantic relationships. Unlike lexical distributions, semantic distributions cannot be constructed directly from a corpus. In order to derive a semantic distribution, observers have to make judgments as to what each combination means. Procedures for making such judgments, introduced by Bloom (1970) and Schlesinger (1971), are known as the method of "rich interpretation" (Bloom, 1970, 1973; Brown, 1973). An observer relates certain aspects of the utterance's immediate context to its contents. By considering the meanings of the individual words and the roles played by their referents it is often possible to infer a particular semantic interpretation of the relationships between the words of a child's utterance.

The challenge of the method of rich interpretation is not only to make specific judgments but to demonstrate their validity as well. Bloom's (1970, 1973) important insight concerning semantic interpretations was to specify how the validity of such interpretations could be evaluated by independent evidence from the corpus. Supporting evidence includes the following observations. The child's choice of word order is usually the same as it would be if the idea were being expressed in the canonical adult form. In some cases, word order is also used contrastively, and in at least one child, intonational differences were observed that were associated with differences in meaning (Bloom, 1973; Bowerman, 1973a; Brown, 1973). As the child's MLU increases, semantic relationships identified by a rich interpretation develop in an orderly fashion. The relationships expressed in 2-word combinations are the first ones to appear in the 3- and 4-word combinations. Many longer utterances appear to be composites of the semantic relationships expressed in shorter utterances. For example, action-object, agent-action, and agent-object relationships merge into an agent-action-object relationship. New semantic relationships are first expressed in short utterances. These are often imitations and reductions of the adult's prior utterance. The initial difficulty of expressing new semantic relationships apparently results in their expression in utterances that are the least taxing for the child (Bloom, 1973; Brown, 1973).

Studies of an ape's ability to express semantic relationships in combinations of two or more signs have yet to advance beyond the stage of unvalidated interpretation. The Gardners interpreted 294 types of Washoe's 2-sign combinations and concluded that 78 percent of these combinations were interpretable in categories similar to those used to describe 2-word utterances of children (Gardner & Gardner, 1971). A similar analysis was performed by Patterson (1978) on 2-sign combinations emitted by the gorilla Koko. No data are available as to the reliability of the interpretations that the Gardners and Patterson have advanced. Because of the paucity of combinations of 3 or more signs it has not been possible to observe, in combinations of more than 2 signs, the elaboration of semantic relationships used to describe Washoe's and Koko's 2-sign combinations.

Without prejudging whether Nim actually expressed semantic relationships in his combinations, 1,262 of his more recent 2-sign combinations were analyzed by the method of rich interpretation. Three of Nim's teachers examined the 2-sign combinations which they recorded in their session reports between mid-December 1976, when Nim was 25 months old, and early June 1977, when Nim was 31 months old (Joyce Butler, 48 reports; Dick Sanders, 58 reports; Bill Tynan, 48 reports). After interpreting the utterances of their own sessions, each teacher interpreted the utterances of one of the other two teachers. They agreed in their interpretations of 717 utterances (57 percent of the original corpus). Disagreements resulted as frequently from different judgments about whether an utterance could be interpreted at all (and, if so, interpreted unambiguously) as from different semantic judgements per se. The disagreements resulted in part (23 percent) because of differences in semantic interpretations and in part (20 percent) because of differences in judgments regarding the interpretability of an utterance. An attempt was made to resolve disagreements through discussions between the two relevant teachers and reference to their records. If a disagreement could not be resolved, the utterance was considered ambiguous and disregarded. Contextual notes in the teachers' records included sufficient information for the teachers to agree as to the interpretation of 967 2-sign combinations (77 percent of the original corpus). In the remaining cases (N = 295), no interpretation could be made (N = 260), or two or more equally reasonable interpretations were made which could not be disambiguated (N = 35). It should be noted, however, that none of our conclusions would be altered if we used either of the interpretations of the 35 combinations which could not be resolved.

Table XII contains 20 categories of semantic relationships which account for 895 (93 percent) of the 967 interpretable 2-sign combinations. Brown (1970) found that there were eleven semantic relationships which account for about 75 percent of all combinations of the children he studied. Similarly, the Gardners (1971) reported that nine categories account for 78 percent of a sample of Washoe's 2-sign combinations, and Patterson (1978) reported that eleven categories accounted for 75 percent of Koko's 2-sign combinations. Table XII compares our semantic categories with those used by Brown, the Gardners, and Patterson. It should be apparent that the number of categories used for interpreting a child's or an ape's early combinations is arbitrary. Our twenty categories could be collapsed roughly into seven in Brown's, with two left over; into eight in the Gardners' system, with two left over; and into eleven in Patterson's system, with one left over.

The results of our semantic analysis are shown in Figure 8-25. In several instances there were significant preferences for placing signs expressing a particular semantic role in either the first or the second positions. Agent, attribute, and recurrence (*more*) were expressed by signs in the first position in 80 percent, 67 percent, and 84 percent of the respective 2-sign combinations in which they occurred. Place and beneficiary roles were expressed by second-position signs in 73 percent and 64 percent of the respective 2-sign combinations in which they occurred.

At first glance, the results of our semantic analysis appear to be consistent with the observations of the Gardners and Patterson. But even though our judgments were shown to be reliable, there are several features of our

## Table XII
## Semantic Categories

| Brown | Patterson | Gardners | Terrace et al. |
|---|---|---|---|
| Nomination | Nomination | — | — |
| Notice | — | — | — |
| Recurrence | Recurrence | Appeal-object | Recurrence-entity<br>Recurrence-attribute of entity<br>Recurrence-action<br>Recurrence-beneficiary<br>Recurrence-place |
| Nonexistence | Nonexistence | — | — |
| Attribute-entity | Attribute-entity<br><br>Attribute-person-state | Object-attribute<br><br>Agent-attribute | Attribute-entity |
| Possessive | Genitive | Agent-object<br><br>Object-attribute | |
| Locative: N + N | | (not applicable) | Agent-place<br>Entity-place<br>Attribute of entity-place |
| | Locative | Action-location | Action-place<br><br>Locative prep.-place |
| Locative: N&V | | Action-object<br><br>Object-location | Entity-locative prep. |
| — | Dative | — | Action-beneficiary<br>Object-beneficiary<br>Attribute of object-beneficiary |
| Agent-action | Agent-action | Agent-action | Agent-action |

*(continued)*

**Table XIII** (*Continued*)
**Semantic Categories**

| Brown | Patterson | Gardners | Terrace et al. |
|---|---|---|---|
| Action-object | Action-object | Action-object | Action-object<br><br>Action-attribute of object |
| Agent-object | Agent-object | Agent-object | Agent-object |
| — | Appeal | Appeal-action<br><br>Appeal-object | (Various) |
| — | — | — | Two propositions |

results which suggest that our analysis may exaggerate the level of semantic competence (as may the analyses of the Gardners and Patterson). Our results also call into question the validity of a rich interpretation of the semantic contents of an ape's 2-sign combinations.

One problem rests on the subjective nature of semantic interpretations. That problem can be remedied only to the extent that evidence corroborating the psychological reality of our interpretations is available (Brown, 1973; Fodor, Bever, & Garrett, 1974; Macnamara, 1972). Neither our study, nor any of the other studies which present "semantic" analyses of an ape's 2-sign combinations, have produced such corroborative evidence. In some cases, utterances were inherently equivocal in our records. Accordingly, somewhat arbitrary rules were used to interpret these utterances. Consider, for example, combinations of *Nim* and *me* with an object name (for instance, *Nim banana*). These occurred when the teacher held up an object that he or she was about to give to Nim who in turn would ingest it. We had no clear basis for distinguishing between the following semantic interpretations of combinations containing *Nim* or *me* and an object name: agent-object, beneficiary-object, and possessor-possessed-object. An additional complication was that in many of these cases, *Nim* or *me* was combined with *eat* or *drink*. Not only was it impossible to determine whether Nim was an agent, beneficiary, or possessor in these cases, but it was also impossible to determine whether *eat* and *drink* referred to consumable objects or to actions. An arbitrary decision was made to assign these cases to the object-beneficiary category, a category which showed a preferred sign order in the clear instances and which also accounted for eighteen percent of the utterances shown in Figure 8-25. This decision may have also contributed to the absence of genitive relationships in our data.

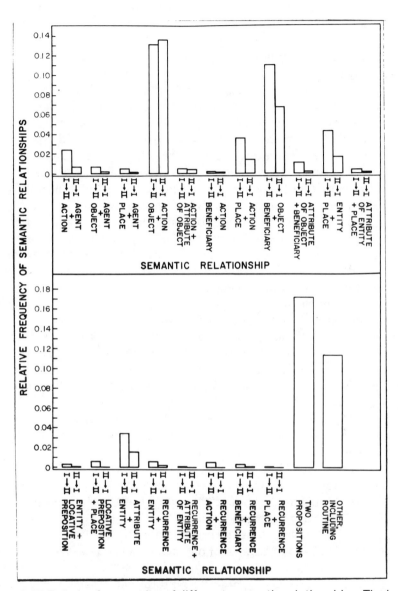

*Figure 8-25.* Relative frequencies of different semantic relationships. The bars above I ⟶ II show the relative frequencies of 2-sign combinations expressing the relationship in the order specified under the bar; e.g. an agent followed by an action. The bars above II ⟶ I show the relative frequencies of 2-sign combinations expressing the same relationship in the reverse order, an action followed by an agent.

An equally serious problem is posed by the very small number of lexical items used to express particular semantic roles. Only when a semantic role is represented by a large variety of signs is it reasonable to attribute position preferences to semantic rules rather than to lexical position habits. Ninety percent of the combinations interpreted as an expression of location contained only one exemplar of that semantic role: the sign *point* (including *up* and *down;* see note 9 for details). A similar state of affairs exists in the case of combinations interpreted as expressions of recurrence. That role was represented exclusively by *more.* In combinations presumed to relate an agent and an object or an object and a beneficiary, one would expect agents and beneficiaries to be expressed by a broad range of agents and beneficiaries; for example, *Nim, me, you,* and names of other animate beings. However, 99 percent (N = 297) of the beneficiaries in utterances judged to be object-beneficiary combinations were *Nim* and *me,* and 76 percent (N = 35) of the agents in utterances judged to be agent-object combinations were *you.* In both agent-object and object-beneficiary combinations, *Nim* and *me* occurred predominantly in the second position (in 64 percent and 68 percent of these combinations, respectively). Accordingly, it is difficult to decide whether the positional regularities favoring agent-object and object-beneficiary constructions (cf. Figure 8-25) are expressions of semantic relationships or idiosyncratic lexical position habits.

In contrast with those cases, combinations describing an action and an object contained a considerable variety of terms in both semantic roles. Even though overall position effects were not found in the case of combinations describing an action and an object, idiosyncratic order effects involving particular signs were noted[14]. *Tickle* was in the first position in all 11 utterances containing *tickle* that were judged as action-object combinations; *play* was in the first position in all but one of the 10 such combinations containing *play. Me* occurred in the second position on 12 occasions, and never in the first position. *Nim,* on the other hand, was in the first position in 16 of the 21 action-object combinations containing *Nim. Drink* and *hug* were in the first position in 11 out of 15 cases and 13 out of 16 cases respectively, while *out* occurred in the second position in 17 out of 23 cases. Even though the number of combinations in these examples is not large, many of the regularities we observed are statistically significant. It is also of interest that similar idiosyncratic orders involving particular signs were apparent in the large corpus we collected in order to perform our distributional analysis. For example, in 313 combinations of the signs *eat* and *me, me* occurred in the second position in 76 percent of the cases, while *Nim* occurred in the second position in about half (59 percent) of the 511 combinations of *eat* and *Nim.* In the 186 combinations of *drink* and *Nim, Nim* occurred in the second position 77 percent of the time, while *me* occurred in the second position with *drink* in about half (44 percent) of 116 cases. In combinations of *eat* and *drink* and food nouns, there were no overall position preferences. There were, however, individual cases showing strong position preferences: *gum* occurred in the first position with *eat* in 83 percent of the 95 cases, and *tea* occurred in the first position with *drink* in all of the 77 cases. As far as we can tell, there is no common thread running through these apparently idiosyncratic patterns that would justify their description by semantic rules rather than by lexical position habits.

In addition to the relational combinations we observed (cf. Table X), 166 combinations were assigned nonrelational interpretations, apparently expressing the conjunction of elements from two propositions; for example, *tickle hug, dirty run, apple nut,* and *in play.* Such expressions have not been reported in previous ape studies. In children, the development of two proposition elements does not occur generally until the MLU passes 2.0, when clauses begin to appear. Prior to that, what appear to be two propositions are actually chained single utterances occurring within the same speech event (Bloom & Lahey, 1977; also see Bloom, Lightbown, & Hood, 1975).

An analysis of video transcripts revealed yet another spurious source of the semantic look of Nim's combinations: the extent to which Nim's utterances were initiated by his teacher's signing and were imitations of his teacher's preceding utterance. An utterance can be considered to be imitative if it contains some or all of the signs of the teacher's prior utterance. In many cases, Nim's teachers were able to judge whether a combination was spontaneous or an imitation of an immediately prior teacher's utterance. Nevertheless, *all* 2-sign combinations were included in the semantic analysis. Since imitations were included in the corpus, it is possible that the semantic relationships and position preferences we observed are to some extent reflections of teachers' signing habits that were imitated, in full or in part, by Nim. Those that were imitated should not be regarded as comparable to a child's nonimitative constructions. In order to provide a general picture of the relationship between Nim's utterances and those of his teacher, we analyzed a corpus of Nim's utterances recorded on videotape, for which we could specify the linguistic as well as the nonlinguistic context.

Painstaking transcriptions of our videotapes revealed certain aspects of Nim's signing that were not apparent to his teachers in the course of normal observation. None of Nim's teachers, nor the many expert observers who were fluent in sign language, detected either the extent to which the initiation and contents of Nim's signing were dependent upon the teacher's signing or the degree to which Nim interrupted his teachers. Having convinced ourselves that Nim's signing was not *simple* imitation, our limited powers of attention were directed more to the contents of his signing and its nonverbal context than to the precise relationship between the teacher's input and Nim's output of signs. The contrast between the conclusions that might be drawn from our distributional analyses and those that follow from our discourse analysis poses an important methodological lesson. In the absence of a permanent record of an ape's signing, and the context in which that signing occurred, an objectively assembled corpus of the ape's utterances does not provide a sufficient basis for drawing conclusions about the grammatical regularities of those utterances.

## Discourse analysis

During recent years there has been increasing interest in the way parents speak to their children (Newport, 1976; Snow, 1972) and in the ways children adjust their speech to aspects of the prior verbal context (Bloom, Rocissano, & Hood, 1976). In its early discourse, a child relates to its parents' speech by often relying on imitation and on contextually obvious topics. That type of discourse appears to be the crucible in which the child's knowledge of pragmatics, semantics, and syntax of its language is formed.

Fillmore (1973) has likened adult conversations to a game in which two participants take turns moving a topic along. Children learn quite early that conversation is such a turn-taking game (Stern, Jaffee, Beebe, & Bennett 1975). Our discourse analysis reveals that the relationship between Nim's and his teacher's utterances is fundamentally different from the one that obtains between a child's utterances and those of its parents. All of the available data concerning Washoe's discourse with her teachers (which will be described below) reveal a similar difference between a chimpanzee's and a child's conversations with their adult teachers.

In our initial analysis of some of the ways in which the signs used by Nim are related to the prior verbal context, we transcribed and analyzed three-and-one-half hours' of videotapes from nine sessions recorded between February 1976 and July 1977, when Nim was between 26 and 44 months old[15]. Each tape was transcribed by the teacher who worked with Nim. Only single signs and linear combinations were used in our discourse analysis. They accounted for 95 percent of the transcribed utterances. An initial check of the remaining 5 percent of the utterances (simultaneous combinations and contraction) indicated that the results of our discourse analysis would remain the same if all of Nim's utterances were included in the analysis.

In order to check the reliability of our transcripts, short segments of five tapes were transcribed by two independent transcribers, both of whom were teachers from the project. The most conservative analysis of reliability we performed included all of the following categories: (1) Unambiguous signs: Both transcribers perceive a clearly interpretable sign and agree as to its designation. (2) Equivocal signs: Transcriber 1 cannot decide between the sign specified by transcriber 2 and one other sign. (3) Nonverbal gestures: These include hand movements that are part of the chimpanzee's natural repertoire of movements. The topographies of these movements overlap with certain signs; for example, scratching the head (similar to *Nim*), pointing (similar to *point*), or waving an arm (similar to *hurry*). (4) "X" signs: These are gestures which look like signs but which are not part of Nim's otherwise attested expressive vocabulary. (5) Molded signs: These are molded by the teacher. (6) Not visible: The transcriber believes a sign occurred but Nim was not sufficiently visible to allow a clear interpretation of it. (7) Nonreport of a sign: One transcriber fails to perceive a sign which the other transcriber reported. (8) Nonreport of a repeated sign: This is the same as (7), but the sign in question was an immediate repetition of a sign about which both transcribers agreed.

In his transcripts, transcriber 1 made 231 entries that Nim had signed. The transcript of transcriber 2 agreed with that of transcriber 1, 104 times, or in 71 percent of the cases in which both transcribers stated that a sign occurred. Transcriber 2 made 209 entries of signs in his transcript. Transcriber 1 agreed with transcriber 2's entries of signs 104 times, or in 78 percent of the cases in which both transcribers stated that a sign occurred. The average of these values, 74.5 percent, underestimates the degree of agreement concerning the data used in our discourse analysis. Molded signs, "X" signs, and nonverbal gestures did not enter into our discourse analysis. The failure to detect a repetition of an immediately preceding sign also did not alter the outcome of our discourse analysis. A final correction of our estimate of reliability has to do with the status of entries in the "equivocal" category as sources of disagreement. In these cases, one transcriber reported sign $X$ and the other transcriber reported sign $X$ or sign $Y$. It was not the case, however, that each of the transcribers reported different signs. Accordingly, it is reasonable to assign a weight of 0.75 to the entries in the "equivocal" category [0.5 for transcriber 1, who reported only $X$, plus 0.25 for transcriber 2, who reported $X$ or $Y$. The above corrections of the reliability estimate yielded a transcriber 1–transcriber 2 agreement of 80.4 percent (176 agreements/219 observations) and a transcriber 2–transcriber 1 agreement of 81.3 percent (165 agreements/203 observations)]. The average agreement between the two transcribers was 81 percent.

A comparison of Nim's discourse with his teachers and children's discourse with adults (cf. Bloom, Rocissano, & Hood, 1976) is shown in Figure 8-26. Adjacent utterances are those which follow an adult utterance without a definitive pause. The most appropriate stage of development for comparing Nim's and a child's utterances is when their MLU's are the same. At 21 months (MLU = 1.4), the average proportion of a child's utterances that are adjacent is 69.2 percent (range 53–78 percent). A somewhat higher percentage (87 percent) of Nim's utterances were classified as adjacent (range 58.7–90.9 percent).

Adjacent utterances were assigned to one of four mutually exclusive

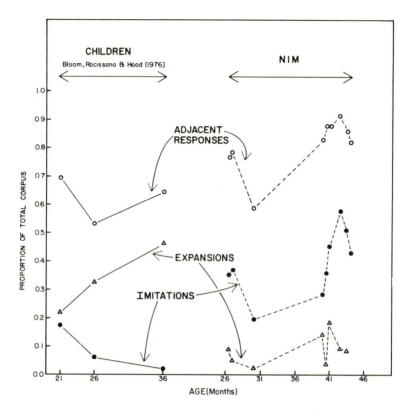

*Figure 8-26.* Proportion of utterances emitted by children (left-hand functions) and by Nim (right-hand functions) which are adjacent to. imitative of, or expansions of, an adult's prior utterance.

categories: (1) *imitations* were those utterances which contained all of the lexical items of the adult's utterances, and nothing else; (2) *reductions* were those utterances which contained some of the lexical items of the adult's utterance and nothing else; (3) *expansions* were those utterances which contained some of the lexical items of the adult's utterance along with some new lexical items; and (4) *novel utterances* were those utterances which contained none of the lexical items of the adult's utterance.

How do Nim's responses to an immediately prior teacher's utterance, on the 509 occasions when he produced an adjacent utterance, compare with the adjacent utterances of children? Among the children studied by Bloom and her colleagues, imitations and reductions accounted for 18 percent (cf. Figure 8-26) of all of the children's utterances at Stage I (MLU = 1.3). That figure decreased with increasing MLU, accounting for only 2 percent of the children's utterances at Stage V (MLU = 3.9). On the average,

39.1 percent adjacent utterances of Nim's adjacent utterances were imitations or reductions (range 19.5–57.1 percent).

At Stage I, 21.2 percent of a child's utterances were expansions of the adult's prior utterance (range 10–28 percent). On the average, only 7.3 percent of Nim's utterances were expansions of his teacher's prior utterance (range 1–15 percent). As the child gets older, the proportion of its utterances that are expansions increases. Bloom and her colleagues (1976) noted that many of the child's utterances were systematic expansions of verb relations contained in the adult's prior utterance. No such pattern was discernable in Nim's expansions. Indeed, a preliminary analysis of Nim's expansions indicates that aside from the teacher's signs, his utterances contain only a small number of additional signs; e.g., *me, Nim, you, hug,* and *eat.* In the sense that Nim's signs are not specific to particular contexts, these signs do not add new information to the teacher's utterance. In fact, the sole function of the teacher's signs seems to be to provide a model which tells Nim what signs are appropriate for particular requests. Unlike the adjacency of children's utterances, the adjacency of Nim's signs to his teacher's signs does not appear to result in informative communication between Nim and his teacher.

Adjacent utterances which follow a prior adult utterance would constitute evidence of turn-taking in discourse. On the other hand, a child who interrupts by beginning to talk during a parent's utterance would provide evidence against an understanding of the principle that the speaker and the listener alternate their messages to one another.

By definition, adjacent utterances may include interruptions of a teacher's or an adult's utterance. Such interruptions detract from true discourse since they result in utterances which are simultaneous rather than successive. We know of no data on the relative frequency or duration of simultaneous utterances that occur in dialogues between children and adults in either spoken or sign language. However, both Bloom (1977) and Bellugi (1977) have reported that interruptions are virtually nonexistent in their videotapes of children learning vocal and sign languages.

Simultaneous signing by Nim and his teacher occurred in 71 percent of the utterances which have been examined (425 out of 585). Seventy percent of these simultaneous utterances occurred when Nim began an utterance while the teacher was signing. When the teacher interrupted one of Nim's utterances, it was generally the case that Nim had just interrupted the teacher and the teacher was, in effect, asserting his or her right to hold the floor. Nim's interruptions showed no evidence that they were in response to the teacher's attempts to take the floor from him.

Our analysis of Nim's discourse with his teachers has revealed that the vast majority of Nim's utterances were occasioned by the teacher's signing and that many of Nim's signs were identical with those of his teacher's most recent utterance(s). Nim imitated what his teacher signed more than twice as frequently as a Stage-I child would in similar circumstances. Nim interrupted his teacher's signing quite frequently and thereby deviated from the pattern of give and take which characterizes discourse between a child and its parents. It is also the case that as a child gains experience in discourse, its frequency of imitation decreases. No such trend was observed in Nim's discourse.

An unanticipated, but instructive, example of the influence of the teacher's signing on Nim's signing can be seen in Figure 8-21, which presents a series of still photographs (taken with a motor-driven camera) of Nim signing *me hug cat.* A careful examination of Figure 8-21 (which was prompted by the results of our discourse analysis) reveals that Nim's teacher signed *you* while Nim was signing *me;* and *who?* while Nim was signing *cat.* Because these were the only four photographs taken of this discourse, we cannot specify just when the teacher began her signs. It is not clear, for example, whether the teacher signed *you* simultaneously or immediately prior to Nim's *me.* It is, however, unlikely that the teacher signed *who?* after Nim signed *cat.* Inspection of Figures 8-9, 8-17, 8-18, and 8-19 also reveal similar patterns of discourse between Nim and his teachers. In Figure 8-9, Nim's teacher is signing *no* in response to Nim's prior utterance, a poorly formed *more* sign (not shown). In Figure 8-17, Nim is signing *Nim* in response to his teacher's query *who?* In Figure 8-18, Nim is signing *hug* in response to his teachers's prompting of that sign. In Figure 8-19, Nim is signing *me* in response to his teacher's signing *mine.* At the very least, these photographs demonstrate the importance of discourse analysis for revealing the extent to which Nim's utterances were influenced by his teacher's signing.

## Comparison of Nim's discourse with that of other signing apes

One valuable source of information which suggests that Nim's discourse with his teachers was not specific to the conditions of our project is a 59-minute film produced by Nova, entitled, *The First Signs of Washoe*[16]. This film, which is mainly about Washoe's signing, also presents brief scenes showing Ally (Nim's full brother) signing with Fouts at the Oklahoma Primate Center, and Koko signing with Patterson in Koko's trailer home. Another film, *Teaching Sign Language to the Chimpanzee: Washoe* (Gardner & Gardner, 1973), which was produced by the Gardners, shows somewhat longer versions of a number of conversations presented in the Nova film. Both films provide good examples of discourse between Washoe and her teachers. A comparison of the longer and the shorter versions of the same conversation provides an instructive example of the importance of capturing as much of the teacher's prior utterance as possible in performing a discourse analysis.

In one scene of the Nova film, Washoe is shown signing *time eat* to B. Gardner. The discourse between Washoe and B. Gardner is presented in the transcript that follows below. Since the films we analyzed were edited, it was not possible to establish a fixed temporal point of reference for the occurrence of each sign. In this and in ensuing transcripts, the time of occurrence of each sign was specified with respect to the first sign of that portion of the transcript (arbitrarily designated 00:00). Time in the film was measured by counting the number of frames from the beginning of each scene.[17] The beginning and the end of each utterance are marked by slashes. Other behavior is described in parentheses.

Consider the following complete scene from *First Signs of Washoe:* In this conversation, Washoe's utterances either followed or interrupted B. Gardner's utterance. It is also the case that the sign *time* was uttered by B. Gardner just prior to Washoe's utterance *time eat.* (In passing, we should note that the Gardners have yet to present detailed evidence that Washoe understood the meaning of the sign *time.* In this and in other examples of its usage it seems as if Washoe learned that it was an appropriate response when requesting food or some other incentive.)

*Teaching Sign Language to the Chimpanzee: Washoe* presents a longer version of the same conversation:

*Time*
*(Seconds)*

| | | | | | |
|---|---|---|---|---|---|
| 00.00 | BG.: | */eat* | | | |
| 00.42 | | *me/* | | | |
| 02.38 | | */more* | | | |
| 02.80 | | *me* | | *(mine)/* | |
| 03.34 | | (W | feeds | BG) | |
| 07.09 | | /thank | | you/ | |
| 10.92 | | */what* | | | |
| 12.38 | | *time/* | | | |
| 12.88 | | | | W: | */time* |
| 13.17 | | *now?/* | | | *eat/* |
| 15.42 | | | | | */ t i m e* |
| 15.76 | | | | | *eat/* |

· · · · · · · · · · · · · · · · · · · · · · · · · · · · · splice · · · · · · · · · · · · · · · · · · · · · · · · · · · ·

| | | | | |
|---|---|---|---|---|
| 00.00 | BG: | */what* | | |
| 00.46 | | *now?/* | | |
| 00.29 | | */what* | W: | */in* |
| 04.79 | | *now* | | *in/* |
| 05.33 | | | | */me* |
| 05.67 | | | | *eat* |
| 06.17 | | | | *time* |
| 06.38 | | | | *eat/* |

The film reveals that both signs of Washoe's utterance *time eat* were signed by B. Gardner immediately prior to Washoe's having signed them.

*Time eat* cannot be considered a spontaneous utterance for two reasons. It was a response to a request to sign by B. Gardner, and it imitated some of the signs just signed by her.

The significance of a full record of discourse between a chimpanzee and its teacher is also revealed by the segment which follows the splice. Suppose that one considered Washoe's combination *me eat time eat* in isolation. Without knowledge of the teacher's prior utterances it would be all too easy to interpret Washoe's utterance as one that signifies a description of future behavior and a knowledge of time. Our analysis of discourse between B. Gardner and Washoe also shows that three out of Washoe's four utterances interrupted B. Gardner's utterances.

Another instructive example of the influence of the teacher on the production of Washoe's signs is provided by the utterance, *baby in my drink,* a combination of four signs described in both films as a creative use of sign language by Washoe. In this sequence, the order of Washoe's signs reflect the order in which the teacher first signed about the referents of Washoe's signs. The actual exchange between Washoe and her teacher, Susan Nichols, is shown below:

| Time (Seconds) | | | | |
|---|---|---|---|---|
| 00:00 | SN: | /that/ (points to cup) | | |
| 00:29 | | (brings cup and doll closer to W. SN allows W to touch it; SN slowly pulls it away) | W: | /baby/ |
| 05:37 | SN: | /that/ (points to cup) | W: | /in/ |
| | | | | (looks away from SN) |
| | SN: | (Brings the cup and doll closer to W) | | |
| | | | W: | (looks back at cup and doll) |
| 08.17 | | | | |
| | | | W: | /baby/ |
| | SN: | (Brings cup closer to W) | | |
| 10.58 | | | W: | /in/ |
| 11.46 | SN: | /that/ (points to cup) | W: | /my |
| 11.42 | | | | drink/ |

In this example of what was actually a "run-on" sequence, two of Washoe's four signs were prompted. It is important to note that the sequence of the promptings (pointing to the doll and then pointing to the cup) follows the order called for by an English prepositional phrase. Only the last two signs, *my* and *drink,* occurred without intervening prompting on the part of the teacher. For these reasons alone, Washoe's actual sequence of signs, *baby in* (pause) *baby in my drink,* cannot be regarded as a clear instance of a spontaneously generated utterance.

   In the immediate preceding scene of the film, Susan was shown drilling
Washoe extensively about a *baby in shoe* and an *apple in hat*. In both cases
Washoe was trying to grab the desired object from the teacher. This suggests that Washoe's sign *my,* in *baby in baby in my drink* was signed to
convey to her teacher that she wanted the doll. Given this type of drill, and
the teacher's pointing to the objects to be named in the appropriate sequence, it seems unwarranted to claim that the utterance is a creative,
spontaneous juxtaposition of signs that conveyed the meaning "a doll in
Washoe's cup."
   As a final example of Washoe's discourse with her teachers, consider
the following conversation about Washoe's intelligence:

*Time
(Seconds)*

| | | | | |
|---|---|---|---|---|
| 00.00 | SN: | *who stupid?* | | |
| 00.42 | | | W: | *Susan, Susan* |
| 05.30 | SN: | *who stupid?* | | |
| 05.58 | | | W: | *stupid* |
| 06.42 | SN: | *who?* | | |
| 06.72 | | | W: | *Washoe* |
| 07.04 | SN: | *Washoe* | | |
| 07:36 | | (tickles Washoe) | | |

   This sequence also appears to be a drill. The important question it
raises, however, is whether Washoe actually understood the meanings of
*stupid* (and *smart*). Her usage of *stupid* was clearly prompted by the
teacher. The exchange between Washoe and Susan also terminated at the
point at which the teacher got Washoe to make the signs *stupid* and
*Washoe*. The circumstances under which this sequence of signs occurred
raises questions about the validity of the Gardner's semantic analysis of
combinations such as *Naiomi good* (Gardner and Gardner, 1971). That
combination was presented as an example of attribution, an interpretation
which would be appropriate only in the absence of the kinds of prompting
and reward shown in the films of Washoe signing.
   This film (*The First Signs of Washoe*) shows 156 of Washoe's utterances. One hundred and twenty are single-sign utterances. These occurr mainly
in vocabulary testing sessions. Each of Washoe's multisign sequences (24
2-sign, 6 3-sign, and 5 4-sign sequences) are preceded by a similar utterance
or prompting from her teacher. Thus, Washoe's utterances often are adjacent to and imitative of her teachers'.
   The short segments of the Nova film showing Ally and Koko signing
reveals a similar relationship between the ape's and the teacher's signing. In
each case, the teacher signed first to initiate the "conversation." Ninety-
two percent of Ally's, and all of Koko's, signs are imitations of the
teacher's prior sign.

The data provided by a single film are admittedly much more limited in scope than data we obtained from our nine videotapes. It seems reasonable to assume, however, that the segments shown in these films, the only films publicly available of apes signing, present some of the best examples of Washoe's, Ally's, and Koko's signing at the time when the films were made. Even more so than our transcripts, these films showed a consistent tendency for the teacher to initiate signing and for the signing of the ape to mirror the teacher's signs.

## OTHER EVIDENCE BEARING ON AN APE'S GRAMMATICAL CAPACITY

Our evaluation of an ape's grammatical capacity has focused exclusively on the production of sequences of signs. We have yet to consider other evidence which has been used to substantiate the claim that apes can produce and understand sentences. In evaluating this evidence it is important to keep in mind the lack of a single decisive test to indicate whether a particular sequence of words qualifies as a sentence or whether a particular performance qualifies as an instance of grammatically guided sentence comprehension (Bloom, 1973; Brown, 1973).

It has been widely observed that the early sequences of words uttered by a child do not necessarily qualify as sentences (Bloom & Lahey, 1977; Braine, 1976; Brown, 1973). Indeed, if a child's initial utterances and his responses to his parents' utterances constituted the only evidence of his linguistic ability, there would be little reason to conclude that a child's production and comprehension of words are governed by a grammar (Bloom, 1973). A "rich interpretation" of a child's early utterances assumes that they are constrained by structural rules (Bowerman, 1973b; Bloom, 1970, 1973; Brown, 1973). It is difficult, however, to exclude simpler accounts of such utterances. A child's isolated utterance of a sequence of words could be a haphazard concatenation of words which bear no structural relationship to one another (Brown, 1973). Even frequently occurring sequences of words may be interpreted as routines that the child learned by rote as imitations of his parents' speech (Braine, 1976).

As children get older, the variety and complexity of their utterances increase gradually. Especially telling is the observation that children pass through phases in which they produce systematically incorrect classes of utterance. During these phrases the child "tries out" different sets of rules before arriving at the correct grammar. Children are also able to discriminate grammatically correct from incorrect sentences (Bever, 1975). Accordingly, explanations of their utterances which are not based upon a grammar become too unwieldy to defend (Bloom & Lahey, 1977).

## Production of Sequences

As is the case with a child, the mere occurrence of a sequence of words uttered by a chimpanzee does not warrant its designation as a sentence. Before regarding such utterances as sentences, it is necessary to discredit simpler interpretations. Consider some examples of sequence production on the part of Sarah and Lana. As a result of rote training, both Sarah and Lana learned to produce specific sequences of words; for example, *please machine give apple* (Rumbaugh, 1977), or *Mary give Sarah chocolate* (Premack, 1976). Subsequently both Sarah and Lana learned to substitute certain new words in order to obtain other incentives from the same or from other agents (for example, *Randy give Sarah apple, please machine give drink,* or *please machine show slide*). In the last sequence, Lana showed evidence that she could use a different "verb" (*show*) in conjunction with a different category of incentives. These incentives were *slide, window,* and *music* (Rumbaugh, 1977).

Sarah's and Lana's multisign utterances are interpretable as rotely learned sequences of arbitrary symbols arranged in particular orders; for instance, *Mary give Sarah apple,* or *please machine give apple.* There is good reason to doubt whether Lana and Sarah understood the meaning of all of the "words" in the sequences they produced. Except for the names of the objects they requested, Sarah and Lana showed little evidence of being able to substitute other symbols in each of the remaining positions of the sequences they learned (Terrace, 1979a). Accordingly it seems more prudent to regard the sequences of lexigrams glossed as *please, machine,* and *give* or plastic chips glossed as *Mary, Sarah,* and *give* as sequences of nonsense symbols rather than as sequences of words.

Consider comparable responding to nonsense symbols in a fixed order by a pigeon. Terrace, Straub, Bever & Seidenberg (1977) and Straub, Seidenberg, Bever, & Terrace (1979) have shown that pigeons can learn to peck arrays of four colors in a particular sequence: green — white — red — blue, irrespective of the physical position of the colors. In this experiment, all of the colors were presented simultaneously and there was no step-by-step feedback following each response. Evidence that the subjects learned the overall sequence, and not simply the specific responses required by the 15 training arrays, was provided by performance which was considerably better than chance on four novel arrays. Such performance demonstrates that pigeons can master serial learning tasks comparable to those mastered by Sarah and Lana. It has yet to be shown that pigeons can master ABC$X$

problems (where X1 could refer to one type of grain, X2 to a different type of grain, X3 to water, X4 to the opportunity to see or to attack another pigeon, and so on). If a pigeon can learn such sequences (a not unlikely outcome) one wonders what is to be gained by assigning "names" to each member of the sequence; for example, referring to the sequence green, white, red, blue, as *machine give R-42 grain.*

Sequences of symbols produced by an ape may seem grammatically related to one another in the eyes of human observers. It does not, however, follow that the chimpanzee had any knowledge of the relationships inferred by a human observer (Limber, 1977; Mounin, 1976; Seidenberg & Petitto, 1979b). As difficult as it may be to train an ape, or any organism, to produce a sequence of arbitrary responses which may look like a sentence, it is even more difficult to show that those sequences have the structural properties of human sentences (Bloom & Lahey, 1977; Dale, 1976).

## Comprehension of Multisymbol Sequences

An inherent difficulty in using apparent comprehension as an indicator of a child's syntactic competence is the frequent presence of nonsyntactic cues to meaning (Bever, 1970; Brown, 1973; Fodor, Bever, & Garrett, 1974; Macnamara, 1972). This can be controlled if sentence comprehension experiments are designed to exclude semantic and extralinguistic cues. However, many purported examples of sentence comprehension by chimpanzees can be explained as nonsyntactic problem-solving behavior. For example, when Sarah was given two pieces of colored paper, she learned to arrange them in response to instructions such as *color 1 on color 2.* Premack (1976) interpreted this behavior as evidence that Sarah comprehended the preposition *on.* Two extra-linguistic cues render this interpretation questionable. As was generally true, *all* of the problems of the relevant training and testing sessions focused on one feature of language, in this case, *on.* During each trial, Sarah was required to put one piece of paper on the other. She could have learned to solve this problem simply by attending to the symbol, *color 1.* That color was *always* to be placed on top of the other color. This rather simple strategy requires no understanding of the relationship between the symbol glossed as *on* and the symbols for the other two colors. When three choices of color were available, the problem was somewhat more difficult because Sarah had to attend to both color names. The context, however, still sufficed to define the task of putting one piece of paper on another. Similar considerations reveal that more complex problems, which seem to require an understanding of the syntactic structure of the instruction (for example, conditional instructions and instructions presented in hierarchical form), could be solved by applying nonsyntactic rules (Terrace, 1979a).

Demonstrations by Premack, Rumbaugh, and the Gardners that their chimpanzees can answer *wh*-questions correctly is evidence of the memory capacity of a chimpanzee. There is little reason, however, to conclude that these chimpanzees comprehend *wh*-questions. In each case, the chimpanzees were drilled extensively on the correct answers to questions such as *color that? what that?,* and so on (Gardner & Gardner, 1975b). The only alternatives present when Sarah was asked *color that?* were the symbols designating various colors (Premack, 1976). For most tests, only two alternative color names were provided. On similar problems, alternating questions were presented to Lana which asked her first to identify the color and then the name of certain objects. Even though this type of problem was slightly more complex than those posed to Sarah, correct performance does not imply an understanding of the interrogative. Lana simply had to match the lexigram shown to her (*name of* vs. *color of*) with the appropriate subset of alternatives available on her console. If, for example, *name of* was presented, she had to restrict her choice to object names, a task on which she had been drilled extensively in earlier problem sets.

Each example of Sarah's and Lana's purported use of language was obtained in a constant setting with repeated problems of the same nature and with a restricted number and variety of answers. These conditions were ideal for the establishment of learning sets and the use of nonsyntactic strategies in solving these problems. Without a greater variety of problems and a greater range of possible answers, the results of such studies should not be interpreted as "linguistic" (Limber, 1977; Mounin, 1976; Seidenberg & Petitto, 1979b; Terrace, 1979a).

In their effort to demonstrate comprehension of *wh*-questions, the Gardners accepted as correct *any* response they designated as being lexically appropriate response. For example, if Washoe signed *blue* in answer to *what color?* when she was shown a red ball, *blue* was considered "correct" because it was a color. The significant correlation the Gardners report between question forms and response forms shows that Washoe learned to respond to category questions with signs from the appropriate category: colors, trainers' names, actions, and so on. However, many of her specific answers were clearly inappropriate. The Gardners nevertheless concluded that Washoe's performance is comparable to that of a child at Stage III in Brown's scheme for describing the development of language in children.

At Stage III, children are not only able to produce correct answers to simple *wh*-questions, but they are also able to produce a variety of constructions whose mean length exceeds 2.75 morphemes. The significance of analyzing child language in terms of stages derives largely from the structural complexities which a child masters, in a cumulative fashion, at each point of its development. The Gardners' conclusion ignores these aspects of a child's language development.

## SUMMARY AND CONCLUSIONS

Taken together, the available data indicate that apes can learn extensive vocabularies of symbols; that is, they can learn that particular symbols are appropriate to particular situations (e.g., *Nim, hug, cat, me* in the presence of a cat). In studies using artificial "languages," chimpanzees are required to solve comprehension or production problems by using certain elements of those languages in order to obtain a reward. Those problems can be solved, however, without an understanding of the semantic relationships which a *human* observer can perceive between the relevant symbols. There is no evidence that apes can *combine* the symbols they learn in order to create new meanings or that they organize semantic relationships between symbols. The function of the symbols of an ape's vocabulary appears to be not so much to identify things or to convey information (cf. Skinner's [1957] concept of "tacts") as it is to satisfy a demand that it use that symbol (cf. Skinner's concept of "mands").

In the present study, more than 20,000 combinations of two or more signs produced by Nim, an infant chimpanzee, were examined for evidence of syntactic and semantic structure. Lexical regularities, in which particular signs tended to occur in particular positions, were observed in the case of 2-sign combinations. It is impossible to explain these regularities as overall position habits or the memorization of many individual sequences. As such, these regularities provide superficial evidence that Nim's 2-sign combinations followed rules of sign order. However, other aspects of Nim's use of sign language suggest that it is erroneous to conclude that his combinations were primitive "sentences."

The mean length of Nim's combinations fluctuated unsystematically between 1.1 and 1.6 during the last 19 months of the project. During that time the size of his vocabulary approximately tripled (from 42 to 125 signs). Nim's combinations of three or more signs showed no evidence of lexical regularities, nor did they elaborate or qualify what he signed when he produced a 2-sign combination.

As has been the practice of other studies of sign language in apes, we performed a "semantic" analysis of Nim's 2-sign combinations. Ninety-three percent of these combinations could be assigned unambiguously to one of 20 semantic categories. Expanding on the results of other studies, we demonstrated the reliability of our semantic judgments and that certain semantic roles were expressed (statistically) in particular orders of signs. In the case of children's utterances, position preferences analyzed by the method of "rich interpretation" can serve as evidence that the children use order rules to express semantic relationships. Certain aspects of our data suggest that it is premature to apply the method of rich interpretation to Nim's utterances. Not only were there too few lexical examples of each semantic role to justify the designation of order regularities as semantic (rather than lexical); there were also too many idiosyncratic order regularities in combinations of particular signs. It would be gratuitous to explain these by categorical semantic rules.

A discourse analysis of Nim's use of sign language, which related Nim's utterances to his teacher's immediately prior use of sign language, produced further evidence that Nim's use of language differed fundamentally from that of a child. Our discourse analysis revealed that Nim imitated and interrupted his teachers' utterances to a much larger extent than a child imitates and interrupts an adult's speech. This suggests that Nim was less creative than a child in producing utterances and that he had not learned the give-and-take aspect of conversation which is evident in a child's early use of language. Instead of conversing, Nim appears to have complied with his teacher's request that he sign when he was unable to acquire a desired object by reaching or grabbing for it, or unable to persuade the teacher to engage in some desirable activity (e.g., a game of chase or tickle) by using a nonverbal gesture. The more rapidly Nim satisfied his teacher's demand to sign, the more rapidly he was rewarded. Accordingly, it is not surprising that Nim's signs often interrupted his teacher's signs.

In general, the teacher's signing appeared to function as a cue informing Nim that only if he signed, would he be rewarded by a desired object or activity. Having learned that many of the signs used by the teacher are acceptable responses, Nim used some of them along with certain generally appropriate signs (e.g., *Nim, me, you*). Analyses of films of other apes signing with their teachers revealed a similar lack of creativity in the apes' utterances, a similar tendency to interrupt and a similar dependence of these utterances on the prior signing of their teachers.

In sum, evidence that an ape can create a sentence can, in each case, be explained by reference to simpler nonlinguistic processes. Sequences of signs produced by Nim and by other apes may bare superficial similarities with the first multiword sequences produced by children in the eyes of a human beholder. But unless alternative explanations of an ape's combinations of signs are eliminated—in particular, the habit of imitating teachers' utterances—there is no reason to regard an ape's multisign utterance as a sentence.

At the level of individual signs, anecdotal evidence suggests that Nim may have learned to use certain signs to express emotional states, and in some instances to use these signs as alternatives to physical action. He also seems to have learned to use certain signs to manipulate the behavior of his teachers by misrepresenting certain body states.

The results of our study are negative in the sense that we have shown that Nim's utterances are not sentences. That is, they do not express well-formed semantic propositions in structured sequences. Our results, however, are positive in that they reveal the strategy that Nim and other apes follow in producing utterances which contain certain superficial properties of sentences.

We are, of course, aware that our results cannot be considered definitely negative concerning an ape's capacity to master the basic features of a natural human language. Even though Nim was subjected to an intensive program of socialization and instruction in sign language, that program was marred by the large number of teachers with which he had to cope. His emotional reactions to the steady replacement of volunteer teachers suggests that his use of sign language may have been limited as much by motivational as by intellectual factors (Terrace, 1979b). As far as we can determine, however, there is no reason to assume that Nim's motivation to sign was affected more adversely by the many teachers he experienced than was Washoe's. Both chimpanzees were taught by a small nucleus of long-term caretakers who were assisted by a larger group of less permanent teachers; both achieved essentially the same level of mastery of sign language.

Our experience suggests that in attempting to extend the mastery of sign language beyond that which we observed in Nim, it is important to guarantee that the subject of this type of study be raised exclusively by a small and stable group of teachers. Our results also show that it is important to have a sufficiently large corpus of utterances, in contexts which can be accurately documented.

For the moment, our detailed investigation suggests that an ape's language learning is severely restricted. Apes can learn many isolated symbols (as can dogs, horses, and other nonhuman species), but they show no unequivocal evidence of mastering the conversational, semantic, or syntactic organization of language.

## NOTES

[1] This research was supported in part by grants from the W.T. Grant Foundation, the Harry Frank Guggenheim Foundation, and NIMH (R01MH29293). We thank Lois Bloom and Roger Brown for their helpful comments on an earlier draft of this manuscript, Stephanie LaFarge for the conscientious care with which she raised Nim during his first 18 months, Drs. B. Stark, S. Lerman, and T. Blumenfeld for their supervision of Nim's medical care, and G.A. Tate for his assistance in producing photographs of Nim. We also wish to thank the more than 100 volunteers who assisted in working with Nim and on data analysis. Particular thanks are extended to Walter Benesch, Ilene Brody, Joyce Butler, Bob Johnson, Susan Quinby, Amy Schachter, and Bill Tynan.

[2] It is often assumed erroneously that all forms of manual-visual communication are American Sign Language. However, sign languages vary along a continuum. At one extreme is ASL, which possesses a unique grammar, expressive devices, and morphology. It is the natural language of North American deaf people which is learned as a first language by many deaf people, especially the deaf children of deaf parents. At the opposite extreme is Signed English; a code for expressing English in a manual-visual mode. In Signed English—but not in

ASL—signs are used in English word order with signed equivalents of morphemes such as -ed and -ly. Pidgin Sign uses ASL signs and some of its expressive devices in English word order without the grammatical morphemes of English. Thus it is derivative of both ASL and Signed English. Hearing persons rarely achieve native-like control over the complex structure and grammar of ASL; their signing skills typically fall somewhere within the Pidgin to Signed English end of the continuum. Pidgin Sign, not ASL, was used in this and all other studies of signing behavior in apes. It is misleading to term their signing "ASL" since it does not exhibit the grammatical structure of that language (see Bornstein, 1900 and Stokoe, Casterine, & Cronberg, 1965).

[3]Yerkish symbols were chosen so to have "no semantic significance at all" (Rumbaugh, 1977, p. 93). In fact, however, the symbols are not semantically arbitrary. Each symbol is composed of one or more of nine design elements, and this symbol appears on one of seven background colors. These colors designate general semantic types; e.g., red for ingestables, blue for activities, green for parts of the body, blue-gray for states and conditions, and so on. Two colors, white and yellow, were used as sentential modifiers; they could occur only at the beginning of a sequence.

[4]The basic structure of a sign is defined by four parameters: location, orientation, hand configuration, and movement. Signs do not inflect in the same manner as words in spoken language; i.e., by adding affixes in a *linear* manner. Rather, ASL accomplishes these same functions by *simultaneously* superimposing the "inflection" on the basic form of the sign. This is generally done by systematically modulating the movement, repetition, and/or spatial parameters of the sign. The structured use of the signing space is an important device for signaling grammatical changes in ASL, particularly pronominal reference in the language. Furthermore, the systematic use of facial expressions, body shifts, and eye gaze are integral parts of the grammar of the language. For these reasons, ASL should be considered as a natural language whose phonology, morphology, syntax, and semantic structure is independent of that of spoken languages. For additional details see Hoemann (1975a).

[5]The son of Pan and Carolyn, both long-term residents at the Institute, Nim is Carolyn's eighth offspring and the fourth to be taught sign language. Ally (a full brother), Tania (a full sister), Onan (a half brother), and Bruno (a half brother), have been subjects of sign language studies conducted at the Institute by Dr. Roger S. Fouts.

[6]Stephanie's household included seven other people: her husband WER; three of Stephanie's children from an earlier marriage, Heather, Jennie, and Joshua Lee (aged 15, 14, and 11, respectively); and on many occasions, WER's four children from an earlier marriage: Louisa, Annik, Albert, and Mathilda (aged 16, 14, 11, and 8, respectively). Another fulltime resident of the house was Marika Moosbrugger, a 28-year-old schoolteacher and close friend of the family. Only Stephanie, Jennie, and Marika could be regarded as proficient in sign language. The other members of the LaFarge household knew a vocabulary of basic signs but had not had formal training in sign language.

[7]Checks of sign order, as opposed to the actual occurrence of signs, were made in too few instances to provide a good estimate of the reliability of sign order. However, two indirect checks of sign order suggested that there were no systematic errors in the teachers' reports: agreement between teachers' reports as to sign order and data from video transcripts.

[8]Two signs originally included in Nim's acquired vocabulary were subsequently deleted. A review of our data suggested that Nim did not understand the meaning of *time* and *what,* and that these signs served as routine event markers: they always appeared in combination with another sign, and were always in the first position. A complete description of the topography of each of Nim's signs and their contexts can be found in Terrace, 1979b, Appendix C.

[9]During the first three years of the project, Nim's teachers varied widely in their sign

language proficiency. At any time, only three or four could be classified as skilled signers. During the final year several factors increased the proficiency of old and new teachers: weekly classes conducted by a native deaf (ASL) signer (Alb Boerwick); weekly informal sessions with skilled Signed English signer (Ronnie Miller), who was the daughter of deaf parents; the addition to the project of an R.I.T.-trained sign-language interpreter (Renee Falitz) and a hard-of-hearing person (Mary Wambach), who was skilled in both Signed English and ASL.

[10]Nim's signing was analyzed during each of the five data periods: Period 1, 6/1/75–12/20/75 (ages 18-25 months); Period 2, 1/5/76-2/28/76 (ages 26-28 months); Period 3, 3/1/76-4/4/76 (ages 29-30 months); Period 4, 4/5/76-7/4/76 (ages 30-33 months); and Period 5, 7/5/76-2/7/77 (ages 33-39 months). These periods were arbitrary and not intended to reflect qualitative changes in Nim's signing. The time of each period was determined by factors such as the availability of volunteers for analyzing data and deadlines for submitting grant proposals.

[11]Initially, when Nim pointed at an object or locations, the point was coded in terms of the interpreted meaning of the point; e.g., *up* if Nim pointed vertically into the air. Eventually it became clear that the majority of points were not easily classifiable, and thus signs that could be glossed such as *up, down, there,* and *that,* were referred to as a single "sign" *point.* Two important exceptions were the signs *me* and *you.* In these instances the contexts justified designation of separate signs. See Hoffmeister (1972) for a discussion of *point* as used by deaf children.

[12]In ASL, repetitions of a sign convey particular meanings. One type of contrast between repeated and nonrepeated signs is exemplified by the contrast between the forms of certain nouns and verbs. Many verbs (e.g., *sweep, fly,* and *drive*) are made with a single motion. Related nouns (e.g., *broom, airplane,* and *car*) are made by repeating a sign twice (the so called "double bounce" form, (cf. T. Suppala & E. Newport, 1978). None of Nim's teachers could distinguish between the meanings of utterances which did and did not contain signs that were repeated successively. Emphasis appears to be their sole function. We saw no evidence that repeated signs were "disfluent," and as is often the case with children who stutter (Colburn, 1979). Overall, less than 5 percent of the linear utterances we observed contained successively repeated signs.

[13]*Run there,* is signed by moving the *run* sign from the signer to a real or previously established location in the signing space. This has been termed "inflecting for location" in ASL and is a regular grammatical device in sign language. Deaf children acquire this process progressively (cf. Seidenberg and Petitto, 1979a). In calculating the child's MLU, however, researchers have labeled constructions such as *run there* as a single sign. Even though a 2-sign count may be warranted, they have counted only 1 sign in order to avoid exaggerating a deaf child's grammatical competence. In addition, *invented signs* and *mimetic depictions* are generally not counted by researchers studying the deaf child's acquisition processes, thus deflating the MLU count even further (Klima & Bellugi, 1972). Accordingly, the deaf child's MLU count might erroneously appear somewhat deflated in comparison with the hearing child's data.

[14]Such isolated effects may be nothing more than what one would expect from statistically random variation. That is, in a certain proportion of the many cases we examined in our semantic analysis (the product of the level at statistical significance and the number of comparisons), we should expect to find statistical evidence of *apparent* structure.

[15]These analyses were performed by the third author as part of his dissertation research. The teachers and the dates on which they were videotaped are Laura Petitto: February 5, 1976, March 18, 1976, and June 24, 1976; Dick Sanders: March 20, 1977, July 13 and 19, 1977; Joyce Butler: April 19, 1977, June 6, 1977; Bill Tynan: April 11, 1977.

[16] *The First Signs of Washoe,* WGBH Nova film, 1976.

[17] Tracings of selected film frames would have been published, but no agreement on film copyright releases was reached with the Gardners. Tracings of signs shown in transcripts below can be seen in Terrace *et al.,* 1979.

## REFERENCES

Bellugi, U. Personal communication, 1977.

Bellugi, U. & Klima, E. S. Two faces of sign: Iconic and abstract. S. R. Harnard, H. D. Steklis, & J. Lancaster (Eds.), *Annals of the New York Academy of the Sciences,* 1976, 280, 514–538.

Bellugi, U. & Klima, E. S. *The signs of language.* Cambridge, Mass.: Harvard University Press, 1979.

Bever, T. G. The cognitive basis for linguistic structures. *In* R. Hayes (Ed.), *Cognition and the development of language.* New York: Wiley, 1970.

Bever, T. G. Psychologically Real Grammar Emerges because of its Role in Language Acquisition. *In* F. Dato, (Ed.), Georgetown University Roundtable on Linguistics, Washington, D.C., 1975.

Bever, T. G., Katz, J., and Langenden, D. T. *An integrated theory of linguistic ability.* New York: Crowell, 1975.

Bloom, L. M. *Language development: Form and function in emerging grammars.* Cambridge, Mass.: M.I.T. Press, 1970.

Bloom, L. M., *One Word at a time: The use of single word utterances before syntax.* The Hague: Mouton, 1973.

Bloom, L. M. & Lahey, M. *Language and development and language disorders.* New York: Wiley, 1977.

Bloom, L. M., Lightbown, P., & Hood, L. Structure and variation in child language. *Monograph of the Society for Research in Child Development,* 1975, 40 (Serial No. 160).

Bloom, L. M. Personal communication, 1977.

Bloom, L. M., Rocissano, L., and Hood, L. Adult-child discourse: developmental interaction between information processing and linguistic knowledge. *Cognitive Psychology,* 1976, 8, 521–522.

Bornstein, H. Sign language in the education of the deaf. *In* I. M. Schlesinger & L. Namir (Eds.), *Sign language of the deaf: Psychological, linguistic and sociological perspectives.* New York: Academic Press, 1978, pp. 338–361.

Bornstein, H. Sign language of the deaf: Psychological, linguistic, and sociological perspectives. *In* I. M. Schlesinger & L. Namir (Eds.), *Current trends in the language sciences.*

Bowerman, M. *Early syntactic development: A cross-linguistic study with special reference to Finnish.* London: Cambridge University Press, 1973a.

Bowerman, M. Structural relationships in children's utterances: syntactic or semantic? *In* T. E. Moore (Ed.), *Cognitive development and the acquisition of language.* New York: Academic Press, 1973b, pp. 197–213.

Braine, M. D. S. Children's first word combinations. *Monograph of the Society for Research in Child Development,* 1976, 41 (Serial No. 164).

Bronowski, J. & Bellugi, U. Language, name and concept. *Science,* 1970, 168, 669 –673.

Brown, E. & Miron, M. S. Lexical and syntactical predictions of the distribution of pause time in reading. *Journal of Verbal Learning and Verbal Behavior,* 1971, 10, 658–667.

Brown, R. *Psycholinguistics: Selected papers by Roger Brown.* New York: Free Press, 1970, pp. 208–231.

Brown, R. *A first language: The early stage.* Cambridge, Mass.: Harvard University Press, 1973.

Burt, M. K. *From deep to surface structure.* New York: Harper & Row, 1971.

Chomsky, N. *Syntactic structures.* The Hague: Mouton, 1957.

Chomsky, N. *Aspects of the theory of syntax.* Cambridge, Mass.: M.I.T. Press, 1965.

Colburn, N. Disfluency behavior and emerging linguistic structures in pre-school children. Unpublished doctoral dissertation, Teachers College, Columbia University, 1979.

Conrad, R. Acoustic confusions in immediate memory. *British Journal of Psychology,* 1964, 55, 78–84.

Dale, P. S. *Language development, structure and function.* New York: Holt, Rinehart & Winston, 1976.

Fillmore, C. *On Deixis.* Bloomington, Ind.: Indiana Linguistics Club, 1973.

Fodor, J. A., Bever, T. G., & Garrett, M. F. *The psychology of language: An introduction to psycholinguistics and generative grammar.* New York: McGraw-Hill, 1974.

Fouts, R. S. Use of guidance in teaching sign language to a chimpanzee (Pan Troglodytes). *Journal of Comparative and Physiological Psychology,* 1972, 80, 515–522.

Fouts, R. S. Capacities for language in great apes. *In* R. H. Tuttle (Ed.), *Society and psychology of primates.* The Hague: Mouton, 1975, pp. 371–390.

Fouts, R. S. & Goodin, L. Acquisition of signs in a chimpanzee: a comparison of training methods. *Bulletin of the Psychonomic Society,* 1974, 4(4a), 264.

Frisch, K. von. *The dancing bees.* London: Methuen, 1954.

Gardner, R. A. & Gardner, B. T. Teaching sign language to a chimpanzee. *Science,* 1969, 165, 664–672.

Gardner, B. T. & Gardner, R. A. Two-way communication with an infant chimpanzee. *In* A. M. Schrier & F. Stollinitz (Eds.), *Behavior of nonhuman primates* (Vol. 4). New York: Academic Press, 1971, pp. 117–184.

Gardner, R. A. & Gardner, B. T. (Producers). *Teaching sign language to the chimpanzee: Washoe.* University Park, Pa.: The Psychological Cinema Register, 1973.

Gardner, B. T. & Gardner, R. A. Comparing the early utterances of child and chimpanzee. *In* A. Pick (Ed.), *Minnesota symposia on child psychology* (Vol. 8). Minneapolis: University of Minnesota Press, 1974a.

Gardner, B. T. & Gardner, R. A. Teaching sign language to a chimpanzee, VII: use of order in sign combinations. *Bulletin of the Psychnomic Society,* 1974b, 4(4a), 264.

Gardner, B. T. & Gardner, R. A. Early signs of language in child and chimpanzee. *Science,* 1975a, 187 (4178), 752–753.

Gardner, B. T. & Gardner, R. A. Evidence for sentence constituents in the early utterances of child and chimpanzee. *Journal of Experimental Psychology: General,* 1975b, 104(3) 244–267.

Gardner, R. A. & Gardner, B. T. Comparative psychology and language acquisition. *Annals of the New York Academy* of Sciences, 1978, *309,* 37–76.

Gross, M., Halle, M., & Schutzenberger, M. (Eds.). *The formal analysis of natural language.* The Hague: Mouton, 1973.

Hayes, C. *The ape in our house.* New York: Harper & Row, 1951.

Hayes, C. & Hayes, K. J. The intellectual development of a home-raised chimpanzee. *Proceedings of the American Philosophical Society,* 1951, 95, 105–109.

Hoemann, H. W. *The American Sign Language: lexical and grammatical notes with translation exercise.* Silver Spring, Md.: National Association of the Deaf, 1975a.

Hoemann, H. W. The transparency of meaning of sign language gestures. *Sign Language Studies,* 1975b, 151–161.

Hoffmeister, R. J. The influential point. *Proceedings of the National Symposium on Sign Language Research 2nd Training,* 1972.

Jenkins, J. J. & Palermo, D. S. Mediation processes and the acquisition of linguistic structure. *In* U. Bellugi & R. Brown (Eds.), *The acquisition of language. Monograph of the Society for Research in Child Development,* 1964, 29(1, 92), 141–169.

Katz, J. & Postal, P. M. *An integrated theory of linguistic description.* Cambridge, Mass.: M.I.T. Press, 1964.

Kellogg, L. A. & Kellogg, W. N. *The ape and the child: A study of environmental influence upon early behavior.* New York: McGraw-Hill, 1933.

Kellogg, W. N. Communication and language in the home-raised chimpanzee. *Science,* 1968, 182, 423–427.

Khouts, N. *Infant ape and human child.* Moscow: Museum Darwinianum, 1935.

Klima, E. S. & Bellugi, U. The signs of language in child and chimpanzee. *In* T. Alloway, L. Krames, & P. Pliner (Eds.), *Communication and affect: A comparative approach.* New York: Academic Press, 1972.

Klima, E. S. & Bellugi, U. Perception and production in a visually based language. *In* D. Aronson & R. Reiber (Eds.), *Developmental psycholinguistics and communication disorders. Annals of the New York Academy of Sciences.* New York: The New York Academy of the Sciences, 1975, 263, 225–235.

Lakoff, G. The global nature of the nuclear stress rule. *Language,* 1972, 48, 76–87.

Lane, H., Boyes-Braem, P., & Bellugi, U. Preliminaries to a distinctive feature analysis of American sign language. *Cognitive Psychology,* 1976, 8, 262–289.

Lane, H. & Grosjean, F. Perception of reading rate by speakers and listeners. *Journal of Experimental Psychology,* 1973, 97, 141–147.

Lenneberg, E. H. Of language, knowledge, apes and brains. *Journal of Psycholinguistic Research,* 1971, 1, 1–30.

Limber, J. Language in child and chimp? *American Psychologist,* 1977, 32(4), 280–295.

Macnamara, J. Cognitive basis of language and learning in infants. *Psychology Review,* 1972, 79, 1–13.

McCawley, J. D. The role of semantics in a grammar, *In* E. Bach & R. T. Harms (Eds.), *Universals in linguistic theory.* New York: Holt, Rinehart & Winston, 1968.

Mounin, G. Language, communication and chimpanzees. *Current Anthropology,* 1976, 17(1), 1–21.

Newport, E. L. Motherese: The speech of mothers to their young children. *In* Castellan, D. B. Pisoni, & G. R. Potts (Eds.), *Cognitive theory* (Vol. 2). Hillsdale, N.J.: Lawrence Erlbaum Assoc., 1976.

Newport, E. L. & Ashbrook, E. F. The emergence of semantic relations in ASL. *Papers and reports on child language development,* 1977, 13, 7 pp.

Patterson, F. G. The gestures of a gorilla: language acquisition by another pongid. *Brain and Language,* 1978, 12, 72–97.

Postal, P. M. The best theory. *In* S. Peters (Ed.), *Goals of linguistic theory.* Englewood Cliffs, N.J.:

Premack, D. A functional analysis of language. *Journal of the Experimental Analysis of Behavior,* 1970, 14, 107–125.

Premack, D. Language in a chimpanzee? *Science,* 1971, 172, 808–822.

Premack, D. *Intelligence in ape and man.* Hillsdale, N.J.: Lawrence Erlbaum, Assoc., 1976.

Rumbaugh, D. M. (Ed.). *Language learning by a chimpanzee: The Lana Project.* New York: Academic Press, 1977.

Schlesinger, H. S. & Meadow, K. P. *Deafness and mental health: A developmental approach.* Berkeley: University of California Press, 1972.

Schlesinger, I. N. Production of utterances and language acquisition. *In* D. I. Slobin (Ed.), *Ontogenesis of grammar.* New York: Academic Press, 1971.

Schlesinger, H. S. Personal communication, 1977.

Seidenberg, M. S. & Petitto, L. A. On the evidence for linguistic abilities in signing apes. *Brain and Language,* 1979a, 8, 162–183.

Seidenberg, M. S. & Petitto, L. A. Signing in apes. *Cognition,* 1979b, 7, 177–215.

Skinner, B. F. The operational analysis of psychological terms, *Psychological Review,* 1945, 52, 270–277.

Skinner, B. F. *Verbal behavior.* New York: Appleton-Century-Crofts, 1957.

Snow, C. E. Mother's speech to children learning language. *Child Development,* 1972, 43, 549–565.

Staats, A. N. *Learning, language, and cognition.* New York: Holt, Rinehart & Winston, 1968.

Stern, D., Jaffee, J., Beebe, B., & Bennett, S. Vocalizing in unison and in alternation: two modes of communication in the mother-infant dyad. *In* D. Arson & R. Reiber (Eds.), *Annals of the New York Academy of the Sciences,* 1975, 263, 89–100.

Stokoe, W. C., Jr., Casterline, D. C., & Croneberg, C. G. *A dictionary of American Sign Language on linguistic principles.* Washington, D. C.: Gallaudet College Press, 1965.

Straub, R. O., Seidenberg, M. S., Bever, T. G., & Terrace, H. S. Serial learning in the pigeon. *Journal of Experimental Analysis of Behavior,* 1979, 32, 137–148.

Supalla, T. & Newport, E. L. How many seats in a chair? The derivation of nouns and verbs in American Sign Language. In P. Siple, (Ed.) *Understanding language through sign language research.* New York: Academic Press, 1978.

Temerlin, M. K. *Lucy: Growing up human.* Palo Alto: Science and Behavior Books, 1975.

Terrace, H. S., Straub, R. O., Bever, T. G., & Seidenberg, M. S. Representation in the pigeon, *Bulletin of Psychonomic Society,* 1977, 9, 269.

Terrace, H. S. Is problem solving language? *Journal of Experimental Analysis of Behavior,* 1979a, 31, 161–175.

Terrace, H. S. *Nim.* New York: Knopf, 1979b.

Terrace, H. S. & Bever, T. G. What might be learned from studying language in the chimpanzee? The importance of symbolizing oneself. *Origins and evolution of language and speech, Annals of the New York Academy of Sciences,* 1976, 280, 579–588.

Terrace, H. S., Petitto, L. A., Sanders, R. J., Bever, T. G. Can an ape create a sentence? *Science,* 1979, *206,* 891–902.

Thorpe, W. H. *Bird song.* London: Cambridge University Press, 1961.

Tinbergen, N. *The study of instinct.* Oxford: Claredon Press, 1951.

## APPENDIX: EXHAUSTIVE LISTING OF NIM'S COMBINATIONS OF 2 OR MORE SIGNS

### Two-Sign Sequences

| Sequence Type | | Tokens | Sequence Type | | Tokens |
|---|---|---|---|---|---|
| Alex | locative/point | 1 | | ball | 1 |
| Andrea | angry | 1 | | bite | 4 |
| | banana | 1 | | cat | 1 |
| | Bill | 5 | | dirty | 2 |
| | cracker | 2 | | handcream | 2 |
| | eat | 4 | | hug | 14 |
| | hug | 2 | | Laura | 1 |
| | Laura | 1 | | me | 6 |
| | locative/point | 2 | | Nim | 4 |
| | me | 1 | | open | 1 |
| | Nim | 6 | | shoe | 1 |
| | peach | 1 | | sorry | 8 |
| | pear | 1 | Anna | eat | 1 |
| | play | 1 | | you | 1 |
| | red | 1 | apple | Andrea | 3 |
| | what | 1 | | baby | 1 |
| | you | 1 | | bite | 1 |
| angry | had | 3 | | bowl | 1 |

*(Continued)*

## Two-Sign Sequences (*cont.*)

| Sequence Type | | Tokens | Sequence Type | | Tokens |
|---|---|---|---|---|---|
| apple (*cont.*) | cracker | 1 | | play | 3 |
| | dirty | 1 | | red | 1 |
| | drink | 6 | | tickle | 1 |
| | eat | 37 | banana | apple | 1 |
| | fruit | 2 | | Bill | 1 |
| | give | 3 | | come | 1 |
| | gum | 3 | | cracker | 1 |
| | hug | 2 | | drink | 4 |
| | in | 1 | | eat | 69 |
| | jump | 1 | | fruit | 1 |
| | locative/point | 2 | | hug | 4 |
| | me | 27 | | locative/point | 4 |
| | more | 5 | | me | 97 |
| | Nim | 65 | | more | 5 |
| | orange | 4 | | Nim | 73 |
| | Out | 2 | | play | 2 |
| | play | 1 | | same | 1 |
| | please | 1 | | sorry | 1 |
| | raisin | 1 | | tea | 1 |
| | red | 1 | | toothbrush | 1 |
| | smell | 1 | | what | 1 |
| | tea | 1 | bed | time | 2 |
| | yogurt | 1 | berry | eat | 3 |
| baby | chair | 1 | | grape | 1 |
| | clean | 2 | | me | 2 |
| | drink | 1 | | Nim | 1 |
| | eat | 3 | Bill | Andrea | 5 |
| | give | 1 | | apple | 1 |
| | hug | 9 | | come | 1 |
| | me | 2 | | groom | 1 |
| | more | 1 | | gum | 1 |
| | Nim | 20 | | hug | 1 |
| | out | 2 | | Nim | 5 |
| | sit | 1 | | play | 1 |
| | tickle | 1 | | shoe | 1 |
| bad | angry | 3 | bite | apple | 2 |
| | bite | 1 | | angry | 6 |
| | dirty | 1 | | bad | 1 |
| | hug | 11 | | down | 1 |
| | me | 1 | | hug | 10 |
| | Nim | 3 | | Joyce | 1 |
| | sorry | 4 | | me | 3 |
| ball | give | 2 | | Nim | 2 |
| | gum | 1 | | no | 2 |
| | in | 1 | | out | 1 |
| | locative/point | 6 | | pear | 1 |
| | me | 7 | | peach | 2 |
| | Nim | 6 | | play | 4 |

## Two-Sign Sequences (*cont.*)

| Sequence Type | | Tokens | Sequence Type | | Tokens |
|---|---|---|---|---|---|
| | please | 1 | | me | 1 |
| | sorry | 7 | | more | 3 |
| | Susan | 1 | | Nim | 2 |
| | tickle | 2 | | play | 1 |
| black | paper | 1 | clean | angry | 1 |
| blue | hug | 1 | | brush | 1 |
| | in | 1 | | bowl | 1 |
| | pants | 2 | | dirty | 2 |
| | sock | 1 | | hug | 3 |
| book | Nim | 2 | | in | 1 |
| | open | 3 | | locative/point | 1 |
| bowl | apple | 1 | | me | 2 |
| bracelet | locative/point | 1 | | Nim | 1 |
| | open | 1 | | open | 1 |
| break | hug | 2 | | toothbrush | 1 |
| | me | 2 | | water | 3 |
| brown | color | 2 | close | light | 1 |
| | eat | 2 | cold | in | 1 |
| | locative/point | 1 | color | black | 4 |
| | Nim | 2 | | blue | 5 |
| | shoe | 1 | | brown | 2 |
| | sweet | 1 | | eat | 2 |
| brush | baby | 2 | | hat | 1 |
| | give | 2 | | Nim | 5 |
| | me | 35 | | orange | 1 |
| | Nim | 13 | | red | 7 |
| | orange | 1 | | yellow | 1 |
| | play | 1 | come | apple | 1 |
| | smell | 1 | | Bill | 5 |
| | toothbrush | 1 | | bug | 2 |
| | what | 1 | | give | 3 |
| | you | 1 | | hug | 14 |
| bug | drink | 2 | | jump | 1 |
| | locative/point | 1 | | kiss | 1 |
| | Nim | 1 | | me | 5 |
| | same | 1 | | Nim | 2 |
| | smell | 1 | | open | 3 |
| cat | apple | 1 | | play | 6 |
| | book | 2 | | tickle | 3 |
| | chair | 1 | cookie | eat | 1 |
| | come | 1 | | nut | 1 |
| | eat | 2 | cracker | eat | 10 |
| | locative/point | 1 | | give | 2 |
| | me | 1 | | locative/point | 1 |
| chair | finish | 1 | | me | 3 |
| | gum | 2 | | Nim | 21 |
| | hug | 1 | | sweet | 2 |
| | locative/point | 6 | | what | 1 |

## Two-Sign Sequences (*cont.*)

| Sequence Type | | Tokens | Sequence Type | | Tokens |
|---|---|---|---|---|---|
| crayon | red | 1 | | grape | 2 |
| cup | in | 1 | | groom | 1 |
| | drink | 2 | | gum | 1 |
| diaper | dirty | 1 | | hat | 1 |
| Dick | bite | 1 | | hot | 1 |
| dirty | chair | 2 | | hug | 6 |
| | down | 1 | | hungry | 1 |
| | eat | 2 | | hurry | 1 |
| | finish | 12 | | in | 3 |
| | hug | 56 | | kiss | 1 |
| | in | 1 | | Laura | 2 |
| | locative/point | 5 | | locative/point | 5 |
| | me | 3 | | me | 51 |
| | Nim | 7 | | more | 14 |
| | orange | 3 | | Nim | 143 |
| | out | 5 | | nut | 1 |
| | pants | 1 | | open | 2 |
| | red | 1 | | orange | 8 |
| | smell | 9 | | red | 1 |
| | sorry | 2 | | smell | 2 |
| | sweet | 2 | | sweet | 12 |
| | toothbrush | 1 | | tea | 44 |
| | water | 1 | | toothbrush | 5 |
| dog | come | 1 | | up | 6 |
| | me | 2 | | water | 7 |
| | play | 2 | | what | 1 |
| | yogurt | 1 | | you | 1 |
| down | come | 1 | eat | angry | 2 |
| | Nim | 1 | | apple | 56 |
| | yogurt | 1 | | baby | 3 |
| draw | black | 1 | | banana | 38 |
| | eat | 1 | | berry | 4 |
| | finish | 1 | | bite | 1 |
| | flower | 1 | | blue | 2 |
| | Nim | 1 | | black | 2 |
| | open | 1 | | brown | 3 |
| | paper | 1 | | bug | 2 |
| | red | 6 | | cat | 1 |
| | tree | 1 | | clean | 1 |
| drink | apple | 6 | | cold | 1 |
| | Bill | 1 | | come | 3 |
| | bite | 1 | | cracker | 6 |
| | cracker | 1 | | drink | 98 |
| | down | 3 | | finish | 2 |
| | eat | 64 | | fruit | 7 |
| | finish | 2 | | give | 12 |
| | flower | 1 | | glass | 1 |
| | give | 7 | | grape | 38 |

## Two-Sign Sequences (*cont.*)

| Sequence Type | | Tokens | Sequence Type | | Tokens |
|---|---|---|---|---|---|
| | green | 2 | | clean | 1 |
| | groom | 3 | | dirty | 7 |
| | gum | 16 | | down | 1 |
| | hug | 15 | | drink | 2 |
| | hungry | 13 | | eat | 7 |
| | in | 2 | | give | 3 |
| | kiss | 2 | | hug | 187 |
| | point | 16 | | me | 1 |
| | me | 76 | | Nim | 7 |
| | locative/point | 16 | | out | 4 |
| | Nim | 302 | | play | 1 |
| | nut | 36 | | Renee | 8 |
| | open | 2 | | shoe | 1 |
| | orange | 10 | | sorry | 7 |
| | out | 1 | | toothbrush | 5 |
| | peach | 5 | | yogurt | 2 |
| | pear | 10 | flower | angry | 2 |
| | play | 1 | | point | 1 |
| | please | 2 | | smell | 1 |
| | raisin | 24 | fruit | eat | 8 |
| | red | 5 | | me | 1 |
| | shoe | 1 | | Nim | 11 |
| | sleep | 1 | | nut | 1 |
| | smell | 2 | | open | 1 |
| | sorry | 1 | gimme | drink | 1 |
| | spoon | 1 | | eat | 2 |
| | Susan | 1 | | handcream | 2 |
| | sweet | 26 | | sweet | 1 |
| | tea | 9 | | toothbrush | 1 |
| | tickle | 1 | | water | 2 |
| | time | 6 | give | apple | 9 |
| | toothbrush | 4 | | baby | 1 |
| | what | 12 | | ball | 14 |
| | work | 3 | | banana | 7 |
| | yellow | 1 | | black | 1 |
| | yogurt | 21 | | blue | 2 |
| egg | banana | 1 | | brown | 1 |
| | clean | 1 | | brush | 3 |
| | eat | 3 | | bug | 2 |
| | me | 2 | | clean | 1 |
| | Nim | 2 | | crayon | 2 |
| | out | 2 | | dog | 1 |
| | pull | 1 | | drink | 15 |
| finish | baby | 1 | | eat | 54 |
| | banana | 1 | | finish | 1 |
| | bite | 1 | | flower | 2 |
| | cat | 1 | | grape | 3 |
| | chair | 2 | | gum | 4 |

## Two-Sign Sequences (*cont.*)

| Sequence Type | | Tokens | Sequence Type | | Tokens |
|---|---|---|---|---|---|
| give (*cont.*) | handcream | 14 | | locative/point | 2 |
| | harmonica | 2 | | me | 12 |
| | hat | 4 | | more | 2 |
| | here | 1 | | Nim | 21 |
| | hug | 3 | | open | 2 |
| | hungry | 2 | | out | 3 |
| | hurry | 2 | | time | 1 |
| | jump | 2 | | up | 1 |
| | key | 1 | green | apple | 1 |
| | kiss | 1 | | sock | 1 |
| | light | 2 | groom | baby | 2 |
| | listen | 1 | | grape | 1 |
| | locative/point | 6 | | handcream | 1 |
| | me | 41 | | me | 21 |
| | more | 3 | | Nim | 6 |
| | Nim | 23 | | peach | 1 |
| | nut | 2 | | you | 2 |
| | open | 2 | gum | apple | 4 |
| | orange | 3 | | Bill | 3 |
| | out | 1 | | bite | 4 |
| | pear | 2 | | drink | 3 |
| | play | 1 | | eat | 79 |
| | raisin | 2 | | gimme | 2 |
| | red | 2 | | give | 3 |
| | rock | 1 | | hug | 1 |
| | smell | 1 | | me | 19 |
| | spoon | 1 | | more | 1 |
| | sweet | 6 | | Nim | 47 |
| | tea | 1 | | pear | 1 |
| | that | 4 | | play | 1 |
| | tickle | 1 | | sweet | 1 |
| | toothbrush | 4 | | tickle | 1 |
| | water | 9 | | what | 1 |
| | what | 1 | | you | 1 |
| glass | eat | 1 | handcream | angry | 1 |
| go | Bill | 1 | | baby | 2 |
| | eat | 1 | | banana | 1 |
| | more | 2 | | Bill | 1 |
| | open | 1 | | brush | 1 |
| good | banana | 1 | | eat | 3 |
| good-bye | cat | 1 | | give | 3 |
| | drink | 1 | | groom | 1 |
| grape | eat | 74 | | hug | 3 |
| | gimme | 1 | | locative/point | 2 |
| | give | 1 | | me | 4 |
| | groom | 1 | | more | 5 |
| | hug | 1 | | Nim | 6 |
| | in | 2 | | open | 1 |

# Two-Sign Sequences (*cont.*)

| Sequence Type | | Tokens | Sequence Type | | Tokens |
|---|---|---|---|---|---|
| | out | 3 | | dirty | 5 |
| | play | 2 | | drink | 5 |
| | sleep | 1 | | eat | 7 |
| | smell | 1 | | finish | 32 |
| | sorry | 1 | | give | 1 |
| | tickle | 1 | | go | 1 |
| happy | me | 1 | | gum | 1 |
| | Nim | 2 | | hungry | 1 |
| harmonica | me | 1 | | in | 1 |
| | Nim | 1 | | Joyce | 1 |
| hat | hug | 3 | | jump | 2 |
| | listen | 1 | | Laura | 2 |
| | me | 20 | | me | 74 |
| | more | 2 | | more | 3 |
| | Nim | 3 | | music | 1 |
| help | Bill | 2 | | Nim | 106 |
| | clean | 1 | | nut | 1 |
| | drink | 1 | | open | 6 |
| | hug | 1 | | orange | 2 |
| | me | 6 | | out | 15 |
| | Nim | 4 | | play | 4 |
| | open | 12 | | please | 5 |
| | out | 4 | | Renee | 34 |
| | pants | 1 | | sorry | 32 |
| | shoe | 2 | | Susan | 8 |
| Herb | eat | 1 | | sweet | 1 |
| | me | 1 | | time | 2 |
| | tickle | 2 | | Tom | 1 |
| | you | 2 | | toothbrush | 1 |
| home | Alex | 1 | | up | 2 |
| hot | cup | 1 | | wash | 1 |
| | drink | 1 | hungry | angry | 1 |
| | light | 1 | | drink | 1 |
| | Nim | 1 | | eat | 13 |
| | tea | 2 | | hug | 5 |
| | water | 2 | | me | 9 |
| hug | Alex | 2 | | Nim | 7 |
| | angry | 1 | | out | 2 |
| | baby | 4 | hurry | drink | 1 |
| | bad | 2 | | eat | 2 |
| | banana | 1 | | gum | 1 |
| | berry | 1 | | more | 2 |
| | Bill | 1 | | play | 1 |
| | bite | 2 | hurt | bite | 1 |
| | clean | 1 | | eat | 2 |
| | come | 5 | | hug | 1 |
| | cracker | 2 | | me | 2 |
| | Dick | 2 | ice | bite | 1 |

## Two-Sign Sequences (*cont.*)

| Sequence Type | | Tokens | Sequence Type | | Tokens |
|---|---|---|---|---|---|
| ice (*cont.*) | Nim | 2 | kiss | baby | 3 |
| in | angry | 1 | | dog | 1 |
| | bad | 1 | | drink | 1 |
| | bite | 1 | | me | 1 |
| | box | 1 | | Nim | 6 |
| | brown | 1 | Laura | bite | 1 |
| | chair | 1 | | bug | 1 |
| | coat | 1 | | grape | 1 |
| | drink | 2 | | listen | 1 |
| | grape | 1 | | locative/point | 1 |
| | hat | 1 | | me | 1 |
| | hug | 1 | | Nim | 1 |
| | listen | 1 | | red | 1 |
| | me | 2 | | you | 2 |
| | Nim | 2 | lie-down | sleep | 2 |
| | out | 5 | light | give | 2 |
| | pants | 70 | | locative/point | 1 |
| | play | 4 | | out | 1 |
| | raisin | 1 | listen | Andrea | 3 |
| | red | 1 | | apple | 1 |
| | shirt | 7 | | Bill | 3 |
| | shoe | 3 | | in | 1 |
| | sock | 1 | | locative/point | 1 |
| | sweet | 1 | | me | 1 |
| | tea | 5 | | Nim | 1 |
| | water | 2 | | sorry | 1 |
| | work | 1 | | you | 1 |
| Joyce | kiss | 1 | locative/point | ball | 1 |
| | me | 1 | | banana | 3 |
| | play | 1 | | bug | 1 |
| | tickle | 1 | | chair | 1 |
| jump | chair | 1 | | clean | 1 |
| | dirty | 1 | | drink | 2 |
| | eat | 1 | | eat | 9 |
| | hug | 11 | | fruit | 1 |
| | me | 7 | | give | 2 |
| | Nim | 6 | | gum | 1 |
| | open | 2 | | handcream | 2 |
| | play | 1 | | in | 1 |
| | rock | 1 | | light | 1 |
| | tickle | 2 | | me | 6 |
| key | hug | 1 | | Nim | 8 |
| | locative/point | 1 | | orange | 1 |
| | me | 3 | | play | 1 |
| | Nim | 1 | | smell | 1 |
| | open | 3 | | spoon | 1 |
| | out | 1 | | tea | 1 |
| | play | 2 | | water | 3 |

## Two-Sign Sequences (*cont.*)

| Sequence Type | | Tokens | Sequence Type | | Tokens |
|---|---|---|---|---|---|
| me | Andrea | 2 | | Renee | 2 |
| | angry | 5 | | shoe | 1 |
| | apple | 17 | | smell | 1 |
| | bad | 2 | | smile | 1 |
| | ball | 10 | | sorry | 17 |
| | banana | 34 | | Susan | 1 |
| | bite | 2 | | sweet | 8 |
| | book | 3 | | tea | 13 |
| | brown | 2 | | tickle | 20 |
| | brush | 9 | | Tom | 4 |
| | clean | 2 | | toothbrush | 1 |
| | come | 2 | | up | 2 |
| | cook | 1 | | Walter | 2 |
| | cracker | 1 | | water | 5 |
| | dirty | 2 | | what | 1 |
| | down | 2 | | work | 3 |
| | drink | 65 | | yogurt | 1 |
| | eat | 237 | | you | 41 |
| | flower | 1 | more | apple | 12 |
| | give | 11 | | ball | 2 |
| | go | 3 | | banana | 62 |
| | grape | 2 | | berry | 2 |
| | gum | 43 | | Bill | 1 |
| | handcream | 3 | | bite | 2 |
| | happy | 2 | | brush | 5 |
| | hat | 26 | | chair | 19 |
| | help | 2 | | drink | 99 |
| | hug | 40 | | eat | 287 |
| | hungry | 2 | | fruit | 2 |
| | in | 5 | | gimme | 1 |
| | jump | 2 | | go | 7 |
| | kiss | 1 | | grape | 11 |
| | Laura | 1 | | groom | 4 |
| | listen | 1 | | gum | 29 |
| | locative/point | 3 | | handcream | 23 |
| | more | 12 | | hug | 16 |
| | Nim | 328 | | hurry | 1 |
| | nut | 4 | | in | 1 |
| | open | 10 | | jump | 1 |
| | orange | 10 | | key | 1 |
| | out | 5 | | listen | 1 |
| | pants | 2 | | locative/point | 1 |
| | peach | 1 | | me | 42 |
| | play | 81 | | Nim | 24 |
| | please | 1 | | nut | 11 |
| | pole | 1 | | open | 1 |
| | raisin | 4 | | orange | 6 |
| | red | 1 | | paint | 1 |

## Two-Sign Sequences (*cont.*)

| Sequence Type | | Tokens | Sequence Type | | Tokens |
|---|---|---|---|---|---|
| more (*cont.*) | peach | 2 | | hungry | 13 |
| | pear | 13 | | in | 3 |
| | play | 41 | | Joyce | 1 |
| | pole | 9 | | jump | 1 |
| | raisin | 1 | | key | 1 |
| | shoe | 2 | | kiss | 2 |
| | smell | 3 | | Laura | 3 |
| | spoon | 2 | | locative/point | 6 |
| | sweet | 14 | | me | 89 |
| | swing | 1 | | more | 7 |
| | tea | 23 | | music | 1 |
| | tickle | 136 | | nut | 9 |
| | toothbrush | 3 | | open | 5 |
| | up | 1 | | orange | 5 |
| | water | 10 | | out | 6 |
| | what | 6 | | pants | 1 |
| | yogurt | 5 | | paper | 1 |
| | hat | 1 | | peach | 1 |
| My | Nim | 1 | | pear | 4 |
| name | Andrea | 2 | | play | 19 |
| Nim | apple | 25 | | raisin | 6 |
| | baby | 6 | | red | 7 |
| | bad | 1 | | Renee | 1 |
| | banana | 18 | | shoe | 1 |
| | Bill | 2 | | sorry | 2 |
| | bird | 1 | | Susan | 1 |
| | bite | 4 | | sweet | 3 |
| | book | 1 | | tea | 7 |
| | brown | 2 | | tickle | 16 |
| | brush | 4 | | toothbrush | 4 |
| | bug | 1 | | Walter | 2 |
| | chair | 2 | | water | 2 |
| | color | 2 | | what | 1 |
| | cracker | 3 | | who | 1 |
| | dirty | 2 | | work | 1 |
| | down | 2 | | yellow | 1 |
| | drink | 43 | | yogurt | 8 |
| | eat | 209 | | you | 4 |
| | finish | 1 | no | break | 1 |
| | fruit | 6 | | climb | 1 |
| | give | 4 | | drink | 1 |
| | go | 4 | nut | cookie | 1 |
| | grape | 5 | | drink | 1 |
| | groom | 1 | | eat | 37 |
| | gum | 21 | | fruit | 1 |
| | handcream | 7 | | give | 2 |
| | hat | 8 | | gum | 1 |
| | hug | 23 | | in | 6 |

## Two-Sign Sequences (*cont.*)

| Sequence Type | | Tokens | Sequence Type | | Tokens |
|---|---|---|---|---|---|
| | me | 16 | | yogurt | 2 |
| | more | 3 | orange | apple | 4 |
| | Nim | 71 | | brown | 1 |
| | open | 6 | | dirty | 4 |
| | out | 3 | | drink | 15 |
| | red | 2 | | eat | 11 |
| | sweet | 2 | | me | 13 |
| | what | 1 | | Nim | 15 |
| off | shoe | 1 | | Renee | 1 |
| on | chair | 1 | | socks | 2 |
| | pants | 1 | | sweet | 3 |
| open | apple | 2 | | out | 1 |
| | baby | 1 | | yogurt | 2 |
| | belt | 1 | | you | 1 |
| | bracelet | 1 | out | baby | 3 |
| | bite | 1 | | banana | 2 |
| | book | 1 | | Bill | 1 |
| | box | 1 | | box | 1 |
| | bug | 2 | | break | 1 |
| | chair | 1 | | chair | 1 |
| | door | 1 | | dirty | 2 |
| | down | 1 | | drink | 5 |
| | draw | 1 | | eat | 6 |
| | drink | 3 | | finish | 2 |
| | eat | 8 | | go | 1 |
| | fruit | 1 | | handcream | 1 |
| | give | 2 | | help | 1 |
| | grape | 3 | | hug | 32 |
| | gum | 1 | | hurry | 2 |
| | help | 3 | | in | 2 |
| | hug | 21 | | key | 1 |
| | in | 1 | | me | 4 |
| | key | 2 | | Nim | 6 |
| | light | 1 | | open | 3 |
| | locative/point | 4 | | pants | 20 |
| | me | 13 | | pear | 4 |
| | Nim | 6 | | plant | 1 |
| | nut | 4 | | play | 3 |
| | orange | 1 | | red | 2 |
| | out | 6 | | shirt | 5 |
| | paper | 1 | | shoe | 19 |
| | pear | 1 | | sock | 1 |
| | play | 2 | | tea | 2 |
| | rock | 1 | | wash | 3 |
| | shoe | 1 | | water | 2 |
| | tickle | 1 | | work | 1 |
| | wash | 1 | paint | yellow | 1 |
| | what | 1 | pancake | eat | 2 |

## Two-Sign Sequences (*cont.*)

| Sequence Type | | Tokens | Sequence Type | | Tokens |
|---|---|---|---|---|---|
| pancake (*cont.*) | me | 2 | | jump | 3 |
| | Nim | 2 | | key | 8 |
| pants | baby | 1 | | locative/point | 4 |
| | hug | 3 | | me | 375 |
| | in | 42 | | more | 7 |
| | locative/point | 1 | | Nim | 67 |
| | me | 4 | | open | 4 |
| | Nim | 2 | | orange | 1 |
| | on | 2 | | out | 4 |
| | out | 26 | | pole | 2 |
| | play | 1 | | shoe | 2 |
| paper | red | 1 | | sorry | 1 |
| peach | apple | 1 | | smell | 1 |
| | eat | 3 | | Susan | 2 |
| | fruit | 2 | | sweet | 1 |
| | Nim | 3 | | tickle | 49 |
| pear | drink | 2 | | Tom | 2 |
| | eat | 8 | | up | 1 |
| | give | 2 | | Walter | 4 |
| | me | 4 | | what | 1 |
| | Nim | 20 | | you | 5 |
| | open | 1 | please | drink | 1 |
| peek-a-boo | come | 1 | | gum | 1 |
| | Nim | 1 | | hug | 9 |
| play | Andrea | 4 | | hurry | 1 |
| | angry | 4 | | me | 1 |
| | ball | 13 | | Nim | 2 |
| | banana | 2 | | open | 1 |
| | Bill | 11 | | tickle | 1 |
| | bug | 3 | pole | me | 2 |
| | clean | 1 | | more | 1 |
| | come | 16 | | Nim | 1 |
| | dirty | 1 | | smell | 1 |
| | dog | 6 | | up | 1 |
| | down | 1 | put | in | 1 |
| | drink | 2 | pull | Nim | 1 |
| | eat | 3 | | out | 1 |
| | finish | 2 | | tickle | 1 |
| | game | 1 | rain | water | 2 |
| | glue | 3 | raisin | apple | 2 |
| | groom | 1 | | eat | 15 |
| | go | 2 | | give | 2 |
| | gum | 4 | | locative/point | 1 |
| | handcream | 1 | | me | 5 |
| | help | 1 | | more | 1 |
| | hug | 23 | | Nim | 23 |
| | in | 1 | | nut | 1 |
| | Joyce | 2 | | open | 1 |

## Two-Sign Sequences (*cont.*)

| Sequence Type | | Tokens | Sequence Type | | Tokens |
|---|---|---|---|---|---|
| really | dirty | 1 | | Nim | 3 |
| red | Andrea | 1 | | off | 7 |
| | apple | 2 | | on | 1 |
| | ball | 2 | | orange | 1 |
| | banana | 1 | | out | 54 |
| | bird | 2 | | pear | 1 |
| | color | 3 | | play | 1 |
| | cup | 1 | | red | 1 |
| | drink | 3 | | tea | 6 |
| | eat | 4 | sleep | apple | 1 |
| | finish | 1 | | hug | 2 |
| | flower | 2 | | lie-down | 1 |
| | fruit | 3 | smell | bug | 1 |
| | hug | 1 | | drink | 3 |
| | Laura | 1 | | eat | 2 |
| | locative/point | 1 | | flower | 1 |
| | more | 1 | | gum | 1 |
| | Nim | 11 | | hot | 2 |
| | orange | 1 | | hug | 1 |
| | out | 1 | | locative/point | 2 |
| | paint | 1 | | me | 1 |
| | shoe | 2 | | Nim | 2 |
| | sweet | 2 | | open | 1 |
| | tea | 2 | | red | 1 |
| | time | 1 | | toothbrush | 1 |
| | up | 1 | socks | in | 1 |
| | work | 1 | | Nim | 1 |
| Renee | cracker | 1 | | out | 1 |
| | eat | 1 | sorry | angry | 3 |
| | finish | 3 | | baby | 1 |
| | hug | 3 | | bad | 3 |
| | Nim | 1 | | Bill | 1 |
| | out | 2 | | bite | 4 |
| | tickle | 1 | | break | 2 |
| rock | give | 1 | | come | 1 |
| | open | 1 | | eat | 1 |
| run | sorry | 1 | | finish | 2 |
| same | me | 1 | | gum | 1 |
| shirt | on | 3 | | hug | 123 |
| | out | 2 | | me | 11 |
| | pants | 1 | | Nim | 13 |
| shoe | chair | 1 | | out | 2 |
| | cracker | 1 | | pants | 1 |
| | give | 1 | | play | 2 |
| | help | 2 | | please | 1 |
| | hug | 1 | | Rene | 1 |
| | me | 4 | | Susan | 1 |
| | more | 1 | | tickle | 1 |

## Two-Sign Sequences (*cont.*)

| Sequence Type | | Tokens | Sequence Type | | Tokens |
|---|---|---|---|---|---|
| spoon | eat | 7 | | apple | 1 |
| | me | 1 | | baby | 1 |
| | Nim | 3 | | ball | 1 |
| stay | toothbrush | 1 | | bite | 2 |
| Susan | me | 1 | | brush | 2 |
| | Renee | 1 | | chalk | 1 |
| | sorry | 1 | | drink | 2 |
| | tea | 1 | | eat | 2 |
| sweet | apple | 3 | | gum | 1 |
| | berry | 1 | | happy | 2 |
| | chair | 2 | | hug | 18 |
| | cracker | 3 | | jump | 1 |
| | drink | 10 | | locative/point | 3 |
| | eat | 27 | | me | 316 |
| | flower | 2 | | more | 23 |
| | handcream | 1 | | Nim | 107 |
| | hug | 2 | | open | 1 |
| | in | 1 | | play | 26 |
| | Laura | 1 | | shoe | 1 |
| | locative/point | 1 | | tea | 2 |
| | me | 23 | | you | 10 |
| | more | 5 | time | eat | 10 |
| | Nim | 85 | | finish | 1 |
| | out | 1 | | give | 1 |
| | open | 1 | | go | 1 |
| | peach | 1 | | hug | 1 |
| | raisin | 6 | | me | 1 |
| | red | 3 | | open | 1 |
| | tea | 1 | | out | 2 |
| | what | 1 | | toothbrush | 1 |
| | yellow | 1 | | work | 6 |
| tea | drink | 77 | Tom | bite | 1 |
| | eat | 11 | | drink | 1 |
| | handcream | 1 | | eat | 2 |
| | hat | 2 | | Nim | 1 |
| | hot | 1 | toothbrush | book | 1 |
| | hug | 2 | | drink | 2 |
| | in | 12 | | eat | 1 |
| | me | 17 | | handcream | 1 |
| | more | 8 | | hug | 2 |
| | Nim | 14 | | me | 6 |
| | nut | 1 | | more | 1 |
| | out | 3 | | Nim | 17 |
| | smell | 1 | | raisin | 1 |
| | tickle | 4 | | time | 1 |
| | time | 2 | tree | break | 2 |
| telephone | in | 1 | up | hug | 1 |
| tickle | Alex | 1 | | open | 1 |

## Two-Sign Sequences (*cont.*)

| Sequence Type | | Tokens | Sequence Type | | Tokens |
|---|---|---|---|---|---|
| | tree | 1 | white | eat | 1 |
| | pole | 2 | who | play | 1 |
| Walter | Nim | 1 | | you | 1 |
| | play | 1 | work | finish | 1 |
| | you | 1 | | grape | 2 |
| wash | diaper | 1 | | hug | 4 |
| | drink | 1 | | out | 2 |
| | water | 1 | | sorry | 2 |
| water | brush | 5 | | time | 8 |
| | clean | 2 | yellow | color | 1 |
| | drink | 8 | | eat | 6 |
| | eat | 2 | | Nim | 3 |
| | gimme | 1 | | toothbrush | 1 |
| | give | 4 | yogurt | apple | 1 |
| | go | 1 | | cracker | 1 |
| | handcream | 1 | | dirty | 1 |
| | hot | 2 | | eat | 16 |
| | in | 1 | | me | 2 |
| | me | 13 | | more | 2 |
| | more | 1 | | Nim | 57 |
| | Nim | 10 | | orange | 2 |
| | open | 1 | | spoon | 1 |
| | toothbrush | 2 | you | banana | 1 |
| | wash | 4 | | Bill | 1 |
| what | ball | 1 | | drink | 2 |
| | bird | 1 | | eat | 8 |
| | book | 3 | | gum | 1 |
| | chair | 1 | | Herb | 2 |
| | clean | 1 | | in | 1 |
| | color | 1 | | me | 20 |
| | drink | 1 | | Nim | 7 |
| | eat | 6 | | open | 1 |
| | fruit | 1 | | orange | 1 |
| | grape | 1 | | Laura | 7 |
| | gum | 1 | | play | 4 |
| | hug | 3 | | shoe | 1 |
| | key | 2 | | Susan | 2 |
| | locative/point | 1 | | sweet | 2 |
| | me | 4 | | tea | 1 |
| | Nim | 4 | | tickle | 9 |
| | open | 1 | | Tom | 1 |
| | raisin | 1 | | water | 2 |
| | smell | 1 | | | |
| | sweet | 1 | Totals: | 1,374 | 9,935 |
| | time | 1 | | | |
| | toothbrush | 1 | | | |
| | you | 1 | | | |
| | work | 2 | | | |

## Three-Sign Sequences

| Sequence Type | | | Tokens | Sequence Type | | | Tokens |
|---|---|---|---|---|---|---|---|
| Andrea | cracker | more | 1 | | Nim | hug | 5 |
| | me | Nim | 1 | | pants | in | 1 |
| | what | play | 1 | bad | hug | me | 1 |
| angry | bite | angry | 1 | | me | eat | 1 |
| | bite | sorry | 1 | | me | Nim | 1 |
| | come | hug | 1 | | Nim | hug | 1 |
| | give | drink | 1 | ball | give | me | 1 |
| | hug | bite | 1 | | in | hat | 1 |
| | hug | sorry | 1 | | Nim | red | 1 |
| | me | angry | 1 | | play | jump | 1 |
| | me | Nim | 1 | | same | eat | 1 |
| | sorry | angry | 1 | banana | Andrea | Nim | 1 |
| | sorry | hug | 1 | | bite | handcream | 1 |
| apple | drink | apple | 1 | | eat | Andrea | 1 |
| | drink | me | 1 | | eat | banana | 3 |
| | drink | Nim | 1 | | eat | drink | 1 |
| | eat | apple | 2 | | eat | me | 11 |
| | eat | drink | 1 | | eat | more | 3 |
| | eat | me | 2 | | eat | Nim | 26 |
| | eat | Nim | 6 | | eat | red | 2 |
| | eat | pear | 1 | | give | hug | 1 |
| | give | me | 1 | | give | Nim | 2 |
| | grape | eat | 2 | | grape | banana | 1 |
| | grape | Nim | 1 | | hug | give | 1 |
| | gum | me | 2 | | hug | me | 2 |
| | hat | me | 1 | | hug | Nim | 1 |
| | in | box | 1 | | Laura | Andrea | 1 |
| | me | apple | 1 | | loc./point | banana | 1 |
| | me | eat | 15 | | me | banana | 10 |
| | me | Nim | 4 | | me | eat | 17 |
| | more | eat | 1 | | me | hug | 1 |
| | Nim | apple | 7 | | me | more | 1 |
| | Nim | eat | 9 | | me | Nim | 18 |
| | Nim | give | 2 | | more | banana | 1 |
| | Nim | gum | 1 | | more | eat | 1 |
| | Nim | out | 1 | | more | me | 1 |
| | orange | apple | 1 | | more | Nim | 3 |
| | orange | eat | 1 | | more | tickle | 1 |
| | out | hug | 1 | | Nim | banana | 6 |
| | peach | bite | 2 | | Nim | drink | 2 |
| | tea | Nim | 1 | | Nim | eat | 33 |
| baby | eat | apple | 1 | | Nim | me | 4 |
| | eat | grape | 1 | | Nim | more | 1 |
| | eat | nut | 1 | | smell | eat | 1 |
| | hug | Nim | 5 | | toothbrush | me | 1 |
| | me | Nim | 1 | | toothbrush | Nim | 1 |
| | Nim | baby | 7 | | wash | pants | 1 |
| | Nim | eat | 3 | berry | give | eat | 1 |

## Three-Sign Sequences (*cont.*)

| Sequence Type | | | Tokens |
|---|---|---|---|
| | grape | berry | 1 |
| Bill | Andrea | eat | 1 |
| | give | gum | 1 |
| | grape | Nim | 1 |
| | gum | eat | 2 |
| | listen | hug | 1 |
| | me | Bill | 1 |
| | Nim | eat | 2 |
| | Nim | nut | 1 |
| | Nim | play | 3 |
| | nut | me | 1 |
| | play | Nim | 1 |
| bird | me | bird | 1 |
| bite | angry | Nim | 1 |
| | apple | bite | 1 |
| | hug | bite | 1 |
| | me | bite | 1 |
| | me | sorry | 1 |
| | me | you | 1 |
| | Nim | bite | 1 |
| black | give | black | 1 |
| book | give | me | 1 |
| | me | Nim | 1 |
| | me | open | 1 |
| break | banana | Nim | 1 |
| | eat | tickle | 1 |
| brown | Nim | more | 1 |
| | shoe | hug | 1 |
| brush | hat | me | 1 |
| | listen | chair | 1 |
| | me | brush | 1 |
| | me | hug | 1 |
| | me | Nim | 1 |
| | me | you | 1 |
| | Nim | baby | 1 |
| | Nim | me | 1 |
| bug | Nim | hug | 1 |
| can't | happy | hug | 1 |
| cat | come | me | 1 |
| | loc./point | book | 1 |
| chair | eat | chair | 1 |
| | me | eat | 1 |
| | more | chair | 1 |
| | smell | red | 1 |
| clean | me | eat | 1 |
| | Nim | out | 1 |
| | out | clean | 1 |
| | out | pants | 1 |

| Sequence Type | | | Tokens |
|---|---|---|---|
| close | out | in | 1 |
| color | Bill | Nim | 1 |
| | brown | groom | 1 |
| | eat | yellow | 1 |
| | Nim | brown | 1 |
| | Nim | color | 1 |
| | Nim | eat | 2 |
| | orange | eat | 1 |
| | orange | Nim | 1 |
| | red | apple | 1 |
| | red | color | 1 |
| | red | Nim | 2 |
| come | drink | eat | 1 |
| | give | sweet | 1 |
| | gum | come | 1 |
| | hug | come | 2 |
| | kiss | hug | 1 |
| | me | come | 1 |
| | me | hug | 1 |
| | me | Nim | 2 |
| | me | Walter | 1 |
| | more | come | 1 |
| | play | hurry | 1 |
| cookie | Nim | eat | 1 |
| cracker | eat | cracker | 2 |
| | eat | Nim | 4 |
| | give | loc./point | 1 |
| | me | cracker | 4 |
| | me | eat | 2 |
| | Nim | cracker | 4 |
| | Nim | eat | 1 |
| | orange | eat | 1 |
| Dick | me | eat | 1 |
| dirty | eat | dirty | 1 |
| | finish | hug | 3 |
| | hug | dirty | 4 |
| | hug | finish | 3 |
| | hug | Nim | 3 |
| | hug | Renee | 1 |
| | in | water | 1 |
| | me | dirty | 1 |
| | me | eat | 1 |
| | Nim | dirty | 3 |
| | Nim | hug | 1 |
| | open | out | 1 |
| | orange | hug | 1 |
| | out | Nim | 1 |
| | pants | in | 1 |

## Three-Sign Sequences (*cont.*)

| Sequence Type | | | Tokens |
|---|---|---|---|
| dirty (*cont.*) | red | out | 1 |
| | sorry | bite | 1 |
| | sorry | hug | 1 |
| draw | hug | pancake | 1 |
| drink | banana | apple | 1 |
| | banana | Nim | 1 |
| | eat | book | 1 |
| | eat | out | 1 |
| | eat | dirty | 1 |
| | eat | drink | 11 |
| | eat | grape | 1 |
| | eat | hurry | 1 |
| | eat | loc./point | 1 |
| | eat | me | 1 |
| | eat | more | 2 |
| | eat | Nim | 4 |
| | eat | nut | 3 |
| | eat | tea | 3 |
| | eat | toothbrush | 1 |
| | give | me | 1 |
| | give | Nim | 1 |
| | groom | eat | 1 |
| | point | Nim | 2 |
| | me | drink | 10 |
| | me | eat | 12 |
| | me | give | 1 |
| | me | loc./point | 1 |
| | me | more | 1 |
| | me | Nim | 14 |
| | me | tea | 1 |
| | more | drink | 1 |
| | more | eat | 3 |
| | more | me | 1 |
| | more | Nim | 1 |
| | more | tea | 2 |
| | Nim | down | 1 |
| | Nim | drink | 10 |
| | Nim | eat | 4 |
| | Nim | loc./point | 4 |
| | Nim | me | 4 |
| | Nim | orange | 1 |
| | Nim | out | 1 |
| | Nim | peach | 1 |
| | Nim | sweet | 3 |
| | Nim | tea | 2 |
| | orange | eat | 1 |
| | red | drink | 2 |

| Sequence Type | | | Tokens |
|---|---|---|---|
| | smell | eat | 1 |
| | sweet | hug | 1 |
| | sweet | hungry | 1 |
| | sweet | me | 1 |
| | sweet | Nim | 3 |
| | sweet | tea | 1 |
| | tea | drink | 1 |
| | tea | eat | 1 |
| | tca | more | 1 |
| | tea | Nim | 2 |
| | toothbrush | clean | 1 |
| | water | drink | 1 |
| | what | drink | 1 |
| eat | apple | eat | 1 |
| | apple | gum | 1 |
| | apple | me | 1 |
| | apple | Nim | 8 |
| | apple | pear | 1 |
| | baby | Nim | 1 |
| | banana | eat | 4 |
| | banana | me | 3 |
| | banana | Nim | 6 |
| | banana | open | 1 |
| | brown | eat | 1 |
| | color | eat | 1 |
| | color | Nim | 1 |
| | cracker | Nim | 1 |
| | drink | Andrea | 1 |
| | drink | banana | 1 |
| | drink | eat | 6 |
| | drink | give | 1 |
| | drink | hug | 2 |
| | drink | me | 5 |
| | drink | more | 1 |
| | drink | Nim | 3 |
| | drink | orange | 1 |
| | drink | red | 1 |
| | drink | sweet | 1 |
| | drink | tea | 2 |
| | finish | down | 1 |
| | finish | eat | 1 |
| | fruit | grape | 1 |
| | fruit | gum | 1 |
| | fruit | me | 1 |
| | fruit | Nim | 2 |
| | give | eat | 3 |
| | grape | drink | 3 |
| | grape | eat | 6 |

## Three-Sign Sequences (*cont.*)

| Sequence Type | | Tokens | Sequence Type | | Tokens |
|---|---|---|---|---|---|
| grape | hug | 1 | Nim | hot | 2 |
| grape | Nim | 6 | Nim | hug | 4 |
| green | Nim | 1 | Nim | hungry | 2 |
| groom | eat | 1 | Nim | loc./point | 2 |
| gum | Bill | 3 | Nim | me | 2 |
| gum | eat | 1 | Nim | more | 2 |
| gum | hurry | 1 | Nim | nut | 4 |
| gum | Nim | 5 | Nim | orange | 2 |
| gum | same | 1 | Nim | peach | 1 |
| hug | drink | 1 | Nim | pear | 1 |
| hug | open | 1 | Nim | play | 1 |
| hug | yogurt | 1 | Nim | raisin | 2 |
| hungry | hug | 1 | Nim | sweet | 5 |
| hungry | Nim | 1 | Nim | tea | 1 |
| in | eat | 1 | Nim | white | 1 |
| jump | tickle | 1 | Nim | yogurt | 7 |
| loc./point | hurry | 1 | nut | eat | 2 |
| loc./point | me | 1 | nut | Nim | 2 |
| loc./point | smell | 1 | nut | raisin | 1 |
| loc./point | sweet | 1 | orange | eat | 1 |
| me | apple | 1 | out | yogurt | 1 |
| me | drink | 3 | pear | apple | 1 |
| me | eat | 16 | pear | drink | 1 |
| me | grape | 1 | pear | eat | 1 |
| me | gum | 2 | pear | handcream | 1 |
| me | hug | 1 | raisin | berry | 1 |
| me | hungry | 1 | raisin | eat | 3 |
| me | more | 1 | raisin | grape | 2 |
| me | Nim | 48 | raisin | me | 1 |
| me | nut | 1 | raisin | more | 4 |
| me | open | 1 | raisin | Nim | 4 |
| me | raisin | 1 | red | Nim | 1 |
| me | tea | 1 | sorry | hug | 1 |
| more | banana | 2 | Susan | hug | 1 |
| more | chair | 1 | sweet | finish | 1 |
| more | drink | 1 | sweet | Nim | 3 |
| more | eat | 11 | sweet | raisin | 1 |
| more | gum | 1 | tea | drink | 2 |
| more | me | 4 | tea | eat | 2 |
| more | Nim | 2 | tickle | me | 1 |
| Nim | apple | 5 | time | eat | 1 |
| Nim | banana | 1 | time | hug | 1 |
| Nim | cracker | 1 | what | Nim | 1 |
| Nim | dirty | 1 | yogurt | eat | 1 |
| Nim | drink | 2 | yogurt | Nim | 1 |
| Nim | eat | 46 | egg | eat | Nim | 1 |
| Nim | give | 1 | finish | angry | Nim | 1 |
| Nim | grape | 1 | | dirty | finish | 1 |

## Three-Sign Sequences (*cont.*)

| Sequence Type | | | Tokens | Sequence Type | | | Tokens |
|---|---|---|---|---|---|---|---|
| finish (*cont.*) | dirty | hug | 1 | | eat | give | 4 |
| | eat | drink | 1 | | eat | loc./point | 1 |
| | eat | hug | 2 | | eat | me | 2 |
| | hug | finish | 3 | | eat | Nim | 6 |
| | hug | give | 1 | | eat | orange | 1 |
| | hug | Nim | 18 | | eat | spoon | 1 |
| | hug | sorry | 2 | | eat | sweet | 1 |
| | me | finish | 1 | | eat | toothbrush | 1 |
| | me | Nim | 2 | | egg | eat | 1 |
| | more | me | 1 | | grape | plate | 1 |
| | Nim | drink | 1 | | jump | ball | 1 |
| | Nim | hug | 3 | | Laura | drink | 1 |
| | out | hug | 1 | | Laura | give | 1 |
| | shoe | out | 1 | | Laura | toothbrush | 1 |
| | sorry | finish | 1 | | me | apple | 2 |
| | wash | hug | 1 | | me | all | 2 |
| flower | bug | flower | 1 | | me | banana | 3 |
| | eat | flower | 1 | | me | brush | 3 |
| | eat | sweet | 1 | | me | color | 1 |
| | smell | flower | 2 | | me | drink | 5 |
| | sweet | eat | 1 | | me | eat | 15 |
| fruit | eat | fruit | 1 | | me | fruit | 1 |
| | eat | Nim | 1 | | me | give | 1 |
| | grape | eat | 1 | | me | gum | 3 |
| | me | eat | 1 | | me | handcream | 4 |
| | me | Nim | 1 | | me | hat | 1 |
| | Nim | Bill | 1 | | me | light | 2 |
| | Nim | eat | 3 | | me | loc./point | 4 |
| | Nim | fruit | 3 | | me | more | 2 |
| | pear | Nim | 1 | | me | Nim | 10 |
| | red | fruit | 1 | | me | nut | 1 |
| gimme | eat | gum | 1 | | me | orange | 1 |
| | eat | me | 1 | | me | raisin | 1 |
| | Nim | eat | 1 | | me | sock | 1 |
| | red | berry | 1 | | me | sweet | 2 |
| | red | drink | 1 | | me | tea | 1 |
| give | apple | hot | 1 | | me | tickle | 2 |
| | apple | me | 1 | | me | water | 2 |
| | ball | give | 1 | | more | drink | 1 |
| | banana | eat | 1 | | more | eat | 1 |
| | drink | give | 2 | | more | gum | 2 |
| | drink | me | 1 | | more | Nim | 1 |
| | drink | Nim | 4 | | more | tea | 2 |
| | drink | tea | 1 | | Nim | color | 1 |
| | eat | banana | 1 | | Nim | cracker | 1 |
| | eat | black | 1 | | Nim | eat | 5 |
| | eat | chair | 1 | | Nim | give | 2 |
| | eat | drink | 3 | | Nim | grape | 1 |

## Three-Sign Sequences (*cont.*)

| Sequence Type | | | Tokens | Sequence Type | | | Tokens |
|---|---|---|---|---|---|---|---|
| | Nim | jump | 1 | | give | Nim | 1 |
| | Nim | loc./point | 1 | | me | ball | 1 |
| | Nim | me | 3 | | me | eat | 10 |
| | Nim | more | 1 | | me | gum | 4 |
| | Nim | pole | 1 | | me | Nim | 8 |
| | Nim | sweet | 1 | | me | smell | 1 |
| | nut | eat | 1 | | more | eat | 1 |
| | raisin | Andrea | 1 | | Nim | eat | 11 |
| | spoon | Nim | 1 | | Nim | me | 1 |
| | sweet | cracker | 1 | | Nim | please | 1 |
| | sweet | eat | 1 | | you | eat | 1 |
| | tea | drink | 2 | handcream | berry | eat | 1 |
| | tea | Nim | 1 | | brown | eat | 1 |
| | toothbrush | hug | 2 | | brush | Nim | 1 |
| | what | Nim | 1 | | give | handcream | 1 |
| | yogurt | Nim | 1 | | give | me | 2 |
| grape | banana | me | 1 | | in | apple | 1 |
| | dick | grape | 1 | | me | give | 1 |
| | eat | Alex | 1 | | more | handcream | 1 |
| | eat | apple | 1 | happy | me | Nim | 1 |
| | eat | baby | 1 | | tickle | more | 1 |
| | eat | drink | 1 | harmonica | drink | hug | 1 |
| | eat | give | 2 | hat | me | drink | 1 |
| | eat | hurry | 1 | | me | hat | 1 |
| | eat | loc./point | 1 | | me | Nim | 3 |
| | eat | me | 2 | | Nim | hat | 1 |
| | eat | more | 1 | | Nim | me | 1 |
| | eat | Nim | 37 | help | shoe | out | 1 |
| | eat | raisin | 1 | Herb | me | play | 1 |
| | eat | sweet | 1 | here | cracker | loc./point | 1 |
| | groom | grape | 1 | hot | give | me | 2 |
| | hug | Nim | 2 | | Nim | eat | 1 |
| | me | eat | 3 | hug | Bill | me | 1 |
| | me | Nim | 5 | | dirty | Nim | 1 |
| | Nim | eat | 13 | | eat | Nim | 1 |
| | Nim | in | 1 | | finish | hug | 4 |
| | out | finish | 1 | | finish | Nim | 2 |
| | peach | pear | 1 | | finish | out | 1 |
| groom | me | loc./point | 1 | | help | up | 1 |
| gum | apple | gum | 1 | | me | finish | 1 |
| | drink | gum | 1 | | me | hug | 6 |
| | eat | Andrea | 1 | | me | more | 2 |
| | eat | drink | 2 | | me | Nim | 17 |
| | eat | gum | 7 | | Nim | eat | 1 |
| | eat | hug | 1 | | Nim | finish | 2 |
| | eat | Nim | 8 | | Nim | hug | 14 |
| | gimme | drink | 1 | | Nim | me | 3 |
| | gimme | Nim | 1 | | Nim | more | 3 |

## Three-Sign Sequences (*cont.*)

| Sequence Type | | | Tokens | Sequence Type | | | Tokens |
|---|---|---|---|---|---|---|---|
| hug (*cont.*) | Nim | sleep | 1 | | angry | sorry | 1 |
| | Nim | sorry | 2 | | apple | gum | 1 |
| | Nim | Susan | 1 | | apple | me | 1 |
| | out | Renee | 1 | | ball | me | 1 |
| | sorry | angry | 1 | | banana | eat | 5 |
| | sorry | hug | 7 | | banana | me | 2 |
| | sorry | me | 2 | | banana | Nim | 1 |
| | sorry | Nim | 1 | | berry | eat | 1 |
| | Susan | Nim | 1 | | brown | in | 1 |
| | tea | drink | 1 | | brush | in | 1 |
| hungry | eat | drink | 1 | | brush | Nim | 1 |
| | eat | hungry | 1 | | cat | Nim | 1 |
| | loc./point | me | 1 | | color | out | 1 |
| | me | Nim | 1 | | cracker | hat | 1 |
| | Nim | eat | 1 | | dirty | sorry | 1 |
| | Nim | hug | 1 | | drink | apple | 1 |
| | Nim | me | 1 | | drink | in | 1 |
| in | give | in | 1 | | drink | loc./point | 2 |
| | grape | Nim | 1 | | drink | Nim | 3 |
| | me | Nim | 1 | | drink | tea | 9 |
| | pants | in | 5 | | eat | apple | 9 |
| Jews-harp | eat | Nim | 1 | | eat | banana | 10 |
| Joyce | jump | me | 1 | | eat | brush | 1 |
| | Nim | me | 1 | | eat | drink | 2 |
| | tickle | me | 1 | | eat | grape | 2 |
| jump | more | tickle | 1 | | eat | gum | 5 |
| | Nim | Jump | 1 | | eat | hug | 1 |
| key | eat | me | 1 | | eat | kiss | 1 |
| | me | key | 1 | | eat | loc./point | 1 |
| | me | Nim | 1 | | eat | me | 4 |
| | Nim | key | 1 | | eat | more | 5 |
| kiss | Joyce | bite | 1 | | eat | Nim | 12 |
| | Nim | eat | 1 | | eat | orange | 12 |
| Laura | apple | give | 1 | | eat | pear | 1 |
| | bite | Laura | 1 | | eat | red | 1 |
| | bite | loc./point | 1 | | eat | toothbrush | 1 |
| | eat | apple | 1 | | finish | hug | 1 |
| | eat | me | 1 | | give | ball | 1 |
| | me | Laura | 1 | | give | eat | 2 |
| | me | orange | 1 | | give | me | 1 |
| | red | give | 1 | | grape | eat | 1 |
| Listen | apple | orange | 1 | | gum | eat | 1 |
| | Bill | Andrea | 1 | | gum | Nim | 1 |
| | hug | hat | 1 | | hat | give | 1 |
| | me | eat | 1 | | hat | in | 1 |
| | me | you | 1 | | hat | me | 1 |
| | Nim | Laura | 1 | | hug | banana | 2 |
| me | angry | peek-a-boo | 1 | | hug | finish | 1 |

## Three-Sign Sequences (*cont.*)

| Sequence Type | | Tokens | Sequence Type | | Tokens |
|---|---|---|---|---|---|
| hug | me | 2 | | play | you | 3 |
| hungry | eat | 1 | | raisin | eat | 1 |
| hungry | grape | 1 | | raisin | nut | 1 |
| hungry | me | 1 | | shoe | play | 1 |
| hungry | pear | 1 | | smell | shoe | 1 |
| jump | hug | 1 | | smell | sweet | 2 |
| jump | play | 1 | | smell | you | 1 |
| listen | tea | 1 | | sorry | bite | 1 |
| loc./point | eat | 2 | | sorry | hug | 2 |
| more | apple | 4 | | sorry | Nim | 1 |
| more | banana | 2 | | Susan | play | 1 |
| more | drink | 2 | | sweet | brown | 1 |
| more | eat | 19 | | sweet | eat | 1 |
| more | give | 1 | | sweet | me | 1 |
| more | orange | 1 | | sweet | Nim | 2 |
| more | tea | 3 | | sweet | what | 1 |
| more | tickle | 1 | | tickle | Andrea | 1 |
| Nim | Andrea | 2 | | tickle | hug | 1 |
| Nim | apple | 1 | | tickle | Nim | 2 |
| Nim | bug | 1 | | tickle | play | 1 |
| Nim | drink | 8 | | toothbrush | hat | 1 |
| Nim | eat | 21 | | up | hug | 1 |
| Nim | gum | 2 | | water | Nim | 1 |
| Nim | hat | 1 | | you | play | 1 |
| Nim | hug | 7 | more | apple | eat | 1 |
| Nim | hungry | 1 | | apple | Nim | 1 |
| Nim | in | 1 | | baby | hug | 1 |
| Nim | kiss | 1 | | baby | Nim | 1 |
| Nim | loc./point | 2 | | banana | eat | 6 |
| Nim | me | 13 | | banana | me | 6 |
| Nim | more | 1 | | banana | Nim | 1 |
| Nim | orange | 1 | | book | handcream | 1 |
| Nim | out | 1 | | chair | eat | 1 |
| Nim | play | 13 | | chair | me | 1 |
| Nim | tea | 3 | | close | hug | 1 |
| Nim | tickle | 1 | | dirty | eat | 1 |
| Nim | time | 1 | | drink | Bill | 1 |
| Nim | up | 1 | | drink | eat | 1 |
| Nim | water | 1 | | drink | give | 1 |
| Nim | what | 1 | | drink | Nim | 3 |
| Nim | you | 3 | | drink | tea | 3 |
| orange | eat | 2 | | drink | toothbrush | 2 |
| out | play | 1 | | drink | water | 1 |
| pants | hug | 1 | | eat | apple | 5 |
| play | Bill | 1 | | eat | banana | 2 |
| play | me | 5 | | eat | Bill | 1 |
| play | Nim | 1 | | eat | drink | 4 |
| play | tickle | 5 | | eat | fruit | 1 |

## Three-Sign Sequences (*cont.*)

| Sequence Type | | | Tokens | Sequence Type | | | Tokens |
|---|---|---|---|---|---|---|---|
| more (*cont.*) | eat | gum | 2 | | tickle | drink | 1 |
| | eat | loc./point | 1 | | tickle | eat | 1 |
| | eat | me | 12 | | tickle | me | 3 |
| | eat | more | 3 | | tickle | more | 8 |
| | eat | Nim | 19 | | tickle | Nim | 5 |
| | eat | nut | 2 | | tickle | play | 3 |
| | eat | red | 1 | | tickle | Susan | 1 |
| | eat | same | 1 | | tickle | you | 1 |
| | eat | sweet | 3 | | what | raisin | 1 |
| | eat | tickle | 1 | Nim | Andrea | Joyce | 1 |
| | grape | eat | 2 | | apple | Nim | 1 |
| | grape | give | 1 | | baby | hug | 1 |
| | grape | hug | 1 | | banana | eat | 3 |
| | grape | Nim | 1 | | banana | fruit | 1 |
| | give | gum | 1 | | banana | more | 2 |
| | gum | eat | 2 | | banana | Nim | 3 |
| | gum | me | 3 | | Bill | Andrea | 1 |
| | gum | Nim | 1 | | Bill | play | 1 |
| | handcream | brush | 1 | | brush | me | 1 |
| | hungry | hug | 1 | | brush | Nim | 1 |
| | loc./point | more | 1 | | clean | baby | 1 |
| | me | banana | 1 | | drink | eat | 2 |
| | me | drink | 1 | | drink | help | 1 |
| | me | eat | 6 | | drink | hug | 1 |
| | me | grape | 1 | | drink | loc./point | 2 |
| | me | more | 1 | | drink | me | 3 |
| | me | Nim | 4 | | drink | Nim | 3 |
| | me | tea | 1 | | drink | you | 1 |
| | me | tickle | 2 | | eat | apple | 1 |
| | me | you | 1 | | eat | banana | 3 |
| | Nim | eat | 9 | | eat | cracker | 1 |
| | Nim | hug | 1 | | eat | drink | 8 |
| | Nim | me | 2 | | eat | fruit | 1 |
| | Nim | play | 2 | | eat | give | 1 |
| | Nim | tickle | 1 | | eat | grape | 9 |
| | nut | ball | 1 | | eat | gum | 1 |
| | nut | give | 1 | | eat | loc./point | 1 |
| | orange | eat | 1 | | eat | me | 8 |
| | peach | eat | 1 | | eat | more | 3 |
| | pear | eat | 1 | | eat | Nim | 17 |
| | play | me | 2 | | eat | nut | 3 |
| | same | more | 1 | | eat | orange | 1 |
| | smell | gum | 1 | | eat | orange | 1 |
| | sweet | more | 1 | | eat | peach | 1 |
| | sweet | Nim | 1 | | eat | pear | 1 |
| | tea | drink | 1 | | eat | raisin | 2 |
| | tea | hug | 1 | | eat | red | 2 |
| | tea | me | 1 | | eat | sweet | 8 |

## Three-Sign Sequences (*cont.*)

| Sequence Type | | Tokens | Sequence Type | | Tokens |
|---|---|---|---|---|---|
| eat | tickle | 1 | | peach | Andrea | 1 |
| eat | water | 1 | | pear | eat | 2 |
| eat | what | 2 | | play | me | 1 |
| eat | yogurt | 3 | | sleep | hug | 1 |
| gimme | gum | 1 | | sorry | Bob | 1 |
| give | water | 1 | | sweet | eat | 1 |
| give | what | 1 | | sweet | gimme | 1 |
| grape | eat | 4 | | sweet | me | 1 |
| grape | me | 1 | | sweet | Nim | 1 |
| groom | baby | 1 | | sweet | you | 1 |
| gum | eat | 1 | | tickle | me | 1 |
| gum | me | 1 | | tickle | more | 1 |
| hug | bad | 1 | | time | me | 1 |
| hug | blue | 1 | | toothbrush | Nim | 1 |
| hug | drink | 2 | | water | down | 1 |
| hug | eat | 1 | | yogurt | Nim | 2 |
| hug | finish | 1 | | you | me | 1 |
| hug | me | 1 | nut | baby | eat | 1 |
| hug | Nim | 1 | | baby | nut | 1 |
| hug | Renee | 1 | | Bill | eat | 1 |
| hungry | Nim | 1 | | eat | drink | 1 |
| hurry | gum | 1 | | eat | me | 1 |
| kiss | baby | 1 | | eat | Nim | 6 |
| Laura | sorry | 1 | | eat | nut | 9 |
| loc./point | eat | 1 | | give | me | 1 |
| loc./point | up | 1 | | help | out | 1 |
| me | drink | 2 | | hurry | eat | 1 |
| me | eat | 27 | | me | drink | 1 |
| me | gum | 2 | | me | eat | 2 |
| me | in | 1 | | me | more | 1 |
| me | Joyce | 1 | | me | Nim | 4 |
| me | Laura | 1 | | more | nut | 1 |
| me | loc./point | 1 | | Nim | eat | 4 |
| me | Nim | 12 | | Nim | me | 5 |
| me | open | 1 | | Nim | nut | 15 |
| me | orange | 1 | | Nim | please | 1 |
| me | play | 3 | | open | hug | 1 |
| me | sorry | 1 | | out | red | 1 |
| me | tickle | 1 | | Tom | eat | 1 |
| more | drink | 1 | | work | out | 1 |
| more | eat | 4 | on | baby | chair | 1 |
| more | Nim | 2 | | baby | Nim | 1 |
| nut | Nim | 2 | open | apple | Nim | 1 |
| open | hug | 1 | | banana | me | 1 |
| orange | eat | 2 | | Bill | open | 2 |
| orange | go | 1 | | color | red | 1 |
| orange | Nim | 1 | | drink | open | 1 |
| pants | in | 1 | | eat | grape | 1 |

## Three-Sign Sequences (*cont.*)

| Sequence Type | | | Tokens |
|---|---|---|---|
| open (*cont.*) | grape | fruit | 1 |
| | grape | in | 1 |
| | grape | Nim | 1 |
| | handcream | tickle | 1 |
| | help | me | 1 |
| | help | open | 3 |
| | hug | me | 1 |
| | Nim | drink | 1 |
| | Nim | eat | 1 |
| | Nim | nut | 1 |
| | Nim | sweet | 1 |
| | please | me | 1 |
| | sorry | open | 1 |
| | toothbrush | open | 1 |
| orange | apple | Nim | 1 |
| | Bill | Andrea | 1 |
| | drink | in | 1 |
| | drink | more | 2 |
| | eat | loc./point | 1 |
| | eat | me | 1 |
| | eat | more | 1 |
| | eat | Nim | 2 |
| | eat | orange | 3 |
| | eat | sweet | 1 |
| | in | hat | 1 |
| | me | eat | 8 |
| | me | Nim | 1 |
| | me | tea | 2 |
| | more | give | 1 |
| | Nim | drink | 1 |
| | Nim | eat | 2 |
| | Nim | me | 1 |
| | Nim | orange | 2 |
| | red | me | 1 |
| | sweet | eat | 1 |
| | tea | drink | 1 |
| | yogurt | orange | 1 |
| orange | Nim | color | 1 |
| orange | Nim | eat | 1 |
| | Nim | orange | 1 |
| | Nim | Renee | 1 |
| out | baby | out | 1 |
| | drink | out | 1 |
| | finish | hug | 1 |
| | gum | Bill | 1 |
| | hug | me | 1 |
| | hug | Nim | 2 |
| | hug | out | 1 |

| Sequence Type | | | Tokens |
|---|---|---|---|
| | hug | Renee | 1 |
| | hug | sorry | 1 |
| | me | Nim | 1 |
| | me | you | 1 |
| | Nim | hug | 1 |
| | Nim | out | 2 |
| | open | hug | 1 |
| | pants | out | 1 |
| | play | finish | 1 |
| paint | yellow | black | 1 |
| | yellow | Nim | 1 |
| pancake | eat | Nim | 1 |
| | me | Nim | 1 |
| pants | in | finish | 2 |
| | in | hug | 1 |
| | Nim | hug | 1 |
| | out | pants | 1 |
| peach | eat | Nim | 1 |
| | grape | banana | 1 |
| | Nim | eat | 2 |
| | pear | apple | 1 |
| pear | apple | eat | 1 |
| | banana | eat | 1 |
| | eat | Nim | 4 |
| | hug | Nim | 1 |
| | hug | pear | 1 |
| | me | Nim | 3 |
| | Nim | eat | 4 |
| | Nim | give | 1 |
| | Nim | grape | 1 |
| | Nim | hug | 1 |
| | Nim | pear | 2 |
| play | Andrea | Bill | 2 |
| | ball | Bill | 1 |
| | Bill | Andrea | 1 |
| | Bill | you | 1 |
| | chair | eat | 1 |
| | come | play | 1 |
| | come | open | 1 |
| | dirty | me | 1 |
| | drink | Bill | 1 |
| | eat | play | 2 |
| | hat | me | 1 |
| | hat | Nim | 1 |
| | hug | Nim | 1 |
| | hug | play | 1 |
| | Joyce | play | 1 |
| | me | Andrea | 3 |

## Three-Sign Sequences (*cont.*)

| Sequence Type | | | Tokens | Sequence Type | | | Tokens |
|---|---|---|---|---|---|---|---|
| | me | angry | 1 | | me | smell | 1 |
| | me | come | 2 | | more | banana | 1 |
| | me | flower | 1 | | Nim | eat | 1 |
| | me | hug | 5 | | Nim | me | 1 |
| | me | jump | 1 | | tea | me | 1 |
| | me | Nim | 81 | | water | handcream | 1 |
| | me | play | 14 | | water | Nim | 1 |
| | me | Susan | 2 | pole | more | pole | 1 |
| | me | tickle | 13 | pull | Nim | pull | 1 |
| | me | you | 3 | | tickle | pull | 1 |
| | more | tickle | 1 | raisin | eat | me | 1 |
| | Nim | Bill | 2 | | eat | more | 1 |
| | Nim | bug | 2 | | eat | Nim | 4 |
| | Nim | gum | 1 | | eat | raisin | 1 |
| | Nim | hug | 1 | | me | Nim | 1 |
| | Nim | me | 3 | | Nim | eat | 3 |
| | Nim | play | 5 | | Nim | raisin | 1 |
| | Nim | tickle | 1 | | nut | raisin | 1 |
| | nut | drink | 1 | red | eat | sweet | 1 |
| | open | tickle | 1 | | gum | Nim | 1 |
| | out | hug | 1 | | Laura | berry | 1 |
| | out | shoe | 1 | | Nim | color | 1 |
| | shoe | play | 1 | | Nim | loc./point | 1 |
| | smell | red | 1 | | Nim | red | 2 |
| | Susan | me | 1 | | Nim | sweet | 1 |
| | Susan | play | 1 | | please | hug | 1 |
| | tickle | groom | 1 | shoe | baby | hug | 1 |
| | tickle | hug | 1 | | handcream | Nim | 1 |
| | tickle | me | 1 | | hug | Nim | 1 |
| | tickle | Nim | 2 | | Nim | eat | 1 |
| | tickle | play | 4 | | out | me | 1 |
| | tickle | water | 1 | | out | tickle | 1 |
| | Walter | Nim | 2 | | play | tickle | 1 |
| | Walter | play | 1 | smell | drink | eat | 1 |
| | water | Nim | 1 | | loc./point | you | 1 |
| | water | tickle | 1 | | me | eat | 1 |
| | you | me | 1 | | me | listen | 1 |
| | you | Nim | 2 | | tea | drink | 1 |
| please | water | drink | 1 | sucks | me | Nim | 1 |
| point/loc. | eat | drink | 1 | sorry | angry | sorry | 1 |
| | eat | what | 1 | | dirty | hug | 1 |
| | give | gum | 1 | | dirty | sorry | 1 |
| | give | me | 1 | | hug | me | 2 |
| | grape | eat | 1 | | hug | music | 1 |
| | hug | me | 1 | | hug | Nim | 5 |
| | listen | me | 1 | | hug | sorry | 5 |
| | me | grape | 1 | | me | sorry | 2 |
| | me | Nim | 1 | | Nim | hug | 1 |

## Three-Sign Sequences (*cont.*)

| Sequence Type | | Tokens | Sequence Type | | Tokens |
|---|---|---|---|---|---|
| sorry (*cont.*) Nim | sorry | 1 | | drink | tea | 7 |
| spoon | eat | drink | 1 | | eat | more | 1 |
| | eat | Nim | 2 | | eat | Nim | 1 |
| | me | drink | 1 | | eat | nut | 1 |
| | me | eat | 1 | | eat | tea | 1 |
| | Nim | eat | 1 | | grape | eat | 1 |
| sweet | apple | Nim | 1 | | in | me | 1 |
| | drink | eat | 1 | | in | spoon | 1 |
| | drink | me | 1 | | me | drink | 3 |
| | drink | Nim | 3 | | me | eat | 1 |
| | drink | sweet | 3 | | me | hug | 1 |
| | eat | me | 3 | | me | in | 1 |
| | eat | Nim | 6 | | me | orange | 1 |
| | eat | sweet | 1 | | me | tea | 1 |
| | fish | Nim | 1 | | more | drink | 1 |
| | give | sweet | 1 | | more | eat | 1 |
| | gum | eat | 1 | | more | Nim | 1 |
| | hungry | me | 1 | | Nim | drink | 2 |
| | in | tea | 1 | | Nim | eat | 1 |
| | Laura | eat | 1 | | Nim | tea | 2 |
| | me | eat | 4 | | play | drink | 1 |
| | me | hug | 2 | | sorry | eat | 1 |
| | me | Nim | 4 | | water | drink | 1 |
| | me | sweet | 2 | | water | hot | 1 |
| | more | me | 1 | | water | tea | 1 |
| | Nim | color | 1 | thirsty | drink | Nim | 1 |
| | Nim | drink | 1 | tickle | banana | Nim | 1 |
| | Nim | eat | 10 | | bite | book | 1 |
| | Nim | me | 5 | | me | give | 1 |
| | Nim | more | 1 | | me | gum | 1 |
| | Nim | open | 1 | | me | hug | 3 |
| | Nim | red | 1 | | me | Laura | 2 |
| | Nim | shoe | 1 | | me | loc./point | 2 |
| | Nim | Susan | 1 | | me | more | 5 |
| | Nim | sweet | 14 | | me | Nim | 44 |
| | pancake | apple | 1 | | me | play | 5 |
| | raisin | Nim | 1 | | me | tickle | 19 |
| | red | Nim | 1 | | me | you | 3 |
| | tea | drink | 1 | | more | me | 7 |
| swing | more | swing | 1 | | more | tickle | 3 |
| tea | bread | give | 1 | | Nim | baby | 2 |
| | cracker | me | 1 | | Nim | eat | 2 |
| | drink | ball | 1 | | Nim | me | 1 |
| | drink | eat | 1 | | Nim | play | 1 |
| | drink | hug | 1 | | Nim | tickle | 4 |
| | drink | me | 4 | | Nim | you | 1 |
| | drink | more | 1 | | pear | grape | 1 |
| | drink | Nim | 9 | | play | me | 2 |

## Three-Sign Sequences (*cont.*)

| Sequence Type | | | Tokens |
|---|---|---|---|
| | play | more | 1 |
| | play | Nim | 1 |
| | play | tickle | 1 |
| | play | you | 1 |
| | shoe | apple | 1 |
| | shoe | grape | 1 |
| | smile | banana | 1 |
| | Walter | Nim | 1 |
| | Walter | play | 2 |
| time | eat | come | 1 |
| | eat | hug | 1 |
| | eat | Nim | 1 |
| | hug | Nim | 2 |
| | hug | time | 1 |
| | Nim | eat | 2 |
| | Nim | hug | 1 |
| | work | Nim | 1 |
| toilet | hug | Nim | 1 |
| toothbrush | banana | Nim | 1 |
| | me | Nim | 2 |
| | me | toothbrush | 1 |
| | Nim | baby | 2 |
| | Nim | eat | 1 |
| | Nim | toothbrush | 3 |
| wash | eat | me | 1 |
| | water | drink | 1 |
| water | drink | Nim | 1 |
| | eat | Nim | 1 |
| | give | eat | 1 |
| | me | drink | 1 |
| | me | you | 1 |
| | Nim | wash | 1 |
| | Nim | water | 2 |
| | tickle | fruit | 1 |
| | tickle | Nim | 1 |
| | what | out | 1 |
| what | book | point | 1 |
| | come | open | 1 |
| | drink | eat | 1 |
| | eat | Nim | 2 |
| | gum | drink | 1 |
| | loc./point | what | 1 |
| | Nim | eat | 2 |
| | Nim | me | 1 |
| | Nim | red | 1 |
| | Nim | you | 1 |
| who | play | me | 1 |
| work | time | Nim | 1 |

| Sequence Type | | | Tokens |
|---|---|---|---|
| yellow | sweet | eat | 1 |
| yogurt | eat | clean | 1 |
| | eat | me | 1 |
| | eat | Nim | 7 |
| | eat | sorry | 1 |
| | eat | yogurt | 2 |
| | grape | Nim | 1 |
| | me | eat | 2 |
| | me | Nim | 2 |
| | me | yogurt | 1 |
| | Nim | eat | 20 |
| | Nim | me | 2 |
| | Nim | yogurt | 4 |
| you | give | nut | 1 |
| | Laura | you | 1 |
| | me | brush | 1 |
| | me | eat | 3 |
| | me | Laura | 1 |
| | me | Nim | 5 |
| | me | play | 8 |
| | me | tickle | 1 |
| | me | you | 1 |
| | play | me | 5 |
| | tickle | hug | 1 |
| | tickle | me | 8 |
| Totals: 1,313 | | | 2,925 |

## Four-Sign Sequences

| Sequence Type | | | | Tokens |
|---|---|---|---|---|
| Andrea | banana | eat | Nim | 1 |
| | hug | me | Nim | 1 |
| angry | bug | Nim | flower | 1 |
| | hug | angry | sorry | 1 |
| | me | sorry | hug | 1 |
| | sorry | hug | angry | 2 |
| | sorry | hug | me | 1 |
| apple | bite | apple | Nim | 1 |
| | eat | apple | eat | 1 |
| | eat | me | Nim | 1 |
| | gum | apple | gum | 1 |
| | me | apple | play | 1 |
| | me | Nim | key | 1 |
| | me | tickle | eat | 1 |
| | more | eat | apple | 1 |
| | Nim | apple | more | 1 |
| | Nim | eat | give | 1 |
| | Nim | me | Nim | 1 |
| | peach | fruit | apple | 1 |
| baby | grape | eat | baby | 1 |
| | hug | Nim | brush | 1 |
| bad | hug | Nim | hug | 1 |
| banana | drink | me | eat | 1 |
| | drink | me | Nim | 1 |
| | drink | me | point | 1 |
| | eat | banana | eat | 2 |
| | eat | banana | give | 1 |
| | eat | banana | Nim | 2 |
| | eat | me | Nim | 4 |
| | eat | more | eat | 1 |
| | eat | more | hug | 1 |
| | eat | Nim | banana | 2 |
| | eat | Nim | me | 1 |
| | me | banana | eat | 1 |
| | me | banana | me | 1 |
| | me | banana | Nim | 2 |
| | me | eat | banana | 4 |
| | me | eat | me | 1 |
| | me | eat | Nim | 2 |
| | me | more | eat | 1 |
| | me | Nim | eat | 1 |
| | me | Nim | me | 4 |
| | more | banana | Nim | 1 |
| | Nim | banana | eat | 2 |
| | Nim | banana | me | 1 |
| | Nim | banana | Nim | 5 |
| | Nim | banana | Susan | 1 |
| | Nim | drink | eat | 1 |

## Four-Sign Sequences (*cont.*)

| Sequence Type | | | | Tokens |
|---|---|---|---|---|
| banana (cont.) | Nim | eat | banana | 2 |
| | Nim | eat | me | 1 |
| | Nim | eat | more | 1 |
| | Nim | eat | Nim | 1 |
| | Nim | loc./point | banana | 1 |
| | Nim | more | banana | 1 |
| | nut | eat | Nim | 1 |
| Bill | Nim | Bill | Nim | 1 |
| bite | angry | bite | hug | 1 |
| | hug | bite | hug | 2 |
| book | me | eat | groom | 1 |
| brown | sweet | Nim | eat | 1 |
| brush | me | Nim | brush | 1 |
| | Nim | cat | hurry | 1 |
| chair | eat | drink | flower | 1 |
| clean | dirty | out | loc./point | 1 |
| | eat | yogurt | eat | 1 |
| color | eat | color | Nim | 1 |
| | Nim | color | orange | 1 |
| | Nim | eat | me | 1 |
| | Nim | eat | orange | 1 |
| | Nim | eat | red | 1 |
| | Nim | me | Nim | 1 |
| come | give | me | come | 1 |
| come | me | Nim | hug | 1 |
| | more | me | eat | 1 |
| | open | me | open | 1 |
| cracker | me | eat | sweet | 1 |
| | Nim | cracker | Nim | 1 |
| Dick | eat | grape | Nim | 1 |
| dirty | eat | grape | Nim | 1 |
| | finish | hug | Nim | 1 |
| | hug | finish | dirty | 1 |
| | hug | me | Nim | 1 |
| | smell | pants | in | 1 |
| | smell | dirty | smell | 1 |
| dog | play | Nim | come | 1 |
| drink | apple | gum | apple | 1 |
| | apple | drink | eat | 1 |
| | brown | give | me | 1 |
| | eat | drink | eat | 3 |
| | eat | give | me | 1 |
| | eat | me | eat | 1 |
| | eat | | Nim | 3 |
| | eat | more | eat | 1 |
| | eat | Nim | me | 1 |
| | eat | sweet | drink | |
| | give | drink | apple | 1 |

## Four-Sign Sequences (*cont.*)

| *Sequence Type* | | | | *Tokens* |
|---|---|---|---|---|
| drink (*cont.*) | give | drink | give | 2 |
| | me | drink | me | 1 |
| | | eat | me | 1 |
| | | more | me | 1 |
| | | | Nim | 1 |
| | me | Nim | eat | 1 |
| | | | me | 2 |
| | | | tea | 1 |
| | | orange | sweet | 1 |
| | | tea | me | 1 |
| | more | drink | Nim | 2 |
| | | | sweet | 1 |
| | | eat | drink | 1 |
| | Nim | drink | eat | 1 |
| | | | Nim | 5 |
| | | eat | drink | 1 |
| | | me | drink | 1 |
| | | | Nim | 1 |
| | sweet | drink | sweet | 1 |
| | | eat | drink | 1 |
| | tea | drink | tea | 1 |
| | | me | Nim | 1 |
| eat | apple | gum | banana | 1 |
| | | me | Nim | 1 |
| | baby | Nim | eat | 1 |
| | bad | eat | sweet | 1 |
| | banana | eat | loc./point | 1 |
| | | | Nim | 1 |
| | | me | eat | 1 |
| | | Nim | banana | 1 |
| | | | eat | 2 |
| | drink | eat | drink | 15 |
| | | | Nim | 1 |
| | | gum | Nim | 1 |
| | | me | eat | 1 |
| | | | Nim | 2 |
| | | Nim | me | 1 |
| | | | orange | 1 |
| | | orange | eat | 1 |
| | | sweet | drink | 1 |
| | finish | hug | Renee | 1 |
| | give | more | eat | 1 |
| | | Nim | eat | 1 |
| | grape | eat | grape | 1 |
| | | | Nim | 3 |
| | | | eat | 1 |
| | | Nim | hug | 1 |
| | gum | Nim | gum | 1 |

## Four-Sign Sequences (*cont.*)

| Sequence Type | | | | Tokens |
|---|---|---|---|---|
| eat (cont.) | hat | me | banana | 1 |
| | hungry | give | Nim | 1 |
| | hurry | eat | nut | 1 |
| | loc./point | banana | Nim | 1 |
| | me | cracker | Nim | 1 |
| | | drink | eat | 1 |
| | | eat | me | 2 |
| | me | Nim | drink | 3 |
| | | | eat | 2 |
| | | | give | 1 |
| | | | hungry | 1 |
| | | | me | 1 |
| | | open | what | 1 |
| | | sweet | eat | 1 |
| | more | drink | sweet | 1 |
| | | eat | Nim | 1 |
| | | me | eat | 1 |
| | | orange | Nim | 1 |
| | Nim | apple | Nim | 1 |
| | | banana | Andrea | 1 |
| | | | eat | 1 |
| | | eat | apple | 1 |
| | | | banana | 1 |
| | | | give | 1 |
| | | | grape | 1 |
| | | | me | 1 |
| | | | Nim | 7 |
| | | | what | 1 |
| | | | yogurt | 1 |
| | | give | Nim | 1 |
| | | me | eat | 1 |
| | | | sweet | 1 |
| | | raisin | Nim | 1 |
| | | red | sweet | 1 |
| | | sweet | eat | 1 |
| | orange | Nim | eat | 1 |
| | raisin | eat | Nim | 1 |
| | | Nim | eat | 1 |
| | smile | Nim | banana | 1 |
| | spoon | me | Nim | 1 |
| | sweet | eat | give | 1 |
| | | | me | 1 |
| | | | sweet | 1 |
| | | me | Nim | 1 |
| | | more | eat | 1 |
| | | Nim | eat | 1 |
| | tea | pear | eat | 1 |
| | yogurt | eat | Nim | |

## Four-Sign Sequences (*cont.*)

| Sequence Type | | | | Tokens |
|---|---|---|---|---|
| eat (*cont.*) | yoghurt | Nim | eat | 1 |
| egg | more | egg | more | 1 |
| finish | dirty | pants | in | 1 |
| | hug | finish | hug | 1 |
| | me | finish | me | 1 |
| | pants | in | clean | 1 |
| fruit | eat | me | Renee | 1 |
| | eat | Nim | eat | 1 |
| | more | Nim | fruit | 1 |
| | nut | drink | Nim | 1 |
| gimme | sweet | Nim | gimme | 1 |
| give | banana | loc./point | banana | 1 |
| | | more | me | 1 |
| | | Nim | banana | 1 |
| | | | eat | 1 |
| | | | me | 1 |
| | crayon | give | crayon | 1 |
| | eat | banana | apple | 1 |
| | | groom | me | 1 |
| | eat | me | eat | 1 |
| | | | give | 1 |
| | | | Nim | 1 |
| | | Nim | me | 1 |
| | grape | Nim | eat | 1 |
| | loc./point | cracker | give | 1 |
| | | tickle | Nim | 1 |
| | me | apple | eat | 1 |
| | | banana | eat | 1 |
| | | eat | apple | 1 |
| | | | banana | 1 |
| | | | nut | 1 |
| | | | orange | 2 |
| | | give | me | 1 |
| | | light | give | 1 |
| | | loc./point | handcream | 1 |
| | | Nim | eat | 2 |
| | | red | eat | 1 |
| | | smell | Nim | 1 |
| | Nim | eat | Nim | 1 |
| | raisin | in | Nim | 1 |
| | sweet | eat | Nim | 1 |
| | tea | drink | eat | 1 |
| grape | dirty | me | Nim | 1 |
| | drink | grape | berry | 1 |
| | eat | me | eat | 2 |
| | | | Nim | 3 |
| | | Nim | baby | 1 |
| | | | eat | 4 |

# Four-Sign Sequences (*cont.*)

| Sequence Type | | | | Tokens |
|---|---|---|---|---|
| grape (cont.) | eat | Nim | give | 1 |
| | | | hug | 1 |
| | | | me | 2 |
| | hug | Nim | eat | 1 |
| | Nim | eat | grape | 1 |
| | | grape | apple | 1 |
| | | me | Nim | 1 |
| | | open | banana | 1 |
| gum | apple | eat | drink | 1 |
| | eat | me | eat | 1 |
| | eat | me | gum | 2 |
| | me | gum | Nim | 1 |
| | | Nim | gum | 1 |
| | | | me | 1 |
| | Nim | eat | grape | 1 |
| | | gum | eat | 1 |
| | | | Nim | 1 |
| handcream | baby | Nim | hug | 1 |
| | give | me | handcream | 1 |
| | Nim | eat | handcream | 1 |
| harmonica | me | Nim | harmonica | 1 |
| hat | play | me | tickle | 1 |
| hug | come | me | open | 1 |
| | me | hug | me | 2 |
| | | sleep | me | 1 |
| | | sorry | Nim | 1 |
| | more | spoon | hug | 1 |
| | Nim | hug | hungry | 1 |
| | | sorry | Renee | 1 |
| | Renee | hug | Renee | 1 |
| hungry | eat | what | hug | |
| | me | eat | Nim | 1 |
| in | dirty | in | dirty | 1 |
| | drink | me | drink | 1 |
| | eat | grape | eat | 1 |
| | pants | dirty | play | 1 |
| | tea | hug | toothbrush | 1 |
| | you | eat | in | 1 |
| key | me | key | drink | 2 |
| | what | red | Nim | 1 |
| Laura | eat | Nim | me | 1 |
| | give | loc./point | me | 1 |
| | me | banana | eat | 1 |
| loc./point | bad | eat | apple | 1 |
| | banana | Nim | eat | 1 |
| | eat | loc./point | eat | 1 |
| | give | eat | Nim | 1 |
| | | Nim | eat | 1 |

## Four-Sign Sequences (*cont.*)

| *Sequence Type* | | | | *Tokens* |
|---|---|---|---|---|
| loc./point (*cont.*) | Nim | eat | gum | 1 |
| | Nim | me | eat | 1 |
| | | water | Nim | 1 |
| | sweet | eat | more | 1 |
| | | eat | Nim | 1 |
| me | Andrea | you | me | 1 |
| | angry | hug | bite | 1 |
| | apple | eat | apple | 1 |
| | drink | Nim | eat | 1 |
| | drink | Nim | red | 1 |
| | eat | banana | eat | 1 |
| | | | handcream | 1 |
| | | | more | 2 |
| | eat | drink | more | 3 |
| | | | sweet | 1 |
| | | me | eat | 3 |
| | | | gum | 1 |
| | | | Nim | 2 |
| | | more | banana | 1 |
| | | Nim | eat | 2 |
| | | | hug | 1 |
| | | tea | drink | 1 |
| | give | gum | me | 1 |
| | grape | Nim | eat | 1 |
| | gum | me | gum | 3 |
| | hug | jump | eat | 1 |
| | | me | Nim | 1 |
| | key | hug | me | 1 |
| | loc./point | Nim | loc./point | 1 |
| | more | eat | loc./point | 1 |
| | Nim | banana | Nim | 1 |
| | | bug | Nim | 1 |
| | | drink | Nim | 1 |
| | | eat | apple | 1 |
| | | | cracker | 1 |
| | | | grape | 1 |
| | | | me | 3 |
| | | | more | 1 |
| | | | orange | 1 |
| | | handcream | eat | 1 |
| | | me | eat | 1 |
| | | | pants | 1 |
| | | | you | 1 |
| | | more | eat | 1 |
| | | play | tickle | 1 |
| | | | you | 2 |
| | | same | gum | 1 |
| | | sweet | me | 1 |

# Four-Sign Sequences (*cont.*)

| Sequence Type | | | | Tokens |
|---|---|---|---|---|
| me (cont.) | Nim | tickle | me | 1 |
| | | | Nim | 1 |
| | play | red | Nim | 1 |
| | raisin | me | raisin | 1 |
| | sweet | me | eat | 1 |
| | | water | me | 1 |
| | tea | drink | more | 1 |
| | tickle | Nim | hug | 1 |
| more | banana | eat | banana | 1 |
| | | | Nim | 2 |
| | | me | Nim | 1 |
| | drink | more | eat | 1 |
| | | Nim | more | 2 |
| | eat | brown | eat | 1 |
| | | drink | me | 1 |
| | eat | gum | me | 1 |
| | | more | drink | 1 |
| | | | eat | 1 |
| | | Nim | more | 1 |
| | | tea | me | 1 |
| | fruit | Nim | raisin | 1 |
| | key | banana | eat | 1 |
| | me | banana | eat | 1 |
| | | drink | eat | 1 |
| | | eat | apple | 1 |
| | | | Nim | 1 |
| | | Nim | more | 1 |
| | | tea | drink | 1 |
| | Nim | eat | grape | 1 |
| | | fruit | raisin | 1 |
| | | more | Nim | 1 |
| | orange | drink | out | 1 |
| | out | fruit | hug | 1 |
| | pear | apple | pear | 1 |
| | sweet | eat | Nim | 1 |
| | tea | drink | tea | 1 |
| | | me | apple | 1 |
| | | more | tea | 1 |
| | tickle | me | Nim | 1 |
| | | more | me | 1 |
| | | Nim | more | 1 |
| | toothbrush | Nim | toothbrush | 1 |
| Nim | banana | eat | drink | 1 |
| | | Nim | banana | 1 |
| | Bill | eat | gum | 1 |
| | bite | Nim | bite | 1 |
| | color | eat | color | 1 |
| | | Nim | me | 1 |

## Four-Sign Sequences (*cont.*)

| Sequence Type | | | | Tokens |
|---|---|---|---|---|
| Nim (*cont.*) | cracker | Nim | cracker | 1 |
| | drink | me | eat | 1 |
| | | | Nim | 1 |
| | | Nim | drink | 1 |
| | eat | banana | eat | 1 |
| | | drink | eat | 1 |
| | | grape | eat | 1 |
| | | | pear | 1 |
| | | hug | Nim | 1 |
| | | hungry | eat | 1 |
| | | | me | 1 |
| | | loc./point | gum | 1 |
| | | me | dirty | 1 |
| | | | eat | 2 |
| | | | grape | 1 |
| | | Nim | drink | 1 |
| | | | eat | 4 |
| | | | grape | 1 |
| | eat | Nim | me | 2 |
| | | | nut | 1 |
| | | orange | grape | 1 |
| | | raisin | eat | 1 |
| | | | grape | 1 |
| | | red | berry | 1 |
| | | sweet | Nim | 1 |
| | | | red | 1 |
| | | what | banana | 1 |
| | | yogurt | eat | 2 |
| | | | more | 1 |
| | | | Nim | 1 |
| | give | loc./point | apple | 1 |
| | grape | eat | Nim | 2 |
| | | Nim | eat | 1 |
| | gum | eat | loc./point | 1 |
| | gum | gimme | gum | 1 |
| | | me | gum | 1 |
| | Herb | tickle | me | 1 |
| | hug | Nim | hug | 1 |
| | loc./point | eat | berry | 1 |
| | me | eat | banana | 1 |
| | | | drink | 1 |
| | | | Nim | 1 |
| | | | peach | 1 |
| | | | raisin | 1 |
| | | Laura | loc./point | 1 |
| | | more | banana | 1 |
| | | Nim | eat | 2 |
| | | | me | 3 |

# Four-Sign Sequences (*cont.*)

| Sequence Type | | | | Tokens |
|---|---|---|---|---|
| Nim (cont.) | more | banana | me | 1 |
| | play | Walter | play | 1 |
| | red | raisin | Nim | 1 |
| | sweet | color | red | 1 |
| | | eat | sweet | 1 |
| | | Nim | color | 1 |
| | | | red | 1 |
| | tickle | chair | go | 1 |
| | you | me | eat | 1 |
| nut | eat | nut | me | 1 |
| | give | me | eat | 1 |
| | | | Nim | 1 |
| | me | nut | eat | 1 |
| | | | me | 1 |
| | Nim | eat | Nim | 2 |
| | | | nut | 1 |
| | | me | Nim | 1 |
| | | nut | Nim | 2 |
| open | open | me | nut | 1 |
| | Alex | hug | Nim | 1 |
| | eat | out | banana | 1 |
| | grape | eat | grape | 1 |
| | | out | grape | 1 |
| | light | me | open | 1 |
| orange | drink | me | eat | 1 |
| | | | Nim | 1 |
| | | orange | Nim | 1 |
| | give | loc./point | orange | 1 |
| | me | eat | drink | 1 |
| | | | give | 1 |
| | | orange | give | 1 |
| | more | me | eat | 1 |
| | | orange | Nim | 1 |
| | shoe | me | Nim | 1 |
| | apple | eat | Nim | 1 |
| | dirty | hug | out | 1 |
| out | shoe | out | shoe | 1 |
| pancakes | me | Nim | eat | 1 |
| pancake | Nim | eat | pancake | 1 |
| | eat | me | pancake | 1 |
| pants | in | hug | Nim | 1 |
| | on | hug | good | 1 |
| | out | pants | in | 1 |
| peach | eat | Bill | Nim | 1 |
| pear | eat | more | give | 1 |
| | | Nim | eat | 1 |
| | | pear | eat | 1 |
| | Nim | apple | eat | 1 |

## Four-Sign Sequences (*cont.*)

| Sequence Type | | | | Tokens |
|---|---|---|---|---|
| pear (*cont.*) | Nim | me | Nim | 1 |
| | | pear | Nim | 2 |
| play | hat | me | hat | 1 |
| | jump | play | Nim | 1 |
| | me | come | me | 1 |
| | | Nim | hat | 1 |
| | | | play | 4 |
| | | | tickle | 1 |
| | | play | Nim | 2 |
| | | | tickle | 1 |
| | more | me | Nim | 1 |
| | Nim | tickle | me | 2 |
| | tickle | me | tickle | 1 |
| | waiter | me | waiter | 1 |
| | waiter | hug | play | 1 |
| raisin | eat | me | Nim | 1 |
| | grape | eat | Nim | 1 |
| | more | raisin | eat | 1 |
| | Nim | me | eat | 1 |
| | | raisin | Nim | 1 |
| red | drink | Nim | give | 1 |
| | Nim | eat | me | 1 |
| same | drink | same | drink | 1 |
| shoe | eat | out | shoe | 1 |
| | out | shoe | out | 1 |
| smell | loc./point | smell | eat | 1 |
| sorry | angry | sorry | hug | 1 |
| | hug | me | toothbrush | 1 |
| | | please | sorry | 1 |
| | | sorry | me | 1 |
| | me | Nim | eat | 1 |
| | Nim | bite | hug | 1 |
| spoon | Nim | eat | Nim | 1 |
| Susan | eat | Nim | eat | 1 |
| sweet | angry | gum | sweet | 1 |
| | banana | sweet | Nim | 1 |
| | drink | Nim | drink | 1 |
| | eat | sweet | Nim | 1 |
| | | me | Nim | 1 |
| | me | eat | red | 1 |
| | | Nim | drink | 1 |
| | | sweet | drink | 1 |
| | | | hungry | 1 |
| | Nim | color | orange | 1 |
| | | drink | sweet | 1 |
| | | loc./point | give | 1 |
| | | me | Nim | 2 |
| | | red | Nim | 1 |
| | | sweet | color | 1 |

## Four-Sign Sequences (*cont.*)

| Sequence Type | | | | Tokens |
|---|---|---|---|---|
| sweet (cont.) | Nim | sweet | me | 1 |
| tea | Andrea | tea | drink | 1 |
| | drink | eat | me | 1 |
| | | | more | 1 |
| | | me | eat | 1 |
| | | | tea | 1 |
| | | Nim | drink | 1 |
| | | tea | drink | 1 |
| | give | me | Nim | 1 |
| | here | tea | here | 1 |
| | hug | eat | drink | 1 |
| | me | eat | drink | 1 |
| | | | Nim | 1 |
| | | loc./point | drink | 1 |
| | | more | tea | 1 |
| | | Nim | drink | 1 |
| | Nim | eat | drink | 1 |
| | shoe | water | Nim | 1 |
| | water | gimme | tea | 1 |
| tickle | eat | gum | cracker | 1 |
| | | Nim | me | 1 |
| | in | tickle | Nim | 1 |
| | loc./point | Nim | me | 1 |
| | me | more | Nim | 1 |
| | me | Nim | cracker | 1 |
| | | | hug | 1 |
| | | | me | 1 |
| | | | more | 2 |
| | | | play | 3 |
| | | | tickle | 2 |
| | | | you | 1 |
| | | play | Nim | 1 |
| | | tickle | hug | 1 |
| | | | me | 1 |
| | more | tickle | more | 1 |
| | Nim | me | Nim | 1 |
| | | tickle | me | 1 |
| | | | Nim | 1 |
| | play | me | Nim | 1 |
| | | Nim | me | 1 |
| | tea | drink | hug | 1 |
| time | banana | me | grape | 1 |
| | out | hug | sorry | 1 |
| toothbrush | eat | toothbrush | eat | 1 |
| | open | more | banana | 1 |
| water | drink | me | drink | 1 |
| | | water | drink | 1 |
| what | eat | me | Nim | 1 |
| | me | gum | eat | 1 |

## Four-Sign Sequences (*cont.*)

| Sequence Type | | | | Tokens |
|---|---|---|---|---|
| what (*cont.*) | tickle | me | play | 1 |
| work | nut | eat | out | 1 |
| yellow | grape | eat | Nim | 1 |
| yogurt | eat | Nim | eat | 1 |
| | | | yogurt | 1 |
| | | yogurt | Nim | 1 |
| | Nim | eat | blue | 1 |
| | | | Nim | 1 |
| you | brush | Nim | out | 1 |
| | Nim | Laura | eat | 1 |
| | play | me | Nim | 1 |

TOTALS:   600                                              708

## Sequences of Five or More Signs

| *Sequence Type* | | *Tokens* |
|---|---|---|
| Andrea | me Nim locative/point Andrea | 1 |
| angry | sorry eat angry me wash finish | 1 |
| | me Nim Nim eat give | 1 |
| apple | eat angry Nim eat | 1 |
| | grape peach in more eat | 1 |
| | hug eat apple Andrea apple | 1 |
| | me eat Nim apple me apple | 1 |
| | me more Nim more Nim | 1 |
| | me Nim gum orange brush gum sweet orange gum | 1 |
| | Nim apple Nim sweet | 1 |
| | Nim eat apple eat | 1 |
| | orange apple orange apple | 1 |
| | tea more eat Nim | 1 |
| baby | eat grape eat Nim | 1 |
| | Nim baby Nim baby | 1 |
| banana | eat banana eat Nim | 1 |
| | eat banana me Nim eat | 1 |
| | eat banana Nim eat | 1 |
| | eat drink more banana | 1 |
| | eat me banana eat | 1 |
| | eat me banana Nim | 1 |
| | eat me eat more | 1 |
| | eat me eat Nim | 1 |
| | eat Nim give banana Nim | 1 |
| | eat Nim more Nim | 1 |
| | give me banana Nim | 1 |
| | give me Nim me | 1 |
| | hug banana me banana | 1 |
| | me banana me Nim me banana eat me | 1 |
| | me banana me tickle | 1 |
| | me banana more banana me eat Nim | 1 |
| | me eat banana Nim | 1 |
| | me Nim eat me | 1 |
| | me Nim more eat Nim | 1 |
| | more eat banana eat | 1 |
| | Nim banana eat me | 1 |
| | Nim banana eat Nim | 1 |
| | Nim banana Nim banana Nim | 1 |
| | Nim banana Nim eat | 1 |
| | Nim eat banana drink Nim banana me | 1 |
| | Nim eat me Nim you | 1 |
| | Nim me banana me | 1 |
| | Nim me Nim banana me Nim | 1 |
| bite | angry bad sorry hug please | 1 |
| color | red color red color red | 1 |
| come | me come me come me | 1 |
| | Nim me Nim me Nim come me Nim Walter come Walter | 1 |
| cracker | more me apple eat | 1 |

## Sequence of Five or More Signs (*cont.*)

| Sequence Type | | Tokens |
|---|---|---|
| drink | eat drink eat drink | 1 |
| | eat drink eat drink tea | 1 |
| | eat drink eat Nim | 1 |
| | eat drink eat Nim locative/point drink | 1 |
| | eat drink eat Nim tea | 1 |
| | eat drink me drink Nim | 1 |
| | eat drink me tea me | 1 |
| | eat drink Nim drink | 1 |
| | eat drink tea eat drink | 1 |
| | eat me eat Nim drink me | 1 |
| | eat me Nim me | 1 |
| | eat Nim drink tea drink | 1 |
| | eat sweet drink give | 1 |
| | give drink give Nim give | 1 |
| | give me eat me eat | 1 |
| | me drink me drink me drink tea | 1 |
| | me drink me drink me Nim drink | 1 |
| | me drink me Nim | 1 |
| | me drink Nim drink me | 1 |
| | me give sweet eat | 1 |
| | me Nim cracker Nim drink | 1 |
| | more drink give drink give | 1 |
| | more drink tea drink | 1 |
| | Nim drink Nim drink Nim | 1 |
| | Nim hug cracker Nim eat | 1 |
| | Nim orange drink eat | 1 |
| | orange locative/point me eat | 1 |
| | tea drink me tea | 1 |
| | tea more drink tea | 1 |
| eat | apple grape raisin pear | 1 |
| | apple Nim apple orange | 1 |
| | apple Nim eat pear | 1 |
| | banana Nim drink Nim | 2 |
| | banana Nim me banana | 1 |
| | come me come eat grape | 1 |
| | drink eat drink eat drink | 1 |
| | drink eat drink eat drink eat drink eat drink | 3 |
| | drink eat drink eat drink eat drink eat drink eat drink eat drink | 1 |
| | drink me eat Nim eat | 1 |
| | drink Nim me eat | 1 |
| | me eat drink eat | 1 |
| | me eat drink Nim | 1 |
| | me eat me banana | 1 |
| | me eat me eat | 1 |
| | me eat me eat me eat me eat me eat me Nim | 1 |
| | me Nim banana eat Nim | 1 |
| | me Nim eat give me | 1 |
| | me Nim eat grape | 1 |

## Sequences of Five or More Signs (*cont.*)

| *Sequence Type* | | *Tokens* |
|---|---|---|
| eat (cont.) | me Nim eat me hug | 1 |
| | me Nim eat yogurt | 1 |
| | me Nim Joyce hug | 1 |
| | me Nim me eat | 1 |
| | me Nim me Nim | 1 |
| | me orange apple orange | 1 |
| | more apple groom pear | 1 |
| | more eat Nim me | 1 |
| | more eat nut me Nim nut give | 1 |
| | more tickle Nim me | 1 |
| | Nim banana eat banana | 1 |
| | Nim eat grape gum apple | 1 |
| | Nim eat grape Nim eat | 1 |
| | Nim eat me Nim eat | 1 |
| | Nim eat me spoon eat | 1 |
| | Nim eat Nim banana | 1 |
| | Nim eat Nim eat | 1 |
| | Nim eat Nim eat blue | 1 |
| | Nim fruit eat Nim eat pear | 1 |
| | Nim locative/point red me | 1 |
| | Nim more eat Nim | 1 |
| | Nim raisin Nim raisin | 1 |
| | Nim sweet more eat | 1 |
| | Nim yogurt eat Nim | 1 |
| | Nim yogurt Nim yogurt | 1 |
| | raisin grape eat raisin | 1 |
| | raisin nut eat raisin drink eat drink eat | 2 |
| | spoon eat Nim spoon | 1 |
| egg | eat egg eat egg eat | 1 |
| finish | out time hug out | 1 |
| fruit | eat Andrea peach Andrea | 1 |
| give | drink give eat Nim eat | 1 |
| | drink me eat tea drink me | 1 |
| | eat cracker me Nim more | 1 |
| | eat give drink eat give | 1 |
| | eat give Nim eat | 1 |
| | eat hug drink give eat drink give banana eat give | 1 |
| | eat toothbrush sweet give banana apple | 1 |
| | locative/point banana drink give | 1 |
| | me banana eat more | 1 |
| | me drink eat Nim | 1 |
| | me eat banana me | 1 |
| | me eat me eat Nim apple | 1 |
| | me eat same eat | 1 |
| | me give me give me | 1 |
| | me Nim drink give | 1 |
| | me Nim eat hug | 1 |
| | me Nim sweet eat | 1 |

## Sequences of Five or More Signs (*cont.*)

| Sequence Type | | Tokens |
|---|---|---|
| give (*cont.*) | me same eat Nim same | 1 |
| | Nim eat banana eat nut | 1 |
| | Nim point Nim me | 1 |
| | Nim play apple gum orange | 1 |
| | orange eat me eat orange me orange | 1 |
| | orange me give eat orange me eat orange give me eat orange give me you | 1 |
| grape | eat fruit Nim pear | 1 |
| | eat me eat grape | 1 |
| | eat me Nim eat | 1 |
| | eat Nim eat Nim | 1 |
| | eat Nim grape eat | 1 |
| | in locative/point Nim eat | 1 |
| | me grape me locative/point | 1 |
| | Nim me grape eat | 1 |
| groom | black Nim spoon eat | 1 |
| gum | come eat gum cracker | 1 |
| | eat banana eat sweet me | 1 |
| | me gum me eat | 1 |
| | more me more eat | 1 |
| | you me you me | 1 |
| hug | finish Nim dirty hug | 1 |
| | Nim hug Nim book | 1 |
| hungry | eat me Nim locative/point | 1 |
| in | hat in hat in hat in hat | 1 |
| jump | me jump me jump | 1 |
| listen | me listen locative/point give listen | 1 |
| locative/point | drink more eat banana | 1 |
| me | apple more banana apple | 1 |
| | banana me eat me | 1 |
| | banana Nim me eat more eat banana eat | 1 |
| | color same Nim give eat Nim eat | 1 |
| | drink eat drink eat drink eat drink eat drink eat Nim | 1 |
| | drink me drink eat drink me drink sweet eat Nim | 1 |
| | eat Andrea apple Andrea apple Andrea apple raisin | 1 |
| | eat drink angry drink eat | 1 |
| | eat drink give eat | 1 |
| | eat fruit ball fruit | 1 |
| | eat me eat water | 1 |
| | eat nut you me nut me eat | 1 |
| | eat same you same me | 1 |
| | give eat apple orange apple me | 1 |
| | give gum me Nim give me | 1 |
| | give Nim you locative/point | 1 |
| | gum me eat gum | 1 |
| | gum Nim eat gum | 1 |
| | more drink tea Nim | 1 |
| | more eat hug eat | 1 |

## Sequences of Five or More Signs (*cont.*)

| Sequence Type | | Tokens |
|---|---|---|
| me (cont.) | more eat more banana brush handcream | 1 |
| | Nim eat drink Nim me | 1 |
| | Nim eat Nim me | 1 |
| | Nim eat sweet red | 1 |
| | Nim groom Andrea key | 1 |
| | Nim me jump tickle me | 1 |
| | Nim me Nim Dick drink eat | 1 |
| | Nim me Nim me | 1 |
| | Nim me Nim me Nim | 1 |
| | Nim me Nim smell Nim | 1 |
| | Nim play locative/point berry | 1 |
| | Nim smell bug me sweet | 1 |
| | Nim sweet Nim sweet | 1 |
| | Nim tickle Nim tea | 1 |
| | Nim tickle what more me | 1 |
| | smell locative/point smell me you | 1 |
| | smell nut smell gum tea | 1 |
| | you me Nim you me you Walter | 1 |
| | banana eat me Nim | 1 |
| | drink more Nim more | 1 |
| | drink Nim drink Nim more drink | 1 |
| | eat please sweet Nim | 1 |
| | eat time give drink tea | 1 |
| | fruit grape Nim eat | 1 |
| | Nim me what tickle | 1 |
| | same eat in me in | 1 |
| | time give drink eat | 1 |
| | what more eat more locative/point | 1 |
| | banana eat banana Nim eat | 2 |
| | drink me drink me | 1 |
| | drink more Nim more | 1 |
| | drink Nim me eat | 1 |
| | eat banana me Nim | 1 |
| | eat drink eat drink | 1 |
| | eat drink more eat | 1 |
| | eat egg eat Nim eat | 1 |
| | eat me locative/point Nim me eat Nim eat me | 1 |
| | eat Nim eat grape Nim | 1 |
| | gum give gum Nim | 1 |
| | gum Nim gum me gum | 1 |
| | Laura banana Nim eat | 1 |
| | locative/point drink me drink | 1 |
| | me banana eat Nim banana | 1 |
| | me eat drink Nim | 1 |
| | me Nim me drink | 1 |
| | me Nim me Nim | 1 |
| | me sweet eat sweet | 1 |
| | more banana eat me | 1 |

## Sequences of Five or More Signs (*cont.*)

| Sequence Type | | Tokens |
|---|---|---|
| Nim (*cont.*) | sweet Nim eat red | 1 |
| | sweet orange sweet Nim | 1 |
| nut | eat Nim give nut | 1 |
| | eat nut me Nim | 1 |
| | me Nim drink Nim | 1 |
| | me nut give me eat Nim nut | 1 |
| | more me eat nut | 1 |
| open | me eat jump me Laura | 1 |
| orange | me Laura orange give | 1 |
| pants | out pants out pants | 1 |
| peach | eat gum eat Nim | 1 |
| pear | Nim give eat Nim | 1 |
| | Nim pear angry pear | 1 |
| | Nim pear Nim pear | 1 |
| play | come me Nim me | 1 |
| | me more me more jump | 1 |
| | me Nim me play ball | 1 |
| | me Nim play me | 1 |
| | me Nim play me jump tickle me Nim tickle play | 1 |
| | me Nim Walter play me Nim | 1 |
| | me play me Nim hat | 1 |
| | me play me play tickle | 1 |
| | me play tickle hat Nim | 1 |
| | me tickle hat tickle me play banana | 1 |
| | me Walter me tickle | 1 |
| | me you Nim play pole | 1 |
| please | hug finish angry please | 1 |
| raisin | eat raisin Nim eat | 1 |
| | Nim more raisin Nim | 1 |
| sorry | angry hug sorry hug | 1 |
| | hug sorry angry sorry | 1 |
| | play me tickle eat open | 1 |
| sweet | cracker more sweet eat sweet me eat | 1 |
| | cracker Nim me give | 1 |
| | drink eat me eat | 1 |
| | drink me sweet drink Nim sweet me sweet eat sweet | 1 |
| | eat me eat sweet Nim give eat Nim me eat sweet | 1 |
| | eat Nim me orange me Nim eat | 1 |
| | give me Nim eat sweet | 1 |
| | me eat Nim you | 1 |
| | Nim eat more red | 1 |
| tea | drink give tea drink Nim | 1 |
| | drink me tea eat | 1 |
| | drink Nim drink tea | 1 |
| | drink tea drink tea drink | 1 |
| | in tea in tea in | 1 |
| | me Nim eat drink Nim | 1 |
| tickle | me Nim tickle Nim | 1 |

## Sequences of Five or More Signs (*cont.*)

| Sequence Type | | Tokens |
|---|---|---|
| tickle (cont.) | me Nim you me Nim | 1 |
| | me tickle me Nim | 1 |
| | me tickle me Nim me | 1 |
| | me tickle me tickle | 1 |
| time | Nim time Nim time | 1 |
| toothbrush | me Nim toothbrush Nim | 1 |
| what | key give me Nim | 1 |
| yogurt | Nim eat yogurt eat yogurt | 1 |
| | Nim me eat Nim | 1 |
| you | locative/point give me eat | 1 |
| | me eat banana eat me eat | 1 |
| | me eat Nim eat cracker | 1 |
| | TOTALS: 300 | 141 |

# 9

# INNOVATIVE USES OF LANGUAGE BY A GORILLA: A CASE STUDY

**Francine G. Patterson**

During the past ten years the behavioral sciences have slowly become acclimated to reports that chimpanzees have mastered the basics of symbolic communication in a visual mode. The assimilation of this new literature has been slow because its acceptance has required the abnegation of a literature and set of expectations which developed in explanation of decades of unsuccessful attempts to teach apes spoken language (Witmer, 1909; Yerkes, 1925; Furness, 1916; Kellogg, 1967; Hayes & Hayes, 1951, 1952; Hayes & Nissen, 1971).

As yet we do not know the limits of this newly discovered symbolic ability in apes; we are still learning how conversing with an ape child is like conversing with a human child and how it is different.

R. Allen and Beatrice Gardner did the pioneering work with two-way (man-ape) visual communication in a gestural mode, American Sign Language (Ameslan) (1969, 1971a, 1971b, 1971c, 1972, 1974a, 1974b, 1975a, 1975b, 1977). Their subject, the chimpanzee Washoe, acquired 132 sign words (to a strict 14-consecutive-day criterion) within a period of 51 months of training. Washoe's acquisition of these signs paralleled the development of language in the human child in several important ways: her early generalizations of signs were based on the same perceptual categories as those of human children, her sign combinations expressed the same basic relational meanings conveyed by children in the early stages of language acquisition, and her answers to questions indicated that she had some knowledge of basic sentence constituents. Further, despite early criticism,[1] her utterances were judged bounded, hierarchic, ordered, and appropriate in context (Watt, 1974).

David Premack initiated a training program with the chimpanzee Sarah in 1969, but employed plastic symbols rather than manual gestures to represent words and concepts (Premack, 1970, 1971a, 1971b, 1975, 1976a, 1976b; Premack & Premack, 1972). Sarah's mode of communication was less flexible than sign language (her use of it was restricted to training sessions and she evidently rarely initiated a conversation), but she showed evidence of mastering complex relations requiring syntaxlike operations: the conditional, locatives, negation, questions, conjunction, and relational terms.

Duane Rumbaugh and his colleagues devised a computer-controlled keyboard console to serve as a communicative interface between man and chimpanzee Lana (Rumbaugh, Gill, & von Glasersfeld, 1973, 1974; Rumbaugh, von Glasersfeld, Warner, Pisani, & Gill, 1974; Rumbaugh & Gill, 1975, 1976a, 1976b; Rumbaugh, 1977; Gill & Rumbaugh, 1974; von Glasersfeld, 1974). The computer was programmed not to deliver goods and services unless Lana's constructions (series of key punches) were acceptable to the grammar imposed by the experimenters. During a five-year period, Lana learned to name objects, identify colors, request activities, ask and answer questions, discriminate grammatical from ungrammatical constructions and truth from falsehood.

Both Premack and Rumbaugh devised artificial symbol systems as media of communication, thus limiting the possibilities for comparison with human children acquiring language. In addition, the subjects were not exposed to the "language" from birth, and their environments differed radically from those of human children. Both studies are susceptible to the criticism that the chimps' accomplishments are not linguistic in the strict sense but merely feats of complex conditional discrimination learning and its generalization. The problems with any critical analysis of this body of research are compounded by the fact that there is not now agreement among linguists as to what language is or when a child can be said to have it. Nevertheless these cautious, yet acclaimed (as well as criticized) reports have provided detailed quantitative, comparative, and analytical data on languagelike behavior in chimpanzees.

Concerned as these early researchers were with establishing early word use, they necessarily could not investigate all aspects of linguistic competence. One aspect neglected was creativity, an indication of the ape's capacity for productive and intentional use of language. There is good evidence that these animals are not merely regurgitating overlearned response patterns to obtain rewards.[2] But is the creative response rare or frequent? Do these animals use language in the subtle ways observed in human children? How much diversity do their utterances reveal? How expressively rich are their productions? What is the nature, extent, and conceptual density of their symbolic innovation? In short, have we similar kinds of evidence for "linguistic genius" in children and in apes?

Although it is too early to answer any of these questions definitively, I would like to begin to give the reader this kind of familiarity with one ape, a female lowland gorilla named Hanabi-Ko (Koko). She has been exposed to to a language environment (including spoken and signed English and Ameslan) from one year of age. During the first 52 months of training, Koko acquired a vocabulary of approximately 250 signs which she spontaneously combined into meaningful and often novel constructions of up to 12 signs in length. She is using this expanding vocabulary of signs to express semantic and possibly grammatical relations similar to those expressed by human children.

# METHOD

## Subject

### Individual history

The subject, a female, captive-born lowland gorilla (*Gorilla gorilla gorilla*) born at the San Francisco Zoo on July 4, 1971, was one year old at the onset of the study. She was named Hanabi-Ko (Japanese for "Fireworks Child") and nicknamed Koko. She remained with her mother in a social group until she was 6 months of age when, suffering from chronic malnutrition and shigella enteritis and septisemia (Lemen, Lemen, Morrish, & Tooley, 1974), she was removed, given intensive care treatment at the University of California, San Francisco Animal Care Facility for 10 days, then returned to the Zoo and reared in the home of the Children's Zoo director for several months before being placed in the Children's Zoo nursery on public display. At the time of her removal from the gorilla group, Koko weighed approximately 4½ pounds, the average birth weight for gorillas. There was a possibility of neurological damage due to the trauma of chronic malnutrition, but Lemen et al. (1973, p. 4) concluded that at one year of age the 20-pound gorilla was "obviously thriving and neurologically normal."

### The gorilla as subject

Behavioral scientists have preferred chimpanzees as subjects in explorations of the capacity of nonhuman primates to acquire language, a bias which reflects the difficulties deriving from the relative scarcity and great size of the gorilla. A further handicap is that the gorilla has not had a particularly positive scientific press: the reports from Africa by early explorers and hunters (e.g., Ford, 1852; Savage & Wyman, 1843) generated a negative stereotype which was altered little by the reputation given to gorillas by Robert Yerkes: "Puzzling, baffling, yet intensely interesting and informing as an object of psychobiological inquiry'' (Yerkes & Yerkes, 1929, p. 525). These words characterize Yerkes's almost love-hate relationship with the gorilla; he suspected, but could not prove, that it might be the most intelligent of the great apes. Unflattering descriptions of the gorilla are not difficult to find in his writings: "Many times in the course of our work it has occurred to us that this giant among apes may represent a natural experiment in which the value of brawn versus brain is being determined" (Yerkes & Yerkes, 1929, p. 523). Terms Yerkes used to describe the gorilla included "aloof," "negativistic," "stubborn," and "uninquisitive." He noted that in direct contrast to the chimpanzee, the gorilla showed a low level of motivation and a positive resistance to imitation. Yet he could not resist speculating that "it is entirely possible that the gorilla, while being distinctly inferior to the chimpanzee in ability to use and fashion implements and operate mechanisms, is superior to it in other modes of behavioral adaptation and may indeed possess a higher order of intelligence than any other existing anthropoid ape" (Yerkes & Yerkes, 1929, p. 512).

We would expect that the primate genetically most closely related to man might also possess cognitive capacities most closely approximating man's. Recent biochemical studies of homologous proteins and nucleic acids in chimpanzee and man (King & Wilson, 1975) suggest that the biological relationship between the two is as close as that between sibling species. This is paradoxical, however, because "sibling species are virtually identical morphologically . . . [but] the substantial anatomical and behavioral differences between humans and chimpanzees have led to their classification in separate families" (p. 115). King & Wilson point out that major anatomical changes usually result from mutations affecting the regulation of genes; and further, that these mutations most often take the form of rearrangements of genes on chromosomes. Thus, one of the most informative genetic comparisons would be to look for correspondences in the exact arrangement of genes on the chromosomes of apes and men. This has been done and the results (summarized by Miller, 1977) of studies of chromosomal regional banding patterns, hybridization, buoyancy, and satellite structure suggest that man is more closely related to the gorilla than to the chimpanzee. Miller speculates that evolutionary paths of man and the gorilla diverged about one million years later than the paths of man and chimpanzee. If this is the case, studies of the gorilla should be most fruitful and revealing in the quest for a fuller understanding of human behavior.

## Environmental Conditions

During the first 11 months (July 12, 1972 to June 20, 1973), this study was carried out in the San Francisco Children's Zoo nursery in view of the public. Koko was accompanied by one or more signing companions for approximately 5 hours daily during this time. From the end of June 1973 onward, the project has been housed in a 5-room, 10-foot-by-50-foot house trailer equipped with standard household items and a variety of sturdy toys.

This relocation, though initially distressing to Koko, permitted more intensive interaction. No longer was she distracted by the public, and I was able to increase her exposure to signing companions and teachers from 5 to between 8 and 12 hours per day. Since August 1972, these teachers have included fluent signers; that is, deaf individuals or persons with deaf parents, for 12 to 20 hours a week, or approximately one-eighth to one-quarter of her waking hours.

I made no attempt to eliminate spoken language from the gorilla's environment, in part because the conditions of the facility housing the project for the first year, San Francisco Children's Zoo nursery, precluded the possibility of such control. Instead, I decided to turn this situation to advantage by adopting a method known as simultaneous or total communication, the use of signs in Ameslan accompanied by spoken English. Ameslan is the gestural language used by the deaf in North America. I provided Koko with native signers (both hearing and deaf) and deaf persons fluent in sign as teachers and companions on a day-to-day basis. Each person communicated with Koko in his or her native language, but deaf individuals were encouraged to use their voices and hearing individuals were required to accompany their speech with sign.

I used sign language as the primary mode of communication because it permitted direct comparison of Koko with both child and chimpanzee. Speech served as a secondary mode of communication. Early research demonstrated that although apes could learn to produce fewer than a half dozen spoken words even after years of training, their comprehension skills were in all cases far superior to their production skills. Koko had for a time been raised by the Children's Zoo director and his wife. When I began to work with her, she was already responsive to several spoken words. I hoped that Koko would eventually comprehend a considerable amount of English even though I doubted that she would ever be able to produce spoken words. Furthermore, it seemed possible that the redundancy of simultaneous sign and speech might facilitate learning (Ferster, 1964). The two modes can, of course, be easily separated for tests of comprehension and production. In summary, the use of simultaneous communication permitted the study of any receptive and productive skills the gorilla might develop in the vocal as well as the manual mode and for the possibility of the transfer of information between modes.

## Approach

Initially Project Koko was structured in form and intention quite similarly to Project Washoe in that I sought to investigate many of the same parameters: vocabulary development, generalization, semantic relations, comprehension, and productivity. My aim was to create a body of data from which direct comparisons could be made between Koko and Washoe and Koko and human children. Consequently certain aspects of my methodology were similar: daily inventories of signs, double blind tests of vocabulary and comprehension, naturalistic observations on the use of sign, and studies of behavioral development. Although similarities in approach and methodology were important for comparative purposes, from its inception, Project Koko diverged from Project Washoe in a number of significant respects:

— the use of deaf personnel as teachers and companions for the gorilla from the beginning of the project;

— the use of spoken English in the presence of Koko, the controlled sampling of the gorilla's productions, and the controlled testing of her comprehension under conditions in which the two modes (sign and English) are separated;

— the collection of extensive samples of the gorilla's signed utterances including descriptions of the context in which they occurred;

— the absence of limits on vocabulary size or content;[3]

— The regular examination of the gorilla's intelligence through the use of standard infant and preschool intelligence tests and Piagetian techniques in order to provide data on her cognitive abilities directly comparable in a quantitative way to those available on human children and apes.

## Training Techniques

Teachers used two different techniques to teach vocabulary and to elicit signing: molding and modeling (imitation). Molding requires the teacher to shape the subject's hands into the appropriate configuration and to guide them through the proper motion. Imitation requires the subject to form the sign after observing its use by the teacher. Both of these techniques are most often used in conjunction with the spoken word, and are used in the initial stages of teaching a vocabulary item. Later on, prompting can be more subtle—pointing to or touching the appropriate body part, or simply voicing the English word alone.

Regimented training procedures proved depressing to Koko's motivation and consequently were used sparingly. Instead I attempted to provide Koko with a stimulating environment replete with objects and activities which might serve as topics of conversation and prompt her to use her developing skills. I found that I could exploit everyday activities to introduce new concepts. Thus Koko learned *large* and *small* and *same* and *different* through the sizes and colors of the glasses she drank from at meal and snack times. Her responses to objects encountered in her environment and her performance on standardized intelligence tests provide evidence that she can generalize from concepts introduced in this manner to other stimuli.

## Data Collection

All project personnel attempt to record every nontrivial linguistic and behavioral response made by Koko during the course of each day in written form in a running journal or diary. I have found this to be perhaps the richest source of information on certain infrequently occurring but significant behaviors. At the end of each session with Koko, her teachers and companions log information about her use of single signs onto a checklist (now consisting of 530 signs) and transcribe her sign combinations and answers to questions, along with context descriptions, onto separate forms.

In addition, repeated samples of Koko's signed utterances have been routinely recorded since week 15 of the project. Initially, several times a week, written records covering a 4- to 5-hour period documented linguistic exchanges between Koko and her companions. These records also included notes on the nonlinguistic context of all utterances. Then, as the gorilla began to sign more frequently, I decided to limit sampling to 8 to 10 hours per month. Each hour of the day between 9 o'clock and 6 o'clock was sampled once each month so that Koko's signing over the spectrum of her activities during the day would be represented. Assignment of sampling hours to days of the month was done on a random basis. Samples on audiotape cassettes replaced written notes after the 40th week. The experimenter dictated an account of all linguistic productions by Koko and her companion(s) along with descriptions of the nonlinguistic context and of any unusual articulation into a compact tape recorder. Unusual articulation includes distortions or inflectional variations of signs by either Koko or her companion(s), and instances in which the simultaneously signed and spoken communications of the companions fail to match.

In order to obtain a more accurate picture of the pace and volume of Koko's signing during the course of a day, one 8-hour-long sample was taken once each month in addition to the eight 1-hour samples from month 12 of the project to the present. When equipment became available (month 16 of the project, November 1973), I collected videotaped samples (from 30 minutes to 8 hours per month, increasing in duration over time as funds became available). These are invaluable in the analysis of certain characteristics of sign form, intonation, and segmentation which only a visual record can fully capture.

## Methodological Problems and Advantages of
## a Case Study Approach

The discussions in this chapter center upon aspects of Koko's sign language use which are based on observations of her behavior in relatively unstructured, uncontrolled circumstances. This approach has its obvious problems and pitfalls, but I believe that the advantages are equally significant.

Problems include the facts that some but by no means all of this type of information has been recorded on videotape or film, and that some is undoubtedly subject to interpretations or explanations alternative to those I have presented. There has been no attempt made in the sign samples from which much of these data were drawn to provide controls for paralinguistic phenomena which may give the gorilla cues as to the intentions of her companions as speakers. But when we humans address each other, we are not isolated by double-blind procedures. It is undoubtedly true that, at least in certain circumstances, a good deal of our comprehension of the spoken message comes from a perfectly natural "Clever Hans" appreciation of nonlinguistic cues to the meaning of the message. To constantly enforce control procedures such as the double blind would disrupt the spontaneity and lessen the potential richness of communication between either human and human or ape and human.

In a discussion of "the perils of the overstructured situation" Fouts (Fouts, Couch, & O'Neil, 1977) restates a point made by Kohler in 1921: Rigorously controlled experimental methodology may restrict the subject's responses to behaviors fitting the preconceived notions of the scientist. Studies thus designed are important and have their place, but it is also vital that we let the "organism demonstrate its linguistic tendencies spontaneously" (Fouts et al., 1977, p. 27).

There is much about language which does not lend itself to reduction to numerical data and statistics. When, for example, Koko once referred to her companion Cathy as a "bird," it would seem that she was making a mistake. And, like the standard test which is incapable of measuring the abilities of the gifted but unmotivated child, a strict scanning of Koko's response in this case would suggest that Koko did not know what she was talking about and was merely randomly generating signs. However, as this conversation unfolds and becomes an argument (see details below), it becomes clear that Koko knows what she is doing but has decided to be uncooperative. Moreover, there are numerous other examples of her negativity that underscore her intent on such occasions. Below is just one illustration.

On January 1, 1978 I wanted to elicit the sign *shell* from Koko. I showed her a sea shell and asked, "What's this?" There was no response. "Forgot?" I asked. Koko did not answer. Finally I sent Koko to her room and closed but did not lock the door. As I did so I said, "Well, I'll just take these goodies to Michael." At this point, Koko edged out of the door and unprompted signed "Shell." That same evening, I wanted Koko to demonstrate the sign for *rock*. This time I did not have a rock to show Koko and so I tried to elicit the sign by saying, "What is the sign for *rock*?" Koko made a number of bizarre gestures with her two fists, but not the sign for *rock* which is made by hitting one fisted hand onto the back of the other hand. Before putting her to bed, I made a final attempt, saying, "I won't give you your night dish [of food] unless you say *rock*." "Rock," signed Koko.

It is through examining in detail such difficult-to-quantify responses and linguistic exchanges that I hope to reveal important qualitative aspects of Koko's signed utterances.

As a preface to the discussion which follows, it is perhaps instructive to provide an example of a typical dialogue between the gorilla and a human companion.

The following is an excerpt from an 8-hour sample taken January 31, 1977 ($ following a word indicates that it was spoken only; otherwise P's utterances are both signed and spoken. Penny is a nickname used in Koko's presence for the author.):

1/31/77 9:00 A.M.
(It is time for Koko's breakfast which normally consists of a square of rice bread and a glass of milk.)

*P:* What do$ you want?

*K:* Apple drink.

*P:* How$ about$ . . . (Penny is about to suggest the usual rice bread but Koko interrupts, signing)

*K:* Apple.

*P:* What time is$ it$? What time? (Penny wants to elicit a new sign in her vocabulary, *breakfast*, Koko is persistently requesting some apple juice—her favorite beverage, which is not a usual breakfast item.)

*K:* Drink.

*P:* Breakfast.

*K:* Breakfast.

*P:* OK$, you want breakfast?

*K:* Good happy.

*P:* What do$ you want for$ breakfast?

(A rhetorical question—Penny is not really going to give her a choice, and gets out rice bread, saying [vocally] as she does so. . . .)

*P:* I've$ got$ something$ good$ for$ gorillas$ . . . right$ here's$ breakfast$.

(Penny offers rice bread to Koko.)

*K:* Bottle there apple.

(Koko indicates a bottle of apple juice in refrigerator.)

*P:* Koko?

(Penny, who does not intend to alter the breakfast menu, firmly closes the refrigerator door and gets the rice bread out of the bag.)

*K:* Mean . . .

(Koko had never before used this sign and Penny did not comprehend her utterance at the time, but recorded its configuration. Koko seemed to be trying to clarify her own intentions.)

*P:* What's this?

*K:* Bottle apple . . . nice there (points to her palm).

*P:* Koko you are$ sign(ing$) wrong things. (Penny wants Koko to sign for the rice bread but Koko rephrases her request.)

*K:* Please milk, please me like drink apple . . . bottle.

*P:* How$ about$ first breakfast?

*K:* Breakfast eat some cookie eat. (Now Koko has either made an error or another unacceptable request — gorillas, like children, do not get sweets for breakfast.)

*P:* No, no bread. (Penny molds "bread" and gives it to Koko. A glass of milk will complete Koko's breakfast. Penny has a glass of water out for powdered milk; Koko touches it and then the container of milk powder.)

*K:* Hurry drink milk.

*P:* Yes, Penny make?

*K:* Glass all milk. (Perhaps Koko is suggesting that Penny put all the milk powder in her glass. Penny molds "make" and makes it.)

*P:* OK$, now what?

*K:* Time milk. (Koko is allowed to drink the glass of milk. Koko, across the counter, hands Penny the empty glass and looks at a new doll a few feet away.)

*K:* Hurry gimme.

*P:* What?

(Koko reaches for new doll, but Penny stops her from getting it.)

*K:* Baby come-on happy. (Penny picks up doll.)

*P:* This is$ baby alive.

*K:* Like baby new.

*P:* Yes! (Penny gives doll to Koko.)

*K:* Good happy.

(Koko lies down on floor with the doll in her arms, signing.)

*K:* Sleep. (Koko seems to have forgotten all about the apple juice . . . .)

## Summary of Koko's Progress

To be considered a reliable part of Koko's vocabulary, a sign must meet a criterion of spontaneous and appropriate use on at least half the days of a given month. This is somewhat different than the criterion Gardner and Gardner (1969) set for the chimpanzee Washoe (spontaneous and appropriate use for a period of 14 consecutive days).

By the end of 1976 when Koko was 5½ years old, 246 signs had met my criterion but the comulative number of different signs Koko had used spontaneously and appropriately was 544. The number of different signs Koko used in this manner each month during 1976 ranged between 284 and 332. These figures indicate that my criterion may underestimate Koko's working vocabulary by between 40 and 80 signs.

In order to directly compare Koko's vocabulary development with that of Washoe, I applied the Gardners' 14-consecutive-day criterion to Koko's data. The Gardners report that after 36 months of training, 85 of Washoe's signs had met their strict criterion. At an identical point in her training, 127 of Koko's signs had met the Gardners' criterion. At the end of her 51 months of training with the Gardners, 132 of Washoe's signs had met the 14-consecutive-day criterion; after 51 months of training, 161 of Koko's signs had met that same criterion. The vocabularies of Koko and Washoe overlap to a considerable extent. Seventy of the 161 signs acquired by Koko within 51 months of training were also acquired by Washoe in the same period of time (see Table I).[4]

### Table I
### Signs in the Vocabularies of Koko and Washoe meeting
### the Gardner and Gardner Criterion within 51 Months of Training
### (5;3 Years of Age)

| | | | | |
|---|---|---|---|---|
| Signs acquired by Koko within 51 months of training not in Washoe's vocabulary at the same point in her training | all | clown | Koko | pinch-skin |
| | alligator | cookie | leg | pink-shame |
| | apple | corn | lip | potato |
| | arm | cracker | lipstick | pour |
| | around | do | match | ring |
| | ask | don't | medicine | rubber |
| | bad | drapes | milk | sandwich |
| | bean | dry | monkey | scratch |
| | bellybutton | ear | mouth | sip |
| | belt | earring | nail | skunk-stink |
| | big | egg | nailclipper | small |
| | blanket | elephant | necklace | soap |
| | blow | eye | nose | sock |
| | bone | feather | on | spice |
| | bottle | finished | onion | sponge |
| | bottom | fish | orange | straw |
| | bracelet | frown | peach | sweater |
| | butter | giraffe | Penny | tape |
| | cabbage | gorilla | pepper | taste |
| | cake | grape | pick-groom | teeth-glass |
| | candy | hair | pig | tiger |
| | carrot | helpmyself | pillow | whistle |
| | chase | | | |

Total:  89

| | | | | |
|---|---|---|---|---|
| Signs in common with Washoe at the same point in her training | baby | cow | light | sleep-bed |
| | bag-purse | different | listen | smile |
| | banana | dirty | look | sorry |
| | berry | drink | me | spoon |
| | bird | eat-food | meat | stamp |
| | bite | flower | mine | string |
| | book | fork | mirror | sweet |

**Table I** (*continued*)

| Signs in common with Washoe at the same point in her training | brush | fruit | more | there-this-that |
|---|---|---|---|---|
| | bug | go | nut | thirsty-swallow |
| | cat | good | open | tickle |
| | catch | grass | out | time |
| | cereal | hat | pen-write | toothbrush |
| | cheese | hug-love | please | tree |
| | clean | hungry(want) | quiet | up |
| | clothes | hurry | red | water |
| | cold | key | ride | white |
| | comb | kiss | same | wiper(bib) |
| | come-gimme | knife-cut | sit-chair | you |
| | | | | Total: 72 |

| Signs acquired by Washoe within 51 months of training not acquired by Koko at the same point in her training | airplane | enough | Larry | run |
|---|---|---|---|---|
| | bath | floor | leaf | shoes |
| | black | funny | Linn | smell |
| | butterfly | goodbye | lock | smoke |
| | can't | green | lollipop | spin |
| | car | Greg | man | Susan |
| | climb | hammer | Mrs. G. | telephone |
| | cover | hand | Naomi | tomato |
| | cry | help | no | Washoe |
| | cucumber | hole | oil | we |
| | Dennis | hose | pants | Wende |
| | dog | hot | pin | who |
| | Don | house | pipe | window |
| | down | hurt | Roger | woman |
| | Dr. G. | in | Ron | yours |
| | | | | Total: 60 |

| | | | | |
|---|---|---|---|---|
| | | | | Total Koko: 161 |
| | | | | Total Washoe: 132 |

Koko's vocabulary has expanded in every conceptual domain, with the greatest increase occurring in the object-name categories (see Table II). This parallels the development of human children (Nelson, 1973).

It is perhaps through this extensive vocabulary development that Koko has been able to directly convey certain abstract ideas never before expressed by a nonhuman: concepts of causality and time, descriptions of internal and emotional states, and assertions of falsehood.

Koko has acquired some words relating to the concept of time (such as now, time, finished) and uses them productively in her communication with us. For example, when rejecting a banana snack, she signed ''Banana later eat, now can't.'' Although Koko's vocabulary at this time did not include any interrogative words, she demonstrated comprehension of them by ap-

**Table II**
**Two Hundred Sixty-four Words Acquired by Koko**
**(P Criterion, 66 Months of Training; Age 6;6)**
**by Semantic Categories**

| Category and Word | Order of Acquisition | |
|---|---|---|
| **Nominals\*** | | |
| *Food and drink* | | |
| eat-food | 2 | (also under verbals) |
| drink | 3 | (also under verbals) |
| bean | 12 | |
| candy | 13 | |
| apple | 17 | |
| nut | 19 | |
| cheese | 26 | |
| orange | 27 | (also under modifiers) |
| egg | 29 | |
| cabbage | 34 | |
| banana | 39 | |
| berry | 45 | |
| butter | 46 | |
| cookie | 47 | |
| cereal | 54 | |
| meat | 55 | |
| potato | 56 | |
| carrot | 57 | |
| corn | 61 | |
| peach | 68 | |
| bread | 74 | |
| gum | 83 | |
| cucumber | 84 | |
| fruit | 100 | |
| prune-raisin | 105 | |
| salad | 106 | |
| salt | 109 | |
| bone | 110 | |
| onion | 116 | |
| spice | 138 | |
| cracker | 145 | |
| grape | 150 | |
| cake | 151 | |
| milk | 153 | |
| sandwich | 154 | |
| water | 158 | |
| pudding | 167 | |
| pepper | 198 | |
| jam | 212 | |
| medicine | 226 | |
| lollipop-ice cream | 227 | |

## Table II (continued)

| Category and Word | Order of Acquisition | |
|---|---|---|
| jello | 229 | |
| lettuce | 244 | |
| breakfast | 249 | |
| tomato | 253 | |
| squash | 259 | (also under verbals and modifiers) |
| coke | 262 | |
| *Total* | 47 | 17.8% |
| *Animals* | | |
| cat | 40 | |
| bird | 90 | |
| bear | 92 | |
| monkey | 94 | |
| dog | 97 | |
| alligator | 104 | |
| skunk-stink | 127 | (also under modifiers) |
| fish | 133 | |
| frog | 134 | |
| tiger | 136 | |
| bug | 140 | |
| cow | 175 | |
| pig | 179 | |
| mouse | 182 | |
| horse | 183 | |
| elephant | 185 | |
| gorilla | 195 | |
| giraffe | 205 | |
| rabbit | 206 | |
| lion | 211 | |
| camel | 219 | |
| *Total* | 21 | 7.9% |
| *Clothes* | | |
| hat | 6 | |
| sweater | 16 | |
| sock | 107 | |
| glove | 152 | |
| pants | 165 | |
| belt | 193 | |
| clothes | 194 | |
| **Total** | 7 | 2.6% |
| *Toys and play equipment* | | |
| swing | 49 | (also under verbals) |
| baby | 69 | |
| ball | 75 | |
| rubber (tire) | 155 | |
| box | 171 | |

# Table II (*continued*)

| Category and Word | Order of Acquisition | |
|---|---|---|
| whistle | 187 | |
| clown | 189 | |
| harmonica | 204 | |
| mask | 213 | |
| *Total* | 9 | 3.4% |
| *Vehicles* | | |
| airplane | 143 | |
| boat | 144 | |
| train | 170 | |
| *Total* | 3 | 1.1% |
| *Furniture and household items* | | |
| blanket | 14 | |
| sit-chair | 44 | (also under verbals) |
| pillow | 66 | |
| light | 88 | |
| soap | 101 | |
| tape | 112 | |
| string | 117 | |
| sleep-bed | 121 | (also under verbals) |
| sponge | 131 | |
| telephone | 161 | |
| toilet | 180 | |
| hammer | 203 | |
| drapes | 224 | |
| *Total* | 13 | 4.9% |
| *Personal items* | | |
| key | 7 | |
| toothbrush | 11 | |
| match | 25 | |
| pen-write | 30 | (also under verbals) |
| brush | 32 | (also under verbals) |
| bracelet | 36 | |
| bag-purse | 48 | |
| time-watch | 70 | (also under time expressions) |
| wiper | 72 | |
| necklace | 77 | |
| lipstick | 85 | |
| cigarette | 87 | |
| book | 95 | |
| stamp | 96 | |
| earring | 102 | |
| hurt | 130 | |
| paper | 142 | |
| nail-clipper | 147 | |
| ring | 149 | |

Table II (*continued*)

| Category and Word | Order of Acquisition | |
|---|---|---|
| stethoscope | 173 | |
| mirror | 174 | |
| comb | 190 | |
| injection | 200 | |
| oil-cream | 218 | |
| toothpaste | 252 | |
| *Total* | 25 | 9.4% |
| | | |
| *Eating and drinking utensils* | | |
| bottle | 24 | |
| teeth-glass | 43 | (also under body parts) |
| straw | 76 | |
| fork | 156 | |
| spoon | 160 | |
| knife-cut | 163 | |
| bowl | 181 | |
| *Total* | 7 | 2.6% |
| | | |
| *Outdoor objects* | | |
| flower | 18 | |
| grass | 35 | |
| leaf | 52 | |
| tree | 64 | |
| feather | 122 | |
| rock | 199 | |
| *Total* | 6 | 2.2% |
| | | |
| *People* | | |
| Koko | 53 | |
| Penny | 91 | |
| man | 197 | |
| Kate | 221 | |
| Mike | 247 | |
| devil | 258 | |
| Cindy | 259 | |
| girl | 261 | |
| *Total* | 8 | 3% |
| | | |
| *Body parts* | | |
| teeth-glass | 43 | (also under eating utensils) |
| hair | 98 | |
| ear | 111 | |
| arm | 114 | |
| pinch-skin | 115 | (also under verbals) |
| head | 120 | |
| leg | 123 | |
| nose | 124 | |

**Table II** (*continued*)

| Category and Word | Order of Acquisition | |
|---|---|---|
| eye | 125 | |
| lip | 128 | |
| mouth | 139 | |
| tongue | 159 | |
| neck | 164 | |
| bottom | 168 | |
| nail | 172 | |
| finger | 184 | |
| foot | 186 | |
| pimple | 196 | |
| bellybutton | 223 | |
| shoulder | 231 | |
| underarm | 254 | |
| *Total* | 21 | 7.9% |
| *Miscellaneous* | | |
| trouble | 265 | |
| *Total* | 1 | .3% |
| *Pronouns* | | |
| me | 42 | |
| you | 78 | |
| myself | 162 | |
| *Total* | 3 | 1.1% |

*Total distinct nominal words included:* 171

| *Modifiers* | | |
|---|---|---|
| more | 4 | |
| clean | 9 | (also under verbals) |
| sorry | 22 | (also under polite words) |
| orange | 27 | (also under food and drink) |
| there | 33 | |
| red | 38 | |
| mine | 50 | |
| cold | 51 | |
| big | 58 | |
| hurry | 59 | |
| this-that | 60 | |
| quiet | 62 | |
| sweet | 63 | |
| small | 67 | |
| hot | 71 | |
| good | 82 | |
| white | 103 | |
| dry | 113 | (also under verbals) |
| skunk-stink | 127 | (also under animals) |
| thirsty-swallow | 132 | (also under verbals) |

**Table II** (*continued*)

| Category and Word | Order of Acquisition | |
|---|---|---|
| dirty | 148 | |
| rubber | 155 | (also under toys and playthings) |
| yellow | 157 | |
| same | 166 | |
| all | 188 | (also under numericals) |
| stupid | 191 | |
| different | 192 | |
| bad | 201 | |
| pink-shame | 207 | |
| hungry | 210 | |
| black | 216 | |
| green | 220 | |
| sad | 233 | |
| mad | 235 | |
| rotten | 238 | |
| now | 241 | (also under time expressions) |
| wrong | 244 | |
| happy | 245 | |
| some | 247 | (also under numericals) |
| fine-polite | 249 | |
| old | 256 | |
| squash | 260 | (also under verbals and food and drink) |
| nice | 262 | |
| *Total* | 43 | 16.2% |
| *Negatives and affirmatives* | | |
| can't | 81 | |
| don't-not | 208 | |
| nothing | 222 | (also under numericals) |
| don-t know | 236 | |
| yes | 239 | |
| no | 251 | |
| *Total* | 6 | 2.2% |
| *Action words* | | |
| eat-food | 2 | (also under food and drink) |
| drink | 3 | (also under food and drink) |
| open | 8 | |
| clean | 9 | (also under modifiers) |
| come-gimme | 10 | |
| catch | 15 | |
| pick-groom | 20 | |
| listen | 21 | |
| tickle | 23 | |
| look | 28 | |
| pen-write | 30 | (also under personal items) |
| brush | 32 | (also under personal items) |
| go | 37 | |

Table II (*continued*)

| Category and Word | Order of Acquisition | |
|---|---|---|
| chase | 41 | |
| sit-chair | 44 | (also under furniture and household) |
| swing | 49 | (also under toys and playthings) |
| blow | 65 | |
| hug-love | 73 | |
| bite | 80 | |
| ask | 86 | |
| taste | 89 | |
| pour | 93 | |
| scratch | 108 | |
| dry | 113 | **(also under modifiers)** |
| pinch-skin | 115 | (also under body parts) |
| smell | 118 | |
| ride | 119 | |
| sleep-bed | 121 | (also under furniture and household) |
| pound | 129 | |
| hurt | 130 | |
| thirsty-swallow | 132 | (also under modifiers) |
| hide-and-seek | 135 | |
| help | 137 | |
| finished | 141 | (also under time expressions) |
| kiss | 146 | |
| knife-cut | 163 | (also under eating utensils) |
| smile | 176 | |
| frown | 177 | |
| sip | 178 | |
| helpmyself | 202 | |
| do | 209 | |
| think | 214 | |
| know | 215 | |
| draw | 217 | |
| make-fix | 225 | |
| break | 228 | |
| want | 230 | |
| like | 232 | |
| play | 234 | |
| have | 237 | |
| cry | 255 | |
| squash | 260 | (also under modifiers and food) |
| tell | 264 | |
| *Total* | 53 | 20% |
| | | |
| *Locatives* | | |
| up | 1 | |
| out | 5 | |
| around | 79 | |
| on | 99 | |
| in | 126 | |

**515**

**Table II** (*continued*)

| Category and Word | Order of Acquisition | |
|---|---|---|
| down | 169 | |
| *Total* | 6 | 2.2% |
| *Time expressions* | | |
| time-watch | 70 | (also under personal items) |
| finished | 141 | (also under verbals) |
| now | 241 | (also under modifiers) |
| night | 254 | |
| *Total* | 4 | 1.5% |
| *Social-expressive* | | |
| sorry | 22 | (also under modifiers) |
| please | 31 | |
| darn | 240 | |
| hi-bye | 242 | |
| *Total* | 4 | 1.5% |
| *Numerical* | | |
| all | 188 | (also under modifiers) |
| nothing | 222 | (also under negatives) |
| some | 247 | (also under modifiers) |
| *Total* | 3 | 1.1% |
| | *Total Distinct Words:* 264 | |

*Nominal categories after Nelson (1973)

propriately responding to *who, what, where,* and *why* questions (Patterson, 1979).

Koko's early signed utterances were similar in form and function to those of young children and chimpanzees. A small set of relational meanings accounted for the majority of her constructions between the ages of 2½ and 3½ years (Patterson, 1978a). And like many children, Koko came up with new words, some with form and meaning all her own, puzzling for a time the adults around her.

## GESTURAL INNOVATION: SINGLE SIGNS

### Generation of Novel Sign-Gestures

Gestures Koko has generated spontaneously (without instruction) fall into two categories: natural gestures and innovative gestures. Almost from the beginning of the project, Koko consistently produced gestures which closely resembled in form and reference the Ameslan signs for *come* or *give-me, go, hurry, up, catch,* and *pound.* These were distinctive because they appeared without direct training at a time when the great majority of Koko's signs were being acquired by molding. Because other young gorillas reared in captive conditions who have not been exposed to sign language use these same gestures, they may be part of the gorilla's natural repertoire (see Table III). Dr. Ronald Cohn, photographer for the project, has recorded

### Table III
### "Natural" Gestures Produced Spontaneously by Koko

| Gloss | Month/ age first observed[a] | Description | Usage | Examples |
|---|---|---|---|---|
| Come-gimme | 1/12 | Flat hand, palm up extended from body, sometimes accompanied by a motion toward body | Requesting objects or the approach of other individuals | 7/27/72 sitting outside, to sun; 3/8/72 consistently used to request food |
| Gorilla | 1/12(42) | Fists alternately strike chest | Excitement; referential use for gorillas or the likeness of gorillas | 7/72 in solitary play, or in response to approach of strangers; 1/17/75 K: Gorilla. B: Who's a gorilla? K: Me |
| Pound | 1/12(28) | Flat hands, palms down simultaneously slap surface | Play invitation or challenge; referential use to request pounding on back | 12/31/72 directed toward iguana Koko is afraid of; 11/23/73 repeated use as request for back pounding; 11/29/73 in response to the query "What?" from a male companion to whom she had just presented |
| That-there | 1/12 | Pointing or contact with index finger | Indicating an object or place | 7/26/72 to pictures of bear and apple in picture book; 9/24/72 indicating spot on mirror where she wants companion to blow "fog" |

## Table III (*continued*)

| Gloss | Month/ age first observed[a] | Description | Usage | Examples |
|-------|------------------------------|-------------|-------|----------|
| Up | 1/12 | One or both arms extended upward | To be picked up, for movement upward | 8/6/72 to be picked up when companion is departing; 9/23/72 for seated companion to get up. |
| Darn | 4/16 | Back of compact hand(s) hit surface or object | Annoyance, frustration | 11/8/72 companion molded sign for horse, Koko pushed toy horse away; sign is molded again and Koko hits toy with backs of both hands; 6/23/76 signed on companion's wrist where missing watch used to be |
| Catch | 9/20(28) | Arms move out and away from body, then quickly and forcefully move back to contact body, crossing over chest | Excitement, invitation to play; for games involving throwing or chasing | 3/10/73 companion repeatedly makes toy dog aproach and retreat; 11/11/73 huge sign to companion about to throw a ball |
| Hurry | 12/23 | Arm extended, open hand shaken at wrist (correct Ameslan configuration: index and second finger are extended together) | Play, excitement; impatience with delay | 4/6/73 companion pretends to struggle to open can containing toy Koko wants |
| Go | 22/33 | Arm moves away from body, extending | Requesting movement of a person, object, or vehicle | 4/26/74 while being carried, or to move in a specific direction |

[a]Month (first number) refers to month of instruction in which gesture was first observed, age (second number) is in months, and number in parentheses is the age of first referential use if later than age first observed.

on film the use of the *come, go,* and *hurry* gestures by captive-born lowland gorillas being reared in a social group at the San Francisco Zoo. In addition, I was fortunate to have the assistance of Ann Southcombe, who had had over 7 years of experience rearing numerous gorillas from infancy to adolescence. She has observed spontaneous use of each of the gestures listed in Table III by one or more young captive-born lowland gorillas at the Cincinnati Zoo. Although Dian Fossey has not reported the use of most of these gestures by wild mountain gorillas, in the film footage of these animals I have seen, gestures resembling *come-gimme* and *pound* did occur.

One interesting gesture Koko produced very early in the study, but did not use productively until years later, is done by hitting the back of one or both fists onto a surface of object (see Figure 9-1). This gestures closely resembles a natural killing motion observed in chimpanzees but which has not been reported in gorillas in the wild (the gesture has, however, been observed in young captive-born gorillas; Ann Southcombe, 1977). Koko uses the sign to express herself in situations in which her goals have been frustrated in some way or in which she seems annoyed by something, and I have translated it as *darn*. The first observed use of this gesture (11/8/72, age

*Figure 9-1. Darn,* Koko's invented expletive, is performed by hitting the back of a clenched fist onto a surface or object. (Credit: Dr. Ronald H. Cohn)

1;4) involved a rejected toy. I held up a toy horse and after molding the sign for *horse* twice, offered it to Koko. She pushed the toy away, but I molded the sign again and placed the horse in front of her. Koko responded by pounding on it with the backs of her fists. Not until June of 1976 did Koko use the sign in combination. In one instance, she signed "Darn bird bird" while a bird outside was giving a cry resembling a distress call for several minutes.

Evidence of Koko's true gestural innovative ability also occurred quite early in the study. She spontaneously generated and used productively (in novel combination) gestures resembling signs, but which were neither standard forms in Ameslan nor gestures observed in untrained gorillas. The intended meaning of some of the gestures was obvious from context (for instance, "tickle"); the meaning of others had to be worked out from the collective records of the contexts of occurrence. For example, during the fifth month of the project (age 1;4), Koko generated a sign which I glossed as *bird* because of its apparent origin, but which seemed to refer more broadly to novel or interesting objects out of reach. In the glass-encased Children's Zoo nursery which was Koko's early environment, my assistants and I spent a good deal of time pointing out and signing about the people and animals that would come into view. On November 18, 1972 a turkey roosting on the window ledge captured Koko's attention. I took advantage of the situation, as I had done on numerous occasions in the past, to teach the sign for *bird*. But this time Koko studied my hand very closely as I signed and subsequently placed her index fingers together on the glass next to the bird at an angle approximating the position of the index finger and thumb in the articulation of the *bird* sign. This gesture, a creation combining both deictic and iconic elements, was used by the gorilla on many occasions after this, often to herself, with reference to a problem involving stacking boxes to reach suspended incentives, and to animals and objects on the other side of the window.

Some of Koko's invented words have been more clearly iconic. For example, the Ameslan sign for *bite* is made by clamping one clawed hand onto the side of the other hand held flat, palm down, Koko's innovated sign for *bite* (open mouth contacting the side of the hand held palm down) originated quite dramatically one afternoon: Koko had play-bitten Ron, one of her companions, just a little too hard and once too often, and he bit her back on the knuckles. Taken by surprise and perhaps even a little shocked, she came to me for comfort. When I asked, "What happened?" Koko cast a woeful glance at the offender and placed her mouth on her hand; the meaning was unmistakable. She has continued to use this form of the sign appropriately ever since (even in imitation of our correctly formed version of the sign) (see Figure 9-2).

Because there is no Ameslan sign for *tickle,* I adopted the sign used by

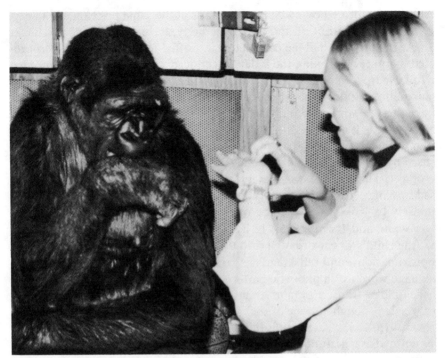

*Figure 9-2.* Koko's invented sign for *bite* is elicited by the standard form done by a companion. (Credit: Dr. Ronald H. Cohn)

the Gardners, which is executed by drawing the index finger across the back of the hand. Although her companions have repeatedly modeled and molded this sign, Koko has consistently used a more graphic gesture—drawing her index finger across her underarm—which I have come to accept as a variant of the *tickle* sign with a perhaps more logical place of articulation.

Although Koko's *bite* and *tickle* signs are highly iconic, other of her invented signs are metaphoric icons; that is, they visually represent only one aspect or part of their referents. This is the nature of most iconic signs in Ameslan (Friedman, 1975). For example, I learned the sign for *stethoscope* (index finger of one hand to the ear; the other hand in a fist on the chest) only after Koko invented her own (in which she placed an index finger to each ear). Two other gestures invented by Koko may also fit into this category. One can only be defined as meaning *walk-up-my-back-with-your-fingers* (both hands are placed palm up on the floor, behind the back, and bounced if a response is not forthcoming or to request repetition). Now that Koko is experiencing estrus periods, she has come up with an interesting variation of this gesture, translatable as *walk-up-my-bottom,* which she first employed during her playful interaction with the gorilla Michael. This gesture is performed by placing both hands in the same position as the earlier form, but in front of and under the body, instead of behind the back.

A final gesture had me completely mystified for some time. It was executed by quickly stroking the index finger across the lips and was preceded or followed by a noun or the pointing gesture, *that.* It was not directed to companions but occurred when Koko was looking through magazines, playing by herself with toys, nesting, or noticing an object in passing. When forced to give it an English equivalent, I called it *note,* and later realized its resemblance to the construction *hi + noun,* found by Bloom (1970), which is used by children not as a greeting, but in taking notice of the presence of an object. This gesture was present only early in the study and is no longer used by Koko. Table IV presents a complete list of invented signs used productively by Koko as of the end of the 69th month of the project.

Winitz and Irwin (1958), in a study of early word acquisition, found that the child's first words fell into three categories: standard words, word approximations, and self-language words. These researchers defined a self-language word as "a phonetic pattern which is interpreted by the observers at the time of transcription as an attempt by the infant to produce a standard word, although not one of the phoenetic elements of the standard word is present" (p. 251). Translating this to sign, a self-language word for Koko was defined as a gestural pattern which was interpreted by the observer(s) as an attempt to produce a sign, although not one of the cheremic elements of the standard sign was present. Between the ages of 13 and 18 months the percentage of self-language words in the child's repertoire ranged from .73 percent to 5.22 percent. Self-language words made up to 22 percent and 26 percent of Koko's vocabulary at these ages (Tables V & VI).

Nonstandard signs were reported to be "prevalent" in samples of deaf children's utterances taken by Hoffmeister (Hoffmeister, Moores, & Ellenberger, 1975); however, these data have yet to be published. Still, an essential aspect of children's early speech or sign is captured in a comment by Menyuk (1971): "The infant seems to have caught on to the principles of the communication game long before he can use the standard rules or models presented to him" (p. 168). The data on Koko indicate that the same may hold true for the infant ape exposed to a visual language environment.

## Modulation of Sign-Gestures

The core meaning of signs may be altered intrinsically by changes in the articulation of one or more parameters (motion, location, configuration, facial expression, or body posture). By actively exploiting the possibilities for simultaneous expression afforded by sign as a visual language, Koko frequently alters the meaning of signs. Such changes in the execution of signs which signal changes in meaning have been identified in standard

**Table IV**
**Signs Invented by Koko**

| Gloss | Month/ age first observed[a] | Description | Usage | Early Examples |
|---|---|---|---|---|
| Blow | 2/13 | Index finger held vertically at mouth (early version done at other's mouth) | Requesting other to blow (onto window, Koko's face) | 8/2/72 Koko puts index finger to companion's mouth for her to continue blowing into Koko's face; 9/18/72 same form, for companion to blow "fog" on window |
| Tickle | 3/14 | Index finger strokes underarm or sole of foot | Requesting tickling | 9/12/72 Koko strokes index finger across sole of foot after being tickled there; 1/13/73 Koko requests repeated play bites by stroking underarm with index finger |
| Bird | 5/16 | Arms in front of of body or on a surface, index fingers held together at tips, 45-degree angle | Interesting objects out of reach | 11/18/72 companion signs "Bird" and points to a turkey at nursery window. Koko looks at bird then at companion's sign **and joins index** fingers on window where bird is; 11/24/72 Koko stacks two boxes in an attempt to reach a suspended banana, then signs |
| Bracelet | 21/32 | Cupped hand pats wrist | Bracelets and other objects covering wrist | 3/8/74 for new bracelet, Koko patted wrist where it would go; 5/1/74 bear puppet on companion's hand |

## Table IV (*continued*)

| Gloss | Month/ age first observed[a] | Description | Usage | Early Examples |
|---|---|---|---|---|
| Bite | 23/34 | Side of hand placed in mouth | Describing, requesting biting | 5/11/74 used as a request for a companion to bite Koko's shoulder |
| Walk-up-my-back | 31/42 | Open hands placed palm up on surface behind back | Requesting tickling game in which companion's fingers move up Koko's back | 1/26/75 to request repetition of back tickling game |
| Clay | 34/45 | Palms of flat hands held horizontally contact; top hand moves back and forth over palm of other | Clay | 4/22/75 Koko requests clay by miming rolling a ball of clay between hands |
| Note | 34/45 | Index finger drawn across lips | **Self-directed, referring to toys and other objects** | 4/15/75 during play with black inflatable chair 5/21/75 "That note that note that" indicating purple towel |
| Stethoscope | 34/45 | Index fingers contact ears | Stethoscopes | 4/18/75 signs "Necklace" then places fingers to ears for a stethoscope the doctor brought; 5/1/75 Koko puts both fists to chest, then both indexes to eyes then signs "Necklace stethoscope" for the instrument |
| Eye-makeup | 35/46 | Index finger(s) strokes eyelid | Eyeshadow, mascara, and other makeup applied to the eye area | 5/16/75 Koko requests eyeshadow with a gesture miming the act of stroking it on over the eyelid; 5/18/75 Koko uses |

## Table IV (*continued*)

| Gloss | Month/ age first observed[a] | Description | Usage | Early Examples |
|---|---|---|---|---|
| | | | | two index fingers as she signs "eye-makeup" to herself while applying it with a makeup brush |
| Sip | 35/46 | Thumb and index finger of compact hand contact mouth | Requesting or labeling food and drink or requesting companion to eat or drink or pretend to | 5/7/75 Koko uses *sip* accompanied by a kissing noise to request a can she had failed to reach from the cupboard; 5/9/75 Koko signs "Mouth you sip" as she offers molasses jar lid to companion |
| Frown | 37/48 | Lower lip folds down over chin; index finger may contact lip | Unpleasant objects or events | 7/2/75 first observed after visit from a chimpanzee with a pendulous lower lip; 7/6/75 companion signs "Forgot?" for hand cream and Koko signs "Frown" (she gives annoyance barks when it is applied) |
| Thermometer | 53/64 | Tucks index finger under arm (where her temperature is taken) | Thermometers | 11/1/76 Koko is ill and has had temperature taken at thigh and underarm. Signs when shown thermometer; 3/28/78 playing doctor, companion gets syringe out of doctor bag, saying, "Let's pretend you're sick. Are you sick?" Koko signs "Thermometer, injection" |

## Table IV (*continued*)

| Gloss | Month/ age first observed[a] | Description | Usage | Early Examples |
|---|---|---|---|---|
| Eyeglasses | 62/73 | Index fingers trace line from eye to back of ears | Eyeglasses | 8/24/77 referring to a spectacled toy tiger "Tiger, tiger, eye, eye, eyeglasses"; 9/9/77 Referring to pair of glasses |
| Nailfile | 63/74 | Index finger extended from compact fist moves back and forth across fingernail | Nailfiles, filing nails | 9/16/77 companion offers nailfile "Want this?" Koko responds "Nail nailfile nice." Companion retrieved nailfile after Koko stole it and asked her what it was |
| Walk-up-my-bottom | 65/76 | Hands placed under bottom, fingers curl up to back | Requesting tickling of bottom | 11/23/77 To gorilla Michael. Koko rests on stomach, presents bottom |
| Away | 69/80 | Hands push forward away from body together, palms held up vertically | | 3/20/77 Koko is shown a toy lamb and asked, "Name of that baby?" Koko kisses it and signs, "Devil away." Companion responds, "No, not name," but Koko signs "Yes." When companion says "Lamb" in English only, Koko signs "Don't-know" |

[a]Month refers to month of instruction in which gesture was first observed and age is given in months.

## Table V
### Number and Percentage of Standard, Approximate, and Self-language Words in the Early Vocabulary of Koko and Human Children* Between 13 and 18 Months of Age

| | 13th month | | | | 18th month | | | |
|---|---|---|---|---|---|---|---|---|
| | Koko[a] | | 23 Children[b] | | Koko | | 35 Children[c] | |
| Category | # | % | # | % | # | % | # | % |
| Standard | 2 | 22 | 22 | 16 | 7 | 37 | 103 | 38 |
| Approximated[d] | 5 | 56 | 114 | 83 | 7 | 37 | 151 | 56 |
| Self-language[e] | 2 | 22 | 1 | 00.7 | 5 | 26 | 14 | 05.2 |

*Figures on human children drawn from Winitz and Irwin, 1958
[a]Figures apply to Koko's emitted, not qualified, vocabulary
[b]Data from 38 samples of approximately 30 minutes each
[c]Data from 58 samples of approximately 30 minutes each
[d]Word approximations were defined for children as utterances containing at least one speech sound that could be found in the standard word; for Koko they were defined as signs in which her hand configuration did not match that of the standard sign
[e]Self-language words were defined for children as utterances in which not one of the phonetic elements of the standard word is present; for Koko they were defined as signs in which all 3 parameters (configuration, motion, and position) differed in some respect from those of the standard sign

## Table VI
### Standard, Approximate, and Self-language Signs in Koko's Early Emitted Vocabulary

| | Emitted signs | |
|---|---|---|
| Category | 13 montns | 18 months |
| Standard | Drink, that | Drink, dog, hat, mouth, nose, out, that |
| Approximate | Come, eat, more, toothbrush up | Come, eat, more, no, pretty, toothbrush, up |
| Self-language | Bird, blow | Bird, blow, darn, scratch, tickle |

Ameslan and labeled *modulations* (Bellugi, 1975). Although Ameslan lacks inflections, modulations can serve grammatical functions which are performed by sequential devices such as word order and inflections in spoken languages. For instance, certain verb signs are executed with reference to a spatial layout of persons or things in relation to the speaker, to signal agent or object. Most modulations in sign language are accomplished primarily by variations in the movement of the hands. Changes in location of the sign and hand configuration play only minor roles.

Emphatic stress is one use to which Koko puts simultaneous modulation. Like the human signer (Friedman, 1975), Koko may use two hands to execute a sign usually articulated with one hand. For example, Koko has signed *rotten* with two hands, with an English translation being *really-rotten* or *very-rotten*.

In addition, Koko varies the place of articulation of several action signs such as *tickle, pinch,* or *pick* to convey slight differences in meaning. At times she will sign *tickle* on her inner thigh instead of her underarm or on both underarms (as a kind of emphasis). The location of the *pinch* sign is highly variable: it may be done on the leg, stomach, arm, neck, and so forth, rather than on the back of the hand, indicating exactly where she wants to be pinched. The sign *pick* is properly done on the index finger, but Koko signs it on her teeth when she needs help dislodging food stuck between her teeth, or as a request for dental floss. Also, Koko has signed *scratch* on her back (to request a back scratching) and on her finger (when confronted with a recently inflicted scratch wound on her companion's finger), as well as on the back of her hand, which is the correct form.

Motion is another parameter of sign which Koko varies to signal qualitative or quantitative differences in the referent. *Alligator* (clapping the palms, horizontally, together) may be done with a small motion to indicate a tiny lizard or other reptile, or with a large motion to indicate a larger specimen. When she has been very bad, Koko enlarges the signing space and increases the speed and forcefulness of the motion of the hand down her face. She may vary the direction of the motion of a sign to indicate a specific actor. *Sip* turned from her own mouth toward that of her companion may be translated as *you-sip*.

Koko uses such variations to mark relations of size, number, location, possession, manner (degree, intensity, or emphasis), agent or object of an action, negation (rejection or denial), to express questions, and as a form of word play akin to wit or humor. Table VII lists 11 relations or functions, modulations used to convey them, and examples of each which have been produced by the gorilla.

This set of modulations intersects but is not identical to the set employed by fluent human signers described by Fischer (in Bellugi & Fischer, 1972). She does not describe anything resembling Koko's modulation for

**Table VII**
**Gestural Modulations Used by Koko**

| Relation or Function | Modulation | Example |
|---|---|---|
| Location | Variation in place of articulation of sign | Bite (on finger) |
| Size | Enlarge or decrease articulatory space | Alligator (big)<br>Alligator (little) |
| Number | Repetition of sign | Bird(s)[a] |
| Manner | | |
| Degree-intensity | Variation in force and/or rapidity of movement or size of sign | (Very) bad |
| Emphasis | Duplication or reduction (number of active hands) or simultaneous production of two versions of the same sign | Tickle (2 hands)<br><br>Yes (nod head & hand) |
| Agent-action | Change in direction of motion of sign | Sip-you? (sign moved from Koko's mouth toward that of companion) |
| Agent-object | Articulation of sign on other's body or object; direction of gaze | Tickle (on Mike)<br>Hungry (on doll) |
| Possession or modification[b] | Simultaneous production of signs; production of sign using object or other | Baby-head<br>Koko-good |
| Question | Facial expression, position of hands held | That pink? |
| Negation-rejection | Headshake or facial expression (frown) | No-gorilla<br>Lemon-frown |
| Humor, word play | Variation in location of articulation | Drink (to ear)<br>Black (on various body parts, persons and objects) |

[a]In Ameslan, only a few nouns are modulated in this way; verbs are most frequently modulated for plural subject or object in this way.
[b]This type of modulation has not been reported for Ameslan.

possession, and the repetition modulation for number is applied by humans mainly to verbs (but also to certain nouns such as *star, friend, enemy,* and *streetlamp*). Further, Koko seems to use changes in position as a modulation more often than human signers. It should be noted that most of these modulations are not mere imitations of sign use by others, but are created by Koko herself.

The result of a certain kind of simultaneous modulation applied by Koko is the creation of compound signs. Here her technique is the merging of two signs to make a new composite. For instance, Koko has made the sign for *coke* with two hands while her arms are in the position of the sign for *love.* An English gloss might be *I-love-coke!* When asked to describe grapefruit, Koko simultaneously made the signs for *frown* and *drink-fruit* (executing *drink* at the position of the sign for fruit, then signing *fruit*). *Love-coke* and *frown-fruit* are used consistently by the gorilla to refer to these foods. Also, certain dolls are frequently labeled "Baby-Koko's" by moving one of the hands used to execute the baby *sign* up to the shoulder. Additional examples are considered below under "Simultaneous Signs."

This discussion of Koko's use of modulation in sign is intended to be illustrative and suggestive rather than complete and analytical; a full account of the development of modulations in the gorilla's signing will be the subject of a future report.

## Gestural Blends

The gestural variations I have described occur frequently, are readily interpretable, and seem to be deliberate and efficient alterations made by Koko to express her desires. In contrast, both Koko and I occasionally generate new simultaneous signs through what we might call slips of the hand.

Two distinct signs are merged by combining the place of articulation of one with the hand configuration of the other. An example produced by Koko was *Chuck-toilet*—a *C* done on the nose. The hand configuration was that of the proper name but the location was that of the *toilet* sign. This occurred after Chuck had emptied her potty. "Good-happy," another instance, was Koko's response when she was asked if she would be good if allowed to come out of her room to meet visitors. The location was that of the *good* sign, the mouth, but the hand configuration was that of *happy,* hand held palm up. I have produced similar gestures unintentionally, usually when I am signing rapidly (for instance, "apple-drink" with the drink sign done at the side of the face instead of at the mouth). This phenomenon fits Hockett's (1959) description of blending, a process exemplified by the word *slithy,* a combination of *lithe* and *slimy.*

Ameslan signs such as *prefer* may have originated in a similar way: the place of articulation is that of the sign for *like* and the hand configuration is that of the sign for *better*. Bellugi (1979) has studied such slips of the hand in human signers and found that the restrictions on movement, location, and configuration which hold for standard signs are maintained. This appears to be true of Koko's gestural slips as well. These occurrences provide evidence that for Koko as well as for human signers, larger linguistic units (signs) are composed of functionally separable elements (Lane, Boyes-Braem, & Bellugi, 1976).

## GESTURAL INNOVATION: SIGN COMBINATIONS

### Simultaneous Signs

An aspect of sign language which has no parallel in spoken languages is simultaneity. Signers can literally say two things at once by executing different signs with each hand (Friedman, 1975). Although adult signers rarely exploit this possibility in daily discourse, they may plan and rehearse simultaneous signing for use in wit or poetry (Bellugi, 1975). Examples of simultaneous signing were also rare in Schlesinger's (1976) samples of deaf children's utterances.

It is unlikely that Koko had been exposed to such sign use when she began signing words simultaneously during the third month of the project. On September 29, 1972, she signed "Food-more" for an additional bite of fruit. During the following month, Koko produced as many as four simultaneous sign combinations per day with an average of 1.3. Data drawn from five 1-hour sign samples at 6-month intervals from 1973 to the beginning of 1978 indicate that incidence of simultaneous signing was greatest early in 1973, with an average of 2.8 utterances per hour. In the following years this behavior decreased in frequency, ranging between .2 and 2.4 simultaneous combinations per sample hour. The number of signs Koko expresses in a given simultaneous combination has averaged two or slightly above (Figure 9-3); but she has used as many as 4 different words at the same time, for example, "Me-up-hurry," and "Hurry-pour-there-drink." Koko uses three different methods to generate simultaneous expressions: executing one sign with each hand (for instance, "Drink-eat"; "You-tickle"), adding the motion or configuration of one sign to the place of articulation of another (as in "Koko-like"; "Hurry-pour"), and adding a facial expression or head movement to a sign (for example, "Fruit-frown"; "No-gorilla"). As noted above, when Koko applies the second and third methods repeatedly and consistently the results are modulations. Additional examples include these: Koko often signs her name (patting the shoulder) simultaneously with the sign for *love* (arms crossed over the chest)

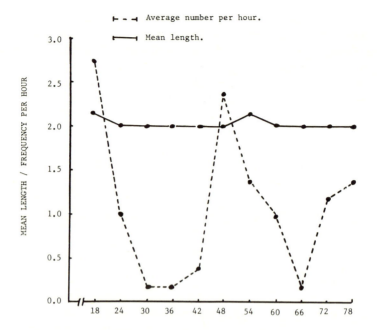

*Figure 9-3.* Mean length and frequency per hour of simultaneously signed combinations by Koko.

and *like* simultaneously with *love* for emphasis (pinching with both hands on crossed arms). "Frown-sad" is a frequent response to scoldings and other unpleasant situations.

Those instances of simultaneous signing which occurred early in the study and those which are not used consistently by Koko (two-handed signing and blends) seem to be the result of excited or hurried signing. One of the deaf assistants on the project reported that his children also signed simultaneously when in a hurry but rarely at other times. Thus early instances of this behavior were most often not deliberate but rather slips of the hand; later instances are less frequent but when they do occur they are most often consistent modulational forms.

## Creation of Compound Names and Metaphor

Koko, like many young children and the chimpanzee Washoe, has, in the face of novel objects or situations and a limited vocabulary, generated new names, often composed of two or more words. Many of these names (especially single-word names) may be classified as errors in reference or overextensions; for example, Koko's labeling such diverse objects as bean sprouts, a dog choke chain, and a variety of green toys, *grass*. Analyses of the contexts of such utterances and of Koko's lexical knowledge at the time of their occurrence indicate that (a) Koko did not know the literal names of the objects or properties, and (b) she was not engaging in symbolic play with them. Other novel word uses by Koko and other signers appear to be deliberate attempts to describe or request an unnamed object—for example, a deaf child's labeling of a mantlepiece as a "Fireplace wall shelf" (Schlesinger, 1976); Koko's labeling pomegranate kernels as "Red corn drink;" Lucy's labeling of a watermelon as "Drink fruit" (Fouts, 1973); or Lana's labeling an orange as "Apple which-is orange" (Rumbaugh, 1977). Still other occasions seem to involve intentional nonliteral word use and may provide examples of early metaphor. In metaphor, a descriptive term is deliberately applied to a referent for which it is not literally appropriate, but to which it bears certain analogies (Gardner, 1973, p. 84). For example, the word *daisy* is metaphoric in origin (from "day's eye": the petals and center resemble an eye; Di Pietro, 1976).

Chukovsky (1963) cites possible examples from the speech of 2- to 5-year-old Russian children: A bald man had a "Barefoot head," and an ostrich was described as a "Giraffe bird." Although it is not possible to determine whether these metaphors were intentional without information on the contexts or on the children's lexical knowledge, they bear a remarkable similarity to Koko's early invented compound names: "Eye hat" for a mask (3;4), "Finger bracelet" for a ring (4;3), "Elephant baby" for a Pinocchio doll (4;10), and "White tiger" for a toy zebra (5;1). In Koko's case these new names referred to objects in her environment for which Koko had either just been given or earlier acquired a literal name. Perhaps more solid evidence of a metaphorical capacity can be found in those instances in which Koko has referred to feelings or emotional states. Koko has described herself as "Red mad" or "Red mad gorilla" on several occasions (5;0) when asked why she behaved aggressively, and spontaneously commented that a nose on a doll she had just labeled as red was "Nose mad." In other cases Koko's responses to direct questioning have supported the linguistic and contextual evidence that she is engaging in deliberate verbal play with relationships between objects and states. The following unusual description may have had humorous intent:

12/23/77
(Assistant Cindy Duggan is holding an almost empty jelly container.)

*K:* Do food.
*C:* Do where, in your mouth?
*K:* Nose.
*C:* Nose?
*K:* Fake mouth.

(Then Koko opens her mouth and licks the jelly container).

*C:* Where's your fake mouth?
*K:* Nose.

The next day I asked Koko what was a fake mouth and she signed "Nose."
    In the following conversation which took place with assistant Barbara Hiller, Koko seemed to label herself as a "Sad elephant" because she had been reduced to drinking water through a thick rubber straw from a large pan on the floor. She had consumed her quota of more interesting drinks that afternoon, and this was Barbara's solution to Koko's repeated requests and complaints of being thirsty.

    2/25/78

*K:* Sad elephant.

    (Koko is sitting on her couch—I'd just told her that I wouldn't give her another drink.)

*B:* What you mean?
*K:* Elephant.
*B:* You a sad elephant?
*K:* Sad . . . elephant me.
*K:* Elephant love thirsty.
*B:* I thought you were a gorilla.
*K:* Elephant gorilla thirsty.
*B:* Are you a gorilla or an elephant?
*K:* Elephant me me.
*K:* Elephant stink.
*K:* Time.
*B:* Time what?
*K:* Time know coke elephant good me.
*B:* You want a drink, good elephant?
*K:* Drink fruit.

    (Koko has been drinking out of a fat rubber sraw—elephant's trunk? I hold up . the rubber straw.)

*B:* What's this?
*K:* That elephant stink.

    (Stink is a sign done on the nose.)

*B:* Is that why you're an elephant?
*K:* That (indicating the straw) there (pointing to her nose).

    (Then Koko wanders off laughing. Later)

*K:* That there (pointing to soda pop).
*B:* Who are you?
*K:* Koko know elephant devil.
*B:* A devil elephant?
*K:* Good, me thirsty.

Intrigued by examples of language use such as these,[5] I am in the process of obtaining empirical evidence for Koko's metaphoric capacity using a test devised by Howard Gardner (1974). For purposes of the test, metaphoric capacity was defined as "the ability to project in an appropriate manner sets of antonymous or 'polar' adjectives whose literal denotation within a domain (sensory modality or other coherent system) is known onto a domain where they are not ordinarily employed" (p. 85). The polar adjectives used were light-dark, happy-sad, loud-quiet, hard-soft, and warm-cold. The corresponding modalities were visual-color, visual-physiognomic, auditory, tactile, and verbal-kinesthetic. In videotaped sessions administered under conditions in which Koko could see only the stimulus and not the experimenter, she had no difficulty identifying literal dark versus light (two shades of green), red (versus blue) as warm, brown (versus blue-gray) as hard, violet-blue (versus yellow-orange) as sad, and lemon-yellow (versus spring green) as loud. Ninety percent of her responses were metaphoric matches as determined by Gardner (1974) and by three adult research assistants on the project who took the same test. Preschoolers in Gardner's study made only 57 percent metaphoric matches; 7-year-olds, 82 percent.

## Noninstrumental and Self-Directed Signing

Will and emotion . . . dominate children's early speech . . . but quite early the child also makes statements which do not aim at the fulfillment of any practical desires. (Leopold, 1949, p. 15)

The use of language for its own sake, when it is not calculated to obtain an external reward or goal of any kind, is another solid indication that Koko has internalized a symbolic system rather than a series of conditioned responses. There are at least three kinds of noninstrumental uses of language in the data compiled on Koko: manual babbling, spontaneous comments about the environment, and self-directed signing.

Manual babbling will be defined here as the use of signs, sign fragments, or gestures resembling signs in situations in which the gestures bear no relationship to the linguistic or nonlinguistic context, and further, are not directed to another individual.

Spontaneous comments about the environment refer to utterances un-

solicited by questions which describe events, objects, or states that are unrelated to the immediate needs or wants of the gorilla. This category of
utterances could be considered to include most utterances in the final category, self-directed utterances.

Self-directed signing will be defined as the use of signs in a meaningful
way, but directed toward no one but the self.

Rumbaugh (1974) states that the learning of language is reinforcing because of the control it provides over the environment. However, we know
that this is not a complete explanation for the acquisition and use of language by children, and it is doubtful that this can be seen as a complete explanation of the acquisition and use of language by apes.

Children babble, talk to themselves, and comment about the state of
the environment without immediately gaining any control over it, and I
have evidence that Koko, too, uses language in these noncontrolling ways.
During the first 11 months of the project, Koko occasionally engaged in
what could most appropriately be termed manual babbling.

She patted, poked, stroked, or pounded various parts of her body,
often rhythmically, either enacting a sequence of different gestures or repeating a particular one, sometimes with variations in tempo or vigor. She
seemed to be playfully experimenting with gestures she had observed or
been taught, or to be exploring the ways in which the hands could contact
the body. When the gestures were signs, they were executed when Koko was
engaged in solitary or play or during a break in activities with a companion;
thus there was no apparent attempt to communicate. The earliest observed
instances of manual babbling included gestures resembling signs: At age
1;2, as Koko lay in bed one evening, she poked one index finger to the palm
of the other hand, ran that finger across the palm, poked it between the
other fingers and clapped.

Babbling was never very frequent. During the first 4 months of the
study, manual babbling was noted in the diary on only 12 occasions. The
frequency per sampled hour during the year 1973 was .31. By the time Koko
was 33 months old, this behavior had disappeared from the language
samples. This is later than the time of the demise of babbling in the human
child, who engages in babbling for approximately the first 18 months of life
(Slobin, 1970). However, the records of child speech development tend not
to mention babbling once the child begins to articulate words. One researcher, Smith (1926), did report babbling in a 27-month-old-girl who while alone
uttered meaningless phrases such as "O bo da," although she used correct
words in communication with others. Smith noted that this girl and other
younger children used many repetitions in their babbling; for instance,
"Dirre dirre dirre oh." For Koko, however, the most frequent form of
manual babbling was the repetition of one sign unit, rather than of strings
of different sign units or variations of one sign unit. Her strings averaged

1.4 units and were never longer than 7 units. Koko's meaningless gestural exercises, then, were quite different in frequency, length, and duration than the meaningless sound exercises in which hearing human children engage (Leopold, 1939; Smith, 1926). Deaf infants who receive no auditory feedback from vocal play have been reported to "babble" manual gestures (Bonvillian & Nelson, in press). Detailed information on the characteristics of manual babbling has not been published, but one might expect the parallels to be closer.

Koko's spontaneous comments about the environment are relatively infrequent in comparison with requests such as "Come tickle," "Me thirsty drink," or "Hurry do that." Nevertheless, Koko's remarks to her companions are not limited to expressing her desires. For example, she signed "Listen quiet" when an alarm clock stopped ringing in the next room (3;6), "Chin red" when I bumped my chin (5.1), and "See bird" when she saw a picture of a crane in a stereo viewer. Table VIII lists 10 examples drawn from the first month of each of the years 1975 through 1978. Most of the statements are brief, averaging only two or three signs in length; some, however, are composed of four or more signs (as, at 5;9, "Bird have stomach white," describing a toy bird with a white breast). In most of her state-

## Table VIII
### Examples of Comments by Koko about the State of the Environment

| Age | Date | Utterance | Context |
|-----|------|-----------|---------|
| 3;6 | 1/1/75 | Listen quiet. | When alarm clock stopped ringing in the next room |
| | 1/7/75 | Me (held) listen. | Music from workman's radio outside |
| | 1/14/75 | Nose stink. | Perfume |
| | 1/21/75 | There cat. | Koko points to window; cat is outside |
| | 1/21/75 | Teeth that. | Teeth in magazine picture of woman's face |
| | 1/23/75 | Listen telephone. | Telephone rings |
| | 1/28/75 | Listen drink listen. | Sound of fizz from carbonated drink |
| | 1/29/75 | Red lipstick red that. | Red pillow on bed |
| | 1/29/75 | Smell stink. | Cooked broccoli |
| | 1/30/75 | Cat that. | Barbara's new leopard ring |
| 4;6 | 1/1/76 | There flower. | Pattern on robe. Barbara kept telling her there were leaves too; Koko kept signing this, always pointing to flowers |
| | 1/2/76 | That red. | Kate's red nail polish |
| | 1/9/76 | That leaf. | Leaf of flower |
| | | That pink. | After selecting pink glass out of a stack of colored glasses |
| | 1/10/76 | That glass. | Glass mirror |

## Table VIII (*continued*)

| Age | Date | Utterance | Context |
|-----|------|-----------|---------|
| | 1/14/76 | Look . . . mouse. | Companion showed Koko a mouse |
| | | Baby. | Mouse |
| | | Moose. | Moose pictured on stamp |
| | 1/17/76 | Pimple look. | Companion had been looking at irritated spot on nose in mirror |
| | 1/27/76 | Bird. | Hears campus bell chimes |
| 5;6 | 1/3/77 | Clean mirror. | After companion cleaned mirror |
| | 1/4/77 | That white. | White sweater |
| | 1/5/77 | There straw. | Points to puppet's mouth where straw had been placed |
| | 1/12/77 | That red. | Puppet's mouth; it is no longer red because Koko removed its tongue |
| | 1/21/77 | This on. | After Koko's sweater has been put on her |
| | 1/22/77 | That candy Mike. | Ron brought candy saying in English that it was for gorilla Mike |
| | 1/24/77 | Cut tree. | As companion cuts celery |
| | 1/25/77 | Good kiss good. | Ann is kissing Mike's ear |
| | 1/27/77 | Bite there red. | Koko indicates spot on her arm at the same place as she bit the gorilla Mike the day before |
| | 1/31/77 | Cry Mike cry. | To deaf assistant as she sweeps floor; Mike is crying |
| 6;6 | 1/2/78 | Good know Mike. | Gorilla Mike finally said Koko's name after many wrong answers |
| | 1/7/78 | Ron you. | To Ron (over one hour earlier she had been asked his name and hadn't responded) |
| | 1/8/78 | Hear bell. | Oven timer rang |
| | 1/10/78 | Hug Koko gorilla. | Drawing of two gorillas hugging; one intended to be Koko, one Mike |
| | 1/12/78 | Write bird there. | Indicates her drawing |
| | 1/12/78 | Pimple there nose. | Spot on companion's nose |
| | 1/15/78 | That soft. | Velvet hat |
| | 1/16/78 | Lady eyemakeup there. | Picture of lady with makeup |
| | 1/28/78 | Nose funny. | P: "Look at Ron." Penny laughs; Ron has toy spider ring on his nose |
| | 1/31/78 | That man. | Picture of adult gorilla |

ments, Koko labels objects or describes attributes. In a few she comments on actions as in (at 4;4) "Kiss you" after kissing a companion and (at 5;6) "Clean mirror" after a companion had done so.

Koko began to sign to herself in the fourth month of the study when she was 16 months old. The first recorded instance of this behavior involved Koko's invented *bird* (out-of-reach) sign. Koko's self-directed signing lacked the rhythmic and carefree expression of her babbled gestures. Instead Koko seemed to be studying the referent possibilities of the sign. She executed the sign on one of her stacking boxes, a toy post office box also used to reach doorknobs and other objects out of reach, a book I was reading while sitting on top of a metal box above her, and the large nursery window. A later example more clearly shows the meaningful relationship of her signing to objects around her:

> (From audiotape of 10/19/76, 10:00 to 11:00 A.M.): While she is nesting, Koko picks up a toy horse, points to her ear, huffs on the toy horse (as she does on the telephone), then throws it down. After rearranging the nest, she picks up a flowered muckluck (slipper), signs "That stink" and throws it out of the nest. She then smells a blanket she's nesting with and signs "That stink."

A subset of five sample hours at 6-month intervals from 1973 to 1978 were inventoried for instances of this behavior. The frequency of self-directed utterances has increased from about .2 per hour to about 6 per hour over this time period; the length of these utterances has increased slightly but inconsistently during this interval (Figure 9-4). My own subjective impression is that the length of Koko's self-directed utterances has gradually increased over the years from length one for the first 2 years to slightly over two recently; perhaps the small sample size does not accurately reflect the incidence and length of these relatively rare utterances.

Honig, Caldwell, and Tannenbaum (1970) report that in a nursery-school setting, self-directed verbalizations in 1-year-old children were twice as frequent as in 4-year-olds. Almost 60 percent of all verbalizations by 1-year-olds in this setting are self-directed, with the proportions dropping to 55, 43, and 27 percent for the 2-, 3-, and 4-year-olds respectively. Koko is directly engaged in activities with a companion during the samples from which the figures in Figure 9-4 are drawn; consequently, fewer self-directed utterances might be expected in a one-to-one teaching situation than in a nursery-school setting where an individual child gets little direct attention from adults. Koko emitted 34 self-directed utterances during the 8-hour sample taken July 26, 1976 (5;0). Approximately 7 percent of her utterances in this sample were self-directed.

During solitary play, Koko's self-directed signing is more frequent.

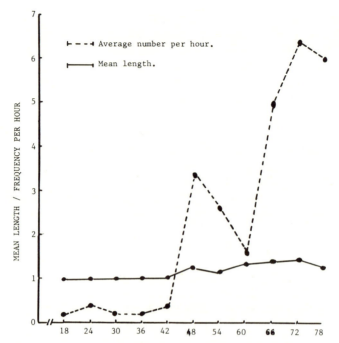

*Figure 9-4.* Mean length and frequency per hour of self-directed utterances by Koko.

While she is engaged in activities such as nesting in clothing or blankets and toys, she will stop arranging the nest momentarily and sign "That red" (indicating a piece of red cloth, 4;11), or "Sleep" and lie down in the nest (5;6). Frequently, while looking through books and magazines, she will comment to herself about what she sees (Fig. 5); for example, "That dry" (to a picture of a girl drying her face with a towel, 4;7), "That toothbrush" (to a toothpaste advertisement, 2;10) and "That apple drink" (to a picture of a bottle of amber-colored cologne, 5;11). She has been observed signing "Bite" or "Teeth" when mouthing objects such as window frames and pens and before catching bugs in her mouth. Other examples include "Lollipop gorilla" after licking a fake ice cream cone, and "Eye, teeth, lip, pimple" while looking into a mirror (6;0). On January 29, 1977 (5;6), I noticed Koko signing "That Koko" to a picture of King Kong depicted on a bowl I bought for her.

At times Koko seems embarrassed when her companions notice that she is signing to herself, especially when it involves her dolls and animal toys. On January 4, 1977 (5;6), while Koko was signing "Kiss" after kissing her alligator puppet, I caught her eye. She abruptly stopped signing and turned away. Occasionally, when her companions have been otherwise occupied, Koko has taken her toy gorillas into the room furthest from them and engaged in sign by herself while playing. On September 14, 1976 (5;2), a trained deaf assistant observed Koko as she seemed to structure an imaginary social situation between two gorilla dolls: she placed the gorillas before her and signed "Bad, bad" while looking at the pink gorilla, then "Kiss" directed to the blue gorilla. Next she signed "Chase tickle" and hit the two of them together (making them play?), then joined in and wrestled them both at once. When the play bout ended, she signed "Good gorilla, good, good." At this point Koko noticed that Cathy, her teacher, was watching and left the dolls. Similar behavior was observed at this time by myself and one other worker, but when the door to the small room furthest from human observers was closed off in order to accommodate the gorilla Michael, the behavior ceased.

Catherine Hayes (1951) reported a similar apparent sensitivity of the chimpanzee Vicki to human observation of her imaginative play.

## Expressions of Intentionality

*P:* I think Mike's smart. Is he smarter than you?
*K:* Think . . . Koko know Mike toilet.

*Figure 9-5.* While looking through books and magazines and while playing alone, Koko frequently signs to herself. Here she signs "Eye" after pointing to the pictured frog's large eye. © National Geographic Society. (Credit: Dr. Ronald H. Cohn)

Intentionality is a multifaceted problem in the study of behavior. When young children or animals are the subjects of study, evidence for intentionality is especially difficult to obtain. Although chimpanzees exhibit intentional behavior in both the field and laboratory, David Premack (1976b) was unable to obtain convincing formal evidence for it in a controlled test situation. Premack operationalized intentionality as having two levels. "At the first level the animal freely controls whether or not it will impart information. At the second level, the animal must, in addition, recognize that it has control over information and be able to infer that others, like it, have a similar capacity" (p. 676). His chimpanzee subjects did not adjust, given an experimenter's undesirable behavior of consuming a reward desired by the chimp by lying to him about the reward (withholding information or pointing to the empty container). In Koko, intentional behavior of the kind observed in chimpanzees under naturalistic conditions has also been observed. At age 1;9 Koko began to engage her companions in behaviors which would distract them so that she could engage in a forbidden activity or stop undesirable behavior on the part of her companion. For example, on March 6, 1973, I had placed Koko's milk and cereal on a ledge while I cleaned her room. Koko pushed my hand to the wall to engage me in grooming activity (picking a spot of dirt off the wall), and then while I was responding to her request, reached for the milk. She uses verbal as well as nonverbal tactics: at age 3;6, during a scolding for stealing a spoonful of butter, Koko signed "Time me toilet go." She didn't use the toilet, however, after being excused.

Although I have not yet obtained formal controlled evidence of intentionality as evidenced by lying (see discussion below), there are other forms of linguistic evidence of intentionality:

"The most obvious way in which language is used intentionally is in the expression of necessity, possibility or propositional attitudes. Examples of the expression of propositional attitudes are statements about beliefs, needs, wants, expectations or fears" (Suppes, 1974, p. 109). Neither Koko nor young children make direct statements of possibility or necessity. They do, however, express propositional attitudes, especially those relating to wants or needs. Koko reached the acquisition criterion for the sign *want* in the 49th month of the project, when she was 61 months old. Examples of her use of the word *want* and those by a human child between the ages of 23 and 39 months are given in Table IX. Koko did not begin to use the sign *want* until she was 49 months of age. In contrast, this word was well established in Nina's lexicon about 20 months earlier: over 1 percent of the items in her 100,000-word corpus were occurrences of some form of *want*. All of Koko's uses of *want* at 61 months are referential (having a concrete reference to a particular object), with the possible exception of the phrase "Attention want." There is no evidence for attributive use (reference of a class of objects). This distinction was definitely being made by Nina by 39

## Table IX
## Use of *Want* by Koko at 61 Months and by Nina from 23 to 39 Months*

| Use | Context |
|---|---|
| **Koko:** | |
| Attention. | K was doing a series of bizarre gestures when asked to sign *Jello*. This was her response when her companion asked her to think |
| Want more. | For firsts of salt |
| Make want teeth. | Box of powdered milk that companion offers. Koko opens it with her teeth |
| Cold want. | Requesting juice ice cubes |
| Make want milk. | Requesting that Penny make formula |
| Bone want Koko eat. | Chicken bone |
| Want prune. | For prune |
| Want eat. | For prune |
| Drink want milk. | Requesting milk |
| Bowl want cold bowl. | For juice cubes in bowl |
| Want eat want eat Koko fruit. | Requesting fruit |
| Want ball want. | For ball |
| Want eat fruit. | For pear |
| Want nut want nut eat. | For nut |
| Jello want. | For Jello |
| Want make open. | In response to "Want out?" To be allowed out of her room |
| Want cake eat. | Requesting cake |
| Cereal want eat Koko. | For cereal |
| Ball want Koko drink. | Wants drink but ball is being offered |
| Want sandwich nut. | For a peanut butter sandwich |
| Mask want. | Requesting a girl mask |
| Mask want. | Requesting a devil mask |
| All eat me want. | For Jello |
| All eat me want taste. | For Jello |
| Want. | In response to "Want out?" To be allowed out of her room |
| All ask red want sip. | For green banana she stole earlier |

| Use | Type |
|---|---|
| **Nina:** | |
| He don't want a Bandaid on. | Attributive |
| I want milk. | Attributive |
| I want some more toys. | Attributive |
| I want another story, ok. | Attributive |
| I want the next page. | Referential |
| I want this. | Referential |
| I want her to wear the blue dress. | Referential |
| Do you want a pink balloon? | Ambiguous |
| Her don't want a cup. | Ambiguous |
| Her want a blanket ok. | Ambiguous |
| I don't want a jersey on. | Ambiguous |
| I want a toy. | Ambiguous |

*Examples of Nina's utterances were drawn from Suppes, 1974.

months (see Table IX). Thus, Koko's expression of this type of proposition-al attitude at this age was limited to concrete reference to specific objects immediately present and not extended to abstract classes of objects removed in time and space.

In addition, Koko's spontaneous comments and responses to ques-tions, while undoubtedly more limited in reference and structurally less complex than those of human children her age, give insight into what and how she thinks about herself and her social and physical environments, and insight into why she responds to these entities in the ways that she does—that is, what her intentions are. The clearest evidence comes from Koko's responses to certain *why* questions, those involving direct inquiry as to her motivations for performing an act. For example, when asked "Why steal milk?" Koko replied "Koko thirsty." On another occasion, a deaf companion pursued her most cherished ball under the project trailer in a game of keep-away, and gained possession of it in violation of Koko's spe-cial rules (which I had failed to adequately explain to her opponent). Koko's response was to give her companion a play bite on the posterior. About 20 minutes later, when asked why she bit her friend, she replied, "Him ball bad." Responses to *why* questions have not yet been reported for chimpan-zees learning in language.

## Displacement and Prevarication

A cardinal characteristic of human language is displacement, the abil-ity to refer to events removed in time and place from the act of communi-cation (Hockett, 1960; Bronowski & Bellugi, 1970). We can use words to construct a surrogate reality in which we can evoke happenings of long ago or far away, or in which we can frame events that have never happened or may never happen.

Koko has often responded to questions about past incidents, some-times long after their occurrence, indicating that she too is capable of dis-placement. The following examples are representative:

1/10/77

*P:* You remember what you had for breakfast?
*K:* Yes, cake.

   (Koko had had baked rice bread—closer to pudding-cake in consistency.)

1/15/77

*P:* Do you remember what happened this morning?
*K:* Penny clean.

(Not the answer I expected, but again accurate. Koko had been upset by something prior to my arrival that morning and had made a mess of her room. It took me the better part of an hour to clean it.)

*P:* Remember yesterday? (Koko had escaped.)
*K:* Koko yesterday forgot.

8/10/77

(Over a month after her sixth birthday, I brought a piece of birthday cake from the freezer.)

*P:* What's this?
*K:* Six.

1/3/77

(The day after Koko bit a companion, she was asked),

*P:* What did you do yesterday?
*K:* Wrong, wrong.
*P:* What wrong?
*K:* Bite.

7/7/76

(The following cross-examination took place 3 days after the event discussed):

*P:* What did you do to P?
*K:* Bite.
*P:* You admit it?

(Previously Koko had referred to the bite as a scratch.)

*K:* Sorry bite scratch.

(P shows the mark on her hand; it really does resemble a scratch).

*K:* Wrong bite.
*P:* Why bite?
*K:* Because mad.

(A few moments later, it occurred to P to ask),

*P:* Why mad?
*K:* Don't-know.

The preceding example is noteworthy because Koko makes reference to a past emotional state, her anger, without actually experiencing it at the moment. This is a clear indication that she is able to separate affect from the context of her utterances, another important feature of displacement.

Perhaps the most telling, yet elusive, evidence that a creature can displace events is lying. Lies are designed to distort another person's perception of reality: language is used to evoke something which never happened or to deny events that did occur.

Although it is difficult to demonstrate intent empirically, I have been accumulating evidence that strongly suggests that Koko possesses and verbally expresses the capacity to dissemble. I have found a few isolated instances at about age 3. In May of 1974 Koko was asked "Who broke this [toy] cat?" Koko's reply was "Kate cat." It is possible that Koko could have misunderstood the question or was avoiding answering by asserting that the cat was Kate's or relating the toy to Kate in some other way, but the cat was Koko's. She had broken it the day before while with Kate. At about the age of 5, more frequent and convincing evidence of her use of the lie to get herself out of trouble appeared: Koko had just tipped the scales at 90 pounds, and when she sat on the kitchen sink it separated from its frame, sinking about 2 inches. Not knowing how it had happened, I asked Koko, "Did you do that?" and Koko signed "Kate there bad," pointing to the sink. Kate, my deaf assistant who had witnessed the incident, defended herself by explaining the situation.

On another occasion Koko was caught in the act of trying to break a window screen with a chopstick she had stolen from the silverware drawer. When asked what she was doing, Koko replied "Smoke mouth" and proceeded to place the stick in her mouth as though she was smoking it (this is a game we engage in frequently with sticks and other cigarette-shaped objects).

Sometimes further questioning can elicit the truth. At age 6;5, Koko scratched a visitor's arm in play. When he discovered the injury he asked Koko, "What's this?" Koko responded, "Dirty." Later he asked, "What is it really?" and she signed, "Hurt . . . you."

The "lipstick" incident was recorded on film in January 1978. While I was busy writing on Koko's checklist of signs, she snatched a red crayon which was on the videotape monitor and began chewing on it. A moment later I noticed and said, "You're not eating that crayon, are you?" Koko signed "Lip" and began moving the crayon first across her upper then her lower lip as if applying lipstick. When I asked her what she was really doing she signed "Bite." When I queried, "Why?" she responded, "Hungry."

The gorilla Michael too has begun to lie. The first recorded instance was on April 22, 1978, when he was approximately 5 years old. Michael had yanked on and ripped a gaping hole in a volunteer's lab coat. When she asked him, "Who did this?" Michael responded, "Penny." He was told that was wrong and asked again, but his response was "Koko." Finally he admitted, "Mike."

## Insult, Swearing, Argument, and Threat

Koko also appears to invent insults. As early as age 2;6, she seems to have used the word *nut* as an insult or expletive. She signed "Nut" to herself after being locked in her room as a punishment for misbehavior. Her companions frequently used the English word in similar ways: "You nut!" when Koko would engage in silly behavior or "Nuts" when something went wrong. There is a group of signs which Koko applies in these nonliteral or figurative ways (Table X). Two, *bird* and *nut,* were originally modulated by a change in position (articulation at the side of the mouth instead of at the

**Table X**
**Signs Koko Uses as Insults, Expletives, and Derogatives**

| Lexical Item | Age | Example of Use | Context |
|---|---|---|---|
| Bad | 5;0 | Bad again. Koko bad again. | Koko tried to use teeth on a visitor a second time during play |
| | 5;7 | Bad bad. | As she watches veterinarian give goats shots |
| | 5;7 | Alligator bad. | P: What are you afraid of? |
| Bird | 5;0 | Kate bird rotten. | Kate won't let Koko open the refrigerator |
| | 5;10 | Bird. | Argument with Cathy |
| | 6;6 | Bird. | P: Be nice to Mike |
| Darn | 5;1 | Darn bird bird. | Prolonged chirping of bird in distress |
| | 5;6 | Darn catch. | Alligator toy caught Koko in a game of chase |
| | 6;6 | Darn Foot. | Her friend, "Foot," leaves without saying goodbye to her |
| Devil | 5;8 | Devil rotten. | P: Do you like Mike? |
| | 6;6 | Think stupid devil. | P: Want Mike in? What think? |
| | 6;7 | Bird devil. | Picture of alligator |
| Dirty | 4;6 | Penny toilet dirty devil. | Koko was gloomy; Penny had punished her yesterday |
| | 4;10 | Dirty mouth dirty taste. | P: What's wrong with milk? |
| | 6;6 | Dirty orange dirty lemon. | P: What's this? (lemon) |
| False-fake | 6;3 | Mad fake fake. | Koko was offered rotten grape |
| | 6;3 | Stink toilet fake think Koko. | Mask |
| | 6;6 | Elephant dirty fake. | Toy elephant Koko was requested to identify |

**Table X** (*continued*)

| Lexical Item | Age | Example of Use | Context |
|---|---|---|---|
| Frown | 4;10 | Frown that pink don't-know. | Kate asks "Why frown?" Koko had earlier forgotten the sign for *pink* (rose) |
| | 4;10 | Frown teeth. | Koko was scolded for biting |
| | 6;6 | Frown fruit. | Grapefruit |
| Mad | 5;8 | Mad rotten. | P: Learning is fun! |
| | 6;2 | Toilet fruit mad. | Koko doesn't want lemon |
| | 6;4 | Mad toilet toilet. | C: What's this? (red spider toy) |
| Nut | 5;6 | Nut nut . . . jealous. | Koko saw Ann and Mike outside; she had asked to go out |
| | 5;7 | Mike nut. | P: Are you jealous of Mike? |
| | 5;10 | Bad gorilla nut. | She sees gorilla Mike outside |
| Old | 6;3 | Old wrong grass. | To King Kong cup |
| | 6;5 | Devil think you old. | C: Name me? K: Love tell you. C: Name? K: Idea. C: Name? |
| | 6;6 | Not old drink. | Penny has milk and Koko gives an annoyance bark. P: Why cranky? |
| Rotten-lousy | 5;1 | Rotten-lousy bird. | Bird chirping in distress outside |
| | 5;6 | Rotten-lousy Mike. | While pulling leash and hitting gorilla Michael |
| | 6;0 | Rotten-lousy. | P: Good? Koko has chewing gum |
| Skunk-stink | 5;0 | That rotten skunk-stink. | Visitor asks "What's that?" Calendar photo of Koko's father |
| | 5;6 | Skunk-stink. | Penny took toys out of Koko's room |
| | 6;6 | That skunk-stink. | Rubber monkey-face puppet |
| Stubborn-donkey | 5;1 | Know that stubborn-donkey. | At Cathy's request, Penny asks Koko to sign about drawings Cathy made to illustrate the numbers one and two |
| | 5;11 | Stubborn-donkey head. | P: Can't say red? What color candy? |
| | 6;4 | Stubborn-donkey do that. | Koko has repeatedly requested the drink Cindy is offering to a doll |
| Stupid | 5;0 | Head stupid. | Penny playfully puts salt shaker on her head |
| | 5;1 | Hat stupid hat on. | Kate's rainhat |
| | 6;7 | Know Mike devil stupid out. | Gorilla Mike has signed "Out out Koko Mike" to come out of his room to play with Koko |
| Toilet | 4;6 | Dirty toilet. | Picture of telephone on vocabulary cards (Koko resents both the test and the telephone) |
| | 6;4 | Think toilet you. | C: Who is rotten? K: Good Koko. C: Cindy rotten? |
| | 6;4 | Rotten toilet. | P: Say *bad* |
| Trouble | 5;1 | Trouble flowers. | After scolding for pulling up flowering plants |
| | 6;3 | Bad trouble. | As Koko is scolded for pinching |
| | 6;7 | Trouble devil. | Gorilla Michael is about to come in and play |

front) to signal their use as insults. After several weeks, when her companions had caught on to the fact that these uses were insults and not errors, Koko stopped consistently employing this modulation. The use of *bird* as an insult was not to my knowledge modeled by Koko's companions; I think that she uses *bird* in a derogatory way because she is annoyed by the raucous noise made by the sparrows nesting in the bushes outside the trailer. It is also possible that one or more of Koko's companions had labeled her "Bird brain."

Koko often combines these signs to make compound insults. For example, one morning I noticed that Koko was glum. The previous morning she had been punished for ripping the rug in her room. The following conversation took place:

1/6/76

*K:* Frown.
*P:* Why frown?
*K:* Penny toilet dirty devil.

On another occasion, when Koko was 5;0, Kate, a research assistant, would not allow Koko to open the refrigerator. Koko responded by signing "Kate bird rotten." One such sequence was recorded on film with a motor-driven camera (Figure 9-6). Koko had ripped the leg off a rag doll (which had earlier lost its other leg when the gorilla Michael was playing with it), and I gathered the pieces (including both legs), sat Koko down in front of them, and scolded her for destroying the doll. She reacted by signing "You dirty bad toilet."

The sign Koko employs as a powerful interjection equivalent to a swearword such as *darn* or *damn* has been described earlier (see section on invented signs). She can sign *darn* very "softly" (whisper) or very "loudly" (shout) by varying the size, forcefulness, location, or number of hands used in articulating the sign.

Most often Koko uses expletives such as *darn* in single sign utterances, but as in the dialogue below, she may use such words in combination:

5/13/77
(Cathy shows Koko a gorilla picture on a benefit poster.)

*K:* Gorilla.
*C:* Who gorilla?
*K:* Bird.
*C:* You bird?
*K:* You.
*C:* Not me, you are bird.
*K:* Me gorilla.

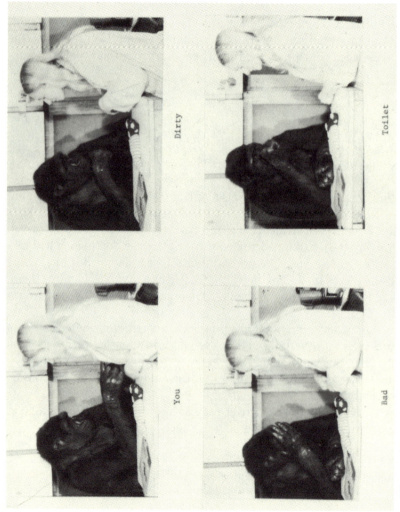

*Figure 9-6.* "You dirty bad toilet." Koko insults her companion who has unjustly accused her of tearing both legs off her rag doll (she was guilty of removing only one). © National Geographic society. (Credit: Dr. Ronald H. Cohn)

*C:* Who bird?
*K:* You, nut.
*C:* Why me nut?
*K:* Gorilla me.
*C:* Not me, me Cathy.
*K:* Nut nut.
*C:* You nut, not me.
*K:* Darn, me good!

(K walks away signing)

*K:* Bad.

The preceding dialogue appears to be a full-fledged argument between Koko and a companion. It demonstrates Koko's capacity for the intentional use of language, for she repeatedly asserts something that is a matter of opinion in the face of assertions to the contrary. Less volatile exchanges involving Koko's correcting rather than arguing with companions occur more frequently:

11/5/77, Barbara Hiller

*K:* Do that (pointing to squash which is on her dinner plate along with a variety of other foods).
*B:* Potato.
*K:* Wrong squash.
*K:* Do hurry that (again pointing to squash).
*K:* Squash eat hurry.

Occasionally, since age 4;5, Koko has "corrected" her human companions when they have labeled her with unfamiliar terms. The first incident, in December of 1975, involved the application of the spoken word *chicken* to Koko by a companion in an attempt to get her attention as she gazed out the window. Koko, still looking out the window signed "No, gorilla." She has made similar responses when the terms *juvenile* and *genius* have been applied to her. In the case of the word *juvenile* the conversation was not even directed to Koko, but was a discussion between Koko's companion and a visitor who had asked if Koko was an adolescent. Her companion replied, "No, she's not an adolescent yet; she's still a juvenile." Koko resounded with, "No, gorilla." The discussion Koko overheard took place exclusively in English. On one occasion, a term was applied to Koko which she apparently through was a mistaken color name: in a sign sample taken January 9, 1977, her companion, Ron, said, "Well, dynamite?" to her in English during a pause in activity as she sat on her toybox with a red blanket. Koko signed, "No, red."

She has also used language to threaten her companions, as a means of obtaining their cooperation. Koko's greatest irrational fear centers around the alligator. Even toothy rubber facsimiles of this creature terrify her. I have taken advantage of this fear to control Koko's behavior. For example, I have placed alligators on forbidden places such as cupboards and the refrigerator. One day, during a teaching session with assistant Cindy Duggan, who worked with Koko through a chain link barrier, the following conversation took place:

11/3/77

*K:* Alligator chase lip. (Lip is Koko's idiosyncratic term for women.)
*C:* Alligator?
*K:* Alligator, do that hurry (pointing to the plate of food). Cindy commented in her notes, ''I think she's threatening me with an alligator if I don't hurry with the food.''

Another similar incident occurred several months later:

1/24/78
(Cindy has spaghetti out but is busy with her notes and is not feeding Koko.)

*K:* Love.
*K:* Have.
*K:* Darn there! (pointing to the spaghetti as Cindy writes).
*K:* Koko have, Koko good there.
*K:* Alligator time that.

Finally, Koko may combine insult, argument, and threat in exchanges with her companions. In the following diary excerpt, Koko appears to be calling Cindy a nut and threatening to use her nails (to scratch).

10/6/77
(Koko is nagging Cindy.)

*K:* Time nails nut.
*K:* Fruit.
*K:* Key key time.
*C:* No, not yet key time.
*K:* Yes time come time nut.
*C:* No, not time!
*K:* Yes time.
*C:* No time.
*K:* Nails . . .
*C:* Why?
*K:* Time!
*C:* Oh!

## Reference to Emotional States

If Koko has fallen from grace by virtue of her lying and insults, she may be partially redeemed by her capacity for empathy. Koko has commented about emotional states of people and animals pictured in magazines and books:

9/24/77
(When shown a picture of the albino gorilla Snowflake struggling against being bathed, Koko, who also hates baths, signed "Me cry there," indicating the picture.

11/3/77

(Koko is looking at a picture of a horse with a bit in its mouth.)

*K:* Horse sad.
*C:* Why?
*K:* Teeth.
*C:* You think horse teeth hurt him?
*K:* Think teeth.

12/27/77
(The gorilla Michael is in the back of the trailer. He has been crying because he can't [refuses to] sign *out* to be allowed out of his room.)

*P·* How feel?
*ʌ:* Feel sorry out.

Spontaneous verbal expressions of emotion appeared relatively late in Koko (at approximately 4 years), as they do in the child (approximately 2½ to 3 years). This contrasts with nonverbal vocal expressions of emotion which in both child and gorilla are either present at birth or appear within the first few months of life.

There is other evidence that Koko can reflect upon and report about her feelings. She has spontaneously informed her companions that she is happy or sad or tired, and regularly answers questions such as, "How are you?" and "How do you feel?" Usually Koko answers in a polite way, as do most people I know, by saying "Fine." But on other occasions she may answer, "Thirsty," or "Hungry," or "Sad." On 1/23/77 (5;6), when I asked her, "How are you this morning?" she signed "Sad feel." On 11/14/77 (6;2), when Koko was recovering from the intestinal flu and had been on a liquid diet for a week, I asked Koko, "How feel?" She responded, "Feel all have" and proceeded to open the refrigerator. When in estrus (March 10, 1978, 6;8), Koko was visited by her human boyfriend (a planned visit, recorded on videotape). As she stood entranced, gazing at him, I asked her how she felt. Without taking her eyes off him, she responded, "Good." Koko has signed "Jealous" while watching Michael and his teacher walking outside (5;6), or Michael and one of her friends playing together (5;7), as well as in food-sharing situations with Michael.

Koko's responses to questions about her feelings are particularly revealing. In a study parallel to one with human children 5 to 13 years old by Wolman, Lewis, and King (1971), I asked Koko a series of questions with these frames: (1) Do you ever have feelings of _____? (2) When do you feel _____? The target feeling states were anger, fear, happiness, sadness, hunger, thirst, sleepiness, and nervousness. Table XI presents Koko's responses. Like the younger subjects mentioned by Wolman et al. (1971) Koko most frequently reported external events as conditions of emotional arousal; for example, when asked, "When do you feel hungry," she answered, "Feel time." A possible explanation of this reply is that when it is time (to eat), she feels hungry.

Several of the replies in Table XI need explanation. The replies to questions about anger and hunger seem to be related to the events of the preceding months. Koko had had great difficulty adjusting to a new teacher, Marjie, and was punished for her objectionable behavior in this woman's presence (aggressive ramming) by being left alone. This involved the lights being turned off and resulted in Koko missing meals. Thus the outcome of Koko's anger was often hunger. Her replies to the questions about nervousness are difficult to interpret. She repeatedly uses the sign *stop,* perhaps because she feels nervous when she is both misbehaving and aware that she will be told to stop or because some events which make her nervous (most often large loud trucks and equipment entering the enclosure in which the trailer is located), she would like to stop. She tries to block out this type of stimuli by requesting, "Drapes up" (to have her companion cover the windows with tarps).

Prior to this study Koko had reported about her fears. She has always been repulsed by lizardlike creatures and toys. One day, several hours after a play session in which she avoided direct contact with the gorilla, Michael, I asked her if she was afraid of him. She made no response, so I rephrased the question:

1/28/77

*P:* What are you afraid of?
*K:* Afraid alligator.

2/25/77, Cathy Ransom

*C:* What are you afraid of? (The purple dinosaur toy is out.)

## Table XI
## Koko's Responses to Questions about Feeling States

**Question 1. Do you ever feel (have feelings of) _____?**
**Question 2. When do you feel _____?**

| Questions | Responses |
| --- | --- |
| 1. Afraid | Afraid polite. |
| 2. Afraid (why) | Trouble devil. |
| 1. Hungry | Hungry. |
| 2. Hungry | Feel time. |
| 1. Sad | Sad-frown. |
| 2. Sad | Sorry cry sad. |
| 1. Mad | Hungry. |
| 1. Mad | Light don't. |
| 1. Angry | Mad. |
| 2. Mad | Hug-Koko please, feel do bad. |
| 2. Mad | Koko mad girl. |
| 2. Mad | Koko-love Marjie bye. |
| 1. Tired | Marjie trouble. |
| 1. Sleepy | Sleep. |
| 2. Sleepy | Go (toward door to trailer). |
| 2. Sleepy | Do sleep. |
| 1. Happy | Feel devil know. |
| 2. Happy | Gorilla polite happy Koko. |
| 1. Thirsty | Thirsty. |
| 2. Thirsty | Love drink. |
| 1. Hungry | Sorry. |
| 1. Hungry | Hungry hungry. |
| 2. Hungry | Feel sorry me hungry. |
| 1. Nervous | Feel nervous. |
| 2. Nervous | Stop with. |
| 2. Nervous | Feel stop. |

*K:* Alligator bad.
*C:* What do you do with bad alligator?
*K:* Gorilla afraid.

Koko has responded to questioning about a feeling state which is psychological rather than physiological, and therefore in a sense more abstract:

5/31/78, Maureen Sheehan

*M:* What do you think is boring?
*K:* Sad.
*M:* Sad?
*K:* Funny.
*M:* What do you think is boring?
*K:* Think eye ear eye nose boring.

Apparently Koko finds drill on overlearned things such as body parts boring.

## SUMMARY AND CONCLUDING REMARKS

In this chapter I have presented a series of cross-sections of data collected over a 6-year period on Koko's use of language in creative and intentional ways. Although these fragments are perhaps representative, they do not present a full picture of her abilities. For example, in the interests of time and space, data included in many of the discussions were drawn from restricted periods of time or from only one type of record (diary or sample); also, discussion of the evidence of humorous intent in Koko's use of language has not been included. At some future time a full exposition of these behaviors will be undertaken.

Consequently I would like to postpone any statements regarding the limits on Koko's development of creative and intentional language and the extent of her abilities as compared with those of a child, and merely summarize the evidence presented here: Koko has generated novel referential sign gestures without instruction, has modulated standard signs in Ameslan to convey slight changes in meaning, has used signs simultaneously, has created compound names some of which may be intentional metaphors, has engaged in self-directed and noninstrumental signing, has used language to refer to things removed in time and space, to deceive, insult, argue, threaten, and express her feelings, thoughts, and desires.

These findings, together with documentation of her sign language acquisition and production capabilities (Patterson, 1978a), and her sign language and spoken English comprehension capabilities (Patterson, 1978b), argue for the conclusion that language acquisition and use by the gorilla, the species perhaps most closely related to man, develops in a manner similar to that of the human child in many respects but at a slower rate and with the requirement of direct intervention, thus paralleling most closely development in the retarded or language-delayed child.

## NOTES

[1]One criticism of the data on Washoe was that the Gardners' records on her sign order were inadequate. It was argued that Washoe was stringing signs together as a complex form of labeling which lacked any internal structure. Although the Gardners subsequently produced evidence that Washoe's signed utterances were not randomly ordered, the rules governing them appear to reflect social more than grammatical considerations (McNeill, 1975). Also, the Gardner's assertion that Washoe's answers to questions demonstrated a knowledge of basic sentence constituents is debatable. It is possible that she learned by rote answers suitable to the subset of questions on which she was quizzed day after day. For example, when asked "Who X?" she could have gradually learned to discriminate the 16 words (which happened to be proper nouns and pronouns) in her vocabulary that were successful as responses from the remaining 116 signs which were not. Hence Washoe's "knowledge of basic sentence constituents" could be reduced to mastery of a set of complex conditional discrimination learning problems—the Gardners' very criticism of concurrent and later research with chimpanzees.

[2]For instance, Washoe's inventions, signs, and compound names; Sarah's identification of the symbol for apple as round and stemmed, not blue and triangular; Lana's invention of names ("Apple which-is orange") and discerning routing of lies told her by humans.

[3]Estimates of the size of the input sign vocabulary to Koko at various points in her development have been made. The numbers of different signs used by Koko's companions during 8 one-hour samples taken during the summers of 1973, 1975, and 1977 were 80, 189, and 353 respectively. Undoubtedly, a larger cross-section of the data would yield somewhat larger figures, but these numbers do indicate that Koko was assimilating a high proportion of the signs to which she was regularly exposed.

[4]After 6 years of testing Koko, I have come to believe that the Gardner and Gardner criterion is arbitrary perhaps to the point of being misleading. For example, Koko used *cucumber* 13 days in a row during two different months in 1975, and she has consistently used the sign in an appropriate manner ever since, but not necessarily on consecutive days. Yet according to the strict Gardner and Gardner criterion, this word and many others like it are not part of Koko's "qualified" vocabulary.

[5]It is quite possible that in the foregoing examples of nonliteral word use, the children and Koko intended not to create metaphor as figurative language use, but rather to alternately describe an object or state given an inability or unwillingness to produce the appropriate standard name. The methodological problems involved in dealing with such a subtle issue as intention in cases such as these are great and are just beginning to be tackled in research with human children (Gardner, Winner, Bechhofer, & Wolf, 1978).

## REFERENCES

Bellugi, U. *The acquisition of sign language and its structure: NIH Progress Report.* San Diego: The Salk Institute for Biological Studies, 1975.

Bellugi, U. *The signs of language.* Cambridge, Mass.: Harvard University Press, 1979.

Bellugi, U. & Fischer, S. A comparison of sign language and spoken language. *Cognition: International Journal of Cognitive Psychology,* 1972, 1(2,3), 173–200.

Bloom, L. *Language development: Form and function in emerging grammars.* Cambridge, Mass.: M.I.T. Press, 1970.

Bonvillian, J. D. & Nelson, K. E. Exceptional instances of language acquisition. *In* K. E. Nelson (Ed.), *Children's language* (Vol. 3). New York: Gardner Press, in press.

Bronowski, J. S. & Bellugi, U. Language, name and concept. *Science,* 1970, 168, 669–673.

Chukovsky K. *From two to five.* Ed. and trans. by Miriam Morton. Berkeley: University of California Press, 1963.

Di Pietro, R. *Language as human creation: First Andrew W. Mellon lecture.* Washington, D.C.: Georgetown University Press, 1976.

Ferster, C. B. Arithmetic behavior in chimpanzees. *Scientific American,* 1964, 210, 98–104.

Ford, H. A. On the characteristics of the *Troglodytes gorilla. Proceedings of the Academy of National Sciences,* Philadelphia, 1852, 6, 30–33.

Fouts, R. S. Acquisition and testing of gestural signs in four young chimpanzees. *Science,* 1973, 180, 978–980.

Fouts, R. S., Couch, J. B. & O'Neil, C. R. *Strategies for primate language training.* Unpublished paper, University of Oklahoma, 1977.

Friedman, L. A. Space, time, and person reference in American Sign Language. *Language,* 1975, 51(4), 940–961.

Furness, W. H. Observations on the mentality of chimpanzees and orangutans. *Proceedings of the American Philosophical Society,* 1916, 55, 281–290.

Gardner, B. T. & Gardner, R. A. Teaching sign language to a chimpanzee, 6: Replies to Wh questions. *Psychonomic Science,* 1971a, 25, 49.

Gardner, B. T. & Gardner, R. A. Two-way communication with an infant chimpanzee. *In* A. M. Schrier & F. Stollnitz (Eds.), *Behavior of nonhuman primates* (Vol. 4). New York: Academic Press, 1971b.

Gardner, B. T. & Gardner, R. A. Comparing early utterances of child and chimpanzee. *In* A. Pick (Ed.), *Minnesota Symposium on Child Psychology* (Vol. 8). Minneapolis: University of Minnesota Presss, 1974a.

Gardner, B. T. & Gardner, R. A. Teaching sign language to a chimpanzee, 7: Use of order in sign combinations. *Bulletin of the Psychonomic Society,* 1974b, 4, 264.

Gardner, H. *The arts and human development: A psychological study of the artistic process.* New York: Wiley, 1973.

Gardner, H. Metaphors and modalities: How children project polar adjectives onto diverse domains. *Child Development,* 1974, 45, 84–91.

Gardner, H., Winner, E., Bechhofer, R., & Wolf, D. The development of figurative language. *In* K. E. Nelson (Ed.), *Children's language* (Vol. 1). New York: Gardner Press, 1978.

Gardner, R. A. & Gardner, B. T. Teaching sign language to a chimpanzee. *Science,* 1969, 165, 644–672.

Gardner, R. A. & Gardner, B. T. Teaching sign language to a chimpanzee, 5: A practical vocabulary test for young primates. *Psychonomic Science,* 1971c, 25, 49.

Gardner, R. A. & Gardner, B. T. Communication with a young chimpanzee: Washoe's vocabulary. *In* R. Chauvin (Ed.), *Modèles animaux du comportement humaine, 198.* Paris: Centre National de la Recherche Scientifique, 1972.

Gardner, R. A. & Gardner, B. T. Early signs of language in child and chimpanzee. *Science,* 1975a, 187, 752–753.

Gardner, R. A. & Gardner, B. T. Evidence for sentence constituents in the early utterances of child and chimpanzee. *Journal of Experimental Psychology,* 1975b, 104(3), 244–267.

Gardner, R. A. & Gardner, B. T. Comparative psychology and language acquisition. *In* K. Salzinger & F. Denmark (Eds.), *Psychology: The state of the art.* New York: Annals of the New York Academy of Sciences, 1977.

Gill, T. V. & Rumbaugh, D. M. Mastery of naming skills by a chimpanzee. *Journal of Human Evolution,* 1974, 3, 483–492.

Hayes, C. *The ape in our house.* New York: Harper & Row, 1951.

Hayes, K. J. & Hayes, C. The intellectual development of a home-raised chimpanzee. *Proceedings of the American Philosophical Society,* 1951, 95(2), 105–109.

Hayes, K. J. & Hayes, C. Imitation in a home-raised chimpanzee. *Journal of Comparative and Physiological Psychology,* 1952, 45, 978–980.

Hayes, K. J. & Nissen, C. H. Higher mental functions of a home-raised chimpanzee. *In* A. M. Schrier & F. Stollnitz (Eds.), *Behavior of nonhuman primates* (Vol. 4). New York: Academic Press, 1971.

Hockett, C. F. Animal "languages" and human language. *In* J. N. Spuhler (Ed.), *The evolution of man's capacity for culture.* Detroit: Wayne State University Press, 1959.

Hockett, C. F. Origin of speech. *Scientific American,* 1960, 203, 88–96.

Hoffmeister, R. J., Moores, D. F., & Ellenberger, R. L. Some procedural guidelines for the study of the acquisition of sign language. *In* W. C. Stokoe, Jr. (Ed.), *Sign Language Studies,* 1975, 7, 121–137.

Honig, A., Caldwell, B., & Tannenbaum, J. Patterns of information processing used by and with young children in a nursery school setting. *Child Development,* 1970, 41, 1045–1065.

Kellogg, W. N. & Kellogg, L. A. *The ape and the child.* New York: Hafner, 1967 (Originally published 1933).

King, M. C. & Wilson, A. C. Evolution at two levels in humans and chimpanzees. *Science,* 1975, 188, 107–115.

Lane, H., Boyes-Braem, P., & Bellugi, U. Preliminaries to a distinctive feature analysis of handshapes in American Sign Language. *Cognitive Psychology,* 1976, 8, 263–289.

Lemen, R. J., Lemen, S. T., Morrish, R., & Tooley, W. H. Marasmus and shigellosis in two infant gorillas. *Journal of Medical Primatology,* 1974, 3, 365–369.

Lemen, R. J., Lemen, S. T., Morrish, R., Tooley, W. H, & Mottram, W. *Marasmus and septisemia in two infant gorillas.* Unpublished paper, University of California, Department of Pediatrics and the Animal Care Facility, 1973.

Leopold, W. F. *Speech development of a bilingual child: A linguist's record.* Vol.

1: *Vocabulary growth in the first two years.* Evanston Ill.: Northwestern University Press, 1939.

Leopold, W. F. *Speech development of a bilingual child: A linguist's record.* Vol. 3: *Grammar and general problems in the first two years.* Evanston, Ill.: Northwestern University Press, 1949.

McNeill, D. *Aspects of induced language in chimpanzees.* Unpublished paper, Institute for Advanced Study, Princeton, N.J., 1975.

Menyuk, P. The acquisition and development of language. *In* J. C. Wright (Ed.), *Prentice-Hall series in developmental psychology.* Englewood Cliffs, N.J.: Prentice-Hall, 1971.

Miller, S. A. Evolution of primate chromosomes. *Science,* 1977, 198, 1116–1124.

Nelson, K. Some evidence for the cognitive primacy of categorization and its functional basis. *Merrill-Palmer Quarterly,* 1973, 19, 21–40.

Patterson, F. G. The gestures of a gorilla: Language acquisition in another pongid. *Brain and Language,* 1978a, 5, 72–97.

Patterson, F. G. Linguistic capabilities of a young lowland gorilla. *In* F. C. Peng (Ed.), *Sign language and language acquisition in man and ape: New dimensions in comparative pedolinguistics.* Boulder, Co.: Westview Press, 1978b.

Patterson, F. G. Linguistic capabilities of a lowland gorilla. Doctoral dissertation, Stanford University, 1979.

Premack, A. J. & Premack, D. Teaching language to an ape. *Scientific American,* 1972, 227, 92–99.

Premack, D. A functional analysis of language. *Journal of the Experimental Analysis of Behavior,* 1970, 14, 107–125.

Premack, D. Language in chimpanzee? *Science,* 1971a, 172, 808–822.

Premack, D. On the assessment of language competence in the chimpanzee. *In* A. M. Schrier & F. Stollnitz (Eds.), *Behavior of nonhuman primates* (Vol. 4). New York: Academic Press, 1971b.

Premack, D. Symbols inside and outside of language. *In* J. Kavanaugh & J. E. Cutting (Eds.), *The role of speech in language.* Cambridge, Mass.: M.I.T. Press, 1975.

Premack, D. *Intelligence in ape and man.* Hillsdale, N.J.: Lawrence Erlbaum Assoc., 1976a.

Premack, D. Language and intelligence in ape and man. *American Scientist,* 1976b, 64(6), 674–683.

Rumbaugh, D. M. Comparative primate learning and its contributions to understanding development, play, intelligence and language. *In* A. B. Chiarelli (Ed.), *Perspectives in primate biology* (Vol. 9). New York: Plenum Press, 1974.

Rumbaugh, D. M. (Ed.). *Language learning by a chimpanzee: The Lana Project.* New York: Academic Press, 1977.

Rumbaugh, D. M. & Gill, T. V. Language, apes, and the apple which-is orange, please. *In* S. Kondo, M. Kawai, A. Ehara, & S. Kawamura (Eds.), *Proceedings from the Symposia of the Fifth Congress of the Internatinoal Primatological Society.* Tokyo: Japan Science Press, 1975.

Rumbaugh, D. M. & Gill, T. V. Language and the acquisition of language-type skills by a chimpanzee (*Pan*). *In* K. Salzinger (Ed.), *Psychology in progress, 270.* New York: Annals of the New York Academy of Sciences, 1976a.

Rumbaugh, D. M. & Gill, T. V. Lana's mastery of language skills. *In* H. Steklis, S. Harnad, & J. Lancaster (Eds.), *Origins and evolution of language and speech, 280.* New York: Annals of the New York Academy of Sciences, 1976b.

Rumbaugh, D. M., Gill, T. V. & von Glaserfeld, E. C. Reading and sentence completion by a chimpanzee *(Pan)*. *Science,* 1973, 182, 731–733.

Rumbaugh, D. M., Gill, T. V. & von Glasersfeld, E. C. A rejoinder to language in man, monkeys and machine. *Science,* 1974, 185, 871–872.

Rumbaugh, D. M., von Glasersfeld, E. C., Warner, H., Pisani, P., & Gill, T. V. Lana (chimpanzee) learning language: A progress report. *Brain and Language,* 1974, 1, 205–212.

Savage, T. S. & Wyman, J. Observations on the external characters of habits of *Troglodytes niger geoff.,* and on its organization. *Boston Journal of Natural History,* 1843, 4, 362–376.

Schlesinger, H. S. The acquisition of sign language. *In* I. M. Schlesinger & L. Namir (Eds.), *Current trends in the study of sign languages of the deaf.* The Hague: Mouton, 1976.

Slobin, D. I. Universals of grammatical development in children. *In* G. Flores d'Arcais (Ed.), *Advances in psycholinguistics.* London: North Holland, 1970.

Smith, M. E. An investigation of the development of the sentence and the extent of vocabulary in young children. *In* University of Iowa: *Studies in child welfare,* 3(5). Iowa City: University of Iowa, 1926.

Southcombe, A. Personal communication, December 28, 1977.

Suppes, P. The semantics of children's language. *American Psychologist,* 1974, 29, 103–114.

von Glaserfeld, E. Signs, communications, and language. *Journal of Human Evolution,* 1974, 3, 465–474.

Watt, W. C. Review of behavior of non-human primates. *In* A. M. Schrier & F. Stollnitz (Eds.), *Behavioral Science,* 1974, 19, 70–71.

Winitz, H. & Irwin, O. C. Syllabic and phonetic structure of infants' early words. *Journal of Speech and Hearing Research,* 1958, 1(3), 250–256.

Witmer, L. A monkey with a mind. *Psychological Clinic,* 1909, 3, 179–205.

Wolman, R. W., Lewis, W. C., & King, M. The development of the language of emotions: Conditions of emotional arousal. *Child Development,* 1971, 42, 1288–1293.

Yerkes, R. M. *Almost human.* New York: Century, 1925.

Yerkes, R. & Yerkes, A. W. *The great apes: a study of anthropoid life.* New Haven: Yale University Press, 1929.

# 10

# A DEVELOPMENTAL STUDY OF THE COMMUNICATION OF MEANING: THE ROLE OF UNCERTAINTY AND INFORMATION

Patricia Marks Greenfield
Cathy Hankins Dent

When a philosopher claims that the meaning of a statement is determined by its use, it is because he takes the meaning to consist in the role it plays in communication between members of a speech community.

—Jay Atlas (1978)

Our concern in this chapter is with the communication of meaning. From the point of view of communication, meaning can be defined as the message which a speaker intends to transmit to a listener (or listeners). A message must be constructed by a speaker and interpreted by a listener. This construction is based on the speaker's perception and cognition of relations. The construction process of the speaker is the focus of the empirical study to be reported. Thus, our concern is with the construction of messages which communicate meaning.

Bates (1976) defines meaning as "the set of mental acts or operations that a speaker intends to create in his listener by using a sentence." This definition specifies the psychological nature of a message. If we broaden Bates's notion to include physical as well as mental acts, the definition covers the type of communication situation we have set up: one in which the goal is to get someone else to *perform* certain acts, not just to *think* them. The definition is useful for a psychological analysis of the communication of meaning because it suggests that we must conceptualize the nature of the operations, mental or physical, which are to be established in the listener. If operations are to be created in the listener, they must first be organized and constructed by the speaker.

The basic communicative situation of our study is one in which a child must explain to another person how to put together a set of objects in a particular way. Thus, the message is a description of what relations must obtain among which things and how to bring about this state of affairs.

In the communication situation of our study, each speaker had to describe three complex action sequences so that a listener who had the same materials but could not see the speaker's actions could build the same construction. The three action sequences are pictured in Figure 10-1, below. For example, the materials for one task consist of a yellow plastic cup and a set of five wooden beads of different colors and shapes. The task is to place three specific beads in the cup one at a time in any order (see Figure 10-1). Because of the nature of the situation, the elements of the message include both verbal description and material entities. In combinations, these represent what the speaker must communicate to the listener.

The concept of the message implies a particular view of the nature of underlying linguistic representation and the relation between language and action. This view, elaborated elsewhere (Greenfield & Smith, 1976; Greenfield, 1978b), is that there is an amodal cognitive system which structures action, the perception of events, and language in the same way. Because of this, preexisting relations structured in perception and action become a

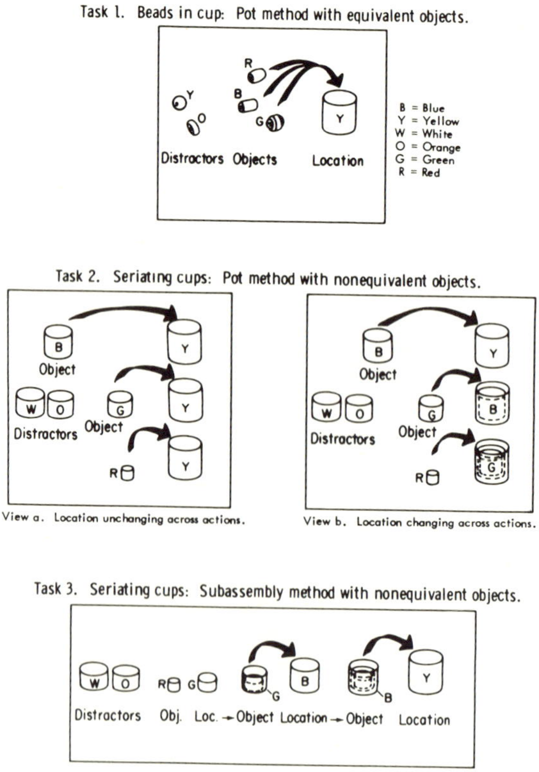

*Figure 10-1.* Combinatorial action tasks.

framework for emergent language at the one-word stage (Greenfield & Smith, 1976; Zukow, Reilly, & Greenfield, in press) and beyond (e.g., Bowerman, 1973; Bruner, Roy, & Ratner, in press; Schlesinger, 1971; Slobin, 1973). Other research indicates that the development and organization of complex action employs principles in common with the grammatical structure of language (e.g., Greenfield, Nelson, & Saltzman, 1972; Goodson & Greenfield, 1975; Greenfield & Schneider, 1977; Greenfield, 1978b).

The action elicited by language structures has been studied (Huttenlocher and Strauss, 1968; Huttenlocher, Eisenberg, and Strauss, 1968; Greenfield and Westerman, 1978), but the language elicited by active construction has not. This approach can be used to investigate systematic differences in descriptive/communicative messages which depend on perceptual features and action possibilities of different construction tasks. Thus, our study is unique in that descriptive messages are used to investigate the developmental relations of language and complex action in communicative situation. This work is consonant with the viewpoint expressed in earlier studies (e.g., Greenfield & Schneider, 1977) that an amodal cognitive organization underlies performance in all modes including language and action.

## A PROPOSITIONAL FRAMEWORK FOR LANGUAGE AND ACTION

In the past we have conceived of this amodal cognitive organization as structured in terms of the propositional form of a case grammar. The idea that knowledge originating in perception can be represented propositionally is proving useful for understanding behavior in a wide range of cognitive tasks apart from language acquisition and the organization of action: memory for prose (e.g., Kintsch, 1972) and verifying information about pictures (e.g., Clark & Chase, 1972) are examples.

A proposition can be conceived as a state or change predicated of a single entity or a relation predicated between two or more entities. In logic, states or relations are called predicates; entities are called arguments. Some propositional notations characterize the internal structure of a proposition simply in terms of the number of arguments it contains. Case grammar, in contrast, specifies the nature of the relation between predicate and argument. Fillmore's (1968) case grammar describes various roles an argument may have in an event: Agent, Object, and Location are the names of the three arguments which are most relevant to the particular situation of our experimental tasks. Whereas Fillmore's original definitions were designed especially for linguistic phenomena, the role definitions will be more suited to an amodal cognitive structure if we eliminate reference to syntactic terms. We can then define Agent as a typically animate instigator of action. Object will be defined as something affected by an action or state. Finally, a

Location is the spatial position or orientation of an action or state. In the situation where someone places three beads in a cup (Figure 10-1, Task 1), the person functions as Agent, each bead has the role of Object, while the cup functions as a Location.

Our conceptualization of the predicate comes from Chafe's (1970) version of case grammar. Whereas Fillmore has a more detailed scheme for the arguments of a proposition, Chafe has a more developed way of treating predicates. In Chafe's view, the act of placing an Object in a Location (e.g., a bead in a cup) would be termed a Locative Action-Process. In this scheme, an Action expresses what someone, its Agent, does; while a Process expresses what happens to something. An Action-Process involves an Agent doing the Action to something. In our experimental situation we call this thing an Object. Locative Action-Processes come about through the combination of a Locative State (the state of being "in," in our example) with an action-process (placing). In Locative Action-Process, an Action-Process results in a change in Location.

Another aspect of our task involves attributes of the Objects or their Location. For instance, the beads in Task 1 (Figure 10-1) are different colors. The predication of a certain color of something is considered a State, or Property, of that thing. Thus, redness is a State, or Property, of one of the beads in our tasks. Finally, there are three discrete events (instances of Locative Action-Process) involved in Task 1. Each one has a place in a temporal sequence. Temporal specification is considered a state of the entire event or proposition.

Thus far, we have used the propositional frameworks of Fillmore and Chafe to describe a way of structuring one of the action sequences used in our study. The framework can also be used to analyze linguistic description of the action sequence. Analysis of language, of course, was the original goal of case grammars. Let us consider the following linguistic description of the first event in the bead task: "First I put the blue bead in the yellow cup". Each element in this sentence can be labeled according to its role in the underlying linguistic proposition.

| First | I | put | the | blue | bead |
|---|---|---|---|---|---|
| Temporal State | Agent | Locative Action-Process | | Property of Object | Object |

| in | the | yellow | cup |
|---|---|---|---|
| Locative State | | Property of Location | Location |

This example of linguistic and action analysis of the beads task shows how the same propositional elements can be used to represent the action and the linguistic description. The reader may have noted that the hierarchical structure of the role relations has not been preserved in this representation of the sentence. What this way of diagramming the sentence accomplishes is to specify the role of surface structure elements (the actual words produced in the order they occur) in the underlying propositional structure. Because this propositional structure represents the event also, this notational system allows the relationship between action structure and linguistic description to be indicated in quite a straightforward manner.

Indeed, the goal of our study is to understand how linguistic elements and elements from the event itself are used in the construction of a message. Another way of putting this problem is to talk about why certain aspects of the action structure are more often given linguistic expression than others. The notion of presupposition is relevant to such an analysis.

## Information, Presupposition, and Linguistic Expression

Our basic hypothesis is that the elements in the message which are relatively certain from the nonverbal context tend to go unstated, while those that are relatively uncertain tend to be expressed linguistically. Here, our use of certainty and uncertainty captures the general sense of these terms as they are used in semantic information theory.[1] That is, a nonverbal element is totally certain when it is the unique possibility in the situation. It becomes relatively more uncertain as the number of alternatives it must be selected from increases. Thus, uncertainty is in the alternatives perceived in the context, and messages are informative to the extent that they allow selection of the element (entity or relation) referred to by the linguistic encoding.

A similar idea is put forth in Stalnaker's (1974) recent discussion of pragmatic presuppositions. He begins by defining pragmatic presuppositions as the background beliefs of the speaker, propositions whose truth he takes for granted or seems to take for granted in making his statement. In another article Stalnaker (1972) adds that the speaker assumes that these background beliefs are shared by the listener. This may not always be the case, but this shared knowledge is a prerequisite for successful communication. Stalnaker goes on to say:

> Which facts or opinions we can reasonably take for granted in this way, as much as what further information either of us wants to convey, will guide the direction of our conversation—will determine what is said. I will not say things that are already taken for granted, since that would be redundant. Nor will I assert things incompatible with the common background, since that would be self-defeating. My aim in making assertions is to distinguish among the possible situations which are compatible with all the beliefs or assumptions that I assume we share. (p. 199)

Thus, Stalnaker sees assertions or statements as functioning to partition alternatives that "are considered live options in the context" (Stalnaker, 1972, p. 388). On the other side of the coin, he views what can be taken for granted as going unstated. Stalnaker's analysis is most compatible with our idea, put forth elsewhere (Greenfield, 1978a; Greenfield & Zukow, 1978), that the state of certainty or the process of taking for granted is the cognitive basis for presupposition, while perception of uncertainty or change is the cognitive basis for assertion. Indeed, we have found that at the very beginning of language development, what is taken for granted goes unstated by the child, while uncertain or changing elements are given verbal expression in the single-word utterance (Greenfield & Smith, 1976; Greenfield & Zukow, 1978).

If communication is to be successful, the speaker should only presuppose elements shared by the listener. In our experimental communication situation, such elements could be the instructions and the array of materials. How would these presupposed elements affect the resulting linguistic description? First, let us identify the components of the linguistic description.

Strawson, a philosopher in the ordinary language tradition, is instructive here. According to him (1950):

> One of the main purposes for which we use language is the purpose of stating facts about things and persons and events. If we want to fulfill this purpose, we must have some way of forestalling the question "what (who, which one) are you talking about?" as well as the question "What are you saying about it (him, her)?" The task of forestalling the first question is the referring or identifying task. The task of forestalling the second is the attributive (or descriptive or classificatory or ascriptive) task. (p. 17)

Thus, the speaker must communicate to the listener: (1) what thing or things he or she is referring to or mentioning, and (2) what is attributed to or predicated of them.

The role of information and certainty in reference has been formulated in Olson's cognitive theory of semantics. Olson posits that "words designate, signal or specify an intended referent relative to the set of alternatives from which it must be differentiated. In the language of information theory we would say that statements reduce alternatives or uncertainty" (Olson, 1970, p. 264). It follows that statements are informative to the extent that they reduce uncertainty or eliminate alternatives. Olson cites Brown's (1958) earlier idea that objects are usually named at the level of generality which allows us to differentiate them from other objects of contrasting function. Thus, the fact that we use the term *ball* more than *baseball* or *sphere* reflects the nature of potential alternative referents: not usually golf balls or cubes, but rather bats, rackets, kites, skateboards. Thus, the very choice of a label reflects the set of alternatives psychologically present in a given context. Olson's analysis moves from word to message, which is defined as "any utterance that specifies the event relative to the set of alternatives" (p. 26q). Olson's formulation suggests the possibility of analyzing the various elements of a statement for their informativeness. This is precisely the task we have set for ourselves in the present study.

Olson goes on to give a specific example most pertinent to our experimental situation:

> The relation of an utterance to an intended referent can best be illustrated by a paradigm case. A gold star is placed under a small, wooden block. A speaker who saw this act is then asked to tell a listener who did not see the act, where the gold star is. In every case the star is placed under the *same* block, a small, round, white, . . . one. However, in the first case there is one alternative block present, a small, round, *black* . . . one. In the second case there is a different alternative block present, a small, *square,* white . . . one. In a third case there are three alternative blocks present, a round black one, a square black one, and a square white one. These three cases are shown in Figure 10-2.
>
> In these situations we would find a speaker saying the following for case one:
>
> It's under the *white* one;
> for case two
> It's under the *round* one;
> for case three
> It's under the *round, white* one (1970, p. 264).

This example shows how a given Property of State of a Location will be expressed verbally if there is an alternative value of the attribute dimension

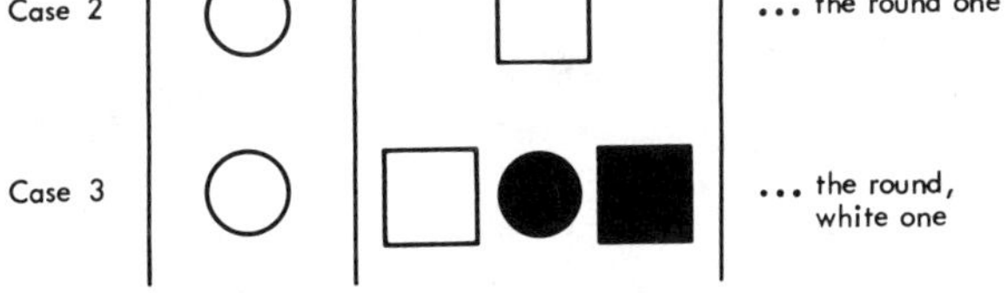

|  | EVENT | ALTERNATIVE | UTTERANCE |
|---|---|---|---|
| Case 1 | ○ | ● | ... the white one |
| Case 2 | ○ | □ | ... the round one |
| Case 3 | ○ | □ ● ■ | ... the round, white one |

*Figure 10-2.* The relation of an utterance to an intended referent. From Olson (1970). Reprinted by permission of the American Psychological Association.

present in the context. Thus, for example, in specifying the Location of the star, a speaker will identify it by color if two Locations, similar in shape but varying in color, are present. In contrast, when two Locations are the same color but different shapes, the speaker will identify the Location by shape rather than color. In both cases, the resulting linguistic expression satisfies a basic requirement for pragmatic presupposition: the existence of a unique referent for each referring expression in an utterance. In each case the resulting linguistic expression is informative; it partitions a set of alternative referents.

Thus, in the second example, if color were the only property to be expressed linguistically, the speaker would not be making unique reference, and the listener could ask, "Which one?". Attributes or States of properties which do not contribute to the specification of a unique referent, by allowing elimination of alternative possibilities, should not receive verbal expression. So, where color is not a relevant attribute, ideally color will not be expressed in the speaker's linguistic description.

## The Development of Referential Communication

A number of studies have looked at the development of the ability to uniquely specify referents by linguistic means. Many of these studies have been summarized by Glucksberg, Krauss, and Higgins (1975). They conclude that adults generally provide information to a listener which discriminates between the referent and potentially confusable nonreferents (Rosenberg & Cohen, 1966; Krauss & Weinheimer, 1967), but that this ability develops with age. Our study will verify this developmental trend by observing verbal descriptions in a variety of complex action contexts. Although one unpublished pilot study looked at communication in an action context (Glucksberg & Kim, 1969), linguistic expression of action was not analyzed. This task is central to our study. By investigating how children describe complex action in a communicative situation, it is possible to see the development of predication as well as reference. It is also possible to see just how cognitive and situational variables influence description.

## OVERVIEW OF THE STUDY

We have four conditions for communication, and the listener's requirements remain constant across all four. Insofar as the speaker is adapting the message to the listener, there should be no difference in performance across conditions. Insofar as cognitive factors unrelated to communication to a listener intervene, there should be differences across conditions. In our study, children described their own actions in two of the experimental conditions, and those of another person in two other conditions. Another variation in conditions was whether the child described the action while it was in progress or afterward. The children represented two age levels, six and ten years.

We are concerned with the construction of messages which communicate meaning and with how this ability develops in children. Both the referential and predication aspects of the description can be analyzed because our study involves children describing action. The manipulative actions and materials of the tasks are analyzed for uncertainty, the verbal elements for informativeness. This analysis allows a discussion of which elements children choose to encode verbally in terms of what is given in the situation and therefore potentially pragmatically presupposed.

## METHOD

### Subjects, Procedure, and Design

A total of 96 children participated in the experiment. They were of varied race and socioeconomic status (all were native English speakers), and they were attending an elementary school in a middle-income neighborhood. There were 48 six-year-olds and 48 ten-year-olds with equal numbers of boys and girls.[2] All participants described a specific series of complex actions to an adult who, the child was told, could not see the action. There were four conditions and three tasks (action sequences) described. The tasks are shown in Figure 10-1. For each child the physical setting was the same. That is, one adult, experimenter $(E_1)$ and the child sat on one side of a table with a second experimenter $(E_2)$ sitting across the table. Between $E_2$ and the child there was a white wooden screen with an opening at the level of $E_2$'s face (see Figure 10-3).

The children in each age group were randomly assigned to one of four conditions with the restriction that sex of the participants was balanced across conditions. Table I presents the four conditions and the instructions given for each task in a given condition. The basic procedure was to present the child with a model of the finished construction and the toys necessary to copy the model (plus distractors). Then $E_1$ either modeled the action and then had the child construct and describe it (active condition), or $E_1$ performed the action and the child described it (passive condition). The methods of combination were modeled to insure that the particular series of actions that were of interest were performed. This modeling also served to clarify the instructions. In addition to the activity dimension, there was a timing dimension. That is, the description was either simultaneous with the action (simultaneous conditions) or after the action (post conditions). If the

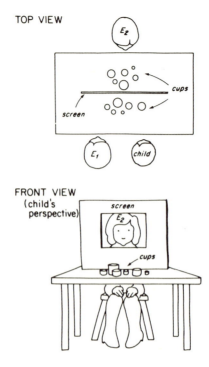

*Figure 10-3.* Schematic drawing of the experimental situation.

child did not understand the instructions, they were repeated, and it was stressed that the child should tell $E_2$ just what each action was. All sessions were audiotaped, and those in which the child performed the actions were videotaped.

As Figure 10-3 shows, all persons could see each other's faces; and the child could see only the face of $E_2$, not her hands or toys ($E_2$ always had the same toys as the child). Each child was told that $E_2$ could see the child's face but not his or her hands or what he or she was doing. In actuality, the $E_2$ could see what the child did and so always produced exactly what the child made. Since from the child's point of view the problem was to tell $E_2$ what she or he was doing so that $E_2$ could build the same thing, the child never failed. Each child described three tasks; the order of tasks was counterbalanced across sex and condition. (See Figure 10-1 for illustration of the tasks.) If a child did not perform the actions as modeled, then the particular construction involved was repeated after all three tasks had been performed. The instructions and modeling were repeated without change, and

## Table I
## Four Conditions of Action Description and
## the Instructions Given in Each Condition

| Time | ACTIVITY | |
|------|----------|---|
| | **Active (child performs action)** | **Passive (child watches E$_1$ perform action)** |
| Simultaneous (description simultaneous with action) | *simultaneous active*<br>E$_1$<br>Here are your toys, and I'll give (name E$_2$) the same toys. This is what I want you to copy (E$_1$ points to model—model always present). E$_2$ can't see this, and she can't see what you're doing, so tell E$_2$ what you're doing while you copy it so that she can build the same thing. She can't see this, and she can't see what you're doing. So remember to tell her what you're doing. OK? Now watch me. (Demonstrates action.) | *simultaneous passive*<br>E$_1$<br>These are my toys, and I'll give E$_2$ the same toys. I'm going to copy this (points to model—model always present). E$_2$ can't see this, and she can't see what I'm doing. You tell her what I'm doing so she can build the same thing. She can't see this and she can't see what I'm doing, so you have to tell her what I'm doing. OK? (E$_1$ performs action.) |
| Post (description after action) | *post active*<br>E$_1$<br>Here are your toys, and I'll give E$_2$ the same toys. This is what I want you to copy (points to model —model always present). E$_2$ can't see this, and she can't see what you're doing. So when you're all done, tell her what you did so she can build the same thing. She can't see this, and she can't see what you're doing, so when you're all done, tell her what you did. OK? Now watch me. (Demonstrates action). | *post passive*<br>E$_1$<br>These are my toys, and I'll give E$_2$ the same toys. I'm going to copy this (points to model—model always present). E$_2$ can't see this, and she can't see what I'm doing. When I'm all done, you tell her what I did so she can build the same thing. She can't see this, and she can't see what I'm doing, so when I'm all done, tell her what I did. OK? (E$_1$ performs action.) |

the language used for the second performance of the tasks was used in the analysis of elements encoded. The simplest task was to put three specific beads out of five (Playskool wooden beads) in a yellow cup in any order (Task 1). The next most complex task was to combine the seriated cups using the pot method (Task 2), and the most complex task was to combine the seriated cups using the subassembly method (Task 3). There were distractor cups and beads so that the child could not simply use "I put the cups together" or "I put the beads in the cup" as a description and be sufficiently informative. For successful communication, a more detailed description was required; the elements to be used had to be differentiated from those not used in the actions.

The task which was most often repeated was the subassembly method of combining seriated cups. Thirteen ten-year-olds and 3 six-year olds did not perform this task correctly the first time, and so they described it a second time. There were 2 ten-year-olds and 2 six-year-olds who had to repeat the pot method of combining the seriated cups. No one performed the beads task incorrectly. The number of children who did not perform the task correctly the *second* time is as follows: 1 ten-year-old and 3 six-year-olds—subassembly task; 3 ten-year-olds and 1 six-year old—pot task. We used their second descriptions even though the task was not correct rather than not use the data at all. This should only provide noise in the data and the patterns that are found are robust to this noise factor.

## Data Analysis

The audio tapes of the children's descriptions were transcribed, and these transcriptions were scored for expression of action elements belonging to the following categories: Agent (Ag), Object (O), Location (L), Action-Process (AP), Temporal State (TS), Property of Object (PO), Locative State (LS), Property of Location (PL). The derivation of these categories from Fillmore and Chafe has already been described. The application of these categories to the linguistic productions in the present study were derived from an "ideal" (maximally complete) description of the actions (see Table II). The categories are defined as follows:

*Arguments*
   Agent (Ag): animate initiator of action-process
   Object (O): inanimate entity affected by the action-process
   Location (L): location or spatial orientation of the action-process

*Predicates*
   Action-Process (AP): action which is performed by the agent and affects the object

## Table II
## Propositional Categories Used for
## Coding Expression of Elements

| Task | | Coding of Maximally Complete Descriptions* | | | | | | | | |
|---|---|---|---|---|---|---|---|---|---|---|
| | | TS | Ag | AP | | PO | O | LS | | PL | L |
| Beads | Pot method | First, | I | put | the | blue | bead | in | the | yellow | cup. |
| | | Then, | I | put | the | green | bead | in | the | yellow | cup. |
| | | Then, | I | put | the | red | bead | in | the | yellow | cup. |
| Cups | Pot method | First, | I | put | the | blue | cup | in | the | yellow | cup. |
| | | Then, | I | put | the | green | cup | in | the | blue | cup. |
| | | Then, | I | put | the | red | cup | in | the | green | cup. |
| Cups | Subassembly method | First | I | put | the | red | cup | in | the | green | cup. |
| | | Then, | I | put | the | green | cup | in | the | blue | cup. |
| | | Then, | I | put | the | blue | cup | in | the | yellow | cup. |

*Type of propositional element Temporal State (TS), Agent (Ag), Action-Process (AP), Property of Object (PO), Object (O), Locative State (LS), Property of Location (PL), Location (L)

Temporal State (TS): modifier of action which indicates sequencing of action
Property of Object (PO): state or condition of object
Locative State (LS): state of object which results from locative action-process
Property of Location (PL): state or condition of location

The verbal encoding scores are based on the total number of combinatorial actions linguistically referred to by the child. A combinatorial action was defined as the putting together of two items from the array of materials; for instance, placing a bead in the cup (Task 1). Since each task is composed of three combinatorial actions with eight elements in each, a child could verbally encode from 0 to 24 elements in a task. Table II illustrates the coding of maximally complete descriptions. The actual frequency of linguistic encoding (0, 1, 2, 3) for each kind of element (e.g., Agent) was divided by the total number of combinatorial actions referred to, yielding a percentage score for each category (Agent, Object, and so on). In most cases, the children linguistically referred to all three actions comprising each task. Seventeen of the 96 children failed to refer to all three component actions for one or more of the tasks they described.

The scoring of a maximally complete and prototypical description is illustrated by the categorizations shown in Table II. Rules for coding less prototypical descriptions are as follows. Spontaneous self-corrections were not coded. Occasionally, a combinatorial action was linguistically encoded in two utterances or two conjoined simple sentences; for example, a ten-year-old began her description of the subassembly method for seriating the cups by saying,

(1) *Take the red one. I put it inside the green one.* Such productions were treated as the verbal encoding of a single combinatorial action. When a type of propositional element occurred in both utterances, it was counted only once. This happened most often with Action-Processes, as in this example (*take* in the first, *put* in the second).

Proforms used to encode the stimuli were counted as the deletion of an argument since such a form indicates that the referent has already been specified by the context, either verbal or nonverbal. (Osgood, 1971, provides empirical support for this interpretation of proform function.) Thus, if a child used pronouns as in *Put it in* or *Put the blue one in,* the Object element was coded as absent. The use of personal pronouns (I, you, she) to encode the Agent was, in contrast, counted because these do, in fact, partition the potential agents in the situation. From a semantic point of view, "thing" seemed equivalent to a pronoun and was coded as such. Similarly, use of a prolocative form such as "there" was coded as the deletion of Location. In general, if a word did not eliminate any alternative possibilities, it was not counted as verbally encoding an element. For this reason certain adjectives (Properties of Object or Location), such as "another," were not coded, but this was an extremely rare phenomenon.

Since most adverbs named the sequencing of actions (for instance, "first," "next"), it was decided to code only for Temporal State adverbs. Thus, some adverbial modification (for example, "together") was not counted in our system. In all but one case the verbs used were the action-process verbs "put," "take," "make," or "build," with "put" used by far the most frequently. One child used the action verb "goes," but this was coded in our action-process category. Locative States were most often the prepositions "in" or "inside," but prepositional phrases such as "on top of" and "on the right side" were also coded as Locative States.

The type of description which was most problematic for coding was that in which the child named only the colors of the cups. In this case the order of mention was used to determine whether the cup was Object or Location. For example, in the Pot task if the description were "blue /green/red" each of these words would be scored as verbally encoding Object since a listing of Locations would have been "yellow/blue/green." The latter never occurred. The Subassembly task was sometimes described as "red/green/blue." These were scored as verbally encoding Object since a list of Locations would be "green/blue/yellow." Again, this latter list did not occur. For the simultaneous active condition it was possible to check videotapes. If the object referred to was in the process of being moved or had just been moved, it was scored as Object. If the object named was not being moved and was a receptacle, it was scored as Location. In addition, when a child named the color of the largest cup, which was always a Location, this was scored as naming the location.

A repeated measures analysis of variance (ANOVA) was performed on these scores in order to ascertain how much of the variance in the scores was due to the effects of age, treatment conditions, and task structure. The propositional categorization of action was used as the repeated factor in the design so that a relatively detailed analysis could be made of the effect of within-task structure on linguistic encoding. Thus, the design was a 2(age) X2(activity)X2(time)X3(task)X8(action element) factorial design with repeated measures. The significant main effects and interactions are given in Table III. The probability levels of the F statistic are corrected using the conservative Geiser-Greenhouse correction (Kirk, 1968), since it is very likely that variance-covariance assumptions underlying the ANOVA were not met (cf. McCall & Applebaum, 1973).

Post-hoc analyses were performed to pinpoint the locus of significant differences. Where only two data points were involved, a $t$-test was used. Where more than two data points were involved, a simple main effects test (which tests for any difference among the points simultaneously) was used first. If this test was significant, then pairs of points were tested using a $t$-test. Since $t$-tests are not conservative and we are using them for post-hoc analyses, we set the alpha level at .01 in order to reduce the likelihood of Type 1 errors.

The results show that there are main effects of age, task, and type of action element. In addition, the following interactions were significant: task by type of action element, time by type of action element, and age by task by type of action element.

### Table III
### Results of the Analysis of Variance

| Source of Variance | F | Corrected Probability Level |
|---|---|---|
| Age | 4.22 | $p = .043$ |
| Task | 17.77 | $p < .001$ |
| Type of action element | 106.78 | $p < .001$ |
| Task X type of action element | 26.92 | $p < .001$ |
| Time of description X type of action element | 6.13 | $p < .001$ |
| Task X age X type of action element | 2.52 | $p < .025$ |

## Task Analysis

The results are interpreted in terms of an analysis of the tasks based on uncertainty. Uncertainty arises when there are alternative entities to choose from or when entities or relations are changing. Thus, we analyzed the tasks in terms of when the entities (arguments) and relations (predicates) occurred in sets of alternatives at one point in time or changed as the task progressed. A summary of this analysis is shown in Table IV and explained below. First features common to all three tasks, and then features specific to each, will be taken up and analyzed with respect to uncertainty.

Table IV shows the patterns of uncertainty in the task analyzed for *alternatives* within each action and *change* across actions, the two basic types of uncertainty. Uncertainty about what is to be done (Action-Process) and the resultant relations among the materials (Locative State) exists within each action for all three tasks. That is, there are a range of possibilities for manipulating the materials. However, Action-Process and Locative State remain constant from action to action within a given task. From the speak-

**Table IV**
**Loci of Uncertainty in Each Task**

|  | Alternatives Within Each Action | Change Across Actions |
|---|---|---|
| *Task 1. Beads: Pot method* | | |
| Arguments | Agent(?) | |
| Predicates | Action-Process | Property of Object |
|  | Locative State | |
|  | Property of Object | |
| *Task 2 (View a). Cups: Pot method* | | |
| Arguments | Agent(?) | |
| Predicates | Action-Process | |
|  | Locative State | Property of Object |
|  | Property of Object | Temporal State |
| *Task 2 (View b). Cups: Pot method* | | |
| Arguments | Agent(?) | |
| Predicates | Action-Process | |
|  | Locative State | Property of Object |
|  | Property of Object | Property of Location |
|  | | Temporal State |
| *Task 3. Cups: Subassembly method* | | |
| Arguments | Agent(?) | |
| Predicates | Action-Process | |
|  | Locative State | Property of Object |
|  | Property of Object | Property of Location |
|  | Property of Location | Temporal State |

er's perspective, the initial uncertainty about Action-Process and Locative State is exaggerated for the listener who, the speaker has been told, cannot see what is being done to the materials. Agent is, in one sense, relatively certain both within and across actions; that is, who will be performing the actions is specified in the initial instructions (Table I) and does not vary from action to action within a task. In another sense, Agent is uncertain within an action, for there exist three potential Agents within the experimental situation, the child and the two experimenters. For this reason, Agent appears in the left-hand column of the table with question marks next to it.

In Task 1, the Beads task (Figure 10-1), the Agent must first select a bead rather than a cup. Therefore, the nature of the Object carries some degree of uncertainty. However, verbally encoding the Object with a noun ("bead") would be uninformative because it does not partition the alternative Objects, all of which are beads. The informative element is the Property of Object, because color or shape differentiates the subset of Object beads from the distractors. Property of Object appears as uncertain in the left-hand column of Table IV (alternatives within each action) because a bead must be selected from alternative possibilities on each move. Property of Object also appears in the right-hand column (change across actions) because a different Object must be selected for each move (Figure 10-1). Once Locative State has been communicated by the word "in," Location is, in contrast to Object, relatively certain, for the cup is, practically speaking, a unique container for the beads. Because there is only one cup in the array, there is no uncertainty about any Property of Location; all properties are determined once it is known that the Location is a cup. Since the beads can be placed in any order, Temporal State of the actions is not a relevant variable.

Task 2, seriation of cups by the pot method (Figure 10-1), differs in that the materials contain only one type of entity (argument), cups. For this reason, the nature of both Objects and Locations is totally certain. As in Task 1, uncertainty lies in the Property of the Object (Table IV) because a particular cup must be chosen as an Object for each move and because Property varies across actions. Unlike Task 1, a particular order of placement (from largest to smallest) is required to complete the task (seriate the cups). Therefore, Temporal State is a relevant variable (right-hand column of Table IV). (Although some children probably interpreted the modeled order in Task 1 as relevant, order would, overall, have been less salient than for the seriation tasks [2 and 3].) Within an action, Property of Location is never uncertain because once the Locative relation (inside of) has been specified and the Object selected, there is only one possible Location in which that Object could fit (see Figure 10-1). This is true because the seriated cups are combined from the largest to the smallest; the largest cup (yellow) is the only container in which the next largest (blue) will fit. In the simpler view of

Task 2, View a (Figure 10-1), the task can be seen as placing a series of cups in the largest yellow cup. Because the yellow cup is always seen as the Location, Property of Location does not vary across actions. The largest yellow cup is seen as the simple receptacle or pot into which all the other cups are placed. The Location is constant. The more complex view of the task (View b, Figure 10-1) involves seeing the last cup placed in the yellow cup as the location for the ensuing action. For example, first the blue cup is placed in the yellow; the next action then takes the blue cup, not the yellow, as its location. Thus, this view produces an additional source of uncertainty: Location, distinguished by its color or size (Property) changes across actions. Thus, it is possible to view the pot method of seriating cups as involving a variable Location for each move.

The task which involves the most uncertainty is Task 3, seriation of cups by the subassembly method (see Figure 10-1). In this task, cups are combined beginning with the smallest cup rather than the largest. Therefore, there not only exist alternatives of Property (color/size) for the Object of each action, but also alternatives of Location, identified by color or size (Property), since the smaller cups can fit into any of the larger ones (reflected in the left-hand column of Table IV). This was not true for the pot method of construction where the larger cups are placed first. As with the pot method, order (Temporal State) is a relevant variable across actions because of the constraints of seriation (right-hand column of Table IV). The Properties of both Objects and Locations also change across actions (also reflected in the right-hand column of Table IV).

If we weight each locus of uncertainty equally, this analysis shows an increasing degree of uncertainty from Task 1 to Task 2 (on either view) to Task 3. These patterns of uncertainty should lead to certain patterns of verbal encoding when the tasks are described. It was hypothesized that uncertain rather than certain elements would be verbally encoded. The resulting linguistic descriptions would thus be informative, for they would partition the alternatives existing for speaker and listener communicating about a particular task structure. In general, it was expected that within-action uncertainty would produce linguistic encoding of a particular element for the *first* action in a task sequence, while between-action variability would motivate the *continued* verbal encoding of an element during the second and third actions in a sequence. How particular patterns of information and certainty are reflected in specific types of linguistic productions will be described in the section that follows.

## RESULTS AND DISCUSSION

The strategy of this section will be to present in detail the results of the analysis of variance, summarized in Table III, and to select concrete examples to illustrate the particular effect being described. In this way, we hope to communicate the linguistic flavor of individual performance, even though the analysis of variance is limited to giving us information about factors affecting the performance of a group as a whole. Because the linguistic descriptions are structured wholes, not a concatenation of elements, it is important to understand how people respond to discrete factors by creating comprehensible, structured descriptions, and examples will be needed for this purpose.

The main effect of age in the analysis of variance reflects the fact that ten-year-olds linguistically realize more than six-year-olds. More specifically, six-year-olds on the average verbally encode 33% of the elements in combinatorial actions they mention, while ten-year-olds verbally encode 43%. Since each overall task sequence contains 24 elements (Table II), these percentages mean that the typical six-year-old who refers to all three component acts is, on the average, realizing eight elements in linguistic form, whereas, a typical ten-year-old realizes ten. Here are two examples which illustrate these typical performances. They come from a six-year-old and a ten-year-old carrying out the same task (pot method for seriating cups) under the same conditions (child describes action while he or she is carrying it out).

First, the six-year-old, with an eight-element description:

(2) *Take a yellow / and then the blue / and then the green / and then the red*

(The convention in this example and the ones that follow is to place a slash between the descriptions of each component combinatorial action.) This six-year-old provides just enough information to specify the entities which will be used (Figure 10-1, Task 2), but fails to indicate relation among them by realizing the Locative State slot with a word such as "in." For this reason, the description can be considered communicatively inadequate.

In the next example, a ten-year-old provides the following ten-element description under the same circumstances (a false start, which the child undoes has been eliminated from the example):

(3) *I'm putting in the blue / putting in the green / putting in red*

This description is more communicatively adequate than (2) as the locative relation has been specified with the word "in" for each component act. While locations are never specified, they are quite certain once the object and relation "in" have been specified because there is at every point in this task only one cup into which a given cup, selected as object, could fit (see Figure 10-1, Task 2). This child does, however, use some redundant information, repeating "putting in" three times. Basically, the same information could have been communicated by, "I'm putting in the blue / the green

/ and the red'' This would have contained only five propositional elements, one fewer than the less adequate communication from the six-year-old. These two examples demonstrate that a less adequate communication may contain either fewer or more linguistic elements than a more adequate one. It is the relation of the verbalized elements to the informational structure of the task which is crucial.

There is additional evidence that the ten-year-olds produced more adequate descriptions from the point of view of the communicative task than did the six-year-olds: there was a lower frequency of complete failure to refer to a component action in a task among the tens than among the sixes. Only 6 ten-year-olds left an action out of their descriptions, and they did so on one task only. In contrast, 11 six-year-olds did so, typically on two out of three tasks.

Discussion of the foregoing examples makes it clear that frequency of linguistic realization varies as a function of the type of element, and the reliability of this effect is confirmed by the analysis of variance (Table III). Figure 10-4 shows the amount of linguistic encoding for Agent, Object, Location, and each of the other categories of element. Looking at these results in relation to the analysis of uncertainty summarized in Table IV, we see

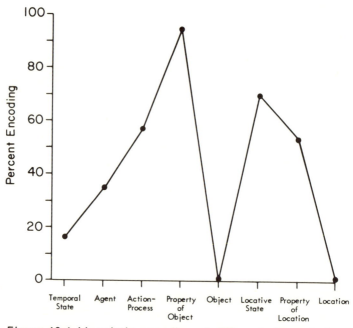

*Figure 10-4.* Linguistic encoding of different elements in a combinatorial action sequence.

that there is an overall correspondence, such that elements categorized most often as uncertain in the table are linguistically expressed most frequently. Thus, Property of Object, the most uncertain element across tasks, according to Table IV, is most often realized in the linguistic descriptions (Figure 10-4). Action-Process, Locative State, Temporal State, and Property of Location fall in the middle in terms of uncertainty as indicated in Table IV, and this middle position is, with the exception of Temporal State, reflected in the graph of Figure 10-4. The anomolous results for Temporal State, which encodes the variable of order, may stem from the possibility of communicating order information through the linear sequence of action and description. That is, the component acts are described in a given order. On the assumption that the listener is carrying out each component act as it is specified by the instructions, references to temporal order like "first," "next," and the like, would be redundant. This interpretation is supported by the nature of the significant interaction between time of description and type of action element, to be discussed below.

The Agent categorization is somewhat complex. By the criterion that the Agent is given in the instructions and is, therefore, certain, it should be linguistically realized only rarely. By the criterion that there are three potential agents present and therefore, there are alternatives, it should be linguistically encoded. The actual position of Agent in the graph just below the other members of the middle group thus seems to reflect both considerations. Finally, in Table IV, two categories never appear as uncertain: Location and Object. The graph in Figure 10-4 shows that these elements are encoded least frequently.

The analysis of another actual description will illustrate how aspects of our informational analysis of the tasks are reflected in the children's linguistic productions. The following example, from a six-year-old girl describing Task 1 (Figure 10-1) while she is doing it, matches the profile of frequency for various action elements shown in Figure 10-4.

(4) *I'm putting the red one in the yellow one / and the green one in the yellow one / and the blue one*

In example 4, as in the graph (Figure 10-4), Agent and Action-Process are mentioned somewhere around one-third of the time; Objects are consistently specified by their Properties rather than by a noun; Location is never specified by a noun and is sometimes omitted altogether; the Locative State is mentioned most, but not all of the time; and Temporal State is not encoded at all. Note that those elements that do not change from action to action (i.e., elements not appearing on the right side of Table IV for Task 1) stop being linguistically encoded as the task progresses. Thus, Agent and Action-Process (*I'm putting*) are encoded for the first action only, while Locative

State and Property of Location (*in the yellow one*) drop out after the second repetition. With respect to Task 1, this description is sufficiently informative to communicate the action to a listener, and even a bit redundant in the initial mention of *yellow* (to refer to cup) and in the repetition of *in the yellow one*. (Compare Example (3), which succinctly communicates the message without making any explicit reference either to "yellow" or to "cup.")

The discussion thus far has implied a different structure of information and certainty for each task and a correspondingly different pattern of linguistic encoding. These differences are manifest in the analysis of variance as a main effect of task, graphed in Figure 10-5. This main effect means that overall the proportion or frequency of elements encoded varies as a function of the task: Task 3, the subassembly method of seriating cups, elicits the highest proportion of linguistically realized elements (45 percent: typically 10 or 11 elements); Task 2, the pot method of seriating cups, elicits an intermediate amount (38 percent: typically 9 or 10 elements); and Task 1, the pot method of placing beads in a cup, elicits the least (31 percent: typically 7 or 8 elements). This order is consistent with our analysis of the uncertainty in the Tasks (Table IV), which shows that the loci of uncertainty become more numerous from Task 1 to Task 2 to Task 3.

This gradient of uncertainty should be, however, specific to certain action elements; Property of Object, for example, does not vary in certainty across tasks; whereas, Property of Location does (see Table IV). A corresponding concentration of the effect of task differences on the linguistic realization of particular elements is manifest in the analysis of variance as a significant interaction between task and type of action element (Table III). This effect is graphed in Figure 10-6. Post-hoc *t*-tests confirm what is clear from visual inspection: that differences are concentrated in the frequency of verbally encoding Locative State and Property of Location. The analysis of

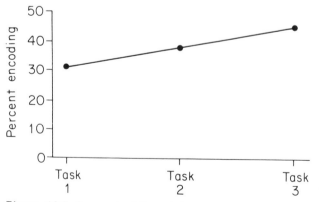

*Figure 10-5.* Amount of linguistic encoding as a function of task structure.

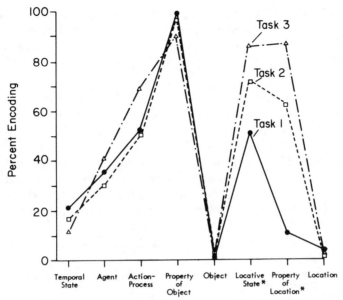

*Figure 10-6.* Effect of task structure on the linguistic encoding of different elements.
*Simple main effect significant.

uncertainty in the tasks (Table IV) shows that the Property of Location element is progressively more informative from Task 1 to Task 3 since it does not vary in Task 1, changes across actions in Task 2 (View b) and involves alternatives within action as well as change across actions in Task 3. This uncertainty pattern is reflected in the results which show that Property of Location is verbally encoded significantly more often in Task 3 than in Task 2, significantly more often in Task 2 than in Task 1 ($p < .001$).[3] The post-hoc *t*-test on the means for each task showed that Locative State was encoded significantly more for Task 3 than for Task 1 ($p < .005$). This is most likely due to the fact that Property of Location is uncertain in Task 3, and to name the Property of Location requires encoding Locative State. That is, for Task 3 children tend to say something like, "Put the red one in the green one," naming both Property of Object and Property of Location since both elements must be selected from an array of alternatives and both change across actions. They would not say, "Put red one / green one" because it is ungrammatical and nonspecific as to the entire Action-Process. However, when the Location is constant as in Task 1, the Locative State can be named once and then left out as in, "Put in the red / the green / the blue."

Specific examples will bear out the reality of this task analysis in terms of their effect on the actual linguistic behavior of individual children. The following examples are from a ten-year-old who described the experimenter's actions after each task had been completed; each description is prototypical in that it contains the mean number of elements used to describe that task, as shown in Figure 10-5. This child's description of the bead task realized 8 elements and goes as follows:

(5) *She put in the red / then a blue / and then a green*

In this description, Agent, Action-Process, and Locative State, constants throughout, are expressed one time each. The Objects, all beads, are specified in terms of their color Property each time an object is manipulated. Order is specified twice with *then,* the only "extra" elements in this communicatially adequate description. This description is similar to that of the ten-year-old presented earlier in Example (3), in that no reference is made to the yellow cup, a totally certain element once the relation "in" has been specified.

Compare her ten-element description of the pot method for seriating cups:

(6) *She put in a yellow one / then a blue / and then a green / and then a red*

One unusual but interesting aspect of this description must first be noted: although the distribution of the elements is consistent with the task structure, one part of the syntax is not; the yellow cup functions as Location, not Object, in the modeled action, yet the child says, *She put in a yellow one.* Essentially, *in* has been misplaced. The description is basically similar to the one elicited by Task 1 Example (5), except that the "pot" or container, identical to the one in the beads task, is verbally specified at the outset (*the yellow one*). This corresponds to a difference in informational structure: in Task 2, the "pot" must be selected from a number of alternative containers, all of them cups; in Task 1, in contrast, there is but a single container present, the yellow cup.

This same child gives the following eleven-element description of the subassembly method for seriating the cups:

(7) *She put the red in the green / the green in the blue / and the blue in the yellow*

Notice in this case that Location, which varies from move to move (Figure 10-1, Task 3) is specified via the color Property for each move. Once again, the uninformative word "cup" does not appear in the description. As we have seen in other examples so far, the absence of repetitive elements yields structures which are, from a syntactic point of view, conjoined.

These examples are a perfect illustration of Figure 10-6, which shows that the locus of task differences lies in the encoding of Property of Location and Locative State: in the Task 1 description, Example (5), no reference is made to Property of Location; the task 2 description, Example (6) mentions Property of Location once (*yellow one*); and the Task 3 description, Example (7) specifies Property of Location three times through mentioning color. The significant difference between Task 1 and Task 3 in frequency of encoding Locative State is also reflected in these examples: the Task 1 description, Example (5), includes the word *in* one time only; the Task 3 description, Example (7) repeats it three times, once for every move.

In contrast to the examples presented so far, some children seem to conceptualize the pot method of seriating cups as involving a variable Location for each move (Figure 10-1, Task 2, View b). This manifests itself in a description which linguistically specifies the Location of each Object as in the Subassembly Task. Here is an example from another ten-year-old who was tested in the identical condition:

(8) *You took the blue; put it in the yellow / took the green; put it in the blue / took the red; and put it in the green*

Thus, the mean amount of linguistic encoding of Locative State and Property of Location for Task 2, the pot method of seriating the cups, may well represent the average of a bimodal distribution in which some subjects linguistically encode it as if Location remains constant (the yellow cup) over moves, while others treat Location as a variable element (yellow, then blue, then green).

While the verbal descriptions of children of both ages reflect the different patterns of uncertainty in the different tasks, those of the ten-year-olds do so to a greater extent. This difference is manifest in the results of the analysis of variance in a significant interaction effect among age, task, and type of action element; this effect is graphed in Figure 10-7. The graph indicates that task variation in the tendency to verbally encode Property of Location and Locative State is greater for the ten-year-olds than for the six-year-olds. Thus post-hoc *t*-tests show a significant difference between six-year-olds and ten-year-olds in verbally encoding Property of Location and Locative State that is specific to certain tasks. Six-year-olds linguistically realize Locative State less often than ten-year-olds for Task 2 ($p < .01$) and for Task 3 ($p < .005$), but not Task 1. Six-year-olds linguistically realize Property of Location less often than ten-year-olds for Task 3 ($p < .005$), but not Tasks 1 and 2. Why this age difference does not manifest itself in the verbal encoding of the other highly informative element, Property of Object, is, however, not clear. It may relate to the greater salience of the moving Object in comparison with the stationary Location. Physical movement, being a type of change, constitutes a basic type of uncertainty. Hence, this

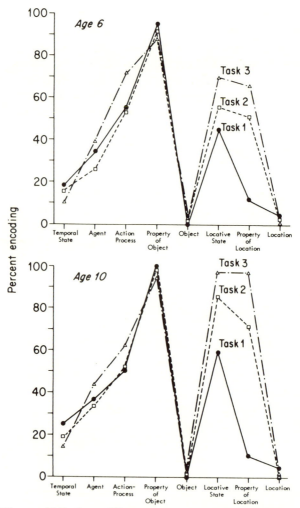

*Figure 10-7.* Age differences in the effect of task structure on the linguistic encoding of different elements.

result can be incorporated within the framework of an informational analysis.

When a task is described after it has been completed (post condition), rather than while it is being performed (simultaneous condition), some elements become more uncertain for the speaker, and others, more certain. This phenomenon is reflected in the results of the analysis of variance by a significant interaction effect between time of description and type of element. This effect is graphed in Figure 10-8. The basic fact revealed by the two curves is that, as we have seen in our other results, elements are linguistically encoded more, the less perceptually obvious (and therefore more uncertain) they are. Temporal State, Agent, and Action-Process, no longer perceptible once the action is over, are encoded more frequently when description takes place *after* the action. Locative State and Property of Location, more perceptually obvious after the action has been completed, show the opposite effect. Two children have been selected to illustrate how certain propositional elements are encoded more frequently when descriptions are simultaneous with action, while others are encoded more frequently when descriptions occur after the completion of the action. One ten-year-old, in describing the pot method of combining seriated cups (Task 2), while he was performing the task (simultaneous condition) said:

(9) *Green into the blue / red into the green / blue into the yellow*

In comparison, another ten-year-old described the same task after he had performed the action (post condition) by saying:

(10) *First I put the blue one in / then the green one / then the red*

These examples are consistent with the results presented in the graph in Figure 10-8, which shows that when description is after action (post condition), Temporal State, Agent, and Action-Process are linguistically realized

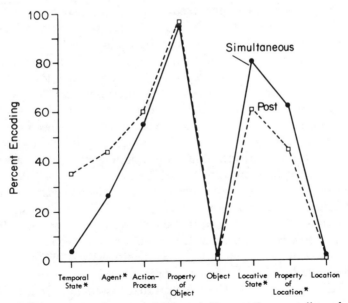

*Figure 10-8.* Effect of time of description on the encoding of different elements.
*t-tests significant.

more often than when action and description are simultaneous (TS, $p < .001$; Ag, $p < .05$, AP, ns.). At the same time, those elements that are less perceptually obvious *during* the action, i.e., Locative State and Property of Location, tend to be linguistically realized more when action and description are simultaneous (LS, $p < .001$; PL, $p < .025$).

## SUMMARY AND CONCLUSIONS

We have presented a theoretical argument and the results of an experiment which relate to the communication of meaning. By approaching the problem of meaning from the perspective of communication, it is possible to analyze the effects of verbal and nonverbal context on the linguistic elements used to construct a meaningful message. This type of analysis is relevant to pragmatics as a branch of linguistics, in which the use of language in a given situation is studied. It is also relevant to psychology since it emphasizes the cognitive abilities which underlie the use of language. We are interested in the development of the ability to combine linguistic elements with elements of the nonverbal event context in order to construct a message. Developmental study of this problem is important because determining something of the progressive growth of the ability to comprehend and communicate can help elucidate some central problems in the study of language and cognition.

More specifically, it is possible to learn of the developmental interaction of the perceptual/cognitive system with the way in which language is used in context to communicate. A first step is to identify the relevant contextual variables and the cognitive abilities required to make use of linguistic and nonlinguistic elements in order to achieve effective communication. We have argued that uncertainty in the nonverbal context, and an amodal cognitive system which can coordinate performance in terms of perception, action and communication, are the important aspects of the communication of meaning. It is posited that this amodal system is structured in the form of propositions such that entities (arguments) are apprehended in terms of states or relations (predicates).

Uncertainty is being used in the information theory sense to refer to the state of affairs in which alternatives exist and choice or selection is called for. In addition, when an element is changing, it is uncertain in the sense that alternatives exist over time. Uncertainty can be seen as the cognitive basis of assertion, and certainty as the cognitive basis of presupposition. Using Stalnaker's (1974) definition of pragmatic presupposition—the background beliefs of the speaker—it is clear that if something is believed to be true, doubt or uncertainty does not exist. Since information, in the sense of allowing selection among alternatives, exists only when there is doubt, something will tend to go unstated unless there is doubt in the mind of the speaker or perceived doubt in that of the listener. The resolution of uncertainty is the function of assertion. Pragmatic presupposition is the matrix of certainty within which uncertainty exists.

In order to further clarify the interrelation of uncertainty (the existence of spatially distributed alternatives or change over time) and language in communication, we performed a study in which children explained how to carry out complex action sequences involving physical objects to someone who could not see the action. Because the action tasks were predetermined, it was possile to do a clear-cut analysis of the various sources of uncertainty in each action task. The concept of a propositional organization of the cognitive system allows a parallel formulation of the organization of action and of the linguistic description.

The experimental situation was such that children of two ages (six and ten years) described construction activities for three tasks (beads into cup, cups seriated in two ways) to someone who supposedly could not see the action. The combinatorial tasks were analyzed for uncertainty in terms of alternatives within actions and change across actions for both entities (arguments) and relations (predicates). The transcripts of descriptions obtained were coded for the lingusitic realization of elements derived from a maximally complete description of the overall action sequence. When the probability of linguistic encoding was analyzed in terms of the factors of age, task, activity, time of description, and kind of element, a complex and interesting pattern of results was obtained. This pattern revealed the perception of uncertainty as a general cognitive process determining selection of elements for linguistic realization.

In general it was found that the descriptions of children of both ages were informative in that they tended more frequently to verbally encode the more uncertain task elements: Property of Object, Property of Location, Action-Process, and Locative State. These four elements were most frequently given verbal expression when type of element was considered independently of the other factors. In addition, when task was considered, it was found that the number of elements verbally encoded increased as uncertainty increased across the three tasks.

The pattern of results is basically the same for both six- and ten-year-olds. However, ten-year-olds generally verbalize more than six-year-olds. This tendency to verbalize more is particularly pronounced for Task 3, which has more uncertainty than the simpler Tasks 1 and 2. Thus, in comparison to the descriptions of the six-year-olds, those of the ten-year-olds reflect to a greater extent patterns of information and certainty inherent in the structure of a complex task. This is evidence that ten-year-olds are better at discerning communicatively important elements over a wider range of conditions. This finding is not inconsistent with those of referential communication studies which have shown that the ability to verbally encode distinguishing features of objects increases with age (Rosenberg & Cohen, 1966; Krauss & Weinheimer, 1967); however, it also indicates that the complexity of the referential situation must be taken into account in describing this ability. Our study extends the range of research on referential communication from the description of isolated object elements to the integrated description of action events.

A final factor which affects the verbal encoding of a message is the time of description relative to the action described. Elements which are not perceptually present to the speaker after the action has been completed (Temporal State, Agent, and Action-Process) are linguistically realized more often in the post condition than in the simultaneous condition where they are perceptually present. Elements which are not as perceptually obvious during action (Locative State and Property of Location) as after the action has been completed are, in contrast, linguistically realized more when description is simultaneous with action. Thus, time of description affects the linguistic message by changing the relative certainty of the various task elements for the speaker. Note that time of description does not affect certainty for the listener, who is always operating under the same conditions. Hence, the effect of time of description is a manifestation of egocentrism: the speaker's message varies to some extent as a function of his or her own informational needs, independent of those of the listener. This variation is not, however, so great as to wipe out the effects of patterns of uncertainty which are operative for listener as well as speaker (note the similarity of the two curves in Figure 10-8). Because of the size and nature of the effects, it seems unlikely that the differences under the two conditions were such as to render any descriptions communicatively inadequate. Thus, even though the speaker, age 6 or 10, is affected by his or her point of view, the message remains sufficiently adapted to the needs of the listener.

By using an experimental approach to studying the communication of meaning, we were able to manipulate contextual variables which influence the construction of messages. We found that age, task, and time of description affected the likelihood of linguistically realizing task elements. The activity factor, whether the child performed the task or watched an adult perform the task, did not produce a statistically significant effect; it seems that the tasks are simple enough that the child's understanding and linguistic encoding are not increased through active manipulation of the materials. By analyzing such variables, we have begun to delineate which aspects of the psychological and physical context predict what is chosen for linguistic realization in the construction of a message to communicate meaning.

Our study is not alone in stressing the importance of contextual uncertainty for the structure and content of what is said. Osgood (1971) reports a study of adults describing simple events involving the manipulation of physical objects. He interprets his findings in terms of the effect of perceptual variables on linguistic descriptions, and discusses presupposition and uncertainty in a manner consonant with our treatment. He stresses that presuppositions are nonlinguistic and dependent on contrasts in the context of the utterances. Uncertainty is used to discuss the choice of specifying adjectives in noun phrases. Osgood's findings with adult parallel ours with children. For example, Osgood concludes "if the perceptual entity must be contrasted with others of its class, then we find an increased likelihood of adjectival modification" (Osgood, 1971, p. 513).

Ford and Olson (1975) did a study of young children's (four to seven years of age) descriptions of objects where the context of alternatives was the major independent variable. They found, as we did, that even young children's utterances reflect the descriptive function of differentiating an event from a set of perceived alternatives. As the referential situation got more complex (more attributes and more stimuli), the performance of the younger children broke down, failing to reflect the informational structure of the situation. Similarly, Dickson (1979) found that referential communication between age four and eight was sensitive to the context of alternatives only when the differentiating attributes were salient. The pattern of these two studies also encompasses our finding that the six-year-olds' communications were less reflective of informational structure, the more complex the task. The fact that the descriptions of our six-year-olds were much less disrupted by the more complex tasks than the subjects in the other two studies probably relates to task differences; only our study involved communication about action.

These findings, like ours, indicate that if the referential situation is within their cognitive capacities, children conform to Stalnaker's (1972) notion that statements function to select from alternatives that are live options in the context. This idea is closely related to Chafe's (1976) notion of contrastiveness. The function of a contrastive sentence is to assert which candidate from an implicit list of possible candidates is the correct one in a particular context of background knowledge. The selected candidate, called the focus of contrast, is distinguished by higher pitch and stronger stress from other elements in the sentence. Our results indicate that linguistic realization per se may also distinguish a focus of contrast from other elements in the message where no set of alternative candidates exist. Take, for example, Tasks 2 and 3, where all the stimuli are cups, but the candidates can be distinguished by color. In this situation, color words are used to select from among the potential candidates, but the word "cup" goes unspoken. Note that this expansion of Chafe's concept is founded in the idea of the message as including both verbal and nonverbal elements. In other words, the entity, cup, is seen as part of the message even though it is not linguistically realized.

The conceptualization of our results is also related to the distinction between given and new information as articulated by Haviland and Clark

(1974; Clark & Haviland, 1977) and, particularly, by Chafe (1976). Chafe defines given information as "knowledge which the speaker assumes to be in the consciousness of the addressee at the time of the utterance" (p. 30). New information, in contrast, "is what the speaker assumes he is introducing into the addressee's consciousness by what he says" (p. 30). Chafe goes on to say that "given information is conveyed in a weaker and more attenuated manner than new information" (p. 31). Our results illustrate this distinction in the fact that elements tended to be linguistically realized the first time they occurred, i.e. when they were new, and drop out on subsequent appearances [see Examples (4), (5), (6), (7)].[4]

Pea (1979) has suggested salience as an alternative to uncertainty in the analysis of word choice by young children first learning language. Pea hypothesizes that children are more likely to mention situational elements which are salient. Greenfield (1980) points out that we must still understand the nature and determinants of salience and that uncertainty (in the sense of alternatives and change over time) helps account for why certain elements are salient. The salience of a given feature shifts as the context changes, and this shift is a function of alternatives and change.

Dent and Rader (1979) also deal with the relation of salience and uncertainty. On their view, salience implies relatively involuntary attention to single discrete aspects of the perceptual field. The perception of uncertainty requires distributed attention to possible alternatives or changes in elements. Thus, the attentional mechanisms that underlie the perception of uncertainty are more complex and structually tuned to the environment than those usually detailed to account for salience effects.

On the side of comprehension, there is evidence of a complementary effect of uncertainty in adults. Greenfield and Westerman (1978) gave verbal instructions to perform various tasks with nesting cups similar to the ones used in this study. Each set of instructions was presented in two different linguistic forms. It was found that where the task was perceptually obvious from the structure of the materials (e.g., instructions to seriate the cups in a nest) the linguistic form did not affect ease of comprehension. Where the task was not obvious from the materials (e.g., instructions to stack the cups in a nonseriated fashion), ease of comprehension was affected by the linguistic form. The implication is that comprehension processes bypass linguistic cues when characteristics of the nonverbal referential situation make them relatively obvious or certain, just as production processes omit what can be taken for granted. Studies of comprehension in children as young as age 2 have also revealed this phenomenon. Where the nonverbal context is such that the child sees fewer alternative interpretations of a set of verbal instructions, his or her use of syntactic cues (e.g., word order) declines (e.g., Bever, 1970; Huttenlocher & Weiner, 1971; Strohner & Nelson, 1974). The younger the child and the less knowledge he or she has of syntax, the more comprehension of the message depends on reduced alternatives, constrained possibilities in the nonverbal referential context (Strohner & Nelson, 1974).

There would seem to be two major directions for future research. One is to perform more fine-grained analyses of nonverbal indices of uncertainty in the type of describing situations used in the research discussed thus far. This would involve measures of attention to various aspects of the situation (cf. Greenfield, 1979). Eye-gaze would seem to be an obvious variable to measure. Possibly, physiological measures of arousal could be used to ascertain what aspects of an event are being attended to. These attention measures would then be used in conjunction with language analyses in an attempt to relate salience and perceived uncertainty to the content and structure of utterances.

The second direction of future research is to delineate at what points in development the requirements of the listener affect the descriptive utterances produced (cf. Ford & Olson, 1975). This research effort should involve both naturalistic and experimental data. All the data discussed in the present paper are experimental. Yet there are situations in real life where a person must describe something to another person who can't see what is being described. For instance, a parent in a separate room and out of sight of their child might call, "What are you doing?". The child then has to describe to the parent something that is only visible to the child-speaker. As for the experimental research, there should be studies that vary not just the events described and the age of the describer, but also differences in background knowledge between listener and speaker. This could be done, for example, by adding a condition in which listeners have a more diverse array of objects than do speakers and speakers are informed about this difference before they communicate.

In our view, meaning is the intended message, and this message is constructed through the coordination of perception, cognition, and language. One of the most important contextual variables to which the perceptual /cognitive system is sensitive is that of uncertainty; the system must be sensitive to the features of objects and actions which are relevant for detecting change and differentiating among alternatives for both self and others. Our study shows how the linguistic communication of children, aged 6 and 10, also functions to mark change and differentiate alternatives in the nonverbal context, thus manifesting the close coordination of language with other modes of cognizing a referential situation.

## ACKNOWLEDGMENTS

The authors would like to express their appreciation to the Spencer Foundation, the source of financial support for our study, and to the children and staff of the Westwood Elementary School, where the study was carried out. We would like to thank Martha Platt, who helped with the first pilot testing; Ann Levy, who persevered from later stages of pilot testing through data collection and coding; and Clyde Dent, who helped analyze the data. This chapter is a revised version of an article in P. French (Ed.) *The development of meaning: Pedolinguistic series.* Japan: Bunka Hyoron Press, 1980 (published in Japanese).

## NOTES

[1]For a more detailed discussion of the relation of our work to information theory, see Pea, 1979 and Greenfield, 1980.

[2]One child in the younger group was seven years, two weeks old. The teacher indicated that the child was six and when we found he had just had his seventh birthday we judged it appropriate to include him in the six-year-old group. Similarly, one child in the ten-year-old group was nine years, eleven months old.

[3]Some children seemed to interpret Task 1 such that the position of the beads in the cup was relevant. Thus, they indicated the position with a prepositional phrase that included an encoding of Property of Location where this Location is another bead (e.g., ''put the blue next to the red''). The number of children who did this is as follows: 5/48 6-year-olds, 10/48 10-year-olds. Otherwise, Property of Location and Locative State would have been verbally encoded even less frequently than they were in this task.

[4]Haviland and Clark's distinction between new and old information in terms of whether or not knowledge is already in memory makes it less applicable to our experiment than Chafe's definition in terms of whether or not knowledge is in consciousness. For example, the fact that Agent is often mentioned for the first combinatorial action in each task does not, after the first task, seem to involve lack of memory of Agent so much as consciousness of Agent. That is, the listener could remember who served as an Agent on the first task, but, because of intervening instructions, be unaware of the relevance of the memory for the second task until brought to his or her conscious attention by the speaker.

## REFERENCES

Atlas, J. D. On presupposing. *Mind,* 1978, 87, 396–411.

Bates, E. *Language and context: The acquisition of pragmatics.* New York: Academic Press, 1976.

Bever, T. The cognitive basis for linguistic structures. *In* J. R. Hayes (Ed.), *Cognition and the development of language.* New York: Wiley, 1970.

Bowerman, M. *Early syntactic development: A cross-linguistic study with special reference to Finnish.* Cambridge, England: Cambridge University Press, 1973.

Brown, R. *Words and things.* Glencoe, Ill.: Free Press, 1958.

Brown, R. *A first language: The early stages.* Cambridge, Mass.: Harvard University Press, 1973.

Bruner, J., Roy, C., & Ratner, N. The beginnings of request. *In* K. Nelson (Ed.), *Children's Language,* Vol. 3. New York: Gardner Press, in press.

Chafe, W. L. *Meaning and the structure of language.* Chicago: University of Chicago Press, 1970.

Chafe, W. Givenness, contrastiveness, definiteness, subjects, topics, and point of view. *In* C. Li (Ed.), *Subject and topic.* New York: Academic Press, 1976.

Clark, H. H. & Chase, W. G. On the process of comparing sentences against pictures. *Cognitive Psychology,* 1972, 3, 472–517.

Clark, H. H. & Haviland, S. E. Comprehension and the given-new contract. *In* R. Freedle (Ed.), *Discourse production and comprehension,* Vol. 1. Hillsdale, N.J.: Lawrence Erlbaum Associates, 1977.

Dent, C. & Rader, N. Perception, meaning and research in semantic development. *In* P. French (Ed.), *The development of meaning: Pedolinguistic series.* Japan: Bunka Hyoron Press, 1979.

Dickson, W. P. Referential communication performance from age 4 to 8: Effects of referent type, context, and target position. *Developmental Psychology,* 1979, 15, 470–471.

Fillmore, C. The case for case. *In* E. Bach & R. T. Harms (Eds.), *Universals of linguistic theory.* New York: Holt, Rinehart & Winston, 1968.

Ford, W. & Olson, D. The elaboration of the noun phrase in children's description of objects. *Journal of Experimental Child Psychology,* 1975, 19 371–382.

Glucksberg, S. & Kim, W. Unpublished study, Princeton University, 1969.

Glucksberg, S., Krauss, R., & Higgins, E. T. The development of referential communication skills. *In* F. D. Horowitz, E. M. Hetherington, S. Scarr-Salapatek, & G. M. Siegel (Eds.), *Review of child development research* (Vol. 4). Chicago: University of Chicago Press, 1975.

Goodson, B. D. & Greenfield, P. M. The search for structural principles in children's manipulative play. *Child Development,* 1975, 46, 734–756.

Greenfield, P. M. Informativeness, presupposition, and semantic choice in single-word utterances. *In* N. Waterson & C. Snow (Eds.), *Development of communication: Social and pragmatic factors in language acquisition.* London: Academic Press, 1978a.

Greenfield, P. M. Structural parallels betwen language and action in development. *In* A. Lock (Ed.), *Action, symbol, and gesture: The emergence of language.* London: Academic Press, 1978b.

Greenfield, P. Going beyond information theory to explain early word choice. *Journal of Child Language,* 1980, 1, in press.

Greenfield, P. M., Nelson, K., & Saltzman, E. The development of rulebound strategies for manipulating seriated cups: A parallel between action and grammar. *Cognitive Psychology,* 1972, 3, 291–310.

Greenfield, P. M. & Schneider, L. Building a tree structure: The development of hierarchical complexity and interrupted strategies in children's construction activity. *Developmental Psychology,* 1977, 13, 299–313.

Greenfield, P. M. & Smith, J. *The structure of communication in early language development.* New York: Academic Press, 1976.

Greenfield, P. M. & Westerman, M. Some psychological relations between action and language structure. *Journal of Psycholinguistic Research,* 1978, 7, 453–475.

Greenfield, P. M. & Zukow, P. Why do children say what they say when they say it? An experimental approach to the psychogenesis of presupposition. *In* K. Nelson (Ed.), *Children's language,* Vol. 1. New York: Gardner Press, 1978.

Haviland, S. & Clark, H. What's new? Acquiring new information as a process in comprehension. *Journal of Verbal Learning and Verbal Behavior,* 1974, 13, 512–521.

Huttenlocher, J., Eisenberg, K., & Strauss, S. Comprehension: Relations between perceived actor and logical subject. *Journal of Verbal Learning and Verbal Behavior,* 1968, 7, 300–304.

Huttenlocher, J. & Strauss, S. Comprehension and a statement's relations to the situation it describes. *Journal of Verbal Learning and Verbal Behavior,* 1968, 7, 527–530.

Huttenlocher, J. & Weiner, S. L. Comprehension of instructions in varying contexts. *Cognitive Psychology,* 1971, 2, 369–385.

Kintsch, W. Notes on the structure of semantic memory. *In* E. Tulving & W. Donaldson (Eds.), *Organization of memory.* New York: Academic Press, 1972.

Kirk, R. *Experimental design: Procedures for the behavioral sciences.* Belmont, Calif.: Brooks/Cole, 1968.

Krauss, R. M. & Weinheimer, S. Effect of referent similarity and communication mode on verbal encoding. *Journal of Verbal Learning and Verbal Behavior,* 1967, 6, 359–363.

McCall, R. & Applebaum, M. Bias in the analysis of repeated measures designs: Some alternative approaches. *Child Development,* 1973, 44, 401–515.

Olson, D. R. Language and thought: Aspects of a cognitive theory of semantics. *Psychological Review,* 1970, 77, 257–273.

Osgood, C. Where do sentences come from? *In* D. Steinberg & L. Jakobovits (Eds.), *Semantics: An interdisciplinary reader in philosophy, linguistics and psychology,* London: Cambridge University Press, 1971.

Osgood, C. & Bock, K. Salience and sentencing: Some production principles. *In* S. Rosenberg (Ed.), *Sentence production: Developments in research and theory.* Hillsdale, N.J.: Lawrence Erlbaum, 1977.

Pea, R. Can information theory explain early word choice? *Journal of Child Language,* 1980, 1, in press.

Rosenberg, S. & Cohen, B. D. Referential processes of speakers and listeners. *Psychological Review,* 1966, 73, 208–231.

Schlesinger, I. M. Production of utterances and language acquisition. *In* D.I. Slobin (Ed.), *The ontogenesis of grammar: A theoretical symposium.* New York: Academic Press, 1971.

Slobin, D. K. Cognitive prerequisites for the acquisition of grammar. *In* C. A. Ferguson & D. I. Slobin (Eds.), *Studies of child language development.* New York: Holt, Rinehart & Winston, 1973.

Stalnaker, R. Pragmatics. *In* D. Davidson & G. Harman (Eds.), *Semantics of natural languages.* Dordrecht, Holland: D. Reidel, 1972.

Stalnaker, R. Pragmatic presuppositions. *In* M. K. Munitz & P. K. Unger (Eds.), *Semantics and philosophy.* New York: New York University Press, 1974.

Strawson, P. F. On referring. *Mind,* 1950, 59, 320–344.

Strohner, H. & Nelson, K. E. The young child's development of sentence comprehension: Influence of event probability, nonverbal context, syntactic form, and strategies. *Child Development,* 1974, 45, 567–576.

Zukow, P., Reilly, J. & Greenfield, P. Making the absent present: Facilitating the transition from sensorimotor to linguistic communication. *In* K. Nelson (Ed.), *Children's language,* Vol. 3, New York: Gardner Press, in press.

# SUBJECT INDEX

# AUTHOR INDEX